Preaching the Inward Light

Studies in Rhetoric and Religion 9

Preaching the Inward Light
Early Quaker Rhetoric

MICHAEL P. GRAVES

BAYLOR UNIVERSITY PRESS

Cover Design by Nicole Weaver, Zeal Design.
Cover image: Frontispiece from *Old Quaker Meeting-Houses*, by John Russell
Hayes, 2nd ed., rev and enlarged, with 166 illustrations. Biddle Press,
Philadelphia, 1911.

Library of Congress Cataloging-in-Publication Data

Graves, Michael P., 1943-
  Preaching the Inward Light : theory and practice of early Quaker
impromptu preaching / Michael P. Graves.
      p. cm. -- (Studies in rhetoric and religion ; 9)
  Includes bibliographical references (p.   ) and index.
  ISBN 978-1-60258-240-8 (hardback : alk. paper)
  1. Quaker preaching--History--17th century. 2. Extemporaneous
preaching--History--17th century. 3. Society of Friends--Sermons--History
and criticism. 4. Sermons, English--History and criticism. I. Title.
  BX7748.P75G73 2009
  252.'096--dc22

                              2009020936

Printed in the United States of America on acid-free paper with a minimum
of 30% pcw recycled content.

CONTENTS

Section IV
A Closer Look at Four Select Quaker Sermons
from the Period 1671 to 1700

PREFACE

This book began with the suggestions and encouragement of two beloved Quaker scholars, T. Canby Jones and Arthur O. Roberts, who counseled me regarding a research topic. Canby Jones actually handed me a copy of all known sermons by George Fox, each of which he had copied from a manuscript during his own research. Later, aided by a Biddle Quaker Leadership Grant from Friends World Committee for Consultation (FWCC), I collected sermons at Friends Historical Library of Swarthmore College and at the Quaker Collection of Haverford College Library, both near Philadelphia. At Haverford, I had the pleasure of meeting Herbert Hadley, of FWCC, and revered Quaker scholar Henry J. Cadbury, both of whom gave me encouragement and sage advice regarding my research. I continued my research at Friends Reference Library, London, which is now known as the Library of the Religious Society of Friends. The encouragement and help of Dorothy Harris (Swarthmore), Edwin Bronner (Haverford), Edward Milligan (Friends), and their colleagues is especially acknowledged and appreciated. Eventually, my thesis project, which involved the rhetorical analysis of seventy-four early Quaker sermons set against the complex milieu of seventeenth-century England, was completed under the scrupulous and learned mentorship of respected rhetorical scholar Walter R. Fisher.[1]

In subsequent years, I have built on my initial research in several ways. In particular, four fellowships in the Summer Seminars for College Teachers program, funded by the National Endowment for the Humanities (NEH), each advanced my thinking and publication program in particular ways at key junctures. First I participated in an NEH seminar titled "Medieval to Modern: Literature, Science, and Religion in England, 1660–1750," held at the University of Florida under the leadership of Aubrey L. Williams, renowned scholar in seventeenth- and eighteenth-century British literature. The seminar deepened my understanding of the time period and particularly of English literary culture. My seminar project centered on the conceptual metaphors of George Fox's surviving sermons.[2]

Subsequently, an NEH Summer Seminar for College Teachers enabled me to study under Richard Bauman, a renowned folklorist who has published significant work on early Quaker communication. The seminar, titled "Oral Literature," was held at the University of Texas at Austin. The first time I met Richard Bauman, he had my dissertation open on his desk—a good omen, I thought. He helped me relate my work on Quaker sermons to the anthropological literature on "key" symbols, a timely and pertinent idea for me, and a shift that resulted in the publication of a revised chapter from my dissertation in the *Quarterly Journal of Speech*.[3]

A third NEH Summer Seminar fellowship took me to Fordham University in New York City for a seminar with the title "The Journey in Medieval Christian Mysticism" under Ewert H. Cousins, editor of the twenty-five-volume *World Spirituality: An Encyclopedic History of the Religious Quest*. In my seminar work I placed Stephen Crisp's sermons, along with his unusual and engaging *A Short History of a Long Travel from Babylon to Bethel*, within the context of medieval Christian writings about the spiritual journey. This project helped me see Crisp's and other early Quaker preachers' sermons in the context of medieval spiritual writings.[4]

Finally, a fourth NEH Summer Seminar for College Teachers found me at the University of London in a seminar titled "Eighteenth Century British Sources of American Rhetoric," directed by distinguished American rhetorical scholar Lloyd F. Bitzer, who encouraged me to keep pursuing my research agenda. The seminar schedule allowed me to divide my research and writing time between the British Library and the Library of the Religious Society of Friends, only blocks apart; to visit Dr. Williams' Library, a short walk away; and to develop an essay that deepened my understanding of Robert Barclay's contributions to the development of a Quaker homiletic theory.[5]

In addition to the NEH seminar fellowships, over the course of my years as a college and university professor, I have enjoyed sabbaticals from both George Fox College (now George Fox University), Newberg, Oregon, and Regent University, Virginia Beach, Virginia, which allowed me to revisit the Quaker Collection at Haverford College, Friends Historical Library of Swarthmore College, and the Library of the Religious Society of Friends. During this time, I also studied at Pendle Hill Quaker Studies Center, Wallingford, Pennsylvania, and the Bevan-Naish Collection of Woodbrooke Quaker Study Centre, Birmingham, England. At Haverford, I was especially helped by Quaker Bibliographer and Special Collections Librarian An Upton. These periods of reflective reading and research deepened and extended this book. In particular, my time at Pendle Hill brought me into contact with William P. Taber Jr., who introduced me to Samuel Bownas' *A Description of the Qualifications Necessary to a Gospel Minister* (London, 1750), an important Quaker preaching manual, hereafter referred to as *Qualifications*, which Taber worked to publish in a modern edition and to which he added an insightful twenty-two-page introduction.[6] At Woodbrooke, I connected with Douglas Gwyn for some helpful, but all too brief, conversation. In the fall of 2005, I traveled again to Woodbrooke, this time to deliver the George Richardson Lecture, which appears here in revised form as chapter 12. On that occasion, I greatly profited from relaxed, humor-filled conversations with Ben Pink Dandelion.

Allow me to state a truism: no book of this kind springs from a single mind. I am deeply indebted to a group of Quaker scholars and thinkers who have profoundly influenced my own thinking about Quaker history and thought, people who challenged my limited view in intellectually rich, yet cordial ways. In addition to T. Canby Jones, Arthur O. Roberts, William Taber, Douglas Gwyn, and Ben Pink Dandelion, mentioned above, I must also add my thanks to Paul Anderson, Ralph Beebe, and Richard Foster for being models of scholarship, good writing, and lives full of "acted truth." In the same light, my former colleagues (at George Fox College) and lifelong friends Ed Higgins and Richard Engnell have consistently encouraged me to study, reflect, and write, and in so many late-night conversations helped me to broaden my perspective.

I was privileged to teach at Regent University during the halcyon days of a new doctoral program in communication studies. Although my colleagues did not always understand why I persisted in researching something as esoteric as early Quaker rhetoric rather than doing rhetorical analysis of contemporary media, they nevertheless supported me in profound ways in my own pursuits. I am indebted to Jack

Keeler, my first dean at Regent, for hiring me to teach on the graduate level, a turn that nudged me into a more consistent research and writing path. Dean William Brown, with whom I served as associate dean for academics, always encouraged my research ventures and set a high standard by his own weighty social-science research. My other Regent University colleagues deserve special thanks for their encouragement toward this project: Benson Fraser, John Lawing, Denis Bounds, Rodney Reynolds, Kathaleen Reid-Martinez, Robert Schihl, Douglas Tarpley, Harry Sova, Cliff Kelley, Michael Smith, Gillette Elvgren, and the late Paul Hunsinger, all of whom comprised a unique scholarly community that, for one brief moment in eternity, was at once deeply spiritual, arrestingly honest, and irrepressibly jovial. For seventeen years, I tried in vain to teach them Quaker silence. Anyone acquainted with the Regent faculty during that period will remember that the most astonishingly honest and raucously jovial colleague of them all was Terry Lindvall, who remains a consistent source of inspiration to me and a persistent goad to my aspirations, a dear friend almost as enthusiastic about historical-critical research as he is witty.

I am also grateful for the encouragement expressed by my Liberty University colleagues and the opportunity Liberty University has made possible to continue an ambitious schedule of scholarly presentations at national and regional conferences, some of which have advanced this book.

I would be remiss if I did not acknowledge my debt to mentors in the academic area of rhetorical studies, begining with Kenneth Hance, who taught me the neo-Aristotelian approach to speech criticism while a visiting professor at California State University at Los Angeles. At CSULA I also studied the history of public address under Anthony Hillbruner and rhetorical criticism under Robert Cathcart and Karlyn Kohrs Campbell, both of whom encouraged me to venture beyond the constraints of strict neo-Aristotelianism. In Campbell's course on great European speakers I first began to deal with early Quaker rhetoric. At CSULA I also met Walter Fisher, who later became my key mentor in the doctoral program at the University of Southern California. At USC I studied public address under James McBath, a meticulous scholar of British and American public address. Also at USC, I had the delight of taking a summer seminar in contemporary rhetorical theory taught by Marie Hochmuth Nichols, who mentored me in innumerable ways and pushed me toward publication.

Through the years, numbers of people in the area of communication studies have encouraged this writing project, but none so consistently as Martin J. Medhurst of Baylor University, who has a unique way of putting practical "feet" to his spiritual gift of encouragement. At significant crossroads in my scholarly life, Marty has been there saying, "This is the way. Walk in it."

In addition, I should like to express my sincere thanks to everyone associated with Baylor University Press who helped to bring this project to completion. I am especially indebted to Carey Newman for his unflaggingly positive attitude and sage advice. Also, Diane Smith and Jenny Hunt enacted their all too often unheralded roles with enthusiasm and grace.

Finally, this project would never have reached completion without the consistent sacrifice and persistent encouragement of my best friend, colleague at four institutions, and beloved spouse, Dr. Darlene Richards Graves, to whom this book is affectionately dedicated.

I bear full responsibility for this book's errors and omissions. On the other hand, any virtues it may exhibit spring from a community of voices composed of friends, mentors, and myself.

INTRODUCTION

Why This Book?

Prolegomena

This book is about seventeenth-century Quaker impromptu preaching, both the development of its theory and its manifestation in practice. Quakers (also known as the Society of Friends, the Friends Church, or simply Friends) are popularly known for their leadership role in social-reform movements, advocacy of pacifism, and development of a worship pattern based on silent waiting for the Spirit's immediate moving. However, it is still not widely understood or acknowledged—even within the Society of Friends—that the early Quakers (c. 1650–1700) were also a vocal, even "revivalistic" sect that sought to put into effect worldwide the moral, spiritual, and practical virtues of what they called "primitive Christianity." In fact, early Quakers can be characterized as a zealous missionary sect, even to the extent of one brave Quaker woman traveling to the sultan of Turkey to witness, a very risky business in the seventeenth century.[1] For a time, Quakerism was the most influential and fastest-growing religious sect in the world. Baptists and Quakers are the only contemporary religious "denominations" to survive from the numerous sects that proliferated during the turbulent seventeenth century in England, and the evangelical fervor of both groups is a partial cause of their vitality and perseverance.[2] Furthermore, it is similarly not well known or acknowledged that, since their appearance in the 1650s, many Quakers who saw and see themselves as acting consistently with the more conservative theological orientation of their earliest progenitors have also placed strong emphasis upon evangelism and the spoken word.[3] This book is about these interesting, peculiar people and their notions of preaching.

1

There are three parts to this introductory chapter. In the first part, "Backgrounds," I will (1) sketch some backgrounds about impromptu preaching, (2) present a working definition of "theory," (3) reveal questions that guide this study, (4) comment on the obstacles to the examination of impromptu preaching, (5) discuss important myths about early Quakers that are implicitly addressed in this book, and (6) present a summary of the book's purpose. In the second part of this chapter, "The Contexts Informing this Book," I will deal with the contexts of rhetorical studies, Quaker studies, and previous scholarship on Quaker preaching and sermons. Finally, in the third section of this chapter, I will preview the book, commenting both on its scope and the content of ensuing chapters.

BACKGROUNDS

Some Backgrounds to Impromptu Preaching

Perhaps surprising to the uninitiated, early Quakers claimed to preach *impromptu*, that is, without prior, contextually situated, intentional preparation, as opposed to *extempore*, where one prepares ahead of time for a specific rhetorical situation but where most of the words themselves are chosen during the speech.[4] Times have changed, of course, and the contemporary Quaker preaching style, at least among today's pastoral Friends (the majority of contemporary Quakers, for whom preaching is still a vital practice), involves advanced planning and is not the same manifestation rhetorically as preaching among the early Friends, who developed their own impromptu practice into an effective and often dynamic rhetorical skill. This book focuses on the earlier, peculiarly Quaker, impromptu preaching tradition.[5]

Impromptu preaching has been a force, or at least has been present, in the life of the church since the first century, yet it has received scant attention from scholars.[6] Not surprisingly, the study of impromptu preaching is potentially significant to the study of all human communication, since so much human communication is not preplanned. Impromptu preaching offers an opportunity to approach some perenial and pertinent topics in rhetorical and communication studies from an interesting and pertinent angle, allowing the investigation of topics that include the nature of oral impromptu invention; the roles of narrative, argument, metaphor, and schemes (such as rhetorical questions) in spontaneous public discourse; the nature and habits of public performance in unrehearsed settings; the operation of memory in the impromptu preaching context; and the spiritual dimensions of communication in public discourse. All of these topics are a part of the Quaker theory of impromptu preaching and its practice.

The Quaker practice of impromptu preaching is the logical extension of the post-Reformation process that moved by stages away from adherence to the church calendar, lectionary, and carefully prepared manuscript or extemporaneous sermons. In his significant recent book, Stephen H. Webb reminds us, "After missionary preaching converted and pacified the barbarian tribes, lectionary preaching became the mainstay of the pulpit."[7] After the Reformation, Webb argues, preaching gradually freed itself from the lectionary because ministers could choose what Scripture to use as a textual base for their sermons. Preaching continued to be "exegetical and evangelical," but delivery began to change so that by the time Whitefield began to preach, it was more "prophetic or exclamatory [in] tone" (115). Webb observes, "If we define rhetoric as the art of listening to an audience so that the message can be adapted even while it is being delivered, then the Protestant sermon becomes an example of pure rhetoric to the extent that the preacher trusts in the Holy Spirit for the success of its delivery" (116). Webb is not writing here of Quakers, but, as we shall see, Quaker preaching went even further and dispensed not only with the lectionary, but also with the necessity to be informed and constrained by a specific Scripture text prior to preaching or to be exegetical at all, for that matter. Quakers also reined in their vocal and gestural expression during the last three decades of the seventeenth century, but also trusted the Holy Spirit for success despite their essentially muted or bland delivery.

A Working Definition of "Theory"

Any book that claims to deal in part with the development of a Quaker *theory* of impromptu preaching ought to offer readers a definition of "theory" suited to this task. For this purpose I turn to Barry Brummett's conversational discussion of theory in the introduction to his *Reading Rhetorical Theory*: "What does it mean to theorize or to have a theory? A quick definition might be that a theory is the assertion of regular, systematic relationships among actions, objects, and events in the world."[8] While it might be urged that early Quakers were not very systematic in their writings about impromptu, "inspired" preaching, this book will argue and illustrate that they nevertheless did *assert* the existence of systematic relationships between beliefs, actions, events, and even objects (if one includes such things as one's clothing). It is this "quick" and somewhat loose conception of theory that will undergird and characterize my discussion of theory in subsequent chapters.

In addition to the investigation of the early Quaker theory of preaching, this book is also about the Quaker practice of impromptu preaching. Of course, we can learn a great deal about their theorizing from their practice, but the practice itself is also worthy of examination. The historical (or contemporary) practice of impromptu preaching by any group initially raises at least three important questions, each with significant theoretical import: (1) Why did the preachers choose the impromptu method and reject the option of preparing ahead of time? (2) How did the preachers accomplish the task of speaking, sometimes at length, without specific preparation? and (3) How was the practice passed on to the next generation? Plausible answers to each of these questions can be developed by attending both to a group's theory and practice. For Quakers, the first question is essentially theological and philosophical in nature, but also bears on the relationship of epistemology to an understanding of rhetoric; the second and third questions, which depend a great deal on answers to the first, are more directly rhetorical and practical in nature. These three questions implicitly undergird the entire book. However, twelve specific questions help frame the chapters and their sequence.

Questions That Guide This Book

The following questions provide an investigative path for the chapters that ensue: (1) What significant features of the intellectual, religious, and sociopolitical milieu of the period 1650–1700 influenced the development of Quaker rhetorical theory and practice? (2) What were the early Quaker presuppositions about human nature, society, epistemology, and preaching that influenced the development of Quaker impromptu preaching theory and preaching practice over the second half of the seventeenth century? (3) How did key seventeenth-century Quaker writers contribute to the development of an early Quaker understanding of impromptu preaching and practice? (4) What were Robert Barclay's key contributions to the Quaker theory and practice of impromptu preaching? (5) How did Samuel Bownas' eighteenth-century ministry manual recapitulate and build upon earlier Quaker preaching theory and practice and contribute to its future? (6) What themes (or topics) are addressed in extant seventeenth-century Quaker sermons, and what are their implications? (7) What key metaphors are discovered in Quaker sermons, and how do they function rhetorically? (8) How is the "incantatory" style manifested in the sermons? (9) How are spatial terms employed in the sermons? (10) To what extent is the guilt appeal present in the surviving sermons? (11) How is personal testimony employed in the sermons? (12) How do George Fox, Stephen Crisp, Robert Barclay, and William Penn individually negotiate the rhetorically challenging impromptu preaching situation and enact Quaker impromptu preaching theory in four specific sermons?

Obstacles to the Study of Impromptu Preaching

The study of historical instances of impromptu or inspired preaching presents formidable challenges. In the first place, complete impromptu sermon texts available for study are rare, and when they do exist, they tell us little about performance (or delivery). Just as frustrating, one discovers a paucity of documents that suggest, let alone develop, a theory of rhetoric or homiletic that pertains to impromptu public address. The same might be said for evidence of a pedagogical practice or ritual for nurturing preachers who work in a culturally specific impromptu speaking tradition. The recent use of audio and video recording devices, along with the continued sophistication of careful field observation and the use of structured ethnographic interviews, has facilitated scholarly investigation of contemporary impromptu preaching, including its rationale(s) and supporting pedagogical system(s).[9] However, the examination of the historical theory and practice of impromptu preaching, in which recording, observation, and interviewing are out of the question, must involve a somewhat different process, which includes (1) the discovery of theoretical writings about the process of impromptu preaching as practiced in the specific historical and cultural setting; (2) the discovery and investigation of journals, tracts, biographies, and other published or unpublished materials for descriptions of the rationale of impromptu preaching in the historical context or collections of advice about its practice and inculcation; and (3) the discovery and analysis of surviving sermon texts, themselves texts that were taken down in shorthand or recalled by auditors in order to deduce from the actual practice a sense of its underlying rationale and stylistic habits and norms. Happily, seventeenth- and eighteenth-century Quakerism constitutes an historical instance of impromptu preaching that is adequately documented in both its theory and practice. Its comparatively accessible records invite scholarly investigation.

Confronting Myths about Early Quakers

Given the discussion above, it should be clear that public, vocal rhetoric was an important part of early Quaker life. However, as alluded to above, there is even today a common stereotype of the Quaker as a quiet individual whose form of worship allows little emphasis upon the spoken word. However correct this description of a Quaker may be when applied to some later historical or contemporary Quakers, it is not an accurate representation of the Quakers during their first fifty years. G. M. Trevelyan presents a more accurate image of early Quakerism when he writes, "In this first period of its power Quakerism . . . was revivalistic in its spirit and methods among the common people, rather than staid and 'Quiet' as it became in later generations."[10] The early Quakers exhibited a tension between silence and speech, but the spoken word was the norm, rather than the exception, for the first two generations of Quakers. In his important examination of the social history of early Quakerism, Arnold Lloyd makes this observation on the importance of public vocal ministry among early Quakers:

> It was the "common" or public preaching meeting rather than the silent meeting which was typical of Quaker ministry throughout our period (1669–1738). The records throughout the country bear witness to the tireless energy of men and women preachers without whose help the Society would have declined into insignificance. The Ministers both men and women were from the first the most potent influence within the fellowship.[11]

William C. Braithwaite, foremost modern historian of the early Quaker period, similarly concludes, "Friends were under a necessity to express themselves. They were continually driven to bear witness in the markets and the churches: they plunged with zest into the controversial debates which were the chief interest of that Puritan age."[12] Quakers were even numbered among the "enthusiasts" who came under attack during the period studied.[13]

As noted above, early Quakers preached "inspired" impromptu sermons, some of which have survived through auditor notetaking. These extant sermon texts can be examined rhetorically to investigate choices made by the preachers under conditions of impromptu speech, but also to discover what their rhetorical practice implies about a theory of preaching. Early Quakers also wrote about preaching in their theological and polemical writings. In addition, many of their numerous tracts, letters, and journals are available for examination to piece together their rationale for impromptu preaching or their advice about preaching practice. This book rises from analyses and interpretations of these surviving primary sources.

At the outset of this book, let me state that I believe that the primary sources reveal to us that early Quakers wanted to rediscover and reinvigorate the reality and vitality of early or "primitive" Christianity, and it is in that context that they also sought to make preaching as vital in their day as it was to the early church. Occasionally, these "evangelical" aspects of the sect's history and development have been de-emphasized or ignored. While the primary objective of this book is to present a rhetorically centered historical interpretation of the early Quaker approach to the theory and practice of impromptu preaching, by implication I will also be addressing misunderstanding and misrepresentation of early Quakers as theologically liberal and uniformly "silent," a belief present among my colleagues in the field of communication and rhetorical studies.[14] For these reasons, in this book I will base my conclusions as much as possible on my interpretations of primary sources discovered from Quakerism's early period rather than relying on conclusions drawn from secondary sources. However, I acknowledge that all analysis and writing of this sort is interpretive at base. I make no claim of scientific objectivity.

Statement of the Book's Purposes

In sum, in this book I aim to elucidate a significant human activity, the practice of self-consciously inspired impromptu speech, through an examination of the documents and surviving impromptu sermons of a particular and significant seventeenth-century Christian sect. Although not my main purpose in this book, I will also implicitly confront scholarship that "misreads" Quaker history, in this case the kind that interprets early Quakers according to a present-day quietistic theologically liberal theology. I acknowledge here the possibility of my committing the equally grievous error of reading Quaker history backwards through the lens of contemporary evangelical and pastoral Quakerism; however, I believe there is a greater tendency in this day, especially among intellectuals, to revise history along secular or theologically liberal lines.[15] In this book I will attempt to pay close attention to primary sources in an attempt to avoid both biases.

THE CONTEXTS INFORMING THIS BOOK

The Context of Rhetorical Studies

This book deals with impromptu preaching, a specific type of public address. However, in today's rhetorical scholarship, public address is but one instance of rhetorical practice that can include everything from public speaking to architecture. The notion of what is "rhetorical" has expanded significantly in the last three decades. To further complicate matters, "rhetoric" can refer to both the practice and theory of persuasion or "influence." One recent undergraduate textbook on rhetorical theory devotes sixteen pages to why it is impossible to state one definition of "rhetoric."[16] Similarly, in their impressive anthology of primary sources in rhetorical theory, Patricia Bizzell and Bruce Herzberg observe, "Rhetoric is a complex discipline with a long history: It is less helpful to try to define it once and for all than to look at the many definitions it has accumulated over the years and to attempt to understand how each arose and how each still inhabits and shapes the field."[17]

While a number of definitions of "rhetoric" might serve this book's purpose, its grounding in a historically situated rhetorical practice suggests the following definition as a logical begining: *"the attempt by one person or group to influence another through strategically selected and stylized speech."*[18] However, I must add that from an early Quaker perspective, the strategic *selection* of language and other aspects of style is as much determined by the preacher's sense of the immediate moving of the Spirit as it is from the recall of Scripture, remembrance of other preachers' exhortations, or any other device for enlarging upon ideas or images at the moment of utterance. In fact, the question of selection is at the heart of the Quaker theoretical project and will be a continuing focus of this book.

The resurgence and importance of historical-critical studies in the field of communication, and specifically the "renaissance" of public address studies, have been discussed at length elsewhere.[19] Here it is important for me to acknowledge that while I wholeheartedly support the vigorous extension of rhetorical studies into novel areas as varied as popular media and culture,[20] visual rhetoric,[21] and the rhetoric of music[22]—I have developed and teach courses in each of these areas—this book is grounded in the historical study of rhetorical phenomena, which continues to be a vital arena of rhetorical studies.[23]

This book ranges over and blends traditional and somewhat non-traditional approaches to rhetorical analysis. At the core of the book, and especially apparent in chapters 1–5, is text in context criticism, with context specifically separated in the first two chapters, which nonetheless employ quotes from Quaker sermon *texts* to illustrate context.[24] Chapters 4 and 5 concentrate on specific "theoretical" texts in their contexts in order to advance an understanding of Quaker homiletic theory. Chapters 9–12 dive more deeply into the close textual analysis of four specific extant sermons.[25] Chapters 6–8 are a bit more difficult to categorize methodologically because their conclusions are drawn from seventy-nine surviving seventeenth-century sermon texts spoken over a span of years by a variety of preachers. Here I trust Stephen E. Lucas' judgment when he includes my essay on Quaker metaphors in a long list of other scholarly works in his fastidiously detailed book review, "The Renaissance of American Public Address: Text and Context." There Lucas writes,

> While we have been concerned in this essay with the close analysis of individual texts with an eye toward explicating their rhetorical artistry, it is important to stress that there are many other important applications of textual study in public address. . . . At the center of rhetorical transactions and, I would argue, properly at the center of the critic's concern, is the text itself. This is true whether the text itself is Jonathan Smith's speech on the federal constitution . . . *a collection of Quaker sermons* . . . or Alain Resnais's classic film *Hiroshima, Mon Amour.*[26]

By Lucas' judgment, chapters 6–8 of this book are *textually based*, but it might be asserted with equal confidence that they employ initial textual analysis as a means of developing a catalogue of rhetorical choices by the preachers across the years, and also employ quotations from texts to illustrate rhetorical characteristics and their variations. Not until chapters 9–12 does the reader encounter analyses of full-text sermons. All of this having been said, in this book, when I am not attempting to ferret out a theory of Quaker-inspired discourse, I am employing close textual analysis to achieve a variety of ends.

The Context of Quaker Scholarship

It may also be helpful for me to situate this book within the burgeoning realm of Quaker studies. During the last fifty years, a number of scholars in the broader fields of history, theology, and English have turned their attention to the turbulent and momentous seventeenth century in England. Religious history of the period has generated considerable interest, and several excellent treatises and shorter monographs, begining in the 1950s and 1960s, dealing particularly with the history and theology of the early Quakers, precipitated what can only be described as a revolution in Quaker studies. These scholars of early Quakerism argued against the formerly accepted early twentieth-century notion that the roots of the sect germinated in the seedbed of continental mysticism. Instead, these revisionists saw the phenomenon of early Quakerism as "a natural, almost predictable outgrowth of Puritanism."[27] Later scholars responded to the Puritan interpretation of Quaker roots, followed by new interpretations, and so forth.[28] This vitality of new thinking about early Quakers led to a general expansion of scholarly activity in Quaker studies.

The implications of any revolution in historical interpretation to the rhetorical scholar are significant. I am reminded that rhetorical theory and practice can neither exist in nor arise out of a vacuum, and the same can be said for historical interpretations of rhetorical theory and practice.[29] P. Albert Duhamel situates himself in that tradition when he observes that rhetoric "canot be adequately interpreted apart from the ideological context in which it occurs."[30] A corollary to this idea is that an interpretation of rhetorical phenomena based solely upon a mystical interpretation of early Quaker underlying ideology must be an inadequate, or at least only a partial, interpretation. On the other hand, viewing Puritanism as a significant sociopolitical factor in Quaker origins would produce a different rationale of rhetoric from that produced by the frame of continental mysticism. Similarly, a mystical origins perspective on the part of the investigator would influence her or him to emphasize some aspects of rhetorical phenomena and de-emphasize, overlook, or discount others. As we have hinted, there are more recent and important historical interpretations beyond mysticism and Puritanism.[31]

More recently, several signs point to the conclusions that (1) Quaker studies have grown exponentially and (2) that multiple interpretations of Quaker origins have been posited and still exist. Let us see if we can quickly illustrate both conclusions at once. Three pieces of evidence are particularly compelling. The first is the publication of numerous books about Quakers, many written by non-Quakers (a possible response to Barry Reay's observation that there is too much "co-religionist" work in

Quaker studies), a selection of which is included in this volume's bibliography. Books are a sign of vitality in any field.[32] Second, the Quaker Studies Research Association was formed in 1992 and began to publish a fully refereed scholarly journal, *Quaker Studies*, in 1995. The international journal has represented a comparatively wide range of scholarly approaches by Quakers and non-Quakers. The third sign is the 2004 publication of a particular volume titled *The Creation of Quaker Theory: Insider Perspectives* (hereafter *Quaker Theory*).[33] Edited by Ben Pink Dandelion, program leader at the Centre for Postgraduate Quaker Studies at Woodbrooke Quaker Studies Centre (Birmingham, England), the book stands as a watershed in Quaker thought. It highlights the variegated contemporary approaches to the scholarly study of Quakers and Quakerism by Quaker scholars ranging from careful historical study to an "activist" position, a challenge to apply principles of Quaker thought and belief to contemporary culture. In his review of the book, Stephen W. Angell, who is clearly skeptical of the term "theory" when applied to Friends, advises, "If you want an introduction to the illuminating turns Quaker scholarship has been taking in the past generation, this book will be a very helpful resource."[34]

As "exhibit A" of Quaker scholarly vitality, the book is more than a resource; it stands as a carefully presented statement about the state of the art in Quaker scholarship produced by Quaker scholars, the "insiders," the "co-religionists." This is not the place to comment extensively on this significant book, but let me remark briefly on two topics that have direct pertinence to this introductory chapter. First, in Pink Dandelion's introduction to *Quaker Theory*, he overviews several modern and contemporary Quaker approaches to "theory." Developing in the nineteenth century and holding sway until the 1950s, the "mystical" interpretation of Quaker history mentioned above, propounded by Rufus Jones and William C. Braithwaite, yielded eventually to the "Puritan" interpretation of Quaker history, also mentioned previously, espoused by Frederick Tolles, Geoffrey Nuttall, Henry J. Cadbury, and Hugh Barbour. Pink Dandelion also asserts that in the 1950s Lewis Benson, an independent scholar, as well questioned the mystical interpretation and argued for "a more prophetic understanding of what Quakerism was about" by concentrating mainly on the writings of George Fox.[35] Pink Dandelion also notes that John Punshon may represent a fourth approach to Quaker theory in his writings because Punshon asserts that "different types of history start from different premises and lead to different results."[36] Feminist studies represent a fifth approach to Quakerism.[37] This list, if anything, points out the impossibility of establishing a predominant or "accepted" theory of Quaker studies and also reveals that "coreligionists" can produce a variety of interpretations.

The plot deepens in Pink Dandelion's conclusion to the volume, in which he presents a visual model of Quaker theory, a tetrahedron, which he constructs from the essays contributed to the book. The three sides of the geometric figure are (1) mainline, (2) metaphysical, and (3) metatemporal. The mainline group represents Quakerism "as one Christian group amongst many who draw their heritage from earlier spiritual insights and who happen to appear at the time of the English Civil War." The metaphysical group emphasizes "the aspect of union, either physically or metaphysically, between God and humanity."[38] For this group, "the mysticism of [Rufus] Jones' interpretation [of Quaker origins] is only a taken-for-granted starting point." Third, the metatemporal group sees "unfolding eschatological realization, or 'realising eschatology,' as central to a reading of Quaker history across time," an approach energized by Douglas Gwyn's writings and seconded by the careful historical scholarship of Rosemary Moore. Finally, on the floor of the tetrahedron is a sociological approach, represented by Gay Pilgrim, an approach that "is interested in the sociological impulses of the group, regardless of their theology," a position that emphasizes sociological description and interpretation and gives "an account of what is going on, theology aside."[39]

The implications of the development in Quaker historical interpretation or "theorizing" are very significant to the present book, as I trust is already apparent or will soon become clear. Here let me point out that the specific rhetorical concerns of this book on Quaker homiletics do not find direct voice in *Quaker Theory*. The view represented in this book perhaps fits into that described by John Punshon, where "different types of history start from different premises and lead to different results," the starting point here being rhetorical studies. As I have stated, this book concerns early Quaker "theorizing" about, and practice of, vocal rhetoric—preaching—and its intellectual, theoretical, pedagogical, and methodological framework. Curiously, the terms "sermon" and "preaching" do not appear in the index of *Quaker Theory*. Quaker rhetorical theorizing is only obliquely addressed in the book but will be central here.[40] On the one hand, this situation is somewhat discouraging because the early Quaker world is, if anything, rhetorical. It is replete with sometimes vigorous and heated struggle over the construction and expression of meaning. The movement is carried through history on the back of street preachers and print propagandists. Allow me to refer again to the definition of "rhetoric" that informs this study: *"the attempt by one person or group to influence another through strategically selected and stylized speech."*[41] Let me also assert from the point of view of Kenneth Burke, whose writings constitute a broader and more comprehensive view of "rhetoric," that early Quaker rhetorical practice is all about how *identification*—Burke's term for the essential goal of rhetorical discourse—may and may not be achieved, both within the group and between the group and the larger culture.[42] In sum, *Quaker Theory* lacks a chapter that directly addresses Quaker rhetorical theory and practice, but on the other hand, the absence of a systematic consideration of early Quaker rhetorical theory and practice is a strong rationale for the book you hold in your hands.

The Context of Previous Scholarship on Quaker Preaching and Sermons

This project builds on the foundation of a small group of writers who preceded me. A few scholars have commented on or presented analyses of Quaker preaching. For purposes of this section, I will briefly mention writers who touch on my topic, but spend the bulk of my time focusing on a select group of writers who move beyond the merely historical framework of early Quaker preaching and speculate about its theory and general practice.

Historians have acknowledged sermons along with tracts to be important historical events and have treated them as data in their historical and biographical accounts. For example, Braithwaite's histories of Quakerism during its first two periods, which remain standard definitive works for the years covered, do not set out a Quaker rhetorical (or homiletic) theory and do not report an analysis of the sermon literature from 1650 to 1700.[43] Likewise, Rufus Jones' *Spiritual Reformers in the 16th and 17th Centuries* and *The Quakers in the American Colonies*, although helpful in presenting one historical interpretation of the roots of Quakerism and its early years, are lacking in any treatment of Quaker theory and practice of preaching.[44] When the topic of preaching is broached by these writers, for example, their approach is to mention the topic of the sermon (where possible) and its relationship to the life of the preacher. A pertinent example of the way in which the sermon literature is reported is Braithwaite's consideration of the last sermon preached by the early Quaker leader William Dewsbury (1621–1688). After quoting a lengthy passage from the sermon, which he says "gives a taste of the earnestness and power of his ministry," Braithwaite remarks, "Such words express the spirit of Dewsbury's own life. Without either the practical genius of Fox or the finely tempered mind of Barclay, he excelled the former in tenderness and the second in depth."[45] Because the historian is not operating as a text in context critic, his remarks do not illuminate the passage for us, nor do they tell us how the language is working toward rhetorical ends; his observations stress that the sermon was expressive of Dewsbury, whom he contrasts with George Fox (1621–1691), the founder of Quakerism, and Robert Barclay (1648–1690), Quakerism's best-known apologist. When Braithwaite puts down his pen, Dewsbury's sermon still awaits the application of rhetorical criticism.

Hugh Barbour, in contrast, must be numbered among writers whose work has moved beyond historical commentary alone toward potentially rich theoretical material about impromptu preaching. His *The Quakers in Puritan England* is a one-volume scholarly account dealing primarily with the years 1652–1665.[46] Barbour provides an important corrective to the mystical view of Quaker beginings espoused by Jones and presents a masterful analysis of Quakerism in the socioreligious climate of pre-Restoration England. His work is particularly germane to this book because, unlike his predecessors, he treats the rhetorical aspects of early Quaker preaching. In an important chapter, which he calls "Debate with Puritan Pastors," he characterizes the rhetorical method of Quaker preachers before 1660 as "a massive assault on any point of guilt in his hearers,"[47] and one in which fierce judgment and condemnation became the rule. Barbour argues that the role of the Quaker minister is that of "matchmaker" rather than priest, in that the preacher felt obligated only to "prepare the way for what God would do."[48] Barbour implies that the Quaker preacher's "take-it-or-leave-it" stance stemmed directly from the presupposition that the "Inward Light" of Christ, not the persuasive effort of the preacher, was the primary instrument of conversion, and that each hearer had the sole responsibility to react to the Light rather than to any use the preacher might make of the arts of discourse. Barbour also contrasts Puritan and early Quaker preaching and concludes that the former more often emphasized God's love, while the latter emphasized God's judgment. Barbour also compares the two groups with regard to their differing epistemology, theology, view of authority, view of education, and additional minor subjects. He exhibits throughout his work an understanding of rhetoric as a tool of persuasion; thus his writings constitute valuable pioneer effort in the analysis of the presuppositions of the earliest period of Quaker rhetoric. His treatment of rhetorical stance, for instance, invites the rhetorician to search for evidence of similar attitude in the years past the Restoration. Following Barbour's lead, I will report an examination of later Quaker sermons for instances of the "massive assault on any point of guilt," which Barbour sees as a hallmark of the earliest period of Quaker preaching. Similarly, attempts by Quakers to develop a theoretical structure for inspired preaching will be examined to see if they reflect the opinion that the Inward Light, rather than the rhetorical strategies of the preacher, serves as the primary persuasive instrument.

Barbour's work is excellent as far as it goes. Inasmuch as only one sermon text, which may itself be a fragment, survives the period prior to the 1670s, Barbour does not offer examples of actual sermon technique except as sermon fragments or as reconstructions reported in Quaker journals. Thus having little to examine in the way of actual full Quaker sermon texts, his concern with rhetoric is weighted toward its theoretical side, particularly its presuppositions, emphasizing its theological roots and implications. He lightly touches on such important areas as style, the relationships of style and presuppositions, and rhetorical strategies in Quaker sermons, other than the "massive assault on guilt," which is itself an important theoretical insight. Furthermore, in Barbour's study we see Quaker rhetoric in terms of its raw beginnings, while the full maturity of some of the significant early leaders came later. George Fox, George Whitehead (1636–1723), Stephen Crisp (1628–1692), William Penn (1644–1718), and William Dewsbury, to name four, are among the early leaders who continued their work to the last decade of the century and, in the case of Penn and Whitehead, into the next. A final observation on Barbour's work is that, despite his sensitivity to the importance of rhetoric, this topic is more peripheral than central to his study, which is to say, his work is that of an accomplished historian of religion, not a rhetorical critic.

Douglas Gwyn must also be acknowledged as an important thinker who has written about some of the rhetorical implications of interpreting the earliest Quakers from the framework of a "realising eschatology" discovered in Fox's writings.[49] By Gwyn's reading, Fox's belief that Christ had come to teach his people himself "meant an end to biblical preaching as such; the Quaker preacher must preach *from the Word's voice within*. Christ himself must preach through the human instrumentality."[50] This preaching, based on immediate revelation, did away with "customary preaching" in weekly set sermons. Gwyn also notes that in Fox's view, true worship is waiting on the Lord in a silent assembly, during which "Christ may move any man or woman to speak his message aloud to the gathered meeting."[51] In the moment of utterance, the gathered people are to experience "the *apocalypse* of the Word of God—an immediate revelation whose content is the end of the world."[52] Such a social and public context produced an intense sense of gravity. Gwyn writes, "to speak when not led or to speak beyond one's leading is to exalt oneself and not Christ; not to speak when one is led to speak is to 'quench the spirit' and 'despise the prophecy' (1 Thess 5:19f)."[53] In this prophetic context, there is not even a hint about rhetorical strategies useful to the impromptu preacher. Gwyn's interpretation is focused largely on Fox's beliefs and influence, and it will be important to trace some of the implications of the notion of realized apocalyptic and its influence across the years and writers dealt with in this book.[54]

Scholars interested in the literary aspects of early Quaker rhetoric have generally neglected, trivialized, or ignored the actual sermon literature, concentrating instead upon the numerous tracts and journals from the period. In 1932 Luella M. Wright published her important study, *The Literary Life of the Early Friends, 1650–1725*, which surveys the period, paying particular attention to the tract, journal, and confessional literature of Friends.[55] Wright's purpose is to "direct attention to a descriptive analysis of the Quakerly and literary qualities dominating the writings of the seventeenth- and early eighteenth-century Friends."[56] She was principally influenced by the mystical interpretation of Quaker origins prominent at the time of her writing and understandably views the works she surveys through a mystical lens. Furthermore, her perspective is that of twentieth-century liberal Quakerism, which often borders on the beliefs of Unitarianism. For example, she characterizes the preaching of Fox in this manner: "George Fox centered his teaching about the *inner Light*—the belief that a spark of divine essence dwells in each human being, and that if obedience is yielded to this inner Light or Word that man can be led into all Truth and thus possess a guide for the intricate problems of daily living and for the conduct of life."[57]

In reality, Fox did not use the term "inner Light" to refer to his spiritual experience. Inner Light as a term came into vogue through the influence of twentieth-century liberal Quakerism.[58] Fox and the "First Publishers-of Truth," as the early Quaker evangelists were called, used the terms "Inward Light," "Seed," or several others, all of which were identified with the working of Jesus Christ in a person's life. As we shall see, the Light was not considered to be an inherent part of the human psyche that shone *outward*, but rather the *inward* enlightening of and from God to every person. Wright's account of this basic presupposition alone reveals a bias that influenced her reading of the early Quakers and puts in question her evaluation of their sermon making. In any case, she does not concentrate on the sermons themselves, although she reports knowledge of the existence of the majority of the published extant sermons. She includes a short chapter on "Sermons, Proverbs, and Advices," which serves to introduce the subject and makes little use of textual analysis. Wright appears to dismiss the sermons with the somewhat curt comment, "these sermons on examination prove to be gospel exhortations, and also like many other sermons of the century, were devoid of incident and illustrative material."[59] Wright does not report an analysis of the sermons against the context of the times, and that task not only remained undone, but her judgment that early Quaker sermons were only "gospel exhortations" without a strong narrative base stood to be further explored or corrected.

Another literary scholar, Jackson I. Cope, published an extensive and provocative monograph titled "Seventeenth Century Quaker Style" in which he posits several characteristics of early Friends' use of language.[60] His work is so important that it demands a more detailed examination. Cope aims to "discover those bedrock aspects of expression which are demonstrably homologous with the profoundest conception of life shared by the first Quakers." Relevant to the early Quaker "conception of life," he discusses "the idea which was even more important than the Light Within, the conception of the 'Name.'"[61] Cope argues that in early Quaker writings, the concept that the proper name of a thing is derived from experiential knowledge of the name of Christ, itself subsumed the concept of the Inward Light. I believe that Cope overstated the case here; that the concept of the name was important to early Quakers, as indeed it was for the writers of the Old and New Testaments, is undeniable, but its overriding preeminence in early Quaker thought is a moot point. However, it is unecessary to accept Cope's view that it was the *essential* presupposition in order to understand or accept his other significant observations on early Quaker style.

Cope's most important contribution is his analysis of the stylistic characteristics of early Quaker discourse. The first, he asserts, is "the essential quality of seventeenth-century Quaker expression, manifesting itself in several guises." That quality is "a tendency to break down the boundary between literalness and metaphor, between conceptions and things." He explains the phenomenon as a situation in which "metaphor has transcended its normal function, and instead of merely indicating a point of resemblances between two differentiable entities, it has totally merged them."[62]

The second stylistic peculiarity Cope observes is a certain function of Quaker discourse, which he believes reflected "the epistemology of verbal incantation." Explaining this quality of discourse, he notes, "it appears when Christ is speaking within the Quaker, and showing forth the Word which is Alpha and Omega, begining and end of understanding the runes of eternity." In point of fact, observes Cope, the incantatory style often produced language characterized by "an incredible repetition, a combining and recombining of a cluster of words and phrases drawn from Scripture." The style was used by both educated and noneducated writers, and often the result was "not ungrammatical, but agrammatical: the intense concentration upon individual words wholly removes the process of expression from a grammatical frame of reference, as the mind is driven on too rapidly to formalize the restraining relationships between sentence elements."[63]

Cope's third observation is essentially the logical extension of blending literalness and metaphor. He maintains that early Quaker writers consistently emphasized the spiritual nature of their concrete experiences, seldom giving detailed descriptions of events: "Scripture phraseology which is inevitably borrowed or adapted for the telling becomes more important than any temporal events it might obscure." Ultimately, Cope writes, "contemporary Quaker experiences seem to have no import to their subjects but as a framework on which to string the language wherein the Scriptures tell the scriptural story of patriarchs and apostles alike."[64]

In addition to analyzing the stylistic characteristics of early Quaker prose, Cope documents a change in Quaker style during the third quarter of the seventeenth century when, he argues, "this mode of viewing life as *scriptura rediviva*, like the 'incantatory' style, withered and disappeared." What became common in the last part of the century was the "self-conscious analogizing through Scripture imagery which sounds only a faint echo of the immediacy of the same phrases on the tongues of the early Publishers of Truth."[65] Cope enumerates the causes of the stylistic change as "the anti-evangelical force of . . . rising Calvinism within the Society [of Friends], . . . the natural anti-enthusiasm of men like Penn," and the establishment of the Second Day's Morning Meeting in 1673, the most important function of which "was to pass upon Quaker manuscripts offered for publication."[66]

Cope's analysis of early Quaker style is restricted to such sources as tracts, letters, and journals, leaving untouched the extant sermon literature from 1674 onward. However, his work offers direction for fruitful analysis of surviving early Quaker sermons. Although he focuses upon style, Cope develops an area of significance to the full study of Quaker rhetoric by characterizing the preachers' customary stylistic habits. His explanation of the qualities of early Quaker style is an excellent statement and suggests three hypotheses that I will apply to the surviving sermon literature: (1) that the style of the sermons exhibits a certain blending of literalness and metaphor, (2) that the style of the sermons can be described as "the epistemology of verbal incantation," and (3) that instances from everyday life in the sermons are used mainly as opportunities for viewing life as *scriptura rediviva*.

Such an extension of Cope's work is valuable for three reasons. First, it will have the obvious value of confirming or qualifying Cope's viewpoint on the change of style in the fourth quarter of the seventeenth century, because the majority of the surviving sermons were preached later in the century. Second, the application will help confirm or qualify Cope's three observations on the characteristics of Quaker style. One would expect the characteristics, especially the incantatory style, to be just as prevalent (if not more prevalent) in impromptu sermons taken down in shorthand as it is in discourse especially composed to be printed, as Cope found it. Finally, the extension of Cope's study is valuable because of the peculiar value of the sermons themselves; that is, they were either printed initially by non-Quakers or never printed, and thus presumably did not come under the initial censoring eye of the Second Day's Morning Meeting."[67] It is important to assess to what extent the incantatory style survived in the sermonizing of the later portion of the century.

In 1962 Maurice A. Creasey published a study that attempted to account for differences in the usage of spatial terms by early Quakers.[68] He notes, "On almost every page of the writings of early Friends the reader feels that he is being challenged to recognize a contrast. This contrast is expressed most frequently in spatial terms by such correlatives as 'inward' and 'outward,' 'within' and 'without,' 'internal' and 'external.'" Creasey compares three groups of writers: (1) that represented by George Fox and James Nayler, from whom "we hear the authentic accents of a profound and vivid evangelical Christian experience, relatively uninfluenced by formal education or theological and philosophical reflection"; (2) that represented by Isaac Pennington, whose "Christian experience is expressed through a profoundly mystical personality possessed of marked ability for religious introspection;" and (3) that represented by William Penn and Robert Barclay, who exhibited a "conscious and explicit intention to relate Quakerism to the theological and philosophical interests of the age."[69] After examining writings from the three groups, Creasey finds that there is a change in the intended meaning of the spatial terms from the earlier, more "primitive" writers such as Fox to the later, more philosophic writers such as Penn and Barclay. He concludes, "particularly at the hands of Robert Barclay, and largely in terms of a confused and illegitimate application of the originally clear and valid distinction between 'inward' and 'outward,' Quakerism became wedded to a prevalent and quasi-Cartesian dualism and, as a consequence, set its feet upon paths which, for many a year, led it into barren places of quietism and formalism."[70]

Creasey's analysis remains an important contribution to the study of early Quaker rhetoric because it identifies the contrast of spatial terms as a significant characteristic of Quaker style, and, more importantly, because it describes the differences in usage with reference to underlying philosophical presuppositions. Like Cope's work, Creasey's contains no direct mention of surviving sermons. Nevertheless, his brief but important study suggests two directions of fruitful analysis of the sermon literature. It intimates first that the contrast of spatial terms will be found in the sermons with some frequency, and second that the differences in usage which he found would also be apparent in the sermons.[71]

Among scholars who have concentrated on the history of the preaching ministry, only Lucia K. Beamish has published a work dealing particularly with Quaker ministry. She studied Quaker ministry from 1691 to 1834.[72] Her work, unlike that of Cope and Creasey, makes use of some sermon texts and is especially valuable for insights into Quaker preaching during the eighteenth century. Beamish, however, only briefly considers preaching before 1690. Her treatment of the roots of the Quaker conception of a minister is informative, and her characterization of Quaker ministry as both deliberate and spontaneous, depending upon the circumstances, moves toward a conceptual model for the analysis of two modes of Quaker preaching.[73] Beamish herself does not present such an analysis. Her consideration of Stephen Crisp's preaching, for example, consists of quoting from his sermons to illustrate "His Faith in the triumphant power of the Gospel," or again, "Crisp's understanding of the aim and value of ministry."[74] She does not examine how Crisp used language strategies to accomplish the rhetorical ends arising from the exigencies of a rhetorical situation. Occasionally she identifies the use of imagery and cites a passage from a sermon as illustration. Because of her wider aim and time frame, Beamish does not present a comprehensive examination of either the development of Quaker homiletic theory or Quaker sermons from the seventeenth century.

A perusal of the standard histories of preaching indicates an obvious lack of research on the rhetoric of the early Quakers. Thomas H. Pattison does not include any Quakers among the preachers he considers, although he devotes limited space to early Quaker preaching as a part of the development of lay preaching in England.[75] Edwin C. Dargan, although generally more extensive than Pattison, does not deal at all with Quaker preaching.[76] His work is valuable, however, for his treatment of Anglican and Puritan preaching in seventeenth-century England. F. R. Webber's work follows Dargan's very closely both in organization and illustrative material for the seventeenth century in England, and it, like Dargan's, does not mention Quaker preaching.[77]

Two standard works on English preaching are worthy of mention because they illustrate the manner in which Quaker preaching has been overlooked in works that focus on the seventeenth century. Caroline Richardson's *English Preachers and Preaching, 1640–1670* is a helpful book, now unfortunately out of print, which provides valuable information on the importance of preaching in its customary form for the period covered.[78] Fox is the only Quaker preacher briefly mentioned by Richardson. W. Fraser Mitchell's *English Pulpit Oratory from Andrewes to Tillotson: A Study of Its Literary Aspects* is likewise out of print.[79] This work deals with the "achievements or shortcomings of the better-known preachers."[80] Mitchell includes no Quakers, and his extensive bibliography cites no extant Quaker sermons.

Horton Davies' important study of English worship and theology in the seventeenth century treats Quaker worship, noting the similarities between Quakers and early Baptists.[81] Although Davies devotes attention to "Quaker Worship: Its Characteristics," stressing helpfully that silence was not an "absolute requirement,"[82] disappointingly, he also refers to the "inner light," rather than the accurate "inward light," an unfortunate linguistic choice he must have habituated through his secondary sources. More significantly, at his hands, Quaker impromptu inspired preaching merits no detailed description or analysis.[83]

Richard Bauman has produced the most important scholarship dealing with the seventeenth-century Quaker rhetorical world. Beginning with an important 1970 essay appearing in *Quarterly Journal of Speech*, he has cracked open early Quaker rhetoric like none other. In the early essay, he considers "certain distinctive patterns of language usage" among the seventeenth-century Friends and concludes that "the rhetoric of the early Quakers was not simply a rhetoric of words, but a unified rhetoric of symbolic action."[84] Bauman emphasizes the idea of "truth" as being fundamental to Quaker thought and considers the Quaker rejection of "you" in the second-person singular—the well-known peculiar pronominal usage—as a manifestation of the Quaker tenet of truth. He speculates upon its effect on English society and the Quaker movement itself and also ponders the Quaker distrust of human-motivated effort, concluding that this attitude resulted in the Quaker concept of silence. In this essay he does not, however, distinguish among the early Quakers, as did Creasey, nor between the early and late seventeenth-century Quakers, as did Cope, Creasey, and Beamish,[85] a development that he takes up in subsequent publications.

In 1974 Bauman published an important essay titled "Speaking in the Light: The Role of the Quaker Minister," where he focuses on the tension between speaking and silence as experienced by the earliest Quaker vocal ministers.[86] He explores the early development of Quaker meetings, differences between praying and preaching, postures of delivery and gesture, and differences between Quakers speaking in a Quaker meeting and Quakers speaking among non-Friends, and, most importantly, he provides a lengthy consideration of the preacher's inner struggle over whether or not to speak. Bauman concludes, "This was a mixing of speaking and silence within a single behavioral frame in which both components, otherwise contradictory, were indispensable."[87]

Bauman's most important contribution to an understanding of early Quaker rhetoric, especially Quakers' understanding of the place and role of preaching, is his book *Let Your Words be Few: Symbolism of Speaking and Silence among Seventeenth-Century Quakers*.[88] In the volume Bauman explores "the role of speaking and silence in Quaker ideology and action."[89] Silence, he maintains, became a metaphor for the suppression of self and self-will in an effort to hear the voice of the Spirit (the Inward Voice or the Inward Light). Speaking was suspect, thus the often repeated injunction, "Let your words be few." The exception to the rule was "properly motivated" speaking, both within Quaker meetings and for evangelistic efforts outside them as well. In chapter 3, the core of his book for purposes of this project, Bauman illustrates how the Quaker form of impromptu speaking rested on a theory of rhetoric: "true communication and persuasion were effected by the reaching of the Light in another person. Truth was felt in the resonant chord struck within one's conscience by another's message." Bauman argues that for Quakers, "religious practice was systematically reduced to the Word. . . . [L]egitimate speaking was not only important to Quaker ministerial practice, for the Quaker ministers it was their sole *raison d'être* and the only basis and means of their authority."[90]

In chapter 5 Bauman develops concepts he first introduced in 1974. Here he analyzes the contexts of Quaker preaching in terms of Quaker agrarian imagery: there were meetings for "plowing," "sowing," "cultivating," and "harvesting." Plowing and sowing occurred when the ministers confronted non-Quakers and attempted to evangelize them. Cultivating and harvesting occurred largely at "threshing" meetings, where attempts were made to separate non-Quakers from their prior sectarian ties. Here Bauman considers matters of style and delivery. Following an ethnographic format developed by Dell Hymes, Bruce Rosenberg, and Denis Tedlock, Bauman discusses style by reconstructing a passage from one of Fox's sermons. The result is a demonstration of Fox's ability to employ "formulaic" devices "to enhance fluency in spontaneous oral composition,"[91] a strategy we will look for in chapter 9, which focuses on one of Fox's sermons.

The tension between silence and speaking surfaces again in Bauman's chapter 8, this time with a specific focus on the Quaker preacher. He summarizes the tension in this way: "Any speaking during worship must emerge from the inward silence of the speaker and be directed toward bringing the auditors to silence or enhancing the condition of silence in which they already reside."[92] Bauman also catalogues the growing tendency among Quakers to scrutinize and control vocal ministry as the movement matured toward the end of the seventeenth century.

The final chapter of Bauman's book traces, in Max Weber's terms, Quakerism's change from "charismatic" movement to "sect." Bauman illustrates the process of "conventionalization" and the broader process of "routinization" by focusing on how Quaker ministerial performance was formalized. He considers how ministers became accountable to "elders," a principle to which the earliest Quakers would not have adhered. By 1689, Bauman maintains, the formerly "unfettered prophetic ministry" had been routinized and "brought under corporate control." Always conscious of his primary subject—"that speaking is fundamentally constitutive of social life"[93]—Bauman discovers the change in developments in Quaker preaching style.

In my *Quarterly Journal of Speech* review of Bauman's book, I assert, "[Bauman] has produced a first-rate piece of careful scholarship that richly illuminates the life of a rhetorically-energized social movement. His work deserves a place in the canon of rhetorical scholarship,"[94] a position I still hold. It stands as the only book-length consideration of seventeenth-century Quaker rhetoric.[95]

PREVIEW OF THIS BOOK

Scope of the Book

This book is divided into four sections which, taken together, set out the early Quaker theory of impromptu, inspired preaching; illustrate its practice; and critically explore the preaching of four important preachers through focus on four significant sermons. The first section sets out some contextual considerations spaning the period 1650–1700. With respect to my consideration of the development of a Quaker theory of inspired discourse, the second section of the book begins with Fox's *Journal* in 1646 and ends in 1750, with my exploration of Samuel

Bownas' eighteenth-century manual of inspired ministry, a book that reflects the century-long period since the beginings of Quakerism. As regards the sermon texts themselves, which are the focus of the book's third and fourth sections, because of my determination to deal with full texts, and because only one sermon text survives the first two decades of the early Quaker period, this book best reflects the years 1671–1700, the period after the years of most vitality and growth in early Quakerism. Authorities record an enlivened and geometric growth of Quakerism after 1652.[96] By the late 1690s, however, many of the early leaders were gone. Fox died in 1691, and Crisp followed in 1692. Penn lived until 1718, but he was increasingly involved in the problems of Pennsylvania and endured a series of strokes, and perhaps these reasons account for the fact that none of his sermons after 1700 have survived. Scholars, notably Bauman, also have observed and documented a change in the activities and beliefs of Quakers in the mid-1690s.[97] With good reason we may conclude that after the period covered in this study, the emphasis on preaching among Quakers was either non-existent, in some cases, or different, in others, from what it had been in most of the last half of the seventeenth century. G. M. Trevelyan noted in this respect that the Quakers of the early eighteenth century "left to Wesley the task of popular revivalism, wherein they themselves had laboured fervently in the days of their founder."[98]

The majority of this book is centered on extant sermon texts. Indeed, that is one of its unique contributions. In truth, the bulk of the sermons from which I draw inferences about Quaker preaching theory and practice were delivered during the waning years of the early period. No sermons for which dates can be accurately established survived the tumultuous 1660s, and only eight sermons are represented from the 1670s. With the exception of Penn's 1699 Farewell Sermon, the majority of sermons studied—all of Crisp's and the remainder of Penn's—were delivered in the 1680s and early 1690s. The sermons, then, give us a picture of the maturity of early Quaker sermon rhetoric, rather than its birth and adolescence. The period the sermons truly represent also reflects the cumulative effects of various attempts to ensure Quakerism's survival through organization, the influence of elders, and control of expression.[99]

The scope of this book is necessarily limited by the availability of primary sources and particularly by the actual number of surviving sermon texts for chapters 6–8. The corpus of sermons omits several figures in early Quakerism known to be powerful preachers, from whom no sermons have survived.[100] However, the sermons are representative of the later period of early Quaker preaching, its more mature period prior to Quakerism's "quietistic" era. Twenty-three men are represented by sermons ranging from the spirited and unlettered Fox to the courtly and learned Barclay and Penn.[101] The majority of the sermons issued from the minds of Fox, Crisp, and Penn, men different enough in temperament and language usage to provide interesting contrasts in Quaker rhetorical *modus operandi*.

Geographically, chapters 6–12 (third and fourth sections) are limited to the places at which the sermons were delivered: (1) eight locations in and about London; (2) Chester, England; (3) Bristol, England; (4) two unspecified locations on Barbados; and (5) one unknown location in the American colonies.[102] This seeming limitation is insignificant when one considers that Quakers, from the first, relied upon traveling ministers who eventually, in most cases, made their way to London at one time or other, and many made voyages to America. Although the majority of the sermons, and all four sermons in chapters 9–12, were delivered in London and its environs, the ministers delivering them represented a much larger geographic area. In sum, the surviving sermons, despite the limitations they place upon this project, are a remarkable collection, representative of Quaker impromptu preaching from 1671 to 1700.[103]

Preview of Chapters

The first section of this book includes two chapters that sketch the contextual background out of which Quaker impromptu preaching emerged. Chapter 1 deals with cultural constraints and sets out in broad brushstrokes the intellectual, religious, and sociopolitical milieu of later seventeenth-century England. It also attempts to capture a still shot of rhetorical and homiletic theory in that age, all with a view toward determining the constraints within which early Quaker rhetoric developed and was practiced. The second contextual chapter reconstructs the early Quaker worldview, with particular attention to the presuppositions that directly underlie their rhetorical theory and practice, including their views on the nature of human beings, their outlook on society, and their view of epistemology.

The second section includes three chapters that trace the development of the early Quaker theory of impromptu preaching. Chapter 3 focuses on the development of early Quaker conceptions of the purposes and instrumentalities of preaching. The discussion considers writings and commentaries by a number of significant seventeenth-century Quaker commentators on preaching, including George Fox, Margaret Fell, Rebecca Smith, George Whitehead, Charles Marshall, Stephen Crisp, and Benjamin Coole. Chapter 4 concentrates solely on Robert Barclay's significant contributions to an understanding of immediate revelation and inspired speech discovered in his *An Apology for the True Christian Divinity* and *The Possibility and Necessity of the Inward and Immediate Revelation of the Spirit of God* (hereafter referred to as *Apology* and *Immediate Revelation*, respectively). Chapter 5, the third and final chapter of the second section, focuses on Samuel Bownas' *A Description of the Qualifications Necessary to a Gospel Minister*, an eighteenth-century homiletic manual for Quaker itinerant ministers, the full expression and culminating statement of the earlier Quaker impromptu preaching tradition.

The third section reports in three chapters an examination of the seventy-nine surviving sermons from the period 1671–1700. Chapter 6 describes the concepts or themes that were actually mentioned or developed in the surviving sermons. The chapter notes the sermons' recurrent terms or themes, which stood for concepts also developed in other sermons, tracts, letters, and "epistles." Three categories of "themes" are examined: (1) theological themes, (2) themes which discuss guidance for individual behavior, and (3) themes dealing with Quaker attitudes toward current society. Each theme is identified, a quantitative estimate of its role in the sermons is established, and illustrations of its manifestation in the sermons are provided through quotations.

Key metaphors discovered in the sermons are the subject of chapter 7. Five significant conceptual metaphors (or clusters) are identified: (1) the light-dark metaphor, (2) the guiding voice metaphor, (3) the seed metaphor, (4) the hunger-thirst metaphor, and (5) the journey or pilgrimage metaphor. In each case, the quantitative significance of the metaphor is estimated, and its functional role in Quaker sermons is illustrated and analyzed.

Four salient characteristics of early Quaker sermons, in addition to themes and key metaphors, are identified and illustrated in chapter 8. The characteristics include (1) the development of the "catechital" style, which employed rhetorical questions, dialogues, and "queries"; (2) the extensive use of spatial terms; (3) the use of the guilt appeal;

and (4) the use of personal testimony. Cope's argument that both the blending of literalness and metaphor—*scriptura rediviva*—and the incantatory style waned during the last quarter of the century is tested in light of evidence from the surviving sermons from the later period. Creasey's argument that Barclay's and Penn's use of spatial terms differed significantly from that of Fox and the earliest Quakers is, likewise, examined in light of the evidence presented in the surviving sermons. Finally, I also examine, with reference to the sermons of the period 1671–1700, Barbour's conclusion that the preaching of early Quakers was characterized by a massive assault on guilt.

The fourth section of this volume applies a text-in-context approach to four important sermons by four significant early Quaker "publick Friends." In each case, the sermon text is included at the end of the chapter. Chapter 9 concentrates on a sermon by Quaker founder George Fox and his need to achieve legitimacy with his hearers through articulate impromptu speech during the 1674 Yearly Meeting in London. As always, Fox faced an "audience" of Quakers who expected him to speak only if immediately moved by the Spirit. On this occasion, he believed that he had a calling to organize the radical Christian sect in ways that would offer succor to its members who keenly experienced persecution in British society, but he also sought to enlist the full skills of women in ministry by insisting on the organization of separate business meetings for men and women, a somewhat controversial move among Quakers. If he chose not to speak, he would likely lose legitimacy in the eyes of his hearers. Similarly, if he spoke poorly, was not perceived as speaking under the impulse of the Inward Light of Christ, or did not offer a clear direction, he would also be viewed as illegitimate. His surviving sermon text constitutes a record of his rhetorical choices in both the challenging impromptu preaching context and the turbulent political environment of the mid-1670s.

Chapter 10 focuses on a significant sermon that Stephen Crisp delivered at a typical London Friends meeting in 1687. Specifically, I will examine the sermon both as a verbal response to an interesting (but not unique) rhetorical situation precipitated by the preacher's intent and implicit claim to be speaking "in the Light" as an "oracle" of God. In fact, the sermon is noteworthy both because of its explication of a Scripture passage, unusual for Friends, and its self-reflexivity. Its topic is the possibility of God speaking directly to people, thus becoming at

the moment of utterance the "Word of God" to them, all simultaneously delivered in a sermon that implicitly claims to be inspired.

Chapter 11 focuses on the only surviving sermon by Robert Barclay, the seventeenth-century Scottish Quaker intellectual and apologist who had outlined an impromptu approach to sermonizing based
on the notion of immediate revelation in his *Apology* (1676) and other
writings, and whose theorizing is discussed in chapter 4. Barclay's own
sermon offers the rhetorical analyst the opportunity to see in action
Barclay's own application of the approach to impromptu preaching
he so much advanced.

William Penn, the widely known and significant seventeenth-
century political figure and writer, was also an important preacher,
but his role as a public speaker has received little attention, though at
least two of his speeches and eleven of his impromptu sermons have
survived. Chapter 12 argues that Penn's sermonic work is noteworthy
through an examination of his 1688 public response to the death of
Rebecca Travers, an important first-generation Quaker leader. Penn's
funeral sermon reveals his struggle to come to grips with the vicissitudes of his own life through reflection on Travers' life and journey.
The chapter focuses on Penn's use of the journey metaphor.

Finally, the book ends with an epilogue drawing together some
implications of the book.

SECTION I

Contextual Background of Quaker Impromptu Preaching

Chapter 1

CULTURAL CONSTRAINTS ON EARLY QUAKER PREACHING

There is no such thing as a "spontaneous" rhetorical theory or practice; that is, no one practices a type of rhetorical discourse or invents a rhetorical theory uninfluenced by the intellectual and societal currents of the culture surrounding it and of which it is a part. The situation is similar to the natural phenomenon that we call spontaneous combustion: it occurs in the presence of combustible materials, and then only when the conditions are present that cause ignition. Rhetorical theory and practice are as much products of their own time as they are a part of the matrix of causes that lead to alterations in society.

To understand the development of the rhetorical or homiletic theory and practice of seventeenth-century Quakers, it is useful for us to first consider some of the conditions and events of seventeenth-century England. By all accounts, the seventeenth century in England was tumultuous. Christopher Hill writes, "The transformation that took place in the seventeenth century is . . . far more than merely a constitutional or political revolution, or a revolution in economics, religion or taste. It embraces the whole way of life. Two conceptions of civilisation were in conflict."[1] Similarly, J. R. Jones comments, "It was as if a whole generation of Englishmen had been subjected to the traditional Chinese curse, that they should 'live in interesting times.' Politically, they inhabited a world of change and uncertainty, of sensational plots and conspiracies, of endless personal intrigue and manoeuvring, of widespread corruption and almost universal cynicism."[2]

This chapter will sketch the significant features of the intellectual, religious, and sociopolitical milieu of the period 1650–1700, characteristics that bear directly or indirectly on the development of Quaker rhetorical theory and practice. The chapter will also characterize the nature and extent of rhetorical thought of that period. I will not deal with these topics in as much detail as might the philosopher or historian of rhetoric, both of whom would perhaps find this account overly brief. Instead, I will be conscious of a specific task, that of determining the nature of the intellectual, religious, sociopolitical, and rhetorical forces that acted as constraints on early Quaker sermon rhetoric.[3]

INTELLECTUAL CURRENTS: A NEW LOOK
AT THE HUMAN BEING AND THE WORLD

The period during which Quakers began to deliver impromptu sermons witnessed a revolution in thought. The signs of intellectual change are sometimes easily perceived. Wallace Notestein concludes regarding the first part of the century that the "world of Elizabeth's reign and even up into the early Stuart period was still medieval in its fundamental concepts."[4] By the late seventeenth century, however, one could see clearly that "an era of science, mathematics, and physical experiment had arrived."[5]

C. John Sommerville observes that after the restoration of the monarchy, many things could not be "restored": "The English mind had been unsettled as never before . . . there was something like a seismic disturbance in the very ground of discourse and scholarship. Radically new approaches to the study of nature, history, economics, politics, and society became possible."[6] Basil Willey helps pinpoint the difference between the medieval and late seventeenth-century mind when he notes that the medieval mind tended to concentrate on final causes, on the why of phenomena, but the new science focused on the *how*. He observes that the intellectual revolution in process "was a general transference of interest in metaphysics to physics, from the contemplation of Being to the observation of Becoming."[7]

While tracing the shift in intellectual perspective is not the concern of this chapter, it may be valuable to establish some of the trends through an examination of two proponents of the "new philosophy": Rene Descartes and Francis Bacon. Descartes and Bacon exemplify the two forces of the new science: Descartes the proponent of mathematics, and Bacon the expounder of the experiment and sensory observation.

In 1649 an English translation of Descartes' treatise *A Discourse on Method* was published. A French thinker writing amid the intellectual freedom of Holland, Descartes attempted to construct what Bertrand Russell called a "complete philosophic edifice *de nova*."[8] A. B.

Gibson sees Descartes' writings exhibiting two characteristics of the late Renaissance: (1) the mathematical method and (2) the personal approach to philosophy. Specifically, the truths of mathematics are not dependent upon events in time; therefore, Descartes' method reflects a general apathy toward history. On the other hand, the personal method places responsibility on the individual who must "live through each turn of the argument reflecting methodically on the implications of his [*sic*] own experience."[9] The first characteristic led to the development of science, while the second tied Cartesian philosophy to the Reformation emphasis on personal religion.

Descartes' philosophy, for our purposes, may be summarized by a consideration of three major tenets. Disenchanted with the learning of his day, Descartes began his own search for truth by doubting all that he possibly could. The purpose of this "Cartesian doubt" was, to use Descartes' own analogy, to find if "it is but a little copper and glass, perhaps, that I take for gold or diamonds." He initially rejected all written knowledge when he noted, "I entirely abandoned the study of letters, and resolved no longer to seek any other science than the knowledge of myself."[10] His introspection led him to make the most remembered statement of his philosophy, "I think, hence I am."[11]

The second tenet of Descartes' philosophy follows naturally from philosophic doubt. If one employs doubt to find the "gold and diamonds" of knowledge, one must have a criterion to test the results of the search. Clarity became the criterion of truth under Descartes' system. On this point he concluded, "I might take, as a general rule, the principle, that all things which we very clearly and distinctly conceive are true, only observing, however, that there is some difficulty in rightly determining the objects which we distinctly conceive."[12]

Although he realized that there were problems with the criterion of clarity, Descartes maintained that the logic of intuition was superior to the deduction involving the syllogism. In Descartes' view, the syllogism could not be used to discover new truth. He grudgingly admitted that the syllogism could be useful in "the communication of what we already know," but it was most often used "in speaking without judgment of things of which we are ignorant."[13] Descartes concluded that the syllogism, the engine of Scholasticism, could not be used to investigate the unknown.

To replace the syllogism, and to provide guidance for his intuitive method, Descartes provided four rules: (1) to avoid precipitancy and prejudice, (2) to divide each of the difficulties under examination into as many parts as possible, (3) to deal with the simplest and ascend to the more complex, and (4) to make complete enumerations and reviews.[14]

The third major tenet of Cartesian philosophy is the use of linear inferences to deduce new propositions. Beyond intuition and the application of his method, Descartes recognized a form of deduction. His nonsyllogistic concept of deduction can probably be reduced to a general process of reasoning from previously intuited propositions.[15]

Descartes, although making a significant break from medieval philosophy, did not rule out religious belief. Instead, he drew a picture of the world far different from the medieval one, in which "it was the function of natural science to serve theology."[16] Frederick L. Nussbaum writes of Descartes, "he succeeded in defining a universe in which the human reason was supreme. In the world beyond experience it led to the knowledge of God. In the world of experience, by wholly different methods, free from involvement with tradition and authority, it could lead to the mastery of the material world."[17]

Descartes had a profound influence in English intellectual circles, but spearheading the new perception of the world among the English were the writings of Francis Bacon, which seemed to capture the fancy of the new age after the 1640s. Although his influence during the early part of the century was minimal, he exerted an undoubted influence during the last half of the century. Born at the high tide of the English Renaissance, he, like Descartes, saw the limitations of what Aristotelianism had become at the hands of the Scholastics. Direct observation of the world had not been the habit of the medieval Schoolmen. Before an interest in science could blossom, it was necessary that a different philosophical attitude be developed. While Descartes began with skepticism, Bacon began with curiosity about the world humans inhabited. Furthermore, human curiosity could only be satisfied by looking directly at the world, and like Descartes, Bacon rejected the need to look into the works of the ancients. William T. Jones sums up the characteristic attitude needed for science to develop when he writes, "There had to be, in a word, a drastic change in the conception of authority, from that of the written word . . . to that of nature and empirical fact."[18] This "drastic change" became Bacon's raison d'être.

Bacon's inquiry into the logic of the ancients led him, like Descartes, to reject the syllogism as "acting too confusedly and letting nature slip out of its hands." He pointed to the shortcomings of the syllogism as residing in its very nature: "the syllogism consists of propositions—propositions of words; and the words are the signs and tokens of notions. Now if the very notions . . . be improperly and overhastily abstracted from facts, vague, not sufficiently definite . . . the whole edifice tumbles."[19]

The system proposed by Bacon to replace that of the ancients was "a form of induction which shall analyze experience and take it to pieces, and by due process of exclusion and rejection lead to an inevitable conclusion."[20] Bacon thought that his form of induction would guard against the errors that could result from relying upon the senses alone. The senses fail in two ways, according to Bacon. First, they often overlook information, for there are many subtleties in nature that can escape them. The senses also fail in that they often convey false information. Bacon discussed at some length what he called the "idols," which were "errors of apprehension to be recognized, allowed for, and circumvented if possible."[21] The "Idols of the Tribe" had their foundation "in human nature itself, and in the tribe or race of men. For it is a false assertion that the sense of man is the measure of things." The Idols of the Cave were "the idols of the individual man. For everyone . . . has a cave or den of his own, which refracts and discolors the light of nature."[22] Bacon recognized that language had the power to "force and overrule the understanding, and throw all into confusion, and lead men away into numberless empty controversies and idle fancies," and he called these misapprehensions the "Idols of the Market." Finally, he noted that "there are Idols which have immigrated into men's minds from the various dogmas of philosophies,"[23] and these were denominated the "Idols of the Theatre." To counteract drawbacks of sense perception and errors of apprehension, Bacon formulated the discipline of an "experiment."

Bacon's inductive method has been criticized as being "cooked up" and "oversimplified,"[24] but his attitude of mind stands, despite the criticism, as a significant departure from that of the medieval philosophers. Bacon went beyond empiricism to the beginnings of scientific experimentalism.

Descartes and Bacon wrote in an age that relied fundamentally upon deduction as its characteristic form of reasoning, and upon ancient and medieval authorities who supplied the basic premises of its syllogisms. The syllogism was at once the foundation of educational method in the universities, where syllogistic disputation held forth,[25] and the philosophic groundings of biblical authority. Notestein reminds us that people at the begining of the century were still dealing with the Bible and its expositors in the old way: "They found premises and then reasoned deductively from them. It was the habit taught then at the university."[26] The new emphasis upon induction and observation was clashing with the old habits and logic. Preparations were being made for the all-out epistemological war of the eighteenth century, which Wilbur Samuel Howell describes so well.[27] In the future lay a time when people would begin to realize that deduction is analogous to the flail, which beats propositions to get at the kernels of truth, while induction is closer to the plow, which turns over the ground to bring forth new propositions.[28] By the mid-decades of the seventeenth century, the new ways of thinking had established more than a foothold. The Royal Society was established in 1660 and began exerting itself in the intellectual life of Britain. The scientific tour de force of the century, however, came with the publication of Isaac Newton's *Principia Mathematica* in 1687. Newton brought together the two forces of the new science, which Descartes and Bacon represented. Nussbaum observes, "For his own and succeeding generations Newton converted the world into formulas of measurement. It became a world in which the physical and the mathematical appeared as the two essential and complementary aspects of reality. The empirically observed and the mathematically deduced were given factitious identity."[29] Newton ushered in the mechanistic view of the universe, in which natural events were seen as governed by natural laws, mathematical in nature. In sum, the new perception of the universe, of nature, of the human, which was in its adolescence in the last half of the seventeenth century, was "reasonable" from every angle. It depended upon human reason at every juncture and exuded confidence that, given unbiased observation and the right application of human reason, the secrets of all creation would be revealed. Trust in the ancients had been shaken, and the quake registered on the seismographs of religion, politics, and rhetoric.

Religious Currents: Puritanism in Apex and Decline

To assume that science overshadowed religion in the last half of the seventeenth century would be a gross oversimplification. If the seventeenth century can be characterized at all, it was at heart a century full of considerable religious fervor. Indeed, Richard F. Jones, in his important study of the growth of the scientific movement in England, concludes that there was a tie between religion and science. He points out that the new learning owed much to the fact that it was accepted by the great intellectual-religious movement of post-Elizabethan England, Puritanism:

> The importance of the Puritans in making Bacon's works popular and in disseminating and advocating his ideas, values, and attitudes is perhaps greater than we realize. Before 1640, he seems to have made no remarkable impression upon men's minds; at the Restoration he had become by far the greatest influence of the time. His name and works were the subject of endless adulation and unvarying tribute. Furthermore, Puritan support of experimental science is seen not only in educational treatises . . . but also in the small group of experimenters at Oxford, . . . These men were in no way fanatical Puritans, but their allegiance was definitely to the Puritan side.[30]

In order to understand the religious situation in the period, Puritanism must be examined, at least briefly, for it permeated the religious milieu of the time. As a religious and political process in England, the Puritan Revolution covered at least the period from the Petition of Right in 1628 to the Restoration in 1660,[31] but the period of Puritan influence extends well beyond these years in both directions, especially into the modern period. In the past, Puritanism, like Quakerism, has suffered from stereotyped images. The writings of William Haller, Perry Miller, and others did much to correct impressions of the Puritans gathered from fictional stereotypes.[32] More recent "revisionist" treatments of Puritanism have increased our understanding of these complex people.[33] As Charles Lloyd Cohen has observed, "Of making many books on Puritans there is no end, a testimony to their significance in Anglo-American culture."[34]

Appearing in the mid-sixteenth century, English Puritanism existed as a recognizable religious group until roughly the time of the Restoration, when it ceased to have a distinct identity. Kristen Poole observes that the very term "Puritan" is in constant tension among scholars and "invokes compromised and sliding categories, is metamorphic and inherently contradictory."[35] Its power, regardless of its definition, spawned new groups at its periphery, which may be called "Puritan" or not, and it infused many English people with its virtues, whom some would not label "Puritan."[36] Enlivened by the effects of the Reformation, Puritans set out to "preach an evangelical Christianity, a religion of prayer and the reading of Scriptures, of meditation and self-examination."[37] Many English citizens had fled England under the bloody reign of Mary, had found shelter in Geneva and other Protestant strongholds, and returned to England with a will to "purify" the Church of England.

Although Puritanism was never universally solidified into a catechism of belief acceptable to all,[38] we can discern the existence of some basic principles that most Puritans held in common. First and foremost, the Puritan believed in the personal experience of God's sovereignty working salvation in one's life. "They insist," writes Alan Simpson, "that the natural man canot grow in grace; he has to be reborn. They explain the rebirth as a personal experience in which the individual encounters the wrath and redemptive love of God."[39] Cohen writes, "Few topics so occupied Puritan preachers as did explicating the pangs of the 'new birth,' and few activities so engrossed believers as did scrutinizing themselves to discover how far regeneration had proceeded."[40]

Second, the Puritan believed that a life of good works was the expected response to salvation. One did not live a moral life in order to attain salvation, but as a result of God's grace. Marshall Knappen summarizes the importance of this tenet of Puritanism: "The mainspring of the Puritan's mechanism was his moral consciousness. . . . By the fruits we are to know the reality of faith."[41] Above all, the Puritan outlook on life was characterized by discipline.

The third basic principle of Puritanism was the belief that Scriptures were the ultimate authority, "the sole source of authority—the complete rule by which men must live."[42] In the words of William Perkins, the Scriptures are "of sufficient credit in and by themselves, needing not the testimony of any creature, not subject to the censure of either men or angels, binding the consciences of all men at all times, and being the only foundation of our faith and the rule and canon of all truth."[43]

The final principle of Puritanism is the belief that the state should be remade for God's glory.[44] Richard Baxter, whom historian Paul Chang-Ha Lim says "epitomizes the godly Puritan tradition,"[45] one of the ablest of Puritan writers and a strong critic of the early Quakers, went so far as to say that "it is this Theocratical Policy or Divine Common-wealth, which is the unquestionable reign of Christ on earth, which all Christians are agreed may be justly sought; and that temporal dignity of Saints, which undoubtedly would much bless the world."[46] Baxter's position was not far-fetched for many Puritans, who generally believed that "the chief end of government is the glorification of God and the welfare of souls. . . . Religion is the essential business of the State."[47]

Given the lack of definitive definition, noted by Poole, and the tide of revisionist and reactionary scholarship on Puritanism presented by Knoppers (see n. 33), it is difficult to be definitive about Puritans, but it is probably safe to say that Puritanism differed substantially from mainstream Anglicanism. Simpson summarizes the essential differences between the opposing views: the Puritan, he writes,

> believed in the total depravity of nature; he was told [by Anglicans] that men were not so fallen as he thought they were. He believed that the natural man had to be virtually reborn; he was told that he could grow in grace. He believed that the sermon was the only means of bringing saving knowledge and that the preacher should speak as a dying man to dying men. He was told that there were many means of salvation, that sermons by dying men to dying men were often prolix, irrational, and socially disturbing, and that what they had to say that was worth saying had usually been better said in some set form that could be read aloud. He demanded freedom for the saints to exercise their gifts of prayer and prophecy, only to be told that the needs of the community were better met by the forms of common prayer. He felt instinctively that the church was where Christ dwelt in the hearts of the regenerate. He was warned that such feelings threatened the prudent distinction between the invisible church of the saved and the visible church of the realm. He insisted that the church of the realm should be judged by Scripture, confident that Scripture upheld him, and prepared to assert that nothing which was not expressly commanded in Scripture ought to be tolerated in the church. He was told that God had left much to the discretion of human reason; that this reason was exercised by public authority, which in England was the same for both church and state; and that whatever authority enjoined, in its large area of discretion, ought to be loyally obeyed.[48]

The Anglican view was derived largely from Richard Hooker's work *Of the Laws of Ecclesiastical Polity*, the thesis of which was that in all things not essential to Christianity or the salvation of souls, "it was permissible and indeed desirable to follow tradition, authority, and, above all, reason, which the Puritans distrusted."[49] Many scholars see Hooker's position as a reconstruction of the Roman Catholic Church within the culturally situated framework of Protestant England.

After years of frustration and repression, especially under the ecclesiastical rule of Archbishop William Laud, two phenomena began to take shape in English Puritanism: fragmentation and migration. Little need be said in this context about the latter, since it does not bear directly upon the development of Quakerism in England or the Quaker theory and practice of preaching. Suffice it to say that many persecuted Puritans migrated to Holland and ultimately to North America to set up their ideal theocracy.

The fragmentation of Puritanism is more germane to this study because, according to Barbour (*Quakers in Puritan England*), Quakerism emerged alongside radical Puritanism, which emanated as the left wing of English Puritanism. Puritans were not tightly organized as a "sect" and did not exhibit an abounding sense of unity during their years of development. Moreover, with the coming and passing of the civil wars (the last in 1648), Puritanism had taken on several guises covering major divergences of viewpoint. John Marlowe pinpoints the branch of Puritanism most influential on early Friends: "On the left wing were the Sectarians, the Zealots of Puritanism. The Sectarians derived their strength and influence from those Bible-reading, psalm-singing, lay-preaching habits which formed the most deeply-rooted and most widespread manifestation of Puritanism in England."[50]

With the passage of time, especially after the rise of Oliver Cromwell, the more radical Puritans became increasingly separatist in their behavior. The phenomenon seems the logical result of the disestablishment of the Episcopacy and the fact that Presbyterianism was not established in its place. During the Commonwealth period, Barbour observes, two themes began to emerge in the radical ranks of Puritanism: social justice and inspiration.[51] The extreme expressions of social justice were found in the movements of the Diggers and the Levelers. In 1649 Gerrard Winstanley attempted to set up a farm on the common at Kingston Hill, activated with "warmly and pantheistically religious" motives.[52] His act was a social protest against the policy of land enclosure by the gentry. Buchanan Sharp notes that the Diggers were the "only apparent supporters in print of the rural laboring poor."[53] The Levelers, on the other hand, under the leadership of John Lilburne, were a political party drawn from the lower middle class, who made religious toleration and the cure of other social injustices the core of their platform.[54] According to Barbour, Leveler politics were largely the political extensions of the idea that the "Elect were equal before God and that God's love and free grace were offered to all men universally."[55] Peter Burke calls the Levelers "an instance of the popularization of radical values" who also "had links with the separatist congregations," maintained a "secret press," and had ties to the theatre.[56]

Barbour also sees "inspiration," or an emphasis upon the Holy Spirit, as a second emphasis taking place among Puritans during Cromwell's time in power. Although more orthodox Puritans believed in the presence of the Holy Spirit in the believer's life, the "radical puritans pushed the link of conversion and the Spirit much further, stressing the emotional fruits of the Spirit in conscious experience."[57] This new emphasis found expression in the insistence upon ministers having a personal "conversion," an acknowledgment of direct "leadings" of the Spirit in the believer's life, and a freedom from any fixed forms in worship. Groups such as the Etheringtonians, Muggletonians, Grindletonians, and many others, including the Quakers, appeared on the scene.[58]

With Cromwell's passing, and the subsequent restoration of the monarchy, the religious picture changed dramatically. The Church of England, once again in the seat of power, was anxious to bring the kingdom back into conformity with Anglicanism. Persecution of Dissenters during the years between the Restoration and the Act of Toleration in 1689 is a matter of historical record and will be mentioned only briefly below.

After religious toleration was achieved under William and Mary, all religious groups in England suffered gradual decline. Sommerville reminds us that "the period 1660–1711 may be seen as falling between two periods of religious assertiveness" and suggests that the Restoration is characterized by "concentration and conservation of energies."[59] The influence of rationalism, deism, and the new science made inroads in Anglican and nonconformist circles alike. For all their depth of religious experience, Puritans, like the majority of thinkers of their age, increasingly tried to reconcile what Basil Willey calls "two inconsistent worldviews": "Two principal orders of Truth were present to the consciousness of the time: one, represented by Christianity, which men could not but reverence, and the other, represented by science, which they could not but accept."[60] Science, which Puritanism had to an extent embraced earlier in the century, was causing it grave concern toward the century's close. However, science did not triumph over religion as the century wore on, but without oversimplifying the complexity of events, we can conclude that the scientific attitude helped change religion, as it did politics and rhetoric. Seventeenth-century English men and women were caught up in the birth pains of an age characterized by shifting epistemological bases; and to a great extent we are not yet through the postpartum trauma in the twenty-first century.

Sociopolitical Currents: The Aristocracy Challenged

The seventeenth century saw extraordinary changes in the social and political life of English people. Ideas which we connect with relatively recent times were debated in alehouses and drawing rooms of seventeenth-century England. We have already noted the appearance of such radical religious-political movements as the Diggers and the Levelers. We can also discern the roots of democracy in such publications as Milton's *Areopagitica* and John Locke's *Two Treatises of Government* and *An Essay Concerning Human Understanding*.[61] Yet democracy, for all its naive, idealistic expression by Diggers and Levelers, was barely in its formative stages. By the time William and Mary ascended the throne, the English, by and large, had had their fill of radical politics. They had also been disillusioned with the theocracy of the Protectorate on the one hand, and blatant rule by divine right on the other. They only knew for sure that they did not want a popish ruler or a tyrant, or one tinged by radicalism.

Historians divide seventeenth-century English history into two periods. The first was an "uneventful prolongation of the Elizabethan era, under conditions of peace and safety instead of domestic danger and foreign war."[62] G. M. Trevelyan sums up both the surface and the subsurface conditions of the first period when he writes, "No industrial, agricultural or social change of importance took place in England during the forty years when the Parliamentary and Puritan Revolution was germinating beneath the soil of an apparently stable and settled society."[63] The picture in the first period is one of a largely rural society with primitive industry and commerce. On the surface, all looked calm, but the roots of rebellion were finding nourishment below the surface.

Although William Caxton had introduced movable type printing to England in the fifteenth century, it was not until the mid-seventeenth century that booksellers were flooded with the tools of their trade. Tracts, books, and pamphlets, following the ferment of religious controversies, produced a veritable plethora of printed broadsides.[64] In terms of lasting influence, none of these matched the publication of the King James Bible as a prime factor in the creation of a revolutionary spirit. After its appearance in 1611, it became at once the most important and best-known book in England. Notestein writes, "Men were reading the Bible in translation and taking to heart its injunctions, and gaining thereby a new zeal for active and personal Christianity."[65] If a man or woman could read and interpret the Scriptures himself or herself, of what use was the priest? The Bible infused Puritanism, as we have seen, and took the place of the Church and tradition as its ultimate authority.[66] False interpretations of prophetic passages even became the authority for powerful political movements such as the Fifth Monarchy Men.[67]

Cromwell's reign climaxed the slow rise of antiaristocratic feeling during the first period of the century. Lawrence Stone goes so far as to call the period 1558–1641 "The Crisis of the Aristocracy."[68] His observation is echoed by Godfrey Davies, who states, "The keynote of the seventeenth century was revolt against authority."[69] Stone synthesizes the revolutionary passions beneath the surface of the English social scene and describes them as they were about to break forth:

> [T]he middle of the seventeenth century saw the eclipse of the monarchy which lost its head; of the peerage, which lost its special privileges, its grasp on the executive, and its influence over the electorate; and of the Anglican Church, which lost its monopoly of patronage and pulpit. It saw the brief emergence into the open of radical ideas about social, economic, sexual, and political equality. Admittedly all this did not last, and by the end of the seventeenth century the peers, like the Anglican clergy and the King, were firmly back in the saddle. But it should be noted that the bit and the curb, the stirrup and the whip, were now of a different design.[70]

Under Cromwell's Protectorate, many extremists in both politics and religion appeared on the scene and were persecuted or tolerated, often at the discretion of local officials. Not surprisingly, during these years Quakerism began to congeal in the northern counties of

England. Cromwell treated the new group with moderation, and it spread and gained adherents.[71]

The second period of the seventeenth century began with the Restoration in 1660. The restoration of the monarchy brought with it a return of the Anglican attitude toward religion, along with a resurgence of Cavalier aristocracy in government. Dissenting religious congregations began to suffer persecution. Former followers of Cromwell reaped the seeds of persecution they had sown. Trevelyan writes, "For a generation after 1660 the Puritans were often bitterly persecuted . . . to avenge the wrongs suffered by the Anglicans and Cavaliers."[72]

The Episcopacy was reestablished in 1661, and the Act of Uniformity was passed, which required all clergymen to conform to the Prayer Book of the Church of England. Webber reports that approximately two thousand men, including independents, Baptists, Presbyterians, and other Dissenters, lost their congregations.[73]

All Dissenters, but especially the Quakers, were singled out for the severe penalties of a series of laws known collectively as the "Clarendon Code," although subsequent scholarship has shown that Lord Clarendon had been pressured into its enactment.[74] The Code included penalties for those who obstinately "refused to hear divine service or attended conventicles or encouraged others to do so."[75] A Conventicle Act, intended to suppress meetings of Dissenters, had been nominally in force until 1669. The ways in which it was circumvented, especially during the plague and fire of London, brought passage of the Second Conventicle Act in 1670.[76]

The Clarendon Code also provided, under the Five Mile Act, that "no clergyman, or schoolmaster was to come within five miles of a city or corporate town, unless he declared that he would not 'at any time endevour any alteration of government either in Church or State.'"[77] Few Dissenters would submit to the oath.

Quakers were singled out by an act passed expressly against them, appropriately called the Quaker Act, which provided penalties for anyone who would maintain "that the taking of an oath in any case whatsoever (although before a lawful magistrate) is altogether unlawful and contrary to the word of God."[78] This provision struck at the Quakers' belief in the literal interpretation of James 5:12, "swear not, neither by heaven, neither by the earth, neither by any other oath: but let your yea be yea; and your nay, nay; lest ye fall into condemnation."

The second part of the act forbade Quakers to leave their homes and assemble, five or more, for unauthorized worship.

Magistrates used a far more severe method of persecution, particularly against Quakers. Braithwaite describes the use of praemunire as a weapon by authorities: "The term *praemunire* . . . denoted a punishment originally devised in the fourteenth century for use against those who acknowledged foreign jurisdiction by paying to Papal process an obedience due the King's Courts alone. The person found guilty was to be put out of the King's protection, his estate was forfeited to the crown, and he was imprisoned during life or at the royal pleasure."[79] Praemunire involved an oath of allegiance and denial of the Pope's authority, which the Quakers, of course, would not take simply because it was an oath. Thus, this weapon proved the most effective against Quakers, surpassing even the Quaker Act and the Clarendon Code in favor by the authorities.[80]

Persecution of Quakers has been emphasized not only because it relates directly to the sermons later dealt with in this book, but also because Quakers bore the brunt of persecution during the perilous days from the Restoration in 1660 to the Act of Toleration in 1689, almost thirty years.[81] Even Baxter, one of the most effective opponents of Quakerism, had praise for the manner in which Quakers bore their persecution:

> [T]he fanatics called Quakers did greatly relieve the sober people for a time: for they were so resolute, and gloried in their constancy and sufferings, that they assembled openly, at the Bull and Mouth near Aldersgate, and were dragged away daily to the Common Gaol, and yet desisted not, but the rest came the next day nevertheless, so that the Gaol at Newgate was filled with them. Abundance of them died in prison, and yet they continued their assemblies still! . . . Yea, many turned Quakers, because the Quakers kept their meetings openly and went to prison for it cheerfully.[82]

The "Glorious Revolution" of 1688, which saw the deposition of James II and the coming of William and Mary to the throne, eventually brought a settlement of England's political struggles that lasted, with minor interruptions, through the coming struggles against France. Toleration for Dissenters was the law of the land, although they were still barred from holding political or military office. The Church of

England remained Anglican but, important for Quakers, lost its power to persecute.[83] The opposing powers of Parliament and absolute monarchy seemed to be resolved in what often approached a state of cooperative effort, with the weight of power now more firmly in the hands of the former. Political parties began to take shape, with the Tories (Cavaliers) representing largely the aristocracy and the Whigs representing the class of tradesmen and merchants now coming into prominence.[84]

Seventeenth-century England, observed as a whole, was a paradox. Beyond the fact of conflicting intellectual, religious, and political views, it was the "heyday of the trading companies, merchant adventurers, and the like,"[85] while at the same time the overall atmosphere of the country was rural and agricultural. Nothing that could accurately be called an "Industrial Revolution" took place in England during the century.[86] "London," writes Trevelyan regarding immense urban areas, "which numbered half a million inhabitants by the end of the century, was the only place in England that could answer that description."[87] Yet medieval civilization was begining to break down with increased communication between people of similar occupation in neighboring shires. It was an age in which the attitude of respectful subservience toward the aristocracy was falling off, and yet the Quakers were persecuted for not doffing their hats in deference to authority.[88] Reay reminds us that seventeenth-century England "was a hierarchical society . . . a society in which the values of the elite, the gentlemen, were dominant."[89]

The period during which the majority of the sermons dealt with in this book were preached—the 1680s and 1690s—saw the culmination of many of the conflicting trends I have already mentioned. Increased rationalism in religion, lessened persecution, movement toward Parliamentary government, increased economic prosperity—all of these factors correlated with and perhaps helped produce an era of spiritual decline. As Hill observes, "After 1689 Dissenters had to face the perils of worldly prosperity, to which their higher code of business ethics and their more single-minded application both contributed."[90] Medievalism was gradually giving way, divine right was superseded by social contract, authority was being questioned, and religious enthusiasm was gradually being made obsolescent by the emerging deism of the Enlightenment.[91]

RHETORICAL CURRENTS: FROM INGRATIATION TO THE PLAIN STYLE

Rhetorical knowledge and belief in the seventeenth century were in the midst of changes that were fast carrying rhetoric from Renaissance to modern thought. The ancients, who first speculated on the nature of rhetoric and its constituents, had viewed the subject primarily as the art of persuasion. Classical theory, in its fully developed form, saw rhetoric as divided into five constituents, or "canons"—invention, arrangement, style, memory, and delivery—each of which was developed into a sometimes complex and variegated set of subcategories. Douglas Ehninger interpreted Renaissance rhetoric as having taken a different bent by emphasizing the canon of style and viewing the speaker's craft as "an aesthetically oriented art of ingratiation—a form of conscious flattery or supplication."[92] A society largely built upon hierarchy of social strata demanded language usage that fostered and reflected social standing. Specifically, it demanded a theory of communication which emphasized "that true excellence is achieved only by a departure from the natural pattern of everyday speech."[93] For purposes of this book, my interpretation, or "reading," follows Ehninger's as well as Wilbur Samuel Howell's *Logic and Rhetoric in England: 1500–1700.*[94]

There are alternate "readings" of the history of rhetorical theory, as the title of Brummett's *Reading Rhetorical Theory* implies. One reading provided by Brummett is surprisingly consonant with the subtext of position or power inherent in Ehninger's reading of the dominant Renaissance rhetoric. Brummett indicates that various definitions of "rhetoric" are "concealing a subtext of struggle over power."[95] In his brief but cogent "Introduction to the Middle Ages and Renaissance," he notes two contradictory developments regarding power: (1) a "diffusion of power that had previously been concentrated in the church," and (2) the "concentration of power in increasingly centralized governments."[96] He also notes that with the growth of the print medium, "privileged classes of most nations began to learn to read and write." In England, it was more than the privileged class that became literate, and literacy helped fuel many of the changes in the seventeenth century.[97]

During the Renaissance, style was emphasized above the other rhetorical offices, and rhetoric became less concerned with the large audience and more involved with the individual. Modern rhetorical concepts began to take shape in the late seventeenth century with the writings of John Locke[98] and blossomed with the thinking of Adam Smith, George Campbell, and Joseph Priestly during the eighteenth-century Enlightenment. These writers, unlike the ancients, saw rhetoric as the art or science of adapting means to ends, of "managing" discourse with a view to addressing a "faculty" in the hearer's mind.[99]

Our period, 1650–1700, witnessed the decline of the Renaissance stylistic view and anticipated the new turn in the study of rhetoric, which to an extent had found expression in the theories of the French educator Peter Ramus, the resurgence of the ancient theory newly revised by the influence of Ramus, and the emergence of a new rhetoric enlivened by the writings of Descartes and Bacon.[100]

The changes that eventually produced modern rhetorical theory were not sudden. It is possible to discern a number of theories operating simultaneously during the seventeenth century. For example, Howell points out that the classical Renaissance stylistic and the beginings of a modern school of rhetoric existed and overlapped in the years 1650–1700.[101] For the limited purposes of this chapter, this discussion will concentrate on the influences of Peter Ramus and Francis Bacon. I will also touch upon the prevailing homiletic theories during the period.

Before Descartes influenced philosophy, the work of another Frenchman was prominent. Peter Ramus, a sixteenth-century French Protestant martyr, had shaken the educational world with his rearrangement of the liberal arts according to three laws. The law of justice prohibited a learned treatise from dealing with more than one field of knowledge. The law of truth prohibited a learned treatise from containing statements true only on occasion or only partly true. The law of wisdom prohibited a treatise from being a mixture of general principles, particular statements, and specific cases arranged in a disorganized fashion.[102] Under Ramus' system, rhetoric and dialectic were compartmentalized from each other and given subject matter that, theoretically, did not overlap. Rhetoric was assigned the province of style and delivery; dialectic was entrusted with invention and arrangement. The resultant theory of discourse is important for several reasons, but I should like to concentrate on its role in associating rhetoric with style alone, and its influence on the development of Puritan sermon form.

The Ramistic compartmentalization of dialectic and rhetoric helped lead to a preoccupation by rhetoricians with just a part of what the classical writers had considered essential to rhetoric. Although Ramus assigned both style and delivery to rhetoric, the second was never developed to any great extent. In fact, in the 1548 edition of the Ramistic *Rhetoric* (actually written by Ramus' friend and colleague, Omer Talon, or Audomarus Talaeus), Talon admits that delivery amounts to the same thing as style.[103] With regard to style, Ramistic rhetoric developed only two conceptions, tropes and figures. Tropes were "a garnishing of speache, whereby one worde is drawen from his firste proper signification to another."[104] Under this Ramistic classification, all tropes became a subspecies of metaphor. Figures, on the other hand, were "a garnishing of speache, wherein the course of the same is chaunged from the more simple and plaine manner of speaking, unto that whiche is more full of excellencie and grace."[105] In this definition one readily sees some affinity of Ramistic rhetoric with the stylistic tradition, which also implied a repudiation of everyday speech patterns.

William P. Sandford's study of English rhetorics from 1530 to 1828 includes the Ramistic rhetoric as a significant part of the period 1577–1600—the period he called the "rhetoric of Exornation."[106] Sandford sees Taleus' *Rhetoric*, along with the work of Richard Sherry,[107] as establishing the vogue of ornamentation. "Later works," Sandford tells us, "copy freely from one or the other, or both."[108] Ong concludes that Ramistic theory "relies more on ornamentation theory than perhaps any other rhetoric ever has."[109] The influence of the Ramistic rhetorical tradition in England has been the subject of inquiry by both Howell and Sandford. Each writer asserts that Ramism flourished in early seventeenth-century England through the writings of Abraham Fraunce, Charles Butler, and others.[110] We gain a sense of Ramistic rhetoric's popularity by recognizing that Butler's translation of Talaeus' *Rhetoric* was widely used as a text for English schoolboys during the entire seventeenth century.[111]

Many scholars see the Ramistic system of thought as an important influence on the development of Puritan sermon form, although the extent of Ramistic influence is a point of contention, which is a topic to which we will later return. The most striking evidence of Ramistic influence is seen in the area of "method." Ramus' original conception of method was twofold. The first method he concerned himself with he calls the "natural" method, characterized by discipline and economy on the part of the writer. Furthermore, it stipulates that things be arranged according to their importance in nature: "that shall be set downe in the first place which is first absolutely cleare; that in the second, which is second; that in the third, which is third; and so forward. Therefore Method doth always goe from the generalls to the particulars."[112] Ramus also recognizes a second kind of method, which was characterized by arrangement according to the importance of the items with reference to the psychology of a particular audience. He refers to orators who employed the following mode: "that which is strongest, is always placed first by them; yet so that those things, which are excellent, are kept for the last place, and those that are but so so are thrust into the middle of the Troupe and Battayle."[113] Ramus prefers the first method, if his own treatises are to be taken as evidence. He not only followed the method of descending order of generality, but he had the habit of dividing his subjects by twos. This can be a workable system as long as the subject with which one is dealing is amenable to this kind of division. Ramus' followers often took his practice to be a characteristic of the "natural method." A second misinterpretation of the natural method occurred because Ramus saw the method as being applicable to all kinds of discourse—scientific, rhetorical, and poetic—and gradually it was assumed that Ramus was solely an advocate of the natural method.

The method of descending order of generality according to dichotomies became a standard method in educational institutions.[114] The prevalence of the natural method in early seventeenth-century England led Bacon to single it out for attack: "whatever does not conveniently fall into these dichotomies, they [Ramists] either omit or pervert beyond nature, so that, so to speak, when the seeds and kernels of science are springing forth, they gather so many dry and empty husks."[115]

Ramism became associated with Puritanism largely through the educational system that trained the clergy. We have already noted the influence of Butler's translation of Talon's *Rhetoric* on lower levels of education. John Milton encountered Ramism in his early education at St. Paul's School, where he memorized Talaeus' *Rhetoric*.[116] Ramism held sway at Cambridge through the influence of Gabriel Harvey, William Perkins, William Ames, and others.[117] Perkins and Ames, as we shall see, produced the primary homiletical sources of Puritanism. Even at Oxford, which Howell argues never accepted Ramism, Thomas Worrall instructed his students to read the works of Ramus.

One of his pupils, Richard Mather, came under Ramistic influence at Oxford, and Howell considers him to be a link between Ramism and the Puritan leadership in early New England.[118]

Babette May Levy has made a weighty study of the sermons that survive the first fifty years of Puritanism in New England. On Ramus' influence on sermonizing, she concludes,

> Ramus's simplified approach to a problem, with the emphasis always upon dichotomies, encouraged any Puritan follower to see his world as composed of opposites. . . . The continued approval of arguing from general theories to singular cases . . . also limited Puritan thinking in many ways, prohibiting any scientific approach to a problem; and the Ramist advocacy of arguing from the familiar or known to the strange or unknown encouraged a preacher to make his points by homely illustrations. . . . The wording of texts was analyzed or "opened"; the results were combined, by the Ramist method of genesis, to form the doctrine. Every statement was followed by its reasons or proofs—a direct method of procedure relying much upon axiomatic truth rather than upon syllogistic reasoning.[119]

Puritanism had found in Ramus a man who was martyred for his Protestantism, a theorist with a no-nonsense method easily adapted to their needs. Miller observes that in England, Ramism "prospered along with Puritanism, with which, by the begining of the seventeenth century, it became almost synonymous."[120]

Some revisionist scholars have seen Ramistic influence differently from the scholars to whom I have been referring. Eugene E. White persuasively argues that "the Puritans were not the thoroughgoing Ramists that Perry Miller and Wilbur Howell have contended" and reveals the extent to which Puritans were also influenced by classical sources.[121] Based on his research, grounded in primary sources, especially Puritan sermons, White believes that "Puritans blended Ramism, Aristotelianism, and neo-Ciceronianism, and they brilliantly coalesced that blend with their concepts of the psychological nature of man and the morphology of conversion."[122] It appears that the argument is about the *extent* of the influence Ramistic thinking had on the Puritans and the extent to which the Puritans felt free to deviate from its precepts. Perhaps Conley's views can help us balance the picture. He holds the Ramistic rhetoric, written by Talon, in high regard, remarking that it is "a very perceptive book composed by someone thoroughly grounded in Classical oratory and poetry."[123] In this view, Ramus' rhetoric is already infused with a depth of classical learning. Conley also offers a balanced conclusion of Ramistic influence: "Ramistic dialectic and rhetoric made their greatest impact on Protestant readers, and almost none at all on Catholic populations. This pattern is evident also in England and Scotland, where . . . Ramus was most influential in Calvinist Puritan circles."[124]

By the mid-seventeenth century, Ramism was waning in England, but Ramistic thought also influenced a group of rhetoricians who Howell has called "Neo-Ciceronians." These writers, who included Charles Butler, John Newton, Thomas Vicars, Thomas Farnaby, William Pemble, and Obadiah Walker, attempted to reach a compromise between Ramistic and traditional rhetoric between 1586 and 1700, according to Howell.[125] These rhetoricians also serve as an indication that the traditional classical pattern continued to be influential throughout the period of the last half of the century. The Neo-Ciceronians gradually supplanted the Ramists and finally obtained dominance.

Although the traditional pattern was predominant during the first fifty years of Quakerism, toward the close of the seventeenth century the outlines of a new rhetoric were taking shape. During the early part of the century, Bacon had set in motion ideas that would culminate in the writings of Locke, and later those of Adam Smith and George Campbell.

Although Bacon did not write a rhetoric as such, his theory is scattered throughout his philosophical works. In the *Advancement of Learning*, he states that "the duty and office" of rhetoric is "to *apply Reason to Imagination* for the better moving of the will."[126] "His entire system of thought," writes Karl Wallace, is "founded on the gradual extension and dominance of reason over emotion."[127] The end of Baconian rhetoric "is to fill the imagination to second reason, and not to oppress it."[128] Bacon, accepting the presuppositions of faculty psychology, distrusted the faculty of *imagination*, yet believed that it was needed to work along with *reason* in order to move the sometimes recalcitrant *will* to act. The imagination becomes, for Bacon, a messenger, a go-between, operating in the gap between human reason and human will. Wallace observes that in Bacon's works, "the sole function of the imagination in speaking or writing is to render logical argument attractive and pleasing; the imagination merely translates logical inferences into pictures. . . . rhetorical address must be, always and foremost, logically sound; imaginative dress, although highly desirable, is not fundamental."[129]

Bacon thought that the imagination could be a detriment when language becomes an end in itself. His famous reaction to stylistic excesses is an illustration of his attitude:

> [T]he admiration of ancient authors, the hate of the schoolmen, the exact study of languages, and the efficacy of preaching, did bring in an affectionate study of eloquence and copie of speech, which then began to flourish. This grew speedily to an excess; for men began to hunt more after words than matter; and more after the choiceness of the phrase, and the round and clean composition of the sentence, and the sweet falling of the clauses, and the varying and illustration of their works with tropes and figures, than after the weight of matter, worth of subject, soundness of argument, life of invention, or depth of judgment.[130]

Bacon's system of rhetoric is based upon a realignment of learning into four intellectual arts: "man's labour is to invent that which is *sought* or *propounded*; or to *judge* that which is *invented*; or to *retain* that which is *judged*; or to *deliver over* that which is *retained*. So as the arts must be four: Art of Inquiry or Invention; Art of Examination or Judgment; Art of Custody or Memory; and Art of Elocution or Tradition."[131] Thus, the five canons of the ancients are reduced to four, style and delivery being subsumed under a single term, "tradition." Although tradition stands for Bacon's concept of communication, the other three arts, he believed, were necessary for rhetorical discourse. Bacon did not strictly divide the subject matter of logic from that of rhetoric, as had Ramus. Instead, he thought that the two arts would operate in different communication settings: logic with the learned, and rhetoric with the popular audience.

Particularly significant to the development of a new rhetoric were Bacon's conceptions of invention and tradition. He emphasized that invention should be the discovery of something new, instead of recalling what one already knows.[132] His view of tradition returned rhetoric to an overriding interest in persuasion through reasoned discourse, instead of concerning itself with ingratiation through style. George Williamson brilliantly summarizes Bacon's notion of rhetoric: "It involves all that may be added to bare argument or logic in order to make it persuasive, including the turn or shape of the argument itself;

ornament is not decorative, but persuasive; it is, or gives, a persuasive form of proof."[133]

Bacon helped move the English language toward the "plain style" of the late century. His influence on the Royal Society is undeniable. Thomas Sprat, writing in 1667, would have the audacity to state the goal of the new scientific rhetoric as "a constant Resolution, to reject all the amplifications, digressions, and swellings of style: to return back to the primitive purity, and shortness, when men delivered so many *things*, almost in an equal number of *words*."[134] These sentiments would not have been uttered by the scientific community a century before. The plain style had moved out of the confines of Puritanism, which had accepted Ramus' logic but rejected the full-blown stylistic tradition, into learned society at large. A new rhetoric was emerging.

There is not a consistent line of division between homiletics and rhetoric during our period. Many of the writers included preaching among the types of speaking they covered. Thomas Wilson, for example, makes frequent references throughout his *Arte of Rhetorique* to preaching. Other writers wrote both for secular and sacred audiences. Furthermore, the trends I have referred to in this discussion of the rhetorical currents apply with consistency to homiletic theory. One finds a strong restatement of classical values, a movement toward Ramism, and a trend toward a "new homiletic," all within the confines of our period.

A discussion of the major homiletical writers of the seventeenth century would not advance this book, nor fit the limits of this chapter, since Quaker preachers and writers ignored them.[135] However, it is important that I point to the significance of works by William Perkins, John Wilkins, and Joseph Glanvill.

William Perkins' *The Art of Prophesying* was the preeminent homiletical handbook of Puritan preachers. The work is divided after the manner of Ramus into a dichotomous pattern. The book considers two subjects: preaching and praying. Preaching is then divided into preparing the sermon and uttering it. These topics are again divided by twos. Although not a thoroughgoing disciple of the master, according to Howell there is sufficient evidence in Perkins' works to place him among the English Ramists.[136]

Perkins distrusted "eloquence," for he believed that "hearers ought not to ascribe their faith to the gifts of men, but to the power of God's word." Although human wisdom was allowed in the preparation of the sermon, it "must be concealed, whether it be in the matter of the sermon or in the setting forth of the words."[137] He specifically cautions the preacher against the use of Greek or Latin phrases in the sermon, because "1. They disturb the minde of the auditors, that they canot fit those thinges which went afore with those that follow. 2. A strange word hindereth the understanding of those things that are spoken. 3. It draws the minde away from its purpose to some other matter. . . ." He summarizes his advice for preachers in four rules:

1. To reade the Text distinctly out of the Canonicall Scriptures.
2. To give the sense and vnderstanding of it being read, by the Scripture it selfe.
3. To collect a few and profitable points of doctrine out of the natvrall sense.
4. To apply (if he have the gift) the doctrines rightly collected, to the life and manners of men in a simple and plaine speech.[138]

In effect, Perkins directly reflects the practical, simplified approach to problems advocated by Ramus. Puritan sermons were most often begun by an "opening" of the Scripture, by which the doctrines were developed; then reasons were offered in proof of the doctrines; finally, the sermon contained a long section on the "uses" or application of the doctrine. The form had been popularized by Perkins.[139]

John Wilkins' *Ecclesiastes, Or A Discourse concerning the Gift of Preaching as it fals under the rules of Art* is mentioned here not only because it was a popular handbook during the seventeenth century, being often reprinted, but also because Wilkins was a prime influence in the criticism of preaching, which occurred during the third quarter of the seventeenth century.

Wilkins believed the preacher should have a broad training in theology, science, languages, and rhetoric. He specifically recommends the use of "heathen writers." He also warns, however, that "To stuff a Sermon with citations of authors, and the witty sayings of others, is to make a feast of vinegar and pepper." On style, Wilkins maintains that the composition should be "plain and natural, not being darkened with the affectation of *Scholastical* harshness, or *Rhetorical* flourishes. . . . The greatest learning is to be seen in the greatest plainness."[140] With regard to method, Wilkins proposes a system not unlike that of Perkins. The preacher is to explicate the passage, confirm its truth, and apply it to his audience. Wilkins' thought found expression

twenty-five years later in James Arderne's *Directions Concerning the Matter and Stile of Sermons* (1671), and Arderne, in turn, became a prime
source for Joseph Glanvill's *An Essay Concerning Preaching: Written for the
Direction of a Young Divine* (1678).[141]

Glanvill, who "brought the doctrine of plainness from the new
theory of scientific exposition and planted it in the ancient theory of
persuasion,"[142] asserted that preaching "ought to be *plain, practical,
methodical, affectionate.*"[143] Glanvill explains that there is "a bastard kind
of eloquence that is crept into the Pulpit which consists in affections
of wit and finery, flourishes, metaphors, and cadences."[144] Yet he does
not condemn all use of the arts of discourse:

> I do not by this reprehend all Wit whatever in Preaching, nor any-
> thing that is truly such: For true Wit is a perfection in our faculties,
> chiefly in the understanding and imagination; Wit in the understand-
> ing is a sagacity to find out the nature, relations, and consequences
> of things: Wit in the imagination, is a quickness of the phancy to
> give things proper Images; now the more of these in Sermons, the
> more judgment, and spirit; and life: and without Wit of these kinds,
> Preaching is dull and unedifying. The Preacher should endeavor to
> speak sharp and quick thoughts, and to set them out in lively colours;
> This is proper, grave, and manly wit, but the other, that which con-
> sists in inversions of sentences, and playing with words, and the like,
> is vile and contemptible fooling.[145]

To Glanvill, a sermon should actually improve the conduct of its
listeners; proceed by a method "not strain'd and forced, but such as the
matter, and the capacities, and wants of the auditors, require"; and "be
spoken with such schemes of speech as are apt to excite the affections
of the most vulgar, and illiterate."[146] Glanvill fittingly concludes our
abbreviated discussion of the homiletic trends of the period, for he,
perhaps more dramatically than others, reveals that the turn toward
more practical, less ornamental messages in rhetorical theory was also
evident in the writing about homiletics.

CONSTRAINTS ON EARLY QUAKER RHETORIC

The constraining influences of the century that witnessed the rise of
Quakerism were different, decidedly different, at the end from what
they had been at the begining. The century was a watershed in Western
history. Everywhere we turn we see the sometimes gradual, frequently
sudden shift from former ways of perceiving—whether in philosophy,

religion, politics, or rhetorical theory. The Quakers themselves became a manifestation of the general movement of growing distrust of tradition, whether it appeared in philosophy, church, or government.

The dogmatic authoritarianism of Scholastic "science" was giving way as the Quakers appeared on the scene. Although Quakers initially produced few scientists, they could not avoid the influences of the new scientific age.[147] By the time Quakerism was firmly established, after the persecution of the Restoration period had ebbed and during the years of the majority of the sermons on which much of this book focuses, the medieval concept of the universe was on its way out; reason and science were begining their long rule, and religious enthusiasm was waning.[148]

Papal authority had been questioned a century earlier in England, but the period of early Quakerism saw the culmination of a religious movement, Puritanism, which ultimately questioned the authority of any nonbiblical church tradition. The Quakers took their cues from this movement, and went farther and subordinated even the authority of Scripture to direct revelation, the Inward Light of Christ.

In politics, the rule of the aristocracy had been questioned during the years of our concern. The theory of rule by divine right had been soundly challenged. The authority of the aristocracy had not been cataclysmically overthrown as it would be in France a century later, but it had been jolted. The Quakers also revolted against authority whenever they believed it to be contrary to the spirit of Christ. Their refusal to doff the hat, to use speech that differentiated between classes, to wear the ruffles and ribbons of the aristocracy, were all signs of their rejection of any hierarchy not established by Christ's authority. Furthermore, their willingness to disobey what they considered to be unjust laws, and to suffer the persecution that followed, is another manifestation of the spirit of the age, albeit an extreme form.

A similar spirit of revolt from the ancient ways, which we espied in philosophy, religion, and politics, also gathered momentum in the rhetorical and homiletical trends of the period. In the sixteenth century, even Ramus considered himself to be reacting to entrenched Scholasticism. Eventually, the Baconian spirit invaded theories of discourse, helping change the predominant theory of style from ingratiation to the plainer style of the Age of Reason. It is difficult to find direct evidence of the influence of this trend upon Quakerism because most of the early Quaker preachers and writers were not formally educated.

Robert Barclay and William Penn received formal education and had access to excellent libraries. Penn, in particular, was both a member of the Royal Society and a lifelong friend of John Locke, thus the influence of the secular trend toward "scientific" speech may have been influential in his writings. Clearly, though, as the century drew to a close, the Quakers strove more for a plainer style of speech. Quakers were probably influenced indirectly by Ramistic rhetoric through the specific homiletic theories of Perkins reflected in Puritan practice, although they roundly rejected the "doctrine-use" format. Many of the so-called lay ministers of early Quakerism grew up on Puritan preaching of the style Perkins advocated.

In short, the situation was ripe for a new movement of radical Christianity, one that would manifest the spirit of change in the intellectual, religious, and political spheres. Old moorings were rejected before new ones were fashioned, and in the years that England drifted, a group of religious voyagers thought they had discerned the bare outlines of the promised land.

Chapter 2

PRESUPPOSITIONS OF EARLY QUAKER PREACHING

The way in which an individual or group characteristically communicates, or thinks about communication, both reveals and depends upon a worldview, for it emanates from human ends, which it may be said to reflect. Allowing for individual, isolated, idiosyncratic deviations from a group's belief structure, most group members communicate a core of common beliefs, which constitute the philosophical underpinings of its rhetoric. This chapter will lay out the framework of seventeenth-century Quaker presuppositions about human nature, society, and epistemology, each comprising a part of the contextual background helpful to a full understanding of the development of Quaker rhetorical theory and preaching practice over the second half of the seventeenth century.

Immature groups differ from mature groups in that the latter set more rigid parameters around the individual's attempts to communicate, while the former accept a great deal of dynamic and mutual influence between the individual's communication and the group's worldview. This book examines Quaker writings about preaching and their preaching practice during their first fifty years. This scope of years bridges the initial period of individual experimentation within the group and a later period when more consistency was expressed and stressed. By the time the sermons dealt with later in this book were presented, the dynamic, idiosyncratic effect of individuals' rhetorical expression upon the group had abated, and the dampening effect of the group belief structure on the individual had become more obvious. It is, therefore, not surprising that the actual sermon texts present a fairly consistent picture of Quaker belief.[1]

This abbreviated examination of Quaker presuppositions will be illustrated, as far as possible, from primary sources, including the sermon texts themselves. The reader should bear in mind, however, that my purpose is not to present a definitive or detailed statement with regard to the topics of this chapter, but to provide further contextual background for better understanding the rationale and development of Quaker impromptu preaching theory and practice.

HUMAN NATURE: FALLEN, ENLIGHTENED, AND SANCTIFIED

Early Quakers accepted the account of the fall of the first man and woman through temptation and disobedience as presented in the Old Testament Scriptures. They saw humans as having been created in the image of God but having marred that image through an act of willful disobedience. In the words of George Fox, Adam and Eve "came into ye Curse, Lost ye Light, & came into Darknesse: Sould under Sin in Transgression."[2] Each individual human, according to Barclay, "is fallen, degenerated, and is subject unto the power, nature, and seed of the serpent. . . . Man, therefore, as he is in this state, can know nothing aright; yea, his thoughts and conceptions concerning God and things spiritual, until he be disjoined from this evil seed . . . are unprofitable both to himself and others."[3]

Rejecting the view of extreme Calvinism, which saw some humans as elected by God to salvation and others to damnation, the early Quakers argued for the existence of "an evangelical, saving Light and grace in all."[4] They took literally the teaching of the Apostle John when he referred to Christ as "the true Light, which lighteth every man that cometh into the world"(John 1:9).[5] According to early Friends, every person could come to the knowledge of God through the Light.

The concept of the Light merits some consideration, since it infuses Quaker thought and directly defines the early Quaker conception of human nature and also human language use. The nature of the Light was a constant topic of contention between early Quakers and their religious competitors. It continues to be of interest and debate among today's Friends.[6] Examination of early Quaker literature reveals that early Friends understood that the Light was wedded to the basic Christian tenet that grace was bestowed to humans through Christ. They often use the phrase "light and grace" in their sermons to indicate that the Light is a phenomenon which works *upon* humans, rather than existing as a part of human nature. Light is a gift of God to humans in the same sense that grace and faith are seen as God's gifts. "Light" is repeatedly used in their sermons along with "Christ,"

"Seed," "Word," "truth," and other terms to signify the same basic phenomenon—God's work in persons. Stephen Crisp often refers to the Light as a "Manifestation of the Spirit." He counsels his audience in 1691 to "embrace the Light, and believe in the Light, in the Lord Jesus Christ."[7]

Among early Quakers, the concept of the Light is not confused with an innate quality of human nature—a so-called "spark of divinity." Barclay, for example, denies human divinity when he asserts, "we certainly know that this light of which we speak is not only distinct, but of a different nature from the soul of man, and its faculties."[8] He and other early Friends expressly separate the Light from the conscience or reason, both of which operate through human faculties. Crisp addresses this topic in a 1692 sermon: "God hath bestowed something upon us, that wars and fights against Sin and Iniquity: How came we by it? Is it any Faculty in Nature? No, Nature is Corrupted and Defiled. . . . Yet there is something in me that answers the pure Law of God, that which makes me to hate things that are Reprovable; that is, Light: How came I by it? It is not Natural; for then it would run Parallel with that Natural Inclination that is in my Soul, to lead me further and further from God." Later in the same sermon, Crisp ties the inward principle to the presence of Christ: "if a Holy Divine Life is in thee, it is He; if a Principle of Truth stir in thee, it is He. . . . This is he that God hath ordained to be the Captain of our Salvation."[9]

The principle of the Inward Light of Christ that enlightens every person is the essential distinguishing factor that sets the early Quaker view of human nature apart from the then-widespread Calvinistic, Puritan viewpoint. The Inward Light presupposes a quality in persons, which would either submit to it or resist it. Early Quakers place strong emphasis on the exercise of human will in the process of salvation. They speak of a personal "Day of Visitation" by God's spirit, during which *every* individual person is touched and wooed by the Inward Light. They enthusiastically maintain that "God doth give to every Man a measure of Grace that brings Salvation," but they also assert, "too many People have not had regard to the Grace of God given to them, but rather trample upon it."[10] Through the exercise of the will, John Bowater reminds his listeners, "many hearken not to the Reproof of the Spirit of the Lord, but they harden their Hearts, and Rebel against the Light, against Gods [sic] Spirit that striveth with them." The will to resist the Light is often strong, yet "if man resist it not," Barclay concludes, "but close with it, he comes to know salvation by it."[11]

In 1670 John Furly addressed the townspeople of Colchester concerning the necessity of responding to the Light: "This Light will deal impartially with you, it will flatter none of you, nor will it accuse any of you falsely; its Voice is God's Voice in you: and speaks one and the same Language with the Lord of Heaven; it will never justify you when you do evil . . . nor never condemn you when you have done well."[12]

Thus far I have argued that the early Quakers held hope for the redemption of fallen human nature through the Inward Light of Christ. Human nature, according to Quaker preachers and apologists, is first fallen and degenerated, yet enlightened by Christ. Assuming a person does not exercise his or her will against the Light, that person enters into salvation. However, salvation alone does not complete the total picture of the human situation reflected in the preaching of the early Quakers. With remarkable consistency, early Friends asserted that humans could attain a state of purity and holiness in which they do not continue willfully to sin. Viewed from the perspective of the Inward Light, this position holds that it is possible for a person to obey the Light of Christ in every single instance.

George Fox's ministry was characterized by a radical belief that holiness could be achieved on earth. His opponents, the "professors" of faith, had strong negative responses to this idea, which are obvious in Fox's account of a 1647 incident, early in his ministry:

> I stayed awhile and declared truth among them. . . . But the professors were in a rage, all pleading for sin and imperfection, and could not endure to hear talk of perfection, and of an holy and sinless life."[13] Fox believed that Christ "brings to ye State of Adam & Eve before they fell, & to ye Image of God in Righteousness, & Holyness; they sitting down in Christ yt never fell."[14]

Here Fox echoes a truth that was "opened" to him early in his ministry and that he recorded in a famous passage in his *Journal*:

> I was come up to the state of Adam which he was in before he fell.
> . . . But I was immediately taken up in spirit, to see into another or more steadfast state than Adam's in innocency, even into a state in Christ Jesus, that should never fall. And the Lord showed me that such as were faithful to him in the power and light of Christ, should come up into that state in which Adam was before he fell.[15]

Fox also believed that the holy and righteous state could not be achieved without the inward, spiritual "Circumcision, & Baptism to plunge down Sin, & Corruption: this must be known before Man & Woman come up into ye Image of God."[16]

Emphasis on achieving holiness is repeated in the later sermons and indicates that early Quakers accepted the possibility that every person could be restored into a state devoid of sin. In 1688, Crisp elaborates this theme and declares that Christ can gradually help a person live righteously: "Resolve upon this, and then the Grace of God will be at work, we shall soon see that we must leave off sining: There is such a thing I must leave, God hath set up a judgment in my Mind against it; though it bring Profit and Pleasure, away it must go. Here is a step, a following step, to follow Christ. He that will deny himself, will follow Christ. . . . Here the Soul is led step by step, even by Christ, the Captain of our Salvation, 'till it is gradually cleansed from sin."[17] In this sermon quotation, we see the theme of perfection coupled with the act of self-denial, a persistent theme in Crisp's sermons.

Following Crisp, Francis Camfield, another "publisher of truth," charges his hearers to "go on to Perfection. . . . Christ is *the Way, the Truth, and the Life*; and every one that comes into this way, and walketh in it, they are going towards Perfection."[18]

Many other examples of the perfection theme could be produced from the sermons of the period.[19] However, over the years from Fox's early ministry to the last decade of the century, there appears to have been a departure from the radical position on perfection held by Fox. The sermons of the late decades emphasize a spiritual conflict, the necessity of self-denial, and a continual process of perfection. Most of the later preachers fit quite comfortably within the confines of Barclay's theological proposition on the subject: "yet doth this perfection still admit of a growth; and there remaineth always in some part a possibility of sining, where the mind doth not most diligently and watchfully attend unto the Lord."[20] Humans are still perfectible, but they are not in Adam's state before he fell, as Fox had envisioned.

Implied in the foregoing discussion is the belief held by early Quakers that humans, far from being mere puppets whose strings are pulled by God, are beings with a free will. For example, a person could either reject or accept the Inward Light; and once a "convinced" Quaker, he or she could move toward perfection only by willfully attending to the Lord.[21] Arguably, the early Quakers saw the will as a dominant faculty of human nature, and one that was best addressed by reason. For all their professed distrust of human reason, which we shall discuss later, early Quaker preachers could use arguments to persuade hearers to will themselves to follow the Light.[22] Paradoxically, although it is human free will that the Quaker preacher most often addressed in sermons, it is the will that could produce the wrong kinds of religion, worship, and preaching, what Barclay calls "will-worship and abominable idolatry."[23] The will, if exercised without the guidance of the Inward Light, could lead people into dark pathways.

In sum, the early Quaker view of human nature offers a strong measure of hope. Humans are not uncharitably destined to hell on the grounds that they are not among the "elect." Although the early Quaker view admits of human degradation through disobedience, it boldly asserts that anyone can overcome the effects of the fall through the Light of Christ. The two most striking features of the early Quaker concept of human nature are that the Inward Light enlightened all persons, and that through the Light anyone could overcome sin in his or her life.

QUAKER VIEW OF SOCIETY

From the "Lamb's War" to the Preservation of the "Remnant"

During the period from the first emergence of Quakerism to the last decade of the seventeenth century, the Quaker outlook on society underwent a process of change. Whereas in the begining Quakers saw themselves as soldiers in the conquering army of Christ the Lamb, after the Interregnum and during the Restoration they began to see themselves increasingly as the remnant to be preserved by God.

Barbour points to the importance of the concept of the "Lamb's War" in early Quakerism: "The Lamb in the Book of Revelation is the conquering Christ who destroys the Anti-Christ, Rome, and Satan and sets up his world dominion for the millenium."[24] The Lamb's War signified both an outward and inward struggle of light against darkness, good against evil, the Lamb against the serpent. Early Friends saw themselves as a part of "primitive Christianity Revived," a new age when Christ would return to set up his kingdom. Barbour's observation that "The early days of the Lamb's War had seemed to them to be the begining of a conquest of the world"[25] expresses the confusion inherent in the metaphor that seems to subsume the aspects of both inward as well as outward struggle. The language used by many of the first-generation Quakers led some of their contemporaries to believe that they, along with other radical Puritans, believed that "for the saints to judge the world and to possess the kingdom was possible."[26] Hence, it was not inappropriate for Henry Cromwell to remark in 1656, "Our most considerable enemy now in our view are the Quakers."[27]

Although laced with militant imagery, the rhetoric of the Lamb's War was primarily inward and spiritual in nature, but the inward changes in attitude also contributed to behavioral changes. The conquest of which the earliest Quaker preachers spoke began internally with subjection to the Light and then moved outward.[28] Early Friends saw themselves as separated from the established government. They took their orders from a different authority. Where the Inward Light contradicted the outward authority of the government or the traditions of church or society, there was no question in their minds regarding which to obey.[29] Many of the behaviors of early Friends separated them from society, but rarely could the actions of early Quakers be described in all fairness as "militant."[30]

Three particular phenomena among early Friends bear mention because they relate their concept of the believer's place in and relationship to society to Quaker language use: (1) their stand against oaths, (2) their insistence upon calling things by their "true" names, and (3) their use of the "plain" speech. These peculiarities of usage were prompted by a principle exemplified in other socially alienating Quaker practices, the principle of acted radical truth.

Quakers refused to take oaths because the Bible forbade it (James 5:12) and because oaths implied a double standard of truth telling whereby one could be held to tell the truth only when under oath. Barclay understood that Christ "abrogated oaths, as a rudiment of infirmity, and in place thereof established the use of truth."[31] The result of holding to a single standard of truth telling, which meant refusal of oaths, was persecution by the government.

Cope is justified in maintaining that the concept of the "name" was important in early Quakerism.[32] For example, Friends were careful to avoid the use of titles, which often bestowed honor on a person who did not merit it. They also were careful to call their places of worship "meetinghouses," not "churches." The term "church" was reserved for members of the body of Christ, not the place where the body met. They took care to choose the proper word, often with a resultant social alienation or suspicion from society at large.

Perhaps the best-known early Quaker language choice, which stood as a witness to their view of society, is their refusal to use "you" for the singular. They argued relentlessly that the common usage was ungrammatical and that it tended to give unwarranted distinction and honor to individuals addressed as "you" rather than "thou." This peculiar pronominal usage had, for many seventeenth-century English people, the same effect as refusal to doff the hat.[33]

As the century drew to a close, Friends viewed themselves less as a conquering army and more as a remnant that had been preserved by God through persecution and peril. "Remnant," like "Lamb's War," was a biblically inspired image calling to mind the preservation of the remnant of Israel by the hand of God during the Babylonian captivity of Old Testament times. The Quaker social peculiarities—plain speech, refusal to take an oath, etc.—originally performed as a means of witness, were becoming mere customs as the new century dawned. Barbour writes that the original Quaker testimonies "were no longer expected to offend or convert anyone and were left by the passing of time and the end of conflict as a former shoreline cut by the high tide of the Spirit before it shifted to new beaches."[34]

Belief waned regarding the triumphant effect of the Lamb's War on society. The solemn warning of God's judgment to the nation, so common during the early years, persisted in some of the later sermons, but its appearance was much rarer. Francis Stamper warned London as late as 1694 that the "vials of my wrath shall be poured upon the Transgressor."[35] But Quakers, by then, regarded themselves differently than they had in earlier decades. Whitehead better illustrated the new Quaker outlook than Stamper when he prayed in 1693, "This is the Belief and Confidence that thou hast raised in the Hearts of a Remnant. Therefore O Lord, we have cause to wait upon thee, and continually to trust in thee, and breath[e] and cry unto thee, for thy whole Heritage, for all them whom thou hast gathered by the Arm of thy Power, that they may be preserved faithful to the end of their Days, that they may be saved from the Evils and Pollutions and Corruptions of the World."[36]

Whitehead set the tone for the next century, which saw the culmination of toleration, acceptance, even respect from the society at large for Friends. Elbert Russell remarks that Quakerism was "passing over from a movement charged with potential energy to a stage of arrested development and cooling enthusiasm."[37] Braithwaite best describes the situation at the close of the century: "The Quaker Church effectively organized as a State within the State, was now mainly concerned with preserving its own quiet way of life; and, driven by the growth of a narrowing discipline, was no longer aflame with a mission to the world."[38]

The sermons examined later in this book illustrate the change in Quaker attitude toward society—"the world"—from that expressed in the powerful metaphor, the Lamb's War, to the overpowering exclusivity of the remnant. Both terms conote separateness from society at large, but the first possesses an apocalyptic sense of victory so strong that it was often confused with revolutionary politics; that same power is strangely repressed in the latter term, having been replaced with an attitude of survival or preservation.

Early Quaker Epistemology: The Pervasiveness of the Inward Light

Prior to the period focused on in this book, Christendom had emphasized various aspects of God's work with humans, but it was the "spiritual Puritans"—the seedbed of Quakerism—who rediscovered the Holy Spirit.[39] Early Friends pushed the concept of the Holy Spirit to its logical extreme. What resulted was an epistemology based almost exclusively upon immediate supernatural revelation, which they called by many names, but most often the Inward Light. I have already alluded to the Quaker understanding of the Light as a vehicle of redemption and perfection in the previous discussion of the early Quaker view of human nature. I also alluded to its influence in motivating the social "witnesses" of Friends. It remains now to see in what sense the Inward Light was viewed as the primary means of knowledge, and what place other means of acquiring knowledge played in the early Quaker epistemology. This topic will be addressed again in the context of the development of a Quaker homiletic theory in chapter 3, but I will begin the discussion here.

We turn initially to the experience of George Fox because he illustrates the radical dependence early Quakers placed on the Light. Fox had a thorough knowledge of the Scriptures and a background acquaintance with doctrine and church tradition, but this fund of knowledge proved unsatisfying to his innermost needs. He records in his *Journal* that as a youngster he believed that God had directly communicated to him that he should "be faithful in all things, and to act faithfully two ways, viz. inwardly to God and outwardly to man, and to keep to 'yea' and 'nay' in all things." In 1643 he left home "at the command of God" to begin to search for an authentic experience in religion. In 1646 Fox had numerous openings, or revelations. The first dealt with the commonly accepted notion that all Christians were believers. On this topic Fox wrote, "the Lord opened to me that, if all were believers, then they were all born of God and passed from death to life, and that none were true believers but such; and though others said they were believers, yet they were not." Later it was opened to him "that being bred at Oxford or Cambridge was not enough to fit and qualify men to be ministers of Christ." His third important opening was that "God, who made the world, did not dwell in temples made with hands."[40] These openings were prior to Fox's often quoted direct encounter with Christ, about which he writes, "And when my hopes in them and in all men were gone, so that I had nothing outwardly to help me, nor could tell what to do, then, Oh then, I heard a voice which said, 'There is one, even Christ Jesus, that can speak to thy condition,' and when I heard it my heart did leap for joy. . . . And this I knew experimentally."[41]

The Light became Fox's prime instrument of knowledge. He asserts, "The divine light of Christ manifesteth all things."[42] As already noted, Friends did not always use the term "Light" to refer to the immediate revelation of Christ.[43] Consequently, when Fox speaks of the experience in which the creation is "opened" to him and he sees how "all things had their names given them according to their nature and virtue,"[44] he explains that the source of the experience is the "Spirit," the "divine Word of wisdom and power," and the "Lord." From Fox's use of these terms and others such as "Light," "Light of Christ," "Seed," etc., to refer to the same phenomenon, we understand that the terms equivalently signify *immediate revelation* from Christ. Because the phenomenon of immediate revelation preceded and produced Fox's opening about the importance of the "name," we must reject Cope's conclusion that the concept of the name overshadows that of the Light in early Quakerism. Fox always maintained, "in his [Christ's] day are all things seen, visible and invisible, by the divine light of Christ."[45]

In Fox's experience, the Scriptures were very important, but secondary to the Light as a source of knowledge. In his *Journal*, he tells the reader that he sees "how people read the Scriptures without a right sense of them, and without duly applying them to their own states." He boldly proclaims that no one could "know the spiritual meaning of

Moses', the prophet's, and John's words . . . unless they had the Spirit and the light of Jesus; nor could they know the words of Christ and of his apostles without the Spirit."[46] By maintaining that the Spirit must illuminate the Scripture, Fox was aligning himself with the spiritual Puritans of the day who believed the same thing,[47] but Fox went further and claimed he "saw in that Light and Spirit which was before Scripture was given forth, and which led the holy men of God to give them forth."[48] In essence, Fox claimed the same type of inspiration from the Spirit that had moved the apostles.

Fox's constant use of the Scriptures in his writings and preaching presents a strong argument that he believed in their efficacy for a range of purposes, and makes good his claim: "I had no slight esteem of the Holy Scriptures, but they were very precious to me . . . and what the Lord opened to me I afterwards found was agreeable to them."[49]

After extensive study that revealed the centrality of faith in Christ's saving work in Fox's total message, T. Canby Jones concludes the following regarding Fox's position on the Scripture:

> The Bible . . . remained finally authoritative as a record of Christ's coming and a declaration of the Spirit's power. Fox also regarded it as the ultimate criterion in controversy. In a negative sense, too, Fox was certain that Scriptures were final authority, since nothing inwardly revealed could be true if it contradicted Scripture. Further, as moral law in matters of outward conduct, for example on oath taking, Scripture represented literal and final authority to Fox. In addition, Fox showed his belief in the authority of Scripture by his view of himself as the defender of the pure Scripture against the perverse interpretations of others. Finally, Fox was sure that there were no better terms to confess Christ, His life, death and resurrection, than those found in the Scriptures. In all these senses the Bible remained ultimately authoritative, even though in general Fox asserted the superior authority of the Holy Spirit.[50]

If we contrast Fox's view on the Bible versus inward revelation with that of other radical Puritans of his day, we find that Fox represents a religion of the Spirit, which placed *high* esteem on the Bible, while the "spiritual Puritans" represent a religion of the Spirit, which placed *highest* esteem on the Bible.

Fox's experience and viewpoint are repeated with frequency in the lives and writings of other early Quakers. Their quintessential position lies not in derogating the Bible, but in insisting that simply knowing the "Book" is not the same as experiencing the grace of God through Christ. Francis Howgill, one of the most powerful of the early Quaker preachers, was raised in Puritan ways. He often prayed, read his Bible, and preached. But when he heard Fox preach that the Light of Christ was the way to salvation, he witnessed that he "believed the eternal word of truth . . . we were all seen to be off the foundation, and all mouths were stopped in the dust."[51]

By the time Barclay pened his *Apology*, the experience of two decades of Quakers had produced an epistemology that amounted to a dynamic tension between the Spirit and the Bible. Whereas Reformation theology begins with the Scriptures as final authority in all matters of faith and practice, Barclay begins with the Spirit: "the testimony of the Spirit is that alone by which the true knowledge of God hath been, is, and can be only revealed. . . . these divine inward revelations, which we make absolutely necessary for the building up of true faith, neither do nor can ever contradict the outward testimony of the Scriptures, or right and sound reason."[52]

Barclay's proposition makes explicit two additional sources of knowledge other than the Spirit: the Scriptures and reason. The Scriptures, sent forth by the Spirit, are "a *secondary rule, subordinate* to the *Spirit*, from which they have all their excellency and certainty." The apologist considers the great work of the Scriptures to be the ability to "witness them fulfilled in us." He also specifically appoints them to be "the only fit outward judge of controversies among Christians; and that whatsoever doctrine is contrary unto their testimony, may therefore justly be rejected as false."[53] The essential early Quaker position on revelation and the Bible amounts to an injunction to obey both the Spirit *and* the Scriptures, since the two are never in contradiction. What I have described as a "dynamic tension" between Spirit and Scripture is illustrated in a 1694 sermon by Benjamin Coole:

> Now the Way whereby God discovers his Mind to Man, is twofold, *without*, and *within*.
>
> 1. The Holy Scriptures without.
> 2. The Holy Spirit within.
>   1. We may learn from without what a Vail there hath been over the Understanding of the Children of Men.
>   2. But there is a further Discovery made to us from within, the Spirit of the Lord convinceth us of Sin.[54]

Barclay also acknowledges the place of reason as a guide primarily in the "natural" world. He queries, "Why need we set up our own carnal and corrupt reason for a guide to us in matters spiritual, as some will needs do?" He later maintains that "the great cause of the apostasy hath been, that man has sought to fathom the things of God in and by this natural and rational principle, and to build up a religion on it, neglecting and overlooking this principle and seed of God in the heart." Nevertheless, he affirms that reason is fit to "order and rule man in things natural" and "may be useful to man even in spiritual things, as it is still subservient and subject to the other [the 'Seed' or 'Light']."[55]

Although the earlier preachers might have been uncomfortable with Barclay's emphasis upon the dualism of nature and spirit, they also tended to give some place to reason in their epistemology.[56] T. Canby Jones has shown that Fox's writings reveal a sense of respect for reason. He points out that Fox believed that, through Adam's fall, human will and mind are perverted, but that the fall did not rob humans of the ability to perceive and reason. Reason, for the unbeliever, according to Fox, is the source of wrong notions and carnal knowledge. Jones notes, "Fox believed, after the experience of salvation it [reason] becomes a noble faculty worthy of great confidence. Reason guided by direct revelation and seasoned with the truth as taught by Christ fills men with wisdom and leads them up into the image of God."[57] However, for Fox, reason never attains a prominent place in his epistemology, and its position is always subservient to that of inward revelation.

Later Friends in the seventeenth century, especially Barclay and Penn, assigned a greater role to reason than did the earlier Friends. Barclay, we have seen, found it an appropriate guide in "natural" things. Penn took this position in hand and particularly in his political writings began to appeal to non-Quakers on the basis of reason. As early as 1670, in a treatise on freedom of religion, he maintains, "The understanding can never be convinced nor properly submit but by such arguments as are rational, persuasive, and suitable to its own nature, something that can resolve its doubts, answer its objections, enervate its propositions."[58] In 1693 he writes, "We must not be . . . raised above reason, in maintaining what we think reasonable."[59] A year later, in a sermon, he asserts, "God hath made men Reasonable," but he also questions why most people "live in a Contradiction to their own rational Natures?"[60] In Penn's mind, this apparent conflict over the place of reason in human deliberation and action seems resolved in 1702, when he writes, "In all Things Reason should prevail: . . . Beasts act by Sense, Man should by Reason. . . . If my own Reason be on the Side of a Principle, with what can I Dispute or withstand it? . . . Reason, like the Sun, is Common to All; and 't is for want of examining all by the same Light and Measure, that we are not all of the same Mind: For all have it to that End, though all do not use it So."[61] Apparently, Penn reaches the point where he can, without hesitation, apply the great Quaker metaphor for divine revelation—the Light— to a function inherent in strictly natural human capabilities. Here it is important to note that Penn's extant sermons do not show the great faith in reason that his other writings come to attain. In his preaching he still maintains that his hearers should "submit to the authority" of God manifested in the "ingrafted Word, in which is Light and Life, that is able to save our Souls."[62] Penn's position on the place of reason was arrived at over a long period of time and under the influences of a cultural turn toward science and rational thought.[63]

Throughout the period of this study, a strong distrust of "worldly learning" continues in the tradition of Fox and the first-generation Friends. Crisp, for example, argues that the learning of the schools led to knowledge that would not aid one in pursuit of God's kingdom: "Men can never attain to the saving Knowledge of God by Study, and by Disputation and reading Books, and Commentators, and Observators of matters of Religion." In the same sermon, however, he admits that being "Men of Parts, Men of Courage, Men of Understanding, Learned Doctors, Masters of Liberal Arts and Sciences: These may help to make them Men." In the realm of the Spirit, on the other hand, people "must come to Christ for Divine Knowledge, Theology, the Knowledge of God, and Divine and Heavenly things are from Christ." The important knowledge, after all, being discovered in the spiritual realm, Crisp held that "worldly" knowledge not only could not produce authentic religious experience, but could actually prevent one from attaining it because "Men think by Reading and Learning, and hearing this and the other Mens Notions and Opinions, they may be edified and profited, and come to the true Knowledge of God."[64] Even Penn speaks with the same driving dependence upon God's power in the spiritual realm when he says, "It is not by Strength and Humane Wisdom, not by Arts and Parts, and Academical Acquirements . . . but by the *Spirit of the Lord*, that we are enabled to overcome the Enemies of our Salvation."[65]

Thus far, this inquiry into the epistemological foundations of early Quaker rhetoric has revealed a threefold pattern. Although the primary source of knowledge for early Quakers was inward revelation, the Light, with which all humans were endowed, and which not only illuminated unregenerate persons with the knowledge of right and wrong but also would lead them to the knowledge of God through Christ if not resisted or perverted, they also acknowledged two additional "secondary" sources of knowledge. First, they affirmed the knowledge contained in the Scriptures, which was valid as a code of moral conduct, as a record of Christ and the events of the early years of Christianity, and as a judge of controversies among Christians. Second, they also attended to knowledge brought about through "right reason," which the earlier Friends saw as valid for the believer when it was guided by the Light, and which Friends toward the close of the century began to see as fit to guide people in the natural realm just as the Light was appropriate to guide in the spiritual realm.

There is one additional source of knowledge for early Quakers that must be discussed. The group, the "community" of believers, or the "Meeting," as Friends preferred, offered collective wisdom and knowledge to individual Friends. Each of the three epistemological principles mentioned above fed into the group experience. The group acted as a check against false leadings of the Spirit, false interpretations of Scripture, and false reasoning. In this sense, the "meeting" may be viewed as a critical epistemological principle, a means of testing the truth.

When testing the truth or spiritual validity of a belief or action, early Quakers trusted the ability to discern a sense of "unity" in the meeting. They believed that the Light of Christ leads people into a sense of unity.[66] In Fox's first sermon for which we have a text, he stresses that the Light will "bring you into unity, and it will draw your mind up into God, and in it you will see more light."[67] Twenty-eight years later, he still insists that his hearers "all drink into one pure Spirit; ye Holy Spirit of God; drink in it; here is unity."[68] In 1688 Crisp expounds on the same theme: "all God's People have been guided by the Spirit of Christ, that universal Spirit, that is one with God. . . . there was a Concord and Unity among them."[69] The concept of unity as a criterion to assess the Spirit's leading emphasizes once again the closeness with which the Quakers identified their secondary sources of knowledge with their primary one, the Light.

CONCLUSION

In this chapter, we have seen how early Quakers viewed the human fallen condition, how they saw themselves against the backdrop of English society, and, most significantly, we have seen how pervasive the early Quaker epistemology became in the life of Friends. The Inward Light was their primary source of knowledge. It produced and empowered the Scriptures; it was seen as superior to reason, yet might enlighten it for the believer; it validated itself in the meeting through a sense of unity; and, ultimately, it produced a potentially powerful form of spoken discourse based on immediate revelation.

Clearly, the early Quaker worldview possessed a unifying principle. Taking in hand the discovery of the spiritual Puritans that the Holy Spirit was a reality in their age, Quakers refined and extended what had been the spiritual Puritan's experience and made inward revelation their guiding principle. The Inward Light of Christ, their most common name for the direct action of God's grace, truth, power, and revelation to humanity, was the source of their optimistic view of human destiny; it infused and empowered the Lamb's War; it became the foundational tenet of their epistemology; and it was also the foundation of their theory of impromptu preaching.

SECTION II

The Evolution of Quaker Impromptu Preaching Theory

CHAPTER 3

THE DEVELOPMENT OF SEVENTEENTH-CENTURY QUAKER IMPROMPTU PREACHING THEORY

Many people assume intuitively that impromptu preaching does not (and perhaps canot) have an underlying rationale that carefully spells out its assumptions and implications and speculates about the way it works and ought to work—in essence, that it has produced no "theory."[1] But that is a naive view, at least with respect to early Quakers. Admittedly, the account of how Quaker rhetorical or homiletic theory eventually developed in the last half of the seventeenth century must be assembled from numerous documents of several types, including journals, tracts, pamphlets, books, letters, and the surviving sermons themselves; the labor is nevertheless rewarding. The result is a bricolage of a theory, a developmental, yet surprisingly consistent, rationale together with a collection of reflective advice about impromptu preaching, all of which could be passed on to ensuing generations. This chapter's collection of accounts about impromptu preaching constitutes the outlines of Quaker homiletic theory and anticipates much of what will follow in the next two chapters. The best systematic expression of the seventeenth-century Quaker rationale for and theory of impromptu preaching is found in the writings of Robert Barclay, the subject of chapter 4. Quakers did not possess a manual of impromptu preaching until 1750, with the publication of Samuel Bownas' *A Description of the Qualifications Necessary to a Gospel Minister*, the focus of chapter 5, a book that both reflects the groundwork laid in this chapter and significantly extends some of the key concepts toward more full expression.

In this chapter, I will examine writings by George Fox, Margaret Fell, Rebecca Smith, George Whitehead, Charles Marshall, Stephen Crisp, and Benjamin Coole, all key seventeenth-century Quaker writers who each contributed to the development of an early Quaker understanding of impromptu preaching and offered advice to fellow Quaker preachers and their descendents.

Contributions of George Fox

George Fox's contributions to the development of a uniquely Quaker theory of preaching are very significant. Here I will deal with his writings that make clear his opinions about the nature and roles of impromptu preaching. His *Journal* is an obvious place to begin, since it both constitutes a record of his life and contains a selection of his epistles (or quotations from his epistles) regarding the ministry. I will approach this section by focusing on some significant early passages written prior to the geometric growth of Quakerism in the 1650s. Then I will elaborate on Fox's significant contributions to a theory of inspired preaching.[2]

Before Quakerism exploded on the scene in 1652, Fox revealed some significant openings in his *Journal* that indirectly or directly relate to his perspective on preaching. In 1647 he notes, while walking in a field, "the Lord opened unto me that being bred at Oxford or Cambridge was not enough to fit and qualify men to be ministers of Christ; and I stranged at it [thought it strange] because it was the common belief of people." Later he writes, "The knowledge which the world hath of what the prophets and apostles spake is a fleshly knowledge."[3] By these two quotations, we see that Fox repudiated the necessity of the formal knowledge base of theology and higher learning that had buttressed both Puritan and Anglican clergymen. His position would be universally embraced by later writers, including Barclay and Penn, both of whom had university educations. In these initial openings, Fox rejects a ministry based on hierarchy of learning and paves the way for a radically egalitarian ministry based on an immediate sense of the Spirit's inspiration by the preacher.

Another of Fox's early openings attacks the dominant use of the terms "temple" and "church": "it was opened to me that God, who made the world, did not dwell in temples made with hands. This . . . seemed a strange word because both priests and people used to call their temples or churches, dreadful places, and holy ground, and the temples of God. . . . his people were his temple, and he dwelt in them."[4] In this opening, Fox implies the lack of necessity for a church building but also the linguistic habit of referring to buildings as temples or churches, instead of calling the people the church, and the body the temple of the Lord. In 1651 he complains, "the steeplehouses and pulpits were offensive to my mind, because both priests and people called them 'the house of God,' and idolized them, reckoning that God dwelt there in the outward house. Whereas they should have looked for God and Christ to dwell in their hearts, and their bodies to be made the temples of God."[5] To Fox, words should not be misused nor go beyond their original scriptural meaning. Truth was at stake. On another occasion, he records, "The priest told me Matthew, Mark, Luke and John were the Gospel, I told him the Gospel was the power of God."[6] Incipient in this powerful verbal response is the idea that the gospel itself transcends Scripture, a precept that will become well explicated and defended by Friends. Later writers and speakers repeat and amplify Fox's rejection of the dominant culture's language norm and also the rituals that accompanied the "idolatry" of the church. Fox sums up the purpose of his early ministry in these words: "I was to bring people off from Jewish ceremonies and from heathenish fables, and from men's inventions and windy doctrines."[7]

Early on, Fox also set another pattern for later writers with his realignment of the relationship of the Scriptures and the Spirit, with the Spirit now assuming the dominant position, as discussed in chapter 2. In a key passage from 1647, Fox contrasts the "true ministry, which produces liberty," and "the ministry that is of man," which results in bondage. Only true ministers operate "in the eternal Spirit, which was before the Scriptures were given forth."[8]

In the same year, Fox writes that the Spirit was the true source of what rhetorical theorists would call "audience analysis." He asserts, "the Lord shewed me that the natures of those things that were hurtful without [evil acts] were within, in the hearts and minds of wicked men." He puzzles why the Lord had revealed these insights to him, "seeing [he] was never addicted to commit those evils." He concludes, "the Lord answered that it was needful I should have a sense of all conditions, how else should I speak to all conditions."[9] Fox, then, believed that both audience analysis and the very words spoken were the result of revelation.

As early as 1648, Fox anticipates some of Margaret Fell's later well-developed arguments in favor of women speaking. In a Leicestershire debate between Presbyterians, Independents, Baptists, and Anglicans, he records that a woman in the congregation asked a question on a point of doctrine. A minister replied, "'I permit not a woman to speak in the church'; though before he had given liberty for any to speak."[10] Fox then takes on the minister and argues for a distinction between the two types of women in the Bible: the woman that was not to speak and "the woman . . . that might prophesy and speak." Fox takes up this topic once again in his 1657 *An Epistle to all People on the Earth*. There he writes about the tension between silence and speaking that characterized the Quaker meeting for worship. In this important work, he specifically includes women in the vocal ministry: "First, the Spirit leading, then words from the Spirit, and thus the Spirit is not quenched in son nor daughter, in handmaid, nor servant."[11] His defense of women preachers figures prominently in my later analysis of one of Fox's sermons in chapter 9.

Fox also strenuously resists the paid ministry and insists that preaching be done without honorarium or "tithe": "I was moved to declare against them all, and against all that preached and not freely, as being such as had not received freely from Christ."[12] He peppers his journal with denunciations of the "hireling ministry," and this powerfully worded position against the established clergy characterizes the writing of most later contributors to Quaker homiletic theory.

Perusal of Fox's *Journal* indicates that, in addition to his early positions already mentioned (i.e., rejecting systematic theological education for clergy; questioning tradition with the reinterpretation and revitalization of common terms like "church," "temple," and "gospel"; elevating the Spirit above Scripture as a guide for the spiritual life; emphasizing the role of the Spirit in audience analysis; defending women's right to speak and prophesy; and rejection of a ministry paid by tithes), he also sets out a number of additional positions that would prove significant in the development of a community who would practice inspired impromptu preaching. Fox's additional contributions include (1) his defense of a preaching ministry totally dependent on a sense of divine, immediate inspiration; (2) his insistence on waiting in the Spirit and not speaking in haste; (3) his concern that ministers live holy lives; (4) his further advice and directions to hearers; and (5) his emphasis on scriptural interpretation seen through the lens of figures and types.

Dependence on Inspiration

Fox's belief in immediate, divine inspiration has already been illustrated by his early openings, discussed above. However, Fox had a specific scriptural base on which he developed the notion of inspiration.

He believed that those who "were faithful to him [Christ] in the power and light of Christ, should come into that state in which Adam was before he fell, in which the admirable works of the creation, and the virtues thereof, may be known, through the openings of that divine Word of wisdom and power by which they were made." In other words, the Light of Christ held the power to reverse the effects of the fall and opened the doors to direct knowledge of the creation to believers. Regarding his personal calling, he writes, "I was to direct people to the Spirit that gave forth the Scriptures, by which they might be led into all Truth, and so up to Christ and God, as they had been who gave them [the Scriptures] forth."[13]

In his own practice, Fox claimed that he spoke only under the direct moving of the Spirit. In a familiar passage from 1651, Fox relates, "I sat of a haystack and spoke nothing for some hours for I was to famish them from words. . . . And at last I was moved of the Lord to speak, and they were all reached by the Lord's power and word of life."[14] In his *Journal* entries about his own preaching, he prefaces his recollections of sermons with phrases such as these: "I was made to open to the people," "I was moved to declare to the people," "the power of the Lord sprang through me," and "the Lord opened my mouth."[15] Fox was never reticent to claim divine inspiration for his own impromptu messages.

In another key passage from the *Journal*, Fox writes about an encounter at Swarthmore, Judge and Margaret Fell's home, with "four or five priests." Fox asks them "whether any of them could say they ever had a word from the Lord to go and speak to such or such a people and none of them durst say so." What follows epitomizes Fox's position that Quaker preaching is utterly dependent on divine inspiration: "But one of them burst out into a passion and said he could speak his experiences as well as I; but I told him experience was one thing but to go with a message and a word from the Lord as the prophets and the apostles had and did, and as I had done to them, this was another thing."[16]

In his 1657 "An Epistle to All People on the Earth," included in his *Journal*, he asserts, "you must witness silence before you come to speak."[17] Along this same line, in a 1658 sermon partly reported in his *Journal*, Fox addresses "those Friends who had received a part of the ministry"—in other words, those called to ministry.[18] He warns his hearers, "In the unmovable word of the Lord God dwell, for whosoever goes out from the pure [ministry] and ministers not in that, comes to an end; though he was serviceable for a time while he lived in the thing." For those traveling in ministry, he cautions, "There is a great danger to Friends travelling abroad in the world, except a man be moved of the Lord by the power of the Lord; for then keeping in that power, he is kept in his journey and in his work." Later in the sermon, he advises, "When any shall be moved to speak in a steeplehouse or market, turn in to that which moves and be obedient to it."[19] He further advises, "If any have been moved to speak and have quenched that which moved them, let them not go forth afterwards into words until they feel the power arise and move them thereto again." In a 1669 epistle, he alludes to the delicate balance between making the choice to speak and going too far in your message: "do not quench the Spirit, nor abuse the power: when it moves and stirs in you, be obedient; but do not go beyond, nor add to it, nor take from it."[20] It is not surprising, given these words of counsel, that Fox raises strong cautions to preachers. Yet we also see that he offers advice for preachers who have gone beyond their inspiration and charts for them a road to recovery of the gift.

Insistence on Waiting and Cautions Regarding Speaking

As seen in the discussion above, inspiration and silent waiting were inextricably woven in Fox's vision. In his 1654 "Epistle to Friends in the Ministry," quoted from in the *Journal*, Fox advocates a generally cautious and conservative stance for potential vocal ministers. He writes, "Friends, be not hasty; for he that believes in the Light makes not haste." He also stresses the concept of waiting: "This is the word of the Lord God to you. Everyone in the measure of life wait, that . . . your minds may be guided up to the Father of life." Later, in the same epistle, he declares, "All Friends that speak abroad, see that it be in the life of God. . . . In that [life] wait to receive power. . . . Waiting in the Light, you will receive the power of God."[21] In a 1656 epistle, also reported in the *Journal*, Fox specifically addresses Friends who are "young and tender in the Truth," those who might "sometimes utter a few words of thanksgiving and praise to God." Here Fox becomes even more pointed in his cautions not to outrun the Spirit: "You will hear and feel and see the power of God, as your faith is all in it, preaching when you do not hear words, to bind, to chain, to limit, to frustrate, that nothing shall rise nor shall come forth, but what is in the power.

And with that you will let up, and open every spring, plant, and spark, in which will be your joy and refreshment."[22] He goes on to direct his hearers to "be patient and still in the power and still in the Light that doth convince you, to keep your minds to God; in that be quiet. . . ." In the 1658 sermon to ministers mentioned above, Fox plainly states, "Take heed of many words."[23] Fox never advocates a quick or hasty decision to speak—or any approval of histrionic presentation.

Perhaps the clearest statement of the relationship between waiting in silence and knowing when to speak appears in Fox's "An Epistle to all People on the Earth" (1657). In this document, he declares,

> Keep to that of God in you . . . when you are still from your own thoughts and imaginations, and desires and counsels of your own hearts, and motions, and will; when you stand single from all these, waiting upon the Lord is strength renewed; He waiting upon the Lord feels his Shepherd, and he shall not want: And that which is of God within everyone, is that which brings them to wait upon God in every particular, which brings them to unity, which joins their hearts together up to God. So as this moves, this is not to be quenched when it is moved to pray or speak; for there is the power of the Lord, this is the arm of the Lord, the dominion, the victory over death.[24]

Fox had set the model of waiting early on in his ministry, waiting even to the point of "famishing" his hearers for words. Fox believed that the source of powerful speech comes from a divine impulse, a "moving" to pray or speak, a motivation that arose from the context of calm, silent waiting.

Insistence on Holy Lives

As noted in chapter 2, Early Quakers believed in the possibility of people attaining sanctification and living holy lives; thus it is not surprising that Fox insisted preachers ought to live holy lives and, specifically, should not give their hearers any excuse to sin. In a 1650 dispute with "professors" [of faith], whom Fox tells us in his *Journal* "came to plead for sin and imperfection,"[25] he stings them with these words: "I bid them keep from talking of the Scriptures, 'the holy men's words, for the holy men pleaded for holiness in heart and life and conversation here; and you plead for impurity and sin which is of the Devil, what have you to do with holy men's words?'" Thus, he chides non-Quaker preachers for making allowances for sin contrary to Scripture and for ministering themselves from impure lives.

On the other hand, when Fox addresses Quaker preachers, as he did in 1656, he reminds them, in a famous passage from the *Journal*,

> [T]his is the word of the Lord God to you all, and a charge to you all in the presence of the living God, be patterns, be examples . . . that your carriage and life may preach among all sorts of people. . . . Then you will come to walk cheerfully over the world, answering that of God in everyone. . . .
>
> Spare no deceit. Lay the sword upon it; go over it; keep yourselves clear of the blood of all men, either by word, or writing, or speaking. And keep yourselves clean . . . that nothing may rule nor reign but power and life itself, and that in the wisdom of God ye may be preserved in it.[26]

Possibly alluding to the extremely negative "public relations" fallout to Friends over James Naylor's 1656 indiscreet "triumphal entry" into Bristol, Fox warns, "Take heed of destroying that which ye have begotten. . . . In the living unmovable word of the Lord God dwell, for whosoever goes out from the pure and ministers not in that, comes to an end; though he was serviceable for a time while he lived in the thing."[27] "Serviceable" indeed. Naylor had been one of the most effective early Quaker pamphleteers, preachers, debaters, and evangelists.

Advice to Hearers Regarding Novice Vocal Ministers

In a key 1656 epistle, quoted in his *Journal*, Fox advises readers about the appropriate response to novice preachers and about their responsibility to mentor fledglings:

> But such as are tender, if they should be moved to bubble forth a few words, and speak in the Seed and Lamb's power, suffer and bear that, that is, the tender. And if they should go beyond their measure, bear it in the meeting for peace sake, and order, and that the spirits of the world be not moved against you. But when the meeting is done, then if anything should be moved of anyone to speak to them between yourselves or one or two of you that feel it in the life, do it in the love and wisdom that is pure and gentle from above.[28]

This piece of advice reveals a great deal about the development of a culture determined to nurture or "elder" novice preachers in their early steps down the formidable path of the oral impromptu tradition: the hearer confronts the novice preacher only if moved by the Spirit, and then only *outside* the meeting for worship. Any confrontation must be accomplished in love, for, as Fox adds, "love is that which doth edify, and bears all things, and suffers, which doth fulfill the force of the law." Similarly, in 1657 Fox advises, "Friends, be careful how that you do set your feet among the tender plants, that are springing up out of God's earth; lest you do hurt them and tread upon them, and bruise them, or crush them in God's vineyard."[29]

Emphasis on Types and Figures

In Fox's view, the Scriptures as explicated in sermons would come alive as they were revivified and lived out in believers' lives. He asserts, "I saw . . . how people read the Scriptures without a right sense of them, and without duly applying them to their own states."[30] Interpreting the Scriptures by means of analysis and application of "figures and types" became one of Fox's habits in his own preaching, and thus a model for others. This emphasis is in line with Cope's notion of *scriptura rediviva* mentioned in the introductory chapter. A prime example of this habitual practice occurred in 1652, when Fox sat on a rock at Firbank Fell and addressed "above a thousand people." On that occasion, and others, Fox "opened the prophets and the figures and shadows and turned them to Christ the substance, and then opened the parables of Christ and the things that had been hid from the begining."[31] His preaching, especially in the context outside of Quaker meetings, had an intentionally hermeneutic focus, using the interpretation of scriptural "figures and shadows" with the aim of "turning the people to the spirit of God." If the Old Testament Scriptures taught the coming Christ in figures and types, then the preacher needed to point that out. If the Spirit who inspired those same Scriptures was available to all hearers, then Fox sought to break through the figures and shadows and have listeners encounter the Light of Christ directly. Fox wanted all listeners to "come to know Christ their teacher, their counselor, their shepherd to feed them, and their bishop to oversee them and their prophet to open to them, and to know their bodies to be the temples of God and Christ for them to dwell in."[32] The emphasis on the explication and application of types and figures would be echoed in the writings of subsequent Quaker preachers and commentators. Ultimately the strategy would be reiterated and underscored by Bownas in his eighteenth-century manual on ministry, discussed in chapter 5.

Three Approaches to Preaching Implied by Fox's Preaching Habits

As the prominent leader of Quakers, what might Fox's own preaching imply to those taking up the challenge of impromptu inspired preaching? Fox's *Journal* reports numerous instances of Fox's preaching, sometimes with incomplete indications of what he recalled that he said, or what others are reported to have taken down in notes. Close perusal of the journal reveals that Fox frequently followed three habits that contemporary and later preachers might emulate. This short list is intended as descriptive of typical preaching by the founder of Quakerism, particularly outside Quaker meetings:[33]

1. Most importantly, Fox frequently directs his hearers to the source of life, the Inward Light, "the spirit of God in themselves, by which they might know God and Christ and the Scriptures and to have heavenly fellowship in the spirit."[34]

2. Fox often moves to a discussion of "types and figures": "So opening the first covenant, I showed them the types and the substance, and bringing them to Christ the second covenant. . . . Christ was come to teach his people himself."[35] Fox could go on at some length about types and figures in the Bible, particularly the Old Testament. This is arguably his second most important response to the challenging impromptu situation. For example, in 1656 in Bristol, Fox remarked, "And so for many hours did I declare the word of life . . . [and] I showed them the types and figures and shadows of Christ in the time of the law, and showed them how that Christ was come that ended the types and shadows."[36] Many additional instances from the *Journal* could be cited to illustrate this significant line of biblical explication and application. To be able to comment on "types and figures," Fox, or any Quaker preacher employing this approach, must have had to study these particular Scriptures and hone his or her arguments beforehand. These symbols are not built into the Bible passages. They *require explanation*, and unless the preachers were familiar with this sort of hermeneutic strain, it would be unavailable to them during the moment of utterance when they might employ it.

3. Frequently Fox would interpret Scriptures in such a way as to attack and expose teachings of the established church and other dissenters whom he opposed, as he does in 1655 at Drayton-of-the-Clay: "So I showed them out of the prophet Isaiah, Jeremiah, Ezekiel, Micah, Malachi, and other prophets how they were in the steps of such as

God had sent his true prophets to cry against."[37] In other words, arguments drawn from his familiarity with Scripture, aided by continual thought and perhaps discussion with fellow Quakers outside the immediate speaking situation, provided Fox a ready-to-hand set of arguments based both on his own Scripture memorization and on a developed scriptural hermeneutic available to him in his memory for use when the situation of immediate debate presented itself.[38]

These three rhetorical habits do not exhaust Fox's repertoire of topics or approaches, but they do capture the essence of his preaching, at least outside of Quaker meetings. One of Fox's sermons delivered before the 1674 Yearly Meeting in London will be analyzed in chapter 9. On that occasion, Fox both followed and went beyond his own advice.

There are numerous implications about Fox's writing on inspired, impromptu preaching that might be touched on here, but let me reflect briefly on some possible implications of his teachings on the preachers' ability to thrive in the crucible of impromptu speaking. I believe that Fox struck on some powerful methods to trigger memory in the process of impromptu speaking (without specific preparation for the preaching event). Recent research indicates that the brain operates on the basis of patterns generated or stimulated in several of its areas and that memory is a complex matter.[39] Peter Atkins, in his important recent book on the place of memory in liturgical worship, after reviewing the current neurophysiological literature on brain function, concludes, "The brain has the ability to record 'information' in such a way that the memory track can be used time and time again. The more we use the track, the sharper the memory becomes. Thus the brain builds up patterns of appropriate responses to a whole variety of thoughts and stimuli." Atkins also remarks that "our new thoughts would seem in reality to be a new combination of old thoughts."[40] Given these observations, it would appear that Fox's knowledge about Scripture, and particularly his extensive *memorization* of the Bible, together with his habit of ferreting out typologies from the Old and New Testaments (applied either to the task of interpreting the New Testament through symbolic references in the Old Testament, or to their own or hearers' lives) helped provide a continuous supply of topics to him during impromptu speech. Additionally, the silence under which the meeting convened had benefits beyond helping him determine if the Spirit was moving him to speak at that moment. I would suggest that during the time of silent waiting, Fox likely would enter a frame of mind in which his previous study of Scripture, conversations about Scripture with ministry colleagues, or memorized Scriptures themselves might come to mind to be employed once the choice to speak had been deter-, mined. Further, I would expect the process to operate in a similar way with other Quaker preachers.

When Fox spoke in a Quaker meeting, the effect on hearers' memories must have been profound. Listeners, who also included persons who might preach on that same occasion (or at another time), heard familiar language and biblical typologies iterated, which must have resulted in the reinforcement of interpretive associational "patterns" in their brains. Add to this the preacher's rehearsal of key metaphors discussed in chapter 7, and you have a storehouse of biblical and spiritual concepts and language that helped bring about a sense of community. For "publick Friends" who were among the hearers, this process helped equip them to speak out of the silence when they were prompted by reinforcing ideas and language in their brains. For those who were not publick Friends, the rehearsal of familiar language and interpretive typologies surely must have helped them become appreciative and discerning listeners into the future.

It is also important to note that I am writing here about the complex process of memory operating in a culture highly influenced not only by literacy but by print. Walter J. Ong's description of how oral memorization operates in a literate culture aptly applies to the early Quaker approach to Scripture memorization: "[V]erbatim memorization is commonly done from a text, to which the memorizer returns as often as necessary to perfect and test verbatim mastery."[41] Misquotation of Scripture would be quickly sensed by Quaker hearers, most of whom were steeped in Scripture accessed primarily through print when they read their Bibles in their own devotional practice. This is a quite different situation from that described by Ong in preliterate cultures, in which memory could operate free from rote memorization.[42]

In sum, Fox's *Journal* and other writings reveal his rationale for immediate, inspired, impromptu preaching based on a self-proclaimed sense of urgency arising from a personal sense of the Spirit's "moving." In this novel model of vocal ministry, the ministers, men and women qualified by their honorable and holy lives, spoke impromptu. They might not be university educated, because that was not seen as a necessary criterion to qualify them for ministry, nor would they be paid like Anglicans or Puritans for their vocal ministry. They would speak out after a period of concentrated and cautious silent waiting, a period during which they might hear the "voice of God" or recall Scriptures they had studied or memorized, having finally sensed that the Spirit was moving them to speak out in the midst of the silence. In their conceptual world, their task was to move their audiences away from false and superstitious religion to real Christianity—from the shadow to the substance, Fox would say. If Fox's advice was heeded, the aspiring novice preacher could count on a tender, sometimes corrective, but thoroughly nurturing response from hearers, whether they considered themselves to be public ministers or not. In Fox's framework, the Spirit was always central and elevated above Scripture, which had its own source in the Spirit, yet his sermons were laced with scriptural quotations and allusions that betrayed habitual, perhaps arduous, study and meditation. Interestingly, in Fox's view, the Spirit might also reveal to the preacher an understanding of the hearers' inward "condition" or frame of mind. In his own preaching, Fox frequently directed his hearers to the Inward Light in their own lives. He also applied biblical types and figures to his hearers' contemporary lives and employed other scriptural explication and application as relevant to the situation—ostensibly, all as immediately brought to mind by the Spirit.

Contributions of Margaret Fell

Margaret Fell (1614–1702) made significant contributions to the development of a Quaker preaching theory through her enormously important *Women's Speaking Justified, Proved and Allowed of by the Scriptures* (hereafter *Women's Speaking*),[43] which she wrote while a prisoner in Lancaster prison.[44] In this key work, Fell uses sophisticated scriptural interpretation to argue that the Scriptures reveal that "God hath put no such difference between the male and female as men would make."[45] Fell refers not only to numerous women in Scripture who "spoke" but to some who were named as "prophets." She reinterprets troubling Pauline Scriptures, such as 1 Corinthians 11:3-13 and 1 Timothy 2:8-14, concluding,

> And what is all this to such as have the power and Spirit of the Lord Jesus poured upon them, and have the message of the Lord Jesus given unto them? Must not *they* speak the word of the Lord because of these undecent and unreverent women that the Apostle speaks of, and to, in these two Scriptures? And how are the men

of this generation blinded, that bring these Scriptures and pervert
the Apostles words, and corrupt his intent in speaking of them and
by these Scriptures endeavour to stop the message and word of the
Lord God in women?[46]

In this quotation, the reader can appreciate Fell's argumentative acumen and facility with written prose. Since this document is now widely
read in both Quaker studies and rhetorical studies circles, for purposes
of this chapter I will move on to focus briefly on two of Fell's lesser-
known published writings that also contribute to the development of
a Quaker impromptu preaching culture beyond the impact of her
important ideological hermeneutic for gender equality in preaching.

In 1665, prior to the publication of *Women's Speaking*, Fell published
A Call to the Universall Seed of God, a seventeen-page tract "[g]iven forth
at Lancaster Castle, about the middle of the 9th. Month, 1664."[47] In
this tract she anticipates some of the positions she would later develop
in *Women's Speaking*. For example, she comments on Jesus' encounter
with the Samaritan woman at the well in Sychar (reported in John
4:4-26). Jesus had revealed to the woman that "they that worship Him
must worship Him in the Spirit and in the Truth." Fell comments,
"This the blessed Messiah was pleased to communicate to a Woman.
. . . and here unto this Woman he opened the Everlasting fountain
and secrets of the great deep which runs freely."[48] Arguably, if Jesus
opened a fount of knowledge to a woman, then knowledge should be
available to women as well as men.

Like Fox, Fell condemns the ministry as practiced in the established church: "[Christ] ended all outward Ministries and Ministrations that preaches for hire, and Ministers in outward things." In the
tract, all "outward" forms of worship are rejected and displaced by
worship "in the Spirit and in the Truth." She asserts, "So here is
the place of publick worship, which Christ Jesus the true Bishop of
the Soules of all his people hath set up, so all that will hear the only
beloved Son of the Living God, they must hear him in their hearts,
they must hear his spirit in their inward parts." This worship would
be achieved only when people "come out of the Apostacy, and out of
all formes, and outside professions and performances, and outward
observations in outward things."[49] Here Fell vehemently reiterates
and stresses some of the ideas we earlier discovered in Fox's writings
from the 1650s, using spatial terms to good effect.

In 1667 Fell published *A Touch-Stone*, written while she was imprisoned in Lancaster Castle and printed along with the second edition of
Women's Speaking.[50] In this tract, Fell effectively articulates the Quaker
objections to preaching as commonly practiced:

> The first thing that I except against in matter and form of their
> Worship . . . is the taking a part or portion of Scripture for a Text,
> and adding thereto their own Inventions, which they study out of
> their own brain, and also bringing other Authors, who have done
> the like; many of them not Christians but Heathens: and thus make
> an Image and set up, and deceive poor peoples souls, and keep them
> ever learning, but never coming to the knowledge of the Truth; and
> are more ignorant of God than many Heathens that never professed
> Christ, nor the Scriptures; and so it is ordinary for them to bring the
> Heathens words in that which they prepare for them, and stir them
> up; and this is quite contrary to Christ and the Apostles practice.[51]

"Christ's ministry," on the other hand, would produce an alternative focus drawn from a different base:

> And this is the matter, and manner, and method of all Christ's
> Ministers, to preach the Resurrection of Christ Jesus, in his Light
> and Spirit, which is a mystery to all carnal men and carnal minds:
> and this is not a deal of Imaginations, and divinations of the brain,
> and studyings of men, who take one verse of Scripture, and add
> unto it what they please, out of other old Authors Writings, Hea-
> then Philosophers, or any thing that will make up an hours talk, till
> their Glass be run, which is quite contrary to the Apostles practice,
> and that which they witnessed, and exhorted against.[52]

Fell's statement rejects any notion of preparation for a specific preaching event and, by implication, all of the prevalent sermon preparation
techniques and strategies employed by Anglicans, Puritans, Baptists,
and other Dissenters. Also, Fell's focus is both a condemnation of
"hireling" preachers speaking "till their [hour]Glass be run"—many
Puritan sermons were about an hour's length—but also a focus on
the proper content of preaching: "the Resurrection of Christ Jesus,
in his Light and Spirit." This focus is an apt example of "realised
eschatology" in that, while not denying the historical resurrection of
Jesus Christ, Fell insists on Jesus' "resurrection" in contemporary times
through the Light. Her focus on Christ also reconfirms Fox's notion

that preaching should direct hearers directly to the source of truth. Fell's condemnation of "imaginations, and divinations of the brain, and studyings of men, who take one verse of Scripture, and add unto it what they please, out of other old Authors['] Writings, [and] Heathen Philosophers" appears to reject the use of biblical commentaries and the consultation of other peoples' sermons. However, her position does not rule out the study of Scripture, per se, but may come close to questioning Fox's hermeneutic of "types and figures" as an "imagination of his brain." If Fell meant to question such Bible study, Fox's practice and advice reveals that he did not concur.

Fell also condemns the oral reading of prayers from the Book of Common Prayer, praying the "Paternoster"—the Lord's Prayer—singing as practiced in the churches, and the habit of calling buildings "churches," which Fell calls "Popish Houses."[53] Fell invokes the standard Quaker objection to "learning" viewed as a prerequisite to pastoral or preaching ministry. She presents a clever and effective argument using the Old Testament priest's "education" for ministry:

> [the priests knew] nothing of Studying, or going to the Universities, nor diving, nor divining into the Body of Darkness, which defiles and polutes: but here was Washing, and Cleansing, and Purifying, and an Offering of two Bullocks, one for a Sin-Offering, another for a Burnt-Offering, the Levites being offered with the Offerings, and they laying ther [*sic*] hands upon the heads of the Offerings, and *Moses* making an Atonement for them, to Cleanse them, before they could be admitted into the Service; and then they were to wait from twenty five years, and upwards unto fifty years, before they might cease waiting, and then they were to minister with their Brethren in the Tabernacle; but they did not wait at the Universities, and at the Schools of Learning, but they waited upon the Service of the Tabernacle of the Congregation; for the Lord had called them for that end.[54]

Here Fell skillfully interweaves a position she shares with Fox and others, that it is absolutely necessary for ministers to be pure and to "wait" before entering into ministry, all within the context of rejecting the notion that a university education was a prerequisite to ministry.

Fell also reiterates belief in immediate revelation:

> [O]ur professed Christian Ministers, in this time of Apostacy . . . will confess the Lord never [s]pake unto them, neither do they expect to

know revelation, nor hear the voice of God, as the Apostle did; for they have preached to all people, that that is ceased. . . . And though it is true, that it hath been ceased among them, in their dark night of Apostacy, yet the holy Spirit of the Lord Jesus Christ, which spake in him, and in all his holy Apostles, *is alive, and lives for evermore.*[55]

As this lengthy quotation reveals, Fell is verbally adept at attacking Anglican, Puritan, and other Dissenter preaching. She observes that non-Quaker preachers "study all their dayes to invent an hour[']s talk to please men, and so they take the Scriptures, and garnish, and adorn, and flourish this dark muddly stuff [from their study] with it, and when they have done, sell it for money." Fell sees the Apostle Paul, a learned man, as having rejected "all his humane Knowledge, and Learning, and filthy Wisdom, and only [choosing] the holy Spirit of the Lord God, the Cross of Christ, whereby he said *he was crucified to the world, and the world to him*; and this is quite contrary to the ministration of men[']s wisdom before mentioned."[56]

Fell ends *A Touch-Stone* with a rhetorically adroit series of "*Queries*" to the Bishops, Minister and Clergy. After arguing indirectly by way of her questions that immediate revelation is still "of the same force and power as ever it was," Fell asks, "Then why is not the ministration of the Spirit, and those that are inspired by the Almighty, the Ministers that are allowed of, and set up by the Powers of the Nation? And why is such a Ministry set up and allowed of by the Powers of the Nation, who deny Revelation, and do not wait for Revelation, but say it is ceased?"[57]

Fell's tenth query includes this stinging question, based on the contrast of inspired impromptu preaching by laypersons to preaching by ordained ministers: "Since that the Spirit is given to every man; how is it that poor people have had one man set up to teach them, it may be thirty or forty years together, and whatsoever was revealed to him that sat by, they were not permitted to speak?"[58]

In sum, Margaret Fell not only presented the best seventeenth-century defense of women preaching, but she also effectively restated the early Quaker rejection of the necessity of university training for ministry, rejection of "bookish" preparation for preaching, and receiving wages for preaching. Fell reiterated the necessity for ministers to be holy and to wait until the Lord directs them to minister. To Fell, worshipping in "Spirit and Truth" *might* involve vocal ministry, but that overt and vocal communication would always be motivated by the immediate moving of the Spirit. She rejects the use of commentaries and other helps for preaching as well as biblical study directed toward the preparation of specific sermons planned in advance.

Contributions of Rebecca Smith

Margaret Fell was not the only seventeenth-century woman to advance the cause of inspired preaching. In 1687 Rebecca Smith of Nailsworth, Gloucestershire, published a twelve-page tract or pamphlet in which she replies to a spurious printed sermon supposedly preached in Southwark Park, London, by a female Quaker preacher.[59] I include this brief work here for three reasons: (1) it is a typical example of the defense of the rationale for Quaker preaching drawn from the corpus of the enormously popular tract wars of the seventeenth century; (2) it reveals further elaboration of the rationale for preaching as laid down by Fox, Fell, and other early Quaker apologists; and (3) Smith's tract constitutes another vigorous defense of impromptu preaching by a woman.[60]

In her preface, Smith informs the reader that she will not attack the counterfeit sermon, which she hopes any reader will spot as a "meer fiction." Instead, she intends "to show the emptiness and vanity of all such preachers and sermons that are not as the oracles of God, and from the ability that God giveth, which is sufficient reproof to this and all that preach without a real call." The "real call," she asserts, following Fox, Fell, and Barclay (the subject of the next chapter), "was not by humane learning, school divinity, or the notions of *Plato* and *Aristotle*, but by the alone power and wisdom of God."[61]

Smith makes it clear that there are two kinds of ministers: (1) those that are produced by "human learning" and (2) those that are produced by "immediate call." She writes, "the true preachers of the gospel of Christ . . . [were] not made ministers thereof by human learning, but by the inward power and virtue of the Spirit of God in their own hearts . . .; such ministers we own as are called immediately by the grace of God, but all those that come in without the call . . . such ministers and preachers we utterly disown and deny."[62] Here Smith restates what was by then the standard Quaker rejection of special theological training for vocal ministry.

In a key section of the tract, Smith borrows from Barclay's previously published (1676) *Apology*, where he elaborates on a passage from Peter's first epistle (1 Pet 4:10-11):[63]

If any man speak, let him speak as the oracles of God, and if any man minister, let him do it as of the ability that God giveth, which is as much as if he had said, they that canot thus speak and thus minister ought not to do it . . . For the particle [if] denotes a necessary condition. Now what this ability is doth appear from the former words, to wit *the gift received,* and the grace whereof they are stewards, as by the immediate concern and dependency of the words doth demonstrate.[64]

Smith's exegesis is based upon her knowledge of grammar and skill at argumentation.

Smith ends her tract with a return to her previous attack on worldly learning and a reiteration of the belief that God chooses "weak instruments, which he hath raised up, and hath furnished . . . with his own power, life, and virtue, though dispised [*sic*] because mean and illiterate."[65] The theme of God's using "weak instruments" will be reiterated by later Quaker commentators and ultimately find full expression in Bownas' *Qualifications* in the next century.[66] Truly, Smith's is a voice from the margin of British society.

She closes with a reference to herself: "therefore, seeing in and amongst them my self with many others, [we] have found that heavenly pearl that giveth contentment, which is the only learning, to be sought after and waited for, forever and ever."[67] By this self-reference, Smith indirectly insinuates the early Quaker position on ministerial gender equity, but chooses not to lay out the arguments to support the position in this tract as Fell had so ably done in 1667.

Smith's *Foundation of True Preaching* repeats some essential themes found in earlier writers: (1) that worldly learning is not a necessary qualification for preaching; (2) that ministers must be called by God, and that the call to preach at any given time must be *immediate*; (3) that the ability to preach to the needs of the moment is a gift from God, not a result of study; (4) that preachers must be God's oracles and not preach their own ideas; and (5) that God's true ministers are "weak instruments," people who are generally ignored or despised by ungodly people.[68] Yet, Smith's tract is important because it is well written and offers novel stylistic treatment of old themes. Her choice to insinuate gender equality, rather than preach it directly, is both clever and effective. It was not lost on her readers that, as a woman, Smith would have been considered a "weak instrument" simply because she was a woman, although she never makes that connection overtly in the tract. The fact that Smith was allowed, perhaps even encouraged, both to preach and to write a pamphlet in defense of preaching in a time and place not conspicuous for an enlightened attitude toward gender equality reveals a great deal about the early Quaker understanding of gender equality and the practice of impromptu preaching.

CONTRIBUTIONS OF GEORGE WHITEHEAD

George Whitehead (1636–1722) inherited Fox's mantle as the key organizer and leader of Quakerism after Fox's passing. He was an ardent tract writer, debater, and effective preacher.[69] In his 1674 tract *Enthusiasm Above Atheism: Or, Divine Inspiration and Immediate Illumination*, he presents an effective defense of inspired preaching, reiterating the ideas that had become commonplace among Friends.[70] He writes with respect to inspired impromptu preaching, "this only is the effectual and powerful preaching, which flows from the Word of Life or Divine Unction within, and not that which comes only by Tradition, Reading and Hear-say, without the Spirit's Guidance."[71] Like other early Quakers, he does not write directly about the possibility that preplanned preaching might also be spoken with the "Spirit's Guidance." Early Quakers were intolerant on this issue and wanted fundamentally to call into question the other forms of contemporary preaching, and the quotation above is a good example of that strongly stated position.

In the document, Whitehead restates important positions regarding the operation of inward revelation dealt with earlier by Robert Barclay, and on which I will comment in the next chapter. Whitehead's main contribution in this document is his clear response to the important question, "Why do you preach if the Light illumines and teaches all people?" Whitehead writes,

> [Quaker preachers] are immediately illuminated and inspired for that work [teaching], and their ministry received from the immediate light and teaching of God within, tends to direct men to him, that they may be taught of him; and therefore are helpful to men: in order to turn them from darkness to the Light, which no ways does imply any defect in the Light within, but an alienation in man's mind, till he be converted. . . . Now the difference between God's immediate illumination or inward work of power, and his working instrumentally by ministers or preaching, lyes here; the one is the cause, and the other an effect; the one is the absolute way or Rule of knowing God, and building up in his knowledge; the other a subordinate help for direction to that way and Rule.[72]

Whitehead, then, follows Fox's essential teaching about the purpose of preaching, that preaching should direct hearers to the inward teacher. Also in agreement with Fox and Fell, Whitehead writes that preaching is useful because it is "a living ministry, both to open the Scriptures, and to show men their duty, both in believing and obeying what is necessary."[73] Whitehead's allusion to a "living ministry" probably lines up with Fell's reference to Jesus telling the woman at the well about the connection between "living water" and worshipping in "Spirit and truth."

This 1674 tract is valuable because it restates in the 1670s the common Quaker belief in immediate revelation and reaffirms its place in Quaker culture, a culture that also prized silence. The tract is less valuable than the contributions of Barclay and Bownas because the document is hardly a dispassionate exposition of Quaker theoretical notions about preaching. In fact, Whitehead is in heated debate and is responding to a tract that attacked the Quaker notion of revelation. Unfortunately, Whitehead's topics and organization are largely laid out for him by the writer he is refuting.

This is not the case, however, with Whitehead's 1704 letter *An Evangelical Epistle to the People of God, in Derision Call'd Quakers*. Here Whitehead expends considerable time offering advice about impromptu preaching, anticipating Samuel Bownas' longer eighteenth-century work. Whitehead inveighs against "Irreverent verbose Discourses to no purpose, to no just, nor true Resolution, but confusion, and also Hurt to our Christian Society." Mindful of Fox's (and later writers') advice to "wait," Whitehead counsels people, particularly in the meeting for business, "let every one concerned therein, reverently mind his Power, and wait to feel his Presence, and to know and receive his Counsel; and when his counsel is open'd and given in any Assembly by any one, it may be in a few words; let none darken, wave, or put by the same, with a multitude of words without Counsel . . . for that bespeaks Ambition and Emulation, which is but a fruit of the Flesh, and favours of a Fleshly mind that looks for Popularity, and a Popular Esteem, which will blow away and vanish like smoak."[74] Whitehead may have been concerned with certain individuals speaking too often and too enthusiastically in meetings, but whatever his motivation, this epistle must have had a dampening effect on impromptu preaching. Whitehead stresses that preachers should "Keep in true Fear and Humility" within their gifts and cautions against getting ahead of "the True Shepherd and safe Guide," by now a well-worn image. He also sees "great danger in any Person striving to inlarge [*sic*] in declaration beyond their ability and gifts."[75] This caution may have made novice preachers more hesitant to speak out because it implies that neophytes will not be given opportunities to expand "their ability and gifts" in the crucible of impromptu address.

On the positive side, there are some new wrinkles in Whitehead's epistle. Here Whitehead carefully draws a distinction between true and false prophets, the former characteristically undergoing "deep Humiliation . . . before they Expose the Matter in publick!" However, he is careful to point out that his caution "is not intended to limit the holy Spirit of Prophecy, nor to discourage any true Prophet, in any divine Commission, or special message from the Lord, as touching *outward Judgments*, or *Calamities*."[76] In other words, there is still a vestige of acceptance for prophecies of God's judgment, but only from a "true Prophet." In his conclusion, Whitehead counsels his readers to achieve unity: "There must be an *Inward* meeting, as well as an *Outward*, to live and keep in this Blessed Unity and Nearness of Spirit in Christ Jesus."[77] This is a classic framing of inward/outward dichotomy to which Creasey has pointed and a reiteration that the unity expressed in the meeting is an important epistemological force. Arguably, the freedom to speak under the claim of inspiration may have encouraged some Quakers to go beyond their sense of calling, especially in business meetings. Clearly, Whitehead is exercising the voice of a powerful elder to rein in practices that he believed were bringing about disunity in meetings. Theologically and rhetorically, he seeks to throttle down, yet maintain, the well-established Quaker belief and practice of inspired speech, as well as the special case of prophetic utterance, including the prediction of judgment and calamity. Thus Whitehead builds upon, clarifies, and expands Quaker notions of inspired speech while raising strong cautions.[78]

CONTRIBUTIONS OF CHARLES MARSHALL

In 1675 Charles Marshall (1637[?]–1698), a colleague of Benjamin Coole from Bristol, whose contributions are discussed later, published late in his ministry an important eight-page tract titled *An Epistle to Friends Coming forth in the Beginning of a Testimony and the Snares of the Enemy therein*,[79] a work full of ministerial advice. As will be mentioned in my consideration of Coole, Marshall's brief work was arguably influential on Coole's later writings. The two apparently had a mutually influential friendship. Both writers had an influence on Bownas' eighteenth-century advice concerning when to initiate and terminate an impromptu, inspired message (as discussed in chapter 5). Marshall introduces the concept of passivity and specifically focuses on the moments when the minister makes a judgment as to whether or not to speak.

Marshall begins with advice to Quakers who "sometimes feel a testimony for the Lord to spring to [their] hearts": "keep your watch in the light, that so none stay behind, neither run before; but let all who open their mouths in the assemblies of the Lord's people, do it as the Oracles of God, in the arising of the eternal pure power. . . . wait diligently, not only to know and savour every motion, but also to know the appointed Time and season when the same motion should be brought forth." In other words, Marshall stresses that the message may be judged as divine, but not *timely* to be shared in that particular meeting. Marshall goes on to employ the metaphor of birth to indicate that a message spoken prematurely amounts to "an untimely birth; which is hurt as to the vessel through which it comes, and the hearers thereof are burdened."[80] The result of "walking in this By-path" can be discouraging to the minister. Marshall writes, "although they may find the true power of God moving in them, yet they never come to be skillful, nor to divide the Word of God aright; and such do not truly grow." Here Marshall stresses the developmental process necessary to become an inspired (impromptu) preacher. Some ministers apparently remain immature. These errant ministers "sometimes bring forth a mixture, sowing the field with two sorts of grain." The mixed-seed metaphor is significant here because it implies that the message, the Seed, is ambiguous and thus produces confusion. Such a result would confuse the hearers' sense of the message's divine inspiration.

To avoid these negative effects on the preacher's psyche and the health of the gathered meeting, when ministers feel "the begining of a testimony," Marshall counsels, they should "wait diligently in that to speak, and when to be silent . . . and when that which is thus scaled to your understanding is offered, retire inward, and sink down into the pure stillness, and keep in the valley."[81] In other words, once the message that you are certain ought to be spoken is delivered, and the seed is thus planted, leave the seed in the ground, "retire inward," and wait silently in the Spirit.

Marshall also warns about the spiritual "Enemy's" presence in the process during which the preacher decides to vocalize the message. To Marshall, the situation is a dynamic spiritual struggle, for "great will be the opposition of the enemy every way."[82] If the Enemy canot provoke the "untimely birth" of a message by seeing it delivered inappropriately and without immediate divine approval, the Enemy "will endeavour to shut up the heart [of the preacher] in disobedience or rebellion, or raise up so many fears, doubts and amazements, if possible to bewilder the soul." Marshall adds a personal note hinting at his own struggle to mature as a preacher: "And here I had perished, if it had not been for the dear love and tender mercy of the Lord."

When the preacher becomes convinced that the message must be shared, Marshall advises, "Then sink down in that in which no vain thought can be hid, and stand single and passive; and the more still, humble and passive thou art . . . the Motion of life will the more live and shew itself, and the power will arise and clear thy understanding; and then, in the power which warmeth thy heart . . . enter into thy service; and when that's done, add not, but sit in the still habitation, and in that humility and passiveness thou wast in before."[83] This piece of advice has implications on how vocal and gestural delivery should be managed. Marshall's approach is extremely conservative and reduces the preacher to a passive, inwardly turned, essentially weak vessel prior to and after delivery of the message. During the spoken word, the preacher will experience the "power" arising and the "understanding" being "cleared," and then speak "in the power which warmeth thy heart." Arguably, in Marshall's view, the message will be emphasized rather than the speaker, whose role even in delivery is passive. Marshall does not acknowledge that the speaker herself or himself is the *instrument* of delivery.

There are important implications to Marshall's emphasis on a passive stance. For example, if the preacher follows Marshall's advice, there will be little conscious consideration of nonverbal messages as an additional path for the Spirit's inspiration. Inspiration is reduced to words alone. The preacher truly is only a conduit. Tarter argues persuasively that messages such as Marshall's helped stifle early Quaker bodily manifestations referred to as "quaking" and also had the effect of dampening "feminine" religious style, thus reducing the power of women in the Friends' organizational structure.[84] This is no small matter, and I concur with her well-constructed argument.

Yet there may be further problems with Marshall's advice, which may have additional implications on the preacher's ability to recall material to mind that would suit the occasion and help fulfill the demands of immediate inspiration—that is, if the evidence linking physical movement and memory is given credence. Ong, for example, notes that the Talmud "is still vocalized by highly oral Orthodox Jews in Israel with a forward-and-backward rocking of the torso" and asserts that "the oral word . . . never exists in a simply verbal context, as a written word does. Spoken words are always modifications of a total, existential situation, which always engages the body."[85] It may be that more active, physically expressive, and emotionally charged delivery by earlier "Quakers" (people who may have actually "quaked" or trembled when speaking under the Spirit's prompting) actually aided their recall of Scripture and other familiar language held in common within the Quaker community.

Early Quakers operated in a culture influenced by what has been called "secondary orality." Primary orality exists "in a culture totally untouched by any knowledge of writing or print."[86] Early Quakers thrived in the enormously important print culture and assimilated the printed Bible into their personal lives, but they also developed an approach to preaching without notes, manuscript, or specific preparation, in many ways similar to discourse practiced in preliterate cultures. They thus practiced preaching in a unique cultural mix that might appropriate approaches to memory emerging from both primary and secondary orality. In a significant recent essay, Bruce E. Gronbeck distinguishes between "recollection," which operates in oral cultures and is the pathway to cultural or societal memory, and "the remembered," which he argues is "the repository of an individual's life events—that person's pleasurable and painful experiences," and which is tied to visual memory, the kind of memory associated with electronic media—but also with print.[87] Using Gronbeck's terms, early Quakers were influenced both by recollection and the remembered. At the point that a preacher stood to speak, his or her prior reading from tracts and other religious literature—but especially Scripture—might be useful if it became the remembered in the particular situation. Simultaneously, recollection was also operating for the preacher by bringing to mind recurrent language patterns, arguments, stories, gestures, movements, tones of voice, etc., that helped develop and form the culture of Friends. Marshall's apparent attempt to "throttle back" Quaker delivery patterns may actually have affected the preachers' ability to "recollect" by altering the body's role in facilitating memory.

Though Marshall's advice to be passive may have had a long-term detrimental effect on delivery, gender roles, and the operation of memory, his advice regarding mentorship was more sanguine. He follows Fox's advice for hearers to be "tender" with fledgling preachers who may stray beyond the constraints of hearers' expectations. Marshall counsels, "when any through want of experience err, in runing before the power, be very tender."[88] More urgently, Marshall tells his readers to "beware how you speak to ease yourselves." In essence, he says, if the preacher is under the command to wait for God's approval before speaking, critical elders ought to be under the same stricture not to "run forth in judgment." In a key passage, Marshall criticizes such hasty and strident negative responses because they "have sometimes hurt, and even destroyed, or at least have become a stumbling-block to such an exercised Friend." Hypercritical elders "have also much hurt themselves; so that they not having a true discerning, between the first moving cause, which is the power, and that which led forth before the power, have judged both, and so have brought a hurt over their own souls, through judging the power of the Lord."

A careful perusal of Marshall's epistle indicates that he believed that discerning the Spirit's leading is fraught with caution for both speaker and listener. Misreading God's leading in either role might provoke disorder and disunity, which may have been present among Friends in Bristol when he wrote the epistle. Marshall ends the letter with an encouragement to readers to "go up to the mountain of the Lord . . . who will teach us more and more of his ways; and here, in all God's holy mountain, is neither hurting nor destroying."[89]

CONTRIBUTIONS OF STEPHEN CRISP

Many early Quakers might be acknowledged for restating or elaborating on a Quaker view of preaching, but the contributions of Stephen Crisp (1628–1692) of Colchester, whose 1687 sermon is examined in chapter 10, are of particular interest, if for no other reason than that an impressive corpus of thirty-two sermons of his have survived.[90]

Crisp's sermons are full of comments about preaching. For example, Crisp testifies in a 1688 sermon, "we were never called of God to Study *Sermons* for you, nor to Preach things that are made ready to our Hands, but as the *Lord our God* hath wrought in us, and as God hath been pleased to make known his Mind to us, and by his Spirit given us Utterance, so we Speak, and so we Preach."[91] Here is the standard Quaker rejection of prior preparation and justification of impromptu sermonizing. Crisp also presents the Light as the source of "understanding," as in this quotation from a 1688 sermon, in which Crisp maintains that the Light of Christ "will open their Understanding far above all Preaching and proving this and the other Doctrine and Tenet, better than any Preaching can."[92]

Furthermore, in 1690, Crisp draws a distinction between rational acceptance of a theological doctrine and true regeneration. He proclaims that Quakers believe that non-Quaker preachers are preaching in error:

> You know there are a great many other Ministers, whose Labour is to perswade People to believe what they say; to lay down a Doctrine, and prove it by Scripture and Reason, and set it home upon their Minds by such Testimony as the Scripture affords, and hereupon they prevail upon the Minds and Judgments of People, to believe what they lay down.
>
> It is easie to lay down a Position, and prove it, and convince People that it must be according to Scripture; but when a Person is convinced of a Principle of Truth, he is not Regenerated thereby.[93]

Many additional quotations from Crisp's sermons might be added to these, but he also wrote about preaching in his other works. In 1690, near the end of his life, Crisp pened *An Epistle of Tender Love and Brotherly Advice*, a lengthy epistle in which he sums up his wisdom, including his observations regarding preaching and listening.[94] Laying the groundwork for Whitehead's 1704 tract discussed above, throughout his 1690 document Crisp stresses that Friends needed to maintain unity in their meetings, whether for business or worship, and seek to achieve a sense of the "order of the Gospel."[95] In business sessions, especially, one might encounter disagreement among the gathered people or meet up with a person whose particular opinion would break the unity. In this circumstance, Crisp advises, "such a one ought to be born with, and cherished, and the supplications of your souls will go to God for him, that God may reveal it to him." He adds, "it is not of absolute necessity that every member of the church should have the same measure of understanding in all things." Crisp counsels patience, to the end that people will be "watchful over their own spirits, and keep in the Lord's power, over that nature and ground in themselves, that would be apt to take an offense."[96] Here is clear affirmation that patience and waiting in the Spirit were still to be greatly prized.

In men's and women's business meetings in which the group determined how "justice and charity" were to be expressed toward poorer members, Crisp advises, "[W]hen ye meet about these things, keep the Lord in your eye, and wait to feel his power to guide and direct you. . . . And beware of all brittleness of spirit and sharp reflection upon each other[']s words. . . . And, therefore, if any man, through want of watchfulness, should be overtaken with heat or passion, a soft answer appeaseth wrath . . . therefore, such a time is fittest for a soft answer."[97] Here Crisp reiterates the prevalent early Quaker counsel to be cautious and to "wait" before the Lord, specifically avoiding angry or "passionate" speech, a word that seems intended to place Quakerism beyond the claim that Friends were mere enthusiasts or histrionic debaters. We have already seen such cautions expressed in the writings of other commentators. They would later find full expression in Bownas' work in the next century.

Crisp also reiterates the classic Quaker rejection of theological study or university education, natural gifts at communication, and "establishment" clergy advantages as prerequisites for "official" ministry in the church: "it is no man's learning, or artificial requirements; it is no man's riches, or greatness in this world; it is no man's eloquence and natural wisdom, that makes him fit for government in the church of Christ; unless he, with all his endowments, be seasoned with the heavenly salt."[98]

Unfortunately, regardless of his speaking acumen in the context of impromptu speech, Crisp did not offer hints about "managing" content or commentary on what verbal strategies might be available to the impromptu preacher.

CONTRIBUTIONS OF BENJAMIN COOLE

In 1696 Benjamin Coole (d. 1717) of Bristol published a pamphlet, *The Quakers Cleared from Being Apostates or the Hammer Defeated*,[99] in which he responds to a "scurrilous pamphlet" titled *William Penn and the Quakers either Apostates or Imposters*," published under the pseudonym "Trepedatious Malleus"—a fearful or hesitant hammer. Despite the fact that Coole's pamphlet was provoked amid the virulent and sometimes very caustic theological debates of the century, it is well written and well argued, lacking any trace of vitriol. Coole was a master of refutation who did not simply follow his rival's line of argument.

Coole presents a defense of the contended and misunderstood concept of the Inward Light or "Light within": "In short, by the Light within we understand not Conscience, nor Natural Reason, but that Light which from the Son of Righteousness Jesus Christ; the Light of the World, shines into the Hearts of the Sons of Men, to give them the knowledge of the Glory of God, or that Spirit of Truth . . . or that still small Voice, that saith, This is the Way, walk in it."[100] This statement is the classic Quaker position on the Light considered in chapter 2. It is also the position earlier developed (in 1676) by Barclay, discussed at greater length in chapter 4.[101] It is significant that Coole thinks it is necessary to begin with a crisply stated theological principle.

Coole similarly restates the Quaker position with regard to the Spirit and Scripture, first articulated by Fox: "For the right understanding [of Scripture] . . . can there be any better method proposed, than for Men to have recourse to that Spirit from whence it did at first flow?" While he denies that Quakers "pretend to infallibility," Coole asserts that a person might "*Infallibly* be led out of all that which is Fallible and Erroneous, both in *Faith* and *Life*."[102] Turning the tables on his opponents, Coole writes, "Yes, they themselves will (I hope) allow the Scripture to be an *Infallible Rule*, and if so, the Spirit of God must be yet more so, since from it the Scripture came."

Interestingly, in the pamphlet, Coole also includes a segment in which he argues that Quaker beliefs are consonant with the Nicene Creed. Here he makes the declaration: "the Quakers believe the substance of the *Nicene* Creed, as truly as any of their adversaries."[103] The affirmation both of Scriptures and of the "substance of" the Nicene Creed appears to be an attempt to position Quaker thought and practice to greater advantage within the larger world of seventeenth-century Christian thought.

After positioning his pamphlet in an interpretive frame that gives credence both to Scripture and to an important Christian creedal statement, Coole moves on to a rebuttal of his opponent's accusation that Quakers liken their "inspiration" to the voice of God "speaking through a cane," implying that it is not the cane's voice and that Quaker preachers see themselves as robotic.[104] This attack metaphorically reinterpreted and marginalized the importance of inspiration, making it seem like a brainless, foolish act of babbling. In response,

Coole clearly advances the understanding of how inspiration works for Quaker preachers by reference to the insightful concepts of "passive" and "active" inspiration:

> [I]n both prayer and thanksgiving, as well as preaching, [Quaker preachers] are partly *passive*, and partly *active*: Passive, in that they submit to the Divine power and Spirit of God, to impress upon their Spirits a grateful sense of the Favours received, for which their hearts are filled with thankfulness: And *Active*, in expressing such thoughts as the Spirit shall suggest to their understanding, as suitable to the present occasion . . . in Preaching the Gospel, it is the Spirit that opens the Understanding, and makes it fruitful in the knowledge of God, and *incites* men, so qualified, to impress the same Image on others, which canot be without being *active* as well as *passive*."[105]

We have encountered the idea of passivity in the previous discussion of the 1675 epistle by Marshall, Coole's Bristol colleague, but Coole counters Marshall's position and deepens the concept of the passive stance by pointing out that inspired preaching involves both passive and active elements, otherwise the words would never become voiced. By this move, Coole divides inward immediate revelation into two stages: the personal or *passive* stage of waiting for and receiving what Fox had earlier called "openings," and the *active* stage of expression through preaching and vocalized prayer. Specifically, publick Friends sitting in a gathered meeting had to "attend the Spirit[']s time . . . to enable them [to speak or pray], when the circumstance of time and place calls for it."[106] Any revealed message or opening might be for the minister alone and not to be shared vocally, as Coole writes regarding vocalized prayer: "[ministers] are not *always* obliged to a vocal Prayer, nor doth God expect it." This significant advice would later find full expression in Bownas' preaching manual, discussed in chapter 5.[107] Additionally, notice how Coole injects the phrase "when the circumstance of time and place calls for it," indicating that some measure of audience analysis and discernment of need on the particular occasion of the meeting might be factored into the preacher's decision to move into a vocalized message. Our early Quaker writers on impromptu preaching rarely comment on the influence of audience and contextual needs as factors prompting a decision to speak, although Fox noted the Spirit as a factor in audience analysis.

CONCLUSION

The early Quaker theory of impromptu, inspired preaching began to take shape in the late 1640s and continued to develop over the course of the century. Contributors to its development held common views initially set in motion by Fox's own practice and writings. His characteristic positions regarding preaching included (1) rejecting formal theological education for clergy, and generally distrusting "learning" as a necessary part of a call to ministry or as preparation for preaching; (2) questioning church traditions, especially as witnessed in rejection of the common Christian vocabulary of the time, which used terms like "church," "temple," and "gospel" in what Fox saw as unbiblical ways, and the rejection of church hierarchy, rituals, etc.; (3) emphasizing the role of the Spirit in audience analysis; (4) defending women's right to speak and prophesy; (5) rejecting the accepted notion of a ministry paid by tithes, or the "hireling" ministry; (6) expressing utter dependence on a sense of immediate revelation before preaching or praying aloud; (7) presenting a cautionary approach to preaching as evidenced by a willingness to wait, sometimes for what on occasion appears to be an excessive period of time, until the Spirit gives utterance; (8) insisting that ministers live holy lives; (9) instructing hearers to be tender with novice impromptu preachers; and (10) relying on a biblical hermeneutic that emphasizes types and figures drawn from Scripture applied to the lives of the hearers. As an admired Quaker leader, Fox's own preaching modeled certain choices and strategies that were inevitably imitated and reinforced among publick Friends, with individual emphases and variations, of course. These choices included the following: (1) directing hearers in a number of settings to the Inward Light, the true source of revelation; (2) both in Quaker Meetings and among non-Quakers, exhibiting a readiness to expand at length on types and figures applied to the audience, an inventional strategy that arguably depended on Fox's biblical knowledge, a necessary product of study and long-term prior preparation; and (3) expressing a willingness to debate, particularly in speaking opportunities outside of Quaker meetings, employing lines of argument and biblical interpretation that also clearly required Fox's immersion in the topic and long-term consideration of how Scripture *should be* interpreted to fit the situation raised in the immediate moments of the debate.

Fell, Smith, Whitehead, Marshall, Crisp, and Coole repeated, extended, and deepened a Quaker understanding of homiletics. The two women included in this chapter are particularly noteworthy. No one matched Fell's power to defend the right of women to speak, but Fell also provided an articulate condemnation of preaching and praying as currently practiced in the church. Furthermore, she defended direct revelation and the necessity of personal holiness. On the other hand, Smith assumed, but did not directly defend, the presence of women in the preaching role. Smith restated Quaker arguments against "worldly learning" being viewed as a necessity for ministry, a requirement that automatically excluded women from the ministry because they were also excluded from the universities. Smith insisted on a direct divine calling to become one of "God's Oracles" and maintained, writing as a self-acknowledged woman preacher, that God chose "weak instruments" for the true ministry.

Whitehead, building on Fox's and Barclay's foundation, defended the necessity of preaching, a "living ministry," to open the Scriptures and "show men their duty." He also wrote against verbosity in sermons and inveighed against personal ambition and pride, stressing instead the virtue of humility.

Marshall, writing in 1675, one year after Whitehead's first tract, discussed earlier, stressed the necessity for preachers to be passive and to discern the Spirit's leading to speak in an attitude of passiveness and stillness. Marshall also viewed the actual delivery of the message as passive, a continual process of the same attitude of humility and passiveness that initially produced the conviction regarding the necessity to speak, but with discernable effects on the dampening of overt bodily expression that sometimes characterized earlier Friends, and with possible immediate effects of the operation of memory in the speakers' minds. However, this same passive and humble attitude would also characterize elders when they criticized what they interpreted as overbearing or rash testimonies by fledgling preachers. Overall, his emphasis on passivity probably had a negative dampening effect on Quaker delivery style, but a positive effect on the process of mentoring tyros.

Crisp, writing in 1690, fifteen years after Marshall (1675) and fourteen years prior to Whitehead's second tract (1704), expressed a similarity both in tone and message to Marshall and Whitehead as he wrote about the necessity of achieving a sense of unity in Quaker meetings, especially within the structure of men's and women's business meetings. Crisp advised caution and a heavy emphasis on waiting before the Lord until a sense of God's leading was clear. Passionately expressed discourse was to be avoided.

At the end of the century, with the cessation of religious persecution and the long-term survival of Quakerism secured, Coole defended the concept of inward revelation, drawing on Barclay's work, but also contributed the concept that immediate revelation was both passive and active, the former constituting inspiration for the individual, and the latter inspiration for the meeting through the shared word. This useful elaboration and corrective on the concept of passivity presented in 1675 by Marshall, fellow resident of Bristol, pointed to the complexity of discovering divine leading for each individual in *every* meeting and helped unpack some of the tensions between passive and active implications of inspired preaching.

The writers dealt with in this chapter present advice with implications on the preachers' ability to thrive in the crucible of impromptu speaking, particularly with respect to the function of memory in the process of speaking without preparation for the specific event. As noted in my discussion of Fox's use of typologies, recent research indicates that the brain operates on the basis of reinforced patterns generated in several of its areas. Given these findings, it would appear that early Quaker preachers' knowledge about, and particularly *memorization* of, Scripture, together with their habit of ferreting out typologies from the Old and New Testaments (applied in the Quaker oral discourse community either to the task of interpreting the New Testament through symbolic references in the Old Testament, or as typologies applied to their own or hearers' lives), arguably helped provide a continuous supply of topics to the preachers in the midst of impromptu sermonizing. Additionally, the silence under which the meeting convened, followed by the subsequent waiting to confirm the Spirit's urging to speak, undoubtedly had additional benefits to the preachers besides helping them determine if the Spirit was moving them to stand and speak. I would suggest that during the time of silent waiting, the preacher likely would enter a frame of mind in which her or his previous study of Scripture, conversations about Scripture with ministry colleagues, or memorized Scriptures themselves might come to mind to be employed once the choice to speak had been determined.

Having now presented a developmental perspective on the initial and relatively unsystematic evolution of Quaker homiletic theory, we now turn to the two writers who contributed the lengthiest and most systematic and in-depth theory and advice of any other early Quakers: Robert Barclay and Samuel Bownas.

CHAPTER 4

ROBERT BARCLAY AND THE GROUNDING OF EARLY QUAKER HOMILETIC THEORY

Robert Barclay (1648–1690), the most important early Quaker intellectual, wrote two works that directly bear on the development of Quaker homiletic theory: *Apology*[1] and *Immediate Revelation*.[2] In this chapter, I will examine pertinent passages from these two works in order to lay out his ideas about the interaction of inward revelation and the Quaker practice of impromptu preaching. By combining reference to these two key works, it is possible to mark the essential outlines of Barclay's notion of the influence of the Inward Light and to discern his key contributions to the development of the Quaker theory and practice of impromptu preaching.

Introduction to *Apology* and *Immediate Revelation*

Prior to embarking on our course, a brief description of these two works by Barclay is in order. Barclay, a Scott who was educated in the schools of Aberdeen and the Scots Theological School of Paris, was twenty-seven in 1676, the year he composed and published his *Apology* in Latin (published two years later in English).[3] Braithwaite observes that the *Apology* is "a direct challenge to much of the Westminster Confession and the Shorter Catechism (1646–1648), which were the maturest and latest formulation of scripture-truth as it appeared to cultured and devout Puritans" (387). Braithwaite also claims that the *Apology* follows the overall organization of the Confession and Shorter Catechism, countering these significant works proposition by proposition.

On the other hand, Barclay's *Immediate Revelation* was composed in the form of a personal address to Heer Paets, a Dutchman highly interested in debating Barclay's theological ideas, whom Barclay describes as a "person of quality."[4] The work was pened in 1676 in Latin, the same year the *Apology* was printed in Latin, but was not published in English until 1692.

In this chapter I will pay particular attention to Propositions I, II, III, V, VI, X, and XI from the *Apology*, as well as significant passages from *Immediate Revelation*, concentrating on their relevance to the development of an understanding of impromptu, inspired preaching.[5]

DEVELOPMENT OF BARCLAY'S EPISTEMOLOGY IN THE *APOLOGY*

In the *Apology*, Barclay's first proposition flatly states, "the height of all happiness is placed in the true knowledge of God" and the "true and right understanding of this foundation and ground of knowledge is that which is most necessary to be known and believed in the first place."[6] With this statement, Barclay rejects at the outset the notion that any other kind of investigation or knowledge is the primary duty or occupation of humankind. He has erected a hierarchy placing the "true knowledge of God" at the top.

His Proposition II, "Of Immediate Revelation," builds on the first: "Seeing 'no man knoweth the Father but the Son, and he to whom the Son revealeth him' [Matt 11:27]; and seeing the 'revelation of the Son is in and by the Spirit'; therefore the testimony of the Spirit is that alone by which the true knowledge of God hath been, is, and can be only revealed." He asserts, "this divine revelation and inward illumination, is that which is evident and clear of itself, forcing by its own evidence and clearness, the well-disposed understanding to assent, irresistibly moving the same thereunto, even as the common principles of natural truths do move and incline the mind to a natural assent."[7] Here we see the suggestion of two sources of knowledge: one inward and the other outward, with the former being absolutely necessary for the knowledge of spiritual matters, and apparently operating only in the presence of a person with a "well-disposed understanding." In addition, we can discern Barclay's assent to the Cartesian criterion of clarity, in this case applied to the immediate revelation of spiritual truths.

In his discussion of Proposition II, Barclay acknowledges the usefulness of other means of knowledge, specifically tradition, works of creation, and Scripture, but he contends that the question with regard to religious knowledge is not "what may be profitable or helpful, but what is absolutely necessary." He asserts, "where the true inward knowledge of God is, through the revelation of his Spirit, there is all; neither is there an absolute necessity of any other."[8]

Clearly, in this section Barclay is not writing about visions, voices, or dreams when he speaks of "immediate revelation." These manifestations, although valid for him, are not the same as the inward enlightenment, but are based on that enlightenment. Of the various scriptural accounts of visions, voices, and dreams that were part of the narratives of the prophets and apostles, Barclay writes, "What made them then give credit to these visions? Certainly nothing else but the secret testimony of God's Spirit in their hearts, assuring them that the voices, dreams, and visions were of and from God." Ultimately, Barclay builds an argument based upon scriptural interpretation: "Christians are always to be led inwardly and immediately by the Spirit of God dwelling in them, and that the same is a standing and perpetual ordinance, as well to the church in general in all ages, as to every individual member in particular."[9]

After several paragraphs of argument involving extensive quotation from the church fathers and reformed theologians—including Calvin—to attest to Proposition II, Barclay concludes, "He in whom the Spirit of God dwelleth, it is not in him a lazy, dumb, useless thing; but it moveth, actuateth, governeth, instructeth, and teacheth him all things whatsoever are needful for him to know; yea, bringeth all things to his remembrance."[10] The operation of the Spirit in the activation of memory will become crucial to impromptu preaching in the recall of Scripture appropriate to the moment or testimonies germane to the topic from the preacher's or another person's life.

How does Barclay believe the Spirit operates on individuals? Certainly not merely by enlightening their understandings so that they may understand the Scriptures. Instead, the Spirit presents the truths *directly* to the mind. He writes, "the Spirit doth not only subjectively help us to discern truths elsewhere delivered, but also objectively present[s] those truths to our minds. For that which teacheth me all things, and is given me for that end, without doubt presents those things to my mind which it teacheth me. . . . Again, That which bringeth all things to my remembrance, must needs present them by way of object; else it were improper to say, It brought them to my remembrance; but only, that it helps to remember the objects brought from elsewhere."[11]

There then follows a lengthy section in which he argues that immediate revelation is superior to tradition (Anglo Catholic) or Scripture (Puritan) as the final rule of faith. He admits that some people claiming divine inspiration have erred, but argues that both tradition and scriptural interpretation have been in error as well. "[T]hose that have their spiritual senses," Barclay insists, "and can savour the things of the Spirit, as it were in prima instantia, i.e., at the first blush, can discern them without, or before they apply them either to scripture or reason . . . [just as] some geometrical demonstrations are by all acknowledged to be infallible, which can be scarcely discerned or proved by the senses."[12]

Barclay believes that the inward revelation is manifested to all people. He ends the discussion of the second proposition with an invitation for his readers to test his ideas personally: "Wait then for this [manifestation] in the small revelation of that pure light which first reveals things more known; and as thou becomest fitted for it, thou shalt receive more and more."[13] Thus a person's ability to receive new revelation depends upon an initial willingness followed by a developmental, even experimental, learning process.

Barclay's third proposition argues that the Scripture is "a faithful historical account," a "prophetical account," and a "full and ample account of all the chief principles of the doctrine of Christ," yet "they are only a declaration of the fountain, and not the fountain itself."[14] Thus the Bible is not to be taken as "the only rule of faith and practice," as the Reformed tradition believed. On the other hand, immediate revelations, he has already argued in Proposition II, "neither do nor can ever contradict the outward testimony of the scriptures, or right and sound reason."[15] Following the trail blazed by Fox, but more astutely, Barclay's proposition clearly reverses the position that Puritans took regarding the Scriptures and the Spirit. They said, Scripture first, then Spirit; Barclay says, Spirit first, then Scripture. Scripture and reason, for Barclay, are reduced to a confirming role in his epistemology of direct revelation. Perhaps the key passage of Proposition III for our purposes is the following: "This is the great work of the scriptures, and their service to us, that we may witness them fulfilled in us, and so discern the stamp of God's spirit and ways upon them, by the inward acquaintance we have with the same Spirit and work in our hearts."[16] Barclay's fifth and sixth propositions identify the Inward Light with Christ and directly counter the hyper-Calvinistic concept of double predestination with this assertion: "this Light enlighteneth the hearts of all for a time, in order to salvation; and this is it that reproves the sins of all individuals, and would work out the salvation of all if not resisted." As noted previously, Barclay further asserts that a Day of Visitation is accorded all persons for their salvation, but that many persons may outlive their individually accorded "day." In these propositions, he distinguishes the Light from human faculties and conscience.[17] The Light is identified as the "spiritual body of Christ," the "vehiculum Dei," yet "neither is Christ in all men by way of union, or indeed . . . by way of inhabitation,"[18] but only as a seed. Following the logic of this metaphor, the seed might sprout and take root if not resisted during an individual's Day of Visitation.

There is a relationship between Proposition II ("Of Immediate Revelation") and Propositions V and VI ("Of Universal and Saving Light"), in that Proposition II sets out the epistemology of immediate revelation and Propositions V and VI apply the epistemology in the context of the theological concept of salvation. Proposition II sets the stage for Propositions V and VI, in which the Light becomes much more prominent. The epistemological principle remains the same for Barclay, whichever term he employs: "Light," "Word," "Voice," or "immediate revelation." The Inward world is superior to the Outward, and the knowledge obtained inwardly is absolutely necessary for spiritual progress.

Development of Barclay's Epistemology in *Immediate Revelation*

In *Immediate Revelation*, Barclay deals with the operations of inward immediate revelation more explicitly than in the *Apology*. He explains that there are both inward and outward senses and that the inward senses are divided into two categories: natural and supernatural. The inward natural senses are comprised of emotions such as anger, love, or hatred; the perception of a "natural truth," such as that the whole is greater than the part; or a deductive leap based on natural reason. He explains the concept with reference to the five "outward senses":

> [A]n example of an inward, supernatural sense is, when the heart or soul of a pious man feels in itself divine motions, influences and operations, which sometimes are as the Voice or Speech of God, sometimes as a most pleasant and glorious illustration or visible object to the inward eye, sometimes as a most sweet savour or taste, sometimes as an heavenly warmness, or (so to speak) melting of the soul in the love of God. Moreover this divine and supernatural operation in the mind of a man, is a true and most-glorious miracle; which when it is perceived by the inward and supernatural sense divinely raised up in the mind of man, doth so evidently and clearly

perswade the understanding to assent to the thing revealed, that there is no need of an outward miracle: for this assent is not because of the thing itself, but because of the revelation proposing it, which is the Voice of God. For when the Voice of God is heard in the soul, the soul doth as certainly conclude the truth of that voice, as the truth of God's being, from whom it proceeds.[19]

Barclay's view of perception begins squarely by rejection of the notion of the tabula rasa:

W]hatsoever is clearly and distinctly known, is known by its proper idea; neither can it be otherwise clearly and distinctly known: For the idea's [*sic*] of all things are divinely planted in our souls; for they are not begotten in us by outward objects, or outward causes (as the better philosophy teacheth) but only are by those outward things excited or stirred up. And this is true not only in supernatural idea's of God . . . and in natural idea's of the natural principles of humane understanding, and conclusions thence deduced by the strength of human reason; but even in the ideas of outward objects, which are perceived by the outward senses.[20]

With Barclay's use of the phrase "clearly and distinctly known," this paragraph amounts to the "smoking gun" of Barclay's alleged Cartesianism. However, it is also the begining of a theory dealing with the operation of the mind and how it responds to inward revelation.

In developing this topic, Barclay writes about the existence of divinely implanted "Supernatural Ideas of Supernatural Beings" in the mind, which, of necessity, must be "stirred up by some Supernatural Operation of God, which raiseth up . . . Supernatural and Spiritual senses."[21] In other words, the mind must have a "wired in" capacity to receive supernatural revelation. He further explains that there is a distinction between natural and supernatural ideas and senses:

As there are natural ideas concerning the things of the natural world [light, color, voice, sounds, etc.] . . . there are ideas of supernatural things. . . . And as the natural ideas are stirred up in us by outward and natural bodies; so those divine and supernatural ideas are stirred up in us by a certain principle, which is a body in naturals in relation to the spiritual world, and therefore may be called a divine body: not as if it were a part of God, who is a most pure spirit; but the organ or instrument of God, by which he worketh in us, and stirreth up in us these ideas of divine things. This is the flesh and blood of Christ.[22]

Here the connection between the "vehiculum Dei," "the Inward Light of Christ," and "immediate divine revelation" come together. For Barclay, all of these terms are different linguistic ways of speaking about the same thing, what amounts to the mystical presence of Christ, not in union, but in sufficient power to "stir up" the "divinely implanted" ideas of divine things. Barclay sees both the "stirring" of inward revelation and its capacity to be received as divine gifts. Barclay is specifically asserting that on the receiving end of immediate divine revelation there must be receptors in the "mind" created specifically to respond to the supernatural ideas generated by the Inward Light. He calls them "senses" or "perceptive faculties" and notes that "in wicked men those senses or faculties do as it were sleep." He reasons that "the objects of the outward senses are not to be confounded, but every object is to have its proper sense; so must we judge of inward and spiritual objects, which have their proper sense, whereby they are to be perceived."[23]

Barclay is not the only Quaker writer to speculate about the need for inward receptors to receive the Inward Light. For example, the Idea of an inward sense of sight is hinted at by Whitehead, who writes, "Now if Christ be to be known within, then that which reveals him, and may be known of God is within; there must be an eye, or else no seeing—and if it be blind or vailed, it must be opened by that which makes manifest things that are reproved, which is light."[24] Whitehead leaves the reader with this brief glimpse, but Barclay goes much deeper and speculates that these inward and spiritual senses "are distinct and distinguishable from all the natural faculties of the soul, whether of imagination, or natural reason," and that it is through these senses alone that "spiritual-minded men do behold the glory and beauty of God. . . . [and] also hear God inwardly speaking in their souls."[25]

Barclay warns that "the devil may counterfeit false likenesses," which can fool the inward and spiritual senses, and that many persons are thus deceived. As we have seen in chapter 3, this idea is later picked up and reinforced in Marshall's important *An Epistle to Friends Coming forth in the Beginning of a Testimony*, published in 1675. But deception can be avoided because Barclay confidently asserts that "divine enjoyments are clearly perceived . . . [by those] in whom the divine and spiritual senses are truly opened, and . . . [in whom] the true supernatural idea's of those things are truly raised up."[26] If a mistake is made, divine illumination is not to blame; the culprit is "some evil disposition of the mind." Here he draws a parallel between the relationship of faulty reasoning to "true reason" and direct divine revelation to "false and pretended revelations, and diabolical inspirations." He likewise counsels that when a person is "deceived by his own imagination" into believing he has a revelation, he is to be directed, presumably by an elder or other discerning and wise person, to turn to the "divine seed" in him, the first and most easily "stirred up" supernatural idea. Barclay says this process is essentially the same as the case of faulty reasoning, in which one would tell the deceived person to "contemplate the first natural ideas of natural things . . . which is a test or touch-stone, by which all the appearances, and likenesses of reason are to be examined." In sum, the inward receptors receive stimuli from both the light and dark sides of the spiritual world, making deception a real possibility for the immature Quaker. Barclay's explanation implies the need for a fully functioning sense of discernment by elders who can direct the errant oracle back to the proper path, thus reinvigorating the plea for careful care previously emphasized by Fox and others.

The principle of hierarchy in both spiritual and natural ideas facilitates the process of growth and development in countering deception in the operation of immediate revelation. Barclay asserts, "as in natural ideas, so in supernatural some are more easily raised up, than others. For there is a certain order both of natural and supernatural idea's, whereby they are gradually excited."[27] One begins with the ideas that are most "easily raised up" as a test for deception. Ultimately, any idea that is thought to be divinely inspired but "is felt to contradict any divine and supernatural idea, which is clearly perceived in the soul, it is a manifest token, that it is not a divine revelation, but either a false imagination, or the wicked suggestion of some evil spirit." Notice that Barclay again implicitly rejects the idea of using Scripture as a test of a deceptive revelation. However, we recall that he has also told the readers of the *Apology* that no true divine revelation will ever contradict Scripture, so the Scripture—interpreted through the Spirit—stands in the wings as a possible corrective to revelatory misjudgment.

Barclay's epistemological system, presented in the *Apology* and later fleshed out in *Immediate Revelation*, is built on the absolute necessity of divine revelation, not only for salvation, but for all "spiritual" knowledge. His view of the mind's operation begins with divinely implanted, innate, natural, and supernatural ideas, which are energized or "stirred up" by means connected naturally to the essence of the ideas. Since the "supernatural ideas" canot be perceived by the operation of the outward senses, they must be perceived by inward and spiritual senses that mirror the work of the physical senses. It is not surprising, then, that Barclay contends that "we [Quakers] need no outward miracles to move us to believe the scriptures."[28]

BARCLAY'S NOTION OF PREACHING

We have now finished a sketch of Barclay's epistemology from which he derives his rationale for early Quaker impromptu preaching and, significantly, posits a theory for how the mind operates before and during the very moments of an impromptu sermon. We may wonder why, given his radical belief in the possibility, indeed the *necessity*, of immediate revelation to all persons, there would still exist any need for preaching in Barclay's schema. He answers this query with a statement found in Proposition III: ". . . though God doth principally and chiefly lead us by his Spirit, yet he sometimes conveys his comfort and consolation to us through his children, whom he raises up and inspires to speak or write a word in season, whereby the saints are made instruments in the hand of the Lord to strengthen and encourage one another."[29] Thus preaching secures a place in his system, but its position is accorded the same weight as Scripture, that is, a secondary place. Reminiscent of Fox, Barclay asserts, "God is teacher of his people himself; and there is nothing more express, than that such as are under the new covenant, need no man to teach them: yet it was a fruit of Christ's ascension to send teachers and pastors for perfecting of the saints. . . . the same work is ascribed to the scriptures as to teachers; the one to make the man of God perfect, the other for the perfection of the saints."[30] Following Fox and others, Barclay asserts in Proposition VI that the goal of preaching is "to preach Christ, and direct people to his pure light in the heart."[31]

While it is clear that Barclay's contemporaries and later Quaker leaders shared his view about revelation, I have uncovered only Whitehead's hint of agreement to Barclay's position on the operation of the human mind with regard to knowledge not derived from the senses—such as revelations from God. Bownas does not discuss the operation of the mind in his later *Qualifications*, discussed in chapter 5. Barclay's position, as laid out in his *Immediate Revelation*, remains a significant, but essentially unacknowledged, rationale for humans, especially preachers, to receive divine knowledge directly. I assert that this layout is as much an epistemologically derived rhetoric based on a type of faculty

psychology as that of Bacon, who preceded him, and George Campbell, who followed him.[32] Ironically, Barclay's layout of the brain's
functioning may be closer to current findings than either Bacon's or
Campbell's. However, to my knowledge, there is no evidence for the
existence of implanted or "prewired" ideas, although Noam Chomsky
has argued that the brain comes with the built-in capacity to learn any
aspect of grammar, regardless of culture or complexity.[33]

In the *Apology*, Barclay was more direct and less philosophical in
his propositions dealing with preaching (or "ministry"). Propositions
X and XI ("Of the Ministry" and "Of Worship," respectively) present most of Barclay's direct observations on preaching. The kernel
of Barclay's position on the ministry is captured in the statement of
Proposition X, which he fleshes out with proofs and illustrations in the
sixty-four pages that follow:

> As by the light or gift of God all true knowledge in things spiritual
> is received and revealed, so by the same . . . every true minister of
> the gospel is ordained, prepared and supplied in the work of the
> ministry; and by the leading, moving, and drawing hereof ought
> every evangelist and Christian pastor to be led . . . both as to the
> place where, as to the persons to whom, and as to the time wherein
> he is to minister. Moreover, they who have this authority may and
> ought to preach the gospel, though without human commission or
> literature; as on the other hand, they who want the authority of this
> divine gift, however learned, or authorized by the commission of
> men or churches, are to be esteemed but as deceivers, and not true
> ministers. . . . Also they who have received this holy and unspotted
> gift, as they have freely received it, so are they freely to give it, with-
> out hire or bargaining, far less to use it as a trade to get money by it:
> yet if God hath called any one from their employment or trades by
> which they acquire their livelihood, it may be lawful for such . . . to
> receive such temporals . . . as are given them freely and cordially by
> those to whom they have communicated spirituals.[34]

The significance of the principles set out in Proposition X canot be
overstressed, since, as we can plainly see, they were erected on a foundation laid by Fox and Fell and provided an articulate rationale for
Quaker writers and preachers to follow. These principles became
a base upon which Rebecca Smith and Samuel Bownas later built.
None of the elements of Proposition X were questioned by either
later writer; thus we can view Barclay's thought as both an accurate

statement and compilation of the Quaker position on ministry at the time he wrote, and a significant undergirding for the work of later Quaker writers such as Crisp, Whitehead, and Coole on the subject of ministry. Not surprisingly, Barclay describes a ministry that is called, activated, and practiced by the authority of the immediate moving of God without reference to "outward human authority" or a person's educational background or intellectual prowess. Furthermore, ministry is to be offered without reference to wages, allowing only that free gifts to meet modest temporal needs may be accepted.

Preaching among early Quakers followed the precepts of ministry in Barclay's Proposition X. The "purified and sanctified person," man or woman, Barclay maintains, "comes . . . to be called and moved to minister to others; being able to speak from a living experience of what he himself is a witness . . . his words and ministry, proceeding from the inward power and virtue, reach to the heart of his hearers, and make them approve of him and be subject unto him." Thus, there is a hoped-for two-way confirmation of spoken ministry prompted by the immediate moving of the Spirit: the minister feels called to speak out of his or her spiritual knowledge and experience, and the words spoken are then approved by the receivers.[35]

Following a trail blazed by Fox and Fell, Barclay decrees that women can minister as readily as men. He cites Luther as saying "that every good Christian (not only men, but even women also) is a preacher." Later in Proposition X, following his stirring defense of untrained, "mechanic" preachers, Barclay asserts, "Seeing male and female are one in Christ Jesus, and that he gives his Spirit no less to one than the other, when God moveth in his Spirit in a woman, we judge it no ways unlawful for her to preach in the assemblies of God's people." Barclay deals with two disheartening Pauline biblical passages often used to silence women (1 Cor 14:34 and 1 Tim 2:11-12), noting that "the same Paul speaks of a woman that labored with him in the work of the gospel," and also notes that the Book of Acts (21:9) records that "Philip had four daughters that prophesied." Finally, on this topic, Barclay points out that "God hath effectually in this day converted many souls by the ministry of women; and by them also frequently comforted the souls of his children; which manifest experience puts the thing beyond all controversy."[36] Barclay does not dwell on the subject of gender as had Fell before him, but she had already done the "heavy lifting," leaving Barclay free to second her motion and develop other areas of concern in more depth, such as the concept of inward receptors of the Light (or revelation).

Barclay argues that the preaching ministry he describes and advocates is not without "learning," although he denies the necessity of "outward" learning. Would-be ministers participate in "true learning . . . from the inward teachings and instructions of the Spirit whereby the soul learneth the secret ways of the Lord, [and] becomes acquainted with the inward travails and exercises of the mind."[37] The preacher's preparation, then, should not consist of study, particularly of philosophy, which Barclay strongly criticizes, but should consist of the deep experience of the Spirit, "because the Spirit and grace of God can make up this want [of learning] in the most rustic and ignorant; but this knowledge can in no ways make up the want of the Spirit in the most learned and eloquent." Later Barclay asserts that "a man of a good upright heart may learn more in half an hour, and be more certain of it, by waiting upon God and his Spirit in the heart, than by reading a thousand of their [divinity school] volumes; which by filling his head with many needless imaginations, may well stagger his faith, but never confirm it."[38]

Barclay, of course, never cautions against studying or meditating on the Bible, but goes out of his way to condemn the study of logic and philosophy, "the root and ground of all contention and debate, and the way to make a thing a great deal darker, than clearer." This position reiterates the standard Quaker objection to "learning," but in Barclay's case, the statement is highly ironic, since he was schooled in philosophy, theology, and logic. Without these intellectual tools, he would not have been capable of pening the *Apology*, a situation he will presently admit. He goes on to advise anyone who knows logic and who becomes a Quaker minister "to forget and lose it . . . it leads into such a labyrinth of contention." On the other hand, Barclay expresses great confidence in common sense and "truth proceeding from an honest heart, and spoken forth from the virtue and Spirit of God." Specifically, Barclay approves of a form of "natural logic": "This secret virtue and power ought to be the logic and philosophy wherewith a true Christian minister should be furnished; and for which they need not be beholden to Aristotle. As to natural logic, by which rational men, without that art and rules, or sophisticated learning, deduce a certain conclusion out of true propositions, which scarce any man of reason wants [lacks], we deny not the use of it; and I have sometimes used it in this treatise; which also may serve without that dialectic art."[39] Despite his disparagement of Aristotle and dialectic, Barclay appears to be affirming the use of an everyday form of logic, what might be described as a practical logic, perhaps the realm of rhetorical syllogism (the enthymeme), which Aristotle presented in book 1 of the *Rhetoric* in his extensive consideration of topics to generate enthymemes.[40]

In a crucial summary passage that is worth quoting at length, Barclay goes on to contrast the typical preaching of his day with the kind of preaching he advocates:

> [The Anglican or Puritan preacher] must learn this art or trade of merchandizing with the scriptures. . . . That he may acquire a knack from a verse of scripture by adding his own barren notions and conceptions to it, and his uncertain conjectures, and what he hath stolen out of books; for which end he must have of necessity a good many by him, and may each Sabbath-day, as they call it, or oftener, make a discourse for an hour long; and this is called the preaching of the word: whereas the gift, grace, and Spirit of God to teach, open, and instruct, and to preach a word in season, is neglected. . . . And so the devil may be as good and able a minister as the best of them; for he has better skill in languages, and more logic, philosophy and school-divinity than any of them. . . . But what availeth all this? Is it not all but as death . . . without the power, life, and spirit of Christianity? . . . And he that hath this, and can speak from it, though he be a poor shepherd or a fisherman and ignorant of all that learning . . . yet speaking from the Spirit, his ministry will have more influence towards converting of a sinner unto God than all of them who are learned after the flesh.[41]

Here we see what is perhaps the most eloquent and biting attack on typical preaching followed by a powerfully worded summary of the traditional Quaker defense of impromptu preaching by so-called laymen. Barclay follows this passage with the specific observation that God chooses "weak instruments" and produces "powerful ministry of illiterate men," ministers "such as the Spirit acts apart for the ministry, by its divine power and influence opening their mouths."[42]

Next Barclay comments on the concept of "prophecy," commonly employed by Puritans as another name for biblical preaching. Barclay allows that prophecy as foretelling remains an active gift from God: "[Prophecy] as it signifies the foretelling of things to come is, indeed a distinct gift, but no distinct office,"[43] which has been given to persons outside the circle of clergy. On the other hand, "Prophecy in the other sense, to wit, as it signifies a speaking from the Spirit of truth, is not only peculiar to pastors and teachers . . . but even a common privilege to the saints." In other words, anyone moved by the Light may "prophcsy" in both senses.

At the end of Proposition X, Barclay summarizes his reflections on the ministry by declaring, "We are for a holy, spiritual, pure and living ministry, where the ministers are both called, qualified and ordered, actuated and influenced in all the steps of their ministry by the Spirit of God; which being wanting, we judge they cease to be ministers of Christ."[44]

We get a more complete image of how Barclay thought this form of vocal ministry ought to operate among early Quakers by examining "Concerning Worship," Proposition XI of the *Apology*, which reads in part,

> All true and acceptable worship to God is offered in the inward and immediate moving and drawing of his own Spirit, which is neither limited to places, times, nor persons. For though we are to worship him always, and continually fear before him; yet as to the outward signification thereof in prayers, praises or preachings, we ought not to do it in our own will, where and when we will; but where and when we are moved thereunto by the stirring and secret inspiration of the Spirit of God in our hearts. . . . All other worship . . . [is] superstition, will-worship, and abominable idolatry in the sight of God.[45]

In Proposition XI Barclay specifically argues for silent group waiting in the presence of God as the only true and acceptable form of worship. Such worship, he declares, normally takes the following course:

> [W]hen assembled, the great work of one and all ought to be to wait upon God; and returning out of their own thoughts and imaginations, to feel the Lord's presence and know a gathering into his name indeed, where he is in the midst according to his promise. And as every one is thus gathered, and so met together inwardly in their spirits as well as outwardly in their persons, there the secret power and virtue of life is known to refresh the soul, and the pure motions and breathings of God's Spirit are felt to arise; from which, as words of declaration, prayers or praises arise, the acceptable worship is known, which edifies the church and is well-pleasing to

God. And no man here limits the Spirit of God, nor bringeth forth his own coned and gathered stuff; but every one puts that forth which the Lord puts into their hearts: and it is uttered forth not in man's will and wisdom; but in the evidence and demonstration of the Spirit and of power.[46]

The silent group waiting Barclay describes produces "an inward travail and wrestling" that sometimes has outward physical signs: "the body will be greatly shaken, and many groans, and sighs, and tears, even as the pangs of a woman in travail, will lay hold upon it," from which outward behaviors arose the name "Quakers." Silence is not the end of such worship, but the begining. Barclay asserts, "as our worship consisteth not in words, so neither in silence, as silence; but in a holy dependence of the mind upon God: from which dependence silence necessarily follows in the first place, until words can be brought forth, which are from God's Spirit . . . there are few meetings that are altogether silent."[47]

Following Fox's early insistence on ministers leading holy lives, Barclay asserts that the first step in preparation for Quaker worship is purgation of the heart, not only of evil, but also of its own inventions—its "inward, natural senses," which he writes about in *Immediate Revelation*.[48] Barclay declares, "it must . . . be purged of its own filth, and all its own thoughts and imaginations, that so it may be fit to receive the Spirit of God, and to be actuated by it."[49] It is not clear from Barclay's description how the potential preacher should discern between the mind's "own inventions" and the implanted ideas that wait for the "stirring" of the Spirit, as Barclay had posited in *Immediate Revelation*.

Barclay describes preaching "actuated" by the spirit of God in a key passage from Proposition XI: "he that ministereth . . . ought to speak forth what the Spirit of God furnisheth him with; not minding the eloquence and wisdom of words, but the demonstration of the Spirit and of power: and that either in the interpreting some part of scripture, in case the Spirit, which is the good remembrancer, lead him to do so, or otherwise words of exhortation, advice, reproof, and instruction, or the sense of some spiritual experiences: all of which will be still agreeable to the scripture, though perhaps not relative to, nor founded upon any particular chapter or verse, as a text."[50] In sum, the preaching Barclay describes would be motivated by a sense of the immediate leading of the Spirit without prior determination to speak;

it would eschew language employed merely as a means of decoration or chosen simply for effect or eloquence; its formal content might be composed, in whole or in part, of commentary on Scripture, exhortation, advice, instruction, or testimony based on personal spiritual experience; and it would need not be based upon a specific text from the Bible, although such textual preaching would be allowed if immediately moved by the Spirit. "Immediately moved" is the key concept in this notion of preaching.[51] Barclay's conclusion to Proposition XI sums up his position succinctly: "The worship, preaching, praying and singing, which we plead for, is such as proceedeth from the Spirit of God, and is always accompanied by its influence, being begun by its motion, and carried on by the power and strength thereof."[52]

CONCLUSION

This consideration of Barclay's *Apology* and *Immediate Revelation* indicates that he developed the philosophical outlines of a rhetorical theory based upon an epistemology with direct revelation as the center of knowledge. Barclay replaces the classical system, with its emphasis on systematic approaches to invention, with a path that relies on the ability of the mind to perceive inward revelation because the mind is prewired to do just that. Ironically, Barclay set forth his notions at roughly the same time the classical system was also being challenged by the rhetoric of the enlightenment, which, as we saw in chapter 1, minimized the classical inventional tools in favor of an epistemological system based on particulars and known primarily through sensation. Whereas, for Barclay, the mind comes preseeded with divinely implanted ideas that are "stirred up" by the Inward Light or by outward sensation, for enlightenment writers, such as Locke, the mind is passive and "clean" as a blank slate until energized by the senses. Language, for Barclay, is dictated by the Spirit so that the speaker becomes a kind of oracle for the eternal Word. The Quaker emphasis on silence translates into a belief that all utterance is fraught with caution, as Fox and the earliest Quakers had maintained. This attitude must have been reinforced by the general belief that the Spirit could, indeed would, speak to *any* person directly. This leads to the question, Where was the need of preaching? Nevertheless, early Quakers did speak, and, according to Barclay, their speaking, when prompted immediately by the Spirit, could help reinforce an inward message and also provide comfort and assurance to hearers.

This examination of Barclay's *Apology* and *Immediate Revelation* also indicates a reluctance on Barclay's part to publish anything beyond a theological and philosophical rationale for impromptu preaching. He wrote nothing about how to prepare for or accomplish the task, or what tools one might be expected to employ while preaching under the impulse of the Inward Light. There is only the barest hint in Barclay's *Apology* regarding the use of memorized Scripture by the preacher as a kind of storehouse of ideas. It is not until Bownas' *A Description of the Qualifications Necessary to a Gospel Minister*, a book published fifty-eight years later, that we discover anything approximating an inventional scheme for impromptu preaching. For Barclay, though, impromptu, inspired preaching was only a tributary to his larger theological river, and he had accomplished the most important part of the task, setting out the best statement of Quaker impromptu preaching's rationale.

That Barclay's *Apology* was influential on generations of Quakers is a commonplace in Quaker histories.[53] Although his view of the mind from *Immediate Revelation* goes essentially unmentioned by later authors, his rationale for impromptu preaching was accepted by Quakers until well into the nineteenth century, when a paid (or "released") pastoral system was adopted by the majority of American Quakers. The pastoral system, although not necessitating the adoption of advanced sermon preparation, helped precipitate a widespread move among Quakers in that direction.[54]

CHAPTER 5

THE FLOWERING OF EARLY QUAKER HOMILETIC THEORY

SAMUEL BOWNAS' MANUAL FOR ITINERANT IMPROMPTU PREACHERS

Samuel Bownas' *Qualifications* is the closest thing to a practical homiletical book produced by Quakers, though the term "homiletics" is never employed by the author.[1] The book is rich in its description of the Quaker rationale for impromptu preaching and full of Bownas' advice to young aspiring Quaker preachers. Although published in the mid-eighteenth century, it reflects earlier Quaker homiletic thought and practice. In this chapter, I will lay out some of the background to *Qualifications* prior to presenting an examination of the book's content that particularly relates to the topic of inspired, impromptu preaching. My discussion of the book itself will deal with the following topics: sanctification, inspiration, advice to "ministers in a state of infancy," and advice on the matter and manner of expression. Finally, I will draw some conclusions about the development of early Quaker impromptu preaching theory in the context of Bownas' significant work.

BACKGROUNDS TO SAMUEL BOWNAS' *QUALIFICATIONS*

Bownas' book builds on the theoretical base for inspired preaching, as well as cumulative advice, set out by earlier Quaker writers, discussed in chapters 3 and 4. As a young preacher, Bownas found himself in a culture highly influenced by strong impromptu ministry, in which the preacher was motivated by a sense of the immediate leading of the Spirit without prior determination to speak; where language was never employed merely as decoration or simply for rhetorical effect; where sermons were about Scripture commentary, exhortation to lead godly lives, advice about the spiritual life, instruction regarding a righteous path, or testimony based on personal spiritual experience; and where sermons may or may not have been based upon a specific text from the Bible. Bownas also came into the vocal ministry when cautions against passionate delivery style or going beyond one's inspiration were circulating among Quakers.

Bownas was born in 1676, the same year Barclay's *Apology* was printed in Latin. By 1696, when he began his speaking ministry, the Quaker tradition of impromptu preaching was already well established. Bownas grew up in a cultural environment that placed strong emphasis on the perpetuation of an "immediately called," basically itinerant, lay ministry, which employed the impromptu sermon exclusively.[2] By the time *Qualifications* saw print in 1750, just three years before his death, Bownas was nearing the end of a long and distinguished ministry as a publick Friend. There is ample reason to believe that his "advices" to young Quaker preachers had been passed along orally long before they reached print. Prior to Bownas' book, printed advice was sparse about how a preacher might actually produce impromptu, inspired discourse, except for the ubiquitous injunction to wait in silence before God until the Spirit offered the words to speak. Fox's use of biblical typologies and figures and his readiness in debate no doubt necessitated serious time spent in study, but that necessity—seen from our perspective—never provoked advice from early Friends for preachers to study in preparation for a specific debate or sermon. Barclay, as we noted, offered some hints regarding materials that would be acceptable in sermons: Scripture interpretation, "words of exhortation, advice, reproof, and instruction, or the sense of some spiritual experiences."[3] Arguably, Bownas began his public life and book with a soup rather thin in printed homiletic instruction, but a repast hearty and thick with accumulated wisdom based on the experience and advice of elders.

As early as 1702, anticipating many of the essential themes he would later develop in *Qualifications*, Bownas had written to the Kendal Meeting of Ministers regarding "this public station of preaching":

> I see great need for us to carefully mind our openings, and go on as we are led by the Spirit; for if we overrun our Guide and opening we shall be confused, not knowing where, or how to conclude. . . .
>
> [L]et us be singly and in sincerity devoted to the will of God . . . whether to preach or be silent; for if we are not sensible of such a resignation, it is doubtful that we may set ourselves at work, when we should be quiet, and so bring an uneasiness upon our friends, and burthen upon ourselves. And this conduct will shut up Friends hearts against our service and ministry . . . every time you appear in the ministry, when it is over, examine yourselves narrowly, whether you

have kept in your places, and to your Guide; and consider whether
you have not used superfluous words that render the matter disagree-
able, or such tones or gestures as misbecome the work we are about,
always remembering, that the true ministers preach not themselves,
but Christ Jesus our Lord. Let us bear this in mind, that neither arts,
parts, strength of memory, nor former experiences will, without the
sanctification of the spirit, do anything for us to depend on.[4]

Here we see Bownas lining up with the cautions of his predecessors,
with regard to both content and delivery, and apparently rejecting the
ancient arts of rhetoric. However, he leaves the door slightly ajar by
adding to his rejection-filled final sentence the key words, "without the
sanctification of the spirit." He appears to realize that some preachers
are better than others in the impromptu situation, and that not all the
differences can be attributed to inspiration alone.

AN EXAMINATION OF THE BOOK ITSELF

Qualifications is 112 pages in length and divided into a seven-page
preface authored by an unknown person, two chapters setting out the
essential "qualifications" for public ministry, six chapters of advice
to men and women in one of the sequential developmental stages
of public ministry, and finally a two-page discourse on the duty of
public prayer.[5]

The first two chapters set out the two essential underlying positions on the ministry, found in the writings of the earliest Friends and
crystallized in Barclay's writings: (1) that the first and ultimate qualification for ministers is to be sanctified or holy persons, and (2) that they
must become ministers and speak in meetings only under the immediate prompting of "Divine Inspiration."

Sanctification

The first chapter treats sanctification as an absolutely necessary first
step toward becoming a public minister. Here Bownas follows the
trail clearly marked by everyone who preceded him. Bownas sensi-
bly writes, "whosoever undertakes the work of the ministry, not being
first reformed themselves, canot justly expect to be inspired by divine
wisdom for the reforming of others." Bownas sees sanctification as a
process, rather than an instantaneous gift, whose developmental process
begins with self-examination and secret prayer. The inevitable discovery of one's rebelliousness from God and the presence of leanings

toward "the pleasures of the flesh and vanities of this life . . . produces uneasiness and melancholy," which some people drown in "their
bottle" or others forget by means of "sports and gaming."[6] Still others
take "a better course." In a key passage, Bownas employs the biblical metaphor of the spiritual journey to capture the link between the
journey toward sanctification and the preparation to receive divine
inspiration:

> [W]e must first expect a being brought from under the bondage of
> corruption to spiritual Pharaoh and Egypt, into the wilderness, e'er
> we can offer acceptably unto God. This state is figuratively called a
> *Wilderness*, a way we have not trod in, showing thereby the necessity
> of depending on our Guide, our spiritual Moses, that must go before
> and take care of our support. For in this Wilderness state we have
> no food, no water, viz. no right refreshment but what this our leader
> provides. . . . In this state we can neither pray, nor do any religious
> act, without the direction of our leader, so that we find the case is
> much altered with us to what it was in time past; for then we could
> pray, sing, preach, and perform other religious duties in our own
> time, feeding and satisfying ourselves.[7]

In the state of utter dependence upon the Guide—the spiritual
Moses—the spiritual traveler, "in the Lord's time," arrives at the "heavenly Canaan." According to Bownas, the pilgrim then comes "to experience the substance of those types and figures . . . to be substantially
and spiritually fulfilled . . . by the operation of the Spirit of our Lord
Jesus Christ, the substance of and foundation of all true religion and
ministry that is really profitable to the hearers."[8] In this preparation
step, the novice minister experiences *scriptura rediviva* and travels across
a threshold between symbol and reality. The preparation thus substantially completed, the fledgling minister "may be qualified to receive a
divine inspiration to minister from to others." In Bownas' use of biblical symbols, we see a profound, but unacknowledged, internalization
of one of Fox's foremost habits of biblical interpretation and preaching: the personal application of biblical "typologies and figures."

Prior to turning to the subject of divine inspiration in the second chapter, Bownas observes that some ministers, for whom it is "but
a short time between . . . begining to be serious and religious" and
their first vocal ministry, may encounter resistance from some of their
hearers. Significantly, one of Bownas' first pieces of practical advice is
directed at *auditors*. We have noted in chapter 3 the cautions to hear-

ers regarding their careful treatment of fledgling ministers. Also, in chapter 4, we noted Barclay's observation that a preacher's ministry is confirmed in the hearers,[9] and that there ought to be a mutual, two-way acknowledgment of the minister's task. Here we see these two threads entwined in Bownas' writing. In the case of overzealous, young preachers who may "a little stretch (at times) beyond their authority," Bownas counsels elders with these words: "Such [preachers] . . . ought to be treated with great charity and meekness, and the good design in them encouraged; and that over-forwardness in them rather shown to them than reproved; and when they see it, they will not need to be told of it, for shame will come fast enough upon them (if they are true ministers) . . . which may hinder some tender spirits from improving in their gifts."[10]

Inspiration

In the second chapter, which deals with the necessity of divine inspiration, Bownas continues his advice to auditors begun in the first chapter, now revealing to them how to sniff out those who are not "true ministers" on the basis of discernment regarding their "inspiration": "[T]hey who conceived themselves to be inspired when they are not, supposing they have a revelation when it is nothing but an imagination of their own brain, are exalted in their minds, being very heady and stubborn, fighting instruction; more apt to teach than learn, being swift to speak but slow to hear, judging everybody that will not receive them as true ministers by foretelling the ruin and downfall of all their opposers." On the other hand, true ministers "are slow to speak and ready to hear and receive instruction, and are known by them that are spiritual to be such."[11]

Bownas devotes the lion's share of the second chapter to presenting a rationale for accepting divine inspiration as absolutely necessary to a minister of the gospel. As we have seen, here he repeats a commonplace iterated by many Quakers before him, especially Fox and Barclay. Bownas argues that inspiration did not end with the development of the biblical canon and, following Fox and others, that just as the Scriptures were inspired by the Spirit, "so by it we must come to a right understanding of them, otherwise they will be as a book sealed."[12]

Early in the second chapter, Bownas disparagingly describes the kind of "uninspired" preaching Quakers often accused their Puritan and Anglican brethren of perpetuating, complete with a direct blow at the Ramus-inspired "doctrine-use" format so popular with American Puritans:[13]

> It is true, men may by study and frequent reading acquire to themselves a form of words, and frame a set and studied speech in a regular way, methodically dividing and subdividing their matter, raising uses and applications from the present subject before them; and all this may be done by the *man*, the *creature*, and *natural part*, having nothing of inspiration or power of the Spirit in it. And pray, what will this ministry do for the hearers? It comes from the head and the contrivance of the man's part, therefore it can reach no further; for no stream can arise higher than its fountain.[14]

Here Bownas reveals acquaintance with the Ramian method of analysis (division and subdivision of topics) and the necessity, following Perkins, for the Puritan preacher to raise "uses and applications" drawn from a doctrinaire interpretation of Scriptures for his hearers. This strong judgment of a dominant approach to homiletics might suggest that Bownas will present a decidedly anti-rhetorical approach to preaching, or avoid writing directly about the *content* of sermons and how the impromptu preacher might put together a sermon, but this is not an accurate account of what we encounter in Bownas' subsequent chapters.

After attacking Puritan homiletics, Bownas defines "inspiration" as "an inbreathing of the divine word into our minds, giving a true understanding of divine things, that we may make choice of, and walk in the paths of wisdom."[15] Here Bownas decisively privileges the more cognitive or rational aspects of human nature rather than the emotional facets then associated with the word "enthusiasm." Having revealed his distrust of imagination, Bownas turns to the rational faculty of understanding, as aided by the Spirit. The preacher is presented as having a measure of rational choice in the impromptu situation. Rather than being sought or manipulated, Bownas writes that this sort of inspiration "ought to be waited for." On this topic, he shares from his own experience: "when I find my understanding inspired and influenced by this blessed gift to minister to others, I give up thereto, speaking to the assembly according to the present ability I receive thereby; and I know this to be the true begining of a right Gospel ministry." There is a strong hint of reluctance, even resignation, in the words "I give up thereto," and Bownas writes about the anxieties associated with the inspired ministry in later chapters.

Divine inspiration, by Bownas' account, produces a "spiritual understanding" akin to that originally experienced when the Holy Spirit revealed to the apostles that Jesus was the Son of God. "[T]his spiritual understanding," Bownas writes, "which they received by revelation, was an undeniable evidence to them, and so it is to us."[16] Spiritual understanding in this scheme is superior to natural understanding, because by natural understanding, "[the apostles] could not perceive the things of the Spirit of God, nor comprehend the light which shined in darkness, which is still the same, even until now." Immediate, direct revelation thus continues unabated from biblical times, just as Bownas' predecessors taught.

Bownas raises the question as to how he can prove this "inspiration" based on revelation to a person who is "in a natural and unenlightened state." His response focuses on the idea we have previously encountered, that not only speakers, but also hearers must be inspired: "It is not possible to do it [prove inspiration] until they who are in unbelief come to believe in the same power, and receive inspiration by the same Spirit to give them a right knowledge of the things of God." Proving your "inspiration" among believers, Bownas asserts, is "no hard task" if one will "endeavor to live according to that doctrine given thee to preach to others."[17] Following early Quaker injunctions against preaching as a mere act of the will, Bownas declares that the preacher should never undertake the work of preaching without the sense of being inspired:

> [N]either in thy own time nor will, nor by thy own contrivance, [should you be] collecting and casting what thou shalt say; for by so doing thou wilt be at a loss and confounded in thyself and give great occasion of offence [*sic*] to them that hear thee; not only to them that are unacquainted with the gift . . . but thy own brethren will be . . . uneasy with thy so appearing; for they will soon find that thou art out of thy place in thy speaking, it not being from inspiration, but imagination of thy own brain.

Thus the speaker "proves" inspiration by speaking under the power of inspiration, not the power of the imagination. Bownas wants preachers to rely on spiritual resources because unbelievers will be more apt to pay attention: "others may perhaps be reached by thy word, and as thou dost minister from a right spirit, and keepest in thy gift, thou mayst be instrumental to beget faith in them that believe not."[18]

There are at least two major problems with Bownas' position on inspiration. First, his argument involves a potentially weak method to prove a message's inspiration. The presence of inspiration is detected and approved by those who already believe in inspiration and now judge the present message to be inspired. These same people may seek approval for their own inspired messages at another or possibly the same meeting. However, if they judge the message to be the result of the preacher's "own contrivance," then the message is not deemed inspired, although, in truth, the message may still be inspired, but merely rejected by the gathered hearers and judged as culturally inappropriate for them, as were, incidentally, many messages delivered by Old Testament prophets. The second problem is that Bownas attempts no explanation of how inward revelation actually occurs, as did Barclay in his *Immediate Revelation* (published in 1692). In fact, Bownas does not respond to, repeat, seek to modify, or in any way indicate an awareness of Barclay's speculations. In so many other ways, Bownas builds on the wisdom of the past, but here he leaves a lacuna.

Advice to Ministers in a State of Infancy

Having followed most of his precursors' tenets and laid the groundwork for a view of ministry based on the absolute necessity of sanctification and divine inspiration, Bownas lays out six chapters of direct advice to ministers. His approach is built on traditional Friends' interest in encouraging novice preachers to grow, but it is also an original contribution in that he is the first writer, to my knowledge, to expand the developmental model of ministry into a systematic and lengthy statement. Bownas considers the case of a maturing minister in three sequential and evolving stages: (1) infancy, (2) a young man's state, and (3) the father's state. The bulk of his advice, fifty-three pages—almost half the book—is aimed at the first stage of development. In the third chapter, Bownas begins, once again, with a word of advice to hearers rather than speakers. He notes that the "infant minister" may often experience intense fear at the initial decision to speak in a meeting for worship: "when they have given up [yielded to the immediate call to speak], it has been in so much weakness and fear, yea, sometimes confusion, that they have hardly known themselves what they have said." At such times, Bownas tells auditors, "exercise charity; and see to thine own gift thou that art a hearer, and try by virtue thereof, whether thou findest not something of God in this infant minister to answer his gift in thy own mind." He continues by invoking an agricultural metaphor to illustrate his point: "give time for proof, and consider the patience of the husbandman, how he waits for a crop after the seed is sown."[19] Fox had used a similar metaphor in an advisory epistle mentioned in chapter 3.

Turning directly to the infant minister, Bownas advises the fledgling preacher to be resigned to the will of God, wait patiently, and depend upon the Spirit "to enlarge thy understanding of divine openings."[20] In a significant passage, Bownas sums up the appropriate response by the infant minister to the impromptu preaching challenge:

> I advise to an inward waiting upon thy gift, to feel the moving thereof in thy own mind, which will by a gentle illumination clear thy understanding and judgment . . . and if thou findest it thy place to minister to others . . . stand up in the meekness of the Spirit which moveth on thy mind, and speak the word thereof according to the present opening that is before thee, regarding strictly on the one hand, by speaking too fast or too loud, thou don't overrun thy natural strength, gift, and opening, which if thou happens to fall into, it will bring thee into confusion, and thou wilt not know when to conclude, and so mayst shut up thy own way in the minds of the brethren, and bring thyself under a just censure; therefore whenever it happens so with thee, *sit down*; for by endeavouring to mend it, thou mayst make it the worse: So on the other hand, be not too low nor too slow in thy speech, so as to lose the matter that way; but carefully keep to thy opening, avoiding both the extremes: Stand up in a calm and quiet frame of mind, as free as possible from either a fear or care how thou shalt come off; but follow thy guide in all circumspection and humility, begining, going on, and concluding in thy gift.[21]

Here Bownas mixes advice regarding both vocal delivery style, which should not be "too fast or too loud," nor "too low nor too slow," and self-conscious monitoring of the Spirit's moving or opening. Delivery volume and pace remain highly subjective, for what is "too fast" or "too low" to one person may be quite different from another. The advice amounts to a call to monitor one's delivery, implying a conscious, rational self-assessment—all on the run. Additionally, Bownas' advice stresses conscious disregard for the outcome or result of the impromptu message, quite a different approach from the "functionalist" perspective of traditional rhetorical teaching.

Bownas also cautions novice preachers not to compare themselves with other speakers, because a favorable comparison may "lift thee up and prove hurtful," while an unfavorable comparison may "cast thee down, and beget too mean an opinion in thee of thy own gift." Furthermore, imitation, the bedrock pedagogical tool of Isocrates, Cicero, and Quintilian, is also to be avoided: "[L]et not the seeming excellency that appears in another's gift above thy own tempt thee to an imitation of either delivery, manner or accent, lest thou insensibly fall into that theft, against which the Lord by his prophet complains, *I am against the prophets* (saith the Lord) *that steal my words, every one from his neighbor*." One should not imitate others, because "there is [*sic*] *diversities of gifts*, and though thine may differ from another's gift, yet mind to keep to it."[22]

Bownas' criterion of success is not to measure one's preaching against someone else's, but to move into inward reflection: "by this thou shalt know that thou art in thy gift, if after thou hast been exercised therein, thou feelest inward satisfaction and comfort to flow in thy mind; but if thou findest trouble and heaviness, consider whether thou hast not been out of thy place, either in the manner of delivering thyself . . . [or] to the matter delivered."[23] Self-monitoring one's inner emotional state bears heavily on the preacher's self-assessment. To my knowledge, this is the first written advice regarding personal discernment of whether or not a delivered message appeared to be fully inspired or not.

In her book on early Quaker ministry, Beamish reminds her readers that in eighteenth-century Quaker preaching, some preachers practiced a "singing tone" of delivery, which, as the century progressed, "became regarded as a special sign of unction . . . [which] speakers were encouraged to cultivate."[24] Bownas forcefully attacks this pretentious style of delivery: "[K]eep to thy own way, both in thy opening and delivering thereof, guarding against all affected tones of singing or sighing and drawing out thy words and sentences beyond their due length, and by speaking too much in a breath and so adding an *Ah!* to the end of them, and drawing thy breath with such a force and groan as will drown thy matter and render thee unacceptable to thy hearers." Regarding vocal delivery, he further advises, "neither lift up thy voice beyond thy natural strength, nor strain thyself beyond due bounds, vainly supposing that when thou makest most noise with an accent and tone that pleaseth thy own imagination, that the power is most with thee; when indeed it is nothing but the heat of thy own spirit, and sparks at thy own kindling."[25] Bownas appears to aver that some aspects of self-monitoring have the potential to be self-delusional.

With regard to kinetic aspects of delivery, Bownas advises, "[A]void all indecent gestures of the body, as throwing thy *arms abroad*, and *lifting up thy eyes*; such gestures not suiting the dignity of the ministry."[26] We canot tell precisely from Bownas' advice whether he is against all eye contact between speaker and audience or whether the preacher should not raise his or her eyes toward heaven in an ecstatic full-body gesture. I suspect it is the former.

In Bownas' comments regarding acceptable vocal and gestural delivery, we observe a concern that the preacher develop a sense of decorum that is modest, self-effacing, message-centered rather than speaker-centered, and perhaps the antithesis of vocal and gestural behavior that initially earned Friends their first nickname, "Quakers."[27] Bownas follows in the moderate path laid out for him by Marshall and Coole in the previous century. This is a thoroughly conservative approach to delivery, probably a response to attacks against "enthusiasm."

On the subject of style, traditional rhetoric's third canon, Bownas is squarely in league with the Puritan and Quaker tradition of "plainness": "guard against superfluous words, impertinently brought it, such as, *I may say, as it were, all and everyone, dear friends*, and *friendly people*, with sundry others of the like kind, which add nothing to thy matter, spoiling its coherence and beauty and expression."[28] Here Bownas seeks to eliminate "filler words," linguistic habits that might easily become the refuge of impromptu preachers in order to "stall for time" while formulating the next thought. I believe Bownas is responding to linguistic choices he personally has heard in Quaker meetings. If readers followed his advice, the effect would be a deepening of the potential effect of each carefully chosen word. In this sparse linguistic environment, words chosen to be uttered tended to gain in weight.

Bownas directly addresses the question of how a young minister can know when to speak and whether he or she needs to know the content of the entire message before rising to speak:

> I . . . advise thee to wait for the descending of the gift of the Spirit, which will bring an exercise over thy mind in which thou mayst be opened with some matter suiting the present occasion; and when thou findest it is thy place to speak, stand up; for it is not to be supposed that all thou mayst have to say on this or that subject can come

before thee e'er thou begins to speak: and if thou should'st suppose it, and so wait, endeavouring to prepare thyself like a school boy, thou wilt be greatly disappointed, not speaking what thou intended, but something else that thou intended not, which may be thy trouble and grief.[29]

Bownas wrote these words within the long tradition of Quaker rejection of traditional learning as a requirement for becoming a minister, applying that notion to a particular instance of preaching without prior conscious preparation for the specific meeting. He also wrote within the long tradition of meetings based on initial silent waiting for the Spirit to move. He follows the moderate, conservative path pointed out by Fox, Marshall, and Coole. The Quaker preacher, after assuring himself or herself of the initial opening, by an intuitive method perhaps beyond Bownas' ability to put into words, must begin speaking without full knowledge of anything but the introductory remarks, speaking "some matter suiting the present occasion." In the experience of speaking, Bownas advises, the preacher will discover a mixture of inspiration (the Spirit) and rational control (understanding). Like those who wrote before him, there is not the slightest indication that Bownas is writing about a kind of "possession" or "ecstasy" over which the speaker has little or no control. There is no hint of "quaking" in Bownas' perspective. The speaker is never "possessed," in any sense.

In Bownas' account of the process of inspiration, understanding plays a dominant role. He writes, "*mind the time* of thy offering, that thou mayst not hinder the service of another, nor hurt thy own, by either standing up too soon or standing too long; all which will be prevented, as thou keep'st in a quiet, cool frame, retaining thy understanding, that thou mayst speak with the Spirit and understanding also."[30] Preachers who followed Bownas' advice could hardly be accused of "enthusiasm."

Similar to Coole, who wrote fifty-four years earlier (1696), Bownas distinguishes between two kinds of inspired messages that might be received by potential public ministers in the meeting for worship: (1) a message intended personally for the minister, and (2) a message intended to be spoken to the assembled group of people. Coole had called the former "passive" and the latter "active." Bownas cautions not to "give that away to others which thou ought to feed upon thyself, and so become a formal and unprofitable minister." The result of such a negative habit is that "the true knowledge of the time when to speak and when to be silent . . . will be lost."[31] As noted in chapter 3, this is an interesting and pertinent distinction among instances of "immediate revelation" discussed by both Marshall and Coole. The preacher would discern not only that the message was from God, but whether or not the message was to be shared in the meeting. In Bownas' framework, if the message was shared vocally, its authenticity would be discovered both in an inward positive sense in the preacher's mind or spirit after the meeting as well as in the responses of hearers.

According to Bownas, some preachers in his circle of acquaintance "delivered themselves more awkwardly and unbecomingly than at other times," the "other times" being their "common affairs" outside the meeting for worship. Bownas maintains that the preacher "should deliver his ministry with a better grace, in pertinent matter to the subject before him, than he does in his discourse in common, according to the degree of assistance received by the Spirit at that time."[32] This is a very important comment, which implies that inspired impromptu preaching might be expected to possess "better grace" than ordinary conversation, because the Spirit would assist the preacher in a more direct organizational and stylistic way during public ministry. Naturally, this expectation of help from a divine muse might have presented a challenge to preachers who nevertheless consistently appeared to be awkward either in their content or delivery, or both, whether in meetings for worship or at "other times" in the outside world. This expectation of divine assistance in content and delivery probably produced a stronger sense of reticence and helped reinforce the decline of Quaker preaching in the eighteenth century.

Bownas advises that once the message is begun, the preacher should continue as he or she sees the way open and the "understanding enlarged." The preacher would be expected to rely on the Spirit to provide "pertinent words to express." He follows with a very practical piece of advice: "Scriptures which will suit thy matter, and confirm it, will be brought in memory that may not have been thought of or read by thee long before; here thou wilt see a reason for what thou sayest."[33] In chapter 3, we noted the implicit necessity for Quaker preachers to assimilate biblical knowledge and language into their brains outside Quaker meetings in order for them to meet their opponents head to head in impromptu debate as well as to develop spiritually. Bownas makes the connection directly to impromptu preaching in the meeting for worship. In his view, Scriptures pertinent to the subject could be interwoven from memory as they appeared to relate to the subject or occasion, and the very phenomenon of memory, the fourth traditional rhetorical canon, could be interpreted as a confirmation of the Spirit's inspiration to speak in the first place. Note that there is no indication in Bownas that the Scriptures are to be used as part of the conscious "preparation" process for speaking at a particular time and place, because there is to be no such specific prior preparation encouraged or "allowed." By implication, scriptural study is to be a natural part of the Quaker's everyday devotional life, including specific Scripture memorization. This process is implicit in all the writers mentioned in the previous two chapters. As noted earlier, memorized Scriptures operated as a potentially huge source of material for early Quaker impromptu preachers in that they could be resident in the memory and "quickened" by the Inward Light at any point in the sermon as it was being delivered. Bownas is simply making this connection explicit.[34]

Bownas concludes his first chapter of advice to "infant ministers" with a reiteration of his admonition to use a restrained style of delivery, a very significant theme for Bownas. He points out that the calm and easygoing style has two advantages: (1) if one's content does not "suit with the sense of some that are thy elders, yet this friendly, cool temper of mind will render thee open to receive . . . kind instruction in the way of the Lord more perfectly"; and (2) the calm delivery will "give thee an advantage to raise thy voice, as thou find'st inward strength and virtue from the Spirit to increase."[35] In this concluding statement, Bownas opens the door slightly to a more vigorous vocal and gestural delivery style, but it is clear that this more oratorical style is not to be a universal or frequent characteristic of Quaker preaching.

ADVICES ON THE MATTER AND MANNER OF EXPRESSION

In the fourth chapter, Bownas provides an important typology of expression relating to the opening, or the moving, of the Spirit. His presentation amounts to a checklist of possible forms of expression that all or part of the impromptu sermon might take, "seeing," as he writes, "there are sundry ways of expressing the same thing."[36] His list includes seven means of expression: (1) parables, (2) allegories, (3) narration or "historical relation," (4) personal testimony of God's goodness in one's life, (5) testimony of God's goodness in another person's life, (6) exposition of a text from Scripture, and (7) the use of typology.

On its face, the list is not composed of distinct categories, but this conclusion is apparent in Bownas' brief explanations.

Bownas treats parables and allegories separately from the other five forms of expression, spending seven pages in their consideration, compared with a total of six pages devoted to the remaining five. Of the seven pages assigned to parables and allegories, six are dedicated to a consideration of parables, leaving allegories in roughly the same position with respect to space allotted as he devotes to the remaining five forms of expression. He offers no direct indication in the text as to why he treats parables at greater length, why he separates allegories from the other five categories, or why he numbers the remaining five separately. I take Bownas' treatment to be indicative of (1) his personal preference among the inventional and presentational tools he lists, and (2) an indication of his belief that preference should be given means of expression that heighten the role of the hearers and the Spirit in the total communication process. I will now turn to a brief examination of each of Bownas' "means of expression."

1. *Parable*. Bownas favors the use of parables because of their emotional impact and because they trigger self-examination through which the Spirit may move: "By parables is . . . truth often set forth in lively and moving terms, producing in the hearers the passions of sorrow, anger, or joy, as the matter set forth affects them, so that hereby they are drawn unawares to pass a severe judgment upon their own doings."[37] He offers four examples from the Bible, begining with the incident of King David and the Prophet Nathan, in which Nathan spoke in a parable to David, and David unwittingly pronounced judgment upon himself (2 Sam 12:1-13). Bownas writes that the parable has the virtue of "gaining great attention; and it is very moving and of good service to them that hear, being given and opened by the Spirit alone." Here Bownas stresses the early Quaker reliance on the immediate working of the Spirit when employing parables. Thus the first choice among several means of expression is the parable left uninterpreted by the preacher. Bownas leaves his consideration of the parable with a warning to infant ministers not to imitate a helpful and effective parable used by another preacher, because it "makes confused work, and instead of edifying the hearers, grieves and loads them with trouble and sorrow to hear solid and divine truths so darkened and perplexed." Here Bownas summarily (and perhaps unecessarily) cuts off

access by novice preachers to a source of proven effective material, with or without acknowledgment of the original source. It is unclear why using a proven device from another preacher may produce confusion or bring about such negative effects. Bownas appears to be saying that the Spirit will stimulate a novel parable in the mind of the preacher in the heat of the moment. I speculate that here Bownas is affirming the standard Quaker notion that specific preparation is to be shuned and that any message prompted by the Inward Light is always superior to any parable borrowed from another preacher. Once again, imitation is to be studiously avoided. Bownas ends with a standard reiteration of the Quaker rationale of impromptu preaching: "I say, if these or any other things be undertaken to be expressed without the Spirit guiding and opening the understanding, it will give too much occasion for that proverb to be renewed, *that comparisons are odious.*"[38] Bownas will advise the fledgling preacher never to provoke the hearers to rate speakers on a hierarchical scale.

2. *Allegory.* Bownas makes short work of allegories without offering anything beyond brief descriptions of the biblical allegories presented by Paul in the Letter to the Galatians, 4, and the author of the Letter to the Hebrews, 7. Bownas includes no advice regarding their use, nor contemporary examples. One may assume that he has heard Quaker ministers employ allegories or has employed them himself on occasion, else why include allegory as one of the means of expression?

3. *Narration or Historical Relation.* Begining with a brief consideration of Stephen's sermon in Acts 7, and Paul's in Acts 13, Bownas asserts that narration, particularly of God's dealing with his people in past ages, is a valuable tool for the preacher. It is unclear from Bownas' account of narration alone whether or not he means to restrict it to the specific narration of historical events from the Bible (as his examples indicate), but his later treatment of testimony from personal or others' experiences indicates that "narration" of contemporary biographical experiences is also encouraged because testimonies are also narrative in format. Narration is lauded for its indirectness in much the same way as the parable: "[Narration] may be compared to the leaf gold which physicians inclose [*sic*] their pills in, they being thereby better concealed from the pallet, that they might go down with the patient more glibly." For this reason, narration is seen as useful in the introductory parts of sermons. Bownas observes, "[I]f one should fall directly upon their present states without a parable,

comparison, allegory, or historical relation [narration], as introductory thereto, it might render our labour useless and ineffectual; but such an introduction, given us by the Spirit, may make way for a more searching and close ministry in setting the states of the hearers in a true light before their eyes"[39] Here Bownas appears close to indicating that, regardless of the Spirit's leading, all impromptu sermons require an attention-getting introduction, and the best ones employ a Spirit-inspired narration. His statement may have prompted a set of expectations for both preachers and auditors. He may also be indicating that when the Spirit has prompted the preacher to deliver a "prophetic" message that may call his or her hearers to repentance, or any other message that might not go down well with the listeners, the preacher is well advised to employ indirection, wrapping the medicine in "gold" for better "ingestion."[40]

4. *Testimony Regarding One's Own Life.* Following a long pattern implied or established by other writers, Bownas allows that the recitation of God's goodness to the preacher in her or his life can be a persuasive vehicle. He cites Paul's own recounting of his life before King Agrippa (Acts 26) with the result that the King was "almost persuaded to be a Christian" (Acts 28). However, use of personal narrative, he warns, "requires great care and caution that boasting may be excluded and the honour of his name, whom we preach, exalted in our ministry." Paul is set forth as the proper model because he "magnified the goodness of God to himself, yet set forth therein that Christ is the true and proper object of faith."[41] Again, anything that appears to breach humility or that exalts the preacher is dismissed and to be avoided.

5. *Testimony Regarding Another's Life.* Here Bownas briefly cites the positive effect of Hebrews 11 "in declaring the great encouragement we have to pursue virtue from the blessings that others have met with thereby."[42] Bownas is silent about whether or not the experiences of others drawn upon by the preacher are limited to those recounted in the Bible.[43]

6. *Exposition of a Text from Scripture.* Here again, Bownas is content to cite two examples from the New Testament in which preaching took the form of expounding from a biblical text: (1) that of Philip to the Eunuch (Acts 8), and (2) Jesus in the Synagogue (Luke 4). We are reminded that Fox's habit included biblical exposition and that Barclay explicitly allowed it. Also, Fox and the earlier writers had rejected the Puritan doctrine-use method, whereby the doctrine would be

extracted or "raised," reasoned from the Scripture text, and its use or application opened to the people. By including Scripture exposition, which Bownas refers to as "expiating," he aligns at least part of Quaker preaching practice somewhat with the great Puritan preaching tradition. However, by making biblical exposition only a part of the means of expression, and by strongly maintaining that such exposition should be presented only under the guidance of the immediate moving of the Spirit, he aligns eighteenth-century Quaker preaching with its own roots in seventeenth-century Quaker practice. Bownas offers no hermeneutical guidance for approaching the Bible other than his earlier counsel for the preacher to follow the Spirit and the following suggestion of elucidating biblical typologies.

7.   *Typology.* Bownas devotes more than two pages to the topic held in high repute by Fox, Fell, and others: attention to the types and figures in the Bible and the application of them to the lives of hearers. This kind of preaching involves a "setting forth [of] the sundry dispensations of God to mankind, as to Abraham and Lot; and in opening the mystery of the Law that came to Moses, as only preparatory to the Gospel, and how the prophets did point out Christ, the substance, which was figured forth by the offerings and shadows under that dispensation." "Things in the history," Bownas writes, "have a meaning to believers in the mystery."[44]

It is clear from his brief discussion of typology that Bownas not only is writing about a hermeneutic that sees the Old Testament in terms of figures that point to events and people in the New Testament, but also that he takes the typology a step further, hearkening back to the process of achieving sanctification in his own first chapter. After a recitation of historical events that brought Israel out of bondage in Egypt, Bownas declares,

> [A]ll these things that happened to Israel in Egypt, through the Red Sea, and in the wilderness have a true resemblance of believers travelling [*sic*] from spiritual Sodom and Egypt, so called; which is no other than coming from a state of fallen nature in the first Adam, in which all are dead and strangers to God . . . unto a state of grace and life through Jesus Christ, our spiritual Moses, being reconciled to God through him who is the second Adam, the Lord from Heaven who never fell. And thus . . . we are opened by the Spirit, in the ministry of the letter, to hold forth the true ministry of the Spirit.[45]

Bownas' position is in line with the early Quaker propensity to view their own lives as spiritual enactments of the tales of the Bible, Cope's *scriptura rediviva*.[46] Bownas' description is also an instance of the early Quaker habitual use of the journey metaphor to describe their personal spiritual experience.

Thus ends Bownas' listing and explanation of the means of expression of the opening. After acknowledging that the means of expression "are of great use and service in the church," he warns that when the means are used to great effect, there is "danger of borrowing one of another and endeavouring to imitate the same."[47] His conclusion to the fourth chapter includes a restatement of the classic Quaker rationale for impromptu preaching:

> [I]t is no more lawful for us to preach what we have read because we have read it, than it is to preach what we have heard because we have heard it. Nay, I may further add . . . that it is not lawful for thee to repeat thy own experience and former openings merely in thy own strength of memory and will. . . . Now a spiritual minister is, and ought every day to be like a blank paper when he comes into the assembly of the Lord's people, not depending on any former openings or experience, either of his own or others that he hath heard or read; but his only and sole dependence must be on the gift of the Spirit to give and bring to his understanding matter suitable to the present state of the assembly before him. Thus will thy words be fitly spoken and like apples of gold in pictures of silver, and thou wilt appear as the oracle of God, ministering out of that ability which God gives.[48]

This extreme statement points out the paradox of Bownas' book on ministry. In reality, the preacher can never be—or be like—"a blank paper," and this is especially the case for Bownas' readers who have just finished his comments about the means of expression. Why would these strategies be suggested, only to be wiped clean from the brain? Any potential preacher in the meeting carried over the meetinghouse threshold the memory of Scripture, much of it memorized; the prior reading of tracts and other theologically oriented books or pamphlets; and the hearing of impromptu sermons from other meetings, etc., none of which could be erased from the mind in preparation for the meeting, even it that were truly advisable. Bownas' simile of the blank paper is very troubling.

Conclusion

The remaining chapters of Bownas' book treat a variety of matters relevant to bringing the "infant minister" along the road toward a "young man's state" and, finally, to the achievement of the "father's state."[49] He deals with ethical conduct in the traveling ministry; cautions against pride, meddling, and gossip; gives advice about finding a proper estimation of one's gifts; advises regarding marriage, trade, and moral conduct; and ends with advice about public prayer. He makes scattered remarks about preaching throughout the remaining chapters, all further elaborations on the rationale and advices we have already considered. One example from the remainder of the book will suffice to illustrate how Bownas reminds his readers about the core of Quaker belief regarding preaching in his remaining chapters:

> [D]o not attempt either to preach or pray without some degree of divine love, begot by the Spirit, to inspire thee to it. . . . Some think, through a mistaken judgment, that they must be doing something every meeting (like the preachers of the *Letter*, who must either be singing, preaching or praying all the time), and by such a conduct they lose their interest and place in the hearts of Friends by too long and too frequent appearing in both preaching and prayer: for the avoiding of which, keep close to thy gift, intently waiting to know thy place, both when to speak and when to be silent; and when thou speakest, begin under a sense of divine influence, whether it be in preaching or praying; and without it, do not either preach or pray; for *Silent Meetings*, though a wonder to the carnal and worldly professors, are of great advantage to the truly spiritually minded; and as thou beginest with the Spirit, keep to it in thy going on and conclude in it, and this will preserve thee from tiring thy brethren and causing them to wish for thy silence.[50]

In summary, Samuel Bownas presents what amounts to the first practical manual for Quaker preachers. Building upon the rationale for impromptu preaching elucidated by Fox, Fell, Barclay, and other seventeenth-century Quakers, Bownas also stresses these considerations: (1) injunctions to hearers to deal gently with fledgling preachers; (2) the presentation of a developmental model of the impromptu preacher; (3) frequent admonishments not to imitate other preachers' delivery, style, or content; (4) criticism of affected delivery and advocacy of a calm and easygoing delivery style; (5) criticism of cliche language; (6) distrust of the imagination and its operation; (7) specific advice to begin speaking without any initial comprehensive sense of the entire message; (8) the injunction to balance "understanding" (rational thought) with the Spirit; (9) the notion that preaching was to be more artful or careful than casual speech because of the work of the Spirit acting as a muse; (10) the idea that memorized Scripture brought to the preacher's mind while preaching was an added confirmation of the topic; and (11) the presentation of a typology of seven overlapping means of expression useful for impromptu preaching, a list favoring those means that held the potential of catching hearers unaware, or of relying on the direct communication of the Spirit with the hearers. Although most of the items had been noted by one or another of the previous writers, the fact that Bownas set them out as a list of choices almost certainly set up an expectation in his readers to employ them, or watch for their use by others, even in the unrehearsed impromptu setting. Whereas with Fox, in chapter 3, we are forced to deduce his typology from his habitual practice, with Bownas, the typology is boldly set out. This is a quite different frame. In a real sense, Bownas proposes an inventional grid within which the Spirit might be likely to move. That is his greatest contribution.

On the other hand, Bownas' book is a disappointment because it is neither systematic nor adequately illustrated or even complete. It is also paradoxical. If the fledgling preacher takes the means of expression to heart and begins to collect and prepare examples for each category, as a speaker following the advice of the ancients might be expected to do, under Bownas' rules, he or she must leave all that potentially useful store of material and approaches at the door of the meetinghouse and enter the meeting like a "blank page."

Additionally, the book does not mention some of the most basic elements of rhetorical lore, some of which might actually help an impromptu preacher. Bownas probably does not include it because he was not acquainted with it. The book is actually a mixture of gold and lead. The easiest way to illustrate what I am saying is to review briefly the five traditional canons of rhetoric and Bownas' consideration of each. Under *invention*, there is no direct mention of audience analysis, although it might be implied that the Spirit does the analysis and provides an apt message attuned to the specific hearers. Bownas does not consider argument as a category, except for the argument by analogy implied in parables, allegories, and typologies, and argument by induction (seen as examples in ancient rhetoric) inherent in testimonies about

actual people's lives. There is no mention of appeals based on arousing hearers' emotions (pathos), and Bownas' remarks about achieving
a calm, staid delivery pattern may imply that preachers ought not to
focus on arousing their own or hearers' emotions. Ethos is especially
stressed through Bownas' insistence that the preacher live a holy life
(possess high moral character). As well, Bownas' discussion of the developmental stages of becoming a mature preacher (the father's state)
implies a gradual growth in competence and goodwill, the other classical components of the speaker's ethos. More importantly, the hearers'
perception of the speaker's competence and goodwill ought to grow
through the years. On the other hand, Bownas neglects to even mention *arrangement*, the second canon of classical rhetoric. Even under the
challenging context of impromptu speech, the preacher must begin
the sermon, follow some sort of path in its content—topical, chronological, problem-solution, cause-effect, etc.—and end the discourse
with a conclusion. Even a reminder of this basic assumption might
have been useful to fledglings. Under *style*, Bownas only mentions what
must be avoided, but this is itself an advance on his precursors. However, he leaves so much unsaid. For starters, he offers no consideration
of word choice, syntax, vivacity, tropes, schemes, or the other standard topics discussed in traditional rhetoric. Some of the important
and useful language strategies found in Quaker sermons of the period,
such as clusters of familiar metaphors drawn from Scripture, or the use
of fairly sophisticated rhetorical questions that forced hearers toward
valued self-examination, are absent from Bownas' discussion. What is
very clear from his comments is that, like his predecessors, he favors a
plain style and, by implication, rejects the concept of *copia*. *Memory*, the
fourth canon, finds some expression in Bownas' work when he mentions that memorized Scriptures might be recalled at the moment most
needed by both the preacher and the hearers. Ironically, effective rhetorical strategies used by other preachers, or by the preacher herself
or himself on another occasion, must not be used and might as well
be forgotten. One might assume, alternatively, that the Spirit might
cause the preacher to recall an apt testimony or narrative, whether
or not it had been employed in a previous sermon. I suspect that this
was often the practice in Quaker preaching, a situation that may have
given rise to Bownas' concern. As stated by Bownas, the stricture on
using material more than once appears to limit to a single use effective
"testimonies," those that truly reflect the preacher's or another godly

person's life, so there does not seem to be a need to remember them. In one fell swoop, the entire ancient educational strategy of *imitatio* is removed from the preacher's consideration. Finally, *delivery*, the fifth canon, comes in for some heavy scrutiny in Bownas' work, with strong advice about what the preacher is to avoid and what to put into effect, all of which emphasized downplay rather than expression, the brake rather than the throttle.

Bownas' *Qualifications* stands as the best compilation of early Quaker perspective and advice about impromptu, inspired preaching. It is unquestionably the lengthiest discussion of the topic by early Quakers. Bownas illustrates better than any other writer the paradox of "theorizing" about a rhetorical phenomenon that claims to be divinely inspired: the more you describe its operation and functions, spelling out all the options (or means of expression) that are open to the preacher, the more the phenomenon may be directed by the preacher's choices rather than the divine muse. One of the disappointments in Bownas' book is his failure to recognize and come to terms with this paradox.

Having now set out an interpretation of the development of Quaker rhetorical or homiletic theory based on many of the key surviving documents, we will now turn to the third section, composed of three chapters that examine the entire corpus of extant seventeenth-century sermons.

SECTION III

The Examination of Seventy-Nine Quaker Sermons from the Period 1671 to 1700

CHAPTER 6

THEMATIC CHARACTERISTICS OF QUAKER SERMONS, 1671–1700

Having traced the development of early Quaker theory about impromptu, inspired preaching, we turn in this section of the book to three chapters that deal with an overview of the practice that reflected the theoretical and justificatory writings. In the following chapters, all seventy-nine surviving sermons will be surveyed, their themes or topics listed and scrutinized, their use of key metaphors explained, and other salient characteristics noted and placed in the context of Quaker preaching theory. We begin with a chapter that considers what these surviving sermons are about, the topics that they address, and the significance of the preachers' choices.

In a description of Peter's early sermons (in Acts 1–2), Ian Ramsey makes this observation: "What a riotous mixture of phrases this is, belonging intrinsically to so many different logical areas with a diversity even greater than that of the Old Testament. This riotous mixing is in effect a rough and ready attempt to secure that special logical impropriety needed to express the Christian message. Each word is logically qualified by the presence of the others, and in this way each word comes to display a suitable measure of impropriety."[1]

Ramsey concludes that the Apostle Peter's purpose, like that of the other early evangelists, "was first and foremost to evoke the distinctive Christian situation, and the logical behavior of his words did not at all interest him."[2] I see a parallel between Ramsey's description and analysis of public discourse in the early church and Quaker sermons of the period between 1671 and 1700. In early Quaker sermons, one sometimes finds a similar "riotous mixture" of themes, terms, and phrases, and one becomes convinced that Quaker preachers were more concerned with evoking a response to their interpretation of the Christian situation than they were in resolving the logical problems inherent in some of their language usage. Ramsey argues that after the first proclamation of the gospel (kerygma), which made no attempt to explain what was preached, "Preaching had to become analysis and teaching."[3]

There is a natural mutation or evolution, it appears, from proclamation to explanation in the history of early preaching. Early Quaker preaching also exhibited the progression from proclamation to explanation, but gravitated toward the former. This tendency toward proclamation, with an occasional slight emphasis on analysis and explanation, is best seen in a survey of the thematic characteristics of the surviving sermons.[4] We shall consider the themes of the sermons in three categories: (1) theological themes, excluding those specifically discussed in chapter 2;[5] (2) themes dealing with guidance for individual behavior; and (3) themes that reveal early Quaker attitudes toward the then-current society. These categories are not mutually exclusive, because theology guided behavior and implied a stance to be taken toward society. The organization of this chapter is intended to provide a degree of structure for the riot of themes occasionally seen in Quaker sermons. My approach will involve identifying the theme, establishing a quantitative estimate of the role it played in the total corpus of extant sermons, and illustrating its expression by means of quotations. Where appropriate, I will briefly discuss changes in use, understanding, or significance of the themes.

THEOLOGICAL THEMES

Close scrutiny of the surviving sermons reveals that they are predominately concerned with theological subjects, or with injunctions to behave in ways that reflect theological positions. In chapter 2, I considered the importance of the Quaker view of human nature, the universal need for salvation, and the possibility of human perfection. I also illustrated the Quaker belief in the principle of the Inward Light, the instrument of God's salvation, inspiration, and perfection. Additionally, I noted the willingness of early Quakers to substitute and combine such words as "Grace" and "Truth" with the term "Light" to signify the same process. It remains now to examine two additional categories of theological themes found in the sermons: (1) theological themes not discussed in chapter 2, which also stress the relationships between God and humans, and (2) theological themes that are tied to religious ritual.[6]

Themes on the Relationship between God and Humans

Two major groups of theological concepts dealing with the relationship between God and humans appear in the sermons. The first is represented by such terms as "faith," "love," "joy," "power," "redemption," and "regeneration" (or "new birth"), all of which were relatively free from controversy in post-Reformation England. Other terms, such as "justification," "sanctification," "judgment," and "second coming of Christ," were debated with considerable vigor during the years of this study. An attempt to separate these two groups of theological terms in a systematic way is beyond the scope of this chapter and lies more within the province of the theologian. The rhetorician is interested primarily in the *use* of the concepts and the manner in which they make their appeal in the sermons. In point of fact, the typical Quaker sermon did not attempt systematically to present one or two themes; instead, the preachers characteristically combined, recombined, and juxtaposed many of the themes in the same sermon, paragraph, or even sentence. Appendix C reveals that many of the theological concepts dealing with the relationship of God and humans are alluded to in the same sermon. This evidence indicates two characteristics of early Quaker preaching. First, it was tied to the bedrock theological language and concepts of Christianity. Second, rather than concentrating their efforts upon the exposition of a single theological theme, the preachers tended to interweave many themes in the same sermon. Obviously, these sermons pay little or no attention to the doctrine-use method.

Two sermons from the 1690s illustrate the combining and recombining of theological themes. John Vaughton exhorts his audience to "keep in this Love of God, and Love to one another, it is the Desire and Breathing of my Soul, that so your Faith may stand not in the Wisdom of Mens Words, but in the Power of God . . . that when we come to die, we lay down our Heads in Peace and be found in him in Peace."[7]

Vaughton does not attempt to define or illustrate "love," "faith," "power," or "peace." This is exhortation, not systematic theology or biblical explication after the manner of Puritans. His audience is expected to be familiar with the concepts, and particularly with Vaughton's exhortation to love one another. Vaughton also implicated several other key concepts in the full passage. In the same way, Coole combined the terms "fear," "love," "peace," and "joy," as well as the concepts of providence, God's favor, and human duty, around an exhortation to love and fear the Lord:

He will provide for those that love and fear him, and hope in his
Mercy, and he will give them all Things to enjoy. . . . Those that Fear
the Lord, he will encompass them with his Favour as with a Shield,
he will speak Peace to them at their down-lying, and fill them with
the joy of his Salvation at their up-rising. It is our great Duty to love
the Lord with all our Hearts, with all our Souls, with all our Mind,
and with all our Might, and to fear the Lord not with a servile Fear,
but with a Filial (Childlike) Fear, that is a concomitant of Love.[8]

Here the concept of loving and fearing God exerts overall control
of the paragraph, but the paragraph itself is a mosaic of theological
terms and concepts bearing on the relationship of God and humans.

Crisp combines the concepts of reconciliation, regeneration, and
justification in a 1687 sermon, in which he maintains, "there is no
other way for People to be reconciled to God, than by coming in to
Christ; to be found in him, to be regenerated and born into his Nature,
and have his Qualities put upon them." He admits that the process he
describes is the "common Profession of Christendom," and confesses,
"If we be justified, we are not justified for a righteous, holy Life, and
for our Obedience; but we are justified through Christ, who worketh a
godly Life in them that believe, so that Man is not justified by any other
way or means."[9] Fox had proclaimed ten years earlier that one must
"come to ye Blood of Jesus Christ to cleanse thee; he is thy Redemption Sanctification & Wisdome,"[10] thus combining three theological
concepts. In a 1690 sermon, Crisp ties the concepts of justification
and sanctification to the personal, experiential aspects of the Light:
"you must have respect to the Principle of Sanctification in your own
Hearts, and turn you to what you may feel an Experience of in your
own Selves, some Principle of Grace and Light in your Hearts, that
can distinguish between good Thoughts and evil Thoughts." In the
same sermon, he emphasizes that "there is no Justification without
Sanctification,"[11] illustrating the Quaker emphasis upon the process
of perfection as the inexorable fruit of true salvation. A similar passage is found in one of Francis Camfield's sermons, in which he ties
the process of perfection to that of regeneration: "who ever expects
Salvation by Christ the only Savior, must be going on to Perfection,
they must begin at the work of Regeneration, and Experience in themselves a New Birth."[12] Many passages could be cited that illustrate the
same habit of combining principles that are never totally explained

or illustrated as doctrines, but simply *rehearsed* as common conceptual coinage in the same context.[13]

There are exceptions to the characteristic combining and recombining of theological terms in Quaker sermons. Fox, Crisp, and Penn exhibit the tendency to blend and juxtapose theological terms, but they were willing, on occasion, to concentrate their efforts on the explication of a single concept in an attempt to instruct their listeners. Fox, for example, distinguishes between live and dead faith at a General Meeting in London: "You se[e] ye world hath a faith, & they have a belief, but there is noe victory (Cry they) So noe faith; he that bruises ye head of ye serpent is ye Author of ye faith, & every man, & woman is to Come, & Look to ye Author, & finisher of that faith (Christ Jesus) that purifies ye heart. . . . So here are ye true witnesses, Them that be of ye true faith: & true hope in Christ in whom they are grafted."[14] Even here, Fox is not able to complete the thought without linking it to the concepts of holiness (purity) and hope. Penn makes the same distinction between live and dead faith twenty years later in a passage that obviously concentrates on the subject of faith, but accomplishes its purpose only after enlisting the aid of the concept of brotherly love expressed by good works: "We must now believe in the Lord Jesus Christ with a *Faith* that worketh *Love*; we canot be saved by a dead Faith, but by a living Faith: And as the *Body* without the *Spirit* is dead, so *Faith* without *Works* is dead also."[15]

Crisp exhibits more propensity to concentrate upon a single theme than most other early Quaker preachers. In a 1687 sermon, he treats the same topic Fox and Penn did in the examples cited above. He begins the section by enunciating the principle that "never was there a true Believer in Christ Jesus, but he received his Faith of God; it was the Gift of God; it was given to him to believe." Crisp argues that true faith "reaches to a compleat Redemption, unto a compleat Sanctification, unto a compleat fitting him for the Kingdom of God." The blending of themes is again evident when Crisp maintains, "the Faith that falls short of Sanctification, and Redemption from Sin, is such a Faith as God never gave his People, it came some other way into the World."[16] Crisp concludes his exposition on faith with an injunction, pointed in its power, which ties faith and perfection together:

> If you keep to Jesus, he will carry on the Work; you did believe in him, for he did work this Faith in you, and he will carry on his own

Work. . . . All others that talk of Faith, and make an empty Profession, they dishonour God; they talk of Perfection, and living without Sin, but never experience it. . . . if you wait to see this work carried on, if you believe and exercise your Faith for the over-coming of your Sins, and *perfecting of Holiness in the Fear of God*, you will hereby bring Glory to God.[17]

The same sense of focus is seen in Crisp's presentation of the importance of attaining peace with God,[18] but the best example is his sermon on God's love, which he begins by elucidating the principle that one of the concerns of humans should be "to help one another to be sensible of the Love of God to us: This is the only thing that can give us true comfort, to have a Sense of the Love of God to us in Christ Jesus." He reasons that "Men do shew forth in their Lives so little Sense of his Love to them." The sermon is a plea to be aware of the manifestation of God's love and to "love him above all, and express our Love, by a willing and persevering Obedience."[19]

Crisp's emphasis on the love of God seems to counter Barbour's observation that Puritan sermons emphasized God's love, while Quaker sermons more often emphasized God's judgment.[20] However, Barbour was writing primarily about the sermons preached during the first two decades of Quakerism. The sermons of concern in this survey show no such preponderance of interest in judgment over love. Out of seventy-nine sermons, fifty-three deal with God's love to humans, and thirty mention human love either to God or one's neighbor. God's judgment is mentioned forty-three times. One must conclude that both themes—love and judgment—are of major importance in the sermons as judged by raw numbers.

Among other preachers who treated love, William Bingley movingly observes that the "Garment of Praise shall Cloath those that Live in the Love of God, and of one another." "God," he proclaims, "will bear us up by his Divine Power, and keep us in a tender sense of his Love to us, while we are living in the daily performance of this great Duty of Love to God, and mutual Love to one another."[21] The more mystical Charles Marshall similarly announces that his sermon is given "unto the Excellency of the Love of God in Christ Jesus; which Love is indeed Incomprehensible and unspeakable, the Love of the Everlasting God through his Beloved Son Jesus Christ." A reader will not discover a more tender affirmation of God's love than that found in this passage from the same sermon: "When the Lord comes to open and manifest to the Children of Men, his great Love, in sending *his Son out of his Bosom* . . . when Men[']s Eyes and Hearts I say, are wonderfully opened to see this Love of God, then their Hearts will be melted and broken, and their prejudice removed."[22]

As noted above, the theme of God's judgment was also treated in the sermons. Judgment appears as a theme in ten fewer sermons (forty-three sermons) than does God's love, but the treatment of the theme is notably robust. Fox, for example, speaks of the fury of God's judgment toward unbelievers and toward believers who continue to sin. In 1674 he asks, "Can you Come to a worse death, than they dyed under the hands of two, or three witnesses, in ye dayes of Moses which was a naturall death, Yes, for they that neglects hearing ye Son, that Speakes from Heaven, this is eternal Death."[23] He warns believers in 1681 "not only to talk of ye Light but walk in it; many talk of Grace & Truth, but walk in unrighteousness, & Unholyness; God is righteous, & Holy, who will judge such."[24] Seven years later, William Dewsbury, in his final sermon, expresses a vivid view of God's judgment. For the faithful as well as unbelievers, he reviewed the awesome Scripture account: "*[H]e will throughly purge his floor, and will gather his Wheat into his Garner, but the Chaff he will burn with unquenchable Fire.*" He follows the Scripture passage with a grim reminder of Christ's image as a refiner's fire: "if you will not yield up your selves to Christ this Day that burns like an Oven, this fire you must dwell with when out of the Body, there will be no quenching of this Fire for ever."[25] Crisp also warns his hearers, "sin not against the Light, lest we die and perish in the midst of those terrible judgments that hang over us."[26] In another sermon, he proclaims, "if your will resist the good things of the Spirit of God . . . then you must all perish, both you and your Fathers; there is no escaping but by being subject to Christ Jesus."[27] Samuel Waldenfield speaks of arrogant men being destined "for Judgment, and for a Day of Slaughter, when God will pour out all his Wrath."[28] Penn's sermons also treat the subject. In one declaration, he warns, "They that will not bow to the Mercy of God, shall bow to his Judgments."[29] In one of his finest sermons, he draws the distinction between the Day of Visitation and the Day of Judgment: "This is the Day of God's Visitation, when God calls Men by his Spirit, and invites them to accept of Mercy. There is a time a coming when he will call them to Judgment: Woe be to them that have not answered the first Call, when the second Call comes." Penn, however, tempers his strong appeal with a peroration that focuses on love:

"This is the Love of God to Mankind. He will bless us in turning us from our Sin to Himself; he will turn us from Darkness to Light . . . if we will hear Him."[30]

Although the Day of Judgment finds expression in the sermons, other topics of eschatology either are not mentioned or are slighted. The second coming of Christ, for example, is treated only twice.[31]

When early Quakers spoke of God's relationship with people, and humans' relationship with God, they interwove the standard terminology of the King James Bible. Briefly stated, they believed that through faith in Christ, persons could attain salvation, which was a gift of God's grace offered to every human being. People could be redeemed (bought back), they maintained, from the powers of evil and regenerated (born again). The process of salvation was accomplished because God loved human beings and was willing to view individuals as though they had never sined (justification), because of Christ's death. The Quaker view demanded a personal salvation on the part of the individual, and Quaker preachers assert that God had revealed himself universally to all humans by his Light—Jesus Christ—through whom perfection and a life of holiness (freedom from the power of sin) could be attained. As a result of salvation and sanctification (the process of God making a believer's life holy and free from sin), the believer would escape God's wrathful judgment. In sum, the theological topics in the sermons that presented the relationships of God and humans express Quaker beliefs that humans are degenerate, enlightened, and capable of both salvation and perfection through Christ.

Theological Themes Related to Religious Ritual

In addition to the theological themes that express and develop the ideas surrounding relationships between God and humans, the preachers also address theological concepts traditionally related to religious ritual. These themes do not enjoy as prominent a place in the sermons as the other theological themes discussed above. Worship, for example, is a theme in thirty-two sermons, baptism in twenty-two, and the Lord's Supper in only two. In each appearance of the Lord's Supper, the preachers emphasize the spiritual nature of the concept, never the physical sacrament. A good illustration of this distinction is the preachers' habit of referring to communion as a fellowship between Christians or between Christ and his Church. The physical act of worship—communion—practiced in some form by most Christian churches, is consistently referred to in the sermons as "the Lord's Supper."[32]

Fox announces in 1674, "There is a standing worshipp in ye Spirit, & in ye Truth, they Receive this worshipp from above."[33] In 1681 he explains this concept more fully: "all Flesh must come to this Spirit of God; & know this Spirit to be poured upon ym . . . all Flesh must come to this Spirit if they will Worship God."[34] Crisp follows the same theme in 1688 when he counsels, "your Worship must be in the Spirit; you must pray in the Spirit and give Thanks in the Spirit." Moreover, he elaborates on the concept of true worship, cautioning his hearers, "There is no Man can truly worship God 'till he comes to a measure of certain Knowledge of him. . . . There must be a Knowledge of God before there can be true Worshipping of him." Crisp thus ties the concept of worship to the Quaker epistemological position that direct revelation—the experiential knowledge of God—trumps historical knowledge or reason in importance. He makes this position more explicit when he says, "you will never come to the Knowledge of God but by the Spirit of God."[35]

Spiritual worship, according to the early preachers, is not only based upon the experiential knowledge of God, but it is also necessarily pure in nature, a virtue that results from "the Knowledge of that Pure Principle of Life and Grace, from whence and out of which, all true Worship doth spring."[36] Quakers rejected the forms and rituals of worship common in Anglican and mainstream Puritan congregations. Crisp perhaps best summarizes the essential Quaker position on worship, at least as found in the extant sermon literature, when he remarks concerning the religions of his age, "They have invented and found out several ways for People to worship and serve God: This and the other Ceremony, this and the other Observation and Method of Preaching and Praying: If all this be without the Assistance and Divine Help of the Mediator [Christ] . . . it is all good for nothing. Therefore the first lesson of a Christian in point of Worship, is that he come to the Knowledge of Christ, by whom and thro' whom he may expect Favour with God."[37] It is apparent here that Crisp is not proclaiming as much as he is justifying the Quaker position. This is an example of apologetical preaching devoid of the interweaving of themes more characteristic of the Quaker proclamation of the gospel in the surviving sermons. Here the terms of the gospel are not at stake, but a particular interpretation of church tradition is being questioned. One may generalize that when the preachers are attacking a commonly held notion of Christian doctrine or practice, they are less inclined to interweave and juxtapose topics, and more inclined to concentrate their efforts on a single topic or theme.

Baptism and communion provide additional examples of themes upon which Quaker preachers become much more direct. As with worship, the spiritual meaning of baptism and communion is stressed. Fox tends to link baptism with the Old Testament Hebrew practice of circumcision. He believed that both rites had lost spiritual meaning after the coming of Christ. For Fox, Christ is "ye Minister of Circumcision & Baptism."[38] Fox believed that the "true Baptism" was spiritual in nature: "People come all to Witness to be Baptized into him & put him on; & to know ye true Baptism yt plunges down ye false Spirit & his Works as ye Apostle saith we are all Baptized by one Spirit into one Body, & here we all drink into one pure Spirit."[39] According to Fox, it is necessary for an individual to experience the true baptism of Christ because "all are baptized into the death of Adam, into death from God, by their unclean spirit:—'Baptized? What is that?' Plunged into Adam's death, and imperfection, and darkness."[40] Ironically, Fox is able to use the term "baptism" to indicate both the entrance of humans into sin and their entrance into salvation.

Crisp strongly defends the Quaker position on "spiritual" baptism in a 1688 sermon. Here he attempts to answer the question about whether Quakers deny baptism: "No, not I, I would have Men and Women Baptized with a Baptism that will do them some good. Some have seen the Vanity and Weakness of this kind of Baptism, and called it Baby Baptism; and therefore would go and be Baptized and plunged in the water over Head and Ears, but they come up again with the same Heart and Mind, and the same Polluted Soul."[41] On the other hand, Crisp declares, "Baptism with *the Holy Ghost and with fire*, is the right Baptism," and he advises people "to be Baptized with this Baptism, Jesus Christ." Waldenfield also uses the term "baptism" to refer to the inward experience of Christ: "The Spirit of Christ came at the begining into our Souls, and we were Baptized by it, and Regenerated by it."[42] In one of the last surviving sermons of the century, Thomas Chalkley reiterates essentially the same position on baptism as expressed by Fox, Crisp, and Waldenfield: "[I]t was not Elementary Water that John spake of, he saith he [Christ] shall wash you, he shall baptize you with the Holy Ghost & with Fire, Now this Fire was spiritual Fire, . . . I would to God, that we might feel his blessed Baptism in our Souls this day."[43]

Much the same interpretation and negative reaction is expressed by early Quaker preachers toward the ritualized observance of communion. Fox speaks of those "that have made Christ so many bodies, and have made hosts, gods, and christs, a body of bread and wine; and whoever will not bow to it, and receive it, must be burned."[44] Early Quakers ask "wherein the Communion of the Saints stands," and answer, "doth it not stand in partaking together of the Bread of Life, which our Father giveth us from Heaven?"[45] In the words of an anonymous Quaker preacher of the late seventeenth century, "Life flows from Vessel to Vessel, and here [is] a Communion, indeed not a communion of Bread and Wine, as the World Receives, which is Carnal; their Wine satisfies not the Soul, it washest not from Sin, nor Cleanseth from Transgression."[46] By far the best apologist among the preachers is Crisp. In reply to the accusation that Quakers deny the Lord's Supper, he rejects its physical necessity and propounds its spiritual truth: "We have never had such a Thought, God knows there is nothing that our Souls long after more but People have been making a kind of World of their own, they have lost a Reality, and make Shadows, as Children do, when they see things made in the House for Service, they will make the like in Sand and Clay: People do not see what a great thing it is to attain to the Supper of the Lord."[47]

The sermons reveal a position on worship, baptism, and communion that not only emphasizes the spiritual nature of these features of Christian ritual but actually eliminates the necessity of their physical expression. "Worship" could be accomplished without oral prayers or sermons; "baptism" was the spiritual filling of the spirit from God; and "communion" was the fellowship of believers partaking of the spiritual "bread" and "wine."

GUIDANCE FOR INDIVIDUAL BEHAVIOR

Although the primary themes of early Quaker sermons are presented for the purposes of exhortation and theological edification, the preachers also present principles for the guidance of individuals into the godly life. An indication of the importance of practical holy living in the sermons is indicated by the realization that sanctification appears in forty-six sermons as a theme, perfection in twenty-nine sermons, and holiness in fifty-four. Among the most significant general attributes that Quaker preachers thought should mark the holy life are love of God and fellow humans,[48] humility, self-denial, order, and simplicity. Injunctions to express love appear in thirty of the sermons; humility and self-denial are themes in forty-one and thirty-six sermons, respectively; and order and simplicity appear twelve and seven times, respectively.

Early Quakers believed that the Inward Light, if obeyed, was sufficient to guide individual behavior, but they were also aware of the excesses of some members of the more radical religious groups of their day who confused their own will with the inward leading of the Spirit.[49] As presented in chapter 2, Quakers tempered their belief in divine revelation with a strict moral code based upon Scripture, common consent of the group, and the leading of the Light.

The Conceptual Foundations of Quaker Life

The early sermons stress the duty of humans to love God and to love their neighbors. Bingley expresses sentiments found in almost half of the sermons when he exhorts his hearers "to walk in Love and have Bowels of Compassion and Love to our Neighbors, that they may be saved, and brought near to God." He explains the principle of love in these terms: "our Duty is, to endeavour to shew forth our Love in Justice, Equity, and Truth in all things, and to be so far from going beyond or seeking to defraud or over-reach our Neighbor, as we should upon all occasions, manifest our care and love to him."[50]

Humility is another foundational tenet (or virtue) of early Quaker behavior. Fox pleads, "In ever[y] motion sink down, keep low, keep to ye Lord."[51] Crisp later affirms the same teaching, adding that a person who truly desires to have something from God "must come in an humble petitioning frame. . . . It is the Lofty, the Proud, those that exalt themselves, the Fat and the Full that want nothing. *These . . . the Lord beholdeth afar off.*"[52] Bingley similarly maintains, "when the Mind is truly humble, and dwells in lowliness, such find Life to spring from God the Fountain of it."[53] John Bowater makes one of the strongest appeals for humility found in the sermons: "Take heed that . . . you do not set up self, but humble your selves to the Dust, and sit at the Feet of Jesus, learn of him to be meek and lowly . . . do not strive for high Places, and for Honour and Dignity, and to be accounted of among Men."[54]

Humility goes hand in hand with the concept of self-denial in the sermons, for self-denial was an outward manifestation of, and means

of achieving, humility. Humility appears as a theme in forty-two of
the sermons, while self-denial appears in thirty-six. Crisp's sermons,
in particular, abound with the image of "the cross" of self-denial. He
reminds his hearers repeatedly that Christ "did absolutely deny that
any Man could be his Disciple, without taking up a Daily-Cross, and
without Self-Denial: Now how should a Man at this day be a Christian, or a Disciple of Christ, without taking up a Daily-Cross, and
without Self-Denial?"[55] In a sermon that I will discuss more extensively in chapter 12, Penn also uses the cross image when he proclaims
that God is with us when "we are following Christ in Patience, Humility, and Self denial, and bearing his Cross, for no Cross no Crown."[56]
Richard Ashby makes the process of self-denial more difficult yet:
"Thou may'st appear to take up a Cross and deny thy self, but there
must be a daily Cross, a denying thy Self continually, not giving way to
our Carnal Wills, to our Carnal Minds, *for to be Carnally minded is Death,
and to be Spiritually minded is Life and Peace.*"[57]

The concept of order is significant primarily because it is a prominent theme in Fox's sermons. Of twelve appearances, eight are in
Fox's sermons, one in Penn's, and two in anonymous sermons. Fox's
concerns to establish a strong, "ordered," organizational structure
for Quakers are discussed in chapter 9. Fox most often contrasts the
"gospel order" with sexual immorality. In a 1671 sermon delivered to
a women's meeting in Barbados, he pleads for chastity so that "God
may be Glorified, & all things kept in Order."[58] Three years later, he
celebrates the power of the gospel in this manner: "In this Gospell:
ye Power of God, Is ye Glorious Order, This joyfull order keeps all
hearts: pure to God, an everlasting order . . . which brings Life, &
Immortality to Light, & Comes to see over that Power of Darkness."[59]
To Fox, the sense of order that should distinguish the believer's life is a
direct result of God's action: "He yt is Heavenly Man [Christ] sets up
a Heavenly Order . . . wch is ye Power yt keeps out of Disorder, out of
Wickedness, out of Unrighteousness, & Ungodliness, & Oppression,
here is an Orderer."[60] Fox believed that the power of God could keep a
person in a sense of order, away from the excesses of Ranterism. Arguably, Penn has the same thought in mind in a wedding sermon when
he speaks about the "Order and Method among us, with Respect to
Nuptial Solemnities." Though the Quaker practice of marriage did
without the ritualized ceremony of the traditional church, or the presence of the priest or pastor, Penn maintains that Quaker marriages

are made in the "Order and Method which is set down in the Holy Scriptures."[61]

Simplicity is a concept (or acted truth) deep in the early Quaker tradition of life. However, although it surfaces as a theme in less than 10 percent of the sermons, it is also implied in the themes of humility and self-denial. Crisp urges his listeners to measure up to the Quaker standard of life with these words: "The Lord preserve and keep you simple, keep you in all Sincerity."[62] He reminds his hearers that Christ had ministered to them because they "lived in Sincerity and Self-denial, loving God above all things; and he taught and conducted us in our Way, this Way of Simplicity."[63]

Specific Behavioral Injunctions

In addition to laying the foundation for life in the concepts of love, humility, self-denial, order, and simplicity, the preachers also provide specific advice as to how the abstract characteristics should be carried out in everyday life. An isolated instance from one of Crisp's sermons shows us that Quakers were expected to be honest in business dealings. In this sermon, Crisp, a businessman himself, is quite pointed in his warning to merchants, tradesmen, and shopkeepers, who "should Pray earnestly that they may *Be kept from the Evil of the World*." Crisp realizes that especially "In Merchandize, and Buying and Selling, there are Snares, and there is Evil we may run into," and he expresses the hope that "When we have bought and sold, we may look back upon what we have done with pure Minds, and clean Consciences in the sight of God."[64]

In another single instance, Fox exhorts his hearers to be generous in helping one another in times of physical need. Fox outlines what is, in essence, a system of community welfare:

> [Y]ou may be serviceable to . . . those yt are in want & necessities in your Generation; that where there are any Children be [*sic*] to be set forth as Apprentices yt herein you assist ym; for such in time may come to help their Parents in their Old Age. . . . & so they being set forth to severall Trades may in a little time come to help their Brothers, & Sisters, & rear up their Families; . . . this will prevent any Poor to be among you; for there should not be.[65]

Quaker families were to practice love and humility. Crisp notes that "In the Government of a Family, there are Occasions and Provocations given to be Passionate and Furious; . . ." "Our profession

obliges us," he asserts, "that when a Child or a Servant gives a Provo-
cation, we are not to behave our Selves unseemly, and unbecoming
our Holy Profession."[66] This injunction is the only one expressed so
directly in the sermon literature.

Eight sermons touch on the subject of sexual morality, either by
defending the sanctity of marriage or by condemning sexual immorality. In 1671 Fox aligns himself with "ye famous Fathers of Truth, &
Saints & Worthyes, & valiants of ye Lord who were Friends of God"
and who "denyed Debauchery, Whoredome Fornication & uncleaness."[67] The same month, he recommended a procedure for Quaker
marriage to a women's meeting in Barbados: "And wn any come to
your meeting about Marriage, let ym bring their Certificates of their
holy Life & conversations from ye meeting in yt City, Town, or Country. whether in England, Ireland, or Scotland, or any of ye Islands
aboard [sic] where lived, & are well known to the Meetings where
they take their Wives; or Wives their Husbands, yt all may be kept,
pure, & clean."[68] Fox teaches the hearers that "if a young woman have
a father, or mother, or guardian, go to them first, and lay the *matter*
before them, that it may go on with their consent, and approbation."[69]
He instructs the local meetings to "query how things be concerning
ye parties, & whether they be free from other Persons." Specifically,
he maintains that the parties of the marriage should "come twice to
ye Men & Womens Meetings, to see yt all things be clear, & well for
decency & Order sake, & also to manifest their Patience, & Chastity."[70]
Early Quakers placed considerable emphasis upon chastity, perhaps
partly because they were accused, along with the Ranters, of partici-
pating in sexual immorality. Fox asserts, "they that profess the truth,
they should know virtue and dominion, and keep themselves clean till
the day of their marriage, and time of their death, that all may be kept
in chasteness and purity, to God's glory."[72] Quakers also maintained
a sense of strictness regarding the proper motives for marriage. Penn
addresses himself to this subject in his 1694 wedding sermon: "[W]e
lay great Stress and Weight upon This, that Married Persons do not
enter into that Relation with a Meer Natural Affection, or for Worldly
Interest, or Advantage; or to gratify a Carnal Fancy: but we must be in
the Exercise of a Divine and Heavenly Affection . . . making the Law
of God our Aim and End."[72]

As mentioned in chapter 2, distinctive language usage became
a significant part of the Quaker approach to life. Considering the

importance of (1) the refusal to take an oath and (2) the use of plain speech (including the strict grammatical usage of "thee" and "thou") in early Quaker life, one might expect great emphasis to be placed on this behavior by the preachers. However, specific references to this set of Quaker linguistic behaviors are comparatively rare in the sermons, appearing only twelve times. An anonymous Quaker assures the listeners, "Quakers are as sound in their yea and nay as ever; as sound in their thee and thou as ever."[73] Perhaps this optimistic observation offers a clue as to the seeming neglect of the preachers to deal with the peculiar Quaker pronominal usage. Refusal to take an oath and the use of plain language marked a person as a Quaker and alienated her or him from the mainstream of society. Arguably, these peculiarities became such a matter of course that they required little emphasis by the preachers. Furthermore, Quaker language usage was a manifestation of the concepts of humility, self-denial, and simplicity, all of which were emphasized in the sermons.

On the topic of oaths, Fox gives us the best examples. In 1678 he reminds the audience at Yearly Meeting in London that the Old Testament provisions for oath taking have been superseded by Christ's teachings: "it is said in Old time they were to perform their Oaths unto ye Lord; but saith Christ Swear not at all."[74] In 1680 he amplifies the same position:

> [W]hat saith Moses? If there be a difference between two, you must go to the high priest, he puts the oath to you, if you be not subject to the high priest it is death. So now this oath is put between you two, and this ends the strife. Now what saith Moses? "Thou shalt keep thy oath." This is the Servant. What saith the Son? Is there any *swearing* in your house?—Nay Christ who is the truth itself, the life itself, he is come. So there is no swearing in his house, for he saith "Swear not at all."[75]

Fox also specifically instructs his hearers in a 1675 sermon regarding the proper use of "thee" and "thou," emphasizing the Quaker view that the use of "you" in the singular unecessarily bestows honor: "Keep your proper language out of ye world, for ye Singular to one, & not ye Plurall out of all Flattering: Go not down again into ye Worlds Language, but keep up in ye Heavenly Power, for ye Truth leadeth into this."[76] The conviction of Quakers to use the plain language, even in the face of social ostracism, was considered to be another manifestation of God's power in the Quaker's life. Obedience to the power brought a sense of joy, as Crisp testifies: "when the Power of the Lord first wrought upon you, and brought you to Yea and Nay, and to plain simple Language and Habit, this was with joy and Delight for Christ's sake."[77]

As previously noted, the Quaker plain language followed the general Puritan distaste for style for style's sake. Six of the sermons specifically repudiate eloquence or the superfluities of style associated with the Renaissance stylistic rhetorics. Bowater, for example, asks why his audience has come to the meeting: "Is it to hear what a Man can say? to hear Eloquence of Speech, to hear some novelties, or is it your end to wait upon God?"[78] Crisp expresses the same strong convictions: "We would preach Christ Jesus the Lord, we would not have you admire Men's Words and Sayings, and charge your Memory with them."[79]

Just as the Quakers' language was to be plain, truthful, even self-denying, Quaker manner of dress was to match the same criteria. Although only four of the sermons reflect this belief, they indicate the importance Quakers placed on the topic. When Fox spoke at the women's meeting in Barbados, he attacked the common attire of the age: "[S]ee yt all walk as becomes ye Truth in modesty . . . so all walk as ye Holy Women of Old were to do as ye Apostle commanded . . . whose adorning let it not be yt of plaiting ye Hair or wearing of Gold, or of putting on of Apparell, but let it be ye hidden Man of ye Heart . . . not in wanton attire."[80]

Not even the "Heathenish Custome of ye Ring in Marriage"[81] escapes Fox criticism in the same sermon. However, none of the rest of the sermons approaches the following extreme viewpoint on dress expressed by an anonymous and rather uncharitable preacher: "[W]hen I go into the Country, and if I meet with any that are called by the Name *Quaker*; before I come to them I look to see if there be a Button upon their Hats, or Lupes, if their Hats be coked, and if they have a fringed Neckcloath, or a long Neckcloath, and if they have great Sleeves, and if they have Flaps upon their Coats. . . . and if any professed Quaker is thus attired, then I go along by him and hardly ask him how he doth."[82]

By the standards of the seventeenth century, the Quaker life was rigid and strict. Crisp best describes, in the form of a dialogue, a common reaction to Quaker life as seen in the sermons: "Hast thou seen Purity, Humility, Sobriety, Meekness, and Self-denial, and an

Heavenly frame of Spirit in thy self or some body else? How dost thou like it? I like it not at all; I love to have Honour and Dignity, Power and Dominion, and my Elbow-Room in the World; I love not this Meekness, Humility and strictness of Life, that a man must have a care what he speaks, and set a Watch upon his Lips, and upon his Heart and Tongue, and Hands, I do not like this kind of Life."[83]

COMMENTARY ON TRENDS AND EVENTS

Turning from evidence in the sermons of the preachers' teachings about specific behavioral choices, we will now survey the seventy-nine sermons for evidence of their commentary on the trends and events of the surrounding English society. The society out of which Quakerism emerged remained to a large extent religiously oriented; thus it is virtually impossible to separate the secular from the sacred in terms of specific trends or events. When a preacher comments on the power of the Roman Catholic Church, for example, he or she is making both a religious and a political statement. Consequently, most of the commentary on trends and events found in the sermons is religious in nature. I have illustrated how early Quaker ministers prefer to proclaim theological themes. Next in order of preference, they choose themes that provide guidance for behavior. Last in quantity of appearance in the sermons are themes that deal with the current society. I shall examine the Quaker reaction to their surroundings in terms of three broad heads: (1) the specifically religious realm, including reaction to their own imprisonment and persecution for religious beliefs, their stance on Roman Catholicism, their attitude on compulsory tithes, and their reaction to the "antienthusiastical" trend; (2) the quasisecular realm, including their response to university education, disputation, the emergence of the new science, and the theatre; and (3) the realm of radically different social norms, including the teaching against participation in war, standing for the equality of women, and taking a stand against the perpetuation of slavery.

The Religious Currents

Perhaps no other themes treated or alluded to in the sermons better illustrate the early Quakers' awareness of their societal environment than the references to persecution and imprisonment. This theme surfaces in thirteen sermons. Fox, for example, warns Friends in 1674 to "be Careful every where as you Travell; There are springings and stirrings abroad."[84] In 1680 he speaks of his own experiences of suffering for his beliefs: "since I came abroad to declare the everlasting truth, I have been a sufferer very much, by times, above these thirty years, in gaols, and prisons. And my body hath been spoiled for the testimony of Jesus. And it was hard for me to come this journey."[85] Crisp uses the redemption of captured Friends in Turkey as an analogy to men who are captives of sin: "We know when our Friends are in Captivity, as in *Turkey*, or elsewhere, we pay down Money for their Redemption; But we will not pay our Money if they be kept in their Fetters still."[86] Here the passing mention of the potentially tragic event of capture is used as a means to make clear a point about the theological concept of redemption—that if you are freed, you are no longer a thrall.

After the coming of toleration in 1688, persecution and prisons continued to be topics in the sermons, usually in moments of praise for past deliverance. Crisp notes in 1688 that the time of suffering has passed, but he warns, "there is now as much Danger and Peril in this time of Liberty and Tranquility, as there was before."[87] Crisp has in mind the "spiritual" peril consisting of the tendency of people to become lax in their faith during times of religious liberty. Later the same year, he observes, "This hath been *London's* Wonder, and *England's* Wonder . . . that such a People's Leaf hath not Withered, nor Faded, as many have done," and he praises God, who "stood by us, and delivered us, when we were compassed about with Dange[r]s, and Distresses."[88] Penn expresses similar praise in 1694, when he exclaims, "Blessed be the Lord, that hath given the Liberty that we see this day."[89] John Vaughton brings to his hearers' memories the day "when the Floods of the Ungodly were muster'd against us, and sometimes halled us out of our Meetings, to Gaols and Prisons, for bearing Testimony to the Truth."[90]

Quakers, like most Puritans, expressed a strong negative stand toward the Roman Catholic Church. Nine of the sermons give expression to these sentiments. Fox, for instance, attempts to identify Quakers as "true Protestants," as against Protestants who are "Popishly affected," probably a reference to Anglicans. He claims, "My suffering hath been . . . for not joining with the relics of Popery." Furthermore, he asserts, "if any say we are Popishly affected, *we are true protestants*, and follow the practice of our forefathers and mothers, the holy men and women."[91]

Early Quakers believed that religious expression outside of Quakerism was based upon the wrong foundation. Crisp condemns the common signs of religious fervor, Roman Catholic or Protestant: "let them spend never so many Hours in Prayer every Day; let them come to Meetings and hear Sermons, and write them and repeat them, and do what they will, here is a Bar of Unbelief that lies in the way, that makes Men *depart from the living God*."[92] Quakers were particularly outraged by the requirement to support the Anglican clergy through compulsory tithes. Fox is particularly denunciatory on this practice: "Now as for these Tithes set up in ye Days of Popery long after Christ of [*sic*] the Apostles decease, here in came these things one after another; This is out of Truth; & ye Life wch ye Apostles were in, who did bear-Testimony against Tithes."[93] Four other sermons, three by Fox and one by Leonard Fell, also reflect the stand against tithes. Ten of the sermons react to the tendency as the century drew to a close to refer to Quakers and other quasi-Puritan sects as "enthusiastical." By the late seventeenth century, the term carried with it the conotation of crass, unthinking emotionalism, added to the original denotation of "inspiration." In the sermons, we view the term in transition from inspiration to emotionalism. We also see the conscious attempt of some Quakers to break the negative identification of Friends with the term. Waldenfield still has in mind the earlier meaning of enthusiasm when he notes that the Quaker doctrine of the coming of Christ by his Light and spirit is "looked upon by many as Anti-christian Doctrine; they call it *Enthusiasm*, and *Quakers Doctrine*, and the Doctrine of the *Spirit*."[94] Penn makes the most forceful statements on enthusiasm found in the sermons. After a disquisition on the omnipresence and inevitable judgment of God, he makes this disclaimer: "These are not *Chimeras* and *Enthusiastical* Fancies, but the great *Realities* of Religion."[95] Distinguishing the concept of the Inward Light from the negative conotations of enthusiasm, Penn both poses and answers a question: "*Am* I turned from that, which would eclipse God's *Light* in my Soul? If thou art turned from Sin to Righteousness, thou art not a *Canter*, thou art not an *Enthusiast*, thou art a true Child of God."[96] Penn's boldest stroke is the identification of enthusiasm with the great psalmist King, David: "When you are panting and breathing after the inward Enjoyment of the Divine Presence, some may ignorantly call it *Enthusiasm*, and say it is meerly the Effect of Melancholly; but holy David, the Man after God's own Heart, was such an *Enthusiast*, he did ardently pant and breathe after the Enjoyment of God's Presence."[97] Here Penn is able to employ Scripture, the foremost tool in the Puritan-Reformed epistemology, to defend a form of enthusiasm still practiced and endorsed by the Quakers.

The Quasisecular Realm

In addition to occasionally commenting on current trends and issues of a specifically religious nature, the preachers also included themes that touch on quasisecular concepts—concepts that were not strictly religious in nature but, because they arose in an age substantially invested in religious disagreements and politicized religion, became linked to religious debate.

In this light, early Quaker sermons first of all reflect the distrust of learning, and especially the refusal to see higher education as a necessity for the understanding of theology and the practice of vocal ministry, that we have seen in their theoretical writings about preaching. Particularly in chapter 3, I addressed the topic of education in the context of the early development of the Quaker theory of impromptu preaching. Early Quaker ministers, with some notable exceptions,[98] were not university trained, so one might expect the preachers to mention this topic with frequency in their sermons, but surprisingly, only eight of them actually allude to or develop the distrust of formal education as a theme. For example, Crisp makes a typical early Quaker slur on the value of university education, when he affirms that anyone may find the way to holiness: "Though he never took a degree at the University, he shall not err in it; though he be a Fool in the account of the World, and never understood Greek or Latin, yet he shall not err in this way."[99]

Turning to a second quasireligious topic, Quakers vigorously entered, yet reacted against, the religious pamphlet and tract wars that proliferated during the century.[100] There is more than a hint in the sermon literature of their stand against contentious debate or disputation. Seven of the extant sermons deal with this theme at least in part. On the issue of disputation, the early Quakers joined in the epistemological struggle of their age. As far as religious knowledge was concerned, they maintained it could not be found through disputation. Crisp follows Barclay's denunciation of contentious debate and urges the flock to "lay aside the Disputes of Doctors and Learn'd Men. . . . Things relating to others, I may let Disputes alone about them; but as for things relating to my Salvation, I must have a certain Knowledge of them." Additionally, in the same sermon, he assures listeners that they can know God's dealings within themselves "by an infallible Evidence of the Spirit of God."[101] A year later. he repeats the theme: "they have been contending, disputing, and jangling and debating one another, and could never agree, and could never come to an understanding . . . by the Holy Spirit."[102]

A third quasireligious topic found expression in the sermons. As the century drew to a close, some preachers appeared to identify the Quaker way with the emerging scientific method. The strategy is not explicit in the sermons, but it is implied by linguistic choices, particularly the adoption of the term "experimental" religion and the use of language tied to the senses. Knowledge gained by disputation is "vain," but as Crisp observed in 1687, God has given "unto a Remnant an *experimental* Knowledge of the Truth."[103] He does not mean by "experimental" what Bacon had in mind, but Crisp does mean that no mere historical knowledge devoid of experience could be adequate in the realm of faith. A year later, Crisp maintains that no one can "have Faith in Christ at a Distance, and thereby be reconciled unto God, but must know his Spirit: I must have an experimental Knowledge of his Power and Wisdom."[104] James Park refers to the same idea in identical terms: "[W]e came to know the Witness of him in our selves, such as know him experimentally, can set their Seals that God is true."[105] I see these references to experiential religion employing the term "experimental" as reflections within the realm of religion of the century's cultural move away from deductive toward inductive epistemological systems. These language choices accurately exemplify what D. Elton Trueblood describes as the "Quaker Way," which is "fundamentally empirical rather than speculative."[106]

The sermons also reveal an attempt to tie experimental religion with the sensory sphere of knowledge, which was an item of investigation in the world of science and philosophy.[107] Eleven of the sermons employ what might be called the "language of the new science." The Quaker belief in the necessity of a religious experience beyond mere rational assent, either to feel the power or to experience the Lord, is expressed in forty-six and thirty-four sermons, respectively. Crisp, for example, attempts to persuade his hearers to know the love of God experimentally, and hints at the dimension of the senses: "every one ought to be acquainted with it, and have the exercise of their minds in it, that so we might know by an experimental and sensible feeling the kindness of God to us."[108] The empirical, sensory identification of Quaker epistemology is complete in this passage from another of Crisp's sermons: "Now where any come to an experimental Knowledge of the Word of the Lord, of this inward Voice, whereby God speaks to the Sons and Daughters of Men, they have received thereby an infallible Feeling of their own State and condition. . . . They come to have a certain infallible Knowledge of their own State."[109] The phrase "infallible feeling" seems to fuse both the empirical and sensory dimensions in one linguistic moment.

The final quasireligious theme deals with the theatre. Although early Quakers were ardent opponents of the theatre, only one reference is made in the sermons to that attitude. Nevertheless, it is strong and follows the conventional Puritan lines of antitheatrical prejudice.[110] Crisp contrasts the comfort, peace, and tranquility that followers of Christ enjoy, with the delights of sin. The former, he asserts, are "an hundred fold better and more delightful than all the Pleasures of Sin, and the Pleasures and Delights of Shows, and Sights, and Plays, and Comedies, which vain Men entertain themselves with in their Carnal State."[111]

Radical Social Proposals

Three themes in the sermons reflect Quaker attitudes toward current society that were unusually radical for the times and for which Quakers became noted in subsequent years. Here particular reference is made to the Quaker opposition to participation in war, the belief in gender equality, and the belief that slavery should not be perpetuated. In a sense, these themes are also quasisecular themes and could legitimately be treated as such. However, they are also a peculiar category of themes because of the extremity of the view expressed and because of subsequent history, which has made these three issues increasingly relevant to Quakers who lived in later eras. Unlike Quaker opposition to the theatre—or the peculiar negative reaction to higher education— convictions about war, gender equality, and the problems of race are still perplexing us today. Significantly, some early Quaker preachers were addressing these topics in the seventeenth century.

Eight of the sermons express antiwar convictions. Crisp looks at war and its roots and concludes, "It is impossible for Nations to make War, and destroy one another, if they would be guided by the unerring Spirit of Christ."[112] Even more distressing to early Quakers was the prospect that wars could be waged in support of one religion or another. The "Holy Church," as Crisp sees it, "comes not out of the Wilderness leaning on Captains, Generals and Armies, but leaning on Christ her well-beloved."[113] Fox specifically taught against the use of carnal weapons. One of his most direct and powerful statements is found in a sermon: "So in Moses's house you had a carnal sword, and weapons of Armour, but have you this armour and carnal weapons in the Son's house? what armour have you there?—'Our armour is spiritual, our weapons are spiritual, not carnal, but mighty through God to the pulling down of strong holds.'"[114]

Though Quakers did not draw the sword in defense of the nation, it is important to note that they expressed in their sermons an affectionate concern for the future of England. Crisp makes it clear that Friends "canot make use of Sword and Spear for the saving of a Nation," but he assures the listeners, "you may do good by your Prayers, and turning to the Lord."[115]

The preachers usually portrayed the current society as wicked, depraved, and far from godly. Typical of the descriptions is this one by Crisp: "Oaths, and Curses, and all manner of Wickedness runs down the Streets like a River; there is Pride, and Wrath, and Envy, and Revenge, and Violence to be found among us."[116] The Quakers' refusal to draw the sword does not prevent Crisp from threatening English society with judgment from God in his sermons: "This Island hath been continually with War and Blood, and Flames and Destruction, and the Cry of the Orphans hath been heard from other Nations: . . . but judgments hang over the Nation."[117] In 1693, midway in the War of the League of Augsburg, in which England was embroiled, Charles Marshall warns of God's displeasure in his prayer: "*[T]hou art at this Day threatening this Nation, and shaking thy Rod over the Land of our Nativity, cause the Inhabitants thereof to humble themselves under thy Mighty Hand.*"[118] Two months later, Francis Camfield prays another prayer, perhaps in lieu of taking up the sword, at the end of his sermon: "*[P]reserve this sinful Land, and let thy continued mercies and blessings, and thy long sufferings prevail upon us, . . . let thy Judgments which are impendent be diverted, and stir up thy People to wrestle with thee with all their Souls, that thou wouldest save this Nation, that England may live in thy Sight.*"[119]

Fox's sermons contain expressions that constitute by far the most radical departures from the norms of English society, Puritan or non-Puritan. He is the only early Quaker preacher whose surviving sermons treat the subjects of women's equality and chattel slavery. With regard to the place of women, Fox argues that before Adam fell, man and woman were equal, but because the woman was the first to sin, the man was appointed to rule over her. However, he asserts that Christ "restores man & woman Into a heavenly order & Government, & so are helps meete in Righteousness, & holyness, truth, & Justice, equity— as they were before they fell."[120] Fox justifies the practice of allowing, even encouraging, women to preach when he says, "The apostle saith, 'I permit not a woman;' yet he appointeth Titus to ordain *Elders*, and the *Elder Women* might be teachers of good things. So he ordains the elder women; then he did not stop them. So the elder women must teach good things: That is their duty, incumbent upon them."[121] The place of women is thus significantly elevated by the founder of Quakers in his sermons. It has taken four centuries for women to be ordained in the Anglican Church.

Fox's position with regard to slavery is equally ahead of his society's practice. Speaking to slave-holding Quakers on Barbados in 1671, he argues that if God set a law for the Jews to release their slaves after a set number of years, then it follows that "it will doubtless be very acceptable to the Lord if so be the Masters of Families here would deal so with their Servants, ye Negroes, & Blacks whom they have bought wth their Money."[122] The specific arrangements for freedom were to be made after approximately thirty years of work by the slave, and the former slave was not to be sent away empty-handed from his or her former master. Fox even goes so far as to advocate interracial marriage to prevent sodomy: "So if a White should lye wth a black, or wth another he should marry her, yea tho she were a beggar, let ym go together to prevent Sodomy."[123]

CONCLUSION

This presentation of the themes in seventy-nine Quaker sermons from the period 1671–1700 demonstrates that the sermons are not merely "gospel exhortations devoid of incident and illustrative material."[124] The majority of the themes are theological, even gospel, but the preachers also treat topics relevant to the *application* of theological principles in everyday life. Arriving on the scene during a religious age and climate, Quakerism focused upon what some modern people might see as obscure, irrelevant doctrinal matters. Of course, this situation may be a more pertinent comment on twenty-first-century people than upon the early Quakers. Yet we have seen another side of the early Quaker mind reflected in the sermons, especially in the preachers' attempts to adapt to a changing epistemological scene by arguing for a religion based upon first-hand experience rather than simply upon tradition. This position may actually be more in line with postmodern thinking. The Quaker use of the "language of the new science" may be interpreted as an attempt to identify with the changing intellectual climate. Furthermore, we have observed a tendency on the part of the preachers to go beyond merely adapting to the conventional confines of the gospel or the norms of English society, to the point of advocating extreme changes in language usage, austere dress codes, and the intention to live scrupulously honest and self-denying lives. The preachers also tended to derogate war, and, at least in Fox's case, to articulate positions on women's equality and slavery that were far ahead of their time.

This survey of thematic characteristics has also revealed Quaker sermons to be different from conventional Puritan sermons of the seventeenth century. The prevailing homiletical theory and practice called for a systematic presentation of doctrine and its application.123 Themes were to be well established and exhaustively presented, not cobbled together in compendious lists or mentioned in the same two or three sentences. Quaker sermons were typically "mosaic" and multithematic. A large number of themes greeted the listener in each sermon. This characteristic is seen in Fox's sermons at the begining of the period, in Crisp's spaning the years 1687–1692, in Penn's from 1688 to 1699, and in other Quaker sermons from 1688 to 1700. Although Quaker preachers could, on occasion, develop a theme with some concentration—especially when the theme was controversial in nature— they more often simply proclaimed its truth in a kind of shorthand and juxtaposed it with another theme to which it seemed related in the moment of utterance. This habit is probably a result of the impromptu approach to preaching rather than any supposed deficiencies in rational or organized thought. Printed tracts and other documents not composed impromptu by the same preachers sometimes show remarkable ability to deal in lengthy, sustained, rational debate.[124]

I have presented an overview of the themes or ideas discovered in the surviving sermons. In the next chapter, I will turn to the recurrent key metaphors found in the sermons, the use of which provided much of the continuity and force by which the ideas were energized.

CHAPTER 7

FIVE KEY METAPHORS IN EARLY QUAKER
SERMONS, 1671–1700

Although many types of rhetorical appeals, including arguments, are discovered in extant early Quaker sermon texts, I believe that the most significant linguistic appeal, what turns out to be the *conceptual essence* of the sermons, is discovered in the preachers' rehearsal of five recurrent key metaphors.[1] Early Quakers tended to see the noumenal world in terms of the phenomenal; the idea in terms of the image.[2] In the idiom of Kenneth Burke, early Quaker preachers "discuss something in terms of something else,"[3] which is to say, they spoke analogically or metaphorically.[4] By this observation, I am not claiming that early Quaker preachers were unique in this characteristic among other religious speakers of their day, or religious speakers of any day, for that matter. Indeed, I. A. Richards argues that "*Thought* is metaphoric, and proceeds by comparison, and the metaphors of language derive therefrom."[5] The most obvious way in which early Quaker sermons differ from those of their contemporaries is that Quaker preachers rejected the doctrine-use sermon structure, which encouraged preachers to raise doctrinal points from a biblical text, present reasons for the doctrines' acceptance, and then apply the doctrine to the listeners' lives, all of which favored rational, tightly constructed argumentative discourse. Consequently, surviving early Quaker sermons do not, and canot, stand or fall on the basis of their argumentative structure, although early Quakers were able debaters, as their tract literature attests.[6] The sermons themselves reveal that their essential linguistic strategy is the use of metaphor.[7] Another way of viewing this difference is to observe that Quaker preachers do not see metaphor as an ornament. In the majority of instances, they do not "tack on" metaphors to amplify or beautify the train of thought as one dons clothing, so that if one were to remove the metaphor, the thought would still stand. Their metaphors are actually conceptual. In most cases, if one removes the metaphor from a sentence of an early Quaker sermon, the sentence is dealt a mortal wound; little substance or appeal remains. Early Quaker sermons thrive on the basis of key recurrent metaphor clusters drawn from Scripture and everyday life, which together become the conceptual analogical system through which they view spiritual truth.[8]

In this chapter, I will first briefly situate the following discussion of the metaphors within the burgeoning scholarly literature on metaphor. Then I will illustrate and examine the five most important and prominent key metaphors that appear in the extant early Quaker sermons: (1) the light-dark cluster, (2) the voice cluster, (3) the seed cluster, (4) the hunger-thirst cluster, and (5) the journey-pilgrimage cluster. Finally, I will focus on the functions these metaphor clusters served in the context of impromptu preaching.

THE BURGEONING STUDY OF METAPHOR

There is neither pause nor paucity in the scholarly discussion of metaphor, and not just in the fields in which one might expect it to occur. Scholars in the sciences, philosophy, linguistics, sociology, anthropology, theology, rhetorical studies, and literature have produced an impressive collection of essays and books on the subject.[9] Here my purpose is not to produce a comprehensive review, but instead to concentrate on a selection of authors who have helped me form the analysis presented in this chapter. I have already mentioned I. A. Richards and Kenneth Burke, to which I must add the name of Richard M. Weaver, all from the ranks of rhetoricians, writers who share the sense that metaphor is more than mere ornament and rhetorical flourish. However, Richards' radical notion that thought itself is metaphoric, which he published in his *Philosophy of Rhetoric* in 1936, lay dormant for quite a while, as well it might, because it was groundbreaking and radical. In one intellectual leap, metaphor went from mere linguistic decoration—a trope that occasionally could and did present all sorts of "problems" in hearers' understanding and also impeded the chain of logical connections—to become the very basis of conceptualization itself. Nineteen years later, Max Black argued that metaphor was not simply "emotive," but could also achieve "cognitive" status.[10] Ted Cohen sees Black's essay as "the pivotal text" in broadening the conception of metaphor.[11] However, it was the 1980 book *Metaphors We Live By* that set the intellectual world on its head. In this book, George Lakoff and Mark Johnson urge that metaphor should be made a *central* concern of philosophy and linguistics, rather than a "peripheral interest." They argue that "metaphor is pervasive in everyday life, not just in language but in thought and action. Our ordinary conceptual system, in terms of which we both think and act, is fundamentally metaphorical in nature." Echoing Richards, whom they neglect to reference in the book, Lakoff and Johnson boldly argue that "human *thought processes* are largely metaphorical."[12] Ensuing articles and books on conceptual metaphors might be described as footnotes to *Metaphors We Live By*.[13] One of the potential problems inherent in Lakoff and Johnson's approach is admitted by them in their preface. There they say they had to reject "the possibility of any objective or absolute truth" and supply "an alternative account in which human experience and understanding, rather than objective truth, played the central role."[14] I do not intend in this chapter to ferret out the truth claims inherent in or implied by the early Quaker preachers' use of metaphors, only to show that their metaphors are not adornments, but conceptual linguistic choices.[15]

In addition to the interests of scholars like Lakoff and Johnson who are investigating the conceptual base of metaphors, this chapter is also influenced by anthropologists and sociolinguists who have also paid significant attention to metaphor and symbols.[16] Because the chapter focuses on "key metaphors," a term that surfaced among anthropologists, some further explanation is warranted. Specifically, I follow Nels Johnson's use of the term "key metaphor,"[17] which is an adaptation of the more inclusive concept "key symbol" used by Sherry Ortner.[18] A key symbol, according to Ortner, is recognized because (1) people in the culture tell you that it is important; (2) people in the culture are positively or negatively aroused by it, rather than indifferent; (3) the symbol comes up in many different contexts; (4) there is greater cultural elaboration surrounding it; and (5) greater cultural restrictions surround it.[19] The metaphors discussed in this chapter are key in seventeenth-century Quaker culture because (1) the metaphors are prominent both in terms of quantity and placement in significant passages in the sermons, and (2) evidence extrinsic to the sermons (from tracts, journals, epistles, etc.) corroborates that the metaphors are among key cultural indicators for early Quakers.[20]

Numerous scholars in rhetoric and public address have analyzed a broad range of artifacts or texts on the basis of their metaphorical strategies;[21] thus, in addition to the influences noted above, this chapter also has roots in a portion of the public-address literature that reflects the rhetorical study of *archetypal* metaphor in public discourse. Michael Osborn, in particular, has contributed in important ways to this approach, but other scholars have also used the approach with skill and insight.[22] Let me observe that key metaphors are not necessarily archetypal, nor are archetypal metaphors always key metaphors for a specific culture. Interestingly, the five key metaphors discovered in early Quaker sermons also exhibit the characteristics of archetypal metaphors cited by Osborn: (1) they are relatively immune to changes in time and culture, (2) they are based on some inexorable part of human experience, and (3) they possess an appeal based upon identification with primal human motivations.[23] While we should expect many cultures to develop key metaphors that, unlike archetypal metaphors, are bound temporally and culturally, Quaker metaphors are both key *and* archetypal (as well as conceptual). In this chapter, where appropriate, either classification is relevant to the analysis.

A last source of influence on my approach to this chapter finds its source in the literature that comes to grips with the challenges related to metaphorical religious language. On this topic, Sallie (TeSelle) McFague has been especially insightful in her published scholarship. In her early book on parable, she begins the chapter on metaphor with these words: "Metaphor is not first of all the language of poets but ordinary language."[24] In her later book on metaphorical theology, she states that in the last two centuries "metaphor has been seen not as a trope but as the way language and, more basically, thought works."[25] McFague is intent on avoiding the "idolatry" of biblical literalism and the "irrelevance" of religious language that is rejected "by many women, blacks, and third-world people."[26] Her answer to both problems is "to understand religious/theological language in terms of metaphors and models." Models are "dominant, comprehensive metaphors with organizing, structural potential." They "can never be taken literally since they are not descriptions but indirect attempts to express the unfamiliar in terms of the familiar." McFague devotes an entire chapter to the question, "God the Father: Model or Idol?" and suggests a "complementary model, that of God as friend" as more appropriate for contemporary people. She further suggests that models (and, by implication, metaphors—out of which models are constructed) that stress relationship—for example, friendship—are the best choices, as long as we realize "we are prohibited from absolutizing any models of

'God."[27] Particularly troubling to McFague are metaphors and models that emphasize male or patriarchal power, as do numerous biblical linguistic choices.

The idea that every religious metaphor, whether patriarchal or not, is inadequate to its task is developed by a number of authors. For example, Earl R. MacCormac observes, "Much of religious language is metaphoric and imprecise, but those qualities may be of advantage rather than indications of failure for as the theologian seeks to speculate about what is difficult to express, he [*sic*] resorts to highly speculative and suggestive language."[28] More recently, Janet Martin Soskice suggests that theologians resort to metaphorical language because the truth behind them is ultimately ineffable: "All the metaphors which we use to speak of God arise from experiences of that which canot adequately be described, of that which Jews and Christians believe to be 'He Who Is' . . . and we are in danger of theological travesty when we forget that this is so."[29] In other words, in religious contexts, metaphors are a linguistic tool for saying something that canot be uttered.

FIVE KEY CONCEPTUAL METAPHOR CLUSTERS

The seventy-nine extant early Quaker sermons provide a rich body of discourse for the study of metaphor in a specific historical and cultural context. As explained in earlier chapters, the early Quaker notion of homiletics placed supreme importance on the immediate revelation of truth from God. The preacher acted as "midwife" or "medium" in the communication of truth to an audience.[30] In this stressed-filled presentational context, the sermon texts reveal that Quaker preachers relied to a great extent on metaphor to tie their sermons together conceptually, having rejected traditional organizational and argumentative approaches such as the doctrine-use format. As we begin this section, we are reminded that Cope identified "the essential quality of seventeenth-century Quaker expression" as "a tendency to break down the boundary between literalness and metaphor, between conceptions and things."[31] For early Quakers, metaphor not only transcended its function as ornament as expressed in Renaissance rhetoric, but became the conceptual underpining of discourse.[32] Let us now examine the five major metaphor clusters used by seventeenth-century Quaker preachers.

The five recurrent clusters of key metaphors are employed throughout the period 1671–1700 and across the twenty-four preachers

included.[33] To reiterate, the five clusters include (1) the light-dark cluster, (2) the voice cluster, (3) the seed cluster, (4) the hunger-thirst cluster,
and (5) the journey-pilgrimage cluster.

The Light-Dark Metaphor

The light-dark metaphor is undoubtedly one of the most important
types of conceptual metaphor. Think of how often we use phrases such
as "Bill shed light on that topic" or "you brightened my day." Clearly,
the metaphor is also archetypal. Osborn writes that it is probably the
prototype of all archetypal qualifiers.[34] Light from the sun is the source
of life on our planet. Photosynthesis, warmth—indeed, sight itself—
are inescapably associated with sunlight. The biblical account lists first
among God's creative acts the creation of light and the separation of
light from darkness. Obviously, the early Quakers were not the first
to discover the strength of associations all people have with light and
darkness. In reality, their immediate sources were biblical, where the
light-dark motif is interwoven with the eternal struggle between good
and evil, and where light is used to signify the coming of Jesus Christ
(John 1:4-9). However, regardless of the source of Quaker usage, one
can make a case that no other religious group has made the light-dark
metaphor so central to their understanding and communication of
God's grace. The light-dark metaphor underlies the early Quaker perception of life to such an extent that it is impossible to treat the other
conceptual metaphors apart from relating them in some way to the
macroscopic and all-encompassing vision of light and dark. Images
of light, or the Inward Light, appear in sixty-nine of seventy-nine sermons; images of darkness or night appear in fifty-seven. Only six sermons do not directly express a variant of either light or dark.[35]

Natural phenomena, such as the sun, moon, stars, clouds, and fog,
become the vehicles of the most characteristic metaphors in the sermons. The light of day, or the dawning sun, is a favorite vehicle from
Fox's time through Penn's. The sun or the day appear in thirty-six of
the sermons. The typical pattern is a variation of that presented by
Fox in 1674:

> They come to se him when ye Day is Come ye Day Spring from
> on high. There is a naturall Day Springs upp—Rise to work lye
> not in bed, till the Sun Rises, as outwardly: so Inwardly, The Day
> Spring from on high:—People have been In Darkness Long enough,
> when Immortality is brought to Light then thei[r] Day Springs from

on high that know, & ye Shadowes & Clouds to fly away, when ye morning breaks, the sun of Righteousness Arises with his heavenly praises, so now this day is Sprung from on high[;] this is witnessed when he comes to Rule in ye Day,—Soe now as every man Comes under God[']s Teaching . . . the[y] Come to know ye Day of God . . . So here is god[']s Day his everlasting day his heavenly Day: his spirituall Day.[36]

The passage is a verbal mosaic of light and dark, which focuses on the dawning of day. It illustrates Cope's description of the incantatory style: "an incredible repetition, a combining and recombining of a cluster of words and phrases drawn from Scripture."[37] If one views beyond Fox's agrammatical, additive style, one can see the strength of the passage lying in the identification of God's teaching, presumably reflecting the tenets of Quakerism, with the "Day spring on high." "Shadows and clouds," along with "darkness," are identified with unrighteousness and, by implication, false teaching. Fox also employs the play on words in which the word "sun" is substituted for "son" in the biblical title "the Sun of Righteousness" (Mal 4:2). The same figure is used almost three decades later by Penn in a passage we will examine presently. A final observation on the quoted passage is that Fox not only identifies the physical dawning of day with the spiritual, he also contrasts the inward day with the outward or natural day. The use of spatial terms has already been noted and will be discussed in detail in chapter 8. Suffice it to say that Fox's passage illustrates the manner in which the early Quaker preachers frequently combine their favorite conceptualizations of reality: the light-dark metaphor family and spatial terms.[38]

In a sermon preached the following year, Fox relies on the same basic image of the sun, but goes further and contrasts the positive effects of the righteous sun with the negative effects of the "Papist[']s Sun," which "scorched ye Blade," and the sun of the "advocates of the common prayer" (Anglicans), which "Scorched & went down." In the same sermon, he maintains that the "Sun of Righteousness . . . shines in your Hearts: As ye Naturall Sun shineth in ye Creation." The ability of the natural sun to scorch the earth is identified with the "persecutor." Those who behold the "Sun of Righteousness," he tells his hearers, "never fear ye Persecutor[']s Sun."[39] The force of the image was apparently so real to Fox that later in the sermon he chooses the identical vehicle to express his interpretation of the Old Testament account regarding the appointment of Aaron as high priest. Aaron's rod budded and produced fruit "in ye Morning Light" as a sign that he was the chosen priest. Fox's application of the story to his hearers is pointed and develops further the lines of association between spiritual daylight and physical daylight: "Now if you be a Royall Priesthood, Offering up Spiritual Sacrifices your Rods have brought forth fruit; bring forth in ye Morning, wn ye Day Springs, God[']s Everlasting Day . . . Rods bud in ye Light in ye Day." In Fox's sermons, the most frequently used vehicle for the concept of light is the sun. The Sun of Righteousness brings light, warmth, growth, and sight, but the false sun only withers the crop.

Fox also uses objects common to the seventeenth-century English household as a part of the light-dark metaphor. Generally speaking, however, he prefers natural phenomena over sources of human-invented light. In the sermon literature, the images of beacons, candles, and lamps (or "lanthorns") appear only ten times compared with thirty-six for sun or day, and twenty-four for sparks and fire. In a memorable passage from a 1677 sermon, the human spirit is compared to a candle and a lamp, both low on the light spectrum compared with the sun. Fox asserts, "Now the Scripture saith ye Spirit of a Man is ye Candle of ye Lord; Christ enlightens ye Candle. . . . Christ Lights this Candle wth his Heavenly Light: so let your Lights shine, your Lamps to burn."[40] Penn elaborates upon a similar point using the lamp image. The oil for the lamp is said to be a "Life of Righteousness and Holiness," and those who have such oil in their lamps are encouraged to see that their "Light continue to shine before Men. . . . that this Light may shine and cover the Nations."[41] Richard Ashby, making the same plea, substitutes the natural vehicle of a star: "you shall be as the Stars shining in a Dark world, and though there be Darkness upon the Earth, yet here is Light."[42] The star image, although a natural phenomenon of light, is employed only eight times in the sermons. Lamps, candles, beacons, even stars, fade in brightness when compared with the sun, but even the lesser lights can, on occasion, conceptualize worthy goals for a Quaker preacher and listeners.

Fox's use of the sun as a symbol for God's light presages its use in later sermons. The power of the light, or rather the early Quakers' faith in its power, is nowhere seen to better advantage than in the following passage from a sermon by Crisp preached sixteen years later:

What if a Company of People should combine together, and say, We will not have the Sun to shine upon the City of *London*; what course must we take? When the Sun is down, we will build a Bank or high Wall to intercept its Light; but notwithstanding all their Endeavours, when the Sun riseth, it will get over their high Banks and Wall; so all their Designs, and all the Contrivances against the Light of the Gospel, and against Christ the Sun of Righteousness, and against the Spirit of Christ, the Light will ascend and get over them, and break through all opposition.[43]

Here, the sun is the vehicle for the "Light of the Gospel," or the "Spirit of Christ." Crisp calls upon the inevitability of the sun's rising in human experience as witness to the inevitable rising of the "Sun of Righteousness."

Sunlight, of course, makes vision possible, illuminating objects and pathways, and this natural characteristic also finds metaphorical expression in the sermons. Samuel Waldenfield, in a classic statement of the core of early Quaker belief, employs this motif for his appeal, "as the Light of the Sun outwardly makes a discovery of Visible Things, so the inward Light of the Son of God makes a Discovery of the invisible Things. . . . When the Light of Christ comes into my Soul, it is to convince me of my Sins."[44] As the sun makes vision possible in the natural world, the "sun" (the Light) enlightens the heart, revealing sin. The image is implied by Crisp, although not by reference to the word "sun," when he alludes to the ability of a source of light to make a path visible: "thou wilt have light from Heaven sent to guide thee and direct thee in the way."[45] Here let me note that there is a natural blending of light-dark and journey-pilgrimage clusters, since travel demands the light of day (or artificial light) to avoid dangers and reckon directions accurately. Penn also implies the sun in a striking passage in which he calls his hearers "Sons and daughters of the Morning": "[T]he Everlasting Day of God hath dawned upon you, and see your Experiences, see the things that your eyes have seen, and your hands have handled."[46]

Whereas the preachers identify light with good in the sermons (with the exception of its use to indicate persecution), they identify all that is dark with evil. Images of darkness or night appear in fifty-seven of the sermons. The preachers refer to the state of the contemporary non-Quaker church as a "long Night of Darkness."[47] Crisp's estimate of the days prior to the advent of Quakerism is captured in this brief quotation: "There hath been a very Dark and Cloudy Day upon our Fore-Fathers, and also upon us, in the Days of our Ignorance."[48] Coole uses "clouds" to illustrate why people reject God's grace: "Man by Sin hath darkened his own Mind, and clouded his Understanding, that he canot see the Glory of God."[49] According to Ashby, people in their natural state "are in the Dark, they are groping for the Wall, they are at an uncertainty."[50] Crisp speaks of a "Veil of Ignorance" that has fallen over people and asks, "what can Darkness see? What can Darkness discover?"[51] For anyone in the meeting who understands but rejects the message of Light, a "Curtain of Darkness"[52] will be drawn between God and his or her soul, and, as Penn concluded, "There is nothing will remain, then, but Chains of Darkness, they that Loved Darkness here, shall be cast into utter Darkness, hereafter, even the Blackness of Darkness for ever."[53]

Light-dark imagery is amplified in psychological force when contrasted in the same context. The quotations cited exhibit the strength of implied or explicit light-dark antithesis. On many occasions, notably during closing prayers, the preachers rely upon the tension. In 1687, Crisp prays that God will "dispel the Clouds of Darkness that hath been upon the Sons and Daughters of Men." He also prays for those "that have been driven away in a cloudy and dark Night," that they be "brought to a glorious and blessed Day, wherein they may enjoy the Gospel that brings Light to dark Souls."[54]

The opposition of light to dark, with unmistakably positive associations for the former and negative for the latter, is the unquestioned primary imagistic appeal of the sermons. Many similar passages could be cited, but these are sufficient to indicate that the opposition of light to dark is the primary metaphor cluster of the sermons.

The Voice Metaphor

Second in importance to the light-dark cluster, and sometimes used in conjunction with or juxtaposed to it, are images drawn from the early Quaker propensity to perceive the world in terms of silence and sound.[55] The image of the guiding voice is a part of a larger cluster of images relating to silence and sound. It is a source of archetypal metaphor because the need for vocal guidance relates to all people in all places and times and because it is tied into our very notions of human communication. Presumably, humans do not choose to be deaf. Many vital responses to the environment and other humans are made on the basis of aural perception. Yet a person may choose to be silent. We have seen that early Quaker culture placed emphasis on silence as a prerequisite to worship, so that in the silence an inward voice could be heard. Quaker belief and practice also placed high importance on weighing one's words and using them with caution. As we have seen, silent waiting was prerequisite to worship. The sermons, arising as impromptu expressions out of the silence, draw on the power of silence practiced as a group discipline. Silence, as such, is mentioned in only six of the extant sermons. However, this fact should not be interpreted to mean that silence is viewed as unimportant by the preachers. Silence is a significant topic in Quaker journals, tracts, and theological writings.[56] Furthermore, the context of silent waiting, which surrounds the sermons, acts as nonverbal reaffirmation of the importance of silence. The voice metaphor, the other polarity from silence, is chosen almost as often as light imagery in the sermons. "Hearing the voice" of God (or Christ, the Spirit, even the Light) is used in forty-one sermons; similarly, Christ or God referred to as the "speaker" or "teacher," implying the voice to be heeded, is used in seventeen sermons.

Fox's sermons are a repository of statements that reiterate the belief that people, if they wait patiently in silence, will experience the silence broken by the voice of Christ. One of his familiar and repeated appeals begins with a recapitulation of the Adam and Eve story, in which God is viewed as the "first Speaker" who communicated with man and woman; Satan is the "second Speaker," who beguiled the two with false words. Christ is seen as the "third Speaker," who "bruises ye head of All false Teachers."[57] The following quotation typifies Fox's use of oral-aural imagery: "God is become ye Speaker againe, that was ye first Speaker in Paradise, God hath spoken to us by his Son. Here doe people come to hear his voice from Heaven."[58] It is, after all, the voice of Christ, not the Light, that Fox uses to describe his own spiritual experience after a long search, and perhaps therein his emphasis on hearing the "voice of the teacher" finds experiential antecedent.[59] According to Fox, if people will shut out the opposing voices, especially that of the second speaker, they will hear the voice of the first speaker once again. Crisp, in 1688, also expresses concern about shutting out the false voices when he observes that those who are under the government of Christ "have been able . . . to make such a Distinction of Voices, and of Sounds, that they have been preserv'd from the Delusions of the Age."[60]

When Quaker preachers use the phrase "Word of God" (or "Word of the Lord"), they do not mean the Bible. In the forty-seven sermons that refer to the Word of God, the usage clearly indicates "Christ the Word" or the "Word as spoken by God." Crisp is typical: "This great Change hath been wrought in many a Soul, by the Operation of the Word of God, of the inward Word, that inward Voice, when the Lord hath taken Men in hand himself."[61] This usage is consistent with early Quaker epistemology, which, as we we have seen, placed secondary emphasis on the Bible and primary importance on direct revelation.[62]

Crisp often uses the imagery of the voice. Sixteen of his thirty-two surviving sermons employ the metaphor. On one occasion, he reveals, "It is Christ they must hear; he is come so near to Men that they hear his Voice, and hear him tell us our very Thoughts."[63] Other preachers rehearse essentially the same imagery. Dewsbury expresses confidence that salvation "is entailed upon such Souls as hear the Voice of Christ."[64] Similarly, Waldenfield hopes "that People might be mindful of the Inward Voice of Christ to their Souls, that when he Speaks, they might hear."[65] In the passages cited thus far, especially those by Fox and Crisp, the blending of literalness and metaphor is striking. In fact, in most of these quotations, the reader canot be certain if a literal or metaphorical voice is implied. Either interpretation is possible.

Given the early Quaker view of humans as creatures who live in darkness prior to "convincement" (the Quaker term for religious conversion), it is almost predictable that their imagery will at some point emphasize not only the importance of light but also the presence of a voice that will guide a person along a dark path. The light-dark and voice clusters are easily mixed, as in this quotation from Crisp: "Blessed be God this Darkness is removed, this Vail [sic] is gone over and taken away; the Brightness of the Glory of the Gospel hath expell'd this Darkness, and thousands now a-days not only hear the Minister reprove them, but they hear a Voice within that doth reprove them for Iniquity. . . . God hath an immediate way of counselling and instructing."[66]

In another sermon by Crisp, the blending of the voice cluster with what I shall presently describe as the journey-pilgrimage cluster occurs: "There is a Voice that calls to People in our Days, to look behind them, for they are out of the way."[67] Thus, the images of light-dark and voice are sometimes interchangeable and easily blended, and either cluster suggests the idea of guidance while traveling on a journey or pilgrimage. The fascinating interaction of light and voice is set forth in a quotation from Crisp summarizing the goal of Quaker preaching: "To persuade all Men every where, that they believe in the Light, and hearken to the Voice of the Light in their own Consciences."[68] In the arresting linguistic juxtaposition "Voice of the Light," Crisp seems to be essaying the limits of these early Quaker concepts through metaphor.

The Seed Metaphor

The third most common key metaphor for the workings of God's grace in the sermons is the Seed. The cluster partakes of sets of interrelated animal and vegetable associations. On the one hand, it refers to the progeny of humans—we are all the "seed" of our ancestors. At the same time, it alludes to botanical germination and growth. The principle of growth according to inherited traits is the same in either case. In the sermons, especially when the word "seed" is used apart from contextual modifiers, the choice evokes a rich integration of associations from both animal and vegetable realms. The metaphor is undoubtedly archetypal. The seed is the first principle, the source from which life springs. Metaphors that draw on the seed call up associations for all humans everywhere. A variation of the seed metaphor appears in twenty-seven of the sermons. It is used in three ways: (1) the Seed as the symbol of good or evil, Christ or Satan; (2) the Seed as the image of the indwelling of good or evil in a person's life; and (3) the Seed as the faithful believers, the progeny of Christ, the remnant, the good seed.

Fox's use of "seed" refers back to the Old Testament promise that God "will put enmity between thee [the serpent] and the woman [Eve], and between thy seed and her seed; it shall bruise thy head, and thou shalt bruise his heel" (Gen 3:15). He identifies the Seed with Christ: "All nations shall come to the blessing of this seed. This seed is Christ, that was promised to break the Serpent's power."[69] According to Fox, one can reject the good seed in favor of the serpent's seed: "They yt Crucifie ye Seed to ym selves a fresh, & quench ye Spirit of God in ym selves . . . entertain ye Evil Seed, and ye Evil Spirit yt brings ye Curse upon ym."[70]

Other preachers also speak of two seeds—one standing for the evil potential in humans, the other standing for the human potential for good through Christ. Crisp says, "there is in every Man by nature the Seed and Root of all Sin and Rebellion against God."[71] On the other hand, John Bowater offers hope "in him that was the promised Seed, whom God promised should break the Serpent[']s head."[72] Crisp talks about the "Persecution, Hatred and Enmity, between the Woman[']s Seed, and the Serpentine Seed. . . . So that it is not to be expected that the Seed of the Serpent . . . can love those that are born of the Woman's Seed."[73]

Eventually, the progeny of the union between Christ and man— the "planting of the Seed"—would come to resemble the parentage. Ultimately, the "child" itself would be called the "Seed." Crisp reminds listeners that the blessing of Abraham is promised "to the Seed, that is, to those that are in Christ." He goes further to refer to the Seed as Christ: "The Faithful are those that are obedient to Christ, who is the Seed of the Promise. . . . They must come to Christ the Seed."[74]

Quotations using the seed thus far reveal a closer affinity to human heredity than to botany. However, many of the sermons employ the seed image in a context explicitly tied to the process of germination and growth in plants.[75] Barclay likens Christ to a seed in the same way that Jesus explained his impending death and resurrection to his disciples: "Every Plant, Seed or Grain that is placed in the Earth, it dies before it grows up. . . . It was necessary that the Son of God (the Prince of Life) should die . . . else he could not finish . . . the Sowing of that Seed . . . whereby we might come to have a share with him."[76] Thus Barclay identifies Christ not only as fulfillment of the seed prophecy in the story of the fall, but also as archetypal reenactment of the life-death cycle in nature.[77]

Quaker preachers also saw the seed in terms dictated by Jesus in the parable of the Sower (Matt 13:3-23; Mark 4:3-20; Luke 8:5-15). Penn, for example, reminds his hearers to keep watch that Satan not "hinder the good Seed (the Word) from taking Root; and bringing forth Fruit."[78] Here we see the blending of the seed and voice clusters through the identification of "seed" and "word."

Although not employed to the extent of the light-dark or voice metaphors, the image of the seed, whether in the context of human progeny or that of agriculture, is an important metaphor in the corpus of the sermons. It becomes a significant way to conceptualize the potential for growth, fruitfulness, life itself, and the life-death-rebirth cycle of Christian teaching. It also allows the preachers to extend the polarizations of light-dark and voice–false voice to the good seed/evil seed, all of which conceptualize the world as enmity between two forces. The growth potential inherent in the seed, however, also introduces the

ominous possibility that, given the proper environment and encouragement, either seed can grow to maturity and bear fruit in any person.

The Hunger–Thirst Metaphor

The need for nourishment is universal. Only when hunger and thirst
are satisfied can we turn to other human concerns such as shelter, clothing, protection from danger, development of relationships, etc. Early
Quaker sermons draw on the primal power of metaphors clustered
around the archetypal pattern of recurrent need for food and drink.
They assimilate the patterns from the Bible and repeat, develop, and
extend them in their sermons. They assert that people should hunger
and thirst for God, just as they experience hunger and thirst for physical nourishment. Furthermore, they maintain, as the Scriptures taught,
that if people do not hunger and thirst after God, they will not find
him: "These Persons are not hungry, and so they are not fed; they are
not thirsty, and so they never obtain that which can satisfy the Soul."[79]

The preachers use several vehicles in the hunger-thirst cluster, but
the two most prominent are "bread" and "water" (also including specific terms relating to water such as "fountain" and "well").[80] The former appears in twenty-three sermons and the latter in nineteen. Either
or both appear in thirty-one sermons.[81]

Passages of simple beauty appear in the sermons when both bread
and water images are combined. Fox announces that when people possess the seed, they "all come to Eat of ye Living Bread yt comes down
from Heaven & drink of ye Living Waters. . . . Here is ye pure standing Fellowship; Meet here, Feed here, Drink here."[82] Relying on concrete and universal experiences such as hunger and thirst, Fox is able
to amplify abstractions such as "peace" and "reconciliation," which
appear prior to the passage just quoted. Butcher later repeats the same
image when he points out that in Quaker meetings, "many a time the
Hungry have been satisfied with Bread, And the Fountain of Living
Water hath been opened, and the Thirsty have been Drinking of it."[83]

In the sermons, God's bread, used apart from water, always implies
the nourishment and comfort of a satiated desire for food. James Park,
for example, explains the result of drawing close to God in terms of
the simple comfort of bread: "Then will your Bread (your Heavenly,
Living Bread) be sure, and you will know the Breaking of it, and the
Eating of it; that Bread which Christ gives, is that whereby we are
Comforted and Refreshed."[84]

Water, employed alone in a sermon passage, is used in a manner paralleling bread that stresses its thirst-quenching rather than its cleansing function. An anonymous preacher uses water imagery to dissuade his hearers from following the preacher instead of discovering the true source of spiritual water: "O come and tast[e] and see, for your selves, don't come to us, to take Water at second-hand, but come to the Springs, where Water runs swiftly and sweetly. Come Friends, Drink of the Stream."[85]

The preachers also blend the hunger-thirst cluster with other key clusters. Crisp, for example, associates "bread" with "Word": "For this is the Nourishment and the Heavenly Bread. . . . The Begotten of God are come to know the Vertue [sic] of the Divine Life, Christ Jesus, their Feeding and their Nourishment is by every Word that proceedeth out of the Mouth of God."[86] Similarly, Fox associates hearing with feeding: "So now feed not on ye Serpent[']s food but feed on God[']s bread, & hear him from heaven:—see what all mankinde, hath gott, by feeding, & hearing of ye serpent."[87]

An incredible blending of light-dark, Seed, and hunger-thirst clusters is discovered in the following passage from Fox, illustrating the ease with which the metaphors were articulated together:

> In ye Old Covenant they had ye Outward Booths, & Feasts of Tabernacles; Now in ye New Covenant they come to be grafted into Christ Jesus, & in him everie Plant grows green allwaies in ye Second Adam. . . . As Christ said her [sic] yt believes in me Out of [his] belly shall flow Rivers of Living Water: Now is this True? Can Rivers Spring out of his Belly? This spake he of ye Spirit: You being [g] rafted into Christ ye Fountain by believing in ye Light. . . . From him ye Living Fountain do these Springs of Living Waters come; this spoke he of ye Spirit, this Spirituall River, & Fountain.[88]

Early Quaker preachers place considerable reliance upon reference to the primal drive to satisfy hunger and thirst. They conceptualize through metaphor the satisfaction and comfort they believe are afforded people who choose to follow their call. The preference for simple food and drink, such as bread, water, milk, or fruit, reflects biblical usage but also implicitly reinforces the Quaker emphasis on living a simple life.

The Journey-Pilgrimage Metaphor

The fifth key metaphor cluster found in early Quaker sermons identified Quaker beliefs with the vision of life as a journey or pilgrimage. The pattern is a reflection of the metaphor of the journey found widely in the literature of many disparate cultures.[89] The journey or pilgrimage, both as an act and metaphor, permeates biblical literature and historical Christianity and is especially significant in medieval and seventeenth-century Christian writings.[90] The sermons reveal variations on the journey metaphor, all involving the conception of life as a journey from an evil to a good place, from Egypt to Canaan, from "Death to Life, and from Darkness to Light."[91] Journey or pilgrimage was either developed or implied in twenty-nine of the extant sermons.[92]

A typical example of the journey-pilgrimage cluster, complete with the identification of the believer's life with the Hebrews in the wilderness, is seen in this passage from Fox: "These that are Come to be Convinced now . . . & that have stood still, & seen salvation, & have been preserved through ye Redd Sea, & have come into ye Wilderness, & out of Egypt, & bondage . . . they finde abundance of trouble, before they Come to Canaan."[93] Just as the journey to the promised land was difficult for the Hebrews, so it is for the seventeenth-century pilgrim, and the early Quakers were reenacting the trek to Caanan on a spiritual or inward plane. Crisp speaks of the people who fled the evil cities of the plains only to be ensnared by the troubles of the wilderness: "We have before our Eyes from day to day, those that have . . . been in great measure brought out of Sodom, and out of the way of Egypt. . . . But at last they have taken and arrogated those Gifts to themselves."[94] Approximately one month after Crisp's sermon, Penn preached an important funeral sermon, which will be analyzed in more depth in chapter 11, in which he contrasts the Land of Promise with the trouble of the present "wandering" life:

> We are Travellers here in this Vale of Tears, in this Earthly Pilgrimage, into the Land of Rest the Heavenly Canaan; Let us follow our blessed Joshua, that is leading us into that Land of Promise, and he will give to every one his Lot. . . . O Blessed are they that are waiting for their Lot and Portion in that Heavenly Country to which Abraham had his Eye, the City, the New Jerusalem.[95]

Six years later, Penn further develops the same image:

> [W]atch against the Enemy of our Souls, that he may not seduce
> us and bewilder us, and make us wander and loose [*sic*] our *Way*,
> while we are travelling through the *Wilderness* of this *World*, toward
> the heavenly Canaan. The same Almighty Arm, that brought us out
> of *Egypt*, will conduct us through the *Wilderness*, and bring us safe
> to Canaan: Our Heavenly *Joshua*, the Lord Jesus Christ, will be our
> Captain and Leader.[96]

The journey-pilgrimage cluster expresses an otherworldliness on
the part of the preachers, especially with regard to life's pleasures. Fox
explains, "Our Religion is Practicall, it brings & bowers [*sic*] down
every mind to seek after things above, as Heirs of another Kingdom, &
not these Outward Transitory things here below; Pilgrims & Strangers
yt are hastning [*sic*] to another Countrey or Kingdom; are not much
affected & taken wth any thing they meet wth as they travell along."[97]
The spiritual journey is so dangerous that, as Crisp maintains, "the
Children of Israel might as well have gone through the Red Sea, without the help of God, as the Christian Traveller can go through the
many difficulties . . . he is to meet with in his Way, without the assistance of God's Holy Spirit."[98]

Penn is, by far, the most frequent and most artful user of the
journey-pilgrimage metaphor. It appears in some form in ten of his
eleven surviving sermons. Penn is also the most innovative in adapting the metaphor to transitory images of the journey in his day. For
example, in one sermon, true believers become not only "pilgrims"
but "tenants": "It becometh us to live as Strangers and Pilgrims on the
Earth: For we are but Tenants *at will* of the Great Lord."[99] In another
sermon, he compared the believer's life to a short stay at a roadside in:
"This World is but an *Inn*, and we must not think to dwell here. We are
Travelling in the way to Heaven, the Undefiled way."[100]

The image of the traveler, whether used by Fox, Crisp, Penn, or
another preacher, is at once familiar and strong because it is built on a
lengthy history of associations from biblical through Puritan times. It is
also related to the "quest" story, which is discovered over a wide cultural
base in both sacred and secular writings as well as in oral literature.
Hermann G. Stelzner has isolated five elements of the quest metaphor,
all of which are found in the journey-pilgrimage cluster used by early
Quaker preachers. Reinterpreted to fit the requirements of the Quaker

metaphor cluster, the five elements become (1) "a precious object and/or Person to be found and Possessed or married"—Jerusalem, Canaan, the Land of Promise (or Christ, God), etc.; (2) "a long journey to find the Object"—the journey or pilgrimage; (3) "a Hero"—the pilgrim-traveler; (4) "the Guardians of the Object who must be overcome before it can be won"—the voice of the second speaker, the lusts of the world, stumbling in the dark, etc.; and (5) "the Helpers who . . . assist the Hero"—the Light, voice, etc.[101] By employing this metaphor, the preachers offer their hearers an archetypal conceptualizing image that informs human experience to such an extent that, in Stelzner's words, "occasionally universal human reactions are elicited."[102]

THREE FUNCTIONS OF THE METAPHORS

The five key metaphor clusters serve three functions, all of which are implicit in the analysis presented above: (1) they provide a means of summarizing and conceptualizing a world that made psychological and theological sense to the speakers and listeners, (2) they stand as means of elaborating the implications of the beliefs in individual Quaker's lives, and (3) they constitute an important inventional tool used by speakers enjoined to preach without preparation.[103]

The Summarizing Function

Quaker preachers spoke against a backdrop of rapid change in England. English society had undergone unprecedented revolutions in politics, religion, and science. Quakers participated to greater or lesser degrees in the liminality of their cultural surroundings, and early Quaker journals attest to the personal confusion, search, and general sense of personal alienation prior to convincement.[104] For these people, then, the telling of religious truth in familiar metaphors with which they could identify and which they could easily share with others in the community became a way to offset the ubiquity of change and flux that surrounded them. The five clusters "summarize" the Quaker's world. They compound and synthesize a complex system of ideas.[105] The preachers could thus avoid having to develop long, systematic, theological arguments or extensive scriptural expositions in favor of rehearsing and combining easily understood yet theologically rich metaphors shared by the Quaker community. In Paul Campbell's terms, the metaphors allowed the preachers and listeners to operate conceptually on the highest stratum, the "poetic-rhetorical" level of the symbological hierarchy.

The metaphors possess an additional advantage inasmuch as they not only summarize positive theological (and, by implication, behavioral) information but also summarize negative theological (and behavioral) information through the process of polarization: light assumes dark (as well as spurious light); the voice stands opposite the false voices or the second speaker; the seed opposes the evil seed or the serpent's seed; the hunger-thirst cluster assumes either the experience of spiritual hunger and thirst for God (and finding satisfaction) or the experience of pseudosatisfaction, which will obviate the drives; the pilgrimage from Babylon to Canaan implies movement from an evil to a holy place and assumes that one can choose *not* to be a pilgrim. Thus, a set of either-or rhetorical options comes to provide structure for the early Quaker's world. They help produce unity through binary opposition.

When the metaphors are used in combination, two forces help bring about a unification of the Quaker's world. First, the metaphors are identified together in the preacher's and hearer's minds through repetition and frequent blending. Second, because the metaphors each implicate one or more of the senses, when the images are combined, an overlapping of the senses—a synesthesia—is suggested metaphorically.[106] In Crisp's arresting phrase "hearken to the Voice of the Light," both sound and sight are invoked in such a way that listeners must be aware, if only subconsciously, that God is not bound to one chanel of sensory input. If light possesses a voice, and if one can feed on the light, then the metaphors indicate that the entire sensorium is vulnerable in a metaphorically unified way to the claims of God mediated through the preachers acting as midwives or oracles.[107] The metaphors also imply that religion is not simply a rational pursuit of the mind detached from the body and that Quakerism, at least, is a commitment that demands participation in a world in which the senses play a vital role.[108]

The Elaborating Function

The five key metaphor clusters not only provide a unifying mosaic of the world for early Quaker preachers and their auditors, they also become a means of extending their thought and, in Burkean terms, "revealing hitherto unsuspected connectives . . . by exemplifying relationships between objects which our customary rational vocabulary has ignored."[109] Ortner calls this process "elaboration" and contends that the end product of the process does not stop short at the level of understanding but ultimately makes the symbol "translatable into orderly action."[110] Both Burke's and Ortner's comments are germane to the elaborating function of metaphors because (1) the naming property of metaphors, by its "connective" nature, reveals new and "extended" relationships in the user's and hearer's mind; and (2) the implications of the metaphor, what may be described as its reinterpretation in personal terms, of necessity assume a personal sorting process that can lead to personal commitment and action. For example, to name life a pilgrimage overlays a gloss of geographic factors that may never have occurred to the person who hears the metaphor applied to life for the first time or in a new context. At the very least, the idea of pilgrimage may call up associations that have lain dormant. Upon assimilating the metaphor, however, the hearer may begin to translate the events in his or her world into the terms of the metaphor (e.g., living in an evil place; finding a straight path; traveling light, and in the Light, etc.), make changes in his or her personal life, or be reaffirmed in changes already made.[111]

It is significant that none of the metaphors differentiate on the basis of gender as do many biblical (and nonbiblical) metaphors, as McFague has remarked. It is axiomatic among early Quakers that women and men are equal in all respects,[112] and, as noted in previous chapters, women were capable and well-respected preachers in early Quaker circles.[113] Thus, all auditors, women and men alike, could easily elaborate and personalize these metaphor clusters into their own spheres of life without having to undergo metaphoric sex change, as one must do in order, for example, to be both "sons of God" and "Brides of Christ" simultaneously, or to be considered as developing into ministers in a "young man's state" or the "father's state," as we noticed Bownas was implicitly suggesting to his readers in chapter 5.

The Inventional Function

Unlike their Puritan and Anglican counterparts, Quaker preachers spoke without assistance of notes, manuscripts, or memorization. Yet they managed to compose sermons on the spot that sometimes approximate the length of many non-Quaker seventeenth-century sermons. The investigator is naturally led to question how they managed the task and to search for mnemonic aids, such as formulaic structures, in the sermons.[114] The key metaphors, although not true formulaic structures in the sense of being predictable in a certain

form in a particular place in a given sermon, nevertheless do function as a basic inventional tool for the preacher. The five metaphors,
with the help of additional rhetorical choices dealt with in chapter
8, allow the preacher several options of acceptable, dense metaphor
clusters, which he or she could build upon, combine, unravel, and
particularize according to the demands of audience or inward sense
of inspiration. The five key clusters are recognized by anyone familiar with the King James Bible as having their roots in its content and
language. The combining of these biblical terms, their elaboration
and particularization, and, most important, the preachers' (and community's) preference for these *particular* metaphors out of a host of
other biblical metaphors, signal the inventiveness of the speakers. The
biblical source also allowed the preachers to string together appropriate Scripture passages from memory as they were suggested by a particular word in a metaphor cluster. Possibly, in this manner they were
able to "gain time" while quoting a passage from the Bible in order to
think ahead to their next point. There is no evidence that the speakers
consciously chose the metaphors because of their advantages in the
process of invention, and it is difficult to imagine one of the preachers
admitting to the use of biblical quotations to fill time while thinking
of the next point. After all, as we have seen, they saw themselves as
God's oracles and were enjoined not to speak unless they were certain
of that role. On the other hand, the argument that the preachers were
not aware of the inventional advantages of the metaphors, or at least
did not choose them for their inventional advantages, is a moot point.
Regardless of their motivation, they chose an adaptable rhetorical
tool that, in addition to its summarizing and elaborating potential,
could also function as a form of invention and, if need arose, as a
"stalling device."[115]

CONCLUSION

Early Quaker sermons offer a provocative example of the use of metaphor. Furthermore, they provide examples of metaphors responding
to knotty theological and rhetorical problems. Early Quakers faced a
paradox: how to encourage a sense of group unity and identity and
maintain a theological stance that stresses the belief that direct revelation from God has not ceased with the canonization of Scripture. Too
much emphasis on the individual's revelation could split the group.
The individual's idiosyncrasy is always potentially at odds with group

unity.[116] Early Quakers met the demands of the paradox on two levels. The first encouraged the impromptu sermon, which allowed the individual to become God's spokesperson, God's oracle. The impromptu format, however, presents its own rhetorical problem: invention. One answer to the demands of the impromptu approach is the use of metaphors functioning as inventional tools.[117] The second-level response to the group-individual paradox also lies in the use of metaphors. The biblically rooted key metaphors allow preachers to stay within the conceptual boundaries of group belief through the presentation of messages that have the earmarks of the word of truth from God, yet have the potential to stretch the conceptual boundaries through elaboration and personalization.

By combining and recombining the five clusters of metaphors, the preachers are able to (1) establish familiar ground by using images acceptable to their audiences' sense of reality, (2) extend their own and their audiences' conceptual worlds through elaboration of the images, and (3) employ an inventional tool that helps deal with rhetorical challenges inherent in the impromptu preaching situation.

CHAPTER 8

OTHER SALIENT CHARACTERISTICS
OF QUAKER SERMONS, 1671–1700

In previous chapters, I examined the themes and key metaphors of early Quaker sermons; it now remains to describe and analyze additional significant characteristics of early Quaker sermons. I shall first discuss the movement away from the incantatory style of the earliest Quakers, described by Cope as "an incredible repetition, a combining and recombining of a cluster of words and phrases drawn from Scripture,"[1] to what I call the "catechital" style, with its use of rhetorical questions, dialogue, and queries, a development that increasingly characterizes the sermons from 1671 to 1700. I will argue that the blending of literalness and metaphor and *scriptura rediviva*, both of which Cope saw as characteristic of early Quaker style, survives in the sermons of our period. In addition, I will argue that the incantatory style does not survive in the later sermons. Second, I will examine the extent and use of spatial terms in the sermons. My position on spatial terms will involve two arguments: (1) that the extensive use of spatial terms in the sermons validates Creasey's observation that spatial terms reveal a contrast between formalized religion and a religion based on personal acquaintance with Christ in the present;[2] and (2) that use of spatial terms in the sermons does not necessarily reveal the extent of dualism between the spiritual world and the natural, which Creasey found in the written works of Quakers in the last part of the seventeenth century. Third, I will discuss the appeal based upon guilt as found in the sermons. Barbour's finding that the earliest Quaker preachers mounted "a massive assault upon any point of guilt"[3] in the hearers will be quantified with regard to the later surviving sermons. Here I will argue that although the guilt appeal is present in the later sermons, it is tempered with the appeal to God's forgiveness. Finally, I will consider the ethical persuasion of the sermons, arguing that the use of personal testimonials became a strong appeal because it placed the preachers themselves on the witness stand. The order in which these four topics is discussed is determined by the relative significance they have in the total picture of Quaker sermon rhetoric as revealed in the seventy-nine surviving texts. The elements that produced the catechital style are more observable than spatial terms, although no complete analysis of the sermons could overlook either factor. Similarly, although the assault on guilt is not the primary appeal in the sermons, it is nonetheless an important one, though balanced by the factor of forgiveness through love. The use of personal testimonials by the preachers appears as the least important characteristic primarily because it is exhibited in fewer sermons. However, personal testimony is undeniably a part of early Quaker rhetoric, not only by its presence in specific sermons but also by Bownas' later argument that it is a powerful means of appeal.

From the "Incantatory" to the "Catechital" Style

Cope examined early Quaker style up to the fourth quarter of the seventeenth century and documented from written sources three stylistic occurrences, which he saw as defining characteristics of Quaker style: (1) the blending of literalness and metaphor, (2) the incantatory style of repetition and combining of scriptural phrases and words, and (3) the reliving of scriptural sagas (*scriptura rediviva*). Whereas Cope's study includes the years prior to the fourth quarter of the seventeenth century, my analysis of surviving sermons focuses on the years of the last three decades of the century. Both the blending of literalness and metaphor as well as *scriptura rediviva* thrive in the surviving sermons, while the incantatory style is very rare. Cope asserts that all three characteristics disappeared as the century neared its close. His documentation on the change of style is generally sparse and does not include mention of the surviving sermons. A close analysis of the extant sermons from 1671 to 1700 argues that Cope's findings must be adjusted. The blending of literalness and metaphor, as Cope describes it, was a theme in chapter 7. There I observe that one significant linguistic strength of the sermons lies in recurrent key metaphors that became analogs between Quaker conceptions of the spiritual and physical worlds. The light, for example, is an excellent instance of the phenomenon that occurs when "metaphor has transcended its normal function, and instead of merely indicating a point of resemblance between two differentiable entities, it has totally merged them."[4] Thus we have already seen that this aspect of Quaker style continues in the later sermons.

Scriptura rediviva is another of Cope's stylistic characteristics displayed in the sermons. The term relates to the reliving of scriptural times in current life. Similarly, we have seen this characteristic emerge as significant in the development of a Quaker theory of impromptu preaching, discussed in chapter 3. This stylistic choice is also implicit in many of the terms used throughout the sermons. Fox, especially, is fond of referring to Quakers as "Inward Jews," with the "inward Ark of the Covenant" and the "spiritual circumcision." These references show that the events and rites of biblical times are being reenacted in a spiritual, inward sense, by true believers. The expression of *scriptura rediviva* is also implicit in the pilgrimage or journey metaphor employed in the sermons and discussed in chapter 7. Cope maintains that after the third quarter of the seventeenth century, Quaker style developed a "self-conscious analogizing through Scripture imagery which sounds only a faint echo of the immediacy of the same phrases on the tongues of the early Publishers of Truth."[5] Yet the continuing popularity of the spiritual journey metaphor in the sermons, often drawn directly from the story of the trek from Egypt to the promised land, is evidence that *scriptura rediviva* had a robust presence in the sermon literature after it apparently waned in the written works (by Cope's reading). I would assert that Penn is not merely analogizing when he says, "It is the Desire of my Soul that you may all be a willing People in the Day of God's Power, and be pressing forward in the Ways of God, towards the Heavenly Canaan. And now that you are brought out of *Sodom* and *Egypt*, you may never hanker after it again, nor go from the narrow Way that leadeth unto Life Eternal."[6]

The "epistemology of verbal incantation," which Cope also calls the "incantatory" style, is not prevalent in the sermons, although one might expect this manifestation to continue in discourse expressly oral and impromptu in nature rather than planned for publication. I have found only eight instances of incantatory style in the sermons, and none match the extremity of expression found in Cope's examples. A quotation from a 1674 sermon by Fox provides the best sermonic instance of the phenomenon, complete with repetition and combining and recombining of scriptural and other phrases:

So now ffriends, all that are in ye Power, & ye Life Come to be heires
of Life, & of a world & kingdom, that hath noe end, so that you
may all keep ye Gospell order, for here comes up his Government,
in ye Heavenly Seed: that bruises ye head of ye serpent, that bruises
ye head of all evill Government: so Now here is ye Government
of ye blessed Righteous Seed, which is a mistery,: This is known
as every one hath Received Christ Jesus, so walk in him, there is ye
Gospell order, that is ye Power of God, which was before ye Devill
was, which brings Life, & Imortality to Light, ye Power of God,
ye Gospell: brings into Life, now in this Power, in this Gospell; is ye
order, ye everlasting order, of ye Gospell, which is a mistery.[7]

Bauman cites this passage from Fox and expertly reconstructs Fox's
words to better reveal "Fox's resort to parallelistic constructions and
to repetitions and recombinations of key words and phrases (power,
life, gospel, order, seed, government), all devices that enhance fluency
in spontaneous oral composition, as demonstrated in the research on
the formal devices that make possible the improvisational composition
of oral poetry in the act of performance, by contrast with the performance of ready-made (written or memorized) oral forms."[8]

Bauman's insightful interpretation is grounded in research that
assumes a previously performed narrative (perhaps dozens or even
hundreds of times) on which the performer can improvise. To the
extent that Fox's (or other preachers') sermons are built on previously performed narratives (in whole or in part), his interpretation
helps answer the question, How did they do it? On the other hand,
early Quaker homiletic theory would reject out of hand the idea of
intentionally using "devices" to generate content or to use previously
delivered content. However, Bauman convinces me that at least Fox is
employing devices that aid the preacher in the immediate impromptu
situation, but I would add that arguably he uses them unconsciously,
given the Quaker strictures about preplanned messages.[9]

The scarcity of the incantatory style in the sermons may be partially accounted for by the reaction among Quakers to the increase
in criticism leveled at enthusiasm and by the somewhat dampening
influence of men like Barclay and Penn, both educated intellectuals.
In addition, Quaker public discourse felt the conservative influence
of the Monday Morning Meeting with its suppression of Jeremiads.
However, my reading of the minutes of that body does not indicate
discussion of any of the sermons or sermon collections consulted in

this study. Regardless of the direct or indirect influence of the Monday Morning Meeting, there were sufficient voices outside that meeting to have a profound effect on style and delivery, and the incantatory style did eventually pass from the Quaker preaching scene in the third quarter of the seventeenth century, as Cope asserted. However, both the blending of literalness and metaphor and *scriptura rediviva* were perpetuated in Quaker sermons of the period.

Now I will turn to the stylistic form that I believe replaced verbal incantation. Examination of the sermons reveals an extraordinary reliance on the use of rhetorical questions. Sixty-four of the sermons use this rhetorical scheme, and most of them actually rely upon it as a key structural component.[10] In forty of the sermons, about half, the questions are put in dialogue form, thus heightening the dramatic impact of the discourse.[11] Eight of the sermons construct questions that are quite similar to the "queries," which later became an integral part of the Quaker discipline.[12] A selection of pertinent examples from the sermons will illustrate the catechital style's use of rhetorical questions, rhetorical questions in dialogues, and rhetorical questions as queries.

Fox often uses short rhetorical questions, either out of idiosyncratic habit or intentionally to add variety and dramatic contact and impact to his sermons. In 1674 he asserts, "God hath spoken to us by his Son: Is God speaking againe? yes, ye same God that was Speaker, in Paradise."[13] A year later, he incorporates longer questions as pointed applications of his theme to the audience: "Do not ye Oxe know his Owner, & ye Ass his Masters Crib? Thy Owner is he yt purchased thee, & bought thee: Dost thou know thy Owner? Dost thou know thy Crib?"[14] In 1678 he is even more direct: "Do you want Wisedom? Do you want Life? Do you want Salvation? from him you mu[s]t have it; So abide in him by belief in ye Eternal Light."[15]

Crisp relies upon the rhetorical question for his organizational structure in many sermons. Of his thirty-two sermons, thirty-one show extensive use of some form of rhetorical question. In a passage that argues against the proposition that the Scriptures are the *only* rule of faith, Crisp asks, "What is the Scripture the Rule of Faith? and may People believe what they find in Scripture? . . . and did Quakers, think you, never find in Scripture that People were to *wait for the Spirit* . . . and that all Religion that is not in Power, is not available, did they not find it in Scripture? And you that are not Quakers, Did you ever read the New Testament? How came it to pass that ye never found these

Texts?"[16] Here Crisp uses rhetorical questions in a confrontational, debate-like context, implying he is addressing a target audience of listeners who are not Friends who are visiting an important London Quaker meeting. A few months later, he once again chides his hearers in a passage that may also indicate he knew there were non-Quakers in the meeting: "How can a People come to the Knowledge of the Truth, without the *Spirit of Truth that reveals it*? Can any come to the Knowledge of Christ unless he that sent him reveals him? Where are People's Books? where are their Bibles? where is their Rule . . . that all their Endeavours for many Ages have proved fruitless in respect of the Knowledge of God?"[17]

The evidence of prolific use of rhetorical questions by other early Quaker preachers is weighty. A quotation from John Butcher is typical: "For what end hath God concluded all under Sin? For what end is it? That we might be destroyed? No, God through Christ . . . hath extended to you the Day of Visitation, that you might come to the knowledge of Life and Salvation: But wherein may we come to this Knowledge? It is in that way which God hath ordained, even by Christ. What is God's end in concluding all under Sin? was it that he might destroy all the Children of Men? No, but that he might have mercy upon all."[18] In the passage, we note the way rhetorical questions actually organize the impromptu rhetorical moment. Clearly, the use of rhetorical questions worked against and controlled the incantatory style. Arguably, rhetorical questions also worked as an important inventional tool in the impromptu situation. Once a Scripture had been placed under consideration in the sermonic moment—through the facility of the preacher's memory of Scripture as prompted by the Spirit (according to Bownas)—the preacher could move easily into a series of questions drawn directly from the words, phrases, tone, total meaning, etc., suggested by the passage or as suggested to the preacher out of sensitivity to audience needs.

The injunction to use plain language kept Quaker preachers from developing to any extent the more elegant, more sophisticated, and perhaps more eloquent figures of speech, but the novelty and directness of rhetorical questions more than compensated for the constraints of "plain language." Rhetorical questions also emphasized the Quaker view of communication because they had a real potential to stir responses in the minds of the listeners, thus placing the focus of the communication situation on the listener rather than the preacher, which is a natural bridge to discussion of the preachers' use of a second and different form of rhetorical question, the dialogue.

As previously noted, in forty of the sermons, about half, the rhetorical questions are presented in minidialogues, a stylistic choice that shifted the focus away from the mind of the listener to an imaginary drama created by the preacher. The sermon's dramatic impact was consequently heightened by the human drama inherent in the dialogue, and the preacher was able to present theological material in an audience-involving format. The dialogue form is well represented in Fox's sermon to a general meeting in 1680: "What saith Moses in the Old Testament? 'The priest's lips shall preserve the people's knowledge': Well said, Moses! What sayest thou in the New Covenant: 'I confess the law served till the seed came.' What seed is that? Christ is the seed of the woman, 'Christ the high priest, made higher than the heavens.'"[19] Here the listener is made to see Moses in dialogue with Fox, and, significantly, the patriarch is articulating the Quaker position that the seed is Christ.

Crisp is a master of the dialogue form among the preachers represented in the sermons. In 1688, he uses dialogue to underscore the difference between Quakers, Puritans, Baptists, and all those who believe that perfection is not possible in this life:

> Go to one place and another place, and ask them what is your way? Our way (say they) is the right way, the most sure and certain way that can be found for People to walk in: But wither will it lead me? It will lead to the Kingdom of God: That is it I would have; but will it lead me to Holiness? No, never in this World, you must never come to Holiness; do the best thou canst do here, it is but Sin. . . . Do you hold out that in your way? Yes; then I have done with that.[20]

During the last two decades of the century, the sermons mirror, or perhaps help lead, the development of a third form of rhetorical question, queries, as an aid to group reflection and discipline. None of Fox's sermons (1671–1681) show this ultimate evolution of the rhetorical question, but the changes begin to appear in Crisp's sermons. Queries reveal a dramatic evolution from traditional rhetorical questions in that they are never intended to be answered by the preacher. Nor are the questions answered by imaginary characters in a dramatic dialogue. Hearers answer the queries in their own minds. Queries work together with appeals for self-examination, which appear in twenty-seven sermons. The appeal for self-examination was well-established in the sermons before the advent of queries and continued throughout the years of this study. Crisp, for example, urges all to "examine their own Hearts, whether they have really received the Gospel."[21] The same appeal is employed by Bowater in 1693: "[L]et every one of you consider with your selves, how far you are broken off from your evil ways." Bowater notes that when the Lord did not seem present at the meetings, "we were willing to reflect upon our selves, and examine within our selves, what was the matter that the Fountain did not send forth its living streams."[22] Quaker preachers also link "waiting" on the Lord to the "experience" of his presence, and the injunction to "feel" his power to the process of self-examination. In the same sermon, Bowater asks, "[W]hat is it that your Souls do desire, you have presented your Bodies here at this time, what is it for? I would have every one of you to wait for your selves, you that have been acquainted with the manifestation of the Spirit, wait in it, feel your minds exercised towards God, wait at his Footstool."[23] The entreaties to wait, experience, and feel appear in fifty-one, thirty-four, and forty-six sermons, respectively.

Queries provide guidelines for the process of self-examination. The beginings of this important self-disciplinary form, as it appears in eight of the sermons, are clearly seen in a typical example from a 1688 sermon by Crisp: "[L]et your Minds be turned inward, search and consider, is there a Light enlightens every Man that comes into the World? Is there a Desire of Eternal Life manifested in me? Is there that in me that puts me upon Obedience to God, and to mend my Life and Conversation, that I might be recommended to God? Is there something in me that speaks to me when I speak amiss, and do amiss?"[24] Here we can sense a shift in the nature of the questions. Crisp responds to none of the queries. These questions put hearers on the spot. Only they as individuals can respond. Perhaps Crisp paused for a moment between each query to allow self-reflection. We do not know how he delivered this message, but we do know that four years later, Crisp has refined the query technique, making it slightly less direct, but still powerful and perhaps more generally applicable: "if Men would, but in every thing they do, answer the Principle of Truth in themselves, they would put the Question to themselves, Shall I take up my Daily Cross, or no? Shall I deny my self those Pleasures that my Conscience doth condemn; and those ungodly Gains that I seek after by Falsehood, by

Lying, Prevaricating and Departing from the Truth? Shall I do this, that I may be Rich and Great in the World, or shall I not?"[25]

Of the sermons represented in this study, Penn's sermons offer the most extensive and skillful use of the query-type rhetorical question. His use is direct and aimed precisely to aid the hearer in self-examination. He tells his listeners at Wheeler Street, "Consider, my Friends, where are your Hearts and Affections this Day? Do you love God above all? Do you love him with all your Hearts, with all your Souls, and with all your Strengths?"[26] Penn offers the best example of the use of queries in another sermon at Wheeler Street. In this passage, the queries constitute a spiritual inventory for his listeners, which is precisely the main function queries eventually came to serve: "[S]ee to it how the Work goes on, the Work of your Redemption and Salvation. Do you feel your selves near to the Lord? Do you find your selves to have more Power over your Souls; Do you know your selves advanced in the Work of God? Are ye come to Die daily to that which is contrary to the Lord?"[27]

We have seen that although the blending of literalness and metaphor, as well as the practice of *scriptura rediviva*, continued in the sermon literature from 1671 to 1700, the incantatory style waned. I call the style of Quaker sermons from 1671 to 1700 catechital because of their reliance upon variations of rhetorical questions. The preachers developed three varieties of forms: (1) the traditional rhetorical question directing the audience toward a specific answer, which the preachers would often provide; (2) the dialogue form, using an imaginary and dramatic question and answer situation; and (3) the query, by which the preachers hoped to stimulate the process of self-examination in their hearers' minds. The first two forms directed the minds of the listeners to specific answers, thus they were catechistic in purpose. The query, although on the surface open-ended in form, directly pointed the hearers to self-examination, which, if undertaken honestly, might lead to prescribed behavioral changes—for example, "repentance," renewal of the spiritual journey, closer adherence to the group's beliefs and behaviors, etc. The catechital style, especially in the form of the query, was better adapted to the more introspective trend of late seventeenth-century Quakerism. Through refinement of the rhetorical question, with the addition of dramatic dialogue and the inwardness and directness of the query, Quaker preachers were able to offset the loss of emotional immediacy resulting from the former incantatory style of the Jeremiads. The queries also allowed the preachers to rein-force group discipline in their sermons.

THE USE OF SPATIAL TERMS

Creasey argued, "On almost every page of the writings of early Friends the reader feels that he is being challenged to recognize a contrast. This contrast is expressed most frequently in spatial terms."[28] His observa-tion holds true for the surviving sermons from 1671 to 1700. Spatial terms appear in sixty-six of the sermons; "inward" and "outward," the terms specifically examined by Creasey in his article, also appear in sixty-six and sixty-three of the sermons, respectively. Although the widespread occurrence of spatial terms in the sermons corroborates Creasey's findings, the manner in which the terms are used neither negates nor substantiates his subsequent argument.

Let me briefly review Creasey's position on the use of "inward" and "outward." Creasey maintains that there are at least two uses of the terms in early Quaker literature. He reports a change in usage between the earliest Quakers, represented by Fox, and the Quakers who came later in the century, represented by Barclay and Penn. Fox uses spatial terms, according to Creasey, to indicate a difference between "on the one hand, a formal or conventional or notional knowledge of Christi-anity as a body of 'revealed truths' and religious and ethical practices and, on the other, a transforming and creative personal acquaintance with and relation to Christ in the Spirit."[29] What had before been only outward knowledge to Fox became inward spiritual experience. At the hands of Barclay and Penn, Creasey argues, "inward" and "outward" not only signified the difference between conventional and spiritual Christianity but "a contrast between two modes of revelation."[30] Creasey writes that with this usage of "inward" and "outward," "it is very difficult to accord any fundamental importance to History or to Scripture." Creasey skillfully illustrates his viewpoint from the apologetical writings of Barclay and Penn.[31] I agree substantially with Creasey's conclusions regarding the apologetical works of Barclay and Penn, but curiously, the usage he points to is not present in Barclay's or Penn's sermons. Whereas Creasey finds a "quasi-Cartesian dualism" between knowledge of the Spirit and the knowledge of history and Scripture, neither interacting with the other, in the apologetical writ-ings of Barclay and Penn, their sermons reveal a use of spatial terms that merely emphasizes the distinction between spiritual and notional Christianity.[32]

My reading of the use of spatial terms in the seventy-nine sermons studied here is that they conform to what Creasey describes as Fox's mode. Fox's use of spatial terms is typified in this passage from a 1678 sermon:

> As the Jews Outwardly were carried to Babilon & Egypt wn they Transgressed ye Outward Law; so plainly wn you Transgress ye New Covenant, & Law of Life wch ye Apostle saith ye Law of Life made me free from Sin & Death; so did not in ye Old Covenant; but ye Law of ye New Covenant this makes People Free: Therefore foreverie one to keep to Christ; & Receive this Law to make ym Gods Free-men, & Free-Women. In ye Old Covenant they had a Law to make People Free Outwardly; In ye New Covenant they have a Law to make free Inwardly, & Outwardly.[33]

To Fox, Old Testament rites, although historical, are mere outward shadows of the inward truth of Christ in the New Testament. Christ is not only the historical personage, however, but also the inward, spiritual truth. Fox observes, "The Jews . . . hung him Outwardly upon ye Tree who had been Inwardly slain from ye Foundation of ye World."[34] He thus incorporates both the historical and spiritual aspects of the death of Christ.

Other early Quaker preachers use the same essential meanings of "inward" and "outward" as does Fox. In a 1688 sermon, Crisp deals with the question of whether the Scripture ("outward evidence") or the indwelling Christ should take precedence, concluding, "The Outward Evidence will do you no good, *'till* you come to lay hold of the Inward Evidence in your own Hearts; *then* the Outward Evidence that God sends, will be serviceable to you."[35] Here Crisp presents two modes of knowing, one inward and the other outward, but the latter is not emasculated at the expense of the former. Crisp clearly opts for both the Christ of experience *and* the Christ of history. In another sermon, he advises his listeners, "be acquainted with the Works of the Lord, *both* inwardly and outwardly."[36] Crisp is really drawing the distinction between the religion of the Spirit, as opposed to that of the letter. A later sermon by Ashby contains this warning: "If any of us are satisfying our selves in sitting down in an Outward Gathering, and only exercising our natural faculties to hear and to understand, and come not to know and be acquainted in our selves, with the Inspiration of the Almighty, the word of Truth, we are Strangers to it." Ashby pleads with the people not to "rest satisfied in outward Form, and in an outward Profession."[37] This is a restatement of the early Quaker position that formal religion is insufficient to transform a life. The same year, Samuel Waldenfield decries the fact that "People have looked for Salvation outwardly many times more than Inwardly; Salvation is an inward Work upon their Souls, by the Spirit and Power of the Lord God."[38] Clearly, the attributes that Creasey discerns in Fox's meaning of the terms "inward" and "outward" characterize these passages. A distinction is being made, in each case, between conventional, lifeless, outward religion and the vital inward experience of the living Christ.

Examination of Barclay's use of spatial terms is hindered by the fact that only one of his sermons is extant, but it, too, shows a usage not even approaching Creasey's interpretation of Barclay's apologetical works. The sermon will be examined in more detail in chapter 11, but in this context let me observe that Barclay desires his hearers to "be Inwardly gathered into this Heavenly Life." After the sermon, Barclay prays in thanksgiving for "those precious Promises which thou hast left upon Record, and impressed upon our Minds and Hearts."[39] After this obvious reference to the Scripture "record," he expresses thanks that God had given an "inward sense of that pure Life of thy Dear Son whereby we may be enabled to live to thy Praise." The quasi-Cartesian dualism between the knowledge of the Spirit and the knowledge of history, between the body and the Spirit, neither interacting with the other, simply is not present in these passages. Barclay seems to say what Fox and others have said, that the only road to the religion of the Spirit is by the Spirit. Barclay, however, says nothing in the sermon that would directly contradict Creasey's position that Barclay wrote about two distinct revelations, that of the Spirit obviating that of the Scripture, in his apologetical works. The sermon is inconclusive evidence with regard to Barclay's use of spatial terms in his sermons.

Penn's sermons, on the other hand, are filled with statements that show the necessity of both the historical *and* the spiritual knowledge of Christianity. He maintains, "They only have the Benefit of what Christ hath done and suffered in his Outward Coming in the Flesh, that believe in him, and see the Necessity of his inward Appearance and Coming in the Spirit."[40] Here Penn does use "inward" and "outward" to refer to two kinds of knowledge, but he does not imply that the "inward appearance" makes the "outward appearance" unnecessary. Penn is, rather, reiterating Fox's position that "people read the Scriptures without a right sense of them, and without duly applying them to their own states."[41] Penn's statement refers as much to the difference between formalized Christianity and spiritual Christianity as it does to two modes of knowledge. The tenor of Penn's usage is clearly seen when we compare passages in his other sermons with the one already cited. In another sermon, Penn uses the phrase "inward freedom" (which Fox also employs in a 1678 sermon): "If thou art made free, thy Knowledge will be accompanied with experience, and not notions only; you want not notions, but Possession of Inward freedom and liberty."[42] Penn here articulates the original meaning of spatial terms: that notional Christianity is inadequate and that personal *experience* of the living God is a necessity. This interpretation infuses such statements as these: "Let us not be Outward but also Inward Christians"[43] and "the Knowledge you have in *Religion*, it must be *experimental*; for *historical* Knowledge only will not do."[44] Neither history nor Scripture is rejected or obviated, but Penn staunchly presents the necessity of going beyond mere historical or scriptural knowledge.

I argue, then, that the surviving sermons present a remarkably consistent usage pattern for spatial terms, the importance of which is plainly manifest in the sermons. The changes in usage that Creasey finds in the apologetical works of Barclay and Penn (works which, in both cases, preceded the dates of the sermons) do not appear in their sermons. Penn does assert that there are two modes of knowledge, Scripture and the Spirit, but I interpret this usage in his sermons to be a reflection of the principle stressed earlier by Fox, that scriptural or historical knowledge of Christ, per se, produces only an outward, notional Christianity; all true Christianity is produced by the work of the Spirit, which also inspired the Scriptures.

The fact that Creasey's findings are not entirely corroborated by an analysis of the sermons may be a result of the small number of sermons that actually survive out of the thousands that were preached. This explanation is especially relevant to Barclay. From Penn, however, eleven sermons survive, none of which obviates Scripture or history as a part of true Christianity. Again, this phenomenon may be due to the relatively small number of extant sermons, but it is more likely a result of the fact that Penn probably did not find it necessary or useful to reveal the totality of his philosophical underpinings in his sermons.

Whatever the case, Penn neither expresses nor implies in his sermons the "embarrassment" at "the Word's becoming flesh" that Creasey found in Penn's apologetics.[45]

THE ASSAULT ON GUILT

Barbour argues that the method of the Quaker preacher prior to 1660 was to mount "a massive assault on any point of guilt in his hearers."[46] This assertion is difficult to establish for the early period of Quaker preaching because only one sermon text survives prior to 1671, and this sermon is not based upon a guilt appeal.[47] However, through a close analysis of other documents of the period, such as reports of preaching in journals, tracts, and meeting reports, Barbour concludes that the primary appeal of early Quaker preachers is on the basis of the hearer's guilt. The seventy-nine sermons examined here, while reflecting the preaching of a later period, arguably one with more interest in maintaining or "preserving" the group order and discipline, also reveal some reliance upon the guilt appeal. In the later sermons, however, the guilt appeal is tempered with an appeal that also stresses God's love and forgiveness.

Forty-three of the sermons deal with God's judgment. The guilt appeal is inextricably connected with the judgment, because judgment implies guilt. On the other hand, love, which implies forgiveness and mercy, infuses the sermons in approximately equal proportions to judgment. I canot characterize the sermons of the post-1670s as reflecting a "massive assault" on guilt.

The causes of this change of tone in the sermons are problematic but perhaps lie in three possible areas. First, we have observed in chapter 2 that the Quaker outlook on society changed from that captured in the image of the Lamb's War—the powerful, overcoming army of the Lamb, which would change society—to that of the remnant, which would be preserved from the evils of the society. The first image calls forth God's righteous judgment; the second image sees God's judgment in perspective with his mercy and preserving love. Second, the sermons of this study were delivered to primarily Quaker gatherings, whereas many of the incidents reported in the early record of the "first publishers of truth" involve evangelistic forays into alien territory.[48] Fully thirty-six of the sermons in this study are primarily intended for the edification of Quaker congregations, while forty-three of the sermons suggest from textual evidence that an audience of both Quakers and non-Quakers is present. None of the sermons studied is intended solely for non-Quakers. These figures do not imply that a guilt appeal was not used for in-group discourse, but they do suggest a reason for the tempering of the appeal to guilt; by and large, those already convinced of the truth of Quaker beliefs presumably needed less direct confrontation with their guilt than did ardent non-Quakers. For the early Quaker, self-examination would reveal guilt apart from the effort of the preacher. The appeal to self-examination is not an "assault on guilt" because whatever guilt results from self-examination is presumably Spirit-induced or self-produced. Third, the emphasis upon judgment and guilt does not present a total picture of God's dealings with humans. The other half of the Quaker message is that guilt can be remedied through Christ; for the believer, God's judgment of sinners is avoided because of Christ's substitutionary atonement. I conclude that the sermons of this study present a better, more mature, and seasoned balance of Quaker belief than do early Quaker writings.

Regardless of the apparent decreased emphasis on guilt appeals in the later sermons, the following examples show that the guilt appeal is, indeed, a salient factor in the sermons, although tempered by positive statements regarding God's love and mercy.

At a men's meeting on Barbados, Fox finds it necessary to threaten God's judgment on those who would not educate their families and slaves in Christian morality: "[L]et not your Families of Whites, & Blacks be like Sodom, & Gomorah . . . lest sudden destruction come upon you, & ye Lord root you out as he did ym."[49] Crisp also alludes to impending death and judgment when he says, "if the Lord should call you this Night to give up your Account, the Lord hath a great deal against you, I am sure."[50] The idea that no evil can be hidden from God is attested to by Bowater, who affirms, "there may be something . . . that doth in secret remain, and though they may seek to hide it from Men in their Profession, yet God will find them out."[51] Even Penn relies on the guilt appeal when he warns, "You must be turned from Sin, or Sin will turn you into Hell."[52]

THE USE OF PERSONAL TESTIMONY

Early Quaker preachers knew the strength of persuasion based on high moral character.[53] At significant moments in their sermons, they discuss experiences that have actually occurred in their own lives and relate them to more abstract theological principles, a rhetorical choice that Bownas later found so effective in his *Qualifications*. It is not surprising, then, that twenty-three of the sermons reveal the speakers relating testimonies of events and changes in their lives. The personal accounts emphasize the high character and competence of the speakers to speak on their topics, but also help establish rapport with their audiences through personal dramatic appeal.

Fox uses the appeal of his personal character to good advantage in 1680 when he addresses a meeting at Wheeler Street. He speaks as the acknowledged leader of the movement, which by then had weathered years of significant persecution. His audience is aware of his personal sacrifices for the Quaker cause. Speaking of the coming new covenant in Christ, as previously quoted in chapter 6, Fox affirms, "[S]ince I came abroad to declare the everlasting truth, I have been a sufferer very much, by times, above these thirty years, in gaols, and prisons. And my body hath been spoiled for the testimony of Jesus. So that I am not able to travel as I have done. And it was hard for me to come this journey: but I was moved of the Lord to come."[54] After this statement, a hearer would have difficulty pressing the charge that Fox was insincere in his beliefs.

At times, the personal testimonies read like pages from a seventeenth-century spiritual journal in which the preacher is as much rehearsing a spiritual autobiography as identifying with the struggles of the hearers. Crisp offers an excellent example:

> [I]n my younger Years, I have Fasted, and Prayed, and spent time in Hearing, Reading, and Meditation, and did all in my own Power, and all to mend my State, but I could not mend it, and as I grew up in Years, Sin and Corruption more prevailed, and there was no help, and I came so far as to believe there was no help, and that if God did not help me, I was undone to all Eternity: I many times wish'd that I had never been born; I went to Ministers and Meetings, and to all sorts of separate People, and to all manner of Ordinances, and to all manner of Means, to mend this bad Heart of Mine. . . . but my Arm was never so long as to reach thereunto, it was far out of my Power and Reach.[55]

Thomas Chalkley, a young preacher on a visit to North America from England, feels the need to defend his knowledge of spiritual matters in this statement: "some persons may say . . . but how doth thou know these things, for thou art but a Youth, I speak nothing Friends, but what I have Experienced. I have felt the word of God enter into my Soul, & . . . I have known what it is, to be born again."[56]

Park also defends himself with a statement of personal conviction in a 1694 sermon, making it clear that belief in the Inward Light does not obviate his personal belief in the historical Jesus: "I never did desire to hear any thing, or speak any thing, that had the least tendency to undervalue the Death, Sufferings, Satisfaction, Mediation, and Intercession of our Lord Jesus Christ; but have always Owned, Believed, and Preached these great Truths."[57]

Even though seventeenth-century Quakers produced a "unified rhetoric of symbolic action"[58] with high ethical standards of life underlining their discourse, they still found it necessary in a number of sermons to make explicit their appeal to personal ethical character.

CONCLUSION

Quaker sermons of the last three decades of the seventeenth century exhibit characteristics that identify them with both an earlier period of Quaker rhetoric as well as a later period. The continued blending of literalness and metaphor, the reference to *scriptura rediviva*, and the appeal to guilt in the sermons provide a link with the earliest Quakers. Conversely, the disappearance of the incantatory style, the increased use of God's love and mercy as an appeal, and the growth of the catechital style, with its use of rhetorical questions, dialogue, and queries, identify the sermons with a later age of Quakerism that was reacting to the attack on enthusiasm and moving toward a period of more introspective quietism. The continued use of spatial terms is an additional sign of continuity in Quaker discourse patterns because it shows a continued emphasis on the spiritual versus the notional approach toward Christianity.

The evidence derived from the sermons delivered from 1671 to 1700 indicates a possible dichotomy between Penn's beliefs that Creasey sees expressed in his apologetical works and those we have seen expressed in his surviving sermons. Penn's sermons show no derogation of the biblical historical record. Generally, the sermons from 1671 to 1700 are transitory. They bridge the gap between the first and third generations of Quakers. One rhetorical constituent that holds fairly constant from the days of Fox through the bulk of the sermons is the explicit use of ethical appeal. Preachers seem more than willing to place their personal experiences and character before their hearers for purposes of defense or as evidence of the Inward Light working in their own lives.

In previous chapters, I identified and illustrated the important themes of Quaker sermons and identified and analyzed their key metaphors and how they functioned as conceptual tools. In this chapter, I identified four additional characteristics of the sermons: (1) the catechital style, (2) the use of spatial terms, (3) the guilt appeal tempered with love, and (4) the use of personal testimony. One might say that in these three chapters, we have looked at the practice of impromptu preaching through the vista provided by a wide-angle lens. Now it is time to take advantage of the detailed view afforded only by a close-up lens. In the next four chapters, I will focus on four select sermons delivered by four very significant early Quaker preachers. I will unpack each sermon rhetorically within the context of its presentation.

SECTION IV

A Closer Look at Four Select Quaker Sermons
from the Period 1671 to 1700

CHAPTER 9

GEORGE FOX FACES THE YEARLY MEETING IN 1674

THE CHALLENGE OF LEGITIMACY IN A CULTURE THAT VALUES IMPROMPTU, INSPIRED DISCOURSE

George Fox (1624–1691), the itinerant firebrand preacher, is acknowledged by historians to be the founder of Quakerism. The vantage of subsequent history and the perseverance of Quakers as a religious and social influence attest to Fox's legacy of more than three hundred years, but it was not Fox's preaching alone, or even that of his contemporaries, that made Quakerism one of the fastest-growing movements in the mid-seventeenth century. Historians also note that Fox's organizational skills helped Quakerism survive and flourish.[1] Quakerism appeared in the mid-1650s and flourished during the Interregnum, but with the restoration of the monarchy under King Charles II, Quakers experienced waves of persecution, which continued until the Act of Toleration in 1689. During this crucial period, most early Quaker leaders, both men and women, including Fox and his spouse, Margaret Fell Fox, spent considerable time in appalling English "gaols" and prisons. In the 1660s and 1670s, Quakers faced a crisis that demanded they accomplish at least two goals: (1) they had to organize themselves so that their work could carry on even in the face of continued persecution and imprisonment, and so that aberrant behaviors by individual Quakers, behaviors that had provoked persecution, might be reined in; and (2) they had to prove to the English people, particularly to the authorities, that they were peaceful folk who did not seek to overthrow the Crown. As an organization, their situation had become perilous principally because of the radical Quaker belief, based on a strict interpretation of Jesus' teachings, that they should never take an oath under any circumstances. An oath simply indicated to Quakers that a person might be lying when not under oath, and Quakers believed in telling the truth at all times. In fact, Quaker refusal to "swear an oath" to the King during judicial proceedings had become the most common way to imprison Friends and thus curb their growth and influence.

This chapter focuses on a sermon Fox delivered in London in 1674, fifteen years before the Act of Toleration, a very crucial time during the Quaker struggle for both organization and public image. Fox, clearly the most important Quaker in the world at that moment, delivered the impromptu address at a significant event known by Friends as a Yearly Meeting. In the sermon, Fox enacts the Quaker impromptu preaching style as described in previous chapters: speaking under the assumed or claimed direct inspiration of the Spirit, presumably unaided by preparation, manuscript, or notes. In Fox's case, we must add that he was aided by his prodigious memory of Scripture passages and buttressed by years of theological debate and previous impromptu preaching in all sorts of settings, some antagonistic, some friendly.

In this chapter, I will first consider the context of the sermon event, including the political situation, the organizational development of Friends to that point in time, and Fox's pertinent biographical circumstances immediately preceding the sermon. Then I will turn to a consideration of the sermon itself seen against the context already set out. The analysis will concentrate on three interrelated features of this complex sermon: (1) Fox's elaboration and application of the "creation-fall-restoration" theme, (2) his treatment of the relationship of "Gospel order" and gender, and (3) his use of the incantatory style. Finally, I will draw some evaluative conclusions about Fox's "performance" within the constraints of the impromptu Quaker sermon tradition.

THE CONTEXT

Context of the Sermon. As already mentioned, Fox's sermon was delivered in the middle of a very turbulent period of English history. With the passing of Oliver Cromwell, and the eventual restoration of the monarchy, the relative freedom of expression for Friends during the Interregnum changed dramatically. The Church of England, once again in the seat of power, was anxious to bring the kingdom back to Anglican conformity. Persecution of Dissenters during the years between the Restoration and the Act of Toleration in 1689 is a well-known matter of historical record and has already been alluded to numerous times. Quakers suffered under the Quaker Act, and the application of praemunire, as described in chapter 1. Persecution, then, is the larger scenic backdrop for Fox's 1674 sermon.

Richard T. Vann notes, "One of the first effects of persecution was the breakdown of the network of traveling ministers, most of whom were confined to prison for considerable periods."[2] Understandably, with many leaders in prison and Friends meetings experiencing waves of disruption, Fox saw that a system of organization would greatly aid Friends during uncertain times. Quaker historian Walter R. Williams writes that in 1666, after three years of imprisonment in Lancaster and Scarborough Castles, Fox, still enduring physical suffering from his confinement, "began the arduous task of nearly four years' duration, of building the widely scattered Friends meetings into a compact body, with suitable rules of procedure in business meetings as well as worship services."[3] Vann describes the types of meetings that were set up to govern Friends: "The most influential was the Meeting for Sufferings, in London, with its network of correspondents in every county to mobilize the whole resources of the group against persecution. Similarly, the [Second Day's or Monday] morning meeting of ministers in London kept a vigilant eye on the morals and doctrine of traveling ministers—and of their books [their writings]. The great annual forum for Friends was the London Yearly Meeting, assembling every Whitsuntide, from which the common concerns of the society emerged."[4]

One of Fox's goals during 1667 and 1668 was to set up local business meetings, "Monthly Meetings" that would parallel the structure of local meetings for worship and also maintain correspondence with the central meetings in London. Vann notes, "All of these meetings, it must be emphasized, were meetings for worship."[5] Thus the "meeting for worship," at which a gathered group fell silent and waited for the Spirit to "move" on individuals to speak, continued to be the standard mode of Friends meeting practice throughout this period of persecution and throughout the period during which Fox strove for organization.

In 1669 Fox married Margaret Fell, who figured prominently in chapter 3, whose important 1666 tract, *Women's Speaking*, asserted, "if the seed of the woman speak not, the seed of the serpent speaks,"[6] thus anticipating some of the language later seen in Fox's sermon, although Fox's *Journal* has him using the image of "Christ, the Word of God, that bruised the head of the Serpent the destroyer" as early as 1647.[7] The interlacing of influence, both conceptual and linguistic, between Fox and Fell is an interesting topic, which this chapter must leave unexplored.[8] However, it is remarkable that in the same year Fell's famous tract was first published (1666), Fox sent an epistle to

all Quaker meetings urging them to establish separate business meetings for women operating in a parallel fashion to business meetings for
men. Fox's most recent scholarly biographer, Larry H. Ingle, carefully
details Fox's growing commitment to separate-gender business meetings throughout the 1660s and into the 1670s.[9] To the casual twentieth-
century observer, the establishment of separate-gender meetings may
seem to be a reflection of gender bias favoring men. In fact, the opposite is true. Russell states the rationale for separate meetings succinctly:
"Before this, women had participated in the existing business meetings
to some extent. Fox realized that lack of experience in public affairs
and modesty alike would prevent the adequate participation of the
women in the Society [of Friends]; and so he violated logical consistency in deference to actualities."[10]

In 1671 Fox had recovered sufficiently from the effects of incar-
ceration that he decided to travel to the West Indies and America,
where he ministered until June 1673, the month when he arrived back
at Bristol.[11] During Fox's absence from England, opposition to the proposed separate-gender meetings for business steadily grew, especially in
Bristol, where an attempt to establish a women's meeting was quashed.
In the Bristol controversy, William Rogers, who, according to Ingle,
"would eventually become the main anti-Fox writer within the Society
of Friends,"[12] led the opposition to separate-gender business meetings.

Meanwhile, back on Barbados at the begining of his journey, Fox
made an announcement in 1671 that any Quaker couple who sought
marriage had to have their plans "examined twice by both men's and
women's meetings, appearing first before the women."[13] Ingle suggests
that Fox strategically delivered this radical news from the relative safety
of a faraway locale, leaving those who remained in England to deal
with the controversy it would inevitably provoke.[14] Whether or not
that was Fox's strategy, upon his return, he faced his opposition twenty
miles outside of Bristol, where a Wiltshireman, Nathaniel Coleman,
"pointed out that the apostle Paul had forbidden women to speak in
church, stressed that women's meetings would lessen the authority of
male elders, and, more basically, insisted that God commanded men to
rule their wives."[15] These key recurrent gender issues became central
to Fox's subsequent public letters and sermons, especially the sermon
delivered at the Yearly Meeting in 1674.

Approximately six months after his return to England, "the notorious George Fox" was arrested and held in jail nearby the Severn

River until his court hearing, at which he was immediately faced with taking the oath of supremacy before a magistrate, which, of course, he refused. Not swearing, as noted earlier, could result not only in continued imprisonment but also in praemunire. Ingle details the interesting, complex, and daunting legal proceedings that Fox underwent over the next fourteen months, after which he was at last released in February 1675.[16] Twice during this period of imprisonment, Fox was released for brief periods on writs of habeas corpus and on both occasions traveled to London to attend to business. On one of those occasions, he addressed the Yearly Meeting with the impromptu sermon that concerns this chapter.

Significant to understanding the context of Fox's 1674 sermon, it is important to note that Fox's physical condition was at a low point. He was already weakened from previous incarcerations and by two long sea journeys that flanked his travels by horseback and foot in America. Ingle writes that "Fox fell ill, for a time becoming so weak he could hardly utter a word and needed air in his closed dungeon."[17] It is impossible for me to describe precisely Fox's physical state at the time he delivered his 1674 sermon, but at the very least, evidence points to a lack of stamina occasioned by continued imprisonment and general physical stress.

When Fox stood to face the Yearly Meeting in 1674, as in all early Quaker meetings, he spoke in a rhetorical situation described in previous chapters, in which any man or woman would have the freedom to speak out in the silence if they believed they were moved to speak by the Inward Light of Christ. As noted above, in practice, there was little if any distinction between meetings for worship and business. Meetings for business always began with silent worship.[18] Any spoken word, as Barclay noted in 1678, "proceedeth from the Spirit of God, and is always accompanied by its influence, being begun by its motion, and carried on by the power and strength thereof."[19] Specifically, when Fox stood to his feet in the meeting, his hearers would be expecting him to speak according to the Quaker mode of impromptu address set out in previous chapters. On that occasion, Fox, as the acknowledged leader of Friends, needed to be plausibly interpreted as an "oracle" of God, motivated by the immediate leading of the Spirit, speaking in an unrehearsed and totally unprepared manner a message composed of language that was chosen at the moment of utterance, not employing frivolous or ostentatious stylistic decoration chosen merely to impress the hearers by calling attention to itself. As at all Quaker meetings for worship, the sermon might take the form of commentary on or application of Scripture, exhortation, advice, instruction, or testimony based on personal spiritual experience. Henry J. Cadbury, writing with reference to Fox's speaking habits later in life, observes that "there is no mention I believe of his having remained silent throughout [the meeting], though he usually spoke only after others had done so, and the meeting closed after he was through. His addresses were long and *extempore* ("impromptu," by my usage). They were often followed by prayer and brief exhortation."[20] Assuming Cadbury's observations apply to Fox's 1674 address, Fox's long impromptu sermon came after a period of waiting and anticipation over what the leader would say, probably at the conclusion of the meeting, and his final words would ring in his listener's ears as they left the meeting.

With this contextual frame in place, I will now turn to an examination of two significant aspects of the 1674 sermon.

CREATION-FALL-RESTORATION

Fox frames the sermon with no hint of the controversy over separate-gender meetings. Instead, he weaves together images drawn from one of his favorite conceptual metaphors and theological frameworks, the creation-fall-restoration sequence. In fact, this cluster of terms represents *the* conceptual underpining of the sermon. Using this theologically rich conceptual pattern in the sermon, Fox tells his hearers that "the Lord alone was the teacher in paradise" and that as long as Adam and Eve—the original humans—"kept under his [the Lord's] teaching," they fared well "in a blessed state." However, when they "hearkened to the false teacher" and "he came to be teacher to Eve and she became teacher to her husband," Adam and Eve "came to be at a loss, and into the fall."[21] Fox's use of this sequential image pattern, frequently employing variations of the very phraseology quoted above, appears repeatedly throughout the 1674 sermon and informs it even when not linguistically present in a given paragraph of the sermon text. It is also important to note that by distinguishing between false and true teachers, he may be insinuating that those who oppose the separate-gender meetings are false and deceptive teachers, sons of the Genesis serpent.

My study of early Quaker sermons indicates that Fox is somewhat unusual among the preachers represented in the seventy-nine surviving early Quaker sermons. At the very least, his considerable reliance on language and word images drawn from the creation-fall-restoration conceptual pattern sets Fox's sermons apart from the others.[22] He drew the terms in this clustered language pattern directly from the Genesis account of the fall, terms and phrases that include "serpent," "Eve," "Adam," "Second Adam," "enmity," "bruise the head," "bruise his heel," "Paradise," and "seed." Fox had been mulling about the catastrophic fall from paradise well before he rose to speak at the 1674 Yearly Meeting. We are here reminded of a familiar passage from the first part of his *Journal*, partially quoted at the end of chapter 2, but quoted in full here, in which he relates a dramatic vision from his youth:

> Now was I come up in spirit through flaming sword into the paradise of God. All things were new, and all the creation gave another smell unto me than before, beyond what words can utter. I knew nothing but pureness, and innocency, and righteousness, being renewed up into the image of God by Christ Jesus, so that I say I was come up to the state of Adam which he was in before he fell. . . . I was immediately taken up in spirit, to see into another or more steadfast state than Adam's in innocency, even into a state in Christ Jesus, that should never fall. And the Lord showed me that such as were faithful to him in the power and light of Christ, should come up into that state in which Adam was before he fell, in which the admirable works of the creation, and the virtues thereof, may be known, through the openings of that divine Word of wisdom and power by which they were made.[23]

The full implications of the Genesis passage took years to ripen in Fox's mind, but three years before the London sermon, he uses the creation-fall-restoration pattern when he addresses a women's meeting on the island of Barbados:

> Friends, in the begining of the creation of God, when God had made all things, he made man and woman, male and female, and created he them in his image and likeness, and set them in dominion above all the works of his hands; and so made the male and female helps meet. The woman was a help meet, a companion, an equal in the holy image of God for the man; a meet help in righteousness and holiness, and to the truth and power of the Lord God; in which they had dominion over all that God made, she was a meet help. There was a service before the fall, but after the fall all was quite out of order. But now in the restoration by Christ the second Adam, the

heavenly man, he renews man and woman, male and female again, and brings them up into God again to be like Him, and redeems them up into God's image that in the fall they lost.[24]

In 1673, upon his return from the West Indies and America, Fox preached in a meeting at Bristol, where he further develops the creation-fall-restoration theme using these words: "They that come to be renewed up again into the divine, heavenly image, in which man was at first made, will know the same God, that was the first teacher of Adam and Eve in Paradise, to speak to them now by his son who changes not." Remarking on that occasion, Fox writes, "Many deep and precious things were opened in those meetings."[25]

In the 1674 sermon at Yearly Meeting, as in the previous two sermons mentioned above, the three terms of the sequence—creation, fall, and restoration—represent three periods or "states" of history: "God was the first teacher in paradise. They that are taught by Him are happy. The serpent was the second teacher. By hearkening unto him, man and woman's unhappiness came. Christ is the third, that bruises the head of all false teachers. So now coming to the head again, the satisfaction of their souls, who is their life, so then they know Him to be a Bishop in his office to rule in their hearts by faith." Under the terms of this tripartite historical sequence, "every man and woman must come to the begining again, God almighty their speaker."[26] Fox links the idea of listening to the first speaker or teacher with a delineation of some of the benefits of this attentive listening. Whereas "professors" (those who "profess" to be Christians, particularly Puritans) "feed on the rudiments of death in the fall," the person who "lives under God's teaching, lives on God's bread." Here we observe the linking of the voice and hunger-thirst metaphor clusters. Using the catechital style, Fox asks his hearers, "Have you heard the serpent?" He responds to his own question, referring to those who listen to the serpent: "They feed on that which he gave, which is dust."[27] Here again Fox directly links the hunger-thirst metaphor with the images of fall and restoration. Hearing the first speaker is identified with eating nourishing food, whereas listening to the serpent results in eating dust in his metaphorical universe where *scriptura rediviva* is common.

Fox then sketches out what is implied by "hearing" or "feeding on" the first speaker or teacher. Once again using the powerful catechital style, Fox asks, "Is God speaking again?" He answers, "Yes, the same God that was speaker in paradise."[28] As we have observed, Quakers taught that the Inward Light of Christ illuminates all people, not just the elect or a select historical few. In the 1674 sermon, Fox moves assuredly into this highly controversial theological territory so hotly disputed by early Quakers and their antagonists. After all, the argument went, if ordinary persons could be in direct contact with the first speaker and feed directly on the bread of life, what was the need of the Bible or, for that matter, preaching? Fox eventually deals with each of these topics directly in the sermon. But first, Fox must reaffirm the concept of the Light of Christ: "The great controversy hath been about the Light, amongst the priests and professors. The great controversy was in Christ's time, about his flesh. 'Is this the Christ the carpenter's son?' etc. The great controversy now is about the Light that is his life." He continues, "You talk of a light. In Him was life, by whom the world was made, and this Light was the life of men." Then he concludes, "There is no man grafted into Christ Jesus but by belief, signified by belief in the Light, in the heart, to the grafted in him, in the life, that is Christ who is Light in you."[29] Here Fox mixes metaphors of light and husbandry or horticulture in a passage on the threshold of incantatory style.

At this point in the sermon, Fox expands the idea of being "grafted" into the "Light" and "Life" of Christ and argues that this process will result in a pure and righteous life, a notion of "perfection" captured earlier in the report of his own experience of going back "through the flaming sword" quoted from his *Journal*: "I knew nothing but pureness, and innocency, and righteousness, being renewed up into the image of God by Christ Jesus, so that I say I was come up to the state of Adam which he was in before he fell." In the sermon, Fox goes on to state,

> He that believes in the Light (which is the life in Christ) is born of God and overcomes the world and believes in him that bruises the serpent's head, that led man into the fall. . . . And so Friends, all that are in the power are in the life—the faith that doth purify—you see the world hath a faith, and they have a belief, but there is no victory (Cry they). So no faith. He that bruises the head of the serpent is the Author of the faith, and every man and woman is to come and look to the Author and finisher of that faith (Christ Jesus) that purifies the heart.[30]

Gwyn observes, "Perfection became one of the most controversial issues of early Quakerism."[31] Gwyn's analysis of Fox's view of perfection begins, appropriately, with an exposition of the three sets of speakers or teachers that we discover in the 1674 sermon, and includes the following summary interpretation that I find to be in total agreement with Fox's position expressed in the sermon: "Christ's salvation is more than a return to Adam's state before the Fall. It establishes believers in 'heavenly places'—a fulfillment which overcomes the ethical separation between God and people. It establishes believers *together* in a way less prone to fall as Adam did."[32]

Fox differs from reformed thinkers who believed that full restoration would not be achieved until the return of Christ and the end of the age. In the sermon, Fox replaces the reformed sequence of creation-fall-redemption with "creation-fall-restoration," which is more than a linguistic change. The choice of "restoration" not only allows the possibility of immediate perfection but also has significant implications on the full restoration of women as equals of men, a significant theme of the sermon discussed later in this chapter.

This description of the creation-fall-restoration cluster in Fox's 1674 sermon has suggested its significance in any attempt to understand Fox's overall theological framework.[33] It stands as one of his most characteristic modes of expression. Actually, when Fox sought to articulate the paradigmatic narrative regarding the meaning of human existence in the most profoundly moving passages of his rhetoric, he chose to rehearse the drama in terms of the creation-fall-restoration sequence. Fox's use of this sequence stressed a cosmic process, a dynamic pattern in which good and evil were polarized in metaphor: "Old Adam" versus the "Second Adam," the "serpent" versus "Christ the seed," "fall" versus "restoration," "chaos" versus "order," "under" and "down" versus "over" and "atop." In this vision, a hearer was positioned between one pole and another. Fox's metaphors conceptualized no neutral ground. Restoration in the order of Second Adam was immediate as well as ultimate, a change in direction with positive results stretching to infinity. The "restored" prefall state was seen as attainable by all persons. Fox's mystical experience of going back through Eden's "flaming sword" more than hinted that men and women live to be restored, to inhabit the creation, now perfected and wise through the work of Second Adam. His personal mystical experience clearly influenced his linguistic choices.

Numerous conclusions can be drawn about Fox's use of the creation-fall-restoration sequence. The most obvious and important is

that Fox jumps into the concept of restoration to the original creation
rather than into the concept of redemption. However, as we have seen
in earlier chapters, the redemption from sins through Christ remained
a necessity within early Quaker theology. In sum, we can say that at
least in Fox's 1674 and other sermons, it was *restoration*, a step beyond
redemption, that he emphasizes.

Let me close this section with this observation: inherent in the
word "fall" is the orientational metaphor in which upward direction
is associated with good and downward with evil.[34] The pattern is very
deep in the linguistic structure of many cultures, especially those that
employ English, but Fox made this conceptual metaphor particularly
significant in this sermon (as well as his other writing and sermons).
Arguably, the fall was perforce downward, and it demanded, in Fox's
words, the "restoration by Christ . . . [who] brings them *up* into God
again . . . and redeems them *up* into God's image," a phrase Fox had
used three years earlier in Barbados.[35] A collage of quotations from
the 1674 and other sermons offers plentiful examples of Fox's preference for up versus down orientational language: "they come *up* in
purity," "religion from *above*," "a power *higher* than the devil," "come
up to the state before the *fall*," "so here is the *top*, and Christ set *above*
all," "feel Him in all who is *over* all," "*plunged* into the death of Adam,"
"go *down* into the pit," "the rock *over* all other foundations," "God hath
the glory who is *over* all," "Ye shall be as Gods, *high, up higher*," "*a-top*
of the serpent's head," "renews *up* into the heavenly image," "come
up to the seed that is blessed," "a *high* priest made *higher* than the heavens," "Jerusalem from *below* and Jerusalem *above*," "*plunges* down the
foul spirit," "look *up* and have the wine of the kingdom," "all looking
upwards and not *downwards* as the ox or cow, to the earth; for those that
look *downwards* look for their bread in the house of old Adam," "in the
truth, *above* the Devil," "[in the fall] death is *uppermost*, death is *on top*,"
"men and women are *under* the death," "sink *down*, keep *low* . . . that all
the faithful may be gathered *up* to God," and so forth.[36]

It is also important to note that not only is Fox establishing an
important Quaker understanding of an apocalyptic theology realized
in the present tense through the creation-fall-restoration sequence, he
is also implicitly claiming "perfection" for himself as he speaks. This
move simply builds his legitimacy with perhaps most of his immediate
hearers. There is no hint of modesty, acknowledgment of personal
sin, or even expression of self-doubt anywhere in the sermon. Also, as

noted in earlier chapters, his impromptu words make an implicit claim
to inspiration.

Having affirmed the promise of restoration through the Second
Adam (Christ), having argued for the possibility of direct Edenic
communication with God (the first speaker), and having planted the
hope of purity and righteousness (perfection) in the present tense, Fox
now turns to the implications regarding the place of Scripture in this
theological schema. Fox takes up this important challenge with these
words: "The Jews professed the scriptures, as the false Christians since
the days of the Apostles do. Here comes two or three witness[es] here.
Didst thou never see Him, hear Him, or handle Him, or touch Him?
How should they that deny the Spirit and power the Apostles were in
be true witnesses? . . . The true witnesses have heard him with their
ears and seen him, and they say God hath spoken unto us by his Son,
hear him that spoke in paradise."[37] Here is an affirmation that experiential, even mystical, religious experience is to be preferred to mere
reverence for or rational understanding of the Scriptures. Although
Fox does not develop the point in this particular sermon, we have seen
in earlier chapters that he did hold the Scriptures in high esteem, but
placed them below the Spirit in the hierarchy of significance. On this
topic, Gwyn writes, "Fox denied the scripture to be the *Word* of God
and touchstone of doctrine, but instead affirmed it to be the *words*
which God inspired the prophets and apostles to write, the *record* of the
Word's dealings in the world."[38]

Regarding the question as to what place preaching might assume
in a system that claims direct access to the first teacher, Fox has this
to say: "The Apostles['] . . . preaching was to bring people to Christ's
teaching: from the false teachers to the true teacher, to God again. So
every one come to be taught of the Lord Jesus Christ, so heirs of Him,
heirs of Life." This is a restatement of Fox's first habitual topic of
preaching, discussed in chapter 3. Toward the end of the sermon, Fox
makes the initial implication even more clear: "The false teachers cry:
'Means, means, ordinances!' God commands thee to hear his son. . . .
Hear the son, the true teacher and feeder that gives life."[39]

GOSPEL ORDER AND GENDER

If the plenteous use of the creation-fall-restoration sequence, with all
its implications, is the skeletal structure of Fox's 1674 sermon, then
the "muscle and sinew" of the sermon is Fox's teaching about "gospel

order."[40] We are reminded that the immediate problem facing Fox in 1674 is the strong negative reaction by some Quakers to his urging to organize separate men's and women's business meetings throughout Quakerdom. There are high stakes in this game. Gwyn reminds us, "The evident hardening of the [political] powers into a new structure of alienated arrangements, the decimation of the ranks of early Quaker prophets through persecution and the need to institute a corporate form of spiritual authority in their place were compelling forces toward consolidation of the movement." Gwyn calls this a "creative moment in Quaker history," wryly noting that "anyone who feels gratitude at inheriting the Quaker spiritual tradition must affirm early Friends for taking this step."[41] In other words, order will pull back on the reigns of prophetic utterance but will also help ensure Quakerism's survival.

In the sermon, Fox positions his first teachings about order, along with their clear implications about the organizational structure of Friends, fully thirteen paragraphs into the sermon. To review, thus far he has (1) set out his assertions about the Edenic creation and the blissful communication between "the First Speaker" and his human creatures; (2) presented the epochal fall of Adam and Eve under the deceitful influence of the "Second Speaker," and (3) insisted that the "Second Adam," Christ the "Seed," who is also the "First Speaker," has restored believers up into the state of Adam before he fell. Fox begins his specific comments on gospel order in this way:

> So now friends, all that are in the power and in the life come to be heirs of life, and of a world and kingdom that hath no end, so that you may all keep the Gospel order, for here comes up his government in the heavenly seed that bruises the head of the serpent, that bruises the head of all evil government. So now here is the government of the blessed Righteous Seed, which is a mystery. This is known as every one hath received Christ Jesus, so walk in Him. There is the Gospel order, that is the power of God, which was before the devil was. . . . Now in this power, in this Gospel, is the order, the everlasting order of the Gospel, which is a mystery.[42]

The gospel order, then, is not simply an organizational structure of meetings, but a mystical, or at least "mysterious," spiritual relationship involving deep and personal enactment of a path back through the "flaming sword." The resulting "government" is to be part and parcel of a personal relationship with the "heavenly seed" that "bruises the head" of the serpent.[43] When a person is "restored," he or she is granted a heritage of life. Fox continues: "Heirs of this power inherit it. Here comes the womens and mens meetings to be in this power. . . . Be heirs of this every man and woman!"[44] This is Fox's first mention of the new order of separately constituted men's and women's business meetings. The gender-separated meetings for business are identified in the sermon with the "order of the Gospel, which is a mystery."

Now Fox links his observation that men and women share in the inheritance of power and life, and also share the responsibility of remaining within the gospel order, to the most important conceptual metaphor employed by early Friends: the light-dark family, discussed in chapter 7. In a significant passage previously quoted in full in chapter 7, Fox says that "restored" men *and* women "go into the vineyard to work. . . . When it is night they canot see. How to work? They come to see Him when the day is come, the day spring from on high. There is a natural day springs up. Rise to work! Lie not in bed till the sun rises, as outwardly. So inwardly, the day spring from on high. People have been in darkness long enough."[45] In this quotation, Fox appears to be rehearsing what was by then standard Quaker imagery, but there is more. After all, the Light can break through and enlighten all people about a variety of matters, including the virtues of separate-gender business meetings.

In paragraph fourteen, Fox details how a person who hears God teaching him or her directly, as Adam and Eve did in the Garden of Eden, comes to know "God's day" and only then is qualified to "work in [God's] vineyard" rather than in the "market" of the world. These workers earn wages—"eternal life"—"which is [*sic*] paid at the end." Also, these laborers, both men and women, become ministers. Fox says, "All men and women that comes [*sic*] into truth. The first work is to convince people of God's truth and turn them from the power of Satan to the power of God." Here Fox specifically includes both genders in the work of ministry. He ends the paragraph with this inclusive and bold statement: "And as for men[s] and womens meetings, after they be convinced of God's eternal truth, and receive His grace and be come to sit under His teaching, and brought to God the first teacher, and to Christ, here is the ground and foundation of these meetings. The order is: the power of God, then heirs of Christ, and of life, and to gather people."

Having established the position of gender equality within the terms discovered in the larger framework of the creation-fall-restoration pattern, Fox is prepared to deal with typical specific prejudices against women. This sequence is probably strategic. If his prejudiced audience members can agree on the theological framework, then half of his battle is won. Fox deals directly with two major objections to women assuming leadership in ministry, objections raised earlier by Wiltshireman Nathaniel Coleman: (1) that the Bible (through St. Paul) instructs that women are not permitted to teach in the church and (2) that the Bible teaches that men are to "rule over" women because Eve "usurped authority over the man and drew man from God's teaching."[46] In answer to the first charge, Fox asserts that St. Paul's teaching is not as clear as some aver. Fox says, "Yet saith the Apostle [Paul]: 'the elder women was [sic] to be teachers of good things,' so such a kind of teaching as this, the Apostle did not forbid." This Scripture had been addressed by Fell in 1667.[47] As for the second charge, Fox asserts that women "were meet helps in paradise before they fell, meet helps in truth, and Righteousness and holiness." His audience must fill in some blanks here, but most are at least familiar with these Quaker interpretations of Paul's pronouncements. Then Fox moves cautiously beyond familiar Quaker conceptual territory, reminding his hearers about the existence of female prophets in the Old Testament but drawing a comparison between their true ministry and Eve's false teaching under the influence of the serpent, the kind of teaching still forbidden women (and men). Now, in a rhetorically adroit move, Fox reminds his hearers, as Fell had written in 1667,[48] that both genders are linked together in the implied biblical metaphor for the church, the "bride of Christ," and interprets St. Paul's teaching that women should be taught at home by their own husbands as applying to *all* Christians because their collective "husband" is Christ. Fox asserts,

> every man and woman is to come under God's teaching, under Christ['s] teaching, to hear Him, their husband at home. The whore is gone from her husband. Therefore: "Learn of me. I am meek and low in heart. I am the way," saith Christ. Here every man and woman that is come into the power of Christ Jesus ·they learn of Him. . . .The woman got over man with false teaching, so now as men and women comes [sic] to hear the head Christ Jesus, the true teacher (that bruises the head of death), who is the head of Life, who saith: "Learn of me," so come to learn of Christ Jesus and receive

the Gospel, the power of God, and so come to be heirs of God, heirs
of Christ, heirs of the Gospel: the Gospel, which is a mystery.[49]

This portion of the sermon is rhetorically masterful, not only
because Fox skillfully interweaves material from his spouse's influential
writings with his own unique argumentative and prophetic style, but
because he also relies on his audience's ability to fill in the missing
pieces of her authorship enthymematically. By leaving Fell unamed, he
could be sure that the majority of his hearers would still recall the allusion, while at the same time he could go beyond his unamed spouse to
advocate for separate women's and men's business meetings from the
viewpoint of a male in leadership. No one could have accused Fox of
hiding behind Fell's articulate rhetoric or expressing only her bias.

In the same paragraph, Fox draws his hearers back to the topic
of separate-gender meetings with these words: "Friends, that men
and womens meetings may be encouraged in all places, for all people
that are come to be heirs of life hear their Teacher, and such as have
received their earnest then go to their work."[50] Clearly, in the metaphorical world created in the sermon,[51] the restoration found in Christ
enables a return to the gender equality of the original creation—the
balance, or parity, discovered in Eden captured in Fox's phrase "meet
helps to one another"[52]—and the suggested organizational structure
of separate business meetings for men and women is the best way
to realize this idealized state within the gender-oppressive culture of
seventeenth-century England.

Fox did not necessarily expect a smooth transition to gender-
separate meetings, and what he had encountered earlier in Bristol could
not have raised his hopes for a conflict-free solution. In the sermon, he
advises the use of tenderness and encouragement, perhaps anticipating continued interpersonal and public strife. Tenderness begins with
God. Those who "inherit Him [Christ]" will experience "tenderness
to every sigh and groan." He continues, "Here is the safety: so not to
hurt any springing, but to encourage all where the buddings and where
the tenderness is." In the next paragraph, he pleads, "O that Friends
may be tender and mind the Gospel order."[53] He is even more pointed
in paragraph 18:

If any difference be in the country speak to one another and not
make a noise abroad, that you may preserve one another, that all
reports that be false may be stopped. Then rise up in the Spirit, dig-

nity, and power of the Lord God, and seek the good one of another in the power of truth, else it defiles many people, and many times people are more ready to hearken to that which is bad than the good, but that is to be kept down. So then feel the heavenly seed of Christ, then here love flourisheth. With one ear hear one. With the other hear the other party.

Similarly, Fox stresses the need for unity, in paragraphs 19 and 20, and peace and reconciliation, in paragraph 21. Importantly, Fox stresses that unity will not be achieved until all parties attend to the Spirit who speaks to them directly: "So, no, there is no unity till they come to Him who is the author of their faith." Fox returns to this idea at the end of his sermon. His listeners, he says, must reject "the false teacher and feeder," "feed on God's bread," and "hear him who was the first speaker in paradise." For the new organizational scheme of separate business meetings to work, everyone "must come all under God's teaching and Christ's teaching, and under God's feeding. Here is God's bread known and fed upon, which is able to nourish and preserve you, and increase you in his power and wisdom."[54]

Conclusion

Fox's answers to the political and organizational constraints facing him and Quakerism at the 1674 Yearly Meeting are remarkable. He chooses not to meet head-on the social unrest provoked by his insistence on moving Friends toward separate-gender meetings. Instead, reaching back into his own mystical spiritual experience, he reminds his hearers of the great cosmic pattern that goes way beyond complete *redemption*, all the way back to *restoration* at the hands of a Creator who seeks to restore all humans back to their prefallen condition. It is not until well into the sermon that he eventually links this broad teaching with the currently controversial topic of separate-gender meetings. By making separate-gender meetings a matter of theological commitment, rather than merely a goad to organizational efficiency or even fairness to women, Fox raises the stakes in the face of the festering threat of schism. His masterstroke is his blending of both Margaret Fell's and his insights, an encompassing of both males and females as "wives" of Christ the "husband," a biblically based hermeneutic founded on feminine identification, which apparently allows him to dispatch rather handily St. Paul's admonition for wives to be taught by their husbands at home (as Fell had argued so capably earlier in the century).

Although in the analysis above I have not directly addressed the question of Fox's legitimacy before this audience, I have considered the topic indirectly, and it is now possible to draw the following conclusions. First, Fox presents himself as "legitimate" by the very act of speaking. By breaking the silence, he claims his initial legitimacy, as would be the case, at least initially, for any Quaker rising to speak in meeting. Second, he establishes his legitimacy by rehearsing a focused and familiar theological position: that of an immediately realized apocalyptic restoration in Christ, a position most of his hearers would find familiar, if not immediately acceptable. Third, he suggests his legitimacy by showing himself to be a resourceful organizer and tying his organizational plans directly to his apocalyptic vision of restoration. In this view, if his hearers practice the gender equality demanded by the apocalyptic vision, they will be enacting the hoped-for gospel order in their own lives, in their own time. For the majority of the audience, this was a legitimate position. For the minority who eventually took part in the Wilkinson-Story separation, this position was illegitimate, and Fox's none-too-subtle argument negatively affected his credibility with them.[55]

Sermon by George Fox Given at a General Meeting, London, April 4, 1674

[1][56] The Lord alone was the teacher in paradise, and while man and woman kept under his teaching, they kept paradise, they kept the image of God. They kept righteousness and holiness, and they had dominion over all that God made while they kept under God's teaching (their Creator). Man and woman were kept in a blessed state, all things were blessed to them, coming from the Lord God, but when they turned from the teachings of the Lord God, and his command, and hearkened to the false teacher, which led them into transgression, there came in the false teacher with his false doctrine, and he came to be teacher to Eve and she became teacher to her husband. It was there, they came to be at a loss, and into the fall, in hearkening to the false teacher who is the head of all false prophets, teachers, and worships. He is the head of them all. While they were under God's teaching, they abode in paradise. So long as they kept under his teaching, man and woman was [sic] happy.

[2] It is said, "the seed of the woman shall bruise the serpent's head," who is the head of all false Teachers, and by hearkening to

this false teacher, they lost their blessed state and came into the curse, lost the light, and came into darkness, sold under sin in transgression. Now there were prophets in the time of the law, and before the flood, that prophesied of Christ the substance, the seed which should come. These were all of the right faith of Abraham.

[3] In short, here you see how man and woman came out of paradise, and came to hearken to a false teacher, and lost the true teacher, and was drove [*sic*] into the earth and buried in the earth. Now "the seed of the woman shall bruise the serpent's head." This is the prophet that is come, Christ, that bruiseth the head of him that brought darkness and {208} the curse. He brings life, and brings the blessing, and brings happiness, renews up into the image of God, and into righteousness as man and woman was in before they fell. Here is the true teacher that taught man and woman in paradise. The Devil was the false teacher that brought man out of paradise. Christ the seed of the woman, bruiseth the head of this false teacher, who is the head of all false teachers, and of all false professions without the possession. There are false Christs, and the true Christ bruises the head of them. This was spoken of the true prophet. He is come on the top of the head of the serpent, who saith: "Learn of me: I am the way." Where?: Into Paradise, into righteousness. "This is my beloved Son, hear him." God that was teacher in paradise, saith "Learn of me, I am the way and the Truth," and again, "I am the Light" (to lead men out of darkness). Here is the way back again. No man comes to the Father's teaching, but by Him, and so comes out of the curse.

[4] So now here are three states. God was the first teacher in paradise. They that are taught by Him are happy. The serpent was the second teacher. By hearkening unto him, man and woman's unhappiness came. Christ is the third, that bruises the head of all false teachers. So now coming to the head again, the satisfaction of their souls, who is their life, so then they know Him to be a Bishop in his offices, to rule in their hearts by faith.

[5] And God was man's teacher in paradise. Then came the false teachers. Christ bruises his head, and brings man again into happiness and peace. Now friends, it is said: "God at sundry time, and after diverse manners, spake to the prophets at sundry times." What times? Before the flood in the world and in the time of Moses, of Ezekiel and Samuel, and unto all the prophets in diverse manners. But now in these {209} last days, God hath spoken to us by his Son. So now here

God Almighty was the first speaker to Adam in paradise, and He is the speaker now to his People. God hath spoken to us by his Son. Every man and woman must come to the begining again, God almighty their speaker. So now, as man hath been under the seed of the serpent and his teaching, now he comes under his teacher Christ Jesus, that bruises the head of the serpent. Now here everyone comes to feed on God's bread from above.

[6] What do the professors feed on? The rudiments of death in the fall. Man that lives under God's teaching, lives on God's bread, bread that comes down from heaven, from above, to feed upon God's bread, bread that comes down from heaven, in a mind, in the Lord's life and power, and above. Here is the heavenly mind and the eye that looks for the heavenly bread from above. So now you are come under God's teaching. "Learn of me," saith Christ. Hear Him! Take heed what you hear. Have you heard the serpent? They feed on that which he gave, which is dust. Now Christ bruises the head of him and God hath spoken to us by his Son. God was the speaker, in paradise. To hear him the professors canot abide, who hearken to old Adam's teacher, the serpent. But Christ the seed bruises the head of him, that was before he was. God hath spoken to us by his Son. Who are the Disciples and Learners of him? Here they came to feed on God's bread and come to walk in Christ Jesus.

[7] Therefore, prize the eternal love of God. See what all mankind hath got by feeding on and hearkening to the serpent's false doctrine, not only hear, but feed. This brought all mankind into the curse and fall. Now hear the true prophet! Hear him: "I am the way, the truth, {210} and the life, and savior, and redeemer, and purchaser." All this is known and read within the Book of Life: And he that bruised the head of the serpent, he is the bread of life. (All is comprehended in these three states.) Though there is abundance more in these things.

[8] Now friends, every man comes to his particular satisfaction, for the Apostles preached to people to hear the beloved Son [and] not to hear him that was the false teacher, the serpent, but to look to him and hear him that crucifies the head of him. This keeps every man's eye and ear to Christ, the heart's home, and every man receives particular satisfaction from Christ. Then with the heart man believes and makes confession with the mouth to salvation. So the seed is come that bruiseth the head of the serpent, and was crucified and is risen. He was made sin for us that knew no sin. Was Christ made Sin? Yes! How? By

debt. He made the debt to be His, and he paid it and set thee at liberty. The world will not believe that he was able to pay old Adam's and his son and daughter's debt. I will make thy debt mine and so made sin to be His, that knew no sin. It is the just, righteous, pure, that pays the debt of the unjust. So He was made sin for us, [He] that knew none, that we through him might be made the righteousness of God, and by receiving of Him, become the sons of God. And so redeemed by him out of the fall, who was before the fall, and so brings under God's teaching again, and the son who says "Learn of me. I am the way to God," God hath spoken to us by His Son. Is God speaking again? Yes, the same God that was speaker in paradise. Here God hath his praise and honor in your hearts.

[9] The great controversy hath been about the Light, amongst the priests and professors. The great controversy was in Christ's time, about his flesh. "Is this the Christ the carpenter's son?" etc. The great controversy now is about the Light that is his life. The {211} devil said Christ was the son of God, nor mark. The controversy then was about Him as he was a man and took flesh upon Him, and was come and suffered according to the flesh, not as he was God, but man. Now the controversy is among Christians about the Light, which is the life of Christ. They may crucify him again as to themselves. He that died once dies no more. You talk of a Light. In Him was life, by whom the world was made, and this Light was the life of men, that all might believe in the light. In him was life. What him? Him by whom the world was made.

[10] The devil nor the professors canot abide the life of Christ Jesus because of their unbeliefs. There is no man grafted into Christ Jesus but by belief, signified by belief in the Light, in the heart, to the grafted in him, in the life, that is Christ who is Light in you. But the Life in Him comes into the life and so grafted into Him by belief, so the root hears you. Hear praises arises [*sic*]! So, here is grafted into Christ by belief, [Here the manuscript breaks off.]

[11] There are several states and growths: as Little Children to whom He says: "that you Sin not," "and if any one sin, we have an advocate with the father, Jesus Christ the Just," etc.; and young men to whom he saith: "because ye are strong: and have overcome the wicked one" and "the Word of God abideth in you"; and "I write unto you fathers because you have known him from the begining," that is in his divinity before he was manifest in flesh. So, be grafted into him,

in the Light, which is Christ. This Light brings into the life of Christ Jesus. No grafting into him, but by belief? So I say to all people they canot crucify Christ no more. He that died once, dies no more. Here is the life of Christ Jesus. All the professors in {212} the world fight against the life, which is the true light that enlightens every man, the life they canot abide. In the life is the unity. There is no grafting into Him in unbelief, in the Light. So there is a belief in Christendom— but no grafting, Pharisee like. Then he that believes in the Light hath the witness in himself. He that believes in the Light (which is the life in Christ) is born of God and overcomes the world and believes in him that bruises the serpent's head, that led man into the fall, and through Christ man comes into the fellowship of God and his son, so into the measure of the stature and fullness of Christ. It is a hidden growth. Glory to God forever! Here His everlasting praises doth abound.

[12] And so Friends, all that are in the power and are in the life— the faith that doth purify—you see the world hath a faith, and they have a belief, but there is no victory (Cry they). So no faith. He that bruises the head of the serpent is the Author of the faith, and every man and woman is to come and look to the Author and finisher of that faith (Christ Jesus) that purifies the heart. In this they please God. So here are the true witnesses: them that be of the true faith and true hope in Christ, in whom they are Grafted. The Jews professed the scriptures, as the false Christians since the days of the Apostles do. Here comes two or three witness[es] here. Didst thou never see Him, hear Him, or handle Him, or touch Him? Dost thou come to bear witness to Him, and no seeing, nor hearing, nor handling, nor tasting of him? How should they that deny the Spirit and power the Apostles were in be true witnesses? Every man that were faithful witnesses, they spake forth from what they had seen, heard, and handled. So every man that speaks from the Holy Ghost, these are the true and faithful witnesses. So every living witness must come to that which gives the true knowledge, {213} being raised up by the Second Adam! before they can be true witnesses to stand before the true Judge, for they are not like to be true witnesses that do not hear nor see God nor Christ. The true witnesses have heard him with their ears and seen him, and they say God hath spoken unto us by his Son, hear him that spoke in paradise. Here comes the true witnesses to witness to Him. So, no[w] look over all the world. Go where the true witnesses are, and let every-one be established upon Him who is the Rock of Ages. Who is your

Rock? Who was yesterday, today, and the same forever, that is always. They that sit under a false teacher and hearken to him, come into misery. God was the speaker to his people that hath spoken to us by his Son, and will be to all Eternity. They see Him that is from everlasting to everlasting, the perfect righteous one, Christ Jesus, that will be, was, and is. He was the teacher in paradise, and happy were they that kept under his teaching. He saith: "Learn of me," and God saith: "This is my beloved Son; hear him." God hath spoken to us by his Son, that God that spoke to Adam in paradise. He is, and was, and is to come. So, praises arise to Him. Here is the exalting [of] His son, He that bruises the serpent's head (that hath brought all into badness and darkness): that Christ doth this, that gives dominion over all. Praises be unto Him forever! {214}

[13] So now friends, all that are in the power and in the life come to be heirs of life, and of a world and kingdom that hath no end, so that you may all keep the Gospel order, for here comes up his government in the heavenly seed that bruises the head of the serpent, that bruises the head of all evil government. So now here is the government of the blessed Righteous Seed, which is a mystery. This is known as every one hath received Christ Jesus, so walk in Him. There is the Gospel order, that is the power of God, which was before the devil was, which brings life and immortality to Light. The power of God, the Gospel, brings into life. Now in this power, in this Gospel, is the order, the everlasting order of the Gospel, which is a mystery. The Gospel brings a man to be a man and to be heirs of the power, which brings life in every particular and life and immortality to light through the Gospel in thee, and before the serpent was, by the power of God. Heirs of this power inherit it. Here comes the womens and mens meetings to be in this power, everyone as heirs of the Gospel, which brought life and immortality to light in you through the Gospel. Be heirs of this every man and woman! Then they go into the vineyard to work and not stand idle in the market, chaffering, buying and selling. And so as people comes [*sic*] to see the power, and to by [be] heirs of the power, these people see how they work. When it is night they canot see. How to work? They come to see Him when the day is come, the day spring from on high. {215} There is a natural day springs up. Rise to work! Lie not in bed till the sun rises, as outwardly. So inwardly, the day spring from on high. People have been in darkness long enough. When immortality is brought to light, then the day springs, the day from on high that know, and the shadows

and clouds to fly away when the morning breaks. The sun of righteousness arises with his heavenly praises. So now this day is sprung from on
high. This is witnessed when He comes to rule in the day.

[14] So now as every man comes under God's teaching, as he
taught in paradise, the[y] comes to know the day of God, as is spoken of in the Apostles' time, till the day dawn and the day spring
from on high. So here is God's day, His everlasting day, His heavenly
day, His spiritual Day. They that come to it, they come to work in
the vineyard, not a bit of God's work done till they come to God's
witness in themselves. He that believes enters into rest and then to
do God's work. Here they have been all buying and selling in the
market till they come to this. There is a state of a servant, and of a
son. When people come to witness the Spirit of God and feel that in
themselves, they turn out of the market and go to work in the vineyard. If thou hire a servant and give him earnest, thou expects his
going to work and bids him go. Thou dost not pay him his wages till
the years or works end. So now Christ, He gives the earnest of the
Spirit. Thy wages is eternal life, thy {216} work which is paid at the
end, when thou hast done thy work. All men and women that comes
[sic] into truth, the first work is to convince people of God's truth
and turn them from the power of Satan to the power of God. Then
they come to receive their earnest and wages, the gift of God. Here
all to work in God's vineyard. All that are convinced, they labor in
that which called them. By the power and grace they were called,
that which brought salvation, and so in the end receive their wages
as Paul was. And as for men[s] and womens meetings, after they be
convinced of God's eternal truth, and receive His grace and be come
to sit under His teaching, and brought to God the first teacher, and
to Christ, here is the ground and foundation of these meetings. The
order is: the power of God, then heirs of Christ, {217} and of life,
and to gather people. Everyone labor that all may walk as becomes
the Gospel. All that have received Christ, so walk in Him. Here God
is honored and glorified.

[15] But now some may object and say: "What work have we, or
what service for women?" They are heirs of life as well as the men.
"I permit not a woman to teach in the Church. As saith the law, is
it not said the man was to rule over the woman?" saith some. They
were meet helps in paradise before they fell, meet helps in truth and
Righteousness and holiness. And after men fell [sic], the woman, she

followed the false teacher, and so got up over the man. She usurped authority over the man and drew man from God's teaching. And they [say] "the man was set over the woman." Yet saith the Apostle [Paul]: "the elder women was to be teachers of good things," so such a kind of teaching as {217} this, the Apostle did not forbid.

[16] In the time of the law, and Gospel there were women prophetesses, but such a kind of teaching as Eve taught her husband in [is] forbidden. Therefore every man and woman is to come under God's teaching, under Christ['s] teaching, to hear Him, their husband at home. The whore is gone from her husband. Therefore: "Learn of me. I am meek and low in heart. I am the way," saith Christ. Here every man and woman that is come into the power of Christ Jesus they learn of Him. They that receive the power, they are heirs of the Gospel and of the power which is able to keep people in order unto the day of salvation. So men and women are to come up into Christ Jesus, into the image of God again, to be meet helps as before the fall. The woman got over man with false teaching, so now as men and women comes [*sic*] to hear the head Christ Jesus, the true teacher (that bruises the head of death), who is the head of Life, who saith: "Learn of me," so come to learn of Christ Jesus and receive the Gospel, the power of God, and so come to be heirs of God, heirs of Christ, heirs of the Gospel: the Gospel, which is a mystery. Friends, that men and womens meetings may be encouraged in all places, for all people that are come to be heirs of life hear their Teacher, and such as have received their earnest then go to their work. Come feed here. I have bread. My master provides me bread, my meat, and my wine and fine linens. I have been barren, and I have {218} been sometime in bitter storms. My master provides me bread, and meat, and wine, and honey to refresh me. And, therefore, mind the power of God in your own particulars. The Apostles speaking preaching was to bring people to Christ's teaching: from the false teachers to the true teacher, to God again. So every one come to be taught of the Lord Jesus Christ, so heirs of Him, heirs of Life. Here no enmity comes. Here they feel his . love and life and Power. All that go abroad in the ministry in countries to encourage Friends that they may be all faithful to truth and righteousness, and so come to be heirs of Christ and life and peace, and so meet helps to one another, as man and woman was in the begining, and so inherit Him that inherits all things in the possession of Christ Jesus; here will be tenderness to every sigh and groan, and that which

springs from the heavenly seed. There is the wisdom in the heavenly seed: here the power of the Lord God is felt. None to go beyond it, but keep in it. With the heart man believes, and with the mouth he makes confession unto salvation. Keep in the salvation, then they keep in the Dominion. Here is the safety: so not to hurt any springings, but to encourage all where the buddings and where the tenderness is, that the Lord may have his glory, who is in all and over all blessed forevermore. {219}

[17] It's said the grace of God, which brings salvation, which teacheth us, it is not sufficient to bring it. All come unto this grace and sit under it's [*sic*] teachings that brings [*sic*] salvation, and they who profess this and are heirs of this, they have comfort and particular satisfaction to themselves. O that Friends may be tender and mind the Gospel order, and heirs of this, of the government of Christ Jesus, possess this, possess all things. This keeps every man to witness which will stand, which was before the world was and will stand when the world is gone. Keep the order of the Gospel, that the Lord may be glorified and exalted over all in you. He is exalted in his power and dominion; and so keep in this which raiseth up the seed in every man where He is exalted, that bruises the head of the serpent in that He is exalted. In Christ all the prophets end, the foundation on the prophets, all the prophets are seen, that all may keep their possessions and live in Him. And as everyone hath received Christ Jesus the Lord, so walk in Him.

[18] If any difference be in the country speak to one another and not make a noise abroad, that you may preserve one another, that all reports that be false may be stopped. Then rise up in the Spirit, dignity, and power of the Lord God, and seek the good one of another in the power of truth, else it defiles many people, and many times people are more ready to hearken to that which is {220} bad than the good, but that is to be kept down. So then feel the heavenly seed of Christ, then here love flourisheth. With one ear hear one. With the other hear the other party: for truth makes a man a man and leads up into the image of God. If thou wouldst know they [their] geneology, look to Adam in the fall—the first birth—where thou maist see they [their] descent and pedigree in the fall and in the transgression of Old Adam; but he that is born of gain [again] of the Womb of the Morning, of the Womb of Eternity, this is beyond all the births in the fall, the Immortal Seed, this is beyond all what must become of the first birth. It must die; thou

must be born again before thou can come to life or be heir of a world without end, which is to be minded. Therefore, come to life! There is dominion over all as you come to this one teacher, through which man comes up into paradise again, the blessed state, and the dominion in the life which is everlasting. Here is an heavenly dominion. Let all walk worthy of this heavenly name. All keep to that which is from everlasting to everlasting. Here they receive virtue and life and refreshment.

[19] All must come to this teacher if ever they come to God. All that come to God's vineyard, they must come out of the market. Some spend their own portions: talk, talk, and so lose their possession. But man that is come to the Spirit of God, he hath his earnest and denies the world's means and saith: "My master is to give me meat, honey, and clothes," also "I have {221} a master that supplies me with all that I need as you are faithful." Here the servants do not come to fall out together, but do dwell together in the unity, that everyone may come to have their wages—everlasting salvation—and so come to be heirs of a world that hath no end. {222}

[20] All that are convinced that you may not always keep under teachings, but that they may be exhorted and brought to Christ their teacher and to walk as becomes the Gospel, as every one hath received Christ, so walk in him and in the truth. All that have received it may honor him in the truth, that is it which the Devil is out of. Here is a worship and a faith that the Devil canot get into, the worship of God in spirit and in truth, which the Devil is out of: in the spirit and truth, which is the perfect standing worship, and is universal. Faith is the gift of God. This worship set up by the heavenly man, this faith that Christ is the author of, men must walk in. By faith thou must walk in that which Christ works in thee. Thou must not walk by sight, but by faith. Christ, who is the author of this, saith it is a mystery: this faith is a mystery. Now we read in the Apostles' days, they that were of this faith—which is a mystery, which Christ was the author of, which was one faith by which they had access to God, in which they had unity—some that had received this faith in some measure, they made shipwreck of faith and a good conscience. You know a shipwreck that breaks all to pieces; that a shipwreck hath been since the Apostles days of faith and a good conscience. One hath made a faith, and another a faith. Hath this faith helped them out of sin that cry no victory, no overcoming? Here is the sea; what a shipwreck is here? So, no, there

is no unity till they come to Him who is the author of their faith, that gives victory and brings to God again. Here is the faith and a shield; here is the unity and a victory over enmity and brings access to God. Here people content themselves in the sea, out of victory and a cry "No victory here!" No man or woman that overcomes to God or Christ Jesus but by that faith which Christ works within. By faith, walk by faith, contend for the faith. It is time which they make shipwreck of it. Look unto Him that is the author of this faith. Contend for the gift of God; contend for the work of God in the heart. Some contend for this man's words and the other man's words, for this sect and the other sect, and so come on heaps; but every man must come to this faith and follow on from faith to faith, and so from glory to glory. So Christ has the honor and the glory. He is the author of faith and hope, and worship here is the faith that keeps from the spots of the world. Christ is the Seed-man. Consider these three things: how man lost paradise, then he forsook God's teachings, and hearkened to the serpent's teaching, the false teacher, then did the false teacher get.

[21] Secondly, now comes Christ Jesus the Second Adam, that bruises the head of the serpent, that destroys him; Christ the head of his Church, who is the true seeds man and plants his hedge about his plants, which is his power. As the outward seedsman sows his seed on the natural ground and makes his fence about it, so here Christ Jesus the heavenly seedsman sows his seed in good ground. Where is it? In the heart of man and woman know this heavenly seedsman. Unbelief hath been so in the heart of man that they say He nor his seed is to be looked for. "My Father," saith Christ, "is the husband-man." He sows his seed in the heart. Look within. There is the power that keeps the seed. Now look within fields and hedges and see how God's blade and seed doth spring up after his rain. As the outward rain causes a fruitful season, so the heavenly rain causes the seed to spring and to become fruitful, and to increase fifty fold: God's seed, God's corn. Where? In the grain after people are dead? No! In this life: sixty fold and an hundred fold. In the world to come: life eternal. People talk of Christ and of no victory here. See how God's plants and vineyards grow. Look into his vineyard and garden and see how it grows in this life. Everyone look into the field and see how God's corn grows, who gathers his wheats into his garner, elect before the world began. Here, all and in truth may see, though this good

seed was sown, the wicked sowed his seed also. The serpent sows his seed. Here came in the apostasy. Now the everlasting Gospel is preached again. Stand up for God's name. There is no salvation in any other, but in this name. Therefore, stand up for that name, the name of Jesus thy savior. They that receive His name, they receive his father's name. He that comes into this name, receives his father's mark in their foreheads in which name, salvation is witnessed, and peace is witnessed, and reconciliation.

[22] The everlasting Gospel comes to be preached again to nations, kindreds, tongues, and people, to the praise and glory of the great God. The false teachers made a world like a wilderness. Christ that bruiseth the head of them all, saith: "Learn of me." There was a false teacher and feeder. Here is come a new teacher and feeder. He alone hath the honor, over all blessed forevermore.

[23] Here is the foundation of God's prophets, who is blessed forever, of whom all are to learn and to be fed of. Keep in the peace and Love of God, then doth every man keep in that which honors God, that you may come to honor God, that you may come to feed on God's bread. Hear him who was the first speaker in paradise. The serpent was the second, that brought death and the curse to all mankind. His image is set up. But Christ saith "Learn of me," so hear Him who renews man up into the image of God and destroys then [the] devil and his image.

[24] The false teachers cry: "Means, means, ordinances!" God commands thee to hear his son. God spake to the fathers by the prophets, but he hath spoken to us by his Son. Glory to God forever! Here is one faith, and one baptism, and one body. Here we sit under his teaching and come into his image. And when they come to hear the serpent, they set up his image in them. As Christ comes to set up his image, the serpent's image is defaced. This know. Then here is salvation—no more here, lo there; no going out, you that have heard his voice, to hear the false teacher and feeder. Hear the son, the true teacher and feeder that gives life. Hear the true teacher and feeder. Know your bread. Know your bread of God. Feed on the bread of God, that bread which is from above. In this the glory of the Lord is over all, that through Him you may be all preserved, through Him that brings the blessing and destroys him that brought the curse. That itching ear that came among people must be turned from, which

brings people on heaps. They must come all under God's teaching and Christ's teaching, and under God's feeding. Here is God's bread known and fed upon, which is able to nourish and preserve you, and increase you in his power and wisdom.

CHAPTER 10

STEPHEN CRISP AND THE BEDROCK
OF EARLY QUAKERISM

Stephen Crisp (1628–1692) was the archetypal middle-class English Quaker preacher of the late seventeenth century. Like John Woolman, the more well-known American Colonial Quaker who lived a century later, Crisp was also a businessman who traveled extensively in the gospel ministry and kept a journal of his travels and spiritual life. Crisp also wrote a literary work with some similarities to John Bunyan's *Pilgrim's Progress*, but in a far more approachable style for today's reader. Like Bunyan, Crisp was an effective preacher, but one who flourished in the challenging early Quaker rhetorical culture described in previous chapters, a culture that eschewed specific preparation before speaking and valorized impromptu sermonizing. Thirty-two of Crisp's sermons—all products of non-Quaker notetakers—survive in print, more than those of any other early Quaker.[1]

This chapter focuses on a significant sermon that Crisp delivered in a London Friends meeting in 1687. Specifically, I will consider first the biographical and other contextual factors that surrounded and compelled Crisp when he spoke. Then I will turn to the sermon text itself, seen as a verbal response to an interesting (but not unique) rhetorical situation precipitated by the preacher's intent and implicit claim to be speaking "in the Light" as an "oracle" of God.

THE MAN AND THE CONTEXT

Stephen Crisp was a very successful businessman, a baize maker born, raised, and educated in Colchester, England. The *Dictionary of Quaker Biography*[2] reveals that at the age of seventeen he became a separatist and later a Baptist. He converted to Quakerism in 1655 and in 1659 became recognized as a Quaker who traveled in the itinerant ministry, a "publick" Friend. Crisp was imprisoned several times for various offenses (refusal to take an oath, "disturber of the peace," etc.). He learned Dutch and German, in addition to Latin, and became a key figure in the establishment of Quakerism in Holland and Germany. His mother and two children died of the plague in 1665–1666. From 1663, Crisp paid numerous visits to Holland that combined business and ministry and also visited many parts of his native land in the ministry. The *DQB* notes that he was also actively engaged in the business affairs of the Yearly Meeting. In 1685, Crisp married his second spouse, Gertrude Dericks Nieson, who died in 1687, the same year he preached the sermon under scrutiny here.

As a businessman, Crisp was known for what today we call "financial planning." As recalled in the "Testimony of the Men's Meeting at Colchester Concerning Stephen Crisp," which is printed as the preface to Crisp's posthumous journal, "He had a large Understanding given him, not only in Spiritual, but also in Temporal things, by which he was very serviceable to many Widows, and Fatherless and others, (as Divers can Testifie) being very ready and free to assist them."[3]

Crisp was one of the most capable early Quaker writers and preachers. He wrote an account of his spiritual journey with the title *A Short History of a Long Travel from Babylon to Bethel.*[4] Published nineteen years after his death, the work immediately became popular among Quakers and was republished twenty times.

A measure of Crisp's preaching ability may be deduced by recalling that more of his impromptu sermons survive (thirty-two) from the early Quaker period than those of any other Friend. The Colchester Men's Meeting in their memorial to him extolled Crisp's gifts at ministry, taking particular notice of his effectiveness at converting people to Quakerism:

> He had a gift of Utterance beyond many, sound in Judgment, Doctrine, and very Convincing to the Understandings of many that heard him; for which cause, his testimony was affecting to many that were not of us, who would come to hear him when he was with us: And he would often call to People to come and try the Sufficiency of the Grace of God, (that a Measure of it was committed to them,) and whether it was not to Save from Sin, (yea, to the utmost,) all such as received and obeyed it. He divided the Word aright, and turned many from Darkness to Light; many Mourners have been comforted by him, and many Tender Hearted helped, through their inward Exercises and Conflicts of Spirit, and have been a Strength to them in their Spiritual Warfare: But his Testimony was as a sharp

Two-edged Sword, to the Rebellious, Obdurate, and Hard-Hearted, to the piercing through them many a time: And his very outward Countenance hath sometimes struck to the Hearts of some, as some have since Confessed: And some that have gotten into a Spirit of Enmity, have been made through the Power that did accompany him, to come and acknowledge the Hurt which that Spirit had done them; and that the Lord was with him.[5]

Not only was Crisp a gifted preacher, but he also took special notice of fledgling impromptu preachers, encouraging and nurturing them in the challenging task at which he excelled. In essence, he was the ideal model for Bownas' and Marshall's conception of passing on the public ministry to the next generation. The Colchester Men's Meeting commented in their testimony, "He was very tender and helpful to divers, who have been of late called forth into a Publick Testimony and into the same Work wherein he was himself imployed [sic] by his great Lord and Master Christ Jesus, being very tender and ready to help forward that which he found to come from the motion of the Seed of Life in any, and would speak a Word in Season to such."[6]

The years leading up to Crisp's 1687 London sermon were tumultuous in the history of England as well as in Crisp's life. As noted previously, Quakers had been persecuted and imprisoned routinely during the 1660s and 1670s, and although King James II proclaimed a pardon for all people imprisoned "for conscience's sake" in 1865, Quakers continued to be persecuted under the "Conventicle Act, which forbade them to meet," until the Act of Toleration was passed in 1689.[7] Thus, a part of the context for Crisp's sermon is the fact that the meeting at which it took place was, strictly speaking, illegal.

The year 1687 was particularly traumatic in Crisp's personal life. In his published journal, he briefly records that his second wife, Gertrude, died, and affirms his confidence in her eternal destiny, "knowing right well her portion is with the Righteous, and her eternal Inheritance is amongst the Just, where Sorrow, Snares and Temptations canot come." His journal implies that he dealt with his grief through the companionship of the London Quaker community and by investing himself with vigor in public ministry. He writes, "And after she was buried, I went up to London, and convers'd among the Brethren three Months, where the Lord was pleased to bless my Service unto many."[8] During this brief period of bereavement, Crisp preached the sermon at the important Quaker meetinghouse located on Grace Church Street.

The Sermon

Crisp builds the sermon around a passage from the Gospel of Matthew's account of the temptation of Jesus. The tempter says, "If thou be the Son of God, command that these stones be made bread." Jesus responds, "It is written, Man shall not live by bread alone, but by every word that proceedeth out of the mouth of God" (Matt 4:3-4 KJV). Although Crisp does not announce the passage as his text, his sermon clearly focuses on the explication and application of this text, an unusual move for Quaker preachers. In a broad sense, Crisp follows the pattern of explicating a Scripture passage and applying it to his hearers, which is essentially the description of the doctrine-use format. However, we will see that Crisp deviates from the dry, lockstep pattern of many Puritan sermons.

In Crisp's hands, the text from Matthew is framed within the context of Quaker belief in the immediate revelation of the "Word" from God. Throughout the sermon, Crisp seeks to direct his hearers to have a personal, immediate experience of revelation, emphasizing that they should experience a contemporary realization of living "by every word that proceedeth out of the mouth of God."[9] Crisp asserts that he is part of a "remnant" group that possesses "experimental knowledge of the truth" and that "have heard, and felt, and tasted of the word of life that was with the Father before the world began." The preacher is ineffectual, unless God himself intervenes. Crisp asserts, "There are many have taken sinners in hand and have gone about to convince them and convert them, but they were not able to do it. But when the Lord hath taken men in hand himself . . . he cries out under the sense of the judgment of God." Crisp continues, "the word that goes out of the mouth of God hath a mighty force and power upon the spirit of a man so that he is converted and changed by it." This "experimental knowledge of the word of God," this "inward voice whereby God speaks to the sons and daughters of men," produces "an infallible feeling of their own state and condition" and provides the hearer with "a certain infallible knowledge of their own state."[10] In fact, according to Crisp, the whole purpose of a Quaker meeting is to make possible this kind of infallible, immediate self-knowledge:

> Now that which is the design of our meeting when we are assembled together is that we may know what the mind and judgment of God is concerning ourselves. How shall we know that unless we ask him

and come to wait upon him and inquire at the oracle of counsel that God hath appointed in the bosom of every man? For he signifies his mind unto the children of men by that light and grace which Jesus Christ hath planted in them. He hath enlightened every man that comes into the world with an undeceiving light, and he hath ministered of his truth and grace to every man.[11]

The result of self-knowledge is "a sense of sorrow, under a weight, under a burden, under an oppression, which signifies [the hearer] is alive and quickened." Thus, the initial sign of immediate revelation is a somber awakening to life, for as Crisp says, "Now lay what load you will upon a dead man, he will neither groan nor grumble at it. But if he comes again to life, he cries: 'Take off the burden, the weight and oppression, that lies heavy upon me!'"[12] This apt analogy presents Crisp's listeners with the paradox that trouble, testing, and woe often initiate the move toward the spiritual life.[13] Crisp asserts that this process of self-awakening continues to be the essential purpose of Quaker meetings: "Hereupon meetings were appointed at first that the word should minister life in them and life to them that attend them. And to this day our meetings are appointed for this purpose: that we may have the ministration of life and virtue from Christ, the fountain of life and virtue."[14]

Clearly, the conceptual center of Crisp's sermon is the assertion that God speaks directly to humans. Every other topic in the sermon radiates from this central axle. In the ninth paragraph, Crisp sets out a key Quaker teaching regarding the operation of the Spirit in a Quaker meeting and how the words of an impromptu preacher work on listeners:

> Therefore, I would have everyone always to have a reverence to the word of life that speaks in themselves. For, if we speak as we are moved by the spirit of God, and utter those things by verbal testimony which God hath made known to us, if you have not an oracle in your bosoms, if you do not at the same time perceive an echo of truth in your own souls, this will do you no good, but be an empty sound which will pass away again. But the mind that is serious and settled, in waiting upon God with an earnest desire that it may receive benefit in going to this and the other meeting, such an one will say: "I pray God bless this opportunity to me that so I may receive benefit to my soul." Where people meet in this manner, they have not only an administration of doctrine from without from this and the

other instrument, but they have a ministration of the word of God in themselves by which a man liveth.[15]

Here Crisp reflects on what Marshall and Coole called the *passive* reception of immediate revelation, the inward perception of a message not necessarily intended to be shared vocally. Obviously, Crisp himself has decided to speak in the meeting and thus enter the *active* phase of immediate inspiration, but he seeks to underscore the necessity for listeners to be part of the total communication process. They will need to echo his message in their minds, thus reaffirming its authenticity. These ideas from the sermon will culminate in his cautionary advice published three years later in *The Christian Experiences, Gospel Labours and Writings, of . . . Stephen Crisp*, when he would write, "[W]hen ye meet about these things, keep the Lord in your eye, and wait to feel his power to guide and direct you. . . . And beware of all brittleness of spirit and sharp reflection upon each other[']s words."[16] In sum, outward words by the preacher are to no avail if the receiver resists the "oracle" within. Earlier in the sermon, Crisp declares, "It canot be by hearing a man preach. Unless the spirit doth cooperate with the word of God, there is no possibility of being quickened [made alive]."[17]

Crisp is now prepared to take on and refute the antagonists of Quaker doctrine. He restates his opponents' claims: "Let us not be led and hurried away with the grand error of the times, the great error of this age and of the ages bypassed, that there is no possibility for people to understand and hear the voice of God, this inward voice. 'There are' (say they) 'no immediate teachings nowadays, no inspirations nowadays.'" In this hypothetical but dramatic dialogue, Crisp responds *indirectly* to his accusers as an aside to his hearers: "They had as well said that there are no conversions nowadays. . . . [T]here is no man in this age is like to be converted to God or redeemed from his iniquity and brought to the knowledge of his maker, unless he have it by the inward working of the eternal God; not by man's preaching and instruction, nor by reading all the good sermons that ever were preached without the cooperation of the holy sanctifying spirit which begets life in them that believe."[18] Here Crisp practices the catechital style in the context of theological debate. His choice probably indicates that non-Quakers are present in the meeting.

Continuing to address his hearers, but now *directly*, Crisp first prods, then concludes with a query: "You that are under any sense of this [inward revelation], that are come to such an inward sense of the operation of the word of God, if you have heard it reprove you, judge you and condemn you, consider that this word proceeded out of the mouth of God and not out of the mouth of any man. You hear the sentence of God upon you in your own consciences. Whence comes it?" Crisp answers his rhetorical question swiftly and decisively, and with a claim of divine inspiration for the inward message his hearers may be "hearing" in the passive mode: "*This is out of the mouth of God.* Every word that comes out of the mouth of God administers life, sense and conviction, and you feel it and receive it, and you may have more familiar acquaintance with it."[19]

Then Crisp reveals to his hearers a part of his motivation for standing to preach, thus moving himself from the *passive* to the *active* mode: "Now there is a great necessity that everyone be persuaded to hearken to this voice, not only at a meeting, but on all occasions they have in the world. I hope I speak to many serious and religious persons that are inquiring about their immortal souls what may be best for their souls."[20]

However, Crisp believes hindrances often prevent people from making deep, religious commitment. In this central portion of the sermon, Crisp develops the idea that "the devil," "the tempter," or "Satan" is "subtle and cuning" and seeks to lead people into acts such as cheating your neighbor, "drunkenness and uncleaness . . . and into the greatest abominations." Crisp strongly advises, "The oracle of God in the heart says: 'Do it not. It is evil. Thou wilt kindle the indignation of the Lord against thee. What will it profit thee to gain the whole world and lose thy own soul? Or what wilt thou give in exchange for thy soul?' Here is one at hand that can give counsel to all of us at all times." In the center of this section, Crisp succinctly reaffirms the radical early Quaker view of perfection: "If there be something that preserves a man from any evil, it can preserve him from all evil."[21] In the world of Crisp's sermon, the polar opposite spiritual forces are no mere anecdote of biblical history, but are powerful forces at work right in the very meeting in which he has risen to speak.

For Crisp, if a person persistently resists the prompting of the inner oracle—the word of God—he or she will eventually reach a point of no return. Crisp flatly states,

> If through custom in sin thou losest the sense of his judgment, it is not because God hath determined to take advantage against thee, but because thou actest against thyself and comest to be past feeling.

Thou wast once under a sense of these things and thou wast not past feeling. If thou at any time told thy parents a lie, thou hadst remorse. But now thou canst tell a lie and not feel it. Whose fault is this? The Lord would have brought thee to love the truth, but thou choosest lying. If thou perish, thy blood will be upon thine own head. The Lord is clear from it.[22]

Crisp then divides his hearers into two potential groups, strongly warning everyone about the dangers of being identified with the first group:

You are sensible of God's speaking this word to you. I exhort you all in the love of God, that you would prize this manner of speaking and look upon it as the greatest mercy that ever you enjoyed, that God hath not given over speaking to you, and that conscience hath not given over speaking to you, and that the spirit of the Lord doth yet strive with you. He will not always strive. You may be of that sort of fools before you die that make a mock of sin, and be as trees twice dead and plucked up by the roots. You that are sensible of this inward voice, prize it above all your mercies. Health and wealth and all other mercies are not worthy to be compared to this voice of God speaking in you.[23]

Thus far in the sermon, Crisp has argued that there exists the possibility for all people to "receive his word." But Crisp warns, "Take heed that this way is not stopped up. You know by what it was opened and what will stop it up again. When you were in much trouble and grief, you cried to the Lord and he delivered you. But 'If I regard iniquity in my heart,' said David, 'the Lord will not hear me.'"[24]

According to Crisp, though the possibility of immediate revelation is open to all, not all will persevere in attending to the inward divine voice or determine to live righteous lives. Crisp avers that God "hath won a remnant, and hath brought them over to believe and trust in his power to remove out of the way that which hindered the intercourse between God and their souls."[25] Speaking to the remnant among his hearers, Crisp captures the collective narrative of their experience:

What a great stir was there in removing out of the way the pride, corruption, enmity, looseness, wantonness, and abundance . . . of evil things that made the soul like a wilderness? What hacking up and burning up was there? God's word, like a hammer and like a fire, did break up and burn up these things. And the same word of

God, like a sword, did cut down those sins and lusts which prevailed over you before. By this means God hath opened a way for you to have access to him and for his word to have access to you.[26]

Here the metaphors for the Word—hammer, fire, and sword—underscore the power of the Word to destroy old habits that once made life a "wilderness." These former behaviors and thoughts have to go to make way for joy, consolation, communion, and fellowship occasioned only by the immediate *passive* reception of the Word.

Nearing his exordium, Crisp once again divides his audience into two potential groups. To one group, the remnant, he says, "You that God hath engaged to be his. . . . O live in a holy fear and watchfulness; and know this . . . you have nothing but what is given you, and what God hath given you he can take away."[27] Remember, at this point, Crisp is no stranger to sudden, irremediable losses of loved ones and is still mourning his second wife's death.

To the other group, he raises another warning: "Those that forget God . . . that forget their brokenness of heart and the subjection of their spirits to God, if they forget this, let them know that . . . they will certainly wither and their inward life will fail."[28] Unlike the Calvinist notion that the elect persevere, the people who "forget God" will wither. In other words, these groups are not eternally fixed; one may cross between them either way. Crisp is presenting the Arminian doctrine that it is possible to lose one's salvation.

This section of the sermon has a direct, persuasive, even "revivalistic" tone, which became popular in the next century with Whitefield and the Wesleys. Crisp is squarely in the lineage of the First and Second Great Awakening preachers who directly plead for their hearers' souls.

After the dire warning, Crisp ends the sermon with these comforting words:

You that have regard to your own souls and do desire heartily (at this time) to be quickened . . . you can say: "I find communion with God and fellowship with my friends and brethren in that one eternal life," I pray God you may continue in it long and lay down you[r] heads in this blessed heavenly life. Now that you may so do, keep yourselves low and humble and in the fear of God, and keep your ears always open to his word, and live as becomes those that are born again and begotten of God and are brought to partake of the divine life. Let temptations surround you, that life will preserve you. He that never

sined is with you to keep you from sin. And he that never deceived
any will keep you from being deceived. To his counsel and conduct,
and to his divine care and protection, I now commit you.[29]

Conclusion

Crisp's sermon is particularly notable because of his skillful use of the
interior dialogue version of the catechital style. As noted in chapter 8,
Quaker preachers had always favored the use of rhetorical questions
as a means to focus hearers' attention and aid their own invention in
the challenging context of impromptu speaking, but it is not until the
end of the century that the sophistication found in Crisp's sermon is
achieved. Crisp offers us absolutely no hint of Cope's "epistemology
of verbal incantation,"[30] displayed occasionally in Fox's sermon discussed in the previous chapter. In Crisp's sermon, the incantatory style
is completely replaced by the catechital.

The sermon is also notable for its organization, which achieves a
sense of movement throughout toward personal commitment on the
part of hearers. Crisp begins with an injunction to live the "experimental knowledge of the word of the Lord," "the inward voice," and
ends with a plea to "keep your ears always open to the word." He
wants his hearers to become a remnant people, who are not deceived,
who resist temptations and persevere to the end. The sermon has a
rare exegetical base that is easy to follow and makes logical sense,
almost as if it is preplanned.

Additionally, Crisp employs language effectively to focus his hearers on a reconsideration of their lives, particularly any non-Quakers
in the congregation. His sermon reveals his use of major conceptual
metaphors. For example, Crisp invokes the standard Quaker metaphorical dichotomy of light versus dark and the typical early Quaker
references to the complex tensions between sound and silence, discussed in chapter 7. In fact, the latter is central to the sermon. His use
of "inward" versus "outward" reflects the standard early Quaker usage
to describe the contrast between the merely earthly or "worldly"—
the "outward"—and the true or real inward experience. Throughout
the sermon, "death" and "dead" are identified with "outward," while
"life" and "quickening" are linked to "inward."

Finally, the sermon is noteworthy because of its self-reflexivity.
Its topic is the possibility of God speaking directly to people, thus
becoming at that moment the Word of God to them. Crisp speaks

directly about the motivation for convening Quaker meetings and his own motivation for preaching on that particular occasion. By rising to speak in the meeting, Crisp, according to Quaker tradition, is claiming to be speaking as an oracle of God with words inspired by the Word. Under this circumstance, it is fascinating that Crisp chooses to speak of the very process whereby he himself came to be a convert to Quakerism and also to stand at that very moment to speak as one of God's messengers.[31]

THE WORD OF GOD A CHRISTIAN'S LIFE: A SERMON PREACHED BY STEPHEN CRISP AT GRACE CHURCH STREET, LONDON, MARCH 14, 1687

[1][32] It was the doctrine of the great master of the Christian religion, the Lord Jesus Christ, while he was preaching and publishing and making known the way of salvation among the sons and daughters of men; he then preached and declared that it was not bread only by which a man lived, but by every word that proceedeth out of the mouth of God. Now the way and means of man's preservation in life in a living state, the method and course that the God of heaven doth open to keep the sons and daughters of men alive, is by this word. Every word that proceedeth out of the mouth of God hath a ministration of life in it; and, therefore, all that are desirous of the enjoyment of the immortal life and of the preserving and increasing of it, they are diligently to wait to be made partakers of this divine ministration. Outward bread is for outward preservation, but man is made inward as well as outward. He hath a soul as well as a body. Now Christ, to signify to us what the inward man is nourished and fed by, tells us that man liveth not by bread alone, but by every word that proceedeth out of the mouth of God.

[2] So now in this our day, as well as in former days, it hath pleased God to give unto a remnant an experimental knowledge of the truth of this; that they have been quickened and made alive by the word of God; that is, they have heard, and felt, and tasted of the word of life that was with the Father before the world began, that hath been divinely ministered to them, by the mercy of God through Jesus Christ. Many that were dead in sins and trespasses he hath said unto them, live. He hath given unto many an inward sense of their state, who sometimes had it not. He hath brought many an one to feel sin to be a burden and an oppressing load, who sometimes before have taken

pleasure and delight in it. This [is] a great change that is wrought in a man's mind that he should come to be loaden with that, burdened and oppressed by that which was before his pleasure and delight. Yet this great change hath been wrought in many a soul by the operation of the word of God, of that inward word, that inward voice, when the Lord hath taken men in hand himself.

[3] There are many have taken sinners in hand and have gone about to convince them and convert them, but they were not able to do it. But when the Lord hath taken men in hand himself, when his creator hath undertaken to deal with him himself, then the man cries out: "I am a worm and no man!" Then he cries out under the sense of the judgment of God. Then he cries out under the indignation of the Lord which he hath kindled by his sins. He cries out for mercy. Then he prays for remission. Then he wishes that he had never provoked the Lord, for the word that goes out of the mouth of God hath a mighty force and power upon the spirit of a man so that he is converted and changed by it. As the prophet said of old: "The word of God is pure, converting the soul."

[4] Now where any come to an experimental knowledge of the word of the Lord, of his inward voice whereby God speaks to the sons and daughters of men, they have received thereby an infallible feeling of their own state and condition. This is the first lesson learned by it. They come to have a certain infallible knowledge of their own state and they are sure that they canot be deceived for it brings an evidence with it in their own consciences so that whatever this word of life signifieth to a man, he hath the knowledge of the same thing evidencing it in his own conscience. As the apostle saith: "If our hearts condemn us, God is greater than our hearts, and knoweth all things." Now here is a way found out for all men to obtain divine knowledge by a divine means, for the Lord speaks by his Spirit, and if men come to hearken to that voice, unto that speaking, they perceive readily what it saith unto them. The Lord tells people now as well as in former ages what he hath against them, and this everyone in the closet of their own hearts come to understand. We read in the Book of Revelations [sic] what our Lord Jesus Christ appointed John to write to the seven churches in Asia, that he had few things against some, and many things against others.

[5] Now that which is the design of our meeting when we are assembled together is that we may know what the mind and judgment of God is concerning ourselves. How shall we know that unless

we ask him and come to wait upon him and inquire at the oracle of counsel that God hath appointed in the bosom of every man? For he signifies his mind unto the children of men by that light and grace which Jesus Christ hath planted in them. He hath enlightened every man that comes into the world with an undeceiving light, and he hath ministered of his truth and grace to every man. Though the man be bad and untrue and in the dark, and there be darkness in him, yet the light shineth in darkness. The man may be a false man, yet there is true knowledge in him if this man hearken to the voice of truth when the God of truth signifies what his mind and judgment is concerning him and his present state.

[6] So that there is an opportunity offered, and if a man believe the word of truth which is administered to his own mind, he canot say such a man hath deceived him, for it is truth itself which is signified to him which he believeth. For the truth is the object of his faith, and he believeth it of himself. He believeth that while he remains wicked in his unrenewed state, he is out of the covenant of God and in the high road to destruction if he doth not get out of it and return to God and mind his duty. He believeth this, and he believeth the truth. It hath been so with many. It hath been so with us all. This is the first kind of faith and belief that ever we receive. For when truth signifieth to us our fallen state, our alienated state, when truth signifies and discovers to us the partition wall of sin and iniquity which we have builded up, whereby the glory and favor of God was hid from the soul, we believed this to be true. We would have been looked upon as heirs of God's kingdom, yet when we are come to hearken to the truth, we find that we are children of the devil and do his works. Shall a man believe this after he hath been forty years a professor of Christianity? If a man believe truth, there is no danger in believing it though it be his own destruction that is threatened.

[7] Now the great thing that I would have ushered into the hearts of men is that they may believe the truth for truth's sake. If men will believe the truth, they must believe many things against themselves which they are not willing to believe. But saith Christ: "No man can be my scholar, my disciple, but by denying himself." I must deny myself, my pretentions to Christianity, my supposed saintship and title to the kingdom of God. Now if I would be convinced that I am a wicked man, a profane man, one that doth not live as becomes the gospel, I must believe truth, the voice of the truth being of infallible

certainty. It is signified divinely by the immortal word that canot deceive us. This ought to be the reason why people should believe the testimony of it though it be against themselves. They that do so presently come to find the effects of it, for they were in their sins and trespasses before, and so are still. They were before in a kind of liberty, in a kind of ease and indulgence of themselves, and still their sins remains [*sic*] in them and they remain in it. But they are now under a sense of sorrow, under a weight, under a burden, under an oppression, which signifies they are alive and quickened. For (if you take an outward comparison) they remain not senseless and dead. Now lay what load you will upon a dead man, he will neither groan nor grumble at it. But if he comes again to life, he cries: "Take off the burden, the weight and oppression, that lies heavy upon me!"

[8] This is the difference between being dead in sins and trespasses and being brought to life and sense again. The word of life that comes from the mouth of God begets a sense in everyone that receiveth it. It is of great service and use to all people to be acquainted with it, that desire to be heirs of life eternal, that desire to be inheritors of the kingdom of God. But how should they come by it? They think by this duty and the other duty, and this and the other temporary performance, to obtain it. No, but if they will have life, they must have it from the God of life that created them. He must create them again to good works. They can have it but by one way. All must be brought to it that way. It canot be by hearing a man preach. Unless the spirit doth cooperate with the word of God, there is no possibility of being quickened, and necessity binds me to hearken and have regard to that one means. Now I say to you, saith Christ, speaking of people's way of living to eternity: "Man liveth not by bread alone, but by every word that proceedeth out of the mouth of God." Now when we come to understand this text, as spoken by our Lord Jesus Christ, we did conclude there was a possibility of understanding and hearing that inward voice and word of truth in our own hearts, that God did speak to us by his son, Jesus Christ, who enlightened us. Hereupon meetings were appointed at first that the word should minister life in them and life to them that attend them. And to this day our meetings are appointed for this purpose: that we may have the ministration of life and virtue from Christ, the fountain of life and virtue, by whom we were to be quickened and strengthened and by whom those who were dead in sins and trespasses were quickened.

[9] Therefore, I would have everyone always to have a reverence to the word of life that speaks in themselves. For, if we speak as we are moved by the spirit of God, and utter those things by verbal testimony which God hath made known to us, if you have not an oracle in your bosoms, if you do not at the same time perceive an echo of truth in your own souls, this will do you no good, but be an empty sound which will pass away again. But the mind that is serious and settled, in waiting upon God with an earnest desire that it may receive benefit in going to this and the other meeting, such an one will say: "I pray God bless this opportunity to me that so I may receive benefit to my soul." Where people meet in this manner, they have not only an administration of doctrine from without from this and the other instrument, but they have a ministration of the word of God in themselves by which a man liveth.

[10] Let us not be led and hurried away with the grand error of the times, the great error of this age and of the ages bypassed, that there is no possibility for people to understand and hear the voice of God, this inward voice. "There are" (say they) "no immediate teachings nowadays, no inspirations nowadays." They had as well said that there are no conversions nowadays. I will prove it from the Holy Scriptures that there is no man in this age is [sic] like to be converted to God or redeemed from his iniquity and brought to the knowledge of his maker, unless he have it by the inward working of the eternal God; not by man's preaching and instruction, nor by reading all the good sermons that ever were preached without the cooperation of the holy sanctifying spirit which begets life in them that believe. And if these men say none can be converted, then we must all go headlong to hell, and they, and all.

[11] "These Quakers may say what they will. There is no immediate teaching nowadays. No man can know the mind of God nor understand the Scriptures. None can open them to you."

[12] But blessed be God, this darkness is removed. This veil is gone over and taken away. The brightness of the glory of the gospel hath expelled this darkness and thousands nowadays do not only hear the minister reprove them, but they hear a voice within that doth reprove them for iniquity, and they find and feel a judgment and tribunal within themselves, and that God hath an immediate way of counseling and instructing them if they will hearken to him.

[13] You that are under any sense of this, that are come to such an inward sense of the operation of the word of God, if you have heard it reprove you, judge you and condemn you, consider that this word proceeded out of the mouth of God and not out of the mouth of any man. You hear the sentence of God upon you in your own consciences. Whence comes it? This is out of the mouth of God. Every word that comes out of the mouth of God administers life, sense and conviction, and you feel it and receive it, and you may have more familiar acquaintance with it. There is not a day or hour that passes over your head, nor mine, but if we attend to this inward voice, we may know what it speaks to us by its counsels, doctrines, reproofs, convictions and illuminations. For the spirit speaketh expressly, with an express signification, unto the spirit of man, and if he be under a temptation to tell a lie, and he comes to a little pause or question whether he shall tell it or no, if he hearken to this inward word he will not pause long about it, but such a sentence will arise in him as that to Joseph: "How can I do this great wickedness and sin against God? How can I speak a lie, tell a lie, when in so doing I sin against God?" Here is a sentence of truth. Wilt thou receive it or no? "No," saist thou, "I will venture to tell a lie." Then shalt thou come into the rank of them that do despite to the spirit of grace and trample underfoot the son of God, and count the blood of the covenant an unholy thing. What sentence such shall have at the latter end you may read at large in the Holy Scriptures.

[14] Now there is a great necessity that everyone be persuaded to hearken to this voice, not only at a meeting, but on all occasions they have in the world. I hope I speak to many serious and religious persons that are inquiring about their immortal souls what may be best for their souls, whether 'tis better to on go in wickedness, or leave off; and that resolve and say: "I would be glad to leave my sins as well as you if I had power and to live a holy life." As for the want of power, that you have not power, I do not wonder at it. For 'til you come to an exercise of faith in that which hath empowered the people of God in all ages, I wonder not that you have not power. You say: "I am so weak that I am overcome before I am aware. The devil is so subtle and cuning with his temptations that I am surprised and snatched into temptations and overcome with evil before I am aware." He is like a roaring lion, going about continually seeking whom he may devour. But who can he devour? Can he devour those that hearken and submit to the word of God? If he could, then none could escape him. If the devil could

pluck out of God's hands, then nobody could go to heaven, nor never shall, if he have power.

[15] Where the devil finds any in their own hands, as suppose a religious person of this and the other religion, who never experienced anything of this power of God, but trusteth to his duties and performances, this man is at his own hand. Now such an one the tempter hath power over. He can make him cheat his neighbor and lead him into drunkenness and uncleaness sometimes, and into the greatest abominations. But if a man come into the exercise of faith and dependence upon God, and hath left trusting in his hands, and saith: "I see I canot preserve myself from sin. I see a necessity of putting my trust in the Lord and of waiting upon God's power to keep me": if the tempter come to such an one, he canot prevail. All the devils in hell canot stir him one jot. The devil may tempt him, but he stands in the power of faith. He knows his name and saith: "Get thee behind me Satan" when the devil comes before him and lays a temptation before him. He casts it behind him. If the devil rise up against him, he can chain him down. He can say in the name of the Lord: "Get thee behind me Satan."

[16] This is the reason why many are tempted and not overtaken; why many are tempted to sin and not overcome. How comes it to pass that we do not do everything that we are tempted to? There is something that keeps us. The devil is not so bad to tempt, but we are as bad in our own inclinations to yield to him: "The heart is deceitful above all things, and desperately wicked. Who can know it?" There is more wickedness in it than can be uttered. If people be tempted and not overcome, something must preserve them. If there be something that preserves a man from any evil, it can preserve him from all evil.

[17] The reason why some people are led into temptation sometimes, and resist it, is because sometimes the temptation suits not their inclination. Sometimes the reputation lies in the way. Sometimes one thing, sometimes another. But when a thing they are tempted to suits their profit and pleasure, then away with the fears of God and nothing shall hinder them: "I will have my pleasure."

[18] But they that understand the keeper of Israel and come to know his power lying in their hearts, these always bring their deeds and temper before him, and they come to him for a verdict and judgment, and they ask: "Doth this tend to the honor or dishonor of God? Is it good or evil?" The oracle of God in the heart says: "Do it not. It is evil. Thou wilt kindle the indignation of the Lord against thee.

What will it profit thee to gain the whole world and lose thy own soul? Or what wilt thou give in exchange for thy soul?" Here is one at hand that can give counsel to all of us at all times. This is he that we must advance. Our labor and work upon the stage of this world among the sons and daughters of men is to advance the virtue and great authority of the mighty counsellor, Christ Jesus. We do say and affirm in the name of God that the same light and God by which God hath brought us out of darkness into his marvellous light, and from the power of the devil into the kingdom of his dear son; the same power is extended to you that you may be sanctified and saved from your sins.

[19] One sect will say: "My tenets are so and so and our ordinances are so and so. Will you come over to us? You shall be a member of our church."

[20] Our duty is to come over to the grace of God that shines in our hearts. Now we are witnesses for God that he doth not desire the death of them that die, but rather that they would turn and live. For his word is gone forth, and his light shines, and his glory is risen upon the nations that they that inhabit the earth may fear him. Fear God and give glory to God. The hour of his judgment is come: do you know that to be true? That you may not be deluded, you shall certainly know that the hour of God's judgment is come.

[21] Thus when anyone suffers himself to be led away with the evil one, when he feels after that a remorse upon his own heart, he finds a secret judgment and tribunal set up in his own bosom against whoredom, lying, drunkenness, fraud and other sins he knows he hath done amiss. He is not going to a confessor that will take off and remove the guilt from his conscience. He hath offended the majesty of the great God, and God hath signified to him. Is not judgment come and hath not God set it up in his own heart? If through custom in sin thou losest the sense of his judgment, it is not because God hath determined to take advantage against thee, but because thou actest against thyself and comest to be past feeling. Thou wast once under a sense of these things and thou wast not past feeling. If thou at any time told thy parents a lie, thou hadst remorse. But now thou canst tell a lie and not feel it. Thou art past feeling. Whose fault is this? The Lord would have brought thee to love the truth, but thou choosest lying. If thou perish, thy blood will be upon thine own head. The Lord is clear from it.

[22] They that receive the word of God have life. For man liveth not by bread only, but by every word that proceedeth out of the mouth

of God. You are sensible of God's speaking this word to you. I exhort you all in the love of God, that you would prize this manner of speaking and look upon it as the greatest mercy that ever you enjoyed, that God hath not given over speaking to you, and that conscience hath not given over speaking to you, and that the spirit of the Lord doth yet strive with you. He will not always strive. You may be of that sort of fools before you die that make a mock of sin, and be as trees twice dead and plucked up by the roots. You that are sensible of this inward voice, prize it above all your mercies. Health and wealth and all other mercies are not worthy to be compared to this voice of God speaking in you. They that prize this will never complain for want of power. They will find power in it. All the power in heaven and earth is contained in this truth that shines unto you. They that come to be exercised in this word receive power from God, for God gives it to them. He gives them power by degrees, from being sons of Belial, sons of the devil, to become sons of God, to as many as believe on his name. They that receive this truth grow tender of a lie, of a vain word. They find themselves grow tender, feeling and sensible. Here is a token that the God of life is quickening them: "I am now tender of speaking a lie to my neighbor. I will not do that thing to another that I would not have another do to me." When you come to a tender state, which is far better than a hard-hearted state, you will have an evidence in yourselves that man liveth not by bread alone, but by every word that proceeds out of the mouth of God.

[23] Blessed are they that God hath brought into acquaintance with his word. Of all nations and people upon the earth, they are a blessed people. Though there are manifold blessings that reach indifferently to all—the sun shines and the rain falls on the evil and the good and on the just and the unjust—yet this is a blessing that can only make the soul happy, that an intercourse between it and its maker is open, that there is an open intercourse for the Lord to hear a man cry and he to receive his word. All those that God hath brought into covenant with himself by Christ he hath made sensible of this intercourse and way of God's speaking to his people which he spake to them by in former days. Take heed that this way is not stopped up. You know by what it was opened and what will stop it up again. When you were in much trouble and grief, you cried to the Lord and he delivered you. But "If I regard iniquity in my heart," said David, "the Lord will not hear me." You cried to the Lord again, it may be, and he did not

answer you. And the Lord cried to you and you answered him not, but hearkened unto your lusts.

[24] Yet the Lord, by his long-suffering and patience, hath won upon a remnant, and hath brought them over to believe and trust in his power to remove out of the way that which hindered the intercourse between God and their souls. What a great stir was there in removing out of the way the pride, corruption, enmity, looseness, wantonness, and abundance more of evil things that made the soul like a wilderness? What hacking up and burning up was there? God's word, like a hammer and like a fire, did break up and burn up these things. And the same word of God, like a sword, did cut down those sins and lusts which prevailed over you before. By this means God hath opened a way for you to have access to him and for his word to have access to you. When you come to the Lord in this way, you know you live by this word. And if you hear the word of the Lord spoken immediately to you, your joy and consolation increaseth and you have sweet communion and fellowship with God and Christ and with one another by this covenant of life. How came you into it? It was by removing a great deal of rubbish out of the way. If you should let this rubbish grow up again, which kept you from the joy of the Holy Ghost, will it not do it again? If your pride, corruption, enmity, prejudice, looseness and wantonness, if these be suffered to grow up in any of you, they will do as they did before: they will separate you from the Lord and from one another. As the truth brought you to God and this heavenly fellowship with him, so if a wrathful mind and wanton spirit get up again, it will separate you from God and scatter you from one another, then you will live in the outward life and die to the inward one and perish. Remember, you were told so.

[25] Everyone that goes from this living word and suffers anything to arise of the old Nature, so much as that riseth, so much will your way of intercourse with God be stopped. Sometimes men cry to God, but they have a bar in their way; and they come for comfort to the throne of grace, but they canot receive those ministrations of joy and peace which they desire. Their foolish hearts are darkened and their minds blinded and they will go on in darkness and be left out of the holy covenant which God hath called his people to.

[26] You that God hath engaged to be his by the operation of his power, O live in a holy fear and watchfulness; and know this, that let your understandings and gifts be what they will, you have nothing but

what is given you, and what God hath given you he can take away: "Thou hast decked thyself with my flax, and my wool, and with my silver and gold, and other ornaments, and followed thy lovers, therefore will I take them away from thee, and strip thee of all thou gloriest in." Those that forget God, of whom they had these things, that forget their brokenness of heart and the subjection of their spirits to God, if they forget this, let them know that, let their parts be what they will, they will certainly wither and their inward life will fail. You that have regard to your own souls and do desire heartily (at this time) to be quickened and find that the Lord hath removed your deadness and quickened and raised you to such a degree and measure of life that you can say: "I find communion with God and fellowship with my friends and brethren in that one eternal life," I pray God you may continue in it long and lay down you [*sic*] heads in this blessed heavenly life. Now that you may so do, keep yourselves low and humble and in the fear of God, and keep your ears always open to his word, and live as becomes those that are born again and begotten of God and are brought to partake of the divine life. Let temptations surround you, that life will preserve you. He that never sined is with you to keep you from sin. And he that never deceived any will keep you from being deceived. To his counsel and conduct, and to his divine care and protection, I now commit you.

CHAPTER 11

"THIS IS MY TESTIMONY UNTO YOU FROM THE LIFE OF GOD"

THE THEORIST TESTS HIS OWN ADVICE

Robert Barclay (1648–1690), the most important early Quaker intellectual and the sect's most capable apologist, delivered a sermon in London on May 16, 1688, the only sermon of his for which a text survives. Being a Scot from Ury, he could be in London only on occasion, and none of his sermons delivered in Scotland have survived.

The existence of this sermon provides a very interesting case, since we have seen in earlier chapters that Barclay wrote specifically and systematically about immediate revelation and inspiration and thus profoundly shaped the development of the theory of Quaker impromptu preaching. In this chapter, I will examine Barclay's sermon against the context of his life and particularly the backdrop of his *Apology* and *Immediate Revelation*. Specifically, I will begin with the context of the sermon, then turn to the sermon itself.

BARCLAY AND THE CONTEXT OF THE SERMON

Barclay, the son of David Barclay, a colonel in the Commonwealth Army, was born in 1648 at Ury, Scotland. After the Restoration in 1665, the elder Barclay was imprisoned at Edinburgh because of his association with Parliament forces. There he came under the influence of a Quaker, a fellow prisoner, as did also Robert when he visited his father. Subsequently, they both became Quakers in 1666. Significantly, Robert Barclay's mother was distantly related to the Royal Family, which connections helped Robert to have a small measure of political influence during the Restoration period, though he also spent a term in prison for his Quaker faith (in Aberdeen from November 7, 1676, until April 9, 1677). However, in later years, through his connection with James II, he was appointed governor of New Jersey, a position he held by deputy from 1682 to 1688. Eventually, he was named Laird of Ury.[1]

As noted in chapter 4, Barclay, then a twenty-seven-year-old Scot, educated in the schools of Aberdeen and the Scots College at Paris, where his uncle was rector, composed and published his *Apology* in Latin in 1676 and two years later published it in English.[2] We are reminded that Barclay's *Immediate Revelation* was composed in 1676 as a letter in Latin to Heer Paets, a Dutch ambassador, and was not published in English until 1686, just two years before the sermon.[3]

My examination of Barclay's *Apology* and *Immediate Revelation* in chapter 4 indicates that he developed the philosophical outlines of a rhetorical theory with direct revelation as the center of knowledge. Barclay replaces the classical system, with its emphasis on inventional machinery, with a system that relies on the perception of inward revelation. For Barclay, the mind comes preseeded with divinely implanted ideas that are "stirred up" by the Inward Light or by outward sensation. Language, for Barclay, is dictated by the Spirit so that the speaker becomes a kind of oracle for the Word. The emphasis on silence translates into a belief that all utterance is fraught with caution. Consequently, the words actually spoken may gain substantially in credibility and become more weighty. Regardless of his cautionary analysis, Barclay nevertheless believed in the efficacy of preaching and that preaching, when prompted immediately by the Spirit, could help reinforce an inward message and provide comfort and assurance.

When Barclay rose to speak on May 16, 1688, at Grace Church Street Meetinghouse, the largest Friends meetinghouse in London, we can assume that he had followed his own advice to wait silently before the Lord in the gathered meeting until he was moved by the Spirit to speak. He was forty years old but would die relatively young in 1690, still in his prime, at the age of forty-two. There must have been an air of expectancy among the gathered Friends, since Barclay was a respected Quaker thinker and writer and also well known as a publick Friend. He was also a visitor from Scotland and a person with a record of publications, public ministry, and missionary work. In sum, he was a person *likely* to be moved by the Spirit to speak at any given meeting. He might also have been expected to draw numerous non-Quakers to the meeting, one of whom took down his sermon in shorthand.

Like most seventeenth-century Quakers, Barclay had suffered imprisonment for his faith, but on that day in May, Friends, especially in London, were already enjoying relative freedom from official repression, and although the meeting was, strictly speaking, illegal, there was probably little likelihood of its being broken up by government officials or a rude crowd, as had been common in earlier days. In fact, the Act of Toleration, for which both Barclay and his friend William Penn had lobbied with James II, was less than a year in the future.

The Sermon in Context

Barclay's sermon is relatively brief, at only 1,473 words, but his prayer that follows the sermon is 1,504 words, making Barclay's sermon the only extant early Quaker sermon in which the prayer surpasses the sermon in length (by thirty-one words). In the volume in which the sermon found print, all but one of the fifteen sermons (preached by fourteen different preachers) includes a prayer following the sermon.[4]

Barclay begins the sermon with the announcement that his sermon is a "testimony" with deep historical roots, a testimony "born of old and . . . also born this day" (paragraph 1). Here he attempts to situate his message not only within the kairotic moment of its utterance but also in the chronological struggle of early Quakers to recapture the reality of primitive Christianity, Christianity stripped of the historical accumulation of what they saw as ineffectual and heathenish rituals and forms, what Barclay called "will worship" in the *Apology*.[5] Instead, he wants "an agreement between the members and the head, the word and the power, the notion and the substance," a balance that will result in "life" for believers, not just ritually expressed belief in creedal doctrines.[6]

Despite the radical begining, the sermon bears many marks of traditional Protestant sermonizing. In theological terms, the sermon deals principally with soteriology, the theological foundation of salvation as effected by Jesus Christ, although that term itself is not used. Barclay launches the sermon from a platform that sets forth an explication and application of a passage from the New Testament, 1 John 5:12: "He that hath the Son hath life; and he that hath not the Son of God hath not life."[7] However, Barclay canot be accused of using the Puritan approach of systematically raising the doctrine from the passage and applying it to the hearers (doctrine-use). Nevertheless, like Crisp's sermon in the last chapter, Barclay's Scripture text is a starting point for his remarks as well as a thread throughout the sermon. In the sermon, "life" is opposed to death. The hearers are enjoined to "receive the Son of God into [their] souls, and by receiving him, partake of his life; and

then let this life produce its action." This is language with a nineteenth-
or twentieth-century "evangelical" ring to it, similar to the language
Crisp had used previously. In paragraph three, Barclay invites his hearers to "examine themselves" and judge "whether they have the Son of
God or not, whether they have Christ or not. If they have Christ, they
have the benefits of his death and of his blood and sufferings. What are
the benefits of "having Christ" to the people who are asked to examine their lives? Barclay answers using standard Protestant theological
terminology: "They are partakers of justification, and sanctification,
and adoption." One of the most important benefits of the conjoin-
ing of "notion" and "substance," or "being made alive in him," is the
ability "to worship him, to glorify him, and to declare of his glory."[8]
Here Barclay makes it clear that "declaring" God's glory—testifying
and preaching—must be preceded by a personal experience—the individual believer having Christ within.

Paradoxically, the life in Christ is obtained only through death, and
not just Christ's death but also the symbolic self-denial and "death" of
the believer. Recall that on a literal level Barclay has "served time" in
a harsh and inhumane Aberdeen "gaol" for his faith. He is not advocating "cheap grace" here. Using the seed metaphor, with its strong
biblical connections, Barclay asserts, "Every plant, seed or grain that is
placed in the earth, it dies before it grows up. There is a dieing before
there is a living. Those that come to the life of the Son of God, they
come to it through dieing, for it was through dieing that he obtained
this life."[9]

For Barclay, there are two kinds of "life." He sets out the biblical
struggle between "that cursed, that corrupt life of unrighteousness"—
the life of Adam—and "the life that springs from the heavenly incorruptible seed." The former Adamic life has a profoundly negative
effect on "the unrighteous." Barclay states, "That [Adamic] life useth
and employeth all their faculties, their understandings, wills, affections
and imaginations, and it useth all the members of their bodies to
please the flesh and fulfill the lusts thereof." Here Barclay uses the lan
guage of the currently prevalent faculty psychology. The Adamic life,
according to Barclay, has an effect on the unrighteous, both *inward*,
through the corruption of their "faculties," and *outward*, through their
depraved physical behaviors. In contrast, those who "have received
Jesus Christ the Son of God . . . have received a new life, another
life." He tells his hearers, "You sit no more in the earthly place nor

live an earthly life, but in the heavenly place where the heavenly life abounds."[10] The sermon relies at key junctures on the orientational metaphor where, as in Fox's sermon, down (earth) is negative and up (heaven) is positive.[11]

Creasey has interpreted Barclay's theological writings as displaying a quasi-Cartesian dualism of body and mind, and the passages cited may be interpreted according to Creasey's view. However, at least from the evidence found in this sermon, Barclay appears to be in good company, because his warnings about the corrupting influence of the flesh are also squarely Pauline (see Romans 8 and Ephesians 2). The begining sentence of Barclay's conclusion is instructive regarding his position on this topic: "[It] is not the things of the earth that we are to remember and to have dwelling in us, but the word of God and that which proceeds from the life of the Son of God."[12] In the sermon's context, Barclay is not pushing a philosophy of dualism here, but instead is nudging his hearers toward an inward spiritual experience rather than settling for a mere set of outward religious practices—in other words, he wants them to have "substance" rather than just "notions."

Having laid out the radical differences between the lives of people "who are dead in sins and trespasses" and those who "sit no more in the earthly place nor live an earthly life, but in the heavenly place where the heavenly life abounds," Barclay is now prepared to spell out some central "consequences that [the life of the indwelling Christ] brings forth amongst the children of God."[13]

In the final paragraph of the sermon, Barclay makes direct proclamations drawn from his previous thinking (and writing) about the implications of the indwelling life of Christ on the practice of preaching in the gathered Quaker meeting. He begins by revisiting his main point: "[It] is not the things of the earth that we are to remember and to have dwelling in us, but the word of God and that which proceeds from the life of the Son of God." He follows this reiteration of the source of inspired speech with language that directly echoes his position on ministry in the *Apology*, noted in chapter 4: "All words and testimonies, preachings, prayer, exhortation, and spiritual counsel, if it be not from the life of the Son of God, it edifies not the Body of the Lord Jesus Christ in love."[14] In other words, authentic preaching—in fact, all authentic verbal expression in ministry—is the result of having the life of Christ within oneself and drawing upon its influence. We may observe here that Barclay appears to be using his memory of what he wrote in the *Apology* to make his point. It was ready at hand in his memory.

Next Barclay directly addresses his listeners as hearers of Quaker impromptu "testimonies," those that ostensibly arise from the life of Christ inwardly dwelling in many of them in the gathered meeting: "Let us receive that which comes from the life of the Son of God, which is manifest amongst us and shed abroad in our hearts. Let us watch and take care that whatsoever is not of this life may not appear, may not be manifest and made known among us."[15] This is Barclay's reminder to his hearers that when they speak, they must only speak under the direct leading of the Spirit, but they must also discern whether the spoken message, presumably including his own sermon, is authentic—that is, whether it "rings true" as proceeding from the "life" of the inward-dwelling Christ. This statement reaffirms the cautionary warnings about inappropriate speech voiced by Whitehead, Marshall, and Coole.[16]

Now Barclay makes a bold move and asserts that his very sermon bears at least some of the marks of authenticity: "This is my testimony unto you from the life of God, which to the glory and praise of his name hath risen in my soul in some measure."[17] Except for the phrase "in some measure," his statement is very close to a claim of immediate inspiration, a rhetorical move rare among the surviving seventeenth-century Quaker sermons.[18] However, this somewhat audacious claim is perhaps no more than a personal restatement of his position expressed in Proposition XI of the *Apology*: "[He] that ministereth, being actuated thereunto by the arising of the grace in himself, ought to speak forth what the Spirit of God furnisheth him with; not minding the eloquence and wisdom of words, but the demonstration of the Spirit and of power."[19]

As Barclay concludes the message, he reaffirms his desire that his hearers "be inwardly gathered into this heavenly life" and specifically "that the fruit thereof may be manifest, that the notice thereof, the sound thereof, the language thereof may be heard in this assembly at all times."[20] In essence, with his specific mention of "sound," he is saying that he hopes sermons like his own will continue to be heard with some frequency at Grace Church Street Meetinghouse. According to the sermon, this continuing manifestation of "heavenly life" is dependent on two things: (1) the life of Christ in each gathered believer and (2) the inward gathering of that life in the specific meeting for worship.

Conclusion

Barclay's sole surviving sermon offers an opportunity to trace some of the effects of the apologist's thinking about impromptu preaching under the direct influence of the Spirit on his own preaching practice. This analysis has argued that Barclay's practice is consistent with his influential published writings on Quaker impromptu preaching. There is no smell of the lamp here; no parading of his considerable breadth of learning; no mention of his aristocratic ethos or position; no Latin, Greek, or Hebrew quotations; and no quotations from theologians, philosophers, or historians. Instead, we are offered a straightforward literal application of the Scripture that indicates that you must have Christ to have life.

The sermon is personal rather than detached and academic. Arguably, Barclay shows courage by claiming his own inspiration. Other preachers avoided the claim. He specifically places himself under scrutiny by reminding his hearers that they are expected to be discerning listeners.

As noted, the sermon's linguistic choices sound surprisingly contemporary and stand as precursors to the revivalistic preaching of the next century in both England and America by Whitefield and the Wesleys. The theological language of personal commitment and the need to "have Christ" anticipates the nineteenth- and twentieth-century evangelical language of "accepting Jesus Christ as your personal savior."

Finally, we may ask why Barclay felt moved to remark about the practice of sermonizing itself, and even to ask boldly "that the fruit [of the heavenly life] may be manifest, that the notice thereof, the sound thereof, the language thereof may be heard" at Grace Church Street Meeting.[21] I would suggest that, in spite of his cautionary tone about vocal ministry, Barclay may actually be fearful that the zeal of the first generation of Quakers is gradually moving toward the reserved, insular "quietism" of the second and especially the third generation of Quakers. By speaking out himself, he affirms that preaching, indeed, has a place. His friend William Penn would preach a funeral sermon on June 19, 1688, one month later, touching on this topic.[22] Apparently Barclay and Penn, like Fox, never required nudging to preach. In former times of persecution, Quakers in general did not need encouragement to preach. It appears that as persecution waned, they now needed prodding from influential publick Friends to keep on the straight and narrow and to speak in the Spirit at meetings.[23]

A Sermon Preached by Robert Barclay at Grace Church Street, London, May 16, 1688

[1][24] This is the testimony that was born of old, and it is also born this day, that there may be an agreement between the members and the head, the word and the power, the notion and the substance: "He that hath the Son hath life, and he that hath not the Son hath not life." [1 John 5:12] So that in this the substance is known whereby men are redeemed to live unto God, and to live for God and to glorify him. This is the end of the testimony of the gospel of our Lord and Savior Jesus Christ, that we may all come to partake of his life, and that by partaking of it we may live upon it, and being made alive in him we shall then be made able to serve him; then shall we be enabled to worship him, to glorify him, and to declare of his glory, and of his power, and of his wisdom, and of his goodness to those that are strangers to him, and to invite all to be partakers thereof. Let all your eyes this day be towards him and to the enjoyment of his life that you may be sensible, and that you may be witnesses of his life.

[2] And this life is not to be obtained but by death; there is a dieing before there is a living. Every plant, seed or grain that is placed in the earth, it dies before it grows up. There is a dieing before there is a living. Those that come to the life of the Son of God, they come to it through dieing, for it was through dieing that he obtained this life. It was necessary that the Son of God, the Prince of Life, should die, that he should be crucified, else he could not finish the work of our salvation, and make way for the revelation and the sowing of that seed, and the dispensation of that grace whereby we might come to have a share with him in that eternal life he obtained for us. They that come to the life of the Son of God, they must obey him; for they must receive the sentence of death to that life which they derive from Adam, that cursed, that corrupt life of unrighteousness, that life of ungodliness, that life wherein self and the will of man delights, wherein the natural man, the animal man, hath a life. We must die, and by dieing come to be partakers of the life of Jesus. He communicates himself to us, and by our receiving him, we receive life: "He that hath the Son hath life,

and he that hath not the Son hath not life," and the consequence is, he that hath not this life, hath not the Son of God.

[3] This is the true way for everyone to try and examine themselves by, and to make a true judgment of themselves, that they may know whether they have the Son of God or not, whether they have Christ or not. If they have Christ they have the benefits of his death and of his blood and sufferings. They that have this life in them, they are in the faith. They are partakers of justification, and sanctification, and adoption; and all those that are under the dispensation of the gospel, that have the benefits of Christ's death, to those he giveth himself, and those to whom he giveth himself, he giveth this life. This is not the life of Adam, a life of unrighteousness, but a life that springs from the heavenly incorruptible seed. Such as partake of it are born again of the word of the Lord that remains forever. This is a life that comes from the Lord from heaven, the quickening Spirit, and this life tends heavenward. It looks heavenward. It carries the affections towards the things that are above. It dwells not in them that have their pleasures in this world. It looks not to the things of this world. It comes from heaven and tends to heaven again. It raiseth the soul that is quickened by it. They that are born of it are made heavenly by it. It makes all heavenly that are quickened by it. By this we may know that we have the Son of God. By this we have an understanding of him and are brought into him that is true.

[4] And this is the living manifestation of Christ whereby he cometh into thy soul, and into my soul. This is the gift of God. We receive God's gift that we may receive life from and by him, that we may live this life. This is that which makes the yoke of Christ easy, and his burden light, and his commandments not grievous to us. The life of Christ doth the work of Christ natually. Those that are in the flesh, mind the things of the flesh. Those that live a carnal life, they mind the works of the flesh. It is their joy, their delight and their pleasure, that which their hearts are carried after. They rise early and lie down late, and all for this end. It is that which their hearts run after all the day long. What is the reason of it? They are in the flesh, in the life of lust. That life moves them, and acts them, and governs them. That life useth and employeth all their faculties, their understandings, wills, affections and imaginations, and it useth all the members of their bodies to please the flesh and fulfil the lusts thereof; these are the consequences of a life of unrighteousness in those that are unrighteous.

[5] But those that have received the Spirit of God, they have received Jesus Christ the Son of God, and this is the consequence: they are become dead to the life of unrighteousness. All that are dead in sins and trespasses he hath quickened. Now when you have received the Son of God, you have received a new life, another life. Then your affections are set upon things that are above, and you are come to sit in heavenly places in Christ Jesus. You sit no more in the earthly place nor live an earthly life, but in the heavenly place where the heavenly life abounds. "For this end the eternal Son of God came into the world that we might have life, and that we might have it more abundantly," that we might abound in the life of Jesus, and in the abundance of it. This is that which is recommended to us, that we might receive the Son of God into our souls, and by receiving him, partake of his life; and then let this life produce its action. Let the word of God dwell richly in you, in all those things that are divine, in all those things, consequences that it brings forth amongst the children of God.

[6] For it is not the things of the earth that we are to remember and to have dwelling in us, but the word of God and that which proceeds from the life of the Son of God. All words and testimonies, preachings, prayer, exhortation, and spiritual counsel, if it be not from the life of the Son of God, it edifies not the Body of the Lord Jesus Christ in love. Let us receive that which comes from the life of the Son of God, which is manifest amongst us and shed abroad in our hearts. Let us watch and take care that whatsoever is not of this life may not appear, may not be manifest and made known among us. And this life that we receive from the Son of God is that which will stand us in stead in the day of trial, and as many as live unto God in this divine life, he is well pleased with them, and the Tempter, the wicked one, canot touch them at all, nor reach them, nor hurt them. This is my testimony unto you from the life of God, which to the glory and praise of his name hath risen in my soul in some measure: It is the desire, and labor, and travel of my soul that you may be inwardly gathered into this heavenly life, that all my dear brethren and sisters who are of the household of faith, may be inward in this life, that the fruit thereof may be manifest, that the notice thereof, the sound thereof, the language thereof may be heard in this assembly at all times, that the Lord our God may be made known to us through this word of life in our hearts, to the praise, honor and renown of his name, who alone is worthy, to whom be glory for ever and ever. Amen.

Prayer after Sermon

[7] O most powerful Lord God of Life, and of glory and blessedness, precious in thy sight are thy people whom with thy power thou hast visited with the day spring from on high, and upon whom thou hast breathed with a divine inspiration and made them alive to thyself through thy tender mercy and goodness which, in the Son of thy love, thou hast freely extended to us, whereby we are made capable of drawing nigh to thee, and of having access into thy blessed presence to enjoy communion with thee through the Lord Jesus Christ.

[8] We desire to wait upon thee and seek fervently after thee. All our expectation is from thee from day to day, and from time to time, that we may receive relief, that we may receive strength from thee, who art the God of all our mercies. Thou hast not been wanting to us in the needful time. Thou hast had regard to the sighing of the poor, to the breathing and supplication of the needy, whose desires have been truly after thee and the sweet enjoyment of thy presence, the feeling of thy blessed power, and the beholding of the light of thy countenance wherein there is life and salvation. Blessed be thy name forever. All living praises and holy thanksgivings be in truth and humility offered up to thee through the dear Son of thy love by all thy children and people, whom thou hast sought out by thy blessed Spirit, and whom thou hast gathered by the arm of thy blessed and mighty power, that they might be a people to thy praise, serving thee in newness of Spirit, worshipping thee in the beauties of holiness and in spirit and truth, and not according to the oldness of the letter, not according to an empty and outward formality, but in the sense of the springings up of that pure life, of that fresh spring of life, that thou hast placed in the hearts of a remnant by thy blessed power. O righteous and holy God, the sense and feeling thereof is beyond words, beyond expression, and beyond utterance.

[9] Therefore, we humbly entreat thee by the blessed arm of thy power, gather thy people more and more into an inward sense of the springings of life, that they may attend upon thee, and feel life in their souls, and breathings after thee in their hearts, that in their daily attendance on thee, they may receive day by day of those living suitable supplies of life, virtue, wisdom, and power whereby they may be supported through all trials and adversities, and through all oppositions and temptations that they may meet withal for the trial of their faith and for the exercise of their patience, that all their afflictions and

exercises may be sanctified to them for the bringing them nearer and nearer to thyself, and into a more lively inward and single dependence on thee and thy divine grace and truth which thou hast made known by Christ Jesus, our only mediator, by whom alone we have access to thee, and whereby we are made capable of beholding the light of thy countenance, and partake of thy divine goodness and blessing, and of those precious promises which thou hast left upon record and impressed upon our minds and hearts. Thou hast poured into us a living and inward sense of that pure life of thy dear Son whereby we may be enabled to live to thy praise; and O blessed powerful Lord God, those that are not convinced and persuaded of thy way and blessed truth, that are not come into it, and to partake of the life of it, that are not yet come to live to thee and to life in obedience to thy blessed Son, the Lord Jesus Christ, who are not come under the power of his cross that they may be crucified to the world and have the world crucified to them: Lord awaken them. Utter thy voice that shakes the mountains. Rend the veil and draw in their hearts and minds and affections from earthly and fading objects, that they may come to breathe after thee, and feel that Spirit in them wherewith thou dost inspire thy people, whereby they may supplicate thee for relief, for strength, and victory over the spirit of the world, and over the temptations of the Devil and the flesh, which do so easily beset men; and whereby many are led captives, who canot yet make mention of thy name and walk in the truth. Lord awaken them by thy powerful voice, and incline their hearts to seek thee while thou art to be found, and call upon thee while thou art near, that thou mayst be known in thy glorious visitation. The chords of thy love thou hast extended, that they may lay hold thereon, that they may be drawn out of the pollutions of the world and of sin and Satan, that have brought death over them. Let the fear of God take place, that they may be afraid to offend thee, as knowing that thou art a jealous God, and thine eyes are upon all the ways of the sons of men. Thou art the heart-searching God. There is no secret can be hid from thine all-seeing eyes. Under that consideration, O Lord, let many come unto thee and reverence thy great name and not provoke thee to displeasure against them.

[11] And O blessed God, thou hast been graciously pleased to begin a good work, a glorious work of righteousness in our days and times. Blessed God and Father, we humbly pray thee carry it on and make it prosper. Prosper the souls of thy people in it that they may be

growing, thriving, and increasing people in thy holy ways and in thy blessed work. And as thou hast sown a precious seed, and planted a noble vine by thine own almighty hand, and given us a root of life, the foundation of our faith, love, and obedience, which foundation thou hast laid in Zion, Lord keep thy people sensible of it, that they may mind it and wait upon thee, and be preserved in that root of life wherein thy blessing is, that thy people may partake of thy blessing and grow up into the nature of that life, to bring forth fruit to thee, to increase in faith and love, in obedience and humility, and meekness, that the life of true Christianity may be promoted and increased among thine heritage, that they may live in it, and shine forth in it as thy workmanship which thou hast created in Christ Jesus unto fruitfulness, unto all good works, that they may walk in them. That so powerful God and living creator, they may live unto thee and act entirely unto thy praise, honor, and glory in their day, age and generation, and that their bright shining forth in the light of truth and righteousness may appear more and more as an invitation to those that are afar off, that in this thy day wherein thou art setting up the tabernacle of David, the kingdom of thy beloved Son, and repairing the ruins and waste places thereof, Lord God eternal, grant that the residue of men may seek after thee, and be sensible that thou art at work, and raising an house for thine honor, and promoting the kingdom of the Son, which is a kingdom of righteousness, that of his government there may be no end, that all those that desire after peace and after happiness in the kingdom of thy dear Son may wait to see him rule and govern, to see him reign whose right it is; that sin may not reign in their mortal bodies, that sinful lusts and vile affections, and an earthly mind may not have power over them and prevail against them, that so their souls may be lifted up to thee; that, blessed eternal God, they may wait upon thee, and renew their strength, and renew their thankfulness for the renewing of thy mercies and the incomes of thy love which are fresh and new every morning; that they may fear thee, and wait upon thee, and diligently seek after thee, and have sweet communion with thee in the enjoyment of thy presence.

[12] And blessed be thou, O Lord God eternal, for all thy mercies, preservations, and encouragements so frequently afforded to thy people, whose eyes and hearts are towards thee. Our souls are deeply engaged to thee, and we have cause to bless, and praise, and honor thy great and excellent name, and through thy dear Son to offer up praise

and thanksgiving to thy great and excellent majesty. For thou alone, O God, art worthy to receive the honor and praise of all thy mercies, benefits and blessings, by all the living here and elsewhere, who art God only over all heaven and the whole earth, blessed and praised for ever, and ever. Amen.

CHAPTER 12

WILLIAM PENN PREACHES AN IMPROMPTU FUNERAL SERMON

William Penn (1644–1718) is perhaps more familiar to contemporary people than any other early Quaker. He is well known as an important seventeenth- and eighteenth-century political figure.[1] What is lesser known is that Penn was also an able preacher. Eleven of his sermons are extant in printed form, each originally a product of unknown but probably non-Quaker listeners with shorthand skills.[2] This chapter will focus on a sermon Penn preached at the London funeral or memorial of important early Quaker minister Rebecca Travers on June 19, 1688. In this chapter, I will (1) place the sermon in the context of both Penn's and Travers' lives; (2) lay out the journey-pilgrimage metaphor for purposes of this chapter; (3) focus on Penn's use of the journey metaphor in response to the immediate rhetorical situation, particularly his choice of language that suggests the differences between the *liminal* journey of the present life and the *status* (or *stasis* in Greek, fixity) of the life to come; and (4) conclude with implications of the sermon with regard to the development of *communitas*.

WILLIAM PENN AND HIS TROUBLES

Born to influence and wealth in the home of a British admiral, Penn's conversion to Quakerism came in 1667, when he was twenty-three years old and tending to his father's affairs in Ireland. By the 1670s, Penn had become one of the acknowledged leaders among Friends, and he used his influence and knowledge of the law to petition Parliament on behalf of Friends, oppose unjust laws, seek an end to religious persecution, and gain the release of imprisoned Quakers. Eventually, upon his father's death in 1670, Penn inherited large landholdings in England and Ireland, and he began to use his wealth and influence in the American colonies.

The period between 1681 and 1684 went exceptionally well for Penn and his colony and has been referred to as "the high point of his life."[3] Penn spent almost two years in Pennsylvania but eventually returned to England to defend the boundaries of his colony in court against Lord Baltimore, a legal battle that Penn could not wage effectively from America. Penn returned to England deeply in debt and left the colony under the care of inadequate absentee leadership.[4]

The four years leading up to Penn's sermon at the memorial of Rebecca Travers were tumultuous in the history of England as well as Penn's life. In Quaker circles, he was beginning to feel the effects of his absence from England, and negative rumors circulated about conditions in the Pennsylvania colony. Similarly, outside Quaker circles, Penn's reputation began to take a turn for the worse, especially with Anglicans and Puritans, among whom he began to be too closely associated with Catholics, especially his personal friend James II, a Catholic, who succeeded Charles II in 1685. Penn began to use his influence with his old friend to attempt to bring about greater toleration for Dissenters.[5] In the process, Penn became identified in many quarters as having Catholic leanings. Penn wrote his famous *Perswasive to Moderation* during this period as part of his campaign for toleration. In 1685, the king proclaimed a pardon for all "imprisoned for conscience's sake," probably due to Penn's influence,[6] and in 1686 Penn traveled to Holland on behalf of the king but also participated in the Quaker traveling ministry while on the continent. In 1688 he sought to offer advice to James about his policies regarding nonconformists.[7]

Penn's political influence ended abruptly after the overthrow of James II by William and Mary in December 1688, five months after his sermon at Travers' memorial. With James now in exile, Penn was summoned as an adherent of the former king, eventually arrested, and accused of treason by the new government.[8] Important to this chapter, late during this period, at a time nestled between his return to England in 1684 and the "Glorious Revolution" in 1688, Penn took time out from his stressful schedule in May 1689 to attend and preach at the memorial service of Travers, ten months before the passage of the Act of Toleration, a law that would usher in "a new era for Friends and other Nonconformists."[9] For a time following his 1688 sermon, Penn actually refused to be seen in public for fear of arrest.[10]

REBECCA TRAVERS AND HER FUNERAL

Travers (1609–1688), the significance of whose memorial drew Penn from seclusion, was an important leader in Quakerism's first generation. Raised as a devout Baptist and student of the Bible, she converted to Quakerism in 1654, at the age of forty-six, after a period of intellectual and spiritual struggle set in motion initially when she attended a public dispute between Baptists and the Quaker firebrand James Nayler, who at that time rivaled George Fox for leadership of the movement and was also one of Quakerism's most controversial public figures.[11] In 1656 Nayler allowed himself to ride into the city of Bristol on a donkey, while women accompanying him spread garments in his path singing "Holy, holy, holy, Lord God of Israel."[12] Braithwaite notes that Nayler was arrested, received 310 lashes with a knotted cord, had his tongue pierced through by a hot iron, and was branded with the letter "B" on his forehead (for "blasphemer"). Travers, who was *not* among the women who attended Nayler on his notorious and misguided "triumphal entry" into Bristol, nevertheless dressed his wounds in prison, remarking, "There was not a space of a man's nail free from stripes and blood from his shoulders near to his waste."[13] Although Nayler subsequently rued his poor judgment and in essence ceded the Quaker movement to Fox, as we have noted previously, the Bristol incident was a public-relations nightmare, which triggered an immediate negative impact on Quakerism, including discouragement, public scandal, increased public disturbances at Quaker meetings, and division among Quakers. Outside of Quaker circles, the affair left "a deep impression of the dangerous tendencies of Quaker principles."[14] Upon Nayler's release from Bridewell Prison in 1659, Rebecca and John Travers (Rebecca's husband) housed Nayler in their London residence through most of the year 1660. Nayler eventually died in October of 1660 after a beating by a highwayman. Travers had a long association with Nayler. Earlier she had written prefaces to some of Nayler's tracts and later petitioned Parliament on his behalf for a cessation of punishment.[15] Her behavior from the time of her convincement, through Nayler's disastrous Bristol affair, to the time of Nayler's extreme punishment and early death, was uniformly marked both by good sense and compassion. These qualities, coupled with what the *DNB* calls her reputation as a "fearless and powerful preacher," marked Travers as a much-sought-after leader among Quakers.[16]

The remainder of Travers' long seventy-nine-year life included two imprisonments at Newgate, ministry of care for the "sick, poor, and prisoners," hosting at her home the very significant "Second Day's Morning Meeting" of Quaker public ministers, and membership (in 1671) on the Quaker court of appeal, the "Six Weeks Meeting."[17] Christine Trevett indicates that Travers authored seven pamphlets, and notes that "The majority of early Quaker women writers produced just one tract or prophetic 'proclamation' of c. 8pp in length," and "the nine who published five or more tracts were little known as preachers or leaders."[18] By this account, Travers was an exceptional person who published at least seven works and was also a powerful preacher and leader.

Travers' memorial probably followed the typical early Quaker format consisting of a meeting during which anyone might speak if they felt moved by the spirit of God. At an early Quaker funeral or memorial, as in all early Quaker meetings, the "ritual" was supremely simple and followed the format set out in chapters 3–5. People gathered initially in silence. Any man or woman would have the freedom to speak out of the silence if they believed they were moved to speak by the Inward Light of Christ. When Penn stood to his feet in the meeting for worship to honor Travers' memory, his hearers would be expecting him, and any other speaker in the meeting, to preach as an oracle of God, speaking by the immediate leading of the Spirit, in an unrehearsed and totally unprepared message.[19]

THE SPIRITUAL JOURNEY METAPHOR

As noted in chapter 7, the journey-pilgrimage metaphor is one of the most significant and pervasive symbols in religious literature and perhaps the central symbol in Christian mystical literature. It has the ability to compress and express many levels of meaning.[20] Ewert H. Cousins, editor of the twenty-five-volume *World Spirituality: An Encyclopedic History of the Religious Quest*, writes, "The [spiritual journey] symbol's main purpose is to express the process of spiritual growth through stages which were charted in the Middle Ages in a number of ways, chiefly as variations of the threefold path of purgation, illumination, and union. The journey usually involves a call, a conversion, divine assistance and guidance, encounters with obstacles, and ultimate success."[21]

Spiritual journeys may take many narrative forms, including (but not limited to) pilgrimage (to a city or shrine), wandering, voyaging, time travel, sojourning, ascent of a mountain or a ladder, and interior exploration (as of a house or castle).

Historical and theological writing on the spiritual journey has been enriched by twentieth-century scholarly work in anthropology. Significant study of historical and modern religious pilgrimages, particularly those involving rituals such as rites of passage, indicates that there are two additional, potentially powerful, aspects of the spiritual journey, which are incipient in medieval narratives, but their naming and elaboration can deepen our understanding of spiritual journeys. Victor Turner writes extensively about the "liminal" state—the state of flux in which the pilgrim finds himself or herself after leaving a "settled" or former life.[22] Turner describes liminality as "an interval, however brief, of margin or limen, when the past is momentarily negated, suspended, or abrogated, and the future has not yet begun, an instant of pure potentiality when everything, as it were, trembles in the balance."[23] Liminal or threshold states can produce exceptional potential for change in an individual's interior world and his or her response to exterior events or persons. One would expect narratives of the spiritual journey to contain some elaboration of the effects of liminality.

On the other hand, the traditional Christian threefold path leads the pilgrim through purgation and illumination to union with the Almighty, which is precisely the opposite of liminality. I will use the Latin term *status* (*stasis* in Greek) to refer to the fixity implied by the experience of unity with the Divine. In sum, the liminal state of life's journey (or pilgrimage) leads to the conclusion of the journey, where the threshold is again crossed and "home" is finally achieved.

Turner also writes about the development of a special kind of community among pilgrims called spontaneous communitas—the unique fellowship of pilgrimage. In spontaneous communitas, conversation occurs that is a "direct, immediate and total confrontation of human identities." Turner notes there is something "magical" about communitas. He asserts, "when the mood, style, or 'fit' of spontaneous communitas is upon us, we place a high value on personal honesty, opennness, and lack of pretensions or pretentiousness."[24] This type of unpretentious communication takes place more readily in the liminal state in which all pilgrims become identified together in some sense as marginal people.

The power of the journey metaphor is perhaps best seen at Christian funerals or other memorials for the dead, when it appears that the departed has passed over a threshold into a mode of existence none of us knows except by resort to familiar biblical metaphors such as "Caanan," "the land of promise," "the other side of Jordan," the "New Jerusalem," and the like.

Having sketched a profile of the spiritual-journey metaphor, I will now turn to an examination of the sermon text itself. After an analytical introduction to the sermon, I will focus on Penn's employment of language that indicates liminality and status.

An Introduction to the Sermon in Context and Penn's Use of the Journey Metaphor

Penn's memorial sermon is not lengthy, consisting of only 1,365 words arranged by a printer into eight paragraphs without a concluding prayer. The printer's paragraph choices actually make good sense, because the sermon does not follow a conventional outline format. Each of the eight paragraphs develops an essential idea, in this sequence: (1) the Word endures, whereas times and seasons change; (2) if we attend to the Word, we will stand before the Lord in the end; (3) travelers on a heavenly pilgrimage set their faces, travel on, and ultimately escape the "second death"; (4) the inner person is changed from mortality into immortality, and, ultimately, those who wait on the Lord are "above changes" of time and mortality; (5) the intent of standing in the eternal Word was the deceased Friend's "reviving cordial," and we should remember God's past help and, like the deceased, persevere as a "peculiar people"; (6) we are travelers on an earthly pilgrimage to a New Jerusalem, a city made by God; (7) if we abide in the Word, which is God, until the end of our days, we will have eternal life, when time shall be no more; and (8) may the Lord preserve you so that you can live, die, and be gathered to eternity. Paragraphs three, four, six, seven, and eight employ the spiritual-journey metaphor.

Initially, the choice and sequence of topics are surprising. If we expect a review of Travers' remarkable life, complete with dramatic and specific highlights of her influence and godly virtues, we are disappointed. Most readers, based on our common experience of funerals and memorials, would expect Penn to begin this memorial sermon with a direct reference to Travers, or at least a reference to her life. Instead, Penn begins with the serious pronouncement, "Time and seasons pass away, but the word of the Lord endureth forever."[25] With the change occasioned by Travers' death weighing heavily on his hearers' minds, at the outset Penn opts to draw their attention away from the relentless wheel of time and mortality that someone's death occasions to a higher and more transcendent level, the realm of the timeless, changeless Word that endures forever. His emphasis on the Word is similar to Stephen Crisp's usage in the sermon analyzed in chapter 10. With this exordium, Penn signals to his hearers that he will be juxtaposing the mutable so-called "real" world of everyday existence against the immutable "true" world of the eternal Word. The contrast of mutable versus immutable is the spine of the sermon, and Penn seizes the occasion of Travers' passing as an opportunity to remind his hearers that she, though herself obviously mutable, likewise believed in the immutable, eternal Word. In effect, Penn reduces Travers and her life's details in light of the awesome face of immutable, ineffable profundity. Penn never mentions Travers by name, and he does not refer to her directly until the fifth paragraph—762 words into the sermon, more than halfway through. Immediately prior to the place in the sermon where Penn speaks directly about Travers, though not by name, he counsels his hearers, "In this eternal word which is God, know your eternal habitation and wait upon God in it. . . . In this the righteous begin, in this they travel on. Blessed are they that walk by faith, that live to the Lord and die in the Lord and shall be forever with the Lord. They are blessed that wait upon the Lord for the sense of this. They are above all the changes of time and mortality." Only after this reminder that people who wait in the presence of the eternal Word gain ground against "time and mortality" does Penn acknowledge Travers' life with these words: "It is this [belief in the eternal Word] that was a reviving cordial to our deceased friend, who received the truth in early days, the days of the dawning of God's power in this land and in this city. The remembrance of it was sweet to her soul." In terms of the spiritual journey, Penn has acknowledged the stress, trials, and tests that Travers has undergone to the point where she required a "reviving cordial." Then, without hesitation, without a hint of sentimental reflection on Travers, Penn acknowledges her personal spiritual experience during the "early days" of Quakerism and applies this biographical kernel directly to his hearers, encouraging them to emulate Travers, who never forgot the spiritual power of the early Friends movement: "Let us remember the love of God and the power and glory of the name of the everlasting God that shined then, that we may be encouraged to keep together as a peculiar people to the praise of him that hath called us out of darkness into his marvelous light, that God over all may be glorified for ever, that we may live to the honor of his blessed name; that Christ's kingdom may be set up among us and that God's great name and power and majesty may be exalted and all flesh abased before him."[26]

To Penn, the brief moment he accords to the remembrance of Travers' life, a long life of commitment and self-sacrifice, becomes an opportunity to call the audience to increased vigilance for the Quaker cause, captured in his phrase, "that Christ's kingdom may be set up among us." The sequence of these quotations is revealing. Penn acknowledges that "waiting" for the "eternal word which is God" is a challenging business to the mourners, because they still walk a spiritual path of pilgrimage in a mutable world where perseverance in the face of darkness is ever required, and where God's kingdom in the New Jerusalem is not yet fully realized, as earlier Quakers might have expected it to be.[27] A new reality has descended on Quakerism, which is now presented as a struggle against the dark side of change, where even the best of persons from time to time may need a "reviving cordial," a "remembrance" of the dawn of God's power. In the end, though the Lamb's War could not achieve much in a cold, hard political environment in which people are imprisoned on a whim, there is still hope of modest gains, achieved by the remnant, and eventual immutability in eternity where Travers now abides.

This theme is picked up later in the sermon when Penn directs his hearers once again to the *source* of immutability: "To this word which is God I commit and commend you and all the flock of God, that you may be preserved to the end of your days, that you may then lay down your heads in peace, that your testimony may not end before your lives end, that the Lord may be with us to shelter and overshadow us in the midst of all our trials and exercises."[28] Penn does not remind his hearers that Travers had been jailed twice at Newgate Prison for her faith, but if they are her fellow pilgrims, they are well aware of her imprisonment and other persecutions. At the moment that Penn speaks, although the gathered group is still under the threat of conventicle laws, in fact Quakers were actually experiencing a lessening of persecution and would eventually achieve a level of relative safety in English society with the passage of the Act of Toleration ten months later. Perhaps Penn's encouragement to his hearers to "keep together as a peculiar people" is an indication of his fear that a measure of "respectability" and freedom from persecution might bring about a gradual lessening of spiritual ardor—that there was a real possibility that their collective and individual testimonies might well "end before their lives," that the dark, mutable forces might triumph over the immutable powers. In any case, these quotations indicate that Penn is intent on reminding his hearers that the spiritual journey is arduous and vulnerable to influences and changes that might drastically affect one's eternal destiny.

PENN'S STRATEGIC USE OF LIMINAL TERMS

From paragraph three on, Penn turns more directly to the powerful metaphor of the spiritual journey. It becomes his primary symbolic means of revealing that human life is changeable, unpredictable, and stressful for the pilgrim but that the journey has a goal that, once achieved, will place the pilgrim traveler in an eternal, permanent place, a "home." It seems an especially apt choice to capture the tension between the mutable and the immutable realms.

In Penn's sermon, the journey's purpose is identification and ultimate union with God, the changeless, eternal Word. This strong teleological element, in this case linked to a sense of both destination and the defeat of time, is what makes the spiritual journey different from aimless wandering or purposeless movement. In the sermon, the tension between the concepts (and images) of "mutable" and "immutable" is poignantly constituted in the journey metaphor. The pilgrim journeys on an unpredictable and changing path in order to attain a permanent, changeless, eternal home.

Penn employs several words and phrases that express the metaphor of the spiritual journey, including "heavenly race," "travelers," "heavenly pilgrimage," "walk," "walking," "travel on," "walk by faith," "vale of tears," and "earthly pilgrimage." These terms emphasize the processual nature of pilgrimage or spiritual journey. Process by definition involves change or mutability, and the journey, as Turner argues, thrusts the pilgrim into a liminal state—the state of flux in which the pilgrim finds himself or herself after leaving a more settled life. Recall that Turner describes liminality as "an interval, however brief, of margin or limen, when the past is momentarily negated, suspended, or abrogated, and the future has not yet begun, an instant of pure potentiality when everything, as it were, trembles in the balance."[29] Liminal circumstances, or threshold states, can produce change in an individual's interior world and his or her response to exterior events or persons. The change may be good, bad, or mixed, but it is unavoidable. Penn employs the process-oriented terms for the journey to emphasize the tentativeness and vulnerability of spiritual commitment. Travers had passed over a threshold into an existence known only to her fellow pilgrims in metaphorical or theological language, or perhaps visions.

Penn's brief references to Travers indicate that she has endured suffering and met challenges she never anticipated when she became convinced under Naylor's ministry. Penn avoids mentioning details of Travers' liminal experience, perhaps because the details are so familiar to his audience and conceivably similar in many ways to their own lives. It is likely that most of the audience could remember some details of Travers' history of suffering, and perhaps some of them could recall this passage from Travers' 1658 tract *A Message from the Spirit of Truth unto the Holy Seed*: "You that have received the earnest of this Spirit, hath he not said, I will dwell in you, and walke in you? Wherefore come out from among them and be you separate. This is the joy that is set before you, to wit, his appearance, and that glory, for the attaining whereof, we endure the present sufferings, and reproach; not to be compared therewith, for glory, immortality, eternall life."[30] The hearers who recalled Travers' words might have regarded them, in the terminology of the spiritual-journey metaphor, as a challenge or reproof by a then-younger woman, with an aura of supernatural prophecy to her words, or perhaps later as guidance from a wise old woman.

We have noted that Penn refrains from speaking directly of Travers' sufferings, but he also avoids mention of his own sufferings, a connection he might have made under the circumstances. However, in paragraph seven, he invokes the title of his significant earlier work *No Cross, No Crown* when he expresses the hope "that the Lord may be with us to shelter and overshadow us in the midst of all our trials and exercises while we are following Christ in patience, humility, and self-denial, and bearing his cross, for no cross, no crown."[31] This sermon's themes and images are strikingly similar to the concluding pages of Penn's original (1669) version of *No Cross, No Crown*, in which he reminds his readers that persecution—"the cross"—naturally follows from a personal decision to turn from "the Sins and Vanities of a perishing World":

> Mind not the difficulties of your March; great and good things were
> never interpriz'd [*sic*] and accomplished without difficulty, and hard-

ship, which always render their injoyment [*sic*] but the more pleasant and glorious in the end. . . . There are among us . . . [those] who have not been without the exercise of suffering the displeasure of their most dear and intimate Relations and Friends; and all those troubles, disgraces, & reproaches, which are accustomed to attend such as forgo the honours, pleasures, ambition, and preferments of the World, and rather chuse to live an humble, serious, and self-denying life.[32]

Penn ends the printed work with a reference to the "crown" to be attained, using some of the same triumphal themes as in the sermon "[A]s for the Redeemed and Sanctified of God, who have followed Jesus in the narrow path of Regeneration, and not loved their lives unto the death, their sorrow shall fly away, every tear shall be wiped from their eyes, and sighing shall be heard no more within their Borders."[33] Here it is important to note, parenthetically, that Penn has apparently employed his own published writing as an aid to memory in the impromptu context and that his strategy does not follow Bownas' dictum never to repeat your previous insight in the present impromptu situation. Penn's reference to his own work is also a rare example of intertextuality in the extant sermons.

Penn's choice to refer to his publication's title was excellent because many of Penn's hearers would have been familiar with his important tract. With his direct verbal reference to *No Cross, No Crown*, Penn appears to be valorizing, justifiably and brilliantly, his own and Travers' suffering for righteousness' sake. Travers' example of perseverance to the end is very much related to Penn's present circumstance. Travers, after all, was Nayler's convert and friend. Because of her Christian principles, she helped a man who had acted foolishly and became a pariah among Friends. She allied herself to a man who was judged as an enemy to Quakerism by many Friends. Eventually, though, Travers herself was judged a just and righteous woman. Likewise, Penn had remained a friend of James II in the face of his overt Catholicism despite the potential ramifications to Penn's reputation. Eventually, Penn, too, might look forward to a day when he would be judged just and righteous by fellow Quakers. The deep, unexpressed, and unacknowledged parallelism between him and Travers surely must have been noted by many in the audience.[34] In the analogous set of personal commitments, we may well discover something of Penn's

motivation to stand in the meeting and speak about Travers, identifying himself rhetorically with her. Clearly, Penn and Travers shared
a belief in the necessity of the temporal cross in order to attain the
immutable crown.

PENN'S STRATEGIC USE OF TERMS FOR STATUS

While the sermon employs the terms from the spiritual-journey metaphor that stress the experience of liminality, Penn also chooses terms
drawn from the metaphor of the journey that stress a fixed, teleological end, a destination, a place, a habitation, a city. The terms that capture status or stasis include "haven of everlasting rest," "land of rest,"
"Zionward," "heavenly Canaan," "Land of Promise," "heavenly
country," "New Jerusalem," "house not made with hands," and "land
of rest." Here the final eternal fixity is captured in words like "home"
or "city," whose "builder and maker is God," and in that marvelously
integrative phrase "eternal kingdom and region where all time shall
be swallowed up."[35] Travers has now crossed a final threshold into a
place of status, the timeless eternal, which for Penn to describe at all
he must resort to metaphorical language. Penn's task is to ensure that
those who remain behind should not seek or attain a premature "rest"
or false status in the face of abating persecution. In effect, he urges
them on across new thresholds, continual instances of *limen*, the familiar trek into the future that culminates when they, too, will cross that
final threshold to join their friend and matriarch, Rebecca, in perpetual communitas.

At journey's end, liminality will be replaced by status, process will be
overcome by place, and mutability will be displaced by the immutable.
For early Quakers, the threefold path was often experienced as enlightenment followed by purgation, with the hope of union. In Travers'
case, she experienced a call under Nayler's ministry; she converted,
received assistance and guidance, encountered formidable obstacles,
and ultimately experienced rest on the other side of Jordan.

CONCLUSION: THE QUEST FOR COMMUNITAS

Having indicated the conceptual spine of the sermon—life's mutability—and the sermon's most pervasive and significant metaphor—the
journey-pilgrimage—I will conclude with some further observations
about the sermon's potential to bring about Turner's concept of
communitas.

Penn's choice of the journey or pilgrimage metaphor is a strategic way to effect communitas among those who remain behind. On the connection of community and the journey or pilgrimage, recall that Turner writes that fellow pilgrims develop a special kind of community while on the journey together: spontaneous communitas—the unique fellowship of pilgrimage. Turner notes that "when the mood, style, or 'fit' of spontaneous communitas is upon us, we place a high value on personal honesty, opennness, and lack of pretensions or pretentiousness."[36] Such communication takes place more readily in the liminal state, in which all pilgrims become identified together in some sense as marginal or even oppressed people.

In the sermon, Penn explicitly reminds his listeners that Quakers have been marginal people who have endured the trials that their faith made inevitable—after all, "no cross, no crown"—and that their community more than ever depends on their commitment to the Word and to each other, "that we may be encouraged to keep together as a peculiar people to the praise of him that hath called us out of darkness into his marvellous light."[37] Viewed against the backdrop of Penn's recent wordly misfortunes, his sermon seems implicitly to argue that his fellow Quaker pilgrims should practice less gossip, engage in a more direct style of communication, and place "a high value on personal honesty, opennness, and lack of pretensions or pretentiousness."[38] A vision of individual mortality, awakened by Travers' recent death, plus a heightened sense of community identification, augers for a community life lived out on a higher plane. The sermon's peroration best captures Penn's communal vision in an eloquent benediction reminiscent of Romans 16:25 and Hebrews 13:20:

> The Lord preserve you by his mighty power in his favor and divine presence, that you may live to his glory and praise, and die in peace and be gathered into that blessed and heavenly assembly and church of the first-born which are written in heaven, and to God the judge of all, and the spirits of just men made perfect, and to Jesus the mediator of the new covenant, and the blood of sprinkling that speaketh better things than that of Abel; that you may eternally magnify and celebrate the praises of the eternal God, to whom be glory for ever and ever. Amen.[39]

Penn was a man of his age, who possessed impressive intellectual and rhetorical gifts, which he used to further what he believed were the best causes and particularly the correct path for Quakers. In spite of his political and business failures, we have seen that he was nevertheless a skilled rhetorical craftsman, as adept in the challenging context of the Quaker impromptu funeral sermon as he was with quill and ink.

A SERMON PREACHED BY MR. WILLIAM PENN UPON OCCASION
OF THE DEATH OF MRS. REBECCA TRAVERS,
AN AGED SERVANT OF GOD; JUNE 19, 1688

[1]⁴⁰ Time and seasons pass away, but the word of the Lord endureth forever. And it is that which hath been the root of life to the heritage of God in all ages and generations, that from whence their joy and hope always sprung, that in which their faith was finished; it was their alpha and it was their omega. In this the righteous begun and set forth, and by this they were preserved in their heavenly race till they came to their great end, the prize of their high calling, the haven of everlasting rest after all the storms and tempests of time; it was this they had their eye to in the begining, and it was their joy that opened in the eternal word, by which they were quickened and revived, and that caused them to endure to the end without fainting, and you shall likewise by patient continuance in well doing, in due time reap if you faint not. It was the word of God to the children of God of old, and it is His word in this day to us: "You shall reap if you faint not." Blessed are you that are called into the vineyard. You shall have an everlasting harvest. If you faint not now, you shall reap then. What shall you reap? Vanity and vexation of spirit, and disappointment? No. You shall reap glory, honor, immortality, and eternal life.

[2] So friends, though every day we have renewed occasions of remembering our latter end, yet there is that which never shall have an end hath dawned unto us, which hath been presented to our view in this glorious day of our visitation; if we lift up our eyes to it and have regard to it, in our rising up and lying down, in our going out and coming in, and in all we put our hands unto, and if we place our interests and portions therein, then our minds will be established, and we shall not be ashamed now, nor blush before the Lord hereafter. If our hearts condemn us not, we shall have boldness before God.

[3] So shall all travelers that have regard to the word of truth while they are in their heavenly pilgrimage; they set their faces Zionward and go on not fainting, not doubting, not desponding. They have an

eye to the Lord Jesus Christ and have their hearts kept by that word that abides forever; their belief and hope is beyond time, fixed upon that which God hath owned to be His word before the world was, and shall be, when time and this world shall be no more; the outward garment which shall be worn while it last, shall then be put off. Blessed are they that know the white linen, that which is whole and all of a piece, that God giveth to His children that love the Lord Jesus in sincerity who is the resurrection and the life. He that comes to know and experience this, the second death shall have no power over him.

[4] Now this change is not only in the outward man, but in the inner man. There is a putting off of that which is fading, mortal, and perishing, and a being clothed upon with immortality and glory. Blessed are they which come to receive that word of God, which hath been the life of God in our souls. This is a day of life to us. Blessed are they that shall be placed in that eternal kingdom and region where all time shall be swallowed up and all tears wiped from their eyes, and fighting and sorrow shall be no more. O friends, lift up your heads for the day of redemption draweth nigh. That you may not be shaken by every wind of doctrine, know that the foundation standeth sure, that is his word that was in the begining with God, that word that was God. In this eternal word which is God, know your eternal habitation and wait upon God in it; it was David's buckler, his shield and strong tower. It was his rock. God set his feet upon a rock that is higher than man's power and all man's wisdom and strength. In this the righteous begin, in this they travel on. Blessed are they that walk by faith, that live to the Lord and die in the Lord and shall be forever with the Lord. They are blessed that wait upon the Lord for the sense of this. They are above all the changes of time and mortality.

[5] It is this that was a reviving cordial to our deceased friend, who received the truth in early days, the days of the dawning of God's power in this land and in this city. The remembrance of it was sweet to her soul. Let us remember the love of God and the power and glory of the name of the everlasting God that shined then, that we may be encouraged to keep together as a peculiar people to the praise of him that hath called us out of darkness into his marvelous light, that God over all may be glorified for ever, that we may live to the honor of his blessed name; that Christ's kingdom may be set up among us and that God's great name and power and majesty may be exalted and all flesh abased before him.

[6] We are travelers here in this vale of tears, in this earthly pilgrimage into the land of rest, the heavenly Canaan. Let us follow our blessed Joshua that is leading us into that land of promise, and he will give to everyone his lot, and they shall stand in that lot in the last day. O blessed are they that are waiting for their lot and portion in that heavenly country to which Abraham had his eye, that city, the New Jerusalem the mother of us all, and that house not made with hands eternal in the heavens, whose builder and maker is God.

[7] This word, which I have been speaking of, is that by which we are humbled and bowed before the Lord and instructed in judgment and righteousness. To this word which is God I commit and commend you and all the flock of God, that you may be preserved to the end of your days, that you may then lay down your heads in peace, that your testimony may not end before your lives end, that the Lord may be with us to shelter and overshadow us in the midst of all our trials and exercises while we are following Christ in patience, humility, and self-denial, and bearing his cross, for no cross, no crown. That which is pleasing to God is walking by faith. What is this faith? A pure resolution of living to God in a holy dependence on him, and a committing our selves entirely to him, that so we may know and enjoy the purifying virtue of his word, that we may not offend God, for "without faith," saith the Apostle, "it is impossible to please him"; "By what means," saith the royal psalmist, "shall a young man cleanse his way? By taking heed according to thy word." This is the blessed word that hath been a root of life in all ages. Let us abide to [sic] this word to the end of our days and we shall then be blessed with that life which shall never end but shall remain when time shall be no more.

[8] The Lord preserve you by his mighty power in his favor and divine presence, that you may live to his glory and praise, and die in peace and be gathered into that blessed and heavenly assembly and church of the first-born which are written in heaven, and to God the judge of all, and the spirits of just men made perfect, and to Jesus the mediator of the new covenant, and the blood of sprinkling that speaketh better things than that of Abel; that you may eternally magnify and celebrate the praises of the eternal God, to whom be glory for ever and ever.

EPILOGUE

At the outset of this book, I remarked that the historical practice of impromptu preaching initially raises at least three important questions: (1) Why did the preachers choose the impromptu method and reject the option of preparing ahead of time? (2) How did the preachers accomplish the task of speaking, sometimes at length, without specific preparation? and (3) How was the practice passed on to the next generation?

In answer to the first question, I have argued that early Quakers chose the impromptu method because they believed in immediate, divine revelation. They professed that the Inward Light of Christ could actually inspire them directly, give them words—words to ponder as messages solely to them, or words to speak aloud in the gathered meeting. They believed the Light would reveal to them when to begin to speak and when to end. They believed all of this so wholeheartedly that they regularly made themselves vulnerable in the impromptu preaching context.

With respect to the second question (How could they speak at length under the condition of impromptu speech?), we have seen that they had many tools at their disposal to accomplish the feat. To begin, they owned Bibles, which they actually read, committing many passages to memory. Furthermore, they lived in a religious subculture in which much of the conversation revolved around and reinforced spiritual topics. Preachers could reach within for scriptural and spiritual material at the moment they were needed in a sermon. Furthermore, they had habituated the catechital style, which put them in the habit of raising questions, phrasing questions as mini-dialogues, or presenting direct queries to their hearers based on the sermon topic or topics. Additionally, they also rehearsed the language of five key conceptual metaphor clusters, any of which they could extend or make particularly vital as the occasion presented itself. As the young minister continued in the vocal ministry, he or she would get better at the task, as noted in Bownas' developmental model, finally achieving full maturity.

I also asked how the practice of impromptu sermonizing was passed on to the next generation. The answer is that Quakers attempted to use a system of "eldering," or the practice of tender responses to fledgling preachers by elders who endeavored, through patience and wisdom, to bring neophyte ministers to maturity. Also, young preachers, although occasionally warned by people like Bownas not to imitate other preachers, could not help but assimilate from other preachers all sorts of useful materials for sermons, plus a notion of what was acceptable content and style for sermons and patterns of appropriate delivery. Later in the century, they could consult advice in writings by Fox, Fell, Smith, Barclay, Whitehead, Crisp, Marshall, and Coole, all contributors to the lore about inspired preaching that culminated in Bownas' work in the eighteenth century.

It may have come as a surprise to some readers that Quakers actually attempted to theorize about their preaching practice, but we have seen in their writings about "immediately inspired" preaching, as well as by drawing theoretical implications from their sermons, that they accomplished the following steps toward a theory. First, they proposed an epistemological framework that took immediate revelation seriously and defended it intelligently. Barclay even went as far as positing a mental mechanism whereby "revelation" might take place. Second, they evolved a set of cautions to help keep a preacher from overstepping her or his inspiration. Third, they viewed hearers as cocontributors to the rhetorical process, hearers who became confirming listeners who either accepted or denied the message as God-breathed. Fourth, they presented a vigorous and articulate biblically based defense of women in the vocal ministry. Fifth, they developed a number of rhetorical appeals, a list of what Bownas came to call the "means of expression." These approaches, such as stress on applying biblical typologies, seemed to work well in the Quaker impromptu situation and might be added to a maturing preacher's repertoire for eventual use on occasions when the Spirit moved. Sixth, they developed their own sense of decorum about linguistic choices and delivery style. Seventh, they developed and shared a common set of infinitely malleable themes. Eighth, they held a community-affirmed fund of metaphors that could be rehearsed when appropriate. Ninth, they had a propensity to view Scripture as a script for their own lives. Tenth, they developed rhetorical questions into the catechital style, a style all its own. Finally, they put in place and encouraged a community-based mentoring system to monitor and perpetuate their oral sermonic practice among the rising new generation. In their theorizing, early Quakers developed a culturally centered approach to preaching that was quite different from that practiced in the surrounding culture by Puritans, Anglicans, or other Dissenters, such as Baptists. Essentially, the Quaker belief in immediate revelation made all the difference.

There is a paradox in Quaker theorizing about an ostensibly Spirit-driven mode of discourse. One might say, "If the Inward Light provides the words, what is the need to theorize?" Although the sources I have examined never say this, perhaps it is the case that the Spirit can employ all the resources and materials in the brain in any impromptu situation. This is close to Barclay's prescient declaration regarding the existence of "inner spiritual ideas" that might be "stirred up" by the Spirit when needed. Similarly, knowledge of Bownas' "means of expression" is pointless unless the means are assimilated by the mind and made ready to be put to use by the preacher. Furthermore, Bownas' warnings not to use other preachers' testimonies or even repeat one's own good material are more than problematic and probably were not followed by most impromptu preachers. Penn's use of material from *No Cross, No Crown* at Travers' funeral probably crossed Bownas' line, but Penn's choice was extremely apt and effective. I believe Bownas' rules were honored more in the breach than in the observance. As mentioned in chapter 5, I find Bownas' *Qualifications* frustratingly incomplete and contradictory in the discussion of "means of expression," but I applaud him for his attempt at theorizing. After all, Bownas was an itinerant Quaker minister, not a theologian or philosopher. If Barclay had written the book, the means of expression would likely have been far more systematic and complete. In sum, my investigation of the Quaker theory of impromptu preaching shows it to be an admirable, often insightful, overwhelmingly spiritual, and sometimes frustrating work in progress, even as late as 1750.

On the other hand, the surviving sermons from 1671 to 1700 sailed bravely on, unimpeded by the waves of sometimes incomplete and unsystematic theorizing. When Luella M. Wright read a selection of early Quaker sermons, she commented that "these sermons on examination prove to be gospel exhortations, and also like many other sermons of the century, were devoid of incident and illustrative material."[1] Her summary statement reveals that she missed the artful and strategic use of rhetorical choices that we have seen at the hands of Fox, Crisp, Barclay, Penn, and a host of others who wove together themes, metaphors, and the catechital style into powerful pieces of rhetorical discourse. Of course, none of these is a "literary" sermon; the preachers had not the luxury to labor over their words ahead of time, as did Anglicans such as Jeremy Taylor. Yet in their own culturally specific realm, judged by standards appropriate to impromptu address, they are remarkably adroit pieces of rhetorical discourse.

Impromptu preaching poses extreme rhetorical challenges to anyone sufficiently brave (or foolish) to attempt it. The pressures on the minister are formidable, especially when the hearers are expected to listen carefully for signs that the preacher may have gone beyond her or his inspiration. In early Quaker meetings, the tension between silence and sound, between the passive and the active, must have been especially challenging for fledgling ministers, as judged by their journals and remarks by Marshall and Bownas. On the other hand, to speak on occasion as God's oracle elevated the preaching task and gave language extra weight, an importance it might not have had in other preaching contexts.

It comes as no surprise to scholars in Quaker studies that early Quaker homiletic theory and practice are conservative theologically and that some of the surviving sermons sound like revival messages. For my fellow scholars in rhetorical studies, this book may have questioned some long-held assumptions about early Quakers but has hopefully reaffirmed an admiration for the art of impromptu speech, however theorized.

APPENDIX A

The Search for Surviving Sermons

My initial search for extant early Quaker sermons revealed a body of printed Quaker sermons, which will be reviewed below in a section dealing with textual considerations. Four standard bibliographic works facilitated my search for citations of sermon collections or individual printed sermons. Donald Wing's *Short-Title Catalogue of Books Printed in England, 1641–1700,* based upon the collections in major libraries in the Western world, together with William Bishop's *American Copies of "Short Title Catalogue" Books* and its *Supplement,* provided sources and lists of libraries holding copies. Two exclusively Quaker bibliographies were indispensable to the search for Quaker sermons: Joseph Smith's *Descriptive Catalogue of Friends Books* (London: Joseph Smith, 1867), which lists 18,000 titles and is still the only exhaustive bibliography of Quakerism, and *Bibliotheca Anti-Quakeriana,* also by Smith, which lists works produced in opposition to Quakerism and books in answer to the attacks published by Quakers.[1]

Subsequent to the development of my initial list of printed sermons, I undertook an extensive (and continuing) search for additional printed sermons and other published literature not mentioned in the important reference books mentioned above, and for manuscript sermons that survived the period 1650–1700. My search focused on finding complete sermons, not quotations from sermons found in letters and journals or incomplete manuscripts. I also eliminated single-paragraph prophecies declaimed on public streets.[2] During the summer of 1970, spring semester of 1986, and summer of 1993, I copied sermons and other materials at Friends Historical Library of Swarthmore College and the Quaker Collection of Haverford College Library, both located near Philadelphia.[3] Similarly, I consulted the extensive collection at the Library of the Religious Society of Friends, London, during the

summers of 1971 and 1993 and the spring semesters of 1991 and
2002.[4] During spring 1991 and fall 2005, I also perused materials catalogued in the 10,000-item Bevan-Naish Collection of early Quaker
material at the Library of Woodbrooke Quaker Study Centre, Birmingham, England.[5]

Textual Considerations. Seventy-nine sermons have survived the
early Quaker period.[6] Given the commitment of early Quakers to
the impromptu, inspired method of preaching and the explicit disdain
for the reading of printed sermons by some Quakers, especially to
prepare for preaching by using another person's words, it is remarkable that so many sermons are actually extant. Samuel Bownas, the
Quaker preacher who bridges the seventeenth and eighteenth centuries and whose manual for Quaker preachers, *Qualifications,* is the
subject of chapter 5, gave us a clear picture of the Quaker attitude
toward sermon preparation, which carried over from the seventeenth
century. Bownas addressed a meeting at Bristol at which he felt himself
"divinely opened with fresh matter, setting forth the service of the spiritual ministry, which was free from all contrivance and forecast of the
creature [the human will], in preparing itself either with former openings, or beautiful collection of texts, or sayings from books or writings,
all which gatherings would bring death, and could be no other in the
best and more favorable construction, though well looked on by some,
than the ministry of the letter, under the pretense of the ministry of
the spirit, which is a deception of the highest nature."[7]

With injunctions similar to Bownas' being common among early
Friends, one may better appreciate the fact that few Quaker sermons
were committed to writing or ever found their way into print, remarkable during an age when printed sermons were important texts of
public discourse.

There was also uneasiness about Quaker sermons being taken down
in shorthand at meetings and later published, though Quaker printers
had reprinted sermons originally published by non-Quaker printers. At
the end of the eighteenth century, prominent and influential Quaker
preacher William Savery complained that the "practice of writing down
Testimonies is become too common, not only in London but in other
places." He went on to declare, "I earnestly desire, that no member of
our religious society will give the least encouragement to any such manuscripts appearing in print, or to the further spreading of those already
printed; or to any more Testimonies being taken down. . . . we shall all

see the practice to be inconsistent with the nature of the worship, ministry, and principles of a people professing as we do."[8] In sum, we can be
thankful that seventy-nine sermons are extant for twenty-first-century
scholars to examine.

The sermons examined in this book are of three categories: (1)
those which exist only in manuscript form, never having been printed,
(2) those which survive both in manuscript as well as in printed form,
and (3) those which are found only in printed form. In any case, the
texts canot be taken as verbatim, but only as very close approxima-
tions of what the speakers actually said. The number of manuscripts
is small, and in no case is a sermon manuscript the product of the
speaker's prior work; it is, instead, the work of a skilled notetaker, and
some may have been recopied from a now lost original. The practice
of taking shorthand notes of sermons was common among Anglicans
and Puritans, and it is likely that the skill was also present to some
extent among Quakers. Some Anglican and Puritan sermons may
have undergone revision prior to publication, involving a comparison
of shorthand notes with a preacher's manuscript.[9] No such possibility
exists with Quaker sermons, for which original manuscripts were lacking as a necessary consequence of the impromptu mode of speaking.
Among Quakers, the printed sermon represents the work of an auditor skilled in shorthand and an enterprising printer. Where possible,
comparisons were made between surviving printed texts, but for the
majority of the sermons, only one text exists. Scholarly criteria commonly used to derive a copy text of a speech for rhetorical examination were not useful in this study, since only minor differences were
discovered between printed texts.[10] Similarly, I found slight variations,
not significant to the purposes and conclusions of this study, when
printed and manuscript texts were compared. In these few cases, texts
were chosen for their readability.

George Fox's sermons offer the greatest variety of sources, although
few have been published. One of the sermons, the only one for which
no date is known, is contained in a volume titled *A Collection of Several Sermons and Testimonies, Spoke or Deliver'd by G. Fox, the Quaker's Great
Apostle.*[11] The collection also contains a sermon by Leonard Fell; two by
Philip Hermon; an anonymous sermon preached at Savoy, London;
and several sermon fragments. In the preface to the volume, the anonymous editor explains that he is one "who sees through the Delusions
of the People call'd Quakers," and has collected the sermons, which

he feels "bear a Contradiction to Truth, and are at Enmity with Sense and Right Reason." An examination of the sermons, and a comparison of them with other extant sermons by Quakers, show them to be substantially in agreement in content, tone, development, and style with other Quaker sermons of the times. Thus, although they were collected and published by an unsympathetic editor, there is little reason to exclude these sermons as nonauthentic.[12]

Nine of Fox's sermons are found in the *Richardson MSS*, which are the best, most complete, and most convenient source of those sermons.[13] As mentioned in the preface, I am indebted to T. Canby Jones, Emeritus Professor of Religion at Wilmington College, Wilmington, Ohio, for texts of several of Fox's sermons also found in the *Richardson MSS*.[14] What appears to be Fox's earliest complete (but brief) sermon is located in an obscure volume titled *Severall Letters to the Saints of the Most High*.[15]

The largest number of sermons survives from Stephen Crisp, the Colchester, England, businessman. The best single source for his sermons is a book printed in 1707, *Scripture-Truths Demonstrated: In Thirty Two Sermons or Declarations of Mr. Stephen Crisp*, printed by a Quaker.[16] The preface of the collection offers an explanation of the notetaker's method and the publisher's motivation for printing the sermons:

> Though the Writer [notetaker] of these Sermons doth out of Modesty decline to Print his Name, yet he is very willing to give all reasonable Satisfaction to any Sober Enquirer, that he has not in the least altered or imposed upon the Author's sense, either in the Taking, or Transcribing of them: And he does further assure the Reader, That he neither is, nor ever was, one of those People called *Quakers*, but always of another Perswasion; yet being willing, according to the Apostle's Rule, to *Try all things*, he has sometimes been present at their Meetings; and having the Art of Short-Writing, he has taken many of their Sermons and Prayers from the Mouths of divers of their Preachers; and, among others, those of Mr. Stephen Crisp, deceased, which upon Review, appeared to him . . . to contain so many Gospel Truths, delivered with such Plainness, Zeal and Demonstration, and generally agreeable to the known Doctrines of Christianity, that it is hoped the publishing of them may be useful to the World.

The publication of Crisp's sermons was doubtless "useful" to Nathaniel Crouch, the original non-Quaker publisher of the sermons and the person whom I take to be the writer of the preface.[17] Publishing the sermons a few at a time, with entrepreneurial flair, Crouch was able to bring out six separate editions of Crisp's sermons. The volume used for this study is a compilation of the three volumes of sermons that Crouch had printed twice, this one printed by the Quaker bookseller J. Sowle and containing two sermons by Crisp that were never before printed.

The bulk of the remaining texts of printed sermons referenced in this book come from two sources, each a volume of "pirated" sermons, the first published by Crouch and later reissued by J. Sowle, the second published by Sowle. In his preface to *The Concurrence and Unanimity; Of the People Called Quakers; . . .*, Crouch explains his motivation for publishing the sermons of prominent Quakers in terms of the success that met his previously published volumes of Crisp's sermons:

> Having lately published several of the Sermons, or Declarations of Mr. Stephen Crisp, Deceased, which have obtained general acceptation with Persons of different Persuasions; I often heard it objected, that though this Person clearly owns, and earnestly recommends the Practise of the Principal Points of the Christian Faith; Yet others of the chief Leaders and Teachers of the People called Quakers, were not of the same Opinion in these Matters; Now the Writer [notetaker] of Mr. Crisp's Sermons, having taken the Declarations of several of their Publick Preachers, at their usual Meetings, I think my self obliged in Truth and Justice, to make some of them publick in this small Volume, to demonstrate their Concurrence and Unanimity.[18]

The remainder of the printed sermons appeared in *The Harmony of Divine and Heavenly Doctrines. . . .*,[19] which was first sold in 1696. This volume notes on the title page, "Taken in Short-hand as it was delivered by them; And now faithfully Transcribed and Published for the Information of those who by Reason of Ignorance may have received a Prejudice against them [Quakers]. By a Lover of that People."

Two additional printed sermons include a 1674 anonymous sermon[20] and William Penn's sermon upon sailing to America in 1699.[21] Additional manuscript sermons include a 1699 prophetic utterance at Chester Meeting by Isaac Alexander,[22] Robert Barrow's "testimony" at George Fox's memorial,[23] Thomas Chalkley's 1698 sermon during a visit to America,[24] and Thomas Wilson's 1694 sermon at Bristol.[25]

APPENDIX B

CHECKLIST OF QUAKER SERMONS, 1650–1700

Preacher	Place	Date	Source
1. Alexander, Isaac	Chester Meetinghouse	12/11/99	1
2. Anonymous	Savoy Meetinghouse	n.d.	2
3. Anonymous	St. Martins le Grand	11/16/74	3
4. Ashby, Richard	St. Martins le Grand	2/16/93	10
5. Barrow, Robert	Grace Church Street	1691	4
6. Barclay, Robert	Grace Church Street	5/16/88	10
7. Bingley, William	Grace Church Street	3/5/93	10
8. Bowater, John	St. John's Street	3/18/93	10
9. Butcher, John	Grace Church Street	3/11/93	10
10. Camfield, Francis	Grace Church Street	5/14/93	10
11. Chalkley, Thomas	American Colonies	6/7/98	5
12. Coole, Benjamin	Grace Church Street	5/12/94	11
13. Crisp, Stephen	Grace Church Street	2/8/87	6
14. Crisp, Stephen	Devonshire House	2/12/87	6
15. Crisp, Stephen	Grace Church Street	3/8/87	6
16. Crisp, Stephen	Grace Church Street	3/14/87	6
17. Crisp, Stephen	St. Martins le Grand	3/26/87	6
18. Crisp, Stephen	Grace Church Street	4/18/87	6
19. Crisp, Stephen	Grace Church Street	4/15/88	6
20. Crisp, Stephen	Grace Church Street	4/25/88	6
21. Crisp, Stephen	Devonshire House	4/29/88	6
22. Crisp, Stephen	Grace Church Street	5/6/88	6
23. Crisp, Stephen	Devonshire House	5/10/88	6
24. Crisp, Stephen	Grace Church Street	5/24/88	6
25. Crisp, Stephen	Devonshire House	5/27/88	6
26. Crisp, Stephen	Grace Church Street	6/3/88	6
27. Crisp, Stephen	Devonshire House	6/10/88	6

Preacher	Place	Date	Source
28. Crisp, Stephen	Grace Church Street	10/10/90	6
29. Crisp, Stephen	Devonshire House	10/12/90	6
30. Crisp, Stephen	St. Martins le Grand	11/9/90	6
31. Crisp, Stephen	Devonshire House	11/12/90	6
32. Crisp, Stephen	Grace Church Street	3/16/91	6
33. Crisp, Stephen	Grace Church Street	7/26/91	6
34. Crisp, Stephen	Devonshire House	7/29/91	6
35. Crisp, Stephen	Grace Church Street	8/2/91	6
36. Crisp, Stephen	Devonshire House	8/5/91	6
37. Crisp, Stephen	Devonshire House	8/9/91	6
38. Crisp, Stephen	Devonshire House	4/6/92	6
39. Crisp, Stephen	Grace Church Street	4/10/92	6
40. Crisp, Stephen	Grace Church Street	5/29/92	6
41. Crisp, Stephen	Grace Church Street	6/19/92	6
42. Crisp, Stephen	Grace Church Street	6/21/92	6
43. Crisp, Stephen	Grace Church Street	7/3/92	6
44. Crisp, Stephen	Devonshire House	7/17/92	6
45. Dewsbury, William	Grace Church Street	5/6/88	10
46. Fell, Leonard	Unknown	Unknown	2
47. Fox, George	Unknown	Unknown	2
48. Fox, George	England	1653	7
49. Fox, George	Barbados	10/71	9
50. Fox, George	Barbados	10/71	9
51. Fox, George	Yearly Meeting, London	6/9/74	9
52. Fox, George	Yearly Meeting, London	6/11/74	9
53. Fox, George	Yearly Meeting, London	5/25 or 5/26/75	9
54. Fox, George	Devonshire House	5/77	9
55. Fox, George	Yearly Meeting, London	5/78	9
56. Fox, George	Wheeler Street	6/1/80	9
57. Fox, George	Yearly Meeting, London	5/24/81	9
58. Hermon, Philip	Longacre	1700	2

APPENDIX B (*CONTINUED*)

Preacher	Place	Date	Source
59. Hermon, Philip	Grace Church Street	1700	2
60. Marshall, Charles	Grace Church Street	3/11/93	10
61. Park, James	Ratcliff	4/19/94	10
62. Penn, William	London	6/19/88	10
63. Penn, William	Grace Church Street	1/16/94	11
64. Penn, William	Devonshire House	1/20/94	11
65. Penn, William	Wheeler Street	1/27/94	11
66. Penn, William	Wheeler Street	4/13/94	10
67. Penn, William	Grace Church Street	8/12/94	11
68. Penn, William	Devonshire House	10/3/94	11
69. Penn, William	Grace Church Street	10/10/94	11
70. Penn, William	Grace Church Street	10/21/94	11
71. Penn, William	Wheeler Street	10/21/94	11
72. Penn, William	Westminster	6/8/99	8
73. Stamper, Francis	Devonshire House	5/3/94	10
74. Vaughton, John	Grace Church Street	4/1/94	10
75. Waldenfield, Samuel	Devonshire House	3/11/93	10
76. Waldenfield, Samuel	Grace Church Street	3/11/93	11
77. Whitehead, George	Grace Church Street	10/4/93	10
78. Whitehead, George	Grace Church Street	10/7/94	11
79. Wilson, Thomas	Bristol	3/20/94	12

Sources

1. Alexander, Isaac. "Issac Alexander's Prophecy delivered at Chester Dec. 12th: 1699." John Thompson MSS. Library of the Religious Society of Friends, London, 16, A slightly different version exists as "Report of Isaac Alexander's Testimony or Message delivered at Chester Meeting ye 11th of 12th mo 1699." *Letters, Dreams & Visions*. Library of the Religious Society of Friends, London. Each of these versions includes a note indicating that the sermon was taken down in shorthand by William Low Jr.

2. *A Collection of Several Sermons and Testimonies*. London: B. Beardwell, 1701.

3. Anonymous. *A Quakers Sermon Preached at the Bull-and-Mouth Meeting-House, In St. Martins-Le-Grand, London, On Sunday the 16th of Nov. 1674*. N.p., 1674.

4. Barrow, Robert. "The Testimony of Robert Barrow 11th Mo 16th 1691 at George Fox Burial, Where Were Supposed to Be Four Thousand Friends Besides Other People, 1691." Copy book, MSS Albums, Friends Historical Library, Swarthmore College, Pa.

5. Chalkley, Thomas. *Mr. T. Chalkley's Sermon & Prayer.* Manuscript at Friends Historical Library, Swarthmore College.

6. Crisp, Stephen. *Scripture-Truths Demonstrated: In Thirty Two Sermons or Declarations of Mr. Stephen Crisp.* London: J. Sowle, 1707.

7. Fox, George. "1653 This Precept was written from the Mouth of George Fox, as he spoke it forth, by a Friend of Truth." In *Severall Letters to the Saints of the Most High.* Sermon. N.p., n.p., 1654.

8. Penn, William. *A Farewell Sermon Preached by Mr. William Penn on Sunday being the 6th instant, at the Quakers Meeting-House at Westminster.* London: for A. B., 1699. For recent scholarly descriptions and contextualization of Penn's printed sermons, see Edwin B. Bronner and David Fraser. *William Penn's Published Writings, 1660–1726: An Interpretive Bibliography.* Vol. 5: *The Papers of William Penn.* Philadelphia: University of Pennsylvania Press, 1986.

9. *Richardson MSS.* 1 vol. Original and typescript, The Quaker Collection, Haverford College Library, Haverford, Pa. For a description of the *MSS* and an account of their contents, including additional sources for Fox's sermons, see Henry Cadbury, "Richardson MSS," *Journal of the Friends Historical Society,* 32 (1935): 34–37.

10. *The Concurrence and Unanimity; Of the People Called Quakers.* London, J. Sowle, 1711.

11. *The Harmony of Divine and Heavenly Doctrines.* London: J. Sowle, 1696.

12. Wilson, Thomas. [Sermon]. *Harvey MSS.* 1/27a. Library of the Religious Society of Friends, London.

APPENDIX C

THEMATIC CHARACTERISTICS OF QUAKER SERMONS

Themes	Sermon Number [1]																	
	1	2	3	4	5	6	7	8	9	10	11	12	13	14	15	16	17	18
Theological [2]																		
Grace			X		X	X	X	X	X	X	X	X	X	X	X	X	X	
Truth	X	X	X	X	X	X	X	X	X	X	X	X	X	X	X	X	X	
Justification					X			X			X		X					
Faith		X	X	X	X	X	X	X	X		X	X		X	X	X	X	
Redemption			X		X	X	X			X		X		X				
Regeneration (New Birth)							X		X		X					X	X	
Repentance			X			X	X		X		X							
Sanctification			X		X	X	X	X	X	X	X	X	X	X	X	X		
Perfection	X						X		X					X	X	X	X	
Preservation		X	X		X	X	X	X	X			X	X	X	X	X		
Remnant						X	X	X			X							
Convincement											X	X	X	X	X	X	X	
Heaven					X						X	X	X		X	X		
Hell			X						X		X		X			X		
Word of Lord		X	X	X		X	X		X	X	X	X	X	X	X	X	X	
Love (God's to Humans)		X	X	X		X	X	X	X	X	X	X	X	X				

Sermon Number

Themes	1	2	3	4	5	6	7	8	9	10	11	12	13	14	15	16	17	18
Peace		X	X	X	X	X	X	X	X		X	X		X	X	X		X
Joy			X	X	X			X	X		X	X	X	X		X		
Power		X	X	X	X	X	X	X	X	X	X	X	X	X	X	X	X	X
Fear (of God)			X	X			X		X			X	X		X	X	X	X
Judgment	X		X	X		X		X	X	X		X				X		X
Worship					X		X								X		X	
Baptism											X							
Lord's Supper—Communion Fellowship		X		X		X								X			X	
Second Coming (of Christ)																		
Behavioral Guidance																		
Love (Human)		X		X	X	X	X	X	X		X	X			X		X	
Holiness			X	X			X	X	X	X	X	X	X		X	X	X	X
Unity							X											
Humility	X		X	X	X	X		X	X	X						X		X
Self-Denial		X	X	X		X		X	X				X			X	X	X
Order		X	X															
Simplicity		X															X	
Sexual Morality																X		

APPENDIX C (continued)

Sermon Number

Themes	1	2	3	4	5	6	7	8	9	10	11	12	13	14	15	16	17	18
Behaviorial Guidance (cont.)																		
Plain Speech		X						X										
Plain Dress		X																
Antieloquence			X					X										
Commentary on Trends and Events																		
Anti-Catholicism																		
Antitithes																		
Distrust of Learning											X							
Antidebate		X	X										X	X				
Language of New Science		X										X			X			
Reaction to "Enthusiasm"																		
Reaction to Persecution		X	X		X					X								
Antiwar											X							
Love of Country										X	X							
Antitheatre																		
Place of Women (Equality)																		X
Antislavery																		

Sermon Number

Themes	19	20	21	22	23	24	25	26	27	28	29	30	31	32	33	34	35	36
Theological																		
Grace	X	X	X	X	X		X	X	X	X	X	X	X	X	X	X	X	X
Truth	X	X	X	X	X		X	X	X	X	X	X	X	X	X	X	X	X
Justification						X	X	X	X		X	X		X				X
Faith	X	X		X	X	X	X	X	X	X	X	X	X	X	X	X	X	X
Redemption	X	X	X		X		X	X	X		X	X	X		X		X	X
Regeneration (New Birth)					X		X	X	X	X	X					X		X
Repentance							X				X	X	X		X	X	X	
Sanctification		X	X		X	X	X	X	X		X	X		X		X	X	
Perfection		X	X				X		X	X	X			X	X			
Preservation					X	X	X	X		X	X	X		X	X	X	X	
Remnant		X			X		X	X	X		X							
Convincement	X	X			X	X	X	X					X			X	X	
Heaven	X	X		X		X	X			X	X				X	X		X
Hell	X						X											X
Word of Lord		X	X	X	X	X	X	X	X	X	X	X		X			X	X
Love (God's to Humans)		X	X	X			X	X	X	X	X	X	X		X	X	X	X
Peace		X	X	X	X	X	X		X	X	X		X	X	X	X		X
Joy			X				X		X	X						X		

APPENDIX C (continued)

Sermon Number

Themes	19	20	21	22	23	24	25	26	27	28	29	30	31	32	33	34	35	36
Theological (cont.)																		
Power	X	X	X	X	X	X		X	X	X	X	X	X	X	X	X	X	X
Fear (of God)						X			X									X
Judgment	X		X	X	X	X	X		X		X	X	X		X	X	X	X
Worship	X	X		X		X	X				X		X					
Baptism	X	X	X				X				X			X				
Lord's Supper—	X																	
Communion/Fellowship	X	X	X	X			X	X		X	X	X		X	X	X		
Second Coming (of Christ)																		
Behavioral Guidance																		
Love (Human)		X	X	X	X	X	X	X	X	X	X	X		X	X	X	X	
Holiness		X		X	X	X		X	X	X	X	X	X	X	X	X	X	
Unity					X		X			X	X			X				
Humility					X			X		X							X	
Self-Denial			X		X				X	X	X		X	X	X		X	X
Order																		
Simplicity															X			
Sexual Morality		X																

Sermon Number

Themes	19	20	21	22	23	24	25	26	27	28	29	30	31	32	33	34	35	36
Plain Speech	X															X		
Plain Dress																		
Antieloquence					X				X									
Commentary on Trends and Events																		
Anti-Catholicism	X		X				X				X							
Antitithes																		
Distrust of Learning					X						X							
Antidebate																		
Language of New Science		X										X						
Reaction to "Enthusiasm"			X															
Reaction to Persecution			X		X		X				X							
Antiwar										X								
Love of Country																		
Antitheatre																		
Place of Women (Equality)																		
Antislavery																		

APPENDIX C (continued)

Sermon Number

Themes	37	38	39	40	41	42	43	44	45	46	47	48	49	50	51	52	53	54
Theological																		
Grace	X	X	X	X	X		X	X	X	X			X	X	X	X		X
Truth	X		X	X	X	X	X	X	X	X	X		X	X	X	X	X	X
Justification		X		X	X	X			X				X			X	X	
Faith	X	X	X		X	X	X	X	X				X	X	X	X	X	X
Redemption	X		X	X	X	X		X	X				X	X	X	X	X	
Regeneration (New Birth)	X	X	X	X		X			X						X		X	
Repentance		X	X	X	X	X	X	X	X									
Sanctification	X	X	X	X			X		X						X	X		X
Perfection									X						X	X	X	X
Preservation		X	X	X	X	X	X	X						X	X	X	X	X
Remnant		X	X	X	X	X	X	X	X									
Convincement	X	X	X	X	X	X	X	X	X					X	X	X	X	X
Heaven		X			X	X	X	X	X						X	X	X	
Hell		X						X										
Word of Lord												X						
Love (God's to Humans)		X	X	X	X	X	X	X	X	X			X	X	X			X
Peace	X	X	X	X	X	X	X	X		X				X	X	X		X

Sermon Number

Themes	37	38	39	40	41	42	43	44	45	46	47	48	49	50	51	52	53	54
Joy	X	X	X		X	X			X					X		X	X	X
Power	X	X	X	X	X	X	X	X	X					X	X	X	X	X
Fear (of God)	X						X		X	X			X	X				
Judgment	X		X		X	X	X	X	X				X	X	X	X		X
Worship		X			X	X	X	X					X		X	X	X	X
Baptism			X						X						X			
Lord's Supper—																		
Communion (Fellowship)					X					X								
Second Coming (of Christ)						X												
Behavioral Guidance																		
Love (Human)	X		X	X	X	X	X	X	X	X			X	X	X	X	X	X
Holiness	X	X	X	X	X	X	X		X			X	X	X	X	X	X	X
Unity		X	X	X	X	X						X		X	X	X	X	X
Humility	X	X	X	X	X		X	X	X									X
Self-Denial	X	X	X	X	X		X	X		X							X	
Order													X	X	X	X	X	X
Simplicity					X	X								X				
Sexual Morality							X						X	X				X
Plain Speech			X			X	X										X	

APPENDIX C (continued)

Sermon Number

Themes	37	38	39	40	41	42	43	44	45	46	47	48	49	50	51	52	53	54
Behavioral Guidance (cont.)																		
Plain Dress							X			X				X				
Antieloquence			X		X													
Commentary on Trends and Events																		
Anti-Catholicism		X								X				X			X	
Antitithes									X									X
Distrust of Learning				X	X		X											X
Antidebate				X	X	X												
Language of New Science					X	X		X										
Reaction to "Enthusiasm"									X							X	X	X
Reaction to Persecution																		
Antiwar	X								X							X	X	X
Love of Country																		
Antitheatre																		
Place of Women (Equality)														X	X	X	X	
Antislavery													X	X				

Sermon Number

Themes	55	56	57	58	59	60	61	62	63	64	65	66	67	68	69	70	71	72
Theological																		
Grace	X	X	X			X	X		X	X	X	X	X	X	X	X	X	X
Truth	X	X	X			X	X	X	X	X	X	X	X	X	X	X	X	X
Justification									X				X		X	X	X	
Faith	X	X	X			X	X	X		X	X	X	X	X	X	X	X	X
Redemption	X						X	X	X		X	X			X	X	X	X
Regeneration (New Birth)	X												X	X	X	X		
Repentance						X					X		X	X	X			
Sanctification		X	X			X	X		X	X	X	X		X	X	X	X	X
Perfection	X					X			X	X	X	X			X	X		X
Preservation	X	X	X			X	X			X	X	X		X	X	X	X	
Remnant							X	X										
Convincement													X					X
Heaven	X	X	X			X	X		X	X	X	X	X	X	X	X		X
Hell							X	X		X	X	X	X			X		X
Word of Lord		X	X		X	X	X	X	X	X	X		X	X	X	X	X	X
Love (God's to Humans)	X		X			X	X	X	X	X	X	X	X	X	X	X	X	X
Peace	X		X			X	X	X	X	X	X	X	X	X	X	X	X	X
Joy			X			X	X	X	X	X	X	X	X	X	X	X	X	X

APPENDIX C (continued)

Sermon Number

Themes	55	56	57	58	59	60	61	62	63	64	65	66	67	68	69	70	71	72
Theological (cont.)																		
Power	X	X	X			X	X	X	X	X		X	X	X	X	X	X	X
Fear (of God)				X							X	X			X	X	X	
Judgment			X	X		X	X		X		X		X	X	X	X		X
Worship	X	X	X			X								X	X			
Baptism	X	X	X				X					X	X				X	
Lord's Supper—																		
Communion (Fellowship)													X		X			
Second Coming (of Christ)																	X	
Behavioral Guidance																		
Love (Human)							X					X		X	X	X	X	
Holiness	X	X	X			X							X	X	X	X	X	X
Unity	X	X	X				X											
Humility	X					X		X	X	X	X		X	X	X	X	X	X
Self-Denial								X	X	X	X				X	X	X	X
Order	X	X	X											X				
Simplicity																		
Sexual Morality		X												X				

Sermon Number

Themes	55	56	57	58	59	60	61	62	63	64	65	66	67	68	69	70	71	72
Plain Speech	X	X	X															
Plain Dress																		
Antieloquence																		
Commentary on Trends And Events																		
Anti-Catholicism		X																
Antitithes	X	X	X															
Distrust of Learning	X										X							
Antidebate												X						
Language of New Science							X								X		X	
Reaction to "Enthusiasm"		X												X	X	X		
Reaction to Persecution		X									X						X	X
Antiwar																		
Love of Country						X												
Antitheatre																		
Place of Women (Equality)		X																
Antislavery																		

APPENDIX C (continued)

Sermon Number

Themes	73	74	75	76	77	78	79	Total
Theological								
Grace	X	X	X		X	X		64
Truth		X	X	X	X	X		72
Justification		X	X			X		28
Faith	X	X			X	X		62
Redemption	X	X	X	X		X		43
Regeneration (New Birth)	X		X	X		X		30
Repentance	X				X	X	X	29
Sanctification		X	X	X		X		46
Perfection			X					29
Preservation		X	X	X	X	X		48
Remnant		X			X	X	X	26
Convincement					X	X		33
Heaven	X		X		X	X		43
Hell	X			X				19
Word of Lord			X			X	X	47
Love (God's to Humans)	X	X		X	X	X		53
Peace	X	X	X	X	X	X		60

Sermon Number

Themes	73	74	75	76	77	78	79	Total
Joy	X					X		43
Power	X	X	X		X	X		68
Fear (of God)		X			X	X		30
Judgment	X		X		X	X	X	43
Worship	X					X		32
Baptism			X	X		X		22
Lord's Supper—								2
Communion (Fellowship)		X				X	X	24
Second Coming (of Christ)					X			2
Behavioral Guidance								
Love (Human)	X	X				X		30
Holiness	X	X	X			X		54
Unity								21
Humility	X		X		X	X	X	42
Self-Denial	X						X	36
Order					X			12
Simplicity								7
Sexual Morality								8
Plain Speech								14

APPENDIX C (continued)

Sermon Number

Themes	73	74	75	76	77	78	79	Total
Plain Dress								4
Antieloquence								6
Commentary on Trends and Events								
Anti-Catholicism								9
Antitithes								5
Distrust of Learning								8
Antidebate								12
Language of New Science								12
Reaction to "Enthusiasm"				X				6
Reaction to Persecution		X						17
Antiwar			X					4
Love of Country			X					5
Antitheatre								1
Place of Women (Equality)								5
Antislavery								2

APPENDIX D

KEY METAPHORS IN QUAKER SERMONS

Sermon Number

Metaphors	1	2	3	4	5	6	7	8	9	10	11	12	13	14	15	16	17	18
Light-Dark																		
Light	X	X	X	X	X	X	X	X	X	X	X	X	X	X		X		X
Sun, Day		X	X	X		X	X	X	X		X	X	X				X	
Sparks, Fire											X	X				X	X	
Star				X														
Beacon, Lamp						X												
Candle		X		X														
Day of Visitation							X	X	X				X		X			
Day of the Lord (God, etc.)	X																	
Voice of the Light																		
Darkness, Night				X	X		X	X	X	X		X	X			X	X	
Clouds, Fog, Mist, Shadows																		
Veil						X										X		
Chains of Darkness							X											
Sound-Silence (Guiding Voice)																		
Silence		X	X					X						X			X	
Hearing the Voice			X			X		X				X	X	X		X	X	

APPENDIX D (continued)

Sermon Number

Metaphors	1	2	3	4	5	6	7	8	9	10	11	12	13	14	15	16	17	18
Sound-Silence (Guiding Voice) (cont.)																		
The Oracle																X		
Christ (God) as Speaker or Teacher		X									X							
Seed																		
Seed		X	X	X	X	X		X										
Tree and Plant			X		X	X	X	X			X							
Vineyard						X	X											
Grafting				X				X										
Hunger-Thirst																		
Water, Well, River, Fountain		X	X	X					X		X	X						
Wine			X								X							
Cup of Life (Salvation)			X															
Cup of Fornication																		
Milk/Nursing	X							X										
Bread				X			X	X	X		X						X	X
Feeding (on Christ)									X									
Journey																		
Pilgrimage			X					X	X								X	

Sermon Number

Metaphors	1	2	3	4	5	6	7	8	9	10	11	12	13	14	15	16	17	18
Wilderness	X							X		X								
Sodom, Egypt			X					X					X					
Canaan, Jerusalem				X				X										

Sermon Number

Metaphors	19	20	21	22	23	24	25	26	27	28	29	30	31	32	33	34	35
Light-Dark																	
Light			X	X	X	X		X	X	X	X	X	X	X	X	X	X
Sun, Day					X			X	X			X			X		X
Sparks, Fire	X										X						
Star	X																
Beacon, Lamp																	
Candle																	
Day of Visitation				X			X										
Day of the Lord (God, etc.)													X	X			
Voice of the Light				X													
Darkness, Night	X		X		X	X	X	X	X	X	X	X	X		X		X
Clouds, Fog, Mist, Shadows	X		X			X	X	X	X	X	X	X					
Veil						X			X	X							
Chains of Darkness																	

APPENDIX D (continued)

Metaphors	Sermon Number																
	19	20	21	22	23	24	25	26	27	28	29	30	31	32	33	34	35
Sound-Silence (Guiding Voice)																	
Silence																	
Hearing the Voice		X	X		X		X	X	X								
The Oracle									X								
Christ (God) as Speaker or Teacher						X	X			X							X
Seed																	
Seed		X		X		X	X				X	X				X	
Tree and Plant		X	X							X	X	X					
Vineyard											X					X	
Grafting																	
Hunger-Thirst																	
Water, Well, River, Fountain																	
Wine																	
Cup of Life (Salvation)																	
Cup of Fornication																	
Milk/Nursing														X		X	
Bread									X	X							

Sermon Number

Metaphors	19	20	21	22	23	24	25	26	27	28	29	30	31	32	33	34	35
Feeding (on Christ)							X							X			
Journey																	
Pilgrimage				X					X	X				X		X	
Wilderness						X											
Sodom, Egypt					X											X	
Canaan, Jerusalem																	

Sermon Number

Metaphors	36	37	38	39	40	41	42	43	44	45	46	47	48	49	50	51	52
Light-Dark																	
Light	X	X	X		X	X	X	X	X	X			X	X	X	X	X
Sun, Day		X	X		X	X	X		X	X					X	X	X
Sparks, Fire	X	X	X							X					X	X	X
Star							X										
Beacon, Lamp						X		X									
Candle																	
Day of Visitation			X						X	X							
Day of the Lord (God, etc.)			X			X											
Voice of the Light																	

APPENDIX D (continued)

Sermon Number

Metaphors	36	37	38	39	40	41	42	43	44	45	46	47	48	49	50	51	52
Light-Dark (cont.)																	
Darkness, Night	X		X	X	X	X	X	X	X	X					X	X	X
Clouds, Fog, Mist, Shadows			X		X	X				X						X	X
Veil					X					X							
Chains of Darkness																	
Sound-Silence (Guiding Voice)																	
Silence													X				X
Hearing the Voice	X		X		X	X	X	X	X	X						X	X
The Oracle				X													
Christ (God) as Speaker or Teacher							X		X							X	X
Seed																	
Seed	X			X				X	X						X		X
Tree and Plant							X	X	X						X		X
Vineyard									X							X	X
Grafting										X						X	X
Hunger-Thirst																	
Water, Well, River, Fountain								X									X

Sermon Number

Metaphors	36	37	38	39	40	41	42	43	44	45	46	47	48	49	50	51	52
Wine																X	X
Cup of Life (Salvation)																	X
Cup of Fornication																	X
Milk/Nursing		X				X											X
Bread																X	X
Feeding (on Christ)								X								X	X
Journey																	
Pilgrimage		X			X					X				X	X		
Wilderness																	X
Sodom, Egypt							X							X			X
Canaan, Jerusalem				X	X					X							

Sermon Number

Metaphors	53	54	55	56	57	58	59	60	61	62	63	64	65	66	67	68	69
Light-Dark																	
Light	X	X	X	X	X			X	X	X	X	X	X	X	X	X	X
Sun, Day	X							X							X	X	X
Sparks, Fire		X	X	X	X			X				X		X			X
Star			X	X								X					X

APPENDIX D (continued)

Metaphors	53	54	55	56	57	58	59	60	61	62	63	64	65	66	67	68	69
Light-Dark (cont.)																	
Beacon, Lamp	X												X				
Candle		X															
Day of Visitation																	
Day of the Lord (God, etc.)										X				X	X	X	
Voice of the Light	X			X													
Darkness, Night	X	X	X	X	X			X				X	X	X	X	X	X
Clouds, Fog, Mist, Shadows	X		X	X	X			X					X		X	X	
Veil				X													
Chains of Darkness																X	
Sound-Silence (Guiding Voice)																	
Silence																	
Hearing the Voice	X	X	X					X			X		X	X	X		X
The Oracle									X								
Christ (God) as Speaker or Teacher	X	X	X	X	X						X						
Seed																	
Seed	X	X	X	X	X												

Sermon Number

Sermon Number

Metaphors	53	54	55	56	57	58	59	60	61	62	63	64	65	66	67	68	69
Tree and Plant	X	X	X	X				X									X
Vineyard			X														X
Grafting		X	X	X	X												
Hunger-Thirst																	
Water, Well, River, Fountain		X	X		X												X
Wine	X	X	X	X													
Cup of Life (Salvation)														X			
Cup of Fornication			X		X												
Milk/Nursing				X								X					
Bread	X	X		X	X				X		X		X	X			X
Feeding (on Christ)	X	X			X												
Journey																	
Pilgrimage				X					X	X	X	X	X	X	X	X	X
Wilderness												X	X			X	X
Sodom, Egypt	X			X								X		X			X
Canaan, Jerusalem			X	X						X	X	X	X				X

APPENDIX D (continued)

Sermon Number

Metaphors	70	71	72	73	74	75	76	77	78	79	Total
Light-Dark											
Light	X	X	X	X	X	X	X	X	X		69
Sun, Day	X	X	X				X				36
Sparks, Fire	X										24
Star			X								8
Beacon, Lamp	X										7
Candle											3
Day of Visitation	X	X				X	X			X	21
Day of the Lord (God, etc.)						X					7
Voice of the Light											2
Darkness, Night	X	X	X		X	X	X	X	X		57
Clouds, Fog, Mist, Shadows									X		27
Veil						X			X		10
Chains of Darkness											2
Sound-Silence (Guiding Voice)											
Silence											6
Hearing the Voice	X	X	X	X		X	X	X	X		41
The Oracle	X	X							X		5
Christ (God) as Speaker or Teacher		X				X					17

Sermon Number

Metaphors	70	71	72	73	74	75	76	77	78	79	Total
Seed											
Seed								X	X		27
Tree and Plant	X	X					X			X	29
Vineyard						X			X		10
Grafting											11
Hunger-Thirst											
Water, Well, River, Fountain	X	X	X			X		X	X		19
Wine		X									8
Cup of Life (Salvation)											5
Cup of Fornication											3
Milk/Nursing											9
Bread		X							X		23
Feeding (on Christ)											8
Journey											
Pilgrimage	X	X	X	X		X		X			29
Wilderness		X									8
Sodom, Egypt	X	X	X					X			18
Canaan, Jerusalem	X		X								15

APPENDIX E

Other Salient Characteristics of Quaker Sermons

Characteristics																		Sermon Number
	1	2	3	4	5	6	7	8	9	10	11	12	13	14	15	16	17	18
Incantatory Style	X	X																
Repetition	X	X	X								X				X			
Parallelism		X						X										
Catechital Style		X	X	X		X	X	X	X	X	X	X	X		X	X	X	X
Rhetorical Questions		X	X	X		X	X	X	X	X	X	X	X		X	X	X	X
Use of Dialogue				X							X		X	X	X	X	X	X
Use of Queries																		
Appeal to Self-Examination				X		X		X		X	X		X			X	X	X
"Wait on the Lord," etc.			X	X		X	X	X	X	X		X	X	X	X	X	X	X
"Experience" the Lord, etc.			X	X			X	X		X					X	X	X	
"Feel" the Power, etc.	X	X	X	X		X	X	X		X	X		X	X		X		X
Spatial Terms																		
Inward		X	X	X		X	X	X	X			X	X	X	X	X	X	X
Outward	X	X	X	X	X	X	X	X	X			X	X	X	X	X	X	X
Two Audiences Clear	X	X		X		X	X	X	X		X	X	X	X	X	X	X	X
In-Group Only			X	X	X					X		X			X			
Personal Testimony	X		X	X	X						X		X					

Sermon Number

Characteristics	1	2	3	4	5	6	7	8	9	10	11	12	13	14	15	16	17	18
Incident in Life Cited											X							
On Specific Biblical Text					X	X		X				X	X			X		
Use of Latin Quotation		X																
Use of "Puritan," Highly																		
Personalized Language		X			X	X	X		X		X	X						X

Sermon Number

Characteristics	19	20	21	22	23	24	25	26	27	28	29	30	31	32	33	34	35
Incantatory Style																	
Repetition		X					X					X					
Parallelism		X						X				X					
Catechital Style	X	X	X	X	X	X	X	X	X	X	X	X	X	X	X	X	X
Rhetorical Questions	X	X	X	X	X	X	X	X	X	X	X	X	X	X	X	X	X
Use of Dialogue	X	X	X		X	X	X	X	X	X	X	X	X	X	X	X	X
Use of Queries				X							X						
Appeal to Self-Examination					X	X			X						X		
"Wait on the Lord," etc.	X	X	X		X			X		X	X	X	X	X	X	X	X
"Experience" the Lord, etc.	X	X							X	X	X	X	X	X	X		X
"Feel" the Power, etc.	X	X			X		X		X	X	X	X		X		X	

APPENDIX E (continued)

Sermon Number

Characteristics	19	20	21	22	23	24	25	26	27	28	29	30	31	32	33	34	35
Spatial Terms																	
Inward	X	X	X	X	X	X	X	X	X	X	X	X	X	X	X		X
Outward		X	X	X	X	X	X	X	X	X	X	X	X	X	X	X	X
Two Audiences Clear	X	X	X	X		X	X	X			X	X	X		X		X
In-Group Only					X				X	X				X		X	
Personal Testimony			X		X		X		X		X				X		
Incident in Life Cited							X										
On Specific Biblical Text	X				X												
Use of Latin Quotation						X					X						
Use of "Puritan," Highly																	
Personalized Language	X						X										X

Sermon Number

Characteristics	36	37	38	39	40	41	42	43	44	45	46	47	48	49	50	51	52
Incantatory Style																	
Repetition	X	X	X									X	X		X	X	X
Parallelism	X	X	X	X					X				X				X
Catechital Style																	
Rhetorical Questions	X	X	X	X	X	X	X	X	X	X	X					X	X
Use of Dialogue	X	X	X	X	X	X	X	X	X	X	X					X	X
Use of Dialogue	X	X	X	X	X	X	X	X	X	X							
Use of Queries					X				X	X							
Appeal to Self-Examination				X	X	·X			X	X							X
"Wait on the Lord," etc.		X	X	X	X	X	X	X	X	X			X		X		
"Experience" the Lord, etc.			X	X	X	X	X		X								
"Feel" the Power, etc.			X	X	X	X	X	X	X						X	X	X
Spatial Terms																	
Inward	X	X	X	X	X	X	X	X	X	X	X	X		X	X	X	X
Outward	X	X	X	X	X		X	X	X	X	X	X		X	X	X	X
Two Audiences Clear	X	X	X	X				X	X	X							
In-Group Only					X	X	X				X	X	X	X	X	X	X
Personal Testimony		X				X			X	X				X			
Incident in Life Cited	X	X								X	X						
On Specific Biblical Text																	

APPENDIX E *(continued)*

Sermon Number

Characteristics	36	37	38	39	40	41	42	43	44	45	46	47	48	49	50	51	52
Use of Latin Quotation																	
Use of "Puritan," Highly			X														
Personalized Language								X		X						X	

Sermon Number

Characteristics	53	54	55	56	57	58	59	60	61	62	63	64	65	66	67	68	69
Incantatory Style					X	X	X	X									
Repetition	X	X	X			X	X					X					
Parallelism	X	X	X									X	X	X		X	X
Catechital Style	X	X	X	X	X			X	X	X			X	X	X	X	
Rhetorical Questions	X	X	X	X	X			X	X	X			X	X	X	X	X
Use of Dialogue				X	X									X	X		X
Use of Queries													X	X			X
Appeal to Self-Examination												X			X	X	
"Wait on the Lord," etc.									X	X	X	X					X
"Experience" the Lord, etc.								X		X	X		X	X	X		X
"Feel" the Power, etc.	X	X		X	X			X					X	X			
Spatial Terms																	

Sermon Number

Characteristics	53	54	55	56	57	58	59	60	61	62	63	64	65	66	67	68	69
Inward	X	X	X	X	X	X				X		X	X	X	X	X	X
Outward	X	X	X	X	X	X				X			X			X	
Two Audiences Clear			X	X				X			X		X		X	X	
In-Group Only	X	X			X	X	X		X	X		X		X			X
Personal Testimony	X	X		X					X		X						
Incident in Life Cited		X		X						X						X	
On Specific Biblical Text				X								X					
Use of Latin Quotation																	
Use of "Puritan," Highly					X				X								
Personalized Language															X	X	

Sermon Number

Characteristics	70	71	72	73	74	75	76	77	78	79	*Total*
Incantatory Style											8
Repetition				X					X		27
Parallelism		X							X		23
Catechital Style	X	X			X	X	X		X		64
Rhetorical Questions	X	X			X	X	X		X		64
Use of Dialogue	X			X						X	40
Use of Queries		X									8

APPENDIX E (*continued*)

Sermon Number

Characteristics	70	71	72	73	74	75	76	77	78	79	Total
Appeal to Self-Examination	X	X									27
"Wait on the Lord," etc.	X	X	X		X	X	X	X	X		51
"Experience" the Lord, etc.	X	X	X					X	X		34
"Feel" the Power, etc.		X	X	X			X	X	X		46
Spatial Terms											
Inward	X	X		X	X	X	X	X	X		66
Outward	X	X		X	X	X	X	X	X		63
Two Audiences Clear	X					X	X	X	X		43
In-Group Only			X	X	X					X	36
Personal Testimony	X										23
Incident in Life Cited	X			X	X						11
On Specific Biblical Text							X				14
Use of Latin Quotation											2
Use of "Puritan," Highly	X	X			X	X					24
Personalized Language											

NOTES

Preface

[1] Michael P. Graves, "The Rhetoric of the Inward Light: An Examination of Extant Sermons Delivered by Early Quakers, 1671–1700." (Ph.D. diss., University of Southern California, 1972) (hereafter cited as "Rhetoric").

[2] Published as Graves, "Mapping the Metaphors in George Fox's Sermons," in *New Light on George Fox, 1624–1691: A Collection of Essays*, ed. Michael Mullet (York, UK: William Sessions, 1994), 45–59.

[3] Graves, "Functions of Key Metaphors in Early Quaker Sermons, 1671–1700," *Quarterly Journal of Speech* 69 (1983). In 1985 the essay was honored with the Publication Award of the Religious Communication Association.

[4] The resulting seminar essay was published as Graves, "Stephen Crisp's *Short History* as Spiritual Journey," *Quaker Religious Thought*, 26, no. 3 (1993).

[5] Later published as Graves, "Robert Barclay and the Rhetoric of the Inward Light," *Quaker Religious Thought* 26, no. 2 (1993).

[6] Samuel Bownas, *A Description of the Qualifications Necessary to a Gospel Minister, London, 1750* (Philadelphia: Pendle Hill Publications and Tract Association of Friends, 1989).

Introduction

Excerpts in the Introduction from "Review of *Let Your Words Be Few: Symbolism of Speaking and Silence among Seventeenth-Century Quakers* by Richard Bauman," *Quarterly Journal of Speech* (November 1984): 482–83 are used by permission.

[1] Mary Fisher's 1657 visit to the sultan, as well as the missionary work of her five colleagues, is discussed in William C. Braithwaite, *The Beginnings of Quakerism*, 2nd ed., ed. Henry J. Cadbury (Cambridge: Cambridge University Press, 1955; repr., 1961), 420. See also Rosemary Moore, *The Light in Their Consciences: The Early Quakers in Britain, 1646–1666* (University Park: Pensylvania State University Press, 2000), 13. For an excellent background on the impact of early Quaker women, see Phyllis Mack, *Visionary Women: Ecstatic Prophecy in Seventeenth-Century England* (Berkeley: University of California Press, 1994).

[2] See T. L. Underwood, *Primitivism, Radicalism, and the Lamb's War: The Baptist-Quaker Conflict in Seventeenth-Century England* (New York: Oxford University Press, 1997), for an excellent account of the Baptist-Quaker disputes. He also notes that a third sect,

the Muggletonians, strong rivals of the early Quakers, "had a continuous [although miniscule] existence until at least 1979" (14).

³ In a helpful table of contemporary Quaker statistics, Ben Pink Dandelion notes that "'Unaffiliated Evangelical' and 'Evangelical Friends International' together account for 39.5% of total Friends membership. Add to this figure the evangelicals (or theologically conservative) members of Friends United Meeting, which account for 48% of Friends, and the total figure of theologically conservative Friends exceeds 50%"; Pink Dandelion, *An Introduction to Quakerism* (New York: Cambridge University Press, 2007), 180. Pink Dandelion's "Part II: Worldwide Quakers Today" charts a straight and fair path through the contemporary Quaker organizational swampland, helping the reader avoid the mire, quicksand, and alligators.

⁴ This distinction between impromptu and extemporaneous speaking will be maintained throughout this book.

⁵ For an excellent account of the turn from "The Free Gospel Ministry" among American Friends, see William F. Rushby, "Cyrus Cooper's Memorial and the Free Gospel Ministry," *Quaker History* 89, no. 1 (2000): 28–46.

⁶ Ostensibly, "inspired," "God-breathed," or "prophetic" impromptu oral discourse is not an aberration in human experience. Claims of inspired impromptu speech dot the landscape of religious traditions across time and geography. For Christians, inspired impromptu preaching is documented in the experience of the early church. For example, the Acts of the Apostles is rife with spontaneous public discourse, which includes Peter's sermon at Pentecost (Acts 2:14-40), Stephen's last sermon (Acts 7:2-53), Peter's public discourse at Caesarea (Acts 10:34-43), Paul's discourse at the Areopagus (17:22-31), and Paul's defense in Jerusalem (Acts 22:1-21).

⁷ Stephen H. Webb, *The Divine Voice: Christian Proclamation and the Theology of Sound* (Grand Rapids: Brazos Press, 2004), 114.

⁸ Barry Brummett, *Reading Rhetorical Theory* (New York: Harcourt College, 2000), 1.

⁹ For example, the rich tradition of impromptu, "inspired" preaching among African Americans has received careful attention. See, e.g., Gerald L. Davis, *I Got the Word in Me and I Can Sing It, You Know: A Study of the Performed African-American Sermon* (Philadelphia: University of Pensylvania, 1985) and Bruce Rosenberg, *Can These Bones Live? The Art of the American Folk Preacher*, rev. ed. (Chicago: University of Chicago Press, 1988). White Appalachian preaching has been explored in insightful ways through the use of observation, interviews, and analysis of audio and video recordings. See Howard Dorgan, *Giving Glory to God in Appalachia: Worship Practices of Six Baptist Subdenominations* (Knoxville: University of Tennessee Press, 1987).

¹⁰ G. M. Trevelyan, *History of England*, vol. 2: *The Tudors and the Stuart Era* (Garden City, N.Y.: Doubleday Anchor, 1953), 217.

¹¹ Arnold Lloyd, *Quaker Social History 1669–1738* (New York: Longmans, Green, 1950), 124.

¹² Braithwaite, *Beginnings of Quakerism*, 132.

¹³ Frederick B. Tolles remarked in his *Quakers and the Atlantic Culture* (New York: Macmillan, 1960) that in the stratum of society from which the early Quakers came, "the highly emotional species of religious experience which contemporaries called *enthusiasm* was indigenous" (91). The term "enthusiasm" propels one immediately into the seventeenth-century epistemological struggles, which involved such notable writers

as Thomas Hobbes, John Locke, and Henry More. For an excellent discussion of the term "enthusiasm"—that is, immediate inspiration—from its Greek origins through the seventeenth century, see Umphrey Lee, *The Historical Backgrounds of Early Methodist Enthusiasm*, Studies in History, Economics and Public Law, no. 339, ed. Faculty of Political Science of Columbia University (New York: AMS Press, 1967), chaps. 1–4. The early Quakers claimed direct inspiration through the Inward Light of Christ; thus they were numbered among "enthusiasts." Their religious experiences were also often emotional. Thus Quakers were "enthusiastic" on both counts. See also Webb, *The Divine Voice*, 119–24.

[14] With perhaps 40 percent of contemporary Quakers espousing a liberal theology and affiliating with silent or unprogrammed meetings (see Pink Dandelion, *Introduction*, 180), it is not surprising that communication scholars pay attention to the liberal and silent image of Friends that has dominated the media and are largely unacquainted with the predominant, more theologically conservative point of view of the Quaker majority. For example, in the mid-1990s I submitted an essay that analyzed the Quaker Tapestry, an impressive contemporary British-inspired artwork about Quaker history and thought, to a flagship communication journal. In part, I presented the point of view that some of the tapestry panels reflected only the theologically liberal part of contemporary Quakerism. In the process of review that resulted in the essay's rejection, an anonymous peer reviewer lectured me on the *real* nature of Quaker theology in words to the effect that the "Light of Christ" was the "universal," cosmic Christ, not the Light of Christ as discovered in the first chapter of John's Gospel, as I had asserted in the essay. I am appreciative that the essay was later published as "The Quaker Tapestry: An Artistic Attempt to Stitch Together a Diverse Religious Community," *Journal of Communication and Religion* 24, no. 1 (2001): 1–42. The essay also seemed to exonerate me for my "error" when it later gained recognition as "2001 Article of the Year" by the Religious Communication Association.

[15] Thomas D. Hamm notes that, despite contemporary Quakerism's miniscule size, "Quakers have attracted considerable scholarly attention, drawn in large part by the prominence of women in Quaker history and the appeal of Quaker commitments to religious freedom and opposition to slavery" (*The Quakers in America* [New York: Columbia University Press, 2003], vi). Such attention by secular scholars in communication studies frequently focuses on the theologically liberal aspects and personages of Quaker history, downplaying, at best, Quakerism's theologically conservative manifestations.

[16] Timothy Borchers, *Rhetorical Theory: An Introduction* (Belmont, Calif.: Thomson Wadsworth, 2006), 5ff.

[17] Patricia Bizzell and Bruce Herzberg, *The Rhetorical Tradition: Readings from Classical Times to the Present*, 2nd ed. (Boston: Bedford/St. Martin's, 2001), 1.

[18] Martin J. Medhurst and Thomas W. Benson, eds. *Rhetorical Dimensions in Media: A Critical Casebook*, 2nd ed. (Dubuque, Iowa: Kendall/Hunt Publishing, 1984), viii (emphasis in original).

[19] See especially Stephen E. Lucas, "The Schism in Rhetorical Scholarship," *Quarterly Journal of Speech* 67, no. 1 (1981): 1–20; Stephen E. Lucas, "The Renaissance of American Public Address: Text and Context," *Quarterly Journal of Speech* 74 (1988): 241–60; Michael C. Leff and Fred J. Kauffeld, eds., *Texts in Context: Critical Dialogues on*

Significant Episodes in American Political Rhetoric (Davis, Calif.: Hermagoras, 1989); Kathleen J. Turner, ed., *Doing Rhetorical History: Concepts and Cases* (Tuscaloosa: University of Alabama Press, 1998); and Martin J. Medhurst, "The Rhetorical Renaissance: A Battlefield Report," *Southern Communication Journal* 63, no. 5 (1998): 309–14.

[20] To my knowledge, the first book that addressed the relationship of rhetorical studies and media was Medhurst and Benson, eds., *Rhetorical Dimensions in Media*.

[21] See, for example, Charles A. Hill and Marguerite Helmers, eds., *Defining Visual Rhetorics* (Mahwah, N.J.: Lawrence Erlbaum Associates, 2004).

[22] See, e.g., James R. Irvine and Walter Kirkpatrick, "The Musical Form in Rhetorical Exchange: Theoretical Considerations," *Quarterly Journal of Speech* 58, no. 3 (1971): 272–85; and Deanna Sellnow and Timothy Sellnow, "The 'Illusion of Life' Rhetorical Perspective: An Integrated Approach to the Study of Music as Communication," *Critical Studies in Media Communication* 18, no. 4 (2001): 395–415.

[23] Similarly, I do not find it necessary to address the question as to whether rhetorical analysis and criticism exist primarily to serve the development and testing of rhetorical theory. For an interesting set of contrasting viewpoints on what has become a sometimes strongly debated issue, see James Darsey, "Must We All Be Rhetorical Theorists: An Anti-Democratic Inquiry," *Western Journal of Communication* 58 (1994): 164–81; and Roderick P. Hart, "Doing Criticism My Way: A Reply to Darsey," *Western Journal of Communication* 58 (1994): 308–12. The topic of theory's place in the writing of rhetorical criticism is also addressed in one of the best theoretical volumes on rhetorical analysis to appear in the last part of the twentieth century: William L. Nothstine, Carole Blair, and Gary A. Copeland, eds., *Critical Questions: Invention, Creativity, and the Criticism of Discourse and Media* (New York: St. Martin's Press, 1994). Nothstine et al. present and illustrate the maxim that "criticism is both served and confined by theory and method" (11).

[24] The important influence of the late Gerald P. Mohrman and his former colleague Michael C. Leff on the development of text in context criticism canot be underestimated. See Leff's "Textual Criticism: The Legacy of G. P. Mohrman," *Quarterly Journal of Speech* 72 (1986), 377–89. The clearest statement of "text in context" criticism may be found in James R. Andrews, Michael C. Leff, and Robert Terrill, *Reading Rhetorical Texts: An Introduction to Criticism* (Boston: Houghton Mifflin, 1998), vi–viii, 5–81. The reader should also consult Michael Leff, "Things Made By Words: Reflections on Textual Criticism," *Quarterly Journal of Speech* 78 (1992): 223–31; the encyclopedic footnotes included in Lucas' "Renaissance," cited above; and Leff and Kauffeld, *Texts in Context*, also cited above.

[25] Close textual analysis sometimes becomes exceptionally detailed, to the point of being referred to as "close reading." For an example of a sophisticated application of close reading, see Michael Leff and Andrew Sachs, "Words the Most Like Things: Iconicity and the Rhetorical Text," *Western Journal of Speech Communication* 54 (1990): 252–73. Leff and Sachs examine paragraphs from Edmund Burke's famous speech on conciliation, a virtuoso (and unsuccessful) rhetorical effort that can bear up under exceptionally "close" scrutiny.

[26] Lucas, "Renaissance," 254 (emphasis added for "a collection of Quaker sermons").

[27] Frederick B. Tolles, "Introduction to Second Edition," *The Second Period of Quak-*

erism, 2nd ed. (Cambridge: Cambridge University Press, 1961), xxvii. Other scholars who have countered the mystical view of Quaker origins, whose works also appear in the bibliography, include Geoffrey Nuttall, Hugh Barbour, T. Canby Jones, and Arthur O. Roberts. These scholars have been succeeded by a new generation of scholars mentioned later in this introduction.

²⁸ On another plane, historian Barry Reay has even applied a "bottoms up" approach to Quaker studies, asserting that we are "forced to see the Quakers through the spectacles of their latter-day co-religionists and sympathizers" who are concerned "with the spiritual rather than the social" (Barry Reay, *The Quakers and the English Revolution* [New York: St. Martin's Press, 1985], 3).

²⁹ An important conceptualization of rhetoric has consistently informed this study, that advanced by P. Albert Duhamel in "The Function of Rhetoric as Effective Expression," *The Province of Rhetoric*, ed. Joseph Schwartz and John A. Rycenga, eds. (New York: Ronald Press, 1965). Duhamel asserts, "The content of the idea 'rhetoric,' or the conception of what constitutes effective expression, is dependent upon the epistemology, psychology, and metaphysics of the system in which it occurs. The rhetorical is determined by the epistemological. The rhetorician's conception of the value of argument, the process of invention by which arguments are to be discovered, the extent to which the devices of elocution are to be employed, is the result of his [*sic*] evaluation of the reliability of the intellect, the nature and availability of truth, and the existence of certitude" (37).

³⁰ Duhamel, *The Province of Rhetoric*, 36.

³¹ Similarly, scholarly interpretations of the Anglo-American Puritan experience have undergone a process of revision in the last three decades. In her introduction to *Puritanism and Its Discontents*, Laura Lunger Knoppers observes that "Puritanism has lost some of its radical political edge in revisionist accounts, other historians have questioned a distinctively Puritan opposition to popular culture in early modern England"; Laura Lunger Knoppers, ed., *Puritanism and Its Discontents* (Newark, Del.: University of Delaware Press, 2003), 10. Her edited book of scholarly essays "reasserts the 'discontents' of Puritanism, both the radical edge that fueled change and reform and the responses that Puritans evoked from discontented contemporaries" (11).

³² Medhurst makes this case for the field of rhetorical studies in "Public Address and Significant Scholarship: Four Challenges to the Rhetorical Renaissance," in Leff and Kauffeld, eds., *Texts in Context*, 35, and continues the argument nine years later in "The Rhetorical Renaissance," 310–11.

³³ Ben Pink Dandelion, ed., *The Creation of Quaker Theory: Insider Perspectives* (Aldershot, UK: Ashgate Publishing, 2004).

³⁴ Stephen W. Angell, review of *The Creation of Quaker Theory: Insider Perspectives*, ed. Ben Pink Dandelion, *Quaker Studies* 10, no. 1 (2005): 116. There is additional evidence of health in Quaker studies. For example, (1) the Quaker Theological Study Group, born in the 1950s, continues to thrive and publish *Quaker Religious Thought*, a significant journal with a strong intellectual focus; (2) Mellon Press continues to publish a series on Quakerism; and (3) several important Web sites devote themselves to serious discussion of Quaker topics. Significant among the latter is the Web site of Quaker Heritage Press, which is responsible for the Quaker Writings Home Page (QWHP) (http://www.qhpress.org/quakerpages/qwhp/qwhp.htm), edited by Larry Kuenning,

a strong Quaker scholar. The QWHP also hosts a significant site for anyone interested in early Quaker sermons, the Quaker Homiletics Online Anthology (http://www. qhpress.org/quakerpages/qhoa/qhoa.htm), edited by Peter Sipple.

[35] Pink Dandelion, "Introduction," *Quaker Theory*, 3.

[36] Pink Dandelion, "Introduction," *Quaker Theory*, 4.

[37] In addition to Phyllis Mack's *Visionary Women*, see also Catie Gill, "'Ministering Confusion': Rebellious Quaker Women (1650–1660)," *Quaker Studies* 9, no. 1 (2004): 17–30; Catie Gill, *Women in the Seventeenth-Century Quaker Community: A Literary Study of Political Identities, 1650–1700*, Women and Gender in the Early Modern World Series (Aldershot, UK: Ashgate Publishing, 2005); Judith Rose, "Prophesying Daughters: Testimony, Censorship, and Literacy Among Early Quaker Women," *Critical Survey* 14, no. 1 (2002): 93–110; Bernadette Smith, "The Testimony of Martha Simmonds, Quaker," *Quaker Studies* 12, no. 1 (2007): 26–38; Julie Sutherland, "Obedience to the Inward Oracle: An Analysis of some Early Quaker Women's Publications," *Quaker Studies* 6, no. 2 (2002): 135–58; Michele Lise Tarter, "Sites of Performance: Theorizing the History of Sexuality in the Lives and Writings of Quaker Women, 1650–1800" (Ph.D. diss., University of Colorado, 1993); Tarter, "The Milk of the Word of God," in *New Voices, New Light: Papers from the Quaker Theology Round Table*, ed. Charles Fager (Wallingford, Pa.: Pendle Hill Publishers, 1995); Tarter, "Quaking in the Light: The Politics of Quaker Women's Corporeal Prophecy in the Seventeenth-Century Transatlantic World," in *A Center of Wonders: The Body in Early America*, ed. Janet Moore Lindman and Michele Lise Tarter (Ithaca: Cornell University Press, 2004), 145–62; Christine Trevett, *Women and Quakerism in the 17th Century* (York, UK: William Sessions, Limited, 1995); and Trevett, *Quaker Women Prophets in England and Wales, 1650–1700* (Lewiston, N.Y.: Edwin Mellen Press, 2000).

[38] Pink Dandelion, "Conclusion," *Quaker Theory*, 232, 233.

[39] Pink Dandelion, "Conclusion," *Quaker Theory*, 234.

[40] Some of the contributors do address rhetorical concerns. For example, in her essay "'Go North!' The Journey towards First-generation Friends and their Prophecy of Celestial Flesh," Michele Lise Tarter deals with the "[disempowerment of] the original Quaker notion of celestial flesh" (93) that formerly called forth the derisive name "Quaker."

[41] Medhurst and Benson, eds. *Rhetorical Dimensions in Media*, viii (emphasis in original).

[42] Kenneth Burke built his approach to rhetoric around the idea of the rhetor identifying himself or herself with the audience and the difficulties experienced when that identification is not achieved. He wrote, "[Y]ou persuade a man only insofar as you can talk his language by speech, gesture, tonality, order, image, attitude, idea, identifying your ideas with his"; Kenneth Burke, *A Grammar of Motives and A Rhetoric of Motives* (Cleveland: Meridian Books/World Publishing, 1961), 579.

[43] Braithwaite, *Beginnings of Quakerism*; and Braithwaite, *The Second Period of Quakerism*, 2nd ed., ed. Henry J. Cadbury (Cambridge: Cambridge University Press, 1961).

[44] Rufus M. Jones, *Spiritual Reformers in the 16th and 17th Centuries* (1914; repr., Boston: Beacon, 1959) and Rufus M. Jones, *The Quakers in the American Colonies* (1910; repr., New York: Russell & Russell, 1962). These works argue that Quaker origins were greatly influenced by the continental mystics.

[45] Braithwaite, *Second Period*, 451.

[46] Hugh Barbour, *The Quakers in Puritan England*, vol. 8, Yale Publications in Religion (New Haven: Yale University Press, 1964).

[47] Barbour, *Quakers in Puritan England*, 129.

[48] Barbour, *Quakers in Puritan England*, 130.

[49] Douglas Gwyn, *Apocalypse of the Word: The Life and Message of George Fox* (Richmond, Ind.: Friends United Press, 1984).

[50] Gwyn, *Apocalypse of the Word*, 210 (emphasis added).

[51] Gwyn, *Apocalypse of the Word*, 211.

[52] Gwyn, *Apocalypse of the Word*, 213 (emphasis in original).

[53] Gwyn, *Apocalypse of the Word*, 211.

[54] To an extent, Gwyn has done this himself in *The Covenant Crucified: Quakers and the Rise of Capitalism* (Wallingford, Pa.: Pendle Hill Publications, 1995). In this book, he traces the evolution of Quakerism from revolutionary movement to an "ordered," domesticated sect. However, Gwyn's frame is history and theology rather than focusing on the investigation of rhetorical theory and practice.

[55] Luella M. Wright, *The Literary Life of the Early Friends, 1650–1725* (New York: Columbia University Press, 1932; New York: AMS Press, 1966). Pages cited are from the 1966 reprint.

[56] Wright, *Literary Life of the Early Friends*, vii.

[57] Wright, *Literary Life of the Early Friends*, 6–7 (emphasis added).

[58] Rushby, "Cyrus Cooper's Memorial," n. 50, 45.

[59] Wright, *Literary Life of the Early Friends*, 146.

[60] Jackson I. Cope, "Seventeenth Century Quaker Style," *Proceedings of the Modern Language Association* 71 (1956): 725–54.

[61] Cope, "Seventeenth Century Quaker Style," 725, 729.

[62] Cope, "Seventeenth Century Quaker Style," 729, 726, 727.

[63] Cope, "Seventeenth Century Quaker Style," 736, 738, 733, 735.

[64] Cope, "Seventeenth Century Quaker Style," 746, 749.

[65] Cope, "Seventeenth Century Quaker Style," 749.

[66] Cope, "Seventeenth Century Quaker Style," 753.

[67] The Second Day's Morning Meeting, or Monday Morning Meeting, was established both as a board of review for Quaker writings and as a meeting to establish order among Quaker ministers in the London area; the *Minutes of Monday Morning Meeting* (Typescript. Transcribed by Edward H. Milligan. 2 vols., 1673–1693, 1694–1700. Library of the Religious Society of Friends, London) for November 24, 1673, records the following: "When bookes comes that are not approved of, the sence of the bretheren to be signified to the Authors" (1). At the May 3 meeting two years later, it was recorded, "It is desired that all freinds [*sic*] about the Citty that have a Publick Testimony . . . doe meet with the Breteren on every first day and second day Morning when they can, otherwise to send a Noat . . . signifying what Meetings they intend to be at on the first dayes" (5).

[68] Maurice A. Creasey, "'Inward' and 'Outward': A Study in Early Quaker Language," *Journal of the Friends' Historical Society*, suppl. no. 30 (London: Friends' Historical Society, 1962).

[69] Creasey, "'Inward' and 'Outward,'" 3, 4.

[70] Creasey, "'Inward' and 'Outward,'" 20.

[71] No sermons survive which could be placed comfortably in the group of writers represented by Isaac Penington (1616–1679).

[72] Lucia K. Beamish, *Quaker Ministry, 1691–1834* (Oxford: By the Author, 76c Woodstock Road, 1967).

[73] Quakers always recognized the calling by God of certain men and women to the public ministry. Thus Quakers supported itinerant evangelists from their earliest years. Friends also maintained that anyone could minister when under the compulsion of the Spirit to do so, without a special calling. See Beamish, *Quaker Ministry*, 16–19.

[74] Beamish, *Quaker Ministry*, 24, 25.

[75] Thomas H. Pattison, *History of Christian Preaching* (Philadelphia: American Baptist Publication Society, 1903), 394–98.

[76] Edwin C. Dargan, *A History of Preaching*, 2 vols. (New York: G. H. Doran, n.d., c. 1905–1912).

[77] F. R. Webber, *A History of Preaching in Britain and America*, 3 vols. (Milwaukee: Northwestern Publishing House, 1957).

[78] Caroline Richardson, *English Preachers and Preaching, 1640–1670* (New York: Macmillan, 1928).

[79] W. Fraser Mitchell, *English Pulpit Oratory from Andrewes to Tillotson: A Study of Its Literary Aspects* (London: Society for Promoting Christian Knowledge, 1932; New York: Russell & Russell, 1962).

[80] Mitchell, *English Pulpit Oratory*, x.

[81] Horton Davies, *Worship and Theology in England from Andrewes to Baxter and Fox, 1603–1690*, vol. 2: *Worship and Theology in England* (Princeton: Princeton University Press, 1975), 492–98. Davies is more sympathetic in his account than is Mitchell, who is uniformly derisive regarding early Quakers and dismisses their preaching in his *English Pulpit Oratory*, 21, 43, and 294. Interestingly, Rolf P. Lessenich, writing forty years after Mitchell, never mentions Quakers in his otherwise painstaking, erudite work on British preaching in the long eighteenth century, *Elements of Pulpit Oratory in Eighteenth-Century England (1660–1800)* (Cologne: Böhlau-Verlag, 1972).

[82] Davies, *Worship and Theology in England*, 511–15.

[83] Davies is an excellent source for two crisp, accurate accounts of Puritan preaching within the larger context of discussions of English and American Puritan worship. See the reprint of his *The Worship of the English Puritans* (Morgan, Pa.: Soli Deo Gloria Publications, 1997; first published in 1948 by Dacre Press), 182–203, and *The Worship of the American Puritans, 1629–1730* (New York: Peter Lang Publishing, 1990), 77–113. The best examinations of Puritan rhetoric remain Eugene E. White, *Puritan Rhetoric: The Issue of Emotion in Religion* (Carbondale: Southern Illinois University Press, 1972); Sacvan Bercovitch, *The American Jeremiad* (Carbondale: Southern Illinois University Press, 1978); Harry S. Stout, *The New England Soul: Preaching and Religious Culture in Colonial New England* (New York: Oxford University Press, 1986); and Teresa Toulouse, *The Art of Prophesying: New England Sermons and the Shaping of Belief* (Athens: University of Georgia Press, 1987).

[84] Richard Bauman, "Aspects of Seventeenth Century Quaker Rhetoric," *Quarterly Journal of Speech* 56 (1970): 74.

[85] Cope observes a change of style among the early Quakers during the third

quarter of the century, which eventually develops into the so-called "plain style" from the incantatory style (Cope, "Seventeenth Century Quaker Style"), 749. Creasey sees a movement toward philosophic dualism and attempted to document it in the apologetical writings of Barclay and Pen with particular reference to the Quaker usage of inward and outward. Both Cope and Creasey see Fox's writings as representative of an earlier style, while Pen exemplifies a later one. Beamish places Fox and Crisp in an earlier period of Quaker ministry, which then changes in character after their deaths in 1691 and 1692, respectively (Beamish, *Quaker Ministry*, 20–22).

[86] Richard Bauman, "Speaking in the Light: The Role of the Quaker Minister," in *Explorations in the Ethnography of Speaking*, ed. Richard Bauman and Joel Sherzer (New York: Cambridge University Press, 1974), 144–60.

[87] Bauman, "Speaking in the Light," 148, 151, 153, 155–60; quote on p. 160. Although not directly germane to the present study, it is worth mentioning that, a year later, Richard Bauman discusses Quaker use of humor, concluding that "Quaker doctrine and practice could simply not accommodate formalized secular humor" ("Quaker Folk-Linguistics and Folklore," in *Folklore: Performance and Communication*, ed. Dan Ben-Amos and Kenneth S. Goldstein [The Hague: Mouton, 1975], 260). This not-so-surprising conclusion perhaps accounts for why surviving early Quaker sermons are devoid of humor.

[88] Richard Bauman, *Let Your Words Be Few: Symbolism of Speaking and Silence among Seventeenth-Century Quakers*, Cambridge Studies in Oral and Literate Culture, no. 8 (New York: Cambridge University Press, 1983). In this section, I will be drawing from my review of Bauman's book in *Quarterly Journal of Speech* (November 1984): 482–83.

[89] Bauman, *Let Your Words Be Few*, 7.

[90] Bauman, *Let Your Words Be Few*, 39, 42.

[91] Bauman, *Let Your Words Be Few*, 77.

[92] Bauman, *Let Your Words Be Few*, 125.

[93] Bauman, *Let Your Words Be Few*, 147, 151.

[94] Graves, review of *Let Your Words Be Few*, 482.

[95] Less important to the concerns of this book, Bauman also deals with the well-known distinctive Quaker speech patterns in chapter 4 and the performance of metaphors (such as "going naked for a sign") in chapter 6; in chapter 7, he considers the Quaker injunction against taking oaths.

[96] Braithwaite, for example, devotes an entire chapter to June 1652, the period following a vision in which Fox saw a "People in white Raiment" waiting to be gathered unto the truth (*Beginnings of Quakerism*, 78–97). See also Barbour, *Quakers in Puritan England*, 45.

[97] Braithwaite treats this period in *Second Period* , 457–96. See also his analysis of the decline of Quakerism, 630–37. In the second volume of *History of English Nonconformity*, Henry W. Clark observed regarding the ebb of Quakerism in the 1690s: "the tide of zeal was going out, leaving bare and rather unlovely shores behind" (New York: Russell & Russell, 1965), 169.

[98] G. M. Trevelyan, *English Social History: A Survey of Six Centuries, Chaucer to Queen Victoria* (New York: Longmans, Green, 1942), 363.

[99] In addition to Bauman's account in *Let Your Words Be Few*, see Gwyn's *The Covenant Crucified* (37–49) and Pink Dandelion's *An Introduction to Quakerism* (53–58) for

excellent accounts of these years and the significant changes among Friends. In addition, see Tarter's "'Go North!,'" in which she discusses the Quaker attempt to reign in the kinds of "enthusiastic" bodily manifestations that originally earned them the name Quakers, a throttling down and censure that, according to Tarter's interpretation, was borne most heavily by Quaker women (see esp. 90–94).

[100] No sermons survive from such important personalities as James Nayler, Edward Burrough, Francis Howgill, Margaret Fell, Rebecca Travers, and others. Their subjects and manner of development may, in some limited instances, be recapitulated through perusal of early documents. An important source for this purpose is Norman Penny, ed., *The First Publishers of Truth* (London: Headley Brothers, 1907); hereafter cited as *FPT*.

[101] In addition, there are two anonymous sermons in which the gender of the preacher canot be known. Although women were active as ministers among Friends, to my knowledge no sermons survive from any of the female Quakers except brief fragments, which are not sermons per se. The names of Elizabeth Hooton, Ane Downer, Sarah Blackbury, and Rebecca Travers are important among Quaker preachers. Women were apparently effective speakers. After hearing Rebecca Collins, John Locke softened his objections to women preaching and wrote, "Women, indeed, had the honour to publish the resurrection of the spirit of love. And let all the disciples rejoice therein, as doth your partner, John Locke" (quoted in Pattison, *History of Christian Preaching*, 398–99).

[102] As noted above, a sermon by Thomas Chalkley is included in this book, although internal evidence indicates that it was preached after his arrival for a visit in the American colonies. Like Fox's preaching at Barbados, I consider this sermon to be representative of the preaching of English Friends from the period. I have extensively analyzed Chalkley's sermon in Michael P. Graves, "'Thou art but a youth': Thomas Chalkley Enacts and Defends the Early Quaker Impromptu Sermon," in *A Rhetorical History of the United States*, vol. 1: *Rhetoric, Religion, and the Roots of Identity in British Colonial America*, ed. James R. Andrews, general ed. Martin J. Medhurst (East Lansing: Michigan State University Press, 2007), 229–74.

[103] The years 1671–1681 are only truly representative of Fox's preaching, since only one additional 1674 sermon by an anonymous preacher is extant from the period.

Chapter 1

[1] Christopher Hill, *A History of England*, vol. 5: *The Century of Revolution 1603–1714*, ed. Christopher Brooke and Denis Mack Smith, 8 vols. (London: Thomas Nelson and Sons, 1961), 4–5.

[2] J. R. Jones, *Country and Court: England, 1658–1714*. The New History of England, ed. A. G. Dickens and Norman Gash (Cambridge, Mass.: Harvard University Press, 1978), 1.

[3] I am using the term "constraints" both in the sense of motivation and of restraint. The intellectual, religious, sociopolitical, and rhetorical environment both compels rhetorical theorizing and discourse and sets limits upon its topics, forms, and effectiveness.

[4] Wallace Notestein, *The English People on the Eve of Colonization* (New York: Harper & Row, 1962), 26.

⁵ Maurice Ashley, *The Pelican History of England*, vol. 6: *England in the Seventeenth Century*, 3d ed. (Baltimore: Penguin Books, 1961), 155.

⁶ C. John Sommerville, *Popular Religion in Restoration England*. University of Florida Monographs, Social Sciences, no. 59 (Gainesville: University Presses of Florida, 1977), 3.

⁷ Basil Willey, *The Seventeenth Century Background: Studies in the Thought of the Age in Relation to Poetry and Religion* (Garden City, N.Y.: Doubleday, 1953), 14, 16.

⁸ Bertrand Russell, *A History of Western Philosophy* (New York: Simon and Schuster, 1945), 557 (emphasis in original).

⁹ A. B. Gibson, *The Philosophy of Descartes* (New York: Russell & Russell, 1967), 4.

¹⁰ Rene Descartes, *Discourse on Method*, in *A Discourse on Method and Selected Writings*, trans. John Veitch (New York: Dutton, 1951), 2, 7.

¹¹ Descartes, *Discourse on Method*, 28.

¹² Descartes, *Discourse on Method*, 29.

¹³ Descartes, *Discourse on Method*, 14.

¹⁴ Descartes, *Discourse on Method*, 15–16.

¹⁵ Rene Descartes, *Rules for the Direction of the Mind*, trans. Laurence J. Lafleur (Indianapolis: Bobbs-Merrill, 1961), 11–12. Norman Smith, in his important treatise *Studies in the Cartesian Philosophy* (New York: Russell & Russell, 1961), sees Descartes' notion of deduction as a type of extended intuition: "Though Descartes adds to intuition deduction, he does not mean by the latter anything really distinct from intuition. We must, he admits, distinguish between the self-evident truths and those others whose certainty can only be discovered by deduction from them. The process, however, by which they are verified is in both cases the same. Deduction is but a long series of intuitions. . . . When the series is too long thus to be gathered into a single fruitful intuition, the memory of the evidence previously verified in intuition has to be relied upon" (32–33).

¹⁶ Frederick L. Nussbaum, *The Triumph of Science and Reason 1660–1685* (New York: Harper & Row, 1962), 1.

¹⁷ Nussbaum, *Triumph of Science and Reason*, 2.

¹⁸ William T. Jones, *A History of Western Philosophy* (New York: Harcourt, Brace, 1952), 591.

¹⁹ Francis Bacon, "Novum Organon," in *The New Organon and Related Writings*, ed. F. H. Anderson (New York: Liberal Arts Press, 1960), 19.

²⁰ Bacon, "Novum Organon," 20.

²¹ Karl R. Wallace, *Francis Bacon on the Nature of Man: The Faculties of Man's Soul* (Urbana: University of Illinois Press, 1967), 125.

²² Bacon, "Novum Organon," 48.

²³ Bacon, "Novum Organon," 48.

²⁴ Karl R. Wallace, *Francis Bacon on Communication and Rhetoric* (Chapel Hill: University of North Carolina Press, 1943), 96.

²⁵ See a brief but informative discussion of this point in David Potter, *Debating in the Colonial Chartered Colleges*, Columbia University Teachers College Contributions to Education, no. 89 (New York: Columbia University Press, 1944), 1–15. Potter includes a description of the typical format of the debate from Isaac Watts, *The Improvement of the Mind, or, A Supplement to the Art of Logic In Two Parts, to Which Is Added, a Discourse on the*

Education of Children and Youth (Boston: D. West, 1793), a popular contemporary manual on disputing.

[26] Notestein, *The English People on the Eve of Colonization*, 32.

[27] Wilbur Samuel Howell, "The Plough and the Flail: The Ordeal of Eighteenth Century Logic," *The Huntington Library Quarterly* 28 (1964): 63–78.

[28] Howell, "The Plough and the Flail," 77.

[29] Nussbaum, *Triumph of Science and Reason*, 26.

[30] Richard F. Jones, *Ancients and Moderns: A Study of the Rise of the Scientific Movement in Seventeenth-Century England*, 2nd ed. (Berkeley: University of California Press, 1965), 117. For a contrasting view, see Marshall M. Knappen, *Tudor Puritanism: A Chapter in the History of Idealism* (Glouchester, Mass.: Peter Smith, 1963), 476.

[31] Braithwaite, *Beginnings of Quakerism*, 1.

[32] See the bibliography for a partial list of pertinent writings by these scholars on the subject of Puritanism.

[33] In the introduction to her significant edited volume, *Puritanism and Its Discontents*, Laura Lunger Knoppers steers her way through published scholarship on Puritanism. She notes that "several decades of historical work have countered the literary stereotype of the interfering Puritan" (9). Works by Patrick Collinson, Peter Lake, Nicholas Tyacke, Alexandra Walsham, and Kristen Poole (included in the bibliography of this book) get her notice as having authored key revisionist works that blunt the "discontent" of Puritans. Her own book is an attempt to "reassert" the strong "discontent" of Puritans "that fueled change and reform" (11). The impressive book by Kenneth Fincham and Nicholas Tyacke, *Altars Restored: The Changing Face of English Religious Worship, 1547–c.1700* (New York: Oxford University Press, 2008), deals with the demise of Puritan influence in England in great detail by reference to hitherto unexplored parish records and artifacts.

[34] Charles Lloyd Cohen, *God's Caress: The Psychology of Puritan Religious Experience* (New York: Oxford University Press, 1986), 3.

[35] Kristen Poole, *Radical Religion from Shakespeare to Milton: Figures of Nonconformity in Early Modern England* (Cambridge: Cambridge University Press, 2000), 5.

[36] Quakerism has been interpreted as an outgrowth of English Puritanism. Barbour observes, "Most of their insights in ethics and worship were in fact the same as those of the puritans. Even characteristically Quaker teachings were often puritan attitudes pushed to severe conclusions. . . . Their conflicts with puritan leaders had the loving desperation of a family feud" (*Quakers in Puritan England*, 2).

[37] Notestein, *The English People on the Eve of Colonization*, 161.

[38] William Perkins made an attempt at this goal in "The Foundation of Christian Religion," *Works* (Cambridge, 1600).

[39] Alan Simpson, *Puritanism in Old and New England* (Chicago: University of Chicago Press, 1961), 5.

[40] Cohen, *God's Caress*, 4–5.

[41] Knappen, *Tudor Puritanism*, 341.

[42] Simpson, *Puritanism in Old and New England*, 6.

[43] William Perkins, *Workes*, 2 vols. (London: 1616–1618), 1:122.

[44] Other generalized principles of Puritanism could be noted, including intellec-

tual toughness, individualism, "zeal," etc. See Knappen, *Tudor Puritanism*, 339–53, for a discussion of these topics.

[45] Paul Chang-Ha Lim, *In Pursuit of Purity, Unity, and Liberty: Richard Baxter's Puritan Ecclesiology in Its Seventeenth-Century Context* (Leiden: Koninklijke Brill, 2004), 8.

[46] Richard Baxter, *A Holy Commonweath*, quoted in Herbert Wallace Schneider, *The Puritan Mind* (Ann Arbor: University of Michigan Press, 1958), 16.

[47] Richard Schlatter, *Richard Baxter & Puritan Politics* (New Brunswick, N.J.: Rutgers University Press, 1957), 21–22.

[48] Simpson, *Puritanism in Old and New England*, 9.

[49] Christopher Morris, Introduction to Richard Hooker's *Of the Laws of Ecclesiastical Polity*, 2 vols. (New York: E. P. Dutton, 1958), viii.

[50] John Marlowe, *The Puritan Tradition in English Life* (London: Cresset Press, 1956), 23–24.

[51] Barbour, *Quakers in Puritan England*, 21.

[52] Barbour, *Quakers in Puritan England*, 24. Winstanley's *The Works of Gerrard Winstanley* was edited and published in 1941 by George H. Sabine (Ithaca: Cornell University Press, 1941; New York: Russell & Russell, 1965).

[53] Buchanan Sharp, "Popular Protest," in *Popular Culture in Seventeenth-Century England*, ed. Barry Reay (London: Routledge, 1988), 299.

[54] See the important study by H. N. Brailsford, *The Levellers and the English Revolution*, ed. Christopher Hill (Stanford: Stanford University Press, 1961).

[55] Barbour, *Quakers in Puritan England*, 24.

[56] Peter Burke, "Popular Culture in Seventeenth-Century London," in *Popular Culture in Seventeenth-Century England*, ed. Barry Reay (London: Routledge, 1988), 51.

[57] Barbour, *Quakers in Puritan England*, 25. Two more recent books focus keenly on the ramifications of Puritan "psychology" on individuals. See Cohen, *God's Caress*, 137–274, and David Leverenz, *The Language of Puritan Feeling: An Exploration in Literature, Psychology, and Social History* (New Brunswick, N.J.: Rutgers University Press, 1980).

[58] In addition to the brief accounts of the varieties of Dissenters by Barbour, *Quakers in Puritan England* (28) and Braithwaite, *Beginnings of Quakerism*, (13, 18–27), one may also profitably consult the work of a later Robert Barclay, *The Inner Life of the Religious Societies of the Commonwealth*, 2nd ed. (London: Hodder & Stoughton, 1876). See also Champlin Burrage, *The Early English Dissenters in the Light of Recent Research 1550–1641*, 2 vols. (New York: Russell & Russell, 1967), a reprint of the 1912 edition, the first volume of which treats the history and criticism, and the second of which contains illustrative documents.

[59] Sommerville, *Popular Religion in Restoration England*, 8.

[60] Willey, *The Seventeenth Century Background*, 117.

[61] Milton's great defense of freedom from censorship was published in 1644. Locke's *Two Treatises* and *Essay* appeared in 1690.

[62] G. M. Trevelyan, *Illustrated English Social History*, 4 vols. (New York: David McKay, 1949–1952), 2:65.

[63] Trevelyan, *Illustrated English Social History*, 2:65.

[64] The Quakers alone produced 2,678 publications during the years 1650–1725 (Rufus Jones, introduction to *The Literary Life of the Early Friends*, by Luella M. Wright [New York: AMS Press, 1966], xiii). See the excellent recent scholarly work on this

topic: Kate Peters, *Print Culture and the Early Quakers*, Cambridge Studies in Early Modern British History (Cambridge: Cambridge University Press, 2005).

[65] Notestein, *The English People on the Eve of Colonization*, 148.

[66] For a consideration of the influence of the King James translation on Puritanism, see Esme Wingfield-Stratford, *The History of British Civilization*, 2nd rev. ed. (New York: Harcourt, Brace, 1949), 542–46. See also Adam Nicolson, *God's Secretaries: The Making of the King James Bible* (New York: HarperCollins, 2003) for the best recent account of the development of the "Authorized" Version.

[67] On the Fifth Monarchy Men, see Louise Fargo Brown, *The Political Activities of the Baptists and Fifth Monarchy Men in England During the Interregnum* (New York: Burt Franklin, 1964); and George Philip Rogers, *The Fifth Monarchy Men* (London: Oxford University Press, 1966).

[68] Lawrence Stone, *The Crisis of the Aristocracy, 1558–1641* (Oxford: Clarendon Press, 1965).

[69] Godfrey Davies, *The Early Stuarts 1603–1660*, vol. 9: *The Oxford History of England*, 2nd ed., ed. George Clark (Oxford: Clarendon Press, 1959), xxi.

[70] Stone, *The Crisis of the Aristocracy*, 9–10.

[71] For scholarly, interesting, and sometimes contrasting accounts of the rise of Quakerism, see Barbour, *Quakers in Puritan England*, 33–71; Moore, *The Light in Their Consciences*, 3–34; Pink Dandelion, *Introduction*, 1–37; and John Punshon, *Portrait in Quaker Grey: A Short History of the Quakers* (London: Quaker Home Service, 1984), 5–79.

[72] Trevelyan, *Illustrated English Social History*, 1:114.

[73] Webber, *A History of Preaching*, 201.

[74] George N. Clark, *The Later Stuarts 1660–1714*, vol. 10: *The Oxford History of England*, 2nd ed., ed. George N. Clark (Oxford: Clarendon, 1955), 21.

[75] Clark, *The Later Stuarts*, 22.

[76] Clark, *The Later Stuarts*, 22.

[77] G. M. Trevelyan, *England Under the Stuarts*, vol. 5: *A History of England*, ed. Charles Oman (London: Methuen, 1965), 327.

[78] Quoted in Braithwaite, *Second Period*, 23.

[79] Braithwaite, *Second Period*, 14 (emphasis in original).

[80] Braithwaite, *Second Period*, 15.

[81] A brief lull in persecution occurred between 1670 and 1673, and it also lessened during the late 1680s, when toleration was about to dawn. See Braithwaite, *Second Period*, 55–87 and 116–50.

[82] Quoted in Braithwaite, *Beginnings of Quakerism*, 41. Scholarly work on Baxter is so voluminous that Paul Chang-Ha Lim began his major work on Baxter's ecclesiology with the wry query, "Another Work on Baxter?" (*In Pursuit of Purity, Unity, and Liberty*, 1). See his extensive bibliography for a sense of Baxter's significance seen by the listing of primary sources, scholarly articles and books, and doctoral dissertations (231–53).

[83] Trevelyan, *History of England*, 2:271.

[84] Ralph Barton Perry, *Puritanism and Democracy* (New York: Vanguard Press, 1944), 70. The parties were in a primitive state of organization. There were always those members of Parliament present who could be counted upon to support whatever government was in power. See Ashley, *England in the Seventeenth Century*, 196.

[85] Carl J. Friedrich, *The Age of the Baroque 1610–1660* (New York: Harper & Row, 1962), 2.

[86] T. S. Ashton, scholar of the Industrial Revolution, dated the begining of the phenomenon at 1760. Of the period 1700–1760, he concludes, "Britain experienced no revolution, either in the technique of production, the structure of industry, or the economic and social life of the people" (*The Industrial Revolution 1760–1830* [London: Oxford University Press, 1964], 41).

[87] Trevelyan, *History of England*, 2:219–20.

[88] Stone describes the Quaker protest against "hat-honor" as a "shattering . . . psychological blow to the conceptual framework of society" based upon the "great principle of subordination" (*The Crisis of the Aristocracy*, 34–35). Refusal to doff their hats became part of the point at issue in the famous trial of William Pen and William Meade, which helped establish the right of juries to arrive at their own verdicts contrary to a judge's instruction (Punshon, *Portrait in Quaker Grey*, 89).

[89] Reay, "Introduction," in *Popular Culture in Seventeenth-Century England*, 18.

[90] Hill, *The Century of Revolution*, 294.

[91] Webb cautions that "the revolt against enthusiasm was not uniform or systematic, but it was widespread" (*The Divine Voice*, 121). See also Michael Heyd, *"Be Sober and Reasonable": The Critique of Enthusiasm in the Seventeenth and Early Eighteenth Centuries* (Leiden: E. J. Brill, 1995).

[92] Douglas Ehninger, "On Rhetorics and Rhetoric," *Western Speech* 31 (1967): 244. See also his "On Systems of Rhetoric," *Philosophy & Rhetoric*, 1 (1968): 131–34.

[93] Wilbur Samuel Howell, "English Backgrounds of Rhetoric," in *History of Speech Education in America*, ed. Karl Wallace (New York: Appleton-Century-Crofts, 1954), 21.

[94] Wilbur Samuel Howell, *Logic and Rhetoric in England: 1500–1700* (Princeton: Princeton University Press, 1956; New York: Russell & Russell, 1961). Although Thomas M. Conley asserts that Howell's work "needs to be superseded by a more careful and balanced account," he nevertheless calls it "the standard account of rhetoric in England for this period" (*Rhetoric in the European Tradition* [White Plains, N.Y.: Longman, 1990], 145).

[95] Brummett, *Reading Rhetorical Theory*, 3.

[96] Brummett, *Reading Rhetorical Theory*, 397, 398.

[97] Another reading is offered by Thomas Conley, who concentrates on theorists who have formerly commanded less attention in standard histories of rhetoric. See his *Rhetoric in the European Tradition*, 114–44.

[98] For an excellent discussion of the influence of John Locke on the development of rhetorical theory in the eighteenth century, see Wilbur Samuel Howell, "John Locke and the New Rhetoric," *Quarterly Journal of Speech* 53 (1967): 319–33.

[99] For a discussion of this rhetorical school, see Ehninger, "On Systems of Rhetoric," 134–37. For an excellent overall introduction to traditional rhetoric, especially as the ancients envisioned it, see R. C. Jebb, *The Encyclopedia Britannica*, 9th and 11th eds., s.v. "Rhetoric"; also E. L. Hunt, "An Introduction to Classical Rhetoric," *Quarterly Journal of Speech* 12 (1926): 201–4. Medieval and Renaissance rhetoric have been the subject of excellent scholarship. One can still profitably read Charles Sears Baldwin, *Medieval Rhetoric and Poetic* (New York: Macmillan, 1928; Glouchester, Mass.: Peter Smith, 1959); and Donald Leman Clark, *Rhetoric and Poetry in the Renaissance* (New

York: Columbia University Press, 1922; New York: Russell & Russell, 1963). Two fine articles also act as good introductions to the subject: Richard McKeon, "Rhetoric in the Middle Ages," *Speculum* 17 (1942): 1–32; and James J. Murphy, "The Arts of Discourse, 1050–1400," *Medieval Studies* 13 (1961): 194–205. For the development of post-Renaissance rhetoric, see especially the writings by Wilbur Samuel Howell in the bibliography.

[100] Wilbur Samuel Howell has observed five changes that were occurring during the period under study that distinguish Renaissance from modern rhetoric ("Renaissance Rhetoric and Modern Rhetoric: A Study in Change," in *The Rhetorical Idiom: Essays in Rhetoric, Oratory, Language, and Drama* [Ithaca, 1958], 53–70): (1) logic aligned itself with scientific investigation, rather than communication; (2) rhetoric became a theory of learned as well as popular discourse; (3) people began to rely more upon factual evidence; (4) simpler methods of arranging material were developed; and (5) language turned from ingratiation to that closely approximating ordinary life.

[101] Howell, in his *Logic and Rhetoric in England, 1500–1700*, has pointed to works that reflected these viewpoints. The classical tradition was restated in English by Thomas Wilson's *Arte of Rhetorique* in 1553, but works in the next century also continued the classical spirit, including Thomas Vicars, *Manuduction to the Rhetorical Art* (London, 1621); Thomas Farnaby, *Index Rhetoricus* (London, 1625; editions to 1767); William Pemble, *Enchiridion Oratorium* (Oxford, 1633); and Obadiah Walker, *Some Instructions Concerning the Art of Oratory* (London, 1659 and 1682); see Howell, 319–26. The stylistic tradition continued in writings by George Puttenham, *The Arte of English Poesie* (London, 1589); Angel Day, *The English Secretorie* (London: Robert Waldegraue, 1586; editions to 1635); and John Hoskins, *Directions for Speech and Style*, which was never printed under Hoskins' name in the seventeenth century but whose ideas found expression in Thomas Blount, *Academie of Eloquence* (London, 1654; editions to 1684) and John Smith, *Mysterie of Rhetorique Unvail'd* (London, 1657; reached the 9th ed. in 1706); see Howell, 327–33. In addition to Bacon's work, Bernard Lamy's *The Art of Speaking* (London, 1676; editions to 1708) also reflected a modern spirit; see Howell, 378–82.

[102] Howell, "English Backgrounds," 30. For a list of Ramus' works, as well as those by his colleague Omer Talon (Audomarus Taleus), the author of the Ramistic *Rhetoric*, see Walter J. Ong, *Ramus and Talon Inventory*. . . . (Cambridge, Mass.: Harvard University Press, 1958). A consideration of the influence of Ramus' dialectic and rhetoric in England, together with a treatment of the major Ramistic works of the period in English, may be found in Howell, *Logic and Rhetoric*, 173–281.

[103] Ong believes that the emphasis away from delivery is a sign of the deflection of rhetoric from the spoken to the written word. See Walter J. Ong, *Ramus—Method, and the Decay of Dialogue: From the Art of Discourse to the Art of Reason* (Cambridge, Mass.: Harvard University Press, 1958), 273.

[104] Dudley Fenner, "The Artes of Logike and Rethorike" (1584), quoted in Howell, *Logic and Rhetoric*, 256. According to Howell, Fenner's work was the first (but unacknowledged) translation of Talaeus.

[105] Fenner, "The Artes of Logike and Rethorike," in Howell, *Logic and Rhetoric*, 256.

[106] William P. Sandford, *English Theories of Public Address, 1530–1828* (Columbus, Ohio: Harold L. Hedrick, 1965), 46.

[107] Richard Sherry, *A Treatise of Schemes and Tropes* (London, 1550).

[108] Sandford, *English Theories of Public Address*, 47.

[109] Ong, *Ramus and the Decay of Dialogue*, 236.

[110] See Howell, *Logic and Rhetoric*, 247–81; and Sandford, *English Theories of Public Address*, 48–76. Their disagreement on the influence of Ramus upon Butler should be noted.

[111] Wilbur Samuel Howell, introduction to *Dialogues on Eloquence*, by Francis Fenelon, trans. Wilbur Samuel Howell (Princeton: Princeton University Press, 1951), 20.

[112] Pierre de la Ramee, *The Art of Logic* (London: Nicholas Bourne, 1626), 182.

[113] de la Ramee, *The Art of Logic*, 189.

[114] See Perry Miller, *The New England Mind: The Seventeenth Century* (Cambridge, Mass.: Harvard University Press, 1954), 127–28.

[115] Found in Miller, *New England Mind*, 127.

[116] Donald Lemen Clark, *John Milton at St. Paul's School: A Study of Ancient Rhetoric in English Renaissance Education* (New York: Columbia University Press, 1948), 13.

[117] Howell, *Logic and Rhetoric*, 211.

[118] Howell, *Logic and Rhetoric*, 193.

[119] Babette May Levy, *Preaching in the First Half Century of New England History*, vol. 6: *Studies in Church History*, ed. Matthew Spinka and Robert H. Nichols (New York: Russell & Russell, 1967), 19. See also Miller, *New England Mind*, 116–53. For a scholarly account of the influence of Puritan preaching on the development of "Civil Religion" in America, see Ronald F. Reid, "Puritan Rhetoric and America's Civil Religion: A Study of Three Special Occasion Sermons," in *Rhetoric, Religion, and the Roots of Identity in British Colonial America*, vol. 1: *A Rhetorical History of the United States*, ed. James R. Andrews, ed., and gen. ed. Martin J. Medhurst (East Lansing: Michigan State University Press, 2007), 65–120. Reid discounts some of the Puritan revisionist historians (84) and concludes that "the Puritan civil religion is still with us, albeit in modified form" (111). In contrast, Patricia Roberts-Miller has argued that the Puritan emphasis on right living and the development of a "person of conscience" has led to contemporary discourse characterized by public pronouncement rather than the true give and take of deliberation. See Patricia Roberts-Miller, *Voices in the Wilderness: Public Discourse and the Paradox of Puritan Rhetoric* (Tuscaloosa: University of Alabama Press, 1999).

[120] Miller, *New England Mind*, 117.

[121] White, *Puritan Rhetoric*, 17–23.

[122] White, *Puritan Rhetoric*, 18.

[123] Conley, *Rhetoric in the European Tradition*, 131.

[124] Conley, *Rhetoric in the European Tradition*, 132.

[125] Howell, *Logic and Rhetoric*, 318–41 (emphasis in original).

[126] Francis Bacon, *The Twoo Bookes of Francis Bacon on the Proficience and Advancement of Learning Divine and Humane*, in *Selected Writings of Francis Bacon*, ed. Hugh G. Dick (New York: Random House, 1955), 309.

[127] Karl R. Wallace, "Bacon's Conception of Rhetoric," in *Historical Studies of Rhetoric and Rhetoricians*, ed. Raymond F. Howes (Ithaca: Cornell University Press, 1961), 119.

[128] Bacon, *Advancenent*, 310.

[129] Wallace, "Bacon's Conception," 181.

[130] Bacon, *Two Bookes*, 285.

[131] Bacon, *Two Bookes*, 285 (emphasis in original).

[132] In his "English Background of Rhetoric," Howell notes that Bacon's view suggested the "ultimate disappearance from rhetorical theory of the elaborate Latin doctrine of postures or positions of argument" (36).

[133] George Williamson, *The Senecan Amble: A Study in Prose Form from Bacon to Collier* (Chicago: University of Chicago Press, 1966), 163.

[134] Thomas Sprat, *The History of the Royal-Society of London*, ed. Jackson I. Cope and Harold Whitmore Jones (St. Louis: Washington University Studies, 1958), 113 (emphasis in original). This is a reprint of the 1667 edition printed in London by F. Martin. For an excellent discussion of Bacon's influence on style, see Williamson, *Senecan Amble*, 150–230 and 275–300. The topic is also treated in Richard F. Jones, "Science and English Prose Style in the 3rd Quarter of the 17th Century," *Publications of the Modern Language Association* 45 (1930): 977–1009.

[135] A listing of homiletical works that influenced seventeenth-century England would include Augustine, *De Doctrina Christiana*; Erasmus, *The Preacher*; Melanchthon, *Institutiones Rhetoricae*; Gerhard Hyperius, *The Practice of Preaching*, trans. John Ludham (London, 1577); Bartholomew Keckerman, *Rhetoricae Ecclesiasticae* (Hanover, 1606); Thomas Granger, *Syntagma Logicum, or The Divine Logike* (London, 1620); William Ames, *Conscience with the Power and Cases Thereof* (London, 1643) and *The Marrow of Sacred Divinity* (London, 1643); Richard Baxter, *The Reformed Pastor* (1655) in *Works*, ed. William Orme (London, 1830); William Chappell, *The Preacher* (London, 1656); John Prideaux, *Sacred Eloquence* (London, 1659); and James Arderne, *Directions Concerning the Matter and Stile of Sermons* (London, 1671).

[136] Howell, *Logic and Rhetoric*, 207.

[137] William Perkins, *The Arte of Prophecying, or, A Treatise concerning the sacred and onely true manner and methode of Preaching*, vol. 2: *Workes*, trans. Thomas Tuke (London: 1613–1616), 670.

[138] Perkins, *The Arte of Prophecying*, 693.

[139] For discussions of the effects of Ramism on Perkins, see Donald K. McKim, "The Functions of Ramism in William Perkins' Theology," *Sixteenth Century Journal* 16, no. 1 (1985): 503–17; and John G. Rechtien, "Logic in Puritan Sermons in the Late Sixteenth Century and Plain Style," *Style* 13, no. 3 (1979): 237–58.

[140] John Wilkins, *Ecclesiastes*, 8th ed. (London: 1704), 20, 199. First edition appeared in 1646.

[141] See introduction to James Arderne, *Directions Concerning the Matter and Stile of Sermons*, ed. John Mackey (Oxford: Basil Blackwell, 1962), ix–xii. For an excellent discussion of the controversy over preaching in the third quarter of the seventeenth century, see Richard Foster Jones, "The Attack on Pulpit Eloquence in the Restoration: An Episode in the Development of the Neo-Classical Standard for Prose," in *The Seventeenth Century* (Stanford: Stanford University Press, 1951), 111–42.

[142] Howell, *Logic and Rhetoric*, 392.

[143] Joseph Glanvill, *An Essay Concerning Preaching: Written for the Direction of a Young Divine* (London: 1678), 11 (emphasis in original).

[144] Glanvill, *An Essay*, 23.

[145] Glanvill, *An Essay*, 71.

[146] Glanvill, *An Essay*, 39, 56.

[147] For discussions of George Fox and William Pen and the Royal Society, see the *Bulletin of the Friends Historical Association* 42:90–91, and 30:8–10, respectively. In later generations, Quakers made contributions to the advancement of science. See *Journal of the Friends Historical Society* 7:30–33, 45, for a list of Quaker members of the Royal Society.

[148] The attack on enthusiasm would reemerge in the next century in response to the preaching of George Whitefield and the Wesleys.

Chapter 2

Portions of this chapter have been adapted from my essay "One Friend's Journey," *Rhetoric & Public Affairs* 7, no. 4 (2004): 513–24. Used by permission.

[1] See Barbour, *The Quakers in Puritan England*, chapters 4–8, for an excellent consideration of Quaker beliefs prior to the Restoration. He considers changes in Quaker outlook after the Restoration in chapter 9.

[2] George Fox, "Sermon at a General Meeting," in *Headley MSS*, 1 vol. (sermon preached in London, 9th, 4th month, 1674) (London: Library of the Religious Society of Friends), 247.

[3] Robert Barclay, *An Apology for the True Christian Divinity* (Philadelphia: Friends' Book-Store, 1867), xi; first English language publication in 1678.

[4] Barclay, *Apology*, xxi. There is controversy among scholars over whether Puritans received their theological underpinings from John Calvin or his successor, Theodore Beza. R. T. Kendall has argued that Calvin taught the doctrine of universal atonement and Beza shifted it to limited atonement (*Calvin and English Calvinism to 1649* [Oxford: Oxford University Press, 1979]). Understandably, this position has been discussed by other writers. See a brief discussion of the controversy of interpretation in Cohen, *God's Caress*, 9–10, n. 15. See also the strong interpretation of limited atonement as espoused by Calvin in Paul Helm, *Calvin and the Calvinists* (Edinburgh: The Banner of Truth Trust, 1982).

[5] Similarly, in John 12:46, Jesus says, "I am come a light into the world, that whosoever believeth on me should not abide in darkness." [All Scripture references taken from the Authorized Version unless indicated.]

[6] See the discussion of the Light in an address by Dean Freiday, "A Common Quakerhood?" in *What Future for Friends? Report of the St. Louis Conference . . . October 5–7, 1970* (Philadelphia: Friends World Committee, n.d.), 27.

[7] Stephen Crisp, "The Excellency of Peace with God," in *Scripture-Truths Demonstrated: In Thirty Two Sermons or Declarations of Mr. Stephen Crisp* (sermon preached at Devonshire House, London, August 5, 1691) (London: J. Sowle), 136, 137.

[8] Barclay, *Apology*, 142. Bauman, in his earlier essay, "Aspects," seems to say that the Light is both a part of man's nature and a gift of grace. He writes that membership in the Society "was to be achieved through the exercise of the *faculty* of the *Inner* Light, present in every man through the grace of the Savior, Jesus Christ" (emphasis added).

[9] Crisp, "The Great Duty of Remembering our Creator," in *Scripture-Truths* (sermon preached at Devonshire House, London, April 6, 1692), 92, 105.

[10] John Bowater, "A Sermon," preached at St. John's Street, London, March 18, 1693, in *Concurrence and Unanimity; Of the People Called Quakers* (London: J. Sowle, 1711), 48, 63.

[11] Barclay, *Apology*, 145.

[12] John Furly, *A Testimony to the True Light*, n.p., 1670, 9. This tract was written as a memorial to Elizabeth Furly, who died in 1669.

[13] George Fox, *The Journal of George Fox*, ed. John L. Nickalls, rev. ed. (Cambridge: Cambridge University Press, 1975), 18. Hereafter referred to as *Journal*.

[14] George Fox, in *Richardson MSS* (sermon preached at Devonshire House, London, 3rd month, 1677) type copy (London: Library of the Religious Society of Friends), 403.

[15] Fox, *Journal*, 27.

[16] Fox, Sermon, 3rd month, 1677, 403.

[17] Crisp, "The Great Mediator of the Everlasting Covenant," in *Scripture-Truths* (sermon preached at Grace Church Street, London, April 25, 1688), 20.

[18] Francis Camfield, in *Concurrence and Unanimity* (sermon preached at Grace Church Street, London, May 14, 1693), 39 (emphasis in original).

[19] Crisp's sermons are especially illustrative of the theme. In a sermon on March 14, 1687, preached at Grace Church Street (*Scripture-Truths*, 38), he makes the observation that "if there be something that preserves a Man from any Evil, it can preserve him from all evil." See also his lengthy examination of the subject in his sermon delivered October 12, 1690, at Devonshire House, in *Scripture-Truths*, 25–28. Other preachers also work the theme into their sermons. Although a complete enumeration is not necessary here, one should note especially William Bingley, in *Concurrence and Unanimity* (sermon preached at Grace Church Street, March 4, 1693), 127; William Pen, in *The Harmony of Divine and Heavenly Doctrines* (sermons preached at Grace Church Street, August 12, 1694, and at Wheeler Street, October 21, 1694) (London: J. Sowle, 1696), 18 and 77, respectively; and Chalkley in *Mr. T. Chalkley's Sermon & Prayer*, manuscript at Friends Historical Library, Swarthmore College (sermon preached on June 7, 1698), 1.

[20] Barclay, *Apology*, 229.

[21] "Convincement" is a term often used by the early Quakers to describe their decision to follow the Light and to become a Friend. It carries with it the conotation of "proof," of argument, but it has a dimension beyond rational assent alone. A "convinced" Quaker had the responsibility to identify his or her speech and actions with the group. By the last decade of the century, the term seems to have referred to mental assent alone, for Pen found it necessary to plead that "those that are Convinced, may be Converted," in *Harmony* (sermon preached at Wheeler Street, January 27, 1694), 115.

[22] See, e.g., William Dewsbury, in *Concurrence and Unanimity* (sermon preached at Grace Church Street, London, May 6, 1688), 18, 19, 22. See also Crisp, "The Divine Monitor: Or Light from Heaven," in *Scripture-Truths* (sermon preached at Grace Church Street, June 19, 1692), 113, 115–17.

[23] Barclay, *Apology*, 322.

[24] Barbour, *Quakers in Puritan England*, 40.

[25] Barbour, *Quakers in Puritan England*, 65.

[26] Geoffrey Nuttall, *The Holy Spirit in Puritan Faith and Experience* (Oxford: Basil Blackwell, 1946), 120.

[27] Quoted in Nuttall, *The Holy Spirit*, 131.

[28] The Lamb's War was the central image of early Quaker "realising eschatol-

ogy," mentioned in the introduction to this book. See, especially, Gwyn, *Apocalypse of the Word* and *The Covenant Crucified*; and Moore, *Light in their Consciences*.

[29] Quakers refused to remove their hats as a sign of honor to authorities, they forsook the ribbons and ruffles so popular in the clothing of their day, they refused to use the pagan names for the months and weekdays, they rejected the barter system in business. See Braithwaite, *Beginnings of Quakerism*, 485–507; Barbour, *Quakers in Puritan England*, 160–80.

[30] The metaphor of war, and related terms, has attracted the attention of rhetorical scholars in several significant articles, including Robert L. Ivie, "The Metaphor of Force in Prowar Discourse: The Case of 1812," *Quarterly Journal of Speech* 68 (1982): 240–53. Of particular interest to the problems raised by religious groups employing war imagery is Michael J. Hostetler's careful use of Kenneth Burke's and Max Black's work on metaphor to call into question some of Carl Wayne Hensley's defense of the war metaphor used by Christians (Michael J. Hostetler, "Rethinking the War Metaphor in Religious Rhetoric: Burke, Black and Berrigan's 'Glimmer of Light,'" *Journal of Communication and Religion* 20, no. 1 [1997]: 49–60).

[31] Barclay, *Apology*, 512.

[32] Cope, "Seventeenth Century Quaker Style," 729.

[33] Fox and two other Quakers published a remarkable book intended to defend the Quaker position on language; George Fox, John Stubbs, and Benjamin Furly, *A Battle-Door for Teachers & Professors to Learn Singular & Plural* (London: 1660). See Braithwaite, *Beginnings of Quakerism*, 496–99, and Bauman, *Let Your Words be Few*, 48–49.

[34] Barbour, *Quakers in Puritan England*, 242.

[35] George Whitehead, in *Concurrence and Unanimity* (sermon preached at Devonshire House, London, May 3, 1694), 36.

[36] Francis Stamper, in *Concurrence and Unanimity* (sermon preached at Grace Church Street, London, October 4, 1693), 36.

[37] Elbert Russell, *The History of Quakerism* (Richmond, Ind.: Friends United Press, 1979), 186.

[38] Braithwaite, *Second Period*, 179.

[39] In *The Holy Spirit*, Nuttall argues that the doctrine of the Holy Spirit "received a more thorough and detailed consideration from the Puritans of seventeenth-century England than it has received at any other time in Christian history," viii.

[40] Fox, *Journal*, 1–2, 7, 8.

[41] Fox, *Journal*, 11. In his recent book, Webb develops what he calls a "Christian Acoustemology." In one section, he deals carefully and sympathetically with the claim by some Christians that they have heard the audible voice of Jesus (Webb, *The Divine Voice*, 33–36).

[42] Fox, *Journal*, 15.

[43] There is not only a confusion of names used to signify similar phenomena but also an overlapping of the functions of the Trinity. Rachel Hadley King asserts, "There is a general identification of the Holy Ghost with the Light" in Fox's theology (*George Fox and the Light Within, 1650–1660* [Philadelphia: Friends Book Store, 1940], 78). In "George Fox's Teaching on Redemption and Salvation" (Ph.D. diss., Yale University, 1956), T. Canby Jones concludes, "Concerning the Holy Spirit Fox demonstrates a tremendous overlapping of concept and function between Christ the

Prophet, the light, the seed and the Holy Spirit. Yet each concept retains some basically unique aspects," 270.

[44] Fox, *Journal*, 27. Cope uses this experience of Fox as a basis for arguing the primacy of the concept of the "name" for early Friends.

[45] Fox, *Journal*, 29.

[46] Fox, *Journal*, 31, 32.

[47] Nuttall, *The Holy Spirit*, 26, 28–30, 33.

[48] Fox, *Journal*, 33.

[49] Fox, *Journal*, 34.

[50] Jones, "George Fox's Teaching," 66–67.

[51] Quoted in Braithwaite, *Beginnings of Quakerism*, 88.

[52] Barclay, *Apology*, 13.

[53] Barclay, *Apology*, 14–15 (emphasis added), 88, 89.

[54] Benjamin Coole, in *Harmony* (a sermon preached at Grace Church Street, London, May 12, 1694), 185 (emphasis in original).

[55] Barclay, *Apology*, 54, 142, 143.

[56] Creasey has pointed to a development in later-seventeenth-century Quakerism, under the influence of Barclay and Pen, toward a quasi-Cartesian dualism. See the introduction to this book. See also a later defense of Barclay's dualism by D. Elton Trueblood in *Robert Barclay: A Portrait of the Life and Times of a Great Quaker Intellectual Leader* (New York: Harper & Row, 1968), 18–19. I am in complete agreement with Trueblood's cogent conclusion: "unless psychophysical dualism . . . has cogency, the Christian hope of life after death is groundless. If consciousness and the body are identical . . . there is nothing that can survive death" (19).

[57] Jones, "George Fox's Teaching," 53–56; quotation on p. 56.

[58] William Pen, *The Great Case of Liberty of Conscience*, in *The Witness of William Penn*, ed. Frederick B. Tolles and E. Gordon Alderfer (New York: Macmillan, 1957), 76.

[59] William Pen, *Some Fruits of Solitude*, in *The Harvard Classics*, ed. Charles W. Eliot (New York: P. F. Collier & Son, 1937), 348.

[60] William Pen, "Two Made One; Or, The Happiness of Marrying in the Lord," in *Harmony* (sermon preached at Devonshire House, London, October 3, 1694), 148.

[61] William Pen, *More Fruits of Solitude*, in *The Harvard Classics*, ed. Charles W. Eliot (New York: P. F. Collier & Son, 1937), 385–86.

[62] William Pen, "The Dying Counsel of the Wonderful Counsellor," in *Harmony* (a sermon preached at Devonshire House, London, January 20, 1694), 110.

[63] In addition to having a year's study at Christ Church, Oxford, there Pen established a friendship with John Locke that was to last a lifetime.

[64] Crisp, "Divine Monitor," in *Scripture-Truths*, 119, 118, 119, 120.

[65] William Pen, "The Great Design of Christianity," in *Harmony* (sermon preached at Wheeler Street, London, January 27, 1694), 121 (emphasis in original).

[66] See Barbour, *Quakers in Puritan England*, 122–23; Jones, "George Fox's Teaching," 68.

[67] George Fox, "1653 This Precept was written from the Mouth of George Fox, as he spoke it forth, by a Friend of Truth," in *Severall Letters to the Saints of the Most High* (sermon, n.p., n.p., 1654), 16. Year of delivery was 1653.

[68] Fox, in *Richardson MSS* (testimony at a Yearly Meeting, London, 3rd Month, 1681), 533.

[69] Crisp, "The Sheep of Christ hear his Voice," in *Scripture-Truths* (sermon preached at Devonshire House, London, May 10, 1688), 145.

Chapter 3

[1] In my use of the word "theory," I am not suggesting that Quakers developed a systematic or elaborate theory of rhetoric like the Greeks or Romans did, or of homiletics, like Reformation Protestants, only that they did theorize about their own practice and defended it. They also speculated about the nature of inspiration and the typical pathways the content of impromptu sermons might take. Inspired speech has been the topic of Western and non-Western rhetoric. See George A. Kennedy, *Comparative Rhetoric: An Historical and Cross-Cultural Introduction* (New York: Oxford University Press, 1998), 39, 134, 192–93. See also Dale L. Sullivan, "*Kairos* and the Rhetoric of Belief," *Quarterly Journal of Speech* 78 (1992): 317–32.

[2] Fox's *Journal* was edited and published after his death in 1691 by Thomas Ellwood, John Milton's secretary.

[3] Fox, *Journal*, 7, 10.

[4] Fox, *Journal*, 8.

[5] Fox, *Journal*, 85. Several aspects of seventeenth-century Quaker linguistic choices were tied to their notion of truth, including rejection of pagan names for months and days of the week, the peculiar pronominal use, the refusal to take an oath, and a general simplicity in speech. See Bauman, *Let Your Words be Few*, and Graves, "Quakerism," in *The Encyclopedia of Language & Linguistics*, vol. 6 (Pergamon Press, 1994), 3416–17.

[6] Fox, *Journal*, 115.

[7] Fox, *Journal*, 36.

[8] Fox, *Journal*, 17.

[9] Fox, *Journal*, 19.

[10] Fox, *Journal*, 24.

[11] George Fox, *An Epistle to all People on the Earth* (London: Giles Calvert, 1657), 15.

[12] Fox, *An Epistle*, 36.

[13] Fox, *Journal*, 27, 34.

[14] Fox, *Journal*, 88.

[15] Fox, *Journal*, 109, 121, 128, 152.

[16] Fox, *Journal*, 123.

[17] Fox, *An Epistle*, 8.

[18] Fox, *Journal*, 340. This "sermon" is not included in discussions that appear in chapters 6–8 because I do not see it as a legitimate sermon text like the seventy-nine included in the later chapters. Arguably, compared with Fox's other extant sermons, this one, and others that appear in part in his *Journal*, bears the heavy hand of editing for publication and is prefaced by this note: "which, being taken in writing by one that was present, was *after this manner*" (340, emphasis added). However, because it appears in the *Journal*, it still reveals the flavor of Fox's early preaching as well as some of Fox's thoughts about the vocal ministry.

[19] Fox, *Journal*, 341.

[20] George Fox, "Epistle CCLXXV, 138," in *Selections from the Epistles of George Fox*, ed. Samuel Tuke (Cambridge, Mass.: Riverside Press, 1879), 23. All subsequent references to Fox's *Epistles* outside the *Journal* are from the same.

[21] Fox, *Journal*, 175, 176.

[22] Fox, *Journal*, 283.

[23] Fox, *Journal*, 340. Bauman has developed this theme in his aptly titled book *Let Your Words Be Few*.

[24] Fox, *An Epistle*, 19.

[25] Fox, *Journal*, 56.

[26] Fox, *Journal*, 263.

[27] Fox, *Journal*, 340. Naylor had entered the city on the back of a donkey. His subsequent trial before Parliament for blasphemy was notorious and injurious to Friends. See Moore, *The Light in Their Consciences*, 30–48, and Gwyn, *The Covenant Crucified*, 161–88. The Naylor affair was particularly injurious to the standing of women in the Quaker movement. See Mack, *Visionary Women*, 210–12.

[28] Fox, *Journal*, 282.

[29] Fox, *Journal*, 312.

[30] Fox, *Journal*, 29–32; quotation on p. 31.

[31] Fox, *Journal*, 108, 109.

[32] Fox, *Journal*, 109.

[33] I am not claiming that Fox followed a rigorous formula when he preached. However, the evidence from his *Journal* does indicate his preference for certain themes and approaches, particularly when he preached outside of Quaker meetings in order to evangelize or debate rival sects.

[34] Fox, *Journal*, 155. Records of the earliest Quaker preachers reveal that they, too, saw themselves as commissioned to turn people to the Light, the inward persuader. For example, an incident from Abbey Holme in the year 1653 reveals that James Langcastr [*sic*] "declared ye truth to the people, and Directed them to ye Light of Christ in there Inward parts, that with the Light they might come to see ye Evill of their ways, and soe come into peace wth that of god in their own conscience." (*FPT*, 72). In 1663 Cristifar Houldar "stod vp, and said, 'Be singell, my frindes, be singell,' and did dereckt vs to the Light and sperit of god in our hartes." (111).

[35] Fox, *Journal*, 155.

[36] Fox, *Journal*, 271.

[37] Fox, *Journal*, 186.

[38] In 1656 Fox made a plea to Cromwell with regard to Quaker persecution. On that occasion, he debated with Edward Pyott and the famous John Owen, vice-chancellor of Oxford, besting both of them, at least by Fox's account (*Journal*, 274–75). See also his 1657 debate with "Priest Tombes," 295–98.

[39] For an excellent review of memory and rhetorical discourse through the years, see Bruce E. Gronbeck, "The Spoken and the Seen: Phonocentric and Ocularcentric Dimensions of Rhetorical Discourse," in *Rhetorical Memory and Delivery: Classical Concepts for Contemporary Composition and Communication*, ed. John Frederick Reynolds (Hillsdale, N.J.: Lawrence Erlbaum Associates, Publishers, 1993), 141–50. See also Sharon Crowley, "Modern Rhetoric and Memory," in *Rhetorical Memory and Delivery*, 36–44.

[40] Peter Atkins, *Memory and Liturgy: The Place of Memory in the Composition and Practice of Liturgy* (Brookfield, Vt.: Ashgate Publishing, 2004), 5, 22.

[41] Walter J. Ong, *Orality and Literacy: The Technologizing of the Word*, New Accents, ed. Terence Hawkes (London: Methuen, 1982; repr., New York: Routledge, 1988), 57.

[42] In *Orality and Literacy*, Ong reviews the work of Milman Parry and Albert Lord, who studied the homeric epics through the lens of twentieth-century Eastern European illiterate oral poets, who employed formulaic structures to achieve feats of memory (58–62).

[43] Margaret Fell, *Womens Speaking Justified, Proved and Allowed of by the Scriptures*, in *Womens Speaking Justified*, ed. Christine Trevett (London: Quaker Home Service, 1989). Originally printed in 1666. In this section I will be referring to the 1667 edition printed with a postscript, as found in *Womens Speaking Justified*, ed. Christine Trevett. Trevett has modernized the original punctuation for contemporary readers.

[44] Feminist scholars have discovered Fell and other Quaker writers as some of the earliest and best rhetors in the struggle for women's rights. Rhetorical scholars now routinely refer to Fell and reprint *Women's Speaking* in anthologies of rhetorical theory. See, e.g., Brummett, *Reading Rhetorical Theory*, 439–47, and Bizzell and Herzberg, *The Rhetorical Tradition*, 748–60.

[45] Fell, *Women's Speaking*, 5.

[46] Fell, *Women's Speaking*, 10.

[47] Margaret Fell, *A Call to the Universall Seed of God*, n.p., 1664.

[48] Fell, *Universall Seed*, 1, 2.

[49] Fell, *Universall Seed*, 7, 13, 15.

[50] Margaret Fell, *A Touch-Stone: or, A perfect tryal by the Scriptures, of all the priests, bishops, and ministers, who have called themselves, the ministers of the Gospel . . . Unto which is annexed, Womens speaking justified, &c.* (London, 1667).

[51] Fell, *A Touch-Stone*, 21–22.

[52] Fell, *A Touch-Stone*, 24.

[53] Fell, *A Touch-Stone*, 28-32.

[54] Fell, *A Touch-Stone*, 35 (emphasis in original).

[55] Fell, *A Touch-Stone*, 38 (emphasis in original).

[56] Fell, *A Touch-Stone*, 39, 42 (emphasis in original).

[57] Fell, *A Touch-Stone*, 84–85 (emphasis in original).

[58] Fell, *A Touch-Stone*, 86.

[59] *Sermon Preached Before the People Called Quakers in the Park of Southwark* (London: printed for N.H., 1688).

[60] Rebecca Smith, *The Foundation of True Preaching Asserted* (London: Andrew Sowle, 1687). As noted in chapter 1, no sermons by seventeenth-century Quaker women have survived (see appendix B). Seventy-nine sermons by early Quaker men are extant.

[61] Smith, *The Foundation of True Preaching Asserted*, 4, 5–6 (emhasis in original).

[62] Smith, *The Foundation of True Preaching Asserted*, 8.

[63] This passage served as a biblical underpining to Barclay's explanation of the minister's call (*Apology*, Proposition X, 284–85), discussed in the following chapter.

[64] Smith, *The Foundation of True Preaching Asserted*, 9 (emphasis in original).

[65] Smith, *The Foundation of True Preaching Asserted*, 9.

[66] Webb develops the concept of God's calling weak instruments in a chapter titled "Stage Fright at the Origins of Christian Proclamation," in which he deals with the topic of speech anxiety exhibited by Moses and the Apostle Paul (*The Divine Voice*, 80–90). He also discusses stage fright in George Whitefield's ministry (96–101).

[67] Smith, *The Foundation of True Preaching Asserted*, 12.

[68] Early Quakers did not use for the terms "clergy" and "laity." Everyone and anyone in the meeting could exercise the right of vocal ministry. They recognized, however, that certain people had a special call of God to vocal ministry—"publick Friends"—but they did not set them aside, show them special honors, ordain them, or even provide a regular living for them. In the *Apology*, Barclay asserted, "That which we oppose, is the distinction of laity and clergy, which in the scripture is not to be found, whereby none are admitted unto the work of the ministry but such as are educated at schools on purpose, and instructed in logic and philosophy, &c., and so are at their apprenticeship to learn the art and trade of preaching, even as a man learns any other art, whereby all other honest mechanic men, who have not got this heathenish art, are excluded from having this priviledge" (305).

[69] Two of his sermons survive. See appendix B.

[70] George Whitehead, *Enthusiasm Above Atheism: Or, Divine Inspiration and Immediate Illumination* [by God Himself] *Asserted.* . . . (n.p., 1674) (hereafter cited as *Enthusiasm*). The complete title of the tract indicates that it was written "*In Answer to a Book, entitled, The Dangers of Enthusiasm Discovered.*"

[71] Whitehead, *Enthusiasm*, 21.

[72] Whitehead, *Enthusiasm*, 44–45.

[73] Whitehead, *Enthusiasm*, 54.

[74] Whitehead, *An Evangelical Epistle to the People of God, in Derision Call'd Quakers* (London: T. Sowle, 1704), 27 (hereafter cited as *Evangelical Epistle*).

[75] Whitehead, *An Evangelical Epistle*, 36, 37.

[76] Whitehead, *An Evangelical Epistle*, 53–54, 55 (emphasis in original).

[77] Whitehead, *An Evangelical Epistle*, 57 (emphasis in original).

[78] Whitehead's cautions appear to be a coda to the late century move away from "revolutionary" or prophetic expressions to a somewhat more restrained form of discourse. Several scholars have written about this development, including Bauman, Cope, Gwyn, Pink Dandelion, and Tarter.

[79] Charles Marshall, *An Epistle to Friends Coming forth in the Beginning of a Testimony and of the Snares of the Enemy therein* (n.p.: 1775; first published in 1675). My references are from the 1775 edition. The document, with slight changes by later editors, may also be consulted on the QWHP, http://www.qhpress.org/quakerpages/qwhp/e2fm.htm. The later publication date indicates the far-reaching influence of Marshall's tract.

[80] Marshall, *An Epistle to Friends*, 1–2, 3.

[81] Marshall, *An Epistle to Friends*, 3–4. Bauman cites Marshall's document as a part of his explication of the early Quaker notion that they could become the oracles or "mouthpieces" of God. See *Let Your Words be Few*, 127.

[82] Marshall, *An Epistle to Friends*, 5.

[83] Marshall, *An Epistle to Friends*, 5–6.

[84] See her interpretation of Marshall's epistle in Michele Lise Tarter, "Prophecy of Celestial Flesh," in *Quaker Theory*, 90–91.

[85] Ong, *Orality and Literacy*, 67.

[86] Ong, *Orality and Literacy*, 11.

[87] Gronbeck, "The Spoken and the Seen," 150–51.

[88] Marshall, *An Epistle to Friends*, 7.

[89] Marshall, *An Epistle to Friends*, 8.

[90] See appendix B.

[91] Crisp, "The First and Great Commandment," in *Scripture-Truths* (sermon preached at Devonshire House, London, May 27, 1688), 63 (emphasis in original).

[92] Crisp, "Christ the Way to Eternal Life," in *Scripture-Truths* (sermon preached at Grace Church Street, London, May 6, 1688), 5.

[93] Crisp, "Pure and Spiritual Worship," in *Scripture-Truths* (sermon preached at Devonshire House, London, November 12, 1690), 67.

[94] Crisp, *An Epistle of Tender Love and Brotherly Advice*, in *The Christian Experiences, Gospel Labours and Writings of . . . Stephen Crisp* (Philadelphia: Benjamin & Thomas Kite, 1822), 263–378.

[95] "Order" was a recurrent theme among Friends in the last decades of the century, seen to good advantage in Fox's *Journal* and his 1674 sermon analyzed in chapter 9.

[96] Crisp, *Epistle of Tender Love*, 368, 369.

[97] Crisp, *Epistle of Tender Love*, 371.

[98] Crisp, *Epistle of Tender Love*, 370.

[99] Coole, *The Quakers Cleared from Being Apostates or the Hammer Defeated* (London: T. Sowle, 1696). One of Coole's sermons is extant. See appendix B.

[100] Coole, *The Quakers Cleared*, 81.

[101] Clearly, Coole was influenced by Barclay. He cited the *Apology* directly in the pamphlet without indicating one iota of dissent from Barclay's views. See especially *The Quakers Cleared*, 76–77, where the reader is directed to the *Apology* for an argument regarding how the Light is not the same as the Conscience.

[102] Coole, *The Quakers Cleared*, 55, 52.

[103] Coole, *The Quakers Cleared*, 59 (emphasis in original).

[104] Coole, *The Quakers Cleared*, 25.

[105] Coole, *The Quakers Cleared*, 26 (emphasis in original).

[106] Coole, *The Quakers Cleared*, 66.

[107] Emphasis in original. Coole's pamphlet ends with a "postscript," which is a defense of the attack on Quakers in an anonymous pamphlet, *The Spirit of Quakerism, and the Danger of their Divine Revelation, Laid Open* (London, 1696). The pamphlet contained accounts of strange behaviors and odd expressions made by Quakers in meetings, all of which Coole either denies or argues for, stating that all Quakers should not be judged on the basis of foolish behavior by a minority (82–95). This brings to mind the cautions raised by Crisp six years earlier.

Chapter 4

This chapter is a revision and extension of my essay "Robert Barclay and the Rhetoric of the Inward Light," *Quaker Reliious Thought* 26 (March 1993) 17–32. Used by permission.

[1] Barclay, *Apology*. Throughout this book, I have employed the 1867 edition published in Philadelphia by the Friends Bookstore. All subsequent references the same.

[2] Robert Barclay, *The Possibility and Necessity of the Inward and Immediate Revelation of the Spirit of God*, in *Truth Triumphant through the . . . Writings of . . . Robert Barclay* (London, 1692).

[3] See the excellent discussion of Barclay's background and influence in Braithwaite, *Beginnings* (385–98) and Wright, *Literary Life of the Early Friends* (55–56). An intelligent biography of Barclay is that by Trueblood (*Robert Barclay: A Portrait of the Life and Times*).

[4] Heer Adrian Paets (1631–1681) was the Dutch ambassador to Spain. According to Peter Sipple, Paets had misrepresented the Quaker view of immediate revelation, giving rise to Barclay's essay or letter (Sipple, "Preface" to Barclay, http://www.geocities.com/quakerpages/rbstuff01.htm). See also John Cunningham, *The Quakers from their Origin till the Present Time: An International History* (Edinburgh: John Menzies, 1868).

[5] The propositions I have omitted from this overview and analysis include the following: IV, "Concerning the Condition of Man in the Fall"; VII, "Concerning Justification"; VIII, "Concerning Perfection"; IX, "Concerning Perseverance, and the Possibility of Falling from Grace"; XII, "Concerning Baptism"; XIII, "Concerning the Communion"; XIV, "Concerning the Power of the Civil Magistrate, in Matters Purely Religious, and Pertaining to the Conscience"; and XV, "Concerning Salutations and Recreations, etc."

[6] Barclay, *Apology*, 13.

[7] Barclay, *Apology*, 28–29.

[8] Barclay, *Apology*, 35. Barclay's division of knowledge into "religious" and everything else appears to be potentially problematic because it seems to imply that divine revelation canot or does not apply to secular knowledge. Later, though, he avers that the Spirit helps discern other types of truth (146).

[9] Barclay, *Apology*, 44, 54.

[10] Barclay, *Apology*, 55.

[11] Barclay, *Apology*, 56.

[12] Barclay, *Apology*, 69–70.

[13] Barclay, *Apology*, 72.

[14] Barclay, *Apology*, 72–73.

[15] Barclay, *Apology*, 28.

[16] Barclay, *Apology*, 88.

[17] Barclay, *Apology*, 110, 131, 135, 142, 143–44.

[18] Barclay, *Apology*, 136, 140–41.

[19] Barclay, *Immediate Revelation*, 897.

[20] Barclay, *Immediate Revelation*, 900. Fourteen years after the *Apology* was published in Latin (1676), John Locke published his *Essay Concerning Human Understanding* (1690), which would deny the existence of innate ideas in the mind and establish a radically different epistemology from Barclay's. Locke's essential foundation is the assumption that all ideas come from sensation or reflection.

[21] Barclay, *Immediate Revelation*, 899.

[22] Barclay, *Immediate Revelation*, 901.

[23] Barclay, *Immediate Revelation*, 902, 898.

[24] Whitehead, *The Light and Life of Christ Within, and the Extent and Efficacy thereof Demonstrated* (London, 1668), 13.

[25] Barclay, *Immediate Revelation*, 902.

[26] Barclay, *Immediate Revelation*, 902.

[27] Barclay, *Immediate Revelation*, 903.

[28] Barclay, *Immediate Revelation*, 903. The controversy over miracles erupted in the seventeenth and flamed in the eighteenth century. Though not pertinent to the purposes of this chapter, Barclay's contribution to the miracles debate, which occupies the last pages of *Immediate Revelation*, is significant because it is necessarily related to his novel position on epistemology. For an excellent perspective on the miracles controversy, which focuses on the types of argument employed by the orthodox apologists and the deists, the major antagonists, see James A. Herrick, "Miracles and Method," *Quarterly Journal of Speech* 75 (1989), 321–34. See also Herrick, *The Radical Rhetoric of the English Deists: The Discourse of Skepticism, 1680–1750* (Columbia: University of South Carolina Press, 1997).

[29] Barclay, *Apology*, 87.

[30] Barclay, *Apology*, 87–88. We are reminded that Barclay employs male pronouns as a matter of convention. It is clear from his writings that he, like the vast majority of early Friends, did not restrict vocal ministry to males.

[31] Barclay, *Apology*, 173.

[32] Both Bacon and Campbell have been classified, along with Hugh Blair, as having developed systems based both on the implications of the new science as well as on faculty psychology, the prevalent notion about the mind's operation. See Craig R. Smith, *Rhetoric and Human Consciousness: A History*, 2nd ed. (Long Grove, Ill.: Waveland Press, 2003), 233–59.

[33] Chomsky, *Language and Mind*, 3rd ed. (New York: Cambridge University Press, 2006), 102ff. and 103–42.

[34] Barclay, *Apology*, 264.

[35] Barclay, *Apology*, 268.

[36] Barclay, *Apology*, 308.

[37] Barclay, *Apology*, 289.

[38] Barclay, *Apology*, 292–93; quotation on pp. 291, 295.

[39] Barclay, *Apology*, 292, 293, 294.

[40] Aristotle, *On Rhetoric: A Theory of Civic Discourse*, trans. George Kennedy (New York: Oxford University Press, 1991), 401–18. Everyday reasoning has experienced extended attention and popularity in the twentieth century, especially following the publication of Stephen Toulmin's *The Uses of Argument* (Cambridge: Cambridge University Press, 1958).

[41] Barclay, *Apology*, 296–97.

[42] Barclay, *Apology*, 297, 298, 300.

[43] Barclay, *Apology*, 302.

[44] Barclay, *Apology*, 321.

[45] Barclay, *Apology*, 321–22.

[46] Barclay, *Apology*, 329.

[47] Barclay, *Apology*, 332, 335, 336.

[48] Barclay, *Immediate Revelation*, 898–902.

[49] Barclay, *Apology*, 353.

[50] Barclay, *Apology*, 360.

[51] Lucia K. Beamish offers a position somewhat different from mine. She argues that "Barclay's use of the word 'immediate' in connection with Revelation was responsible for a profound misunderstanding in the minds of subsequent Quaker ministers, including [Samuel] Bownas. While Barclay had meant by it that the Spirit's teaching came unmediated to the soul of man, his readers understood by the word a sudden, instantaneous revelation, that rendered any previous thought injurious to the message that must be passed on. This misunderstanding had a lamentable effect on eighteenth century Ministry [among Quakers]" (44). Beamish's interpretation of Barclay's position appears to be based on his statements in Proposition II. I argue that his use of the term "immediate" in Proposition XI ("Concerning Worship") justifies the interpretation that preachers should not consciously plan their sermons ahead of time.

[52] Barclay, *Apology*, 380.

[53] For example, the influence of Barclay's quasi-Cartesian dualism, discussed in chapter 1, has been a matter of concern and debate among Quaker scholars. See the writings by Creasey and Hall in the bibliography.

[54] For an account of the effect of the nineteenth-century "holiness" revivals and their influence on American Quakers, see Walter R. Williams, *The Rich Heritage of Quakerism: The Past Speaks to the Present* (Grand Rapids: Eerdmans, 1962), 192–201. See also Hugh Barbour and J. William Frost, *The Quakers* (Richmond, Ind.: Friends United Press, 1994), 203–18, and the recent scholarly volume on the topic by Carole Dale Spencer, *Holiness: The Soul of Quakerism*, Christian History and Thought (Colorado Springs: Paternoster Press, 2007).

Chapter 5

This chapter is an extension of a portion of my essay "'Thou art but a youth': Thomas Chalkley Enacts and Defends the Early Quaker Impromptu Sermon," in *A Rhetorical History of the United States*, vol. 1: *Rhetoric, Religion, and the Roots of Identity in British Colonial America*, ed. James R. Andrews, gen. ed. Martin J. Medhurst (East Lansing: Michigan State University Press, 20007), 229–74. Used by permission.

[1] Bownas, *Qualifications*. I have employed the 1750 edition printed in London by Luke Hinde; all subsequent references the same. Unless indicated, all emphases in quoted material are in the original. A modern edition of *Qualifications*, including an excellent introduction by William P. Taber Jr., was published in 1989 by Pendle Hill Publications and Tract Association of Friends (*A Description of the Qualifications Necessary to a Gospel Minister, London, 1750.* [Philadelphia]).

[2] Although none of Bownas' sermons survive, he wrote an autobiographical piece (*An Account of the Life, Travels and Christian Experiences in the Work of the Ministry* [1756]). See also Taber's introduction to the 1989 edition of *Qualifications* (xvii–xxxviii) and Beamish, *Quaker Ministry* (11–59). Beamish presents an interesting and original analysis of Bownas' *Qualifications*, based in part on a comparison of the book with Richard Baxter's very influential 1656 "Gildas Salvianus," in *The Reformed Pastor*, 2nd ed., ed. John T. Wilkinson (London: Epworth, 1950).

[3] Barclay, *Apology*, 360.

[4] Bownas, "To the Meeting of Ministers at Kendal in Westmoreland," *Friends' Intelligencer* 14 (1857): 210. Found on Kuenning, ed., QWHP, http://www.qhpress.org/quakerpages/qwhp/bownase.htm (accessed April 17, 2008).

[5] Unaccountably, the unsigned preface was not included in the 1989 edition, in spite of the fact that it clearly indicates that, although Bownas employed male pronouns throughout the work, his usage is merely grammatical and conventional and does not *exclude* women from preaching. The author of the preface tells the reader that the book will make clear "how necessary it is for *men and women* to experience the sanctification of the Spirit to procede [*sic*] or go before, that they may be duly qualified to help or advise others" (v, emphasis added).

[6] Bownas, *Qualifications*, 13, 14.

[7] Bownas, *Qualifications*, 15 (emphasis in original).

[8] Bownas, *Qualifications*, 16.

[9] Barclay, *Apology*, 264.

[10] Bownas, *Qualifications*, 20–21.

[11] Bownas, *Qualifications*, 30–31. Here Bownas reveals his distrust of the faculty of imagination because of its possible, even probable negative effects on inspiration.

[12] Bownas, *Qualifications*, 24.

[13] As noted in chapter 2, the doctrine-use format was well established in the homiletical writings of the time but was prominent in Perkins' extremely influential *The Arte of Prophecying*, the primary homiletical source for Puritans.

[14] Bownas, *Qualifications*, 25 (emphasis in original).

[15] Bownas, *Qualifications*, 26.

[16] Bownas, *Qualifications*, 27.

[17] Bownas, *Qualifications*, 28, 32.

[18] Bownas, *Qualifications*, 33.

[19] Bownas, *Qualifications*, 36, 37.

[20] Bownas, *Qualifications*, 37.

[21] Bownas, *Qualifications*, 38 (emphasis in original).

[22] Bownas, *Qualifications*, 39–41 (emphasis in the original). Perhaps the paradigmatic statement of the classical regard for imitation is discovered in these words from Quintilian: "From these authors, and others worthy to be read, a stock of words, a variety of figures, and the art of composition, must be acquired; and our minds must be directed to the imitation of all their excellence; for it canot be doubted that a great portion of art consists in *imitation*" (quoted in Bizzell and Herzberg, *The Rhetorical Tradition*, 400).

[23] Bownas, *Qualifications*, 41.

[24] Beamish, *Quaker Ministry*, 53. I have discovered no evidence of this approach to delivery in the seventeenth century, but such cultural habits often have deep historical roots.

[25] Bownas, *Qualifications*, 41–42 (emphasis in original).

[26] Bownas, *Qualifications*, 41 (emphasis in original).

[27] See Barclay, *Apology*, 335–36.

[28] Bownas, *Qualifications*, 42 (emphasis in original).

[29] Bownas, *Qualifications*, 42–43.

[30] Bownas, *Qualifications*, 44 (emphasis added).

[31] Bownas, *Qualifications*, 44–45.

[32] Bownas, *Qualifications*, 45.

[33] Bownas, *Qualifications*, 46.

[34] Thomas Chalkley (1675–1741), in his 1720 tract, *Some Considerations on the Call, Work, and Wages, of the Ministers of Christ*, which otherwise repeats and reaffirms the prevalent Quaker positions regarding inspired speaking, specifically mentions the value of memory in recalling Scripture: "every true Believer in him, wants this Remembrancer, which must needs be a great Comfort to us, to have [Christ's] excellent Speeches and Divine Doctrine brought by his own Spirit to our Remembrance" (in *A Collection of the Works of Thomas Chalkley in Two Parts* [Philadelphia: B. Franklin & D. Hall, 1749], 537).

[35] Bownas, *Qualifications*, 46.

[36] Bownas, *Qualifications*, 47.

[37] Bownas, *Qualifications*, 48–49.

[38] Bownas, *Qualifications*, 50–51 (emphasis in original).

[39] Bownas, *Qualifications*, 52–53.

[40] The topic of indirection as a discourse strategy appears regularly in scholarly literature. See, for example, Walter Jost, "On Concealment and Deception in Rhetoric: Newman and Kierkegaard," in *Rhetoric Society Quarterly* 24, no. 1/2 (1994): 51–74; Jason Ingram, "Plato's Rhetoric of Indirection: Paradox as Site and Agency of Transformation," *Philosophy & Rhetoric*, 40, no. 3 (2007): 293–310; and Pat J. Gehrke, "The Southern Association of Teachers of Speech v. Senator Theodore Bilbo: Restraint and Indirection as Rhetorical Strategies," in *Southern Communication Journal* 72, no. 1 (2007): 95–104.

[41] Bownas, *Qualifications*, 53, 54.

[42] Bownas, *Qualifications*, 54.

[43] Since none of Bownas' sermons have survived, we canot ascertain what his own practice was in this regard. However, other surviving sermons indicate that Quaker preachers used materials sparingly from their own and others' lives in their sermons, preferring, instead, examples drawn directly from the Bible. As we will see in chapter 12, one of the two surviving funeral sermons from the seventeenth century, this one delivered by William Pen "upon occasion of the death of Mrs. Rebecca Travers, an aged servant of God," manages to turn the occasion to an examination of life viewed as a pilgrimage without direct mention of Travers' name or rehearsal of the essential details of her life (*Concurrence and Unanimity*, 73–77).

[44] Bownas, *Qualifications*, 55–56.

[45] Bownas, *Qualifications*, 56–57.

[46] Cope, "Seventeenth Century Quaker Style," 746.

[47] Bownas, *Qualifications*, 58.

[48] Bownas, *Qualifications*, 58–59.

[49] Bownas, *Qualifications*, 60–112. Here Bownas' choice of the words "young man's state" and "father's state" seem to imply that ministers are to be males, since women canot identify with these male terms as they might be able to sense themselves included in the more generic term "man." Bownas' choice is highly problematic given the presence of effective female Quaker preachers.

[50] Bownas, *Qualifications*, 107 (emphasis in original).

Chapter 6

[1] Ian Ramsey, *Religious Language: An Empirical Placing of Theological Phrases* (London:

SCM Press, 1957), 154. Ramsey's thesis is that religious discourse is characterized by "odd language" and "logical impropriety" because it describes a "religious situation," itself characterized by "discernment." Ramsey claims, "there are situations which are spatio-temporal and more. Without such 'depth'; without this which is 'unseen,' no religion will be possible" (15). The religious situation is also characterized by total "commitment," which "is based upon but goes beyond rational considerations" (17). Religious language, argues Ramsey, exhibits logical peculiarities and contains significant tautologies.

[2] Ramsey, *Religious Language*, 17.

[3] Ramsey, *Religious Language*, 155.

[4] For purposes of this chapter, two notions of "theme" will be included in the discussion: (1) concepts developed by the preachers through amplification, argument, illustration, images, etc.; and (2) recurrent terms in the sermons, which allude to concepts developed in other Quaker sermons or writings, and which the hearers bring to bear upon the term as used in the sermon. For example, the term "justification" is repeated with frequency in the sermons without detailed consideration of the concept it stands for. Yet a sermon such as Crisp's "Christ the Way, the Truth, and the Life" (April 18, 1687), in *Scripture-Truths*, treats justification as a major concept. In this discussion, I will consider as "thematic" both the recurrent mention of the term and its occasional detailed treatment, because even when the term is used without explanation, it implies and assumes the basic knowledge of the concept by the audience.

[5] For a quantitative record of such terms as "perfection," "preservation," "remnant," and "convincement," all of which were discussed in previous chapters, see appendix C. Quaker terms for the indwelling of Christ—"Light," "voice," "Seed"—as well as themes relevant to the satisfaction possible through God and the spiritual pilgrimage will be discussed as key metaphors in chapter 7. See appendix D for a quantitative record of these "imagistic" themes.

[6] These categories roughly approximate Ramsey's distinction between "relational" words and "object" words, *Religious Language*, 179–82.

[7] Vaughton, in *Concurrence and Unanimity* (sermon preached at Grace Church Street, London, April 1, 1694), 174.

[8] Coole, "Christ the Mighty Helper of Poor Helpless Man," in *Harmony* (sermon preached at Grace Church Street, London, May 12, 1694), 190–91.

[9] Crisp, "Christ the Way, the Truth, and the Life," in *Scripture-Truths* (sermon preached at Grace Church Street, London, April 18, 1687), 97, 103.

[10] Fox, in *Richardson MSS* (sermon preached at Devonshire House, London, May, 1677), 405.

[11] Crisp, "Bearing the Cross of Christ," in *Scripture-Truths*, 34.

[12] Camfield, in *Concurrence and Unanimity* (sermon preached at Grace Church Street, London, May 14, 1693), 41.

[13] The list would include the following: Dewsbury, in *Concurrence and Unanimity* (sermon preached at Grace Church Street, London, May 6, 1688), 11–26; Crisp, "First and Great Commandment," in *Scripture-Truths*, 33–68; Bowater, in *Concurrence and Unanimity* (sermon preached at St. John's Street, March 18, 1693), 46–72; and Whitehead, "Preaching of Christ *Crucified*," in *Harmony* (sermon preached at Grace Church Street, October 7, 1694), 155–77.

[14] Fox, in *Headley MSS,* (sermon preached at a general meeting, London, June 9, 1674), 252.

[15] Pen, "The Sure Foundation," in *Harmony* (sermon preached at Grace Church Street, London, October 10, 1694), 29 (emphasis in original).

[16] Crisp, "Saving-Faith, the Gift of God Alone," in *Scripture-Truths* (sermon preached at Grace Church Street, London, March 8, 1687), 149, 150, 151.

[17] Crisp, "Saving-Faith," in *Scripture-Truths,* 153 (emphasis in original).

[18] Crisp, "Excellency of Peace," in *Scripture-Truths,* see especially 127–29, 133–34, 139, and 142.

[19] Crisp, "The Wonderful Love of God to Mankind," in *Scripture-Truths* (sermon preached at St. Martins le Grand, London, November 9, 1690), 175–76, 191.

[20] Barbour, *Quakers in Puritan England,* 134.

[21] Bingley, in *Concurrence and Unanimity* (sermon preached at Grace Church Street, London, March 4, 1693), 130, 131.

[22] Marshall, in *Concurrence and Unanimity* (sermon preached at Grace Church Street, London, March 11, 1693), 88, 92 (emphasis in original).

[23] Fox, in *Headley MSS* (sermon preached at a general meeting, London, June 11, 1674), 281.

[24] Fox, in *Richardson MSS* (sermon preached at Yearly Meeting, London, May 24, 1681), 548.

[25] Dewsbury, in *Concurrence and Unanimity* (sermon preached at Grace Church Street, London, May 6, 1688), 13 (emphasis in original), 23.

[26] Crisp, "Salvation from Sin by Jesus Christ," in *Scripture-Truths* (sermon preached at Devonshire House, London, August 9, 1691), 203.

[27] Crisp, "Christians should be often thinking on the Name of the Lord," in *Scripture-Truths* (sermon preached at Devonshire House, London, July 17, 1692), 245.

[28] Waldenfield, in *Concurrence and Unanimity* (sermon preached at Devonshire House, London, March 11, 1693), 146.

[29] Pen, "The Great Design of Christianity," in *Harmony* (sermon preached at Wheelers Street, London, January 27, 1694), 131.

[30] Pen, "God's Call to the Careless World," in *Harmony* (sermon preached at Grace Church Street, London, October 21, 1694), 49, 60.

[31] See Waldenfield, "Christ Altogether Lovely," in *Harmony* (sermon preached at Grace Church Street, London, March 11, 1693), 210–11 for an account of the second coming, which makes it clear that the immediate experience of Christ is far more important than his future return to earth. See also Pen, "God's Call," in *Harmony,* 54. One strong reason that the Second Coming was not stressed is the belief in "realised eschatology," i.e., that Christ had already appeared to "teach His people Himself." See Gwyn, *Apocalypse of the Word.*

[32] Quakers actually made what Ramsey has called "object" words into "relational" words. See Ramsey, *Religious Language,* 179–85.

[33] Fox, in *Headley MSS* (sermon preached at Yearly Meeting, London, June 11, 1674), 268.

[34] Fox, in *Richardson MSS* (sermon preached at Yearly Meeting, London, May 24, 1681), 544.

[35] Crisp, "No true Worship without the right Knowledge of God," in *Scripture-Truths* (sermon preached at Grace Church Street, London, May 24, 1688), 55, 151, 153.

[36] Crisp, "Pure and Spiritual," in *Scripture-Truths*, 55.

[37] Crisp, "Pure and Spiritual," in *Scripture-Truths*, 58.

[38] Fox, in *Richardson MSS* (sermon preached at Devonshire House, London, May, 1677), 392.

[39] Fox, in *Richardson MSS* (sermon preached at Yearly Meeting, London, May 24, 1681), 539

[40] Fox, A sermon preached at Wheeler Street, June 1, 1680. *A Sermon . . . by Thomas Story*, in *Harmony*, 64.

[41] Crisp, "Baptism and the Lord's Supper Asserted," in *Scripture-Truths* (sermon preached at Grace Church Street, London, April 15, 1688), 85–87.

[42] Waldenfield, "Christ Altogether Lovely," in *Harmony*, 213.

[43] Chalkley, *Mr. T. Chalkley's Sermon & Prayer*, manuscript at Friends Historical Library, Swarthmore College, 3.

[44] Fox, A sermon preached at Wheeler Street, June 1, 1680, *A Sermon . . . by Thomas Story*, in *Harmony*, 68.

[45] Crisp, "The Spirit of Christ the only true Guide," in *Scripture-Truths* (sermon preached at Grace Church Street, London, October 10, 1690), 53.

[46] In *A Collection of Several Sermons and Testimonies* (London: B. Beardwell, 1701), 13.

[47] Crisp, "Baptism," in *Scripture-Truths*, 88. Substantially the same presentation was made by Crisp in "First and Great Commandment," in *Scripture-Truths*, 56, in which he speaks of Christ's visit to each person's heart bearing the bread of life and the wine of the kingdom.

[48] We have already considered God's love to humans as a theological theme. It remains to treat human responsibility to love God and fellow humans.

[49] Ranters were notorious for this practice. Braithwaite wrote that the Ranters "represented the revolt against authority in its extremest form." The essential defect of Ranterism was its refusal to provide a test "by which the individual could distinguish between the voice of the Spirit and the voice of his own will" (*Beginnings*, 22).

[50] Bingley, in *Concurrence and Unanimity* (sermon preached at Grace Church Street), 127, 128.

[51] Fox, in *Richardson MSS* (sermon preached at Devonshire House, May 1677), 409a.

[52] Crisp, "The Acceptable Sacrifice," in *Scripture-Truths* (sermon preached at Grace Church Street, July 3, 1692), 206–7 (emphasis in original).

[53] Bingley, in *Concurrence and Unanimity* (sermon preached at Grace Church Street), 127.

[54] Bowater, in *Concurrence and Unanimity* (sermon preached at St. John's Street), 64.

[55] Crisp, "Bearing the Cross of Christ," in *Scripture-Truths*, 14.

[56] Pen, in *Concurrence and Unanimity* (sermon preached upon occasion of the death of Mrs. Rebecca Travers, n.p., June 19, 1688), 76–77. Here Pen recalled to his hearers the title of his work *No Cross, No Crown*, which he wrote while in the Tower of London, 1668.

[57] Ashby, in *Concurrence and Unanimity* (sermon preached at St. Martins le Grand, February 16, 1693), 105 (emphasis in original).

[58] Fox, in *Richardson MSS* (sermon preached at a Women's Meeting, Barbados, October 1671), 257.

[59] Fox, in *Headley MSS* (sermon preached at Yearly Meeting, June 11, 1674), 271.

[60] Fox, in *Richardson MSS* (sermon preached at Yearly Meeting, London, May 25 or 26, 1675), 453.

[61] Pen, "Two Made One," in *Harmony*, 152.

[62] Crisp, "The Inward Preacher: Or, the Office of Conscience," in *Scripture-Truths* (sermon preached at Grace Church Street, June 21, 1692), 146.

[63] Crisp, "The Necessity of an Holy Life and Conversation," in *Scripture-Truths* (sermon preached at St. Martins le Grand, March 26, 1687), 55.

[64] Crisp, "The undefiled Way to Eternal Rest," in *Scripture-Truths* (sermon preached at Devonshire House, July 29, 1691), 105 (emphasis in original), 106.

[65] Fox, in *Richardson MSS* (sermon preached at a Women's Meeting, Barbados, October, 1671), 206.

[66] Crisp, "The undefiled Way," in *Scripture-Truths*, 105.

[67] Fox, in *Richardson MSS* (sermon preached at a Men's Meeting, Barbados, October, 1671), 206.

[68] Fox, in *Richardson MSS* (sermon preached at a Women's Meeting, Barbados, October, 1671), 256.

[69] Fox, A sermon preached at Wheeler Street, June 1, 1680, *A Sermon . . . by Thomas Story*, in *Harmony*, 74 (emphasis in original).

[70] Fox, in *Richardson MSS* (sermon preached at a Women's Meeting, Barbados, October, 1671), 257.

[71] Fox, A sermon preached at Wheeler Street, June 1, 1680, *A Sermon . . . by Thomas Story*, in *Harmony*, 74.

[72] Pen, "Two Made One," in *Harmony*, 151.

[73] *Collection of Several Sermons*, 7.

[74] Fox, in *Richardson MSS* (sermon preached May, 1678), 463.

[75] Fox, A sermon preached at Wheeler Street, June 1, 1680, *A Sermon . . . by Thomas Story*, in *Harmony*, 72 (emphasis in original).

[76] Fox, in *Richardson MSS* (sermon preached at Yearly Meeting, May 25 or 26, 1675), 437–38.

[77] Crisp, "Inward Preacher" in *Scripture-Truths*, 143.

[78] Bowater, in *Concurrence and Unanimity* (sermon preached at St. John's Street, March 18, 1693), 53.

[79] Crisp, "Divine Monitor," in *Scripture-Truths*, 128.

[80] Fox, in *Richardson MSS* (sermon preached at a Women's Meeting, Barbados), 261.

[81] Fox, in *Richardson MSS*, 257.

[82] *Collection of Several Sermons*, 8.

[83] Crisp, "Acceptable Sacrifice," in *Scripture-Truths*, 218–19.

[84] Fox, in *Headley MSS* (sermon preached at Yearly Meeting, London, June 11, 1674), 278.

[85] Fox, A sermon preached at Wheeler Street, June 1, 1680, *A Sermon . . . by Thomas Story*, in *Harmony*, 73–74. Altogether, Fox was imprisoned eight times.

[86] Crisp, "Captive Sinners set free by Jesus Christ," in *Scripture-Truths*, 120 (emphasis in original).

[87] Crisp, "Sheep of Christ," in *Scripture-Truths*, 148.

[88] Crisp, "First and Great Commandment," in *Scripture-Truths*, 64–65 (emphasis in original).

[89] Pen, "The Great Design of Christianity," in *Harmony*, 135.

[90] Vaughton, in *Concurrence and Unanimity* (sermon preached at Grace Church Street), 174.

[91] Fox, A sermon preached at Wheeler Street, June 1, 1680. *A Sermon . . . by Thomas Story*, in *Harmony*, 74 (emphasis in original).

[92] Crisp, "Salvation from Sin," in *Scripture-Truths*, 193 (emphasis in original).

[93] Fox, in *Richardson MSS* (sermon preached at Devonshire House, May, 1677), 392.

[94] Waldenfield, "Christ Altogether Lovely," in *Harmony*, 211 (emphasis in original).

[95] Pen, "Two Made One," in *Harmony*, 149 (emphasis in original).

[96] Pen, "The Sure Foundation," in *Harmony*, 28 (emphasis in original).

[97] Pen, "God's Call," in *Harmony*, 59–60 (emphasis in original).

[98] Both Barclay and Pen had university experience.

[99] Crisp, "Captive Sinners," in *Scripture-Truths*, 113–24.

[100] See Peters, *Print Culture and the Early Quakers*.

[101] Crisp, "Mighty Work," in *Scripture-Truths*, 11, 3.

[102] Crisp, "Christ the Way to Eternal Life," in *Scripture-Truths*, 11.

[103] Crisp, "The Word of God a Christian's Life," in *Scripture-Truths*, 27 (emphasis added). Fox's *Journal* employed the same language to describe the encounter with Christ. After hearing the voice, Fox tells us, "my heart did leap for joy. . . . And this I knew experimentally" (11).

[104] Crisp, "Great Mediator," in *Scripture-Truths*, 18.

[105] Park, in *Concurrence and Unanimity* (sermon preached at Ratcliff, London, April 1694), 179.

[106] D. Elton Trueblood, *The People Called Quakers* (New York: Harper & Row, 1966), 33.

[107] In the "Novum Organum," Bacon considers the senses to be prone to "dullness, incompetency, and deceptions" and thus proposed the discipline of the experiment to compensate for the detriments of sensory experience alone (see Aphorism L). John Locke also includes a discussion of sensory knowledge in his *Essay on Human Understanding*, in which he maintains that humans come to know of their own existence by intuition, God's existence by demonstration, and the existence of other things by sensation (see book 4, sections 1–4). Quaker preachers use the words "experimental," "feel," and "experience," and their derivatives, in a mental, not physical, sense. In chapter 4, I discuss Barclay's notion of how the senses relate to knowledge.

[108] Crisp, "Wonderful Love," in *Scripture-Truths*, 178–79.

[109] Crisp, "Word of God," in *Scripture-Truths*, 28–29.

[110] See Elbert N. S. Thompson, *The Controversy between the Puritans and the Stage* (New York: Russell & Russell, 1966) for a scholarly account of the Puritan reaction to the theatre. See also Jonas A. Barish, *The Antitheatrical Prejudice* (Berkeley: University of California Press, 1981). Quaker responses to theatre have changed considerably over the years. See my "The Anti-Theatrical Prejudice and the Quakers: A Late Twentieth Century Perspective," in *Truth's Bright Embrace: A Festschrift in Honor of Arthur O. Roberts*, ed. Howard Macy and Paul Anderson (Newberg, Ore.: Barclay Press, 1996).

[111] Crisp, "Spirit of Christ," in *Scripture-Truths*, 50.

[112] Crisp, "Spirit of Christ," in *Scripture-Truths*, 46.

[113] Crisp, "No true Worship," in *Scripture-Truths*, 173.

[114] Fox, A sermon preached at Wheeler Street, June 1, 1680. *A Sermon . . . by Thomas Story*, in *Harmony*, 72.

[115] Crisp, "Salvation from Sin," in *Scripture-Truths*, 203.

[116] Crisp, "Acceptable Sacrifice," in *Scripture-Truths*, 224.

[117] Crisp, "Salvation from Sin," in *Scripture-Truths*, 202–3.

[118] Marshall, in *Concurrence and Unanimity* (sermon preached at Grace Church Street), 97 (emphasis in original).

[119] Camfield, in *Concurrence and Unanimity* (sermon preached at Grace Church Street), 44–45 (emphasis in original).

[120] Fox, in *Richardson MSS* (sermon preached at Yearly Meeting, June 11, 1674), 274.

[121] Fox, A sermon preached at Wheeler Street, June 1, 1680, *A Sermon . . . by Thomas Story*, in *Harmony*, 65 (emphasis in original).

[122] Fox, in *Richardson MSS* (sermon preached at a Men's Meeting, Barbados), 204.

[123] Fox, in *Richardson MSS* (sermon preached at a Women's Meeting, Barbados), 258.

[124] Wright, *Literary Life of the Early Friends*, 146.

[125] See Mitchell, *English Pulpit Oratory*, 396.

[126] See, e.g., Barclay's *Apology* or Pen's *No Cross, No Crown* (London, 1694).

Chapter 7

This chapter is largely adapted from Graves, "Functions of Key Metaphors" and "Mapping the Metaphors in George Fox's Sermons," in *New Light on George Fox, 1624–1691: A Collection of Essays*, ed. Michael Mullet, 45–59 (York, England: William Sessions, 1994). Used by permission.

[1] The preachers make use of traditional kinds of arguments, including cause-effect, effect-cause, sign, definition, and example. By far the most numerous argument form in the sermons, which infuses nearly all of them, is the argument based upon the authority of Scripture (see Crisp, "Word of God," in *Scripture-Truths*, 34, for an example of this argument; see also Crisp, "Mighty Work," in *Scripture-Truths*, 16–17). The sermons also provide examples of such argument forms as dilemma (see Crisp, "Mighty Work," in *Scripture-Truths*, 17; see also Pen, "The Great Design of Christianity," in *Harmony*, 125), *reducto ad absurdum* (Crisp, "Baptism," in *Scripture-Truths*, 86–87), and *a fortiori* (Fox, Men's Meeting, Barbados, October, 1671, in *Richardson MSS*, 200; see also Crisp, "Captive Sinners," in *Scripture-Truths*, 121–22).

[2] Kenneth Burke maintains that "there is a difference between an abstract term naming the 'idea' . . . and a concrete image designed to stand for the idea. . . . [I]f the image employs the full resources of imagination, it will not represent merely one idea, but will contain a whole bundle of principles" (*A Rhetoric of Motives* [Berkeley: University of California Press, 1969], 86).

[3] Burke, *Permanence and Change*, Library of Liberal Arts (Indianapolis: Bobbs-Merrill, 1965), 104.

[4] Richard M. Weaver writes about the importance of analogy, of which family metaphor is a part: "the cosmos is one vast system of analogy, so that our profoundest intuitions of it are made in the form of comparisons. To affirm that something is like something else is to begin to talk about the unitariness of creation. . . . There is a recognition that the unknown may be continuous with the known, so that man is moving about in a world only partly realized, yet real in all its parts" ("Language is Sermonic," in *Language is Sermonic*, ed. Richard L. Johanesen, Renard Strickland, and Ralph T. Eubanks [Baton Rouge: Louisiana State University Press, 1970], 214).

[5] I. A. Richards, *The Philosophy of Rhetoric* (New York: Oxford University Press, 1965), 94 (emphasis in original).

[6] Their verbal duels with the Baptists also reveal their debating skills. See T. L. Underwood, *Primitivism, Radicalism, and the Lamb's War: The Baptist-Quaker Conflict in Seventeenth-Century England* (New York: Oxford University Press, 1997).

[7] There are additional powerful strategies found in the sermons, which will be discussed in chapter 6. I see the strategy of archetypal metaphor in the sermons primarily as a means to develop the "motive" of the discourse, which is the reaffirmation of an image. This terminology and conceptualization of rhetorical discourse is taken from Walter Fisher, "A Motive View of Communication," *Quarterly Journal of Speech* 56 (1970): 131–39, a much-undervalued yet still-insightful essay. Fisher maintains the communicator perceives a rhetorical situation in terms of a motive, and "motives are names which essentialize the inter-relations of communicator, communication, audience(s), time, and place" (132). "Reaffirmation" is a motive "concerned with revitalizing an image" (132), specifically when "a communicator attempts to revitalize a faith already held by his [*sic*] audience" (134). Although the sermons included in this book exhibit evangelistic tendencies, their primary appeal is directed toward Quakers or people on the verge of becoming Quakers; thus the motive is primarily reaffirmation. Just as Fisher found that Lincoln's "Gettysburg Address" and Martin Luther King's "I Have a Dream" speech both used the strategy of archetypal metaphor to accomplish the motive of reaffirmation, early Quaker sermons often similarly employ the strategy of archetypal metaphor.

[8] I follow Kathleen Hall Jamieson in the use of the term "clusters," meaning related metaphors obviously belonging to the same imagery pattern or conceptual structure ("The Metaphoric Cluster in the Rhetoric of Pope Paul VI and Edmund G. Brown, Jr.," *Quarterly Journal of Speech* 66 [1980]: 51–52). More recently, Lyn Cameron has developed a way to study clustering, spontaneous metaphors in interpersonal conversation. See her "Metaphor Clusters in Discourse," *Journal of Applied Linguistics* 1, no. 2 (2004): 107–36.

[9] A helpful review of some of this literature on metaphor, especially that directly pertinent to the larger concept of "religious language," and thus very significant to this

chapter, may be found in Dan R. Stiver, *The Philosophy of Religious Language: Sign, Symbol & Story* (Malden, Mass.: Blackwell, 1996), 1–86, 112–34.

[10] Black, "Metaphor," *Proceedings of the Aristotelian Society* 55 (1954–1955): 273–94. Black more fully developed his conception of metaphor in *Models and Metaphors: Studies in Language and Philosophy* (Ithaca: Cornell University Press, 1962).

[11] Cohen, "Metaphor and the Cultivation of Intimacy," in *On Metaphor*, ed. Sheldon Sacks (Chicago: University of Chicago Press,1979), 3. Sheldon Sacks' edited volume is also a landmark publication, with essays by Paul de Man, Donald Davidson, Wayne C. Booth, Kersten Harries, David Tracy, Richard Shiff, Howard Gardner and Ellen Winner, and Paul Ricoeur (Sacks, ed. *On Metaphor* [Chicago: University of Chicago Press, 1979]).

[12] George Lakoff and Mark Johnson, *Metaphors We Live By* (Chicago: University of Chicago Press, 1980), ix, 3, 6 (emphasis in original).

[13] Both Lakoff and Johnson have followed their coauthored landmark book with subsequent studies, including Lakoff, *Women, Fire, and Dangerous Things: What Our Categories Reveal About the Mind* (Chicago: University of Chicago Press, 1987), and Johnson, *The Body in the Mind: The Bodily Basis of Meaning, Imagination, and Reason* (Chicago: University of Chicago Press, 1987). In the latter, Johnson acknowledges Richards' influence, as well as Philip Wheelright's in *Metaphor and Reality* (Bloomington: Indiana University Press, 1962).

[14] Lakoff and Johnson, *Metaphors We Live By*, x.

[15] Brett A. Miller has written a cogent essay in which he argues that Lakoff and Johnson present a position that is "self-certifying, therefore self-refuting, and is ultimately arbitrary and naively subjective" ("Seeing Through a Glass Darkly: Religious Metaphor as Rhetorical Perspective," *Journal of Communication and Religion* 22 [1999]: 218). Miller goes on to present a new perspective on metaphor that adds "neo-realist ontological and epistemological elements of perspective realism" (232).

[16] See, e.g., James W. Fernandez, "Persuasions and Performance: Of the Beast in Every Body . . . And the Metaphors of Everyman," *Daedalus* 101 (1972): 39–60, and "The Mission of Metaphor in Expressive Culture," *Current Anthropology* 15 (1974): 119–33; Sherry B. Ortner, "On Key Symbols," *American Anthropologist* 75 (1973): 1338–46; Brenda E. F. Beck, "The Metaphor as a Mediator Between Semantic and Analogic Modes of Thought," *Current Anthropology* 19 (1978): 83–88; and David Sapir and J. Christopher Crocker, eds., *The Social Use of Metaphor* (Philadelphia: University of Pensylvania Press, 1977). For examples of applications of metaphorical analysis to specific cultures, see Michele Zimbalist Rosaldo, "Metaphors and Folk Classification," *Southwestern Journal of Anthropology* 28 (1972): 83–99, and "It's All Uphill: The Creative Metaphors of Ilongot Magical Spells," in *Sociocultural Dimensions of Language Use*, ed. Mary Sanches and Ben Blount (New York: Academic Press, 1975), 177–203; Gustav Thaiss, "The Conceptualization of Social Change Through Metaphor," *Journal of Asian and African Studies* 13 (1978): 1–13; and Nels Johnson, "Palestinian Refugee Ideology: An Enquiry into Key Metaphors," *Journal of Anthropological Research* 34 (1978): 524–39.

[17] Nels Johnson, "Palestinian Refugee Ideology."

[18] Ortner, "On Key Symbols."

[19] Ortner, "On Key Symbols," 1329.

[20] See, e.g., Fox's *Journal* and the selections in *Early Quaker Writings*. In addition, the

discussions of Quaker presuppositions in chapter 2 and early development of Quaker homiletic theory in chapter 3 attest to the importance of the five metaphors analyzed in this chapter.

[21] A select list of authors and essays using metaphorical analysis of various artifacts includes William Gribbin, "The Juggernaut Metaphor in American Rhetoric," *Quarterly Journal of Speech* 59 (1973): 297–303; Paul Newell Campbell, "Metaphor and Linguistic Theory," *Quarterly Journal of Speech* 61 (1975): 1–12; Ivie, "Metaphor of Force"; Leff, "Topical Invention and Metaphoric Interaction," *Southern Speech Communication Journal* 48 (1983): 214–29; and Robert L. Ivie, "Metaphor and the Rhetorical Invention of Cold War 'Idealists,'" *Communication Monographs* 54 (1987): 165–82; Simon Barker, "Rigour or Vigour: Metaphor, Argument, and Internet," *Philosophy & Rhetoric* 31, no. 4 (1998): 248–65; Theodore Sarbin, "The Metaphor-to-Myth Transformation with Special Reference to the 'War on Terrorism,'" *Peace & Conflict* 9, no. 2 (2003): 149–58; Lionel Wee, "Proper Names and the Theory of Metaphor," *Journal of Linguistics* 42, no. 2 (2006): 355–71; and Michael L. Butterworth, "Purifying the Body Politic: Steroids, Rafael Palmeiro," *Western Journal of Communication* 72, no. 2 (2008): 145–61.

[22] A partial list of essays that deal with archetypal metaphors would include Michael M. Osborn and Douglas Ehninger, "The Metaphor in Public Address," *Speech Monographs* 29 (1962), 223–34; Michael Osborn, "Archetypal Metaphor in Rhetoric: The Light-Dark Family," *Quarterly Journal of Speech* 52 (1967): 115–26; J. Vernon Jensen, "British Voices on the Eve of the American Revolution: Trapped by the Family Metaphor," *Quarterly Journal of Speech* 63 (1977): 43–50; Michael Osborn, "The Evolution of the Archetypal Sea In Rhetoric and Poetic," *Quarterly Journal of Speech* (December 1977): 347–63; John Adams, "The Familial Image in Rhetoric," *Communication Quarterly* 31, no. 1 (1983): 56–61; Donald Rice, "Order Out of Chaos: The Archetypal Metaphor in Early American Rhetoric," *North Dakota Journal of Speech & Theatre* 9, no. 1 (1996): 18–24.

[23] Osborn, "Archetypal Metaphor," 115–26.

[24] Sallie McFague, *Speaking in Parables: A Study in Metaphor and Theology* (Philadelphia: Fortress Press, 1975), 43. McFague's statement is slightly different but shares a great deal with the position Campbell argues in a series of important publications—that there is a symbological hierarchy in which "language is by definition poetic (employs metaphor, rhythm, *personae*, and the mental/symbolic forms of crescendo, contrast, repetition, etc) . . . *and* rhetorical (presents perspectives, arguments, urges attitudes, actions). . . . Hence, poetic-rhetorical discourse is the primary symbolic form. . . . Understood as the systematic critique of presuppositions, philosophical discourse is the secondary form, resting on poetic-rhetorical bases . . . while the tertiary form, scientific discourse, depends on poetic-rhetorical bases and on presuppositions that can be philosophically explicated" (Campbell, "Symbolical Hierarchy: A Further Word," *Philosophy & Rhetoric* 9, no. 2 [1976]: 116). See also Campbell's earlier essay "Poetic-Rhetorical, Philosophical, and Scientific Discourse," *Philosophy & Rhetoric* 6, no. 1 (1973): 1–29.

[25] Sallie McFague, *Metaphorical Theology: Models of God in Religious Language* (Philadelphia: Fortress Press, 1982), 37. McFague nestles her positions within the influential writings of Max Black, Walter Ong, Paul Ricoeur, and, particularly, Richards (*Philosophy of Rhetoric*).

[26] McFague, *Metaphorical Theology*, 193.

[27] McFague, *Metaphorical Theology*, 145–92, 194.

[28] Earl R. MacCormac, *Metaphor and Myth* (Durham: Duke University Press, 1976), 71. MacCormac's main emphasis is to show that both science and theology are utterly dependent on metaphor.

[29] Janet Martin Soskice, *Metaphor and Religious Language* (Oxford: Clarendon, 1985), 160.

[30] Both metaphors are possible. The preachers were "midwives" because they sought to bring to life the Light that they believed shines in all persons, what they sometimes called "that of God in every man." The term "medium" in this context is Bauman's (personal conversation, University of Texas, Austin, Texas, summer 1982). Bauman argues that Quaker preachers saw themselves as mouthpieces through which the inspiration of God (the Word) flowed. On the other hand, Barbour prefers the term "matchmaker," noting that "human actions of either the preacher or the repentant hearer were intended only to prepare the way for what God would do" (*Quakers in Puritan England*, 130).

[31] Cope, "Seventeenth Century Quaker Style," 79. Cope's work does not cite any of the sermons of this essay and tends to concentrate on an earlier period relying largely upon journals and tracts for his evidence. The sermons reveal that what he concluded about the use of metaphor by Quakers during the 1650s and 1660s is accurate for the only surviving record of spoken language (rather than what was composed for print) in the last three decades of the seventeenth century. Chapter 8 deals with this topic in more detail.

[32] Renaissance rhetoric viewed the speaker's craft as "an aesthetically oriented art of ingratiation—a form of conscious flattery or supplication" (Ehninger, "On Rhetorics and Rhetoric," 244). Quakers consciously avoided verbal ingratiation, preferring the "plain speech" of Puritans and going beyond them in group strictures on language use. For an excellent consideration of Quaker language against the background of other widespread language experimentation, see Hugh Ormsby-Lenon, "'The Dialect of Those Fanatic Times': Language Communities and English Poetry from 1580 to 1660" (Ph.D. diss., University of Pensylvania, 1977), 379–88. The subject of literalness and metaphor has also attracted the attention of philosophers. See, e.g., Michael McCanles, "The Literal and the Metaphorical: Dialectic or Interchange," *Proceedings of the Modern Language Association* 90 (1976): 279–90.

[33] Two of the sermons included in the study are anonymous but may have been preached by one or two of the other named preachers in the study.

[34] Osborn, "Archetypal Metaphor," 117–24. "Qualifiers" are forces that direct association patterns between tenor and vehicle of the metaphor. See Osborn and Ehninger, "Metaphor in Public Address," 228.

[35] Two of the five are by Stephen Crisp and George Fox, in whose other sermons the terms are ubiquitous. The remaining three sermons that do not express light/dark patterns do not employ any of the five clusters (one sermon by Leonard Fell, n.d., and two sermons by Philip Hermon, 1700. These are the only sermons that survive Fell and Hermon.

[36] Fox, *Headley MSS* (sermon preached at Yearly Meeting, May 9, 1674), 253–54.

[37] Cope, "Seventeenth Century Quaker Style," 733.

[38] Creasey, "'Inward' and 'Outward.'"

[39] Fox, *Richardson MSS* (sermon preached at Yearly Meeting, May 25 or 26, 1675), 439, 440, 452.

[40] Fox, *Richardson MSS* (sermon preached at Devonshire House, May, 1677), 392–93.

[41] Pen, "The Great Design of Christianity," in *Harmony*, 130.

[42] Ashby, *Concurrence and Unanimity* (sermon preached at St. Martins le Grand), 116.

[43] Crisp, "Bearing the Cross of Christ," in *Scripture-Truths*, 33 (emphasis in original).

[44] Waldenfield, "Christ Altogether Lovely" in *Harmony*, 206.

[45] Crisp, in *Scripture-Truths*, 50.

[46] Pen , in *Concurrence and Unanimity* (sermon preached at Wheeler Street on April 13, 1694), 80.

[47] Crisp, "Bearing the Cross of Christ," in *Scripture-Truths*, 14.

[48] Crisp, "The Dawning of the Day of Grace and Salvation," in *Scripture-Truths* (sermon preached at Grace Church Street, August 2, 1691), 110.

[49] Coole, "Christ the Mighty Helper of Poor Helpless Man," in *Harmony* (sermon preached at Grace Church Street, May 12, 1694), 184–85.

[50] Ashby, in *Concurrence* (sermon preached at St. Martins le Grande, February 16, 1693), 102.

[51] Crisp, "The Standard of Truth," in *Scripture-Truths* (sermon preached at Grace Church Street, May 29, 1692), 70.

[52] Coole, "Christ the Mighty Helper of Poor Helpless Man," in *Harmony*, 186.

[53] Pen, "Two Made One," in *Harmony*, 146.

[54] Crisp, "Mighty Work," in *Scripture-Truths*, 26.

[55] For excellent discussions of the tension between silence and speech, see Bauman's "Aspects," "Speaking in the Light," and *Let Your Words be Few*.

[56] See, e.g., Barclay's *Apology*, Proposition VII.

[57] Fox, in *Headley MSS* (sermon preached at Yearly Meeting, June 9, 1674), 248.

[58] Fox, in *Headley MSS* (sermon preached at Yearly Meeting, June 11, 1674), 282.

[59] Fox recorded that when his hopes in men were exhausted, "then, Oh then, I heard a voice which said, 'There is one, even Christ Jesus, that can speak to thy condition,' and when I heard it my heart did leap for joy" (*Journal*, 11). In the *Journal*, Fox appears to speak of a literal voice. The sermons are ambiguous as to whether the voice is literal or figurative.

[60] Crisp, "Sheep of Christ," in *Scripture-Truths* (sermon preached at Devonshire House, May 10, 1688), 14.

[61] Crisp, "Word of God," in *Scripture-Truths* (sermon preached at Grace Church Street, March 14, 1687), 28.

[62] Arthur O. Roberts, in his *Through Flaming Sword A Spiritual Biography of George Fox* (Newberg, Ore.: Barclay Press, 1959), has stated the early Quaker position of the "Word" in this way: "He who knows Jesus Christ experimentally knows the revelation of God about which the Scriptures speak authentically. Scriptures are the words of God, Jesus Christ is the Word of God" (92).

[63] Crisp, "Excellency of Peace," in *Scripture-Truths* (sermon preached at Devonshire House, August 5, 1691), 128.

[64] Dewsbury, in *Concurrence and Unanimity* (sermon preached at Grace Church Street, May 6, 1688), 17.

[65] Waldenfield, "Christ Altogether Lovely," in *Harmony*, 203.

[66] Crisp, "Word of God," in *Scripture-Truths*, 35. Crisp, Whitehead, and Pen at times all use an alternative to the "voice"—the "oracle" or "the oracle within"—but these linguistic stand-ins appear in only five sermons (Graves, "Rhetoric," 216–17).

[67] Crisp, "Great Duty," in *Scripture-Truths*, 102.

[68] Crisp, "Christ the Way," in *Scripture-Truths*, 4.

[69] Fox, A sermon preached at Wheeler Street, June 1, 1680. *A Sermon . . . by Thomas Story*, in *Harmony*, 65.

[70] Fox, in *Richardson MSS* (sermon preached at a men's meeting, Barbados, October, 1671), 200–201.

[71] Crisp, "Wonderful Love," in *Scripture-Truths*, 177.

[72] Bowater, in *Concurrence and Unanimity* (sermon preached at St. John's Street, March 18, 1693), 47.

[73] Crisp, "Bearing the Cross of Christ," in *Scripture-Truths*, 30–31.

[74] Crisp, "Excellency of Peace," in *Scripture-Truths*, 140.

[75] Many of the variations of the seed cluster are related to plants and trees and other agricultural images. "Plants" and "trees" appear in twenty-nine sermons, the "vineyard" or the "vine" appears in ten sermons, and "grafting," essential to Paul's letter to the Romans (11:17-24), appears in eleven sermons.

[76] Barclay, in *Concurrence* (sermon preached at Grace Church Street, May 16, 1688), 2. See also John 12:24.

[77] Maud Bodkin notes that the symbol of the seed of wheat transports us "to a world whose less discriminating mode of thought has upon us the power of an inchoate or unconscious poetry. Within that world, the sequence of rain, flood, and springing corn constitutes a holy rebirth wherein man participates and finds an expression of his own nature" (*Archetypal Patterns in Poetry* [London: Oxford University Press, 1934], 274).

[78] Pen, "The Heavenly Race," in *Harmony* (sermon preached at Grace Church Street, January 16, 1694), 97.

[79] Crisp, "Acceptable Sacrifice," in *Scripture-Truths*, 207. See Matt 5:6.

[80] Terms for water are rarely used in the sermons to refer to baptism or cleansing.

[81] Other terms drawing on the hunger-thirst pattern not discussed here include "fruit," "milk," "nursing," and "wine." See appendix D.

[82] Fox, in *Richardson MSS* (sermon preached at Yearly Meeting, May 25, 1681), 538–39.

[83] Butcher, in *Concurrence and Unanimity* (sermon preached at Grace Church Street, March 11, 1694), 163.

[84] Park, in *Concurrence and Unanimity* (sermon preached at Ratcliff, April 19, 1694), 183.

[85] Sermon preached at Savoy Meetinghouse, n.d., in *Collection of Several Sermons*, 11.

[86] Crisp, "Divine Life," in *Scripture-Truths* (sermon preached at Grace Church Street, March 16, 1691), 69.

[87] Fox, in *Headley MSS* (sermon preached at Yearly Meeting, May 9, 1674), 249.

[88] Fox, in *Richardson MSS* (sermon preached at Yearly Meeting, May, 1678), 479.

[89] The journey metaphor is carefully discussed by Georg Roppen and Richard Sommer in *Strangers and Pilgrims: An Essay on the Metaphor of Journey* (New York: Humanities Press, 1964). These authors call the journey the "metaphor of narration, of duration, extension, and purpose. Space and time operate in the metaphor under the control of a single element, a purpose or teleological force" (preface, n.p.). For an excellent overview of the journey metaphor, see Northrop Frye, "The Journey as Metaphor," in *Myth and Metaphor: Selected Essays, 1974–1988*, ed. Robert D. Denham (Charlottesville: University Press of Virginia, 1990), 212–26.

[90] The journey of the Jewish nation from Egypt to the Land of Promise is perhaps the best biblical example of the journey metaphor. In medieval times, there are numerous sources, but one might begin with St. Bonaventure's *The Soul's Journey into God*, ed. Ewert H. Cousins (New York: Paulist Press, 1978). In seventeenth-century England the image of the Pilgrim was immortalized by John Bunyan's *Pilgrim's Progress* (1678). In 1691 Crisp wrote his *A Short History of a Long Travel from Babylon to Bethel* (London: J. Sowle, 1711) (not published until 1711), which paralleled Bunyan's work at several points but also differed from it in very significant ways. See my essay, "Stephen Crisp's *Short History*," 5–23.

[91] Crisp, "Spirit of Christ," in *Scripture-Truths*, 51.

[92] Several of the sermons use the phrases "spiritual journey," "heavenly journey," and "spiritual travel." See appendix D.

[93] Fox, in *Headley MSS* (sermon preached at Yearly Meeting, June 11, 1674), 269.

[94] Crisp, "Sheep of Christ," in *Scripture-Truths*, 147.

[95] Pen, "A sermon preached upon occasion of the Death of Mrs. Rebecca Travers, June 19, 1688," in *Concurrence*, 6.

[96] Pen, "The Sure Foundation," in *Harmony*, 28 (emphasis in original).

[97] Fox, in *Richardson MSS* (sermon preached at women's meeting, Barbados, October, 1671), 273.

[98] Crisp, "The undefiled Way," in *Scripture-Truths*, 97.

[99] Pen, "Two Made One," in *Harmony*, 152.

[100] Pen, "The Great Design of Christianity," in *Harmony*, 129 (emphasis in original).

[101] Hermann Stelzner, "The Quest Story and Nixon's November 3, 1969 Address," *Quarterly Journal of Speech* 57 (1971): 164.

[102] Stelzner, "The Quest Story," 163.

[103] The terms "summarizing" and "elaborating" are borrowed from Ortner. Summarizing symbols "operate to compound and synthesize a complex system of ideas" ("On Key Symbols," 1340). On the other hand, elaborating symbols work by "sorting out complex and undifferentiated feelings and ideas, making them comprehensible to oneself, communicable to others, and translatable into orderly action." Ortner also asserts that she is "distinguishing not only types of symbols, but types of symbolic functions" (1344).

[104] See, e.g., Hill, *Century of Revolution*, 4–5.

[105] See Thomas Ellwood, and Joseph Wyeth. *The History of the Life of Thomas Ellwood*. (Philadelphia: For sale at Friends' Book Store, 1865), 24–36.

[106] Ortner, "On Key Symbols," 1340.

[107] See Fernandez, "The Mission of Metaphor," 124.

[108] Notably, Fox's *Journal* is full of references to the senses. During one of Fox's religious experiences, he records, "I was come up in Spirit through the flaming sword into the paradise of God. All things were new, and all the creation gave another smell unto me than before, beyond what words can utter" (27).

[109] Kenneth Burke, *Permanence and Change*, 104.

[110] Ortner, "On Key Symbols," 1340.

[111] Lakoff and Johnson map major metaphors in Western thought and illustrate their profound effects on our lives in their provocative volume, *Metaphors We Live By*.

[112] Thaiss notes that the metaphors of Iranian rhetoric build upon cultural assumptions regarding distinctions in status and function among the sexes ("Conceptualization," 5–10).

[113] No sermons delivered by women have survived, which possibly reflects a bias of the non-Quaker notetakers who transcribed the sermons.

[114] See Rosenberg, "The Formulaic Quality of Spontaneous Sermons," *Journal of American Folklore* 83 (1970): 3–20.

[115] Rosenberg, "The Formulaic Quality," 9. The "stall formula" as used by African American folk preachers consists of words or phrases repeated, usually in an exaggerated emotional pattern, in order to gain time. Quaker metaphors leading to the recitation of memorized Scripture passages are hardly the same thing, yet they may have served a similar purpose on occasion.

[116] The infamous case of James Nayler is dealt with by Braithwaite in *Beginnings of Quakerism*, 241–78. See also William G. Bittle, *James Nayler 1618–1660: The Quaker Indicted by Parliament* (York, UK: William Sessions, 1986); Gwyn, *The Covenant Crucified*; and Moore, *The Light in Their Consciences*.

[117] Another answer lies in a set of characteristics discussed in the next chapter.

Chapter 8

Portions of this chapter are adaptations or extensions of material in Michael Graves, "'Thou art but a youth': Thomas Chalkley Enacts and Defends the Early Quaker Impromptu Sermon," in *Rhetoric, Religion, and the Roots of Identity in British Colonial America*, ed. James R. Andrews, vol. 1: *A Rhetorical History of the United States*, ed. Martin J. Medhurst (East Lansing: Michigan State University Press, 2007). Used by permission.

[1] Cope, "Seventeenth Century Quaker Style," 733.

[2] Creasey, "'Inward' and 'Outward,'" 5.

[3] Barbour, *Quakers in Puritan England*, 129.

[4] Cope, "Seventeenth Century Quaker Style," 733.

[5] Cope, "Seventeenth Century Quaker Style," 749.

[6] Pen, "God's Call," in *Harmony*, 43 (emphasis in original).

[7] Fox, in *Headley MSS* (sermon preached at Yearly Meeting, London, June 9, 1674), 253.

[8] Bauman, *Let Your Words Be Few*, 77.

[9] In *Let Your Words Be Few*, Bauman appears to agree with my interpretation that occasionally preachers like Fox effect Cope's incantatory style in the post-1670s. See 76–78.

[10] Edward P. J. Corbett has distinguished between figures, tropes, and schemes in this manner: "We will use 'figures of speech' as the generic term for any artful deviations from the ordinary mode of speaking or writing. But we will divide the figures of speech into two main groups—the schemes and the *tropes*. A scheme (Greek *schema*, form, shape) involves a deviation from the ordinary pattern or arrangement of words. A trope (Greek *tropein*, to turn) involves a deviation from the ordinary and principal signification of a word" (*Classical Rhetoric for the Modern Student* [New York: Oxford University Press, 1965], 426–27).

[11] Rhetorical theorists have long recognized the power of rhetorical questions, especially when used in the form of imaginative dialogue. One of the most forceful statements is the ancient observation of Longinus: "the content is quite inadequate, but the inspired, rapid turn of question and answer, the reply to himself as if he were someone else, not only make the passage more successful because the figure is used, but actually more convincing." Again, "Passionate language is more moving when it seems to arise spontaneously and not to be contrived by the speaker, and the rhetorical question answered by oneself stimulates this emotional spontaneity" (Longinus, *On Great Writing*, trans. G. M. A. Grube (Indianapolis: Bobbs-Merrill, 1957), 30].

[12] On the importance of queries, Margaret H. Beacon writes in her *The Quiet Rebels* (New York: Basic Books, 1969), "[the queries were] questions which the monthly meeting asked themselves on a regular basis. The queries were first used as a form of gathering information about the Society, but gradually became a form of self-examination" (81). Queries dealt with whether meetings were convened for worship, whether there was expression of love and unity, whether children were being trained properly, whether trade and business were being conducted in an honest manner, whether vain amusements were avoided, and other factors important in Quaker life. Rufus Jones added that "the 'Queries' called for an examination of the life from at least a dozen moral and spiritual view-points, and tended to present a concrete moral ideal for the daily life at home and in business occupations" (*Quakers in the American Colonies*, 146). Although instances of the use of queries or "advices" by individual Quaker meetings are known before the 1690s, they became more common after the turn of the century.

[13] Fox, in *Headley MSS* (sermon preached at Yearly Meeting, London, June 9, 1674), 250.

[14] Fox, in *Richardson MSS* (sermon preached at Yearly Meeting, London, May 25 or 26, 1675), 451.

[15] Fox, in *Richardson MSS* (sermon preached at Yearly Meeting, London, May, 1678), 480.

[16] Crisp, "Baptism," in *Scripture-Truths*, 73 (emphasis in original).

[17] Crisp, "No true Worship" in *Scripture-Truths*, 153 (emphasis in original).

[18] Butcher, in *Concurrence and Unanimity*, 156–57.

[19] Fox, A sermon preached at Wheeler Street, June 1, 1680, *A Sermon . . . by Thomas Story*, 69.

[20] Crisp, "Captive Sinners," in *Scripture-Truths*, 114.

[21] Crisp, "Dawning of the Day," in *Scripture-Truths*, 111.

[22] Bowater, in *Concurrence and Unanimity*, 52.

[23] Bowater, in *Concurrence and Unanimity*, 53.

[24] Crisp, "Christ the Way," in *Scripture-Truths*, 6.

[25] Crisp, "Standard of Truth," in *Scripture-Truths*, 78.

[26] Pen, "The Promise of God For The Latter Days," in *Harmony*, 66.

[27] Pen, in *Concurrence and Unanimity*, 79.

[28] Creasey, "'Inward' and 'Outward,'" 3.

[29] Creasey, "'Inward' and 'Outward,'" 5.

[30] Creasey, "'Inward' and 'Outward,'" 12.

[31] Creasey cites Barclay's *Apology* (1678) and *Immediate Revelation* (1686) and Pen's *The Christian-Quaker* (1674).

[32] Cartesian dualism lies between mind and matter, soul and body. Descartes begins his philosophy by doubting all but his ability to doubt. The existence of self, matter, natural phenomena, and God are "proven" by the fact that the human mind has an innate knowledge of the existence of a perfect being—God—and since a perfect being would not deceive, humans can take the external world to be an actuality so long as one has clear and distinct ideas of the external world. The soul, therefore, does not derive its knowledge from sensation or experience. The dualism that Creasey sees in Pen's writings is exemplified in Pen's view of history in the Scriptures. Creasey writes, "For Pen, the revelation given by God in and through the vicissitudes of the history of the Hebrew people, and through the discipline of cultus and law, priest and prophet, is not seen as a progressive drawing near by God, revealing and effecting that which, apart from these things, must have remained hidden. It is seen, rather, as a somewhat regrettable intrusion of the inferior 'outward' mode of revelation, made necessary by the people's failure to make right use of an already fully available 'inward' mode of revelation" ("'Inward' and 'Outward,'" 13). Creasey concludes his statement on Pen's position by adding that "Pen does not altogether avoid giving the impression that, in some way, the Word's becoming flesh is almost an embarrassment to him in his apologetic" (13). Barclay, by Creasey's interpretation, goes even further than Pen and distinguishes "within the concept of Revelation, two kinds of Revelation, an 'inward' kind alleged to be without any essential connection with History, and an 'outward' kind, whose existence canot indeed be denied and whose value canot be minimized from the standpoint of Christian faith and experience but which can be accorded only an equivocal and almost marginal status in religious thought. . . . [Barclay also postulates] a 'separate and distinct' organ within man, which yet is no part of man's essential being, dependent in no way upon the constitution of man's mind, whereby alone this inward mode of Revelation is to be received" (22). I see Barclay's position from a different vantage point than Creasey's. This topic is discussed in chapter 4, where I interpret Barclay's *Immediate Revelation* as a theoretical structure in the impromptu preaching environment, a structure that could function in tension alongside revealed truth in Scripture. I have described the position generally taken by early Quakers in their sermons as a "dynamic tension" between the Spirit and the Scriptures, between the indwelling Spirit and the historical Jesus. Arthur O. Roberts has succinctly summarized this position: "Although much of the Quaker preaching proclaimed the immediacy of spiritual experience of Christ, it should never be forgotten that it is the once-offered Jesus Christ who 'speaks to the condition' of searching, sinful man, the real Pascal Lamb, whose blood wet the hillside in Palestine" (*Through Flaming Sword*, 94).

[33] Fox, in *Richardson MSS* (sermon preached at Yearly Meeting, May, 1678), 474.

[34] Fox, in *Richardson MSS* (sermon preached at Devonshire House, May, 1677), 398. Fox maintains that "Christ died for all, as well for blacks as for whites, for every Man" (Women's Meeting, Barbados, 272–73). The necessity of Christ's historical death is made even plainer in this passage from a 1675 sermon: "In ye days of Christ they were mad against him; they warred against him in his Flesh as he was Man. Now he said he was ye Light; & ye Son of God, yt every one should believe in him, & receive him; Now they Crucified him, Buried him, he is risen his Flesh saw no Corruption; ye Heavenly Spiritual Man his Blood purchaseth he who saw no Corruption" (in *Richardson MSS* [sermon preached at Yearly Meeting, London, May 25 or 26], 450).

[35] Crisp, "Christ All in All," in *Scripture-Truths*, 30–31 (emphasis added).

[36] Crisp, "The Kingdom of God Within," in *Scripture-Truths*, 82 (emphasis added).

[37] Ashby, in *Concurrence and Unanimity*, 101, 108.

[38] Waldenfield, "Christ Altogether Lovely," in *Harmony*, 197.

[39] Barclay, in *Concurrence and Unanimity*, 5, 7.

[40] Pen, "God's Call," in *Harmony*, 18.

[41] Fox, *Journal*, 31.

[42] Pen, in *Concurrence* (sermon preached at Wheeler Street, London, April 13, 1694), 83.

[43] Pen, "Two Made One," in *Harmony*, 197.

[44] Pen, "The Sure Foundation," in *Harmony*, 25 (emphasis in original).

[45] Creasey, "'Inward' and 'Outward,'" 13.

[46] Barbour, *Quakers in Puritan England*, 129.

[47] See Fox's brief 1553 sermon in *Severall Letters*, 15–16.

[48] Quakers held three kinds of meetings: (1) public meetings for evangelistic purposes ("threshing" meetings), (2) meetings for worship, and (3) business meetings (see Roberts, *Through Flaming Sword*, 99). The sermons of this study were delivered primarily at worship meetings, although Fox's addresses at yearly meetings fall into the third category.

[49] Fox, in *Richardson MSS* (sermon preached at Men's Meeting, Barbados, October, 1671), 125.

[50] Crisp, "Dawning of the Day," *Scripture-Truths*, 125.

[51] Bowater, in *Concurrence and Unanimity*, 56.

[52] Pen, "God's Call" in *Harmony*, 52.

[53] The concept of "ethos" has been the subject of investigation by rhetoricians from the time of Aristotle, who maintained that the speaker should produce proof in his discourse that he is (1) a person of high moral character, (2) a person competent to speak on the subject, and (3) a person of good will (see *Rhetoric*, book 1, chap. 2, and book 2, chap. 1).

[54] Fox, A sermon preached at Wheeler Street, June 1, 1680. *A Sermon . . . by Thomas Story*, in *Harmony*, 73–74.

[55] Crisp, "First and Great Commandment," in *Scripture-Truths*, 52.

[56] June 7, 1698, handwritten manuscript at Friends Historical Library of Swarthmore College, 9–10. For an extensive text in context analysis of this important sermon, see my "Thou art but a youth."

[57] Park, in *Concurrence and Unanimity*, 183.

[58] Bauman, "Aspects," 74.

Chapter 9

A portion of this chapter adapts and extends material in Michael Graves, "Mapping the Metaphors in George Fox's Sermons," in *New Light on George Fox, 1624–1691: A Collection of Essays*, ed. Michael Mullet, 45–59. (York England: William Sessions, 1994). Used by permission.

[1] See Braithwaite, *Second Period*, 251–89.

[2] Richard T. Vann, *The Social Development of English Quakerism, 1655–1755* (Cambridge, Mass.: Harvard University Press, 1969), 96.

[3] Williams, *Rich Heritage*, 95.

[4] Vann, *Social Development*, 101.

[5] Vann, *Social Development*, 102.

[6] Quoted in Trevett, *Women and Quakerism*, 56. For a scholarly discussion of Margaret Fell Fox's influence, see Trevett, 54–58.

[7] Fox, *Journal*, 13.

[8] It is possible, of course, that the journal was edited at a later date to reflect more of Fell's influence and to reflect a later use of the terms. This is not a viewpoint I hold.

[9] Larry H. Ingle, *First Among Friends: George Fox and the Creation of Quakerism* (New York: Oxford University Press, 1994), 252–55; 261–62.

[10] Russell, *History of Quakerism*, 132.

[11] For an account of Fox's journey, see *Journal*, 580–664.

[12] Ingle, *First Among Friends*, 253.

[13] Ingle, *First Among Friends*, 254 (emphasis in original).

[14] Ingle, *First Among Friends*, 254.

[15] Ingle, *First Among Friends*, 243. See Fox, *Journal*, 666–68.

[16] Ingle, *First Among Friends*, 246–49.

[17] Ingle, *First Among Friends*, 247.

[18] Russell, *History of Quakerism*, 75–76.

[19] Barclay, from Proposition XI, *Apology*.

[20] Henry J. Cadbury, "George Fox's Later Years," in *Journal of George Fox*, ed. John L. Nickalls (London: Religious Society of Friends, 1975), 733–34.

[21] Fox, paragraph 1. This and all subsequent citations of the sermon text are made with reference to paragraph numbers added to and included in the text of the sermon, which appears at the end of the chapter.

[22] Graves, "Mapping the Metaphors."

[23] Fox, *Journal*, 27.

[24] Fox, in *Richardson MSS* (sermon preached at a Women's Meeting, Barbados, October, 1671), 252.

[25] Fox, *Journal*, 666.

[26] Fox (sermon preached at Yearly Meeting, 1674), paragraph 4, paragraph 5.

[27] Fox (sermon preached at Yearly Meeting, 1674), paragraph 6.

[28] Fox (sermon preached at Yearly Meeting, 1674), paragraph 8.

[29] Fox (sermon preached at Yearly Meeting, 1674), paragraph 9, paragraph 10.

[30] Fox (sermon preached at Yearly Meeting, 1674), paragraphs 11–12.

[31] Gwyn, *Apocalypse of the Word*, 77.

[32] Gwyn, *Apocalypse of the Word*, 76 (emphasis in original).

[33] In this section, I have adapted portions of Graves, "Mapping the Metaphors." See particularly 52–54.

[34] The ubiquitous orientational metaphor is discussed in Lakoff and Johnson, *Metaphors We Live By*, 14–21. Mircea Eliade has analyzed the role of celestial symbols in relationship to height and rites of ascent in *The Sacred and the Profane: The Nature of Religion*, trans. Willard R. Trask (New York: Harcourt, Brace, Jovanovich, 1959), 118–29 and idem, *Images and Symbols: Studies in Religious Symbolism*, trans. Philip Mairet (New York: Sheed & Ward, 1961), 47–51.

[35] Fox, in *Richardson MSS* (sermon preached at Women's Meeting, October 1671), 273 (emphasis added).

[36] These examples are from Graves, "Mapping the Metaphors," 52–53 (emphasis added). In that essay, I propose the following: "In Fox's sermons, the orientational metaphor is more than mere habit. He goes out of his way to employ it" (53).

[37] Fox (sermon preached at Yearly Meeting, 1674), paragraph 12.

[38] Gwyn, *Apocalypse of the Word*, 31 (emphasis in original).

[39] Fox (sermon preached at Yearly Meeting, 1674), paragraph 16, paragraph 24. Space does not permit a reconsideration of the paradoxical tension between belief in the possibility of everyone's direct communication with God, and retaining a belief in the validity and necessity of preaching (a topic discussed in earlier chapters), nor does the 1674 sermon exploit this theme. For a scholarly discussion of this topic, see Bauman, *Let Your Words be Few*, 20–42.

[40] For a crisp, clear presentation of the situation facing Fox, Fell, and others, see Gwyn, "From Covenant to Contract: The Quaker Counter-Restoration," in *Heaven on Earth: Quakers and the Second Coming*, ed. Ben Pink Dandelion, Douglas Gwyn, and Timothy Peat (Birmingham, UK: Woodbrooke College and Curlew Publications, 1998), 130–38.

[41] Gwyn, "From Covenant to Contract," in *Heaven on Earth*, ed. Pink Dandelion, Gwyn, and Peat, 130, 132.

[42] Fox (sermon preached at Yearly Meeting, 1674), paragraph 13.

[43] See Gwyn, *Apocalypse of the Word*, 73–74.

[44] Fox (sermon preached at Yearly Meeting, 1674), paragraph 13.

[45] Fox (sermon preached at Yearly Meeting, 1674), paragraph 13.

[46] Fox (sermon preached at Yearly Meeting, 1674), paragraph 15.

[47] Fell, *Women's Speaking*, 8–10.

[48] Fell, *Women's Speaking*, 17.

[49] Fox (sermon preached at Yearly Meeting, 1674), paragraph 16.

[50] Fox (sermon preached at Yearly Meeting, 1674), paragraph 16.

[51] Key metaphors are in abundance. The sermon is an example of Fox's surprising ability to combine key Quaker metaphors with other metaphors into a cyclical, repetitive mosaic. The metaphors are abundant from paragraph 16 until the end of the sermon. Fox uses the good and bad seed, drawn from the Genesis account of the fall, and hunger-thirst metaphors—"Come feed here. I have bread"—in the same context (paragraph 16). Later, the seed becomes the seed sown by Christ, "the

Seed-man" (paragraph 20), "true seeds man," and "heavenly seedsman" (paragraph 21). Hearers are told to "feed on God's bread (paragraph 23) and to "Know your bread. Know your bread of God. Feed on the bread of God, that bread which is from above" (paragraph 24).

[52] Fox (sermon preached at Yearly Meeting, 1674), paragraph 16.

[53] Fox (sermon preached at Yearly Meeting, 1674), paragraphs 16, 17.

[54] Fox (sermon preached at Yearly Meeting, 1674), paragraph 20, 22, 23, 24.

[55] On the separation, see Braithwaite, *Second Period*, 290–323, 360–66, 469–82, and 494. See also Ingle, *First Among Friends*, 261–64.

[56] *Richardson MSS* 208–22. Sermon given at a general meeting, London. April 4, 1674, typed copy at the Library of the Religious Society of Friends, London. Transcribed April 3, 2002, by Michael P. Graves. "{}" indicates page numbers in *Richardson MSS*, typed copy.

Chapter 10

Much of this chapter is reprinted from "Stephen's Crisp's Short History as Spiritual Journey," *Quaker Religious Thought* 26 (1993): 5-23; and "Robert Barclay and the Rhetoric of the Inward Light," *Quaker Religious Thought* 26 (1993): 17-32. Used by permission.

[1] These sermons were published in Crisp, *Scripture-Truths*.

[2] *Dictionary of Quaker Biography*, ed. Edward Milligan, typed manuscript at the Library of the Religious Society of Friends, London. "Crisp, Steven (1628–1692) (Stephen)," unpaginated. Hereafter referred to as *DQB*.

[3] "Testimony of the Mens Meeting at Colchester Concerning Stephen Crisp," August 17, 1692 (unpaginated), in Crisp, *The Christian Experiences, Gospel Labours and Writings, of . . . Stephen Crisp* (London: T. Sowle, 1694).

[4] Crisp, *A Short History*. Written in 1691, the piece was not included among Crisp's works collected and published by John Field under the title *A Memorable Account . . . of . . . Stephen Crisp, in his Books and Writings herein collected*, ed. John Field (London, 1694). This compilation was later published as *The Christian Experiences, Gospel Labours and Writings, of . . . Stephen Crisp* (Philadelphia: Benjamin & Thomas Kite, 1822). The most recent and only twentieth-century publication of *A Short History* was produced by the Tract Association of Friends in the 1970s.

[5] "Testimony of the Mens Meeting at Colchester," in Crisp, *Christian Experiences*, n.p.

[6] "Testimony of the Mens Meeting at Colchester," in Crisp, *Christian Experiences*, n.p.

[7] For a scholarly account of these times, see Braithwaite, *Second Period*, 21–114.

[8] Crisp, *Christian Experiences*, 59.

[9] Crisp, "Word of God," paragraph 1. The sermon is included in Crisp, *Scripture-Truths*, 26–45. This and all subsequent citations of the sermon text are made with reference to paragraph numbers added to and included in the text of the sermon, which appears at the end of the chapter.

[10] Crisp, "Word of God," paragraphs 2, 3, 4.

[11] Crisp, "Word of God," paragraph 5.

[12] Crisp, "Word of God," paragraph 7.

[13] Crisp's *A Short History* features various kinds of "tests" and employs "unburdening" and "stripping" symbols. See my "Stephen Crisp's *Short History*," 17–18.

[14] Crisp, "Word of God," paragraph 8.

[15] Crisp, "Word of God," paragraph 9.

[16] Crisp, *Christian Experiences*, 370.

[17] Crisp, "Word of God," paragraph 8.

[18] Crisp, "Word of God," paragraph 10.

[19] Crisp, "Word of God," paragraph 13 (emphasis in original).

[20] Crisp, "Word of God," paragraph 14.

[21] Crisp, "Word of God," paragraphs 15, 18, 16.

[22] Crisp, "Word of God," paragraph 21.

[23] Crisp, "Word of God," paragraph 22.

[24] Crisp, "Word of God," paragraph 23.

[25] Crisp, "Word of God," paragraph 24.

[26] Crisp, "Word of God," paragraph 24.

[27] Crisp, "Word of God," paragraph 26.

[28] Crisp, "Word of God," paragraph 26.

[29] Crisp, "Word of God," paragraph 26.

[30] Cope, "Seventeenth Century Quaker Style," 736.

[31] Chalkley's 1698 sermon is also significantly self-reflexive.

[32] Stephen Crisp, *Scripture-Truths Demonstrated: In Thirty Two Sermons or Declarations of Mr. Stephen Crisp* (London: J. Sowle, 1707), 28–45.

Chapter 11

[1] I have developed this biographical paragraph through recourse to Trueblood's intelligent biography of Barclay and a helpful entry on Barclay in *The Dictionary of National Biography*, edited by Leslie Stephen and Sidney Lee, 22 vols. (London: Oxford University Press, 1973 [hereafter referred to as *DNB*]). I also perused two Web sites I judge to be reliable, located at http://freepages.genealogy.rootsweb.com/~barclay/HistoryLore.htm ("Barclay Family History & Lore," accessed November 6, 2006) and http://www.mearns.org.uk/stonehaven/barclay.htm ("The Barclay's of Stonehaven," accessed November 6, 2006).

[2] See the discussions of Barclay's background and influence in Braithwaite, *Second Period* (385–98) and Wright, *Literary Life of the Early Friends* (55–56).

[3] Barclay, *DNB*, 1089.

[4] Barclay, *Concurrence and Unanimity*.

[5] Barclay, *Apology*, 321–22.

[6] Barclay, paragraph 1. This and all subsequent citations of the sermon text are made with reference to paragraph numbers added to and included in the text of the sermon, which appears at the end of the chapter.

[7] Barclay, paragraph 1.

[8] Barclay, paragraph 1. Braithwaite accuses Barclay of failing to declare the "coexistence of the Divine and the human in Christ and in human personality" (*Second Period*, 384). Braithwaite notes that Barclay is "cautious" and "is content with affirming the value both of the historic life of Christ in the flesh and of the inward experience of His life, without attempting to explain their relation to one another fully" (385). The

sermon affirms both the historical Jesus as revealed in the Scriptures and the necessity of "having Christ" experientially.

[9] Barclay, paragraph 2.

[10] Barclay, paragraphs 5, 3, 4, 5, 5.

[11] See Lakoff and Johnson, *Metaphors We Live By*, 14–21.

[12] Barclay, paragraph 6.

[13] Barclay, paragraph 5.

[14] Barclay, paragraph 6.

[15] Barclay, paragraph 6.

[16] See chapter 3.

[17] Barclay, paragraph 6.

[18] Chalkley implies that he is speaking under the unction of immediate inspiration in his 1698 sermon. See my "Thou art but a youth."

[19] Barclay, *Apology*, 360.

[20] Barclay, paragraph 6.

[21] Barclay, paragraph 6.

[22] Pen, "A Sermon by William Pen, June 19, 1688," in *Harmony*. This sermon is addressed in chap. 12.

[23] Barclay's prayer addresses these concerns more directly. He prays that "true Christianity may be promoted and increased among thine heritage, that they may live in it, and shine forth in it as thy workmanship which thou hast created in Christ Jesus unto fruitfulness, unto all good works, that they may walk in them. . . . Lord God eternal, grant that the residue of men may seek after thee, and be sensible that thou art at work, and raising an house for thine honor, and promoting the kingdom of the Son, which is a kingdom of righteousness" (paragraph 11).

[24] *The Concurrence and Unanimity; Of the People Called Quakers* (London, J. Sowle, 1711), 1–10.

Chapter 12

Whereas this study focuses on Pen's significant rhetorical choices in the sermon, a lengthier rhetorical analysis of the sermon was previously presented as the George Richardson Lecture at the Quaker Studies Research Association at Woodbrooke Quaker Studies Centre, Birmingham, England, in fall 2005. The paper was later published as Graves, "Travelers Here in this Vale of Tears: William Pen Preaches a Funeral Sermon," *Quaker Studies* 12, no. 1 (2007): 7–25. This chapter draws heavily from the longer essay. The author gratefully acknowledges permission to reprint portions of this.

[1] The entries on Pen in the *DNB* and *American National Biography* [John A. Garraty and Mark C. Carnes, eds. [New York: Oxford University Press, 1999] hereafter referred to as *ANB*) command nine and four pages, respectively, alerting the reader to the fact that Pen was a person of significance on both sides of the Atlantic.

[2] The sermons are found in Pen, *Concurrence and Unanimity*; and *A Farewell Sermon Preached by William Penn on Sunday Being the 6th Instant, at the Quakers Meeting-House at Westminster* (London, 1699).

[3] *ANB* 17:293.

[4] The story of Quaker colonization is told in Braithwaite, *Second Period*, 399–411. For a more popular, but intelligent, rendering of this story, see Catherine O. Peare, *William Penn: A Biography* (Philadelphia: J. B. Lippincott, 1957), 245–83.

[5] Pen, "A William Pen Chronology, 1644–1726," in *William Penn's Published Writings, 1660–1726: An Interpretive Bibliography*, vol. 2: *The Papers of William Penn*, ed. Edward B. Bronner and David Fraser (Philadelphia: University of Pensylvania Press, 1985), 21.

[6] *DNB* 15:759.

[7] Bronner and Fraser, *William Penn's Published Writings*, 21.

[8] Bronner and Fraser, *William Penn's Published Writings*, 21.

[9] Braithwaite, *Second Period*, 160.

[10] For an account of Pen's later years, see Braithwaite, *Second Period*, 151–78, and Peare, *William Penn*, 284–414.

[11] For helpful scholarly background on the momentous effects of Nayler's life on the subsequent development of Quakerism, see Bittle, *James Nayler 1618–1660*; Braithwaite, *Beginnings*, 241–78; and Ingle, *First among Friends*, 119–35.

[12] Braithwaite, *Beginnings*, 252.

[13] Quoted in Braithwaite, *Beginnings*, 263.

[14] Braithwaite, *Beginnings*, 267, 268.

[15] Trevett, *Women and Quakerism*, 39.

[16] *DNB* 16:1089. Regrettably, I have been unable to discover any record of Travers' preaching.

[17] *DNB* 16:1089.

[18] Trevett, *Women and Quakerism*, 39, 151.

[19] Curiously, despite the importance of oral and printed memorials among early Friends, to my knowledge there were only two full-text funeral sermons to survive from the period before 1700. One is the sermon delivered by Pen. The other is a sermon by Robert Barrow titled "The Testimony of Robert Barrow 11th Mo 16th 1691 at George Fox Burial, Where Were Supposed to Be Four Thousand Friends Besides Other People, 1691" (copy book, MSS Albums, Friends Historical Library, Swarthmore, Pa.). There may be additional funeral sermons extant in the individual collections of Quaker meetings that I have not visited, or owned by people I do not know. At any rate, with less than one hundred Quaker sermons of any sort surviving from the seventeenth century, we are fortunate to have even two funeral sermons at hand. For an account of the types of things people said at graveside services, see Braithwaite, *Second Period*, 163, 416, and the following pages.

[20] For a succinct introduction to the subject, see Frye, "The Journey as Metaphor," 212–26.

[21] Ewert Cousins, informational letter describing a National Endowment for the Humanities Seminar for College Teachers (fall 1985), 1. My understanding of the medieval spiritual journey, its patterns, and common episodes has been profoundly influenced by Professor Cousins, under whose guidance I studied as an NEH fellow at a Summer Seminar for College Teachers at Fordham University during the summer of 1986.

[22] See especially "Notes on Processual Symbolic Analysis," in Victor Turner and Edith Turner, *Image and Pilgrimage in Christian Culture: Anthropological Perspectives* (New York: Columbia University Press, 1978) 245–51.

[23] Victor Turner, "Liminal to Liminoid," in *From Ritual to Theatre: The Human Seriousness of Play* (New York: Performing Arts Journal, 1982), 44.

[24] Turner, "Liminal to Liminoid," 47, 48.

[25] Pen, paragraph 1. This and all subsequent citations of the sermon text are made with reference to paragraph numbers added to and included in the text of the sermon, which appears at the end of the chapter.

[26] Pen, paragraphs 4, 5.

[27] This is the argument presented by those who interpret Quaker history in terms of realized eschatology. See writings by Gwyn and Pink Dandelion in the bibliography.

[28] Pen, paragraph 7.

[29] Turner, "Liminal to Liminoid," 44.

[30] Rebecca Travers, *A Message from the Spirit of Truth unto the Holy Seed* (London: Thomas Simmons, 1658).

[31] Pen, paragraph 7.

[32] William Pen, *No Cross, No Crown*, in *William Penn on Religion and Ethics*, ed. Hugh S. Barbour, 39–113, quotation on p. 112.

[33] Pen, *No Cross, No Crown*, 113.

[34] Here Pen follows Bownas' preference for indirection.

[35] Pen, paragraph 4.

[36] Turner, "Liminal to Liminoid," 48.

[37] Pen, paragraph 5.

[38] Turner, "Liminal to Liminoid," 48.

[39] Pen, paragraph 8.

[40] *The Concurrence and Unanimity; Of the People Called Quakers* (London, J. Sowle, 1711), 73–77.

Epilogue

[1] Wright, *Literary Life of the Early Friends*, 146.

Appendix A

[1] As a result of the search initiated for my dissertation in 1971, I compiled a checklist of all Quaker sermons then known to me covering the years 1650–1700. It lists seventy-four authentic sermons delivered by Quakers during the period plus additional sermons that include oral presentations from George Keith's splinter group, the Society of Christian Quakers. Subsequently, the list was published as Graves, "Checklist of Extant Quaker Sermons, 1650–1700," in *Quaker History* 63 (1974): 53–57. The checklist has been updated and included as appendix B.

[2] Some of these prophetic utterances were taken down and preserved in "Letters, Dreams & Visions," in "One Hundred and twenty-seven letters," manuscript, vol. S.78, Library of the Religious Society of Friends, London. "Letters, Dreams & Visions" is a fascinating manuscript collection consisting primarily of letters but also including brief prophetic utterances and descriptions of visions.

[3] Friends Historical Library contains 45,000 volumes of books, pamphlets, and periodicals relevant to the history of Quakerism as well as an extensive collection of more than 400 manuscripts. The Quaker Collection of Haverford College Library

contains more than 32,000 printed volumes on Quakerism, including the 1,600 rare Quaker tracts and pamphlets of the William H. Jenks Collection, most of which are from the seventeenth century. In addition to the Jenks Collection, the Quaker Collection lists more than 2,000 other seventeenth-century printed works. The manuscript collection at Haverford lists 60,000 items, including "Letters and Papers of William Pen" and the *Richardson MSS*, a source of nine of George Fox's sermons. In addition, the Quaker Collection also contains 200 reels of microfilm records, including the Minutes of London Yearly Meeting for the years 1668–1860, and the *Swarthmore MSS* of the Library of the Religious Society of Friends, located at Friends House, London.

[4] The Library of the Religious Society of Friends, London, is the largest repository of Quaker material outside the United States and includes 60,000 books and pamphlets and extensive manuscript sources. Particularly helpful to this project were the manuscript and typescript copies of the "Minutes of Monday Morning Meeting" covering the years 1673–1700, the key records of the meeting of Friends ministers in the London area, and the original copy and typed copy of the *Richardson MSS*.

[5] Between Woodbrooke's regular collection and the Bevan-Naish Collection, Woodbrooke Quaker Library "contains over half of all items published in the 17th century by Quakers" (http://www.woodbrooke.org.uk/index.php?main=pages&page=39, accessed April 27, 2008).

[6] My list of surviving early Quaker sermons has grown from the original seventy-four that comprised the database for my 1972 dissertation to seventy-nine, and I expect that a limited number of sermons may still be extant and lie undiscovered. From my experience, the principal reason that the list is mutable is that many of the surviving sermons not found in print are catalogued as "testimonies," "declarations," "prophecies," etc., instead of as "sermons." To further perplex the researcher, most of the items catalogued as testimonies, declarations, prophecies, etc.—and they are legion—upon examination prove not to be sermons. Cataloging protocols appear to marginalize the significance of preaching among Friends and make it more difficult to discover sermons.

[7] Bownas, "Life," in *Friends' Library*, 3:57, quoted in Wright, *Literary Life of the Early Friends*, 144. Bracketed material is Wright's.

[8] Savery, *Some Remarks on the Practice of Taking Down and Publishing the Testimonies of Ministering Friends* (London: James Phillips and Son, 1797), 6–7.

[9] Mitchell, *English Pulpit Oratory*, 36–37.

[10] See Lester Thonssen and A. Craig Baird, *Speech Criticism: The Development of Standards for Rhetorical Appraisal* (New York: Ronald Press, 1948), 297–311, for the still very relevant protocol for establishing the authenticity of speech texts.

[11] Fox, *Collection of Several Sermons*.

[12] The editor has collected what appear to be examples of faulty style, what could be described as Quaker preachers at their worst moments, as it were, in the impromptu speaking situation. Far from being a justification to exclude these examples, this becomes a prime reason to include them, because they have the potential to provide examples of the range of rhetorical skill exhibited by the preachers.

[13] Fox, *Richardson MSS*, Library of the Religious Society of Friends, London. I have also consulted the identical copy of the manuscript at Haverford College Library, Quaker Collection, Haverford, Pa. The pages cited in this study refer to a typed copy

of the *MSS* found at the Library of the Religious Society of Friends, London. For a description of the *MSS* and a brief historical account of their origin, see Henry J. Cadbury, "Richardson MSS," *Journal of the Friends Historical Society* 32 (1935): 34–37.

[14] Some of Fox's sermons exist in additional manuscript collections and print sources. For example, for Fox's sermon at Yearly Meeting, London, June 9, 1674, there is an incomplete copy in the *Headley MSS*, 247–61, at the Library of the Religious Society of Friends, London. The *Headley MSS* also contain Fox's sermon at Yearly Meeting, London, June 11, 1674, 262–83. Fox's sermon given to a general meeting at Barbados was printed as *Gospel Family-Order, being a Short Discourse Concerning the Ordering of Families both of Whites & Blacks and Indians* (London, 1676). Fox's sermon at Wheeler Street, London, June 1, 1680, is also found in the *Swarthmore MSS* at the Library of the Religious Society of Friends, London, and, in addition, in a volume printed in America, *A Sermon Preached at the Meeting House of the People Called Quakers . . . with an appendix, containing an original Sermon of George Fox* (Philadelphia, Pa., 1825), 18–25. His sermon at Yearly Meeting, London, May 25 or 26, 1675, may be found in the *Penington MSS*, vol. 4, 90–98, located at the Library of the Religious Society of Friends, London. Two of Fox's sermons, Devonshire House, April, 1677, and Yearly Meeting, London, April, 1678, can be found only in the *Richardson MSS*, typed copy, 153–61, and 176–84, respectively.

[15] Fox, "Sermon," in W. Dewsbury, J. Nayler, G. Fox, and J. Whitehead, *Severall Letters to the Saints of the Most High*, (n.p., 1654). The sermon is prefaced with the words "1653 This Precept was written from the Mouth of George Fox, as he spoke it forth, by a Friend of Truth." I am indebted to T. Canby Jones for this reference.

[16] (London: J. Sowle, 1707).

[17] The preface, although unsigned, bore the initials "N. C.," which probably stand for "Nathaniel Crouch." See Wright, *Literary Life of the Early Friends*, 145–46.

[18] (London: J. Sowle, 1711).

[19] (London: J. Sowle, 1723).

[20] Anonymous, *A Quakers Sermon Preached at the Bull-and-Mouth Meeting-House, In St. Martin-Le-Grand, London, On Sunday the 16th of Nov. 1674*, n.p., 1674. The use of "Sunday" and "Nov." indicates a non-Quaker publisher.

[21] Pen, *A Farewell Sermon*.

[22] Isaac Alexander, "Issac Alexander's Prophecy delivered at Chester Dec: 12th: 1699." John Thompson MSS. Library of the Religious Society of Friends, London, 16. A slightly different version of the brief sermon with the title "Report of Isaac Alexander's Testimony or Message delivered at Chester Meeting ye 11th of 12th mo 1699" is found in *Letters, Dreams & Visions*, Library of the Religious Society of Friends, London, 69. Alexander's sermon is the only complete sermon in this collection from the period before 1700. Each of these versions of Alexander's sermon includes a note indicating that the sermon was taken down in shorthand by William Low Jr. (Thompson MSS, 16; *Letters, Dreams & Visions*, 69).

[23] Barrow, "Testimony of Robert Barrow." I have been unable to find the original of this nineteenth-century copy.

[24] Chalkley, *Mr. T. Chalkley's Sermon & Prayer*. This is the only surviving sermon delivered during the seventeenth century by Chalkley. See my "Thou Art but a Youth," 229–74.

[25] Thomas Wilson, *Harvey MSS*, 1/27a, Library of the Religious Society of Friends, London.

Appendix B

Appendix B is an extensive revision of Michael Graves' "A Checklist of Extant Quaker Sermons, 1650–1700," Quaker History 69 (Spring 1974). Used by permission.

Appendix C

[1] The number refers to the sermon number in appendix B, the Checklist of Quaker Sermons, 1650–1700.

[2] The list indicates that the word or its derivative appears or that the preacher discusses the topic.

BIBLIOGRAPHY

PRIMARY SOURCES

A Sermon Preached at the Meeting House of the People Called Quakers . . . with an appendix, containing an original Sermon of George Fox. Philadelphia, 1825.

Alexander, Isaac. "Isaac Alexander's Prophecy delivered at Chester Dec: 12th: 1699." John Thompson MSS. Library of the Religious Society of Friends, London, 16.

————. "Report of Isaac Alexander's Testimony or Message delivered at Chester Meeting ye 11th of 12th mo 1699." *Letters, Dreams & Visions.* Library of the Religious Society of Friends, London.

Annual Catalogue of George Fox's Papers, MSS. Library of the Religious Society of Friends, London.

Anonymous. *A Quakers Sermon Preached at the Bull-and-Mouth Meeting-House, In St. Martins-Le-Grand, London, On Sunday the 16th of Nov. 1674.* N.p., 1674.

————. *The Spirit of Quakerism, and the Danger of their Divine Revelation, Laid Open.* London, 1696.

Arderne, James. *Directions Concerning the Matter and Stile of Sermons.* Edited by John Mackey. Oxford: Basil Blackwell, 1962. First published in 1671.

Aristotle. *On Rhetoric: A Theory of Civic Discourse.* Translated by George Kennedy. New York: Oxford University Press, 1991.

Bacon, Francis. "Novum Organon." In *The New Organon and Related Writings.* Edited by F. H. Anderson. New York: Liberal Arts Press, 1960.

————. *The Twoo Bookes of Francis Bacon on the Proficience and Advancement of Learning Divine and Humane.* In *Selected Writings of Francis Bacon.* Edited by Hugh G. Dick. New York: Random House, 1955.

Barclay, Robert. *An Apology for the True Christian Divinity.* Philadelphia: Friends Book-Store, 1867. First English language publication in 1678.

————. *The Possibility and Necessity of the Inward and Immediate Revelation of the Spirit of God.* In *Truth Triumphant through the . . . Writings of . . . Robert Barclay.* London, 1692.

Barrow, Robert. "The Testimony of Robert Barrow 11th Mo 16th 1691 at George Fox Burial, Where Were Supposed to Be Four Thousand Friends Besides

Other People, 1691." Copy book, MSS Albums, Friends Historical Library, Swarthmore, Pa.

Baxter, Richard. "Gildas Salvianus." In *The Reformed Pastor*, 1656. 2nd ed. Edited by John T. Wilkinson. London: Epworth, 1950.

Blount, Thomas. *The Academy of Eloquence*. London: Ane Mosely, and are to be sold by, 1664.

Bownas, Samuel. *An Account of the Life, Travels and Christian Experiences in the Work of the Ministry*. London: L. Hinde, 1756. Also published and widely available as Samuel Bownas, "Life." In William Evans, and Thomas Evans. *The Friends' Library Comprising Journals, Doctrinal Treatises, and Other Writings of Members of the Religious Society of Friends*. Philadelphia: J. Rakestraw, 1837. Vol. 3, no. 57.

———. *A Description of the Qualifications Necessary to a Gospel Minister*. London: L. Hindeinde, *1750*. Philadelphia: Pendle Hill Publications and Tract Association of Friends, 1989.

Bunyan, John. *The Pilgrim's Progress from This World, to That Which Is to Come Delivered Under the Similitude of a Dream, Wherein Is Discovered the Manner of His Setting Out, His Dangerous Journey, and Safe Arrival at the Desired Country*. London: Printed for Nath. Ponder, 1678.

Chalkley, Thomas. *Mr. T. Chalkley's Sermon & Prayer*. Manuscript at Friends Historical Library, Swarthmore College.

———. *Some Considerations on the Call, Work, and Wages, of the Ministers of Christ* (1720). In *A Collection of the Works of Thomas Chalkley in Two Parts*. Philadelphia: B. Franklin & D. Hall, 1749.

A Collection of Several Sermons and Testimonies. London: B. Beardwell, 1701.

Concurrence and Unanimity, The; Of the People Called Quakers. London: J. Sowle, 1711.

Coole, Benjamin. *The Quakers Cleared from Being Apostates or the Hammer Defeated*. London: T. Sowle, 1696.

Crisp, Stephen. *The Christian Experiences, Gospel Labours and Writings, of . . . Stephen Crisp*. London: T. Sowle, 1694.

———. *An Epistle of Tender Love and Brotherly Advice*. In *The Christian Experiences, Gospel Labours and Writings of . . . Stephen Crisp*. Philadelphia: Benjamin & Thomas Kite, 1822.

———. *A Memorable Account . . . of . . . Stephen Crisp, in his Books and Writings herein collected*. Edited by John Field. London, 1694.

———. *Scripture-Truths Demonstrated: In Thirty-Two Sermons or Declarations of Mr. Stephen Crisp*. London: J. Sowle, 1707.

———. *A Short History of a Long Travel from Babylon to Bethel*. London: J. Sowle, 1711. Reprint, Philadelphia: Friends Tract Society, n.d.

Day, Angel. *The English Secretorie Wherein Is Contayned a Perfect Method for the Indıtıng of All Manner of Epistles and Familiar Letters, Together with Their Diversities, Enlarged by Examples Under Their Severall Tytles*. London: Robert Waldegraue, 1586.

de la Ramee, Pierre. *The Art of Logic*. London: Nicholas Bourne, 1626.

Descartes, Rene. *Discourse on Method*. In *A Discourse on Method and Selected Writings*. Translated by John Veitch. New York: Dutton, 1951.

———. *Rules for the Direction of the Mind*. Translated by Laurence J. Lafleur. Indianapolis: Bobbs-Merrill, 1961.

Farnaby, Thomas. *Index Rhetoricus, 1625*. English linguistics, 1500-1800; a collection of facsimile reprints, no. 240. Menston: Scolar P., 1970

Fell, Margaret. *A Call to the Universall Seed of God*. N.p.: 1664.

————. *A Touch-Stone: or, A perfect tryal by the Scriptures, of all the priests, bishops, and ministers, who have called themselves, the ministers of the Gospel . . . Unto which is annexed, Womens speaking justified, &c*. London: [s.n.], 1667.

————. *Womens Speaking Justified, Proved and Allowed of by the Scriptures*. In *Womens Speaking Justified*. Edited by Christine Trevett. London: Quaker Home Service, 1989. Originally printed in 1666, this is a reprint of the 1667 edition. Citations are to the 1667 edition.

Fenner, Dudley. *The Artes of Logike and Rethorike [Sic] Plainelie Set Foorth in the Englishe Tounge, Easie to Be Learned and Practised: Togeather with Examples for the Practise of the Same, for Methode in the Gouernment of the Familie, Prescribed in the Word of God, and for the Whole in the Resolution or Opening of Certaine Partes of Scripture, According to the Same*. Middelburg: [R. Schilders], 1584.

Fox, George. "1653 This Precept was written from the Mouth of George Fox, as he spoke it forth, by a Friend of Truth." In *Severall Letters to the Saints of the Most High*. Sermon. N.p., 1654.

————. *An Epistle to all People on the Earth*. London: Giles Calvert, 1657.

————. *Gospel Family-Order, being a Short Discourse Concerning the Ordering of Families both of Whites & Blacks and Indianns*. London, 1676.

————. *Journal of George Fox*. Edited by John L. Nickalls. London: Religious Society of Friends, 1975.

————. *Narrative Papers of George Fox*. Edited by Henry J. Cadbury. Richmond, Ind.: Friends United Press, 1972.

————. *"The Power of the Lord Is Over All": The Pastoral Letters of George Fox*. Edited by T. Canby Jones. Richmond, Ind.: Friends United Press, 1989.

————. *Something Concerning Silent Meetings*. Broadside. N.p., n.d.

Fox, George, John Stubbs, and Benjamin Furly. *A Battle-Door for Teachers & Professors to Learn Singular & Plural*. London: 1660.

Furly, John. *A Testimony to the True Light*. London: [s.n.], 1670. In the collection of the British Library.

Glanvill, Joseph. *An Essay Concerning Preaching: Written for the Direction of a Young Divine*. London: 1678.

Harmony of Divine and Heavenly Doctrines, The. London: J. Sowle, 1696.

Harwood, John T., Aristotle, and Bernard Lamy. *The Rhetorics of Thomas Hobbes and Bernard Lamy*. Landmarks in rhetoric and public address. Carbondale, Ill: Southern Illinois University Press, 1986.

Headley MSS. 1 vol. Library of the Religious Society of Friends, London.

Hoskins, John, and Hoyt H. Hudson. *Directions for Speech and Style*. Princeton: Princeton University Press, 1935.

"Letters, Dreams & Visions." In "One Hundred and twenty-seven letters." Manuscript, vol. S.78. London: Library of the Religious Society of Friends.

Locke, John. *An Essay Concerning Human Understanding*. New York: Dover Publications, 1959. First published in 1690.

Longinus. *On Great Writing*. Translated by G. M. A. Grube. Indianapolis: Bobbs-Merrill, 1957.

Marshall, Charles. *An Epistle to Friends Coming forth in the Beginning of a Testimony and of the Snares of the Enemy therein*. N.p., 1775. First published in 1675.

Minutes of Monday Morning Meeting. Typescript. Transcribed by Edward H. Milligan. 2 vols.: 1673–1693, 1694–1700. London: Library of the Religious Society of Friends.

Pemble, William. *Enchiridion Oratorium*. Oxford: J. Lichfield, 1633.

Pennington MSS. Library of the Religious Society of Friends, London.

Penn, William. *The Concurrence and Unanimity; Of the People Called Quakers*. London: J. Sowle, 1711.

———. *A Farewell Sermon Preached by Mr. William Penn on Sunday being the 6th instant, at the Quakers Meeting-House at Westminster*. London: for A. B., 1699.

———. *The Great Case of Liberty of Conscience*. In *The Witness of William Penn*. Edited by Frederick B. Tolles and E. Gordon Alderfer. New York: Macmillan, 1957.

———. *More Fruits of Solitude*. In *The Harvard Classics*. Edited by Charles W. Eliot. New York: P. F. Collier & Son, 1937.

———. *No Cross, No Crown*. In *William Penn on Religion and Ethics*. Edited by Hugh S. Barbour Studies in American Religion 53. Lewiston, N.Y.: Edwin Mellen, 1991.

———. *Primitive Christianity Revived*. London: T. Sowle, 1696.

———. *The Rise and Progress of the People Called Quakers*. Philadelphia: For sale at Friends' bookstore, 1870. Originally printed as the preface to George Fox's *Journal*.

———. *Some Fruits of Solitude*. In *The Harvard Classics*. Edited by Charles W. Eliot. New York: P. F. Collier & Son, 1937.

———. *Urim and Thummim, or, The Apostolical Doctrines of Light and Perfection Maintained Against the Opposite Plea of Samuel Grevill (a Pretended Minister of the Gospel) in His Ungospel-Like Discourse against a Book Entituled A Testimony of the Light Within, Anciently Writ by Alexander Parker*. London: [s.n.], 1674.

———. *William Penn on Religion and Ethics: The Emergence of Liberal Quakerism*. Edited by Hugh S. Barbour. Studies in American Religion 53. Lewiston, N.Y.: Edwin Mellen, 1991.

Perkins, William. *The Arte of Prophecying, or, A Treatise Concerning the Sacred and Onely True Manner and Method of Preaching*. Vol. 2: *Workes*. Translated by Thomas Tuke. London, 1606; London, 1613–1616.

———. "The Foundation of Christian Religion." *Works*. Cambridge, 1600.

———. *Workes*. 3 vols. London, 1616–1618.

Puttenham, George, Richard Puttenham, John Lumley Lumley, Frank Whigham, and Wayne A. Rebhorn. *The Art of English Poesy*. Ithaca: Cornell University Press, 2007.

Richardson MSS. 1 vol. Original and typescript. Library of the Religious Society of Friends. London, n.d.

Savery, William. *Some Remarks on the Practice of Taking Down and Publishing the Testimonies of Ministering Friends*. London: James Phillips & Son, 1797.

["Sermon"] in Dewsbury, W., J. Nayler, G. Fox, and J. Whitehead. *Severall Letters to the Saints of the Most High*. n.p., 1654.

Sermon Preached Before the People Called Quakers in the Park of Southwark. London: Printed for N. H., 1688.

Sherry, Richard, and Desiderius Erasmus. *A Treatise of Schemes and Tropes (1550)*. Delmar, N.Y.: Scholars' Facsimiles & Reprints, 1977.

Smith, John. *Mystery of Rhetoric Unveiled, 1657*. English linguistics 1500–1800: a collection of facsimile reprints, no. 205. Menston (Yorks.): Scolar P., 1969.

Smith, Rebecca. *The Foundation of True Preaching Asserted*. London: Andrew Sowle, 1687.

Sprat, Thomas. *The History of the Royal-Society of London*. Edited by Jackson I. Cope and Harold Whitmore Jones. St. Louis: Washington University Studies, 1958.

Swarthmore MSS. 2 vols. London: Library of the Religious Society of Friends. Also on microfilm at Haverford College, Quaker Collection, Haverford, Pa.

Travers, Rebecca. *A Message from the Spirit of Truth unto the Holy Seed*. London: Thomas Simmons, 1658.

Vicars, Thomas. *Manuduction to the Rhetorical Art*. London, 1621.

Walker, Obadiah. *Some Instructions Concerning the Art of Oratory Collected for the Use of a Friend a Young Student*. London: Printed by J. G. for R. Royston, 1659.

Whitehead, George. *The Authority of the True Ministry*. . . . London: Robert Wilson, 1660.

———. *Christ Ascended above the Clouds*. London printed: [s.n.], 1669.

———. *Enthusiasm Above Atheism: Or, Divine Inspiration and Immediate Illumination* [by God Himself] *Asserted*. London: [s.n.], 1674.

———. *An Evangelical Epistle to the People of God, in Derision Call'd Quakers*. London: T. Sowle, 1704.

———. *The Glory of Christ's Light Within Expelling Darkness*. London: s.n., 1669.

———. *The Light and Life of Christ Within*. London: [s.n.], 1668.

Wilkins, John. *Ecclesiastes*. 8th ed. London: 1704. First edition, 1646.

Wilson, Thomas. *The Arte of Rhetorique, 1553. A Facsimile Reproduction with an Introd. by Robert Hood Bowers*. Delmar, N.Y.: Scholars Facsimiles & Reprints, 1977.

Wilson, Thomas. [Sermon]. *Harvey MSS*. 1/27a. London: Library of the Religious Society of Friends.

Winstanley, Gerrard. *The Works of Gerrard Winstanley*. Edited by George H. Sabine. Ithaca: Cornell University Press, 1941; New York: Russell & Russell, 1965.

Secondary Sources

American National Biography. Edited by John A. Garraty and Mark C. Carnes. New York: Oxford University Press, 1999.

Andrews, James R., Michael C. Leff, and Robert Terrill. *Reading Rhetorical Texts: An Introduction to Criticism*. Boston: Houghton Mifflin, 1998.

Angell, Stephen W. Review of *The Creation of Quaker Theory: Insider Perspectives*. Edited by Ben Pink Dandelion. *Quaker Studies* 10, no. 1 (2005): 116.

Appelbaum, Robert. *Literature and Utopian Politics in Seventeenth-Century England*. New York: Cambridge University Press, 2002.

Ashley, Maurice. *England in the Seventeenth Century*. Vol. 6: *The Pelican History of England*. 3rd ed. Baltimore: Penguin Books, 1961.

Ashton, T. S. *The Industrial Revolution 1760–1830*. London: Oxford University Press, 1964.

Atkins, Peter. *Memory and Liturgy: The Place of Memory in the Composition and Practice of Liturgy*. Brookfield, Vt.: Ashgate Publishing, 2004.

Baldwin, Charles Sears. *Medieval Rhetoric and Poetic*. New York: Macmillan, 1928; Glouchester, Mass.: Peter Smith, 1959.

Barbour, Hugh. *The Quakers in Puritan England*. Vol. 8, Yale Publications in Religion. New Haven: Yale University Press, 1964.

Barbour, Hugh and J. William Frost. *The Quakers*. Richmond, Ind.: Friends United Press, 1994.

Barbour, Hugh, and Arthur O. Roberts, eds. *Early Quaker Writings*. Grand Rapids: Eerdmans, 1973.

Barbour, Reid. *Literature and Religious Culture in Seventeenth-Century England*. New York: Cambridge University Press, 2002.

Barclay, Robert. *The Inner Life of the Religious Societies of the Commonwealth*. 2nd ed. London: Hodder & Stoughton, 1876.

Barish, Jonas A. *The Antitheatrical Prejudice*. Berkeley: University of California Press, 1981.

Barker, Simon. "Rigour or Vigour: Metaphor, Argument, and Internet." *Philosophy & Rhetoric* 31, no. 4 (1998): 248–65.

Bauman, Richard. "Aspects of Seventeenth Century Quaker Rhetoric." *Quarterly Journal of Speech* 56 (1970): 67–74.

———. *Let Your Words Be Few: Symbolism of Speaking and Silence among Seventeenth-Century Quakers*. Cambridge Studies in Oral and Literate Culture, no. 8. New York: Cambridge University Press, 1983.

———. "Quaker Folk-Linguistics and Folklore." In *Folklore: Performance and Communication*. Edited by Dan Ben-Amos and Kenneth S. Goldstein. The Hague: Mouton, 1975.

———. "Speaking in the Light: The Role of the Quaker Minister." In *Explorations in the Ethnography of Speaking*. Edited by Richard Bauman and Joel Sherzer. New York: Cambridge University Press, 1974.

Beacon, Margaret H. *The Quiet Rebels*. New York: Basic Books, 1969.

Beamish, Lucia K. *Quaker Ministry, 1691–1834*. Oxford: By the Author, 76c Woodstock Road, 1967.

Beck, Brenda E. F. "The Metaphor as a Mediator Between Semantic and Analogic Modes of Thought." *Current Anthropology* 19 (1978): 83–88.

Bercovitch, Sacvan. *The American Jeremiad*. Carbondale: Southern Illinois University Press, 1978.

———, ed. *The American Puritan Imagination: Essays in Revaluation*. New York: Cambridge University Press, 1975.

Bittle, William G. *James Nayler 1618–1660: The Quaker Indicted by Parliament*. York, UK: William Sessions, 1986.

Bizzell, Patricia, and Bruce Herzberg. *The Rhetorical Tradition: Readings from Classical Times To The Present.* 2nd ed. Boston: Bedford/St. Martin's, 2001.

Black, Max. "Metaphor." *Proceedings of the Aristotelian Society* 55 (1954–1955): 273–94.

———. *Models and Metaphors: Studies in Language and Philosophy.* Ithaca: Cornell University Press, 1962.

Bodkin, Maud. *Archetypal Patterns in Poetry.* London: Oxford University Press, 1934.

Bonaventure. *The Soul's Journey into God.* Edited by Ewert H. Cousins. New York: Paulist Press, 1978.

Borchers, Timothy. *Rhetorical Theory: An Introduction.* Belmont, Calif.: Thomson Wadsworth, 2006.

Borman, Ernest G. "The Puritan Rhetorical Style." In *The Force of Fantasy: Restoring the American Dream.* Carbondale: Southern Illinois University Press, 1985.

Brailsford, H. N. *The Levellers and the English Revolution.* Edited by Christopher Hill. Stanford: Stanford University Press, 1961.

Braithwaite, William C. *The Beginnings of Quakerism.* 2nd ed. Edited by Henry J. Cadbury. Cambridge: Cambridge University Press, 1955. Reprint, 1961.

———. *The Second Period of Quakerism.* 2nd ed. Edited by Henry J. Cadbury. Cambridge: Cambridge University Press, 1961.

Brayshaw, A. Neave. *The Quakers: Their Story and Message.* 3d ed. London: George Allen & Unwin, 1938.

Brilioth, Yngve. *A Brief History of Preaching.* Translated by Karl E. Mattson. Philadelphia: Fortress, 1965.

Bronner, Edwin B., and David Fraser, eds. *William Penn's Published Writings, 1660–1726: An Interpretive Bibliography.* Vol. 5: *The Papers of William Penn.* Philadelphia: University of Pennsylvania Press, 1986.

Brown, John. *Puritan Preaching in England: A Study of Past and Present.* New York: Charles Scribner's Sons, 1900.

Brown, Louise Fargo. *The Political Activities of the Baptists and Fifth Monarchy Men in England During the Interregnum.* New York: Burt Franklin, 1964.

Brummett, Barry, ed. *Reading Rhetorical Theory.* New York: Harcourt College, 2000.

Burke, Kenneth. *A Grammar of Motives and A Rhetoric of Motives.* Cleveland: Meridian Books/World Publishing, 1961.

———. *Permanence and Change.* Library of Liberal Arts. Indianapolis: Bobbs-Merrill, 1965.

———. *A Rhetoric of Motives.* Berkeley: University of California Press, 1969.

Burke, Peter. "Popular Culture in Seventeenth-Century London." In *Popular Culture in Seventeenth-Century England.* Edited by Barry Reay. London: Routledge, 1988.

Burrage, Champlin. *The Early English Dissenters in the Light of Recent Research 1550–1641.* 2 vols. New York: Russell & Russell, 1967.

Butterworth, Michael L. "Purifying the Body Politic: Steroids, Rafael Palmeiro." *Western Journal of Communication* 72, no. 2 (2008): 145–61.

Cadbury, Henry J. "George Fox's Later Years." In *Journal of George Fox.* Edited by John L. Nickalls. London: Religious Society of Friends, 1975.

———. "Richardson MSS." *Journal of the Friends Historical Society* 32 (1935): 34–37.

Cameron, Lyn. "Metaphor Clusters in Discourse." *Journal of Applied Linguistics* 1, no. 2 (2004): 107–36.

Campbell, Paul Newell. "Metaphor and Linguistic Theory." *Quarterly Journal of Speech* 61 (1975): 1–12.

———. "Poetic-Rhetorical, Philosophical, and Scientific Discourse." *Philosophy & Rhetoric* 6, no. 1 (1973): 1–29.

———. "Symbolical Hierarchy: A Further Word." *Philosophy & Rhetoric* 9, no. 2 (1976): 116–22.

Chang-Ha Lim, Paul. *In Pursuit of Purity, Unity, and Liberty: Richard Baxter's Puritan Ecclesiology in Its Seventeenth-Century Context*. Leiden: Koninklijke Brill, 2004.

Chomsky, Noam. *Language and Mind*. 3rd ed. New York: Cambridge University Press, 2006.

Clark, Donald Leman. *John Milton at St. Paul's School: A Study of Ancient Rhetoric in English Renaissance Education*. New York: Columbia University Press, 1948.

———. *Rhetoric and Poetry in the Renaissance*. New York: Columbia University Press, 1922; New York: Russell & Russell, 1963.

Clark, George N. *The Later Stuarts 1660–1714*. Vol. 10: *The Oxford History of England*. 2nd ed. Edited by George Clark. Oxford: Clarendon, 1955.

Clark, Henry W. *History of English Nonconformity*. New York: Russell & Russell, 1965.

Cohen, Charles Lloyd. *God's Caress: The Psychology of Puritan Religious Experience*. New York: Oxford University Press, 1986.

Cohen, Ted. "Metaphor and the Cultivation of Intimacy." In *On Metaphor*. Edited by Sheldon Sacks. Chicago: University of Chicago Press, 1979.

Collinson, Patrick. *The Birthpangs of Protestant England: Religious and Cultural Change in the Sixteenth and Seventeenth Centuries*. New York: St. Martin's Press, 1988.

———. "Elizabethan and Jacobean Puritanism as Forms of Popular Religious Culture." In *The Culture of English Puritanism, 1560–1700*. Edited by Christopher Durston and Jacqueline Eales. Basingstoke, UK: Macmillan, 1996.

———. *The Elizabethan Puritan Movement*. Berkeley: University of California Press, 1967.

———. *Godly People: Essays on English Protestantism and Puritanism*. London: Hambledon Press, 1983.

———. *The Religion of Protestants: The Church in English Society, 1559–1625*. Oxford: Clarendon, 1982.

Conley, Thomas M. *Rhetoric in the European Tradition*. White Plains, N.Y.: Longman, 1990.

Cope, Jackson I. "Seventeenth Century Quaker Style." *Proceedings of the Modern Language Association* 71 (1956): 725–54.

Cousins, Ewert. NEH Letter. Fall, 1985.

Corbett, Edward P. J. *Classical Rhetoric for the Modern Student*. New York: Oxford University Press, 1965.

Creasey, Maurice A. "'Inward' and 'Outward': A Study in Early Quaker Language." *Journal of the Friends' Historical Society*. Suppl. no. 30. London: Friends' Historical Society, 1962.

"Crisp, Steven (1628–1692) (Stephen)." Typed biographical manuscript. London: Library of the Religious Society of Friends, n.d.

Crowley, Sharon. "Modern Rhetoric and Memory." In *Rhetorical Memory and Delivery: Classical Concepts for Contemporary Composition and Communication*. Edited by John Frederick Reynolds. Hillsdale, N.J.: Lawrence Erlbaum Associates, 1993.

Cunningham, John. *The Quakers from their Origin till the Present Time: An International History*. Edinburgh: John Menzies, 1868.

Dargan, Edwin C. *A History of Preaching*. 2 vols. New York: G. H. Doran, n.d., c. 1905–1912.

Darsey, James. "Must We All Be Rhetorical Theorists: An Anti-Democratic Inquiry." *Western Journal of Communication* 58 (1994): 164–81.

Davies, Godfrey. *The Crisis of the Aristocracy, 1558–1641*. Oxford: Clarendon, 1965.

———. *The Early Stuarts 1603–1660*. Vol. 9: *The Oxford History of England*. 2nd ed. Edited by George Clark. Oxford: Clarendon, 1959.

Davies, Horton. *The Worship of the American Puritans, 1629–1730*. New York: Peter Lang, 1990.

———. *The Worship of the English Puritans*. Morgan, Pa.: Soli Deo Gloria, 1997.

———. *Worship and Theology in England from Andrewes to Baxter and Fox, 1603–1690*. Vol. 2: *Worship and Theology in England*. Princeton: Princeton University Press, 1975.

Davis, Gerald L. *I Got the Word in Me and I Can Sing It, You Know: A Study of the Performed African-American Sermon*. Philadelphia: University of Pennsylvania, 1985.

The Dictionary of National Biography. Edited by Leslie Stephen and Sidney Lee. 22 vols. London: Oxford University Press, 1917; reprint 1973.

The Dictionary of Quaker Biography. Edited by Edward Milligan. Typed Manuscript. London: Library of the Religious Society of Friends, n.d.

Dorgan, Howard. *Giving Glory to God in Appalachia: Worship Practices of Six Baptist Subdenominations*. Knoxville: University of Tennessee, 1987.

Downey, James. *The Eighteenth Century Pulpit: A Study of the Sermons of Butler, Berkeley, Secker, Sterne, Whitefield, and Wesley*. Oxford: Clarendon, 1969.

Duhamel, P. Albert. "The Function of Rhetoric as Effective Expression." In *The Province of Rhetoric*. Edited by Joseph Schwartz and John A. Rycenga. New York: Ronald Press, 1965.

Ehninger, Douglas. "On Rhetorics and Rhetoric." *Western Speech* 31 (1967): 242–49.

———. "On Systems of Rhetoric." *Philosophy & Rhetoric* 1 (1968): 131–34.

Eliade, Mircea. *Images and Symbols: Studies in Religious Symbolism*. Translated by Philip Mairet. New York: Sheed & Ward, 1961.

———. *The Sacred and the Profane: The Nature of Religion*. Translated by Willard R. Trask. New York: Harcourt, Brace, Jovanovich, 1959.

Ellwood, Thomas, and Joseph Wyeth. *The History of the Life of Thomas Ellwood*. Philadelphia: For sale at Friends' Book Store, 1865.

Engnell, Richard A. "Otherness and the Rhetorical Exigencies of Theistic Religion." *Quarterly Journal of Speech* 79 (1993): 82–98.

Evans, Marsee Fred. "A Study in the Development of a Theory of Homiletics in England from 1534 to 1692." Ph.D. diss., University of Iowa, 1932.

Fehrman, Carl. *Poetic Creation: Inspiration or Craft.* Translated by Karin Petherick. Mineapolis: University of Minesota Press, 1980.

Fernandez, James W. "The Mission of Metaphor in Expressive Culture." *Current Anthropology* 15 (1974): 119–33.

―――. "Persuasions and Performance: Of the Beast in Every Body . . . And the Metaphors of Everyman." *Daedalus* 101 (1972): 39–60.

Fincham, Kenneth, and Nicholas Tyacke. *Altars Restored: The Changing Face of English Religious Worship, 1547–c. 1700.* New York: Oxford University Press, 2008.

Fisher, Walter. "A Motive View of Communication." *Quarterly Journal of Speech* 56 (1970): 131–39.

Forbes, Christopher. *Prophecy and Inspired Speech: In Early Christianity and its Hellenistic Environment.* Peabody, Mass.: Hendrickson, 1997.

Fox, Michael V. "Ancient Egyptian Rhetoric." *Rhetorica* 1 (1983): 21–34.

Freiday, Dean. "A Common Quakerhood?" In *What Future for Friends? Report of the St. Louis Conference . . . October 5–7, 1970.* Philadelphia: Friends World Committee, n.d.

Friedrich, Carl J. *The Age of the Baroque 1610–1660.* New York: Harper & Row, 1962.

Frye, Northrop. "The Journey as Metaphor." In *Myth and Metaphor: Selected Essays, 1974–1988.* Edited by Robert D. Denham. Charlottesville: University Press of Virginia, 1990.

Gehrke, Pat J. "The Southern Association of Teachers of Speech v. Senator Theodore Bilbo: Restraint and Indirection as Rhetorical Strategies." In *Southern Communication Journal* 72, no. 1 (2007): 95–104.

Gibson, A. B. *The Philosophy of Descartes.* New York: Russell & Russell, 1967.

Gill, Catie. "'Ministering Confusion': Rebellious Quaker Women (1650–1660)." *Quaker Studies* 9, no. 1 (2004): 17–30.

―――. *Women in the Seventeenth-Century Quaker Community: A Literary Study of Political Identities, 1650–1700.* Women and Gender in the Early Modern World Series. Aldershot, UK: Ashgate, 2005.

Graves, Michael P. "The Anti-Theatrical Prejudice and the Quakers: A Late Twentieth Century Perspective." In *Truth's Bright Embrace: A Festschrift in Honor of Arthur O. Roberts.* Edited by Howard Macy and Paul Anderson. Newberg, Ore.: Barclay Press, 1996.

―――. "Checklist of Extant Quaker Sermons, 1650–1700." *Quaker History* 63 (1974): 53–57.

―――. "Functions of Key Metaphors in Early Quaker Sermons, 1671–1700." *Quarterly Journal of Speech* 69 (1983): 364–78.

―――. "Mapping the Metaphors in George Fox's Sermons." In *New Light on George Fox, 1624–1691: A Collection of Essays.* Edited by Michael Mullett, 45–59. York, UK: William Sessions, 1994.

―――. "One Friend's Journey." *Rhetoric and Public Affairs* 7, no. 4 (2004): 513–24.

―――. "Quakerism." In *The Encyclopedia of Language & Linguistics.* Vol. 6. Oxford: Pergamon Press, 1994.

―――. "The Quaker Tapestry: An Artistic Attempt to Stitch Together a Diverse Religious Community." *Journal of Communication and Religion* 24, no. 1 (2001): 1–42.

———. Review of *Let Your Words Be Few: Symbolism of Speaking and Silence among Seventeenth-Century Quakers*, by Richard Bauman. *Quarterly Journal of Speech* (November 1984): 482–83.

———. "The Rhetoric of the Inward Light: An Examination of Extant Sermons Delivered by Early Quakers, 1671–1700." Ph.D. diss., University of Southern California, 1972.

———. "Robert Barclay and the Rhetoric of the Inward Light." *Quaker Religious Thought* 26, no. 2 (1993): 17–32.

———. "Stephen Crisp's *Short History* as Spiritual Journey." *Quaker Religious Thought* 26, no. 3 (1993): 5–23.

———. "'Thou art but a youth': Thomas Chalkley Enacts and Defends the Early Quaker Impromptu Sermon." In *Rhetoric, Religion, and the Roots of Identity in British Colonial America*. Edited by James R. Andrews. Vol. 1: *A Rhetorical History of the United States*. Edited by Martin J. Medhurst. East Lansing: Michigan State University Press, 2007.

———. "Travelers Here in this Vale of Tears: William Penn Preaches a Funeral Sermon." *Quaker Studies* 12, no. 1 (2007): 7–25.

Gribbin, William. "The Juggernaut Metaphor in American Rhetoric." *Quarterly Journal of Speech* 59 (1973): 297–303.

Gronbeck, Bruce E. "The Spoken and the Seen: Phonocentric and Ocularcentric Dimensions of Rhetorical Discourse." In *Rhetorical Memory and Delivery: Classical Concepts for Contemporary Composition and Communication*. Edited by John Frederick Reynolds. Hillsdale, N.J.: Lawrence Erlbaum Associates, 1993.

Gwyn, Douglas. *Apocalypse of the Word: The Life and Message of George Fox*. Richmond, Ind.: Friends United Press, 1984.

———. *The Covenant Crucified: Quakers and the Rise of Capitalism*. Wallingford, Pa.: Pendle Hill Publications, 1995.

Hall, Francis B. "The Thought of Robert Barclay: An Evaluation." *Quaker Religious Thought* 7 (1965): 2–31.

Hamm, Thomas D. *The Quakers in America*. New York: Columbia University Press, 2003.

Hart, Roderick P. "Doing Criticism My Way: A Reply to Darsey." *Western Journal of Communication* 58 (1994): 308–12.

Harvey, T. Edmund. *Quaker Language. The Presidential Address to the Friends Historical Society, 1928*. London: Friends Historical Society, 1928.

Haviland, Margaret. "'And the King shall answer and say unto them, Verily I say unto you, inasmuch as ye have done it unto one of the least of these my brethren, ye have done it unto me': The Response of Quaker Women to Matthew 25:40." Paper presented to the Philadelphia Center for Early American Studies, March 30, 1990.

Helm, Paul. *Calvin and the Calvinists*. Edinburgh: Banner of Truth Trust, 1982.

Herrick, James A. "Miracles and Method." *Quarterly Journal of Speech* 75 (1989): 321–34.

———. *The Radical Rhetoric of the English Deists: The Discourse of Skepticism, 1680–1750*. Columbia: University of South Carolina Press, 1997.

Heyd, Michael. *"Be Sober and Reasonable": The Critique of Enthusiasm in the Seventeenth and Early Eighteenth Centuries.* Leiden: E. J. Brill, 1995.

Hill, Charles A., and Marguerite Helmers, eds. *Defining Visual Rhetorics.* Mahwah, N.J.: Lawrence Erlbaum Associates, 2004.

Hill, Christopher. *The Century of Revolution 1603–1714.* Vol. 5: *A History of England.* Edited by Christopher Brooke and Denis Mack Smith. 8 vols. London: Thomas Nelson & Sons, 1961.

Hostetler, Michael J. "Rethinking the War Metaphor in Religious Rhetoric: Burke, Black and Berrigan's 'Glimmer of Light.'" *Journal of Communication and Religion* 20, no. 1 (1997): 49–60.

Howell, Wilbur Samuel. "English Backgrounds of Rhetoric." In *History of Speech Education in America.* Edited by Karl Wallace. New York: Appleton-Century-Crofts, 1954.

———. Introduction to *Dialogues on Eloquence,* by Francis Fenelon. Translated by Wilbur Samuel Howell. Princeton: Princeton University Press, 1951.

———. "John Locke and the New Rhetoric." *Quarterly Journal of Speech* 53 (1967): 319–33.

———. *Logic and Rhetoric in England, 1500–1700.* Princeton: Princeton University Press, 1956; New York: Russell & Russell, 1961.

———. "The Plough and the Flail: The Ordeal of Eighteenth Century Logic." *The Huntington Library Quarterly* 28 (1964): 63–78.

———. "Renaissance Rhetoric and Modern Rhetoric: A Study in Change." In *The Rhetorical Idiom; Essays in Rhetoric, Oratory, Language, and Drama.* Edited by Donald Cross Bryant and Herbert August Wichelns. New York: Russell & Russell, 1966.

Hunt, Everett Lee. "An Introduction to Classical Rhetoric." *Quarterly Journal of Speech* 12 (1926): 201–4.

Ingle, Larry H. *First Among Friends: George Fox and the Creation of Quakerism.* New York: Oxford University Press, 1994.

Ingram, Jason. "Plato's Rhetoric of Indirection: Paradox as Site and Agency of Transformation." In *Philosophy & Rhetoric* 40, no. 3 (2007): 293–310.

Irvine, James R., and Walter Kirkpatrick. "The Musical Form in Rhetorical Exchange: Theoretical Considerations." *Quarterly Journal of Speech* 58, no. 3 (1971): 272–85.

Ivie, Robert L. "Metaphor and the Rhetorical Invention of Cold War 'Idealists.'" *Communication Monographs* 54 (1987): 165–82.

———. "The Metaphor of Force in Prowar Discourse: The Case of 1812." *Quarterly Journal of Speech* 68 (1982): 240–53.

Jamieson, Kathleen Hall. "The Metaphor Cluster in the Rhetoric of Pope Paul VI and Edmund G. Brown, Jr." *Quarterly Journal of Speech* 66 (1980): 51–72.

Jebb, R. C. *The Encyclopedia Britannica,* 9th and 11th eds.

Jensen, J. Vernon. "British Voices on the Eve of the American Revolution: Trapped by the Family Metaphor." *Quarterly Journal of Speech* 63 (1977): 43–50.

Johnson, Mark. *The Body in the Mind: The Bodily Basis of Meaning, Imagination, and Reason.* Chicago: University of Chicago Press, 1987.

Johnson, Nels. "Palestinian Refugee Ideology: An Enquiry into Key Metaphors." *Journal of Anthropological Research* 34 (1978): 524–39.

Jones, J. R. *Country and Court: England, 1658–1714*. The New History of England. Edited by A. G. Dickens and Norman Gash. Cambridge, Mass.: Harvard University Press, 1978.

Jones, Phyllis, and Nicholas Jones. *Salvation in New England: Selections from the Sermons of the First Preachers*. Austin: University of Texas Press, 1977.

Jones, Richard F. *Ancients and Moderns: A Study of the Rise of the Scientific Movement in Seventeenth-Century England*. 2nd ed. Berkeley: University of California Press, 1965.

———. "The Attack on Pulpit Eloquence in the Restoration: An Episode in the Development of the Neo-Classical Standard for Prose." In *The Seventeenth Century*. Stanford: Stanford University Press, 1951.

———. "Science and English Prose Style in the 3rd Quarter of the 17th Century." *Publications of the Modern Language Association* 45 (1930): 977–1009.

Jones, Rufus M. *The Later Periods of Quakerism*. 2 vols. London: Macmillan, 1914.

———. *The Quakers in the American Colonies*. New York: Russell & Russell, 1962.

———. *Spiritual Reformers in the 16th and 17th Centuries*. 1914. Reprint, Boston: Beacon, 1959.

Jones, T. Canby. "George Fox's Teaching on Redemption and Salvation." Ph.D. diss., Yale University, 1956.

Jones, William T. *A History of Western Philosophy*. New York: Harcourt, Brace, 1952.

Jost, Walter. "On Concealment and Deception in Rhetoric: Newman and Kierkegaard." In *Rhetoric Society Quarterly* 24, no. 1/2 (1994): 51–74.

Kendall, R. T. *Calvin and English Calvinism to 1649*. Studies in Christian History and Thought. Colorado Springs: Paternoster Press, 2006.

Kennedy, George A. *Comparative Rhetoric: An Historical and Cross-Cultural Introduction*. New York: Oxford University Press, 1998.

King, Rachel Hadley. *George Fox and the Light Within, 1650–1660*. Philadelphia: Friends Book Store, 1940.

Knappen, Marshall M. *Tudor Puritanism: A Chapter in the History of Idealism*. Glouchester, Mass.: Peter Smith, 1963.

Knoppers, Laura Lunger ed., *Puritanism and Its Discontents*. Newark: University of Delaware Press, 2003).

Kuenning, Larry, ed. Quaker Writings Home Page. http://www.qhpress.org/quaker-pages/qwhp/qwhp.htm.

Lake, Peter. *Anglicans and Puritans? Presbyterians and English Conformist Thought from Whitgift to Hooker*. London: Unwin Hyman, 1988.

———. *Moderate Puritans and the Elizabethan Church*. Cambridge: Cambridge University Press, 1982.

Lakoff, George. *Women, Fire, and Dangerous Things: What Our Categories Reveal About the Mind*. Chicago: University of Chicago Press, 1987.

Lakoff, George, and Mark Johnson. *Metaphors We Live By*. Chicago: University of Chicago Press, 1980.

Larson, Rebecca. *Daughters of the Light: Quaker Women Preaching and Prophesying in the Colonies and Abroad, 1700–1775*. New York: Alfred A. Knopf, 1999.

Lee, Umphrey. *The Historical Backgrounds of Early Methodist Enthusiasm*. Studies in History, Economics and Public Law, no. 339. Edited by the Faculty of Political Science of Columbia University. New York: AMS Press, 1967.

Leff, Michael C. "Textual Criticism: The Legacy of G. P. Mohrman." *Quarterly Journal of Speech* 72 (1986): 377–89.

———. "Things Made By Words: Reflections on Textual Criticism." *Quarterly Journal of Speech* 78 (1992): 223–31.

———. "Topical Invention and Metaphoric Interaction." *Southern Speech Communication Journal* 48 (1983): 214–29.

———. "Up from Theory: Or I Fought the Topoi and the Topoi Won." *Rhetoric Society Quarterly* 36, no. 2 (2006): 203–11.

Leff, Michael C., and Fred J. Kauffeld, eds. *Texts in Context: Critical Dialogues on Significant Episodes in American Political Rhetoric*. Davis, Calif.: Hermagoras, 1989.

Leff, Michael, and Andrew Sachs. "Words the Most Like Things: Iconicity and the Rhetorical Text." *Western Journal of Speech Communication* 54 (1990): 252–73.

Lessenich, Rolf P. *Elements of Pulpit Oratory in Eighteenth-Century England (1660–1800)*. Cologne: Böhlau-Verlag, 1972.

Leverenz, David. *The Language of Puritan Feeling: An Exploration in Literature, Psychology, and Social History*. New Brunswick, N.J.: Rutgers University Press, 1980.

Levy, Babette May. *Preaching in the First Half Century of New England History*. Vol. 6: *Studies in Church History*. Edited by Matthew Spinka and Robert H. Nichols. New York: Russell & Russell, 1967.

Lloyd, Arnold. *Quaker Social History 1669–1738*. New York: Longmans, Green, 1950.

Lucas, Stephen E. "The Renaissance of American Public Address: Text and Context." *Quarterly Journal of Speech* 74 (1988): 241–60.

———. "The Schism in Rhetorical Scholarship." *Quarterly Journal of Speech* 67, no. 1 (1981): 1–20.

MacCormac, Earl R. *Metaphor and Myth in Science and Religion*. Durham, N.C.: Duke University Press, 1976.

Mack, Phyllis. *Visionary Women: Ecstatic Prophecy in Seventeenth-Century England*. Berkeley: University of California Press, 1994.

Marlowe, John. *The Puritan Tradition in English Life*. London: Cresset Press, 1956.

McCanles, Michael. "The Literal and the Metaphorical: Dialectic or Interchange." *Proceedings of the Modern Language Association* 90 (1976): 279–90.

McDowell, Nicholas. *The English Radical Imagination: Culture, Religion, and Revolution, 1630–1660*. Oxford English Monographs. New York: Oxford University Press, 2004.

McFague, Sallie. *Metaphorical Theology: Models of God in Religious Language*. Philadelphia: Fortress, 1982.

———. *Speaking in Parables: A Study in Metaphor and Theology*. Philadelphia: Fortress, 1975.

McKeon, Richard. "Rhetoric in the Middle Ages." *Speculum* 17 (1942): 1–32.

McKim, Donald K. "The Functions of Ramism in William Perkins' Theology." *Sixteenth Century Journal* 16 (1985): 503–17.

Medhurst, Martin J. "Public Address and Significant Scholarship: Four Challenges to the Rhetorical Renaissance." In *Texts in Context: Critical Dialogues on Significant Episodes in American Political Rhetoric*. Edited by Michael C. Leff and Fred J. Kauffeld, 29–42. Davis, Calif.: Hermagoras, 1989.

————. "The Rhetorical Renaissance: A Battlefield Report." *Southern Communication Journal* 63, no. 5 (1998): 309–14.

Medhurst, Martin J., and Thomas W. Benson, eds. *Rhetorical Dimensions in Media: A Critical Casebook*, 2nd ed. Dubuque, Iowa: Kendall/Hunt Publishing, 1984.

Miller, Brett A. "Seeing Through a Glass Darkly: Religious Metaphor as Rhetorical Perspective." *Journal of Communication and Religion* 22 (1999): 214–36.

Miller, Perry. *The New England Mind: The Seventeenth Century*. Cambridge, Mass.: Harvard University Press, 1954.

Mitchell, W. Fraser. *English Pulpit Oratory from Andrewes to Tillotson: A Study of Its Literary Aspects*. London: SPCK, 1932; New York: Russell & Russell, 1962.

Moore, Rosemary. *The Light in Their Consciences: The Early Quakers in Britain, 1646–1666*. University Park: Pennsylvania State University Press, 2000.

Morris, Christopher. "'Introduction' to Richard Hooker." In *Of the Laws of Ecclesiastical Polity*. 2 vols. New York: E. P. Dutton, 1958.

Mullett, Michael. *John Bunyan in Context*. Edinburgh: Edinburgh University Press, 1996.

————, ed. *New Light on George Fox, 1624–1691*. York, UK: William Sessions, 1994.

Murphy, James J. "The Arts of Discourse, 1050–1400." *Medieval Studies* 13 (1961): 194–205.

Nicolson, Adam. *God's Secretaries: The Making of the King James Bible*. New York: HarperCollins, 2003.

Notestein, Wallace. *The English People on the Eve of Colonization*. New York: Harper & Row, 1962.

Nothstine, William L., Carole Blair, and Cary A. Copeland, eds. *Critical Questions: Invention, Creativity, and the Criticism of Discourse and Media*. New York: St. Martin's Press, 1994.

Nussbaum, Frederick L. *The Triumph of Science and Reason 1660–1685*. New York: Harper & Row, 1962.

Nuttall, Geoffrey. *The Holy Spirit in Puritan Faith and Experience*. Oxford: Basil Blackwell, 1946.

Ong, Walter J. *Orality and Literacy: The Technologizing of the Word*. New Accents. Edited by Terence Hawkes. London: Methuen, 1982. Reprint, New York: Routledge, 1988.

————. *The Presence of the Word: Some Prolegomena for Cultural and Religious History*. [Yale 1967.] Mineapolis: University of Minesota Press, 1981.

————. *Ramus—Method, and the Decay of Dialogue: From the Art of Discourse to the Art of Reason*. Cambridge, Mass.: Harvard University Press, 1958.

————. *Ramus and Talon Inventory. . . .* Cambridge, Mass.: Harvard University Press, 1958.

Ormsby-Lenon, Hugh. "'The Dialect of Those Fanatic Times': Language Communities and English Poetry from 1580 to 1660." Ph.D. diss., University of Pennsylvania, 1977.

Ortner, Sherry B. "On Key Symbols." *American Anthropologist* 75 (1973): 1338–46.

Osborn, Michael. "Archetypal Metaphor in Rhetoric: The Light-Dark Family." *Quarterly Journal of Speech* 52 (1967): 115–26.

———. "The Evolution of the Archetypal Sea in Rhetoric and Poetic." *Quarterly Journal of Speech* (1977): 347–63.

Osborn, Michael M., and Douglas Ehninger. "The Metaphor in Public Address." *Speech Monographs* 29 (1962): 223–34.

Pattison, Thomas H. *History of Christian Preaching*. Philadelphia: American Baptist Publication Society, 1903.

Peare, Catherine O. *William Penn: A Biography*. Philadelphia: J. B. Lippincott, 1957.

Penny, Norman, ed. *The First Publishers of Truth*. London: Headley Brothers, 1907.

Perry, Ralph Barton. *Puritanism and Democracy*. New York: Vanguard Press, 1944.

Peters, Kate. *Print Culture and the Early Quakers*. Cambridge Studies in Early Modern British History. Cambridge: Cambridge University Press, 2005.

Pink Dandelion, Ben, ed. *The Creation of Quaker Theory: Insider Perspectives*. Aldershot, UK: Ashgate, 2004.

———. *An Introduction to Quakerism*. New York: Cambridge University Press, 2007.

Pink Dandelion, Ben, Douglas Gwyn, and Timothy Peat, eds. *Heaven on Earth: Quakers and the Second Coming*. Birmingham, UK: Woodbrooke College & Curlew Publications, 1998.

Pieper, Josef. *Enthusiasm and Divine Madness: On the Platonic dialogue Phaedrus*. Translated by Richard and Clara Winston. New York: Harcourt, Brace & World, 1964.

Pipes, William H. *Say Amen, Brother!: Old-Time Negro Preaching: A Study in American Frustration*. New York: William-Frederick, 1951.

Pollard, Arthur. *English Sermons*. Writers and Their Works, 158. London: Longmans, Green, 1963.

Poole, Kristen. *Radical Religion from Shakespeare to Milton: Figures of Nonconformity in Early Modern England*. Cambridge: Cambridge University Press, 2000.

Potter, David. *Debating in the Colonial Chartered Colleges*. Columbia University Teachers College Contributions to Education, no. 89. New York: Columbia University Press, 1944.

Punshon, John. *Portrait in Quaker Grey: A Short History of the Quakers*. London: Quaker Home Service, 1984.

Ramsey, Ian. *Religious Language: An Empirical Placing of Theological Phrases*. London: SCM Press, 1957.

Reay, Barry, ed. *Popular Culture in Seventeenth-Century England*. London: Routledge, 1988.

———. *The Quakers and the English Revolution*. New York: St. Martin's Press, 1985.

Rechtien, John G. "Logic in Puritan Sermons in the Late Sixteenth Century and Plain Style." *Style* 13 (1979): 237–58.

Redwood, John. *Reason, Ridicule and Religion: The Age of Enlightenment in England, 1660–1750*. London: Thames & Hudson, 1976.

Reid, Ronald F. "Puritan Rhetoric and America's Civil Religion: A Study of Three Special Occasion Sermons." In *Rhetoric, Religion, and the Roots of Identity in British Colonial America*. Vol. 1: *A Rhetorical History of the United States*. Edited by James R. Andrews. General editor, Martin J. Medhurst. East Lansing: Michigan State University Press, 2007.

Reynolds, John Frederick, ed. *Rhetorical Memory and Delivery: Classical Concepts for Contemporary Composition and Communication*. Hillsdale, N.J.: Lawrence Erlbaum Associates, 1993.

Rice, Donald. "Order Out of Chaos: The Archetypal Metaphor in Early American Rhetoric," *North Dakota Journal of Speech & Theatre* 9, no. 1 (1996): 18–24.

Richards, I. A. *The Philosophy of Rhetoric*. New York: Oxford University Press, 1965.

Richardson, Caroline. *English Preachers and Preaching, 1640–1670*. New York: Macmillan, 1928.

Roberts, Arthur O. *Through Flaming Sword: A Spiritual Biography of George Fox*. Newberg, Ore.: Barclay Press, 1959.

Roberts-Miller, Patricia. *Voices in the Wilderness: Public Discourse and the Paradox of Puritan Rhetoric*. Tuscaloosa: University of Alabama Press, 1999.

Rogers, George Philip. *The Fifth Monarchy Men*. London: Oxford University Press, 1966.

Roppen, Georg, and Richard Sommer. *Strangers and Pilgrims: An Essay on the Metaphor of Journey*. New York: Humanities Press, 1964.

Rosaldo, Michele Zimbalist. "It's All Uphill: The Creative Metaphors of Ilongot Magical Spells." In *Sociocultural Dimensions of Language Use*. Edited by Mary Sanches and Ben Blount. New York: Academic Press, 1975.

———. "Metaphors and Folk Classification." *Southwestern Journal of Anthropology* 28 (1972): 83–99.

Rose, Judith. "Prophesying Daughters: Testimony, Censorship, and Literacy Among Early Quaker Women." *Critical Survey* 14, no. 1 (2002): 93–110.

Rosenberg, Bruce. *Can These Bones Live? The Art of the American Folk Preacher*, rev. ed. Chicago: University of Chicago Press, 1988.

———. "The Formulaic Quality of Spontaneous Sermons." *Journal of American Folklore* 83 (1970): 3–20.

Rosenfield, Israel. *The Invention of Memory: A New View of the Brain*. New York: Basic Books, 1988.

Rushby, William F. "Cyrus Cooper's Memorial and the Free Gospel Ministry." *Quaker History* 89, no. 1 (2000): 28–46.

Russell, Bertrand. *A History of Western Philosophy*. New York: Simon & Schuster, 1945.

Russell, Elbert. *The History of Quakerism*. Richmond, Ind.: Friends United Press, 1979.

Sacks, Sheldon, ed. *On Metaphor*. Chicago: University of Chicago Press, 1979.

Sandford, William P. *English Theories of Public Address, 1530–1828*. Columbus, Ohio: Harold L. Hedrick, 1965.

Sapir, David, and J. Christopher Crocker, eds. *The Social Use of Metaphor*. Philadelphia: University of Pennsylvania Press, 1977.

Sarbin, Theodore. "The Metaphor-to-Myth Transformation with Special Reference to the 'War on Terrorism.'" *Peace & Conflict* 9, no. 2 (2003): 149–58.

Schlatter, Richard. *Richard Baxter & Puritan Politics*. New Brunswick, N.J.: Rutgers University Press, 1957.

Schneider, Herbert Wallace. *The Puritan Mind*. Ann Arbor: University of Michigan Press, 1958.

Scott, Robert L. "Dialectical Tensions of Speaking and Silence." *Quarterly Journal of Speech* 79 (1993): 1–18.

———. "Rhetoric and Silence." *Western Speech* 36 (1972): 146–58.

Sellnow, Deanna, and Timothy Sellnow. "The 'Illusion of Life' Rhetorical Perspective: An Integrated Approach to the Study of Music as Communication." *Critical Studies in Media Communication* 18, no. 4 (2001): 395–415.

Sharp, Buchanan. "Popular Protest." In *Popular Culture in Seventeenth-Century England*. Edited by Barry Reay. London: Routledge, 1988.

Simpson, Alan. *Puritanism in Old and New England*. Chicago: University of Chicago Press, 1961.

Sipple, Peter, ed. Quaker Homiletics Online Anthology. http://www.qhpress.org/quakerpages/qhoa/qhoa.htm.

Smith, Bernadette. "The Testimony of Martha Simmonds, Quaker." *Quaker Studies* 12, no. 1 (2007): 26–38.

Smith, Craig R. *Rhetoric and Human Consciousness: A History*. 2nd ed. Long Grove, Ill.: Waveland Press, 2003.

Smith, Joseph. *Descriptive Catalogue of Friends Books*. 2 vols. London: Joseph Smith, 1867.

———. *Supplement to Descriptive Catalogue of Friends Books*. 2 vols. London: E. Hicks, 1893.

Smith, Norman. *Studies in the Cartesian Philosophy*. New York: Russell & Russell, 1961.

Smyth, Charles. *The Art of Preaching: A Practical Survey of Preaching in the Church of England, 1747–1939*. London: SPCK, 1953.

Sommerville, C. John. *Popular Religion in Restoration England*. University of Florida Monographs, Social Sciences, no. 59. Gainesville: University Presses of Florida, 1977.

———. "Religious Typologies and Popular Religion in Restoration England." *Church History* 45 (1976): 1–10.

Soskice, Janet Martin. *Metaphor and Religious Language*. Oxford: Clarendon, 1985.

Spencer, Carole Dale. *Holiness: The Soul of Quakerism*. Christian History and Thought. Colorado Springs: Paternoster Press, 2007.

Spencer, Jon Michael. *Sacred Symphony: The Chanted Sermon of the Black Preacher*. Contributions in Afro-American and African Studies 111. New York: Greenwood Press, 1987.

Stelzner, Hermann. "The Quest Story and Nixon's November 3, 1969 Address." *Quarterly Journal of Speech* 57 (1971): 163–72.

Stiver, Dan R. *The Philosophy of Religious Language: Sign, Symbol & Story*. Malden, Mass.: Blackwell, 1996.

Stone, Lawrence. *The Crisis of the Aristocracy, 1558–1641*. Oxford: Clarendon, 1965.

Stout, Harry S. *The New England Soul: Preaching and Religious Culture in Colonial New England.* New York: Oxford University Press, 1986.

Sullivan, Dale L. "*Kairos* and the Rhetoric of Belief." *Quarterly Journal of Speech* 78 (1992): 317–32.

Sutherland, Julie. "Obedience to the Inward Oracle: An Analysis of Some Early Quaker Women's Publications." *Quaker Studies* 6, no. 2 (2002): 135–58.

Tarter, Michele Lise. "'Go North!' The Journey towards First-generation Friends and their Prophecy of Celestial Flesh." In *The Creation of Quaker Theory: Insider Perspectives.* Edited by Ben Pink Dandelion, 83–98. Aldershot, UK: Ashgate, 2004.

———. "The Milk of the Word of God." In *New Voices, New Light: Papers from the Quaker Theology Round Table.* Edited by Charles Fager. Wallingford, Pa.: Pendle Hill Publishers, 1995.

———. "Quaking in the Light: The Politics of Quaker Women's Corporeal Prophecy in the Seventeenth-Century Transatlantic World." In *A Center of Wonders: The Body in Early America.* Edited by Janet Moore Lindman and Michele Lise Tarter. Ithaca: Cornell University Press, 2004.

———. "Sites of Performance: Theorizing the History of Sexuality in the Lives and Writings of Quaker Women, 1650–1800." Ph.D. diss., University of Colorado, 1993.

Thaiss, Gustav. "The Conceptualization of Social Change Through Metaphor." *Journal of Asian and African Studies* 13 (1978): 1–13.

Thompson, Elbert N. S. *The Controversy between the Puritans and the Stage.* New York: Russell & Russell, 1966.

Thonssen, Lester, and A. Craig Baird. *Speech Criticism: The Development of Standards for Rhetorical Appraisal.* New York: Ronald Press, 1948.

Tolles, Frederick B. "Introduction to Second Edition." *The Second Period of Quakerism.* 2nd ed. Cambridge: Cambridge University Press, 1961.

———. *Quakers and the Atlantic Culture.* New York: Macmillan, 1960.

Toulmin, Stephen. *The Uses of Argument.* Cambridge: Cambridge University Press, 1958.

Toulouse, Teresa. *The Art of Prophesying: New England Sermons and the Shaping of Belief.* Athens: University of Georgia Press, 1987.

Trevelyan, G. M. *England Under the Stuarts.* Vol. 5: *A History of England.* Edited by Charles Oman. London: Methuen, 1965.

———. *English Social History: A Survey of Six Centuries, Chaucer to Queen Victoria.* New York: Longmans, Green, 1942.

———. *History of England.* Vol. 2: *The Tudors and the Stuart Era.* Garden City, N.Y.: Doubleday Anchor Books, 1953.

———. *Illustrated English Social History.* 4 vols. New York: David McKay, 1949–1952.

Trevett, Christine. *Quaker Women Prophets in England and Wales, 1650–1700.* Lewiston, N.Y.: Edwin Mellen Press, 2000.

———. *Women and Quakerism in the 17th Century.* York, UK: William Sessions, 1995.

Trueblood, D. Elton. *The People Called Quakers.* New York: Harper & Row, 1966.

————. *Robert Barclay: A Portrait of the Life and Times of a Great Quaker Intellectual Leader*. New York: Harper & Row, 1968.

Tuke, Samuel, ed. *Selections from the Epistles of George Fox*. Cambridge, Mass.: Riverside Press, 1879.

Turner, Kathleen J., ed. *Doing Rhetorical History: Concepts and Cases*. Tuscaloosa: University of Alabama Press, 1998.

Turner, Victor. "Liminal to Liminoid." In *From Ritual to Theatre: The Human Seriousness of Play*. New York: Performing Arts Journal, 1982.

Turner, Victor, and Edith Turner. *Image and Pilgrimage in Christian Culture: Anthropological Perspectives*. New York: Columbia University Press, 1978.

Tyacke, Nicholas. *Anti-Calvinists: The Rise of English Arminianism, c. 1590–1640*. New York: Oxford University Press, 1987.

————. *Aspects of English Protestantism c. 1530–1700: Politics, Culture and Society in Early Modern Britain*. Manchester, UK: Manchester University Press, 2002.

————. *The English Revolution c. 1590–1720: Politics, Religion and Communities*. UCL/Neale Series on British History. Manchester, UK: Manchester University Press, 2008.

————. *The Fortunes of English Puritanism, 1603–1640*. London: Dr. Williams's Trust, 1990.

————. "The 'Rise of Puritanism' and the Legalizing of Dissent, 1571–1719." In *From Persecution to Toleration: The Glorious Revolution and Religion in England*. Edited by Ole Peter Grell, Jonathan I. Israel, and Nicholas Tyacke. Oxford: Clarendon, 1991.

Underhill, Evelyn. *Mysticism: A Study of the Nature and Development of Man's Spiritual Consciousness*. New York: New American Library, 1974.

Underwood, T. L. *Primitivism, Radicalism, and the Lamb's War: The Baptist-Quaker Conflict in Seventeenth-Century England*. New York: Oxford University Press, 1997.

Vann, Richard T. *The Social Development of English Quakerism, 1655–1755*. Cambridge, Mass.: Harvard University Press, 1969.

Wallace, Karl R. "Bacon's Conception of Rhetoric." In *Historical Studies of Rhetoric and Rhetoricians*. Edited by Raymond F. Howes. Ithaca: Cornell University Press, 1961.

————. *Francis Bacon on Communication and Rhetoric*. Chapel Hill: University of North Carolina Press, 1943.

————. *Francis Bacon on the Nature of Man: The Faculties of Man's Soul*. Urbana: University of Illinois Press, 1967.

Walsham, Alexandra. "'A glose of godliness': Philip Stubbes, Elizabeth Grub Street and the Invention of Puritanism." In *Belief and Practice in Reformation England*. Edited by Caroline Litzenberger and Susan Wabuda. Aldershot, UK: Ashgate, 1998.

Watts, Isaac. *The Improvement of the Mind, or, A Supplement to the Art of Logic In Two Parts, to Which Is Added, a Discourse on the Education of Children and Youth*. Boston: D. West, 1793.

Weaver, Richard M. "Language is Sermonic." In *Language is Sermonic*. Edited by Richard L. Johanesen, Renard Strickland, and Ralph T. Eubanks. Baton Rouge: Louisiana State University Press, 1970.

Webb, Stephen H. *The Divine Voice: Christian Proclamation and the Theology of Sound*. Grand Rapids: Brazos Press, 2004.

Webber, F. R. *A History of Preaching in Britain and America*. 3 vols. Milwaukee: Northwestern Publishing House, 1957.

Webster, Linda J. "Among Friends: Establishing an Oratorical Tradition among Quaker Women in the Early Colonial Era." In *A Rhetorical History of the United States*, Vol. 1: *Rhetoric, Religion, and the Roots of Identity in British Colonial America*. Edited by James R. Andrews. General editor, Martin J. Medhurst. East Lansing: Michigan State University Press, 2007.

Wee, Lionel. "Proper Names and the Theory of Metaphor." *Journal of Linguistics* 42, no. 2 (2006): 355–71.

Wenzel, Siegfried. *Preachers, Poets, and the Early English Lyric*. Princeton: Princeton University Press, 1986.

Wheelright, Philip. *Metaphor and Reality*. Bloomington: Indiana University Press, 1962.

White, Eugene E. *Puritan Rhetoric: The Issue of Emotion in Religion*. Carbondale: Southern Illinois University Press, 1972.

Willey, Basil. *The Seventeenth Century Background: Studies in the Thought of the Age in Relation to Poetry and Religion*. Garden City, N.Y.: Doubleday, 1953.

Williams, Walter R. *The Rich Heritage of Quakerism: The Past Speaks to the Present*. Grand Rapids: Eerdmans, 1962.

Williamson, George. *The Senecan Amble: A Study in Prose Form from Bacon to Collier*. Chicago: University of Chicago Press, 1966.

Wingfield-Stratford, Esme. *The History of British Civilization*. 2nd rev. ed. New York: Harcourt, Brace, 1949.

Wings of an Eagle: An Anthology of Caroline Preachers with 60 Extracts from Their Sermons. Edited by George Lacey May. London: SPCK, 1955.

Wright, Luella M. *The Literary Life of the Early Friends, 1650–1725*. New York: Columbia University Press, 1932; New York: AMS Press, 1966.

Zulick, Margaret D. "The Active Force of Hearing: The Ancient Hebrew Language of Persuasion." *Rhetorica* 10 (1992): 367–80.

———. "The Agon of Jeremiah: On the Dialogic Invention of Prophetic Ethos." *Quarterly Journal of Speech* 78 (1992): 125–48.

INDEX OF WORKS

INDEX OF NAMES

SUBJECT INDEX

Newgate Prison, 47, 296, 300
Nicene Creed, 107

oath(s), 46–47, 67–68– 71, 172, 180,
227, 231, 258, 363n95, 377n5; James
5:12, 46, 67; "yea" and "nay," 46, 69,
172–73; *see also* truth
obey/obedience: (secular), 41, 47; (theological), 17, 64, 67, 72, 99, 160, 162,
168, 173, 214, 258, 286, 290–91
orality (primary and secondary), 103
ordain ministers/elders, 92, 94–95
order(s): Barclay and, 73; gender, 181,
228, 233, 238–40, 251; Gospel, 105,
169, 210, 239–40, 242, 244, 249,
252, 412n14; increased significance,
381n95; in lives, 169–70, 361n67; in
marriage, 169–70; in meetings, 86,
104, 143, 171, 220, 239, 250; ministers
as orderers, 126; negative effect on
spontaneity, 239, 361n54; persuasion and, 360n42; Ramus and, 52; of
Second Adam, 236; of truth or ideas,
43, 120; vs. chaos, 236, 395n22
organization: (of Friends), 21, 25, 28, 69,
98, 102, 169, 227–29, 239, 242–44,
35; (rhetorical structure–arrangement),
50, 99, 113, 143, 182, 186–87,
211–12, 266
Oxford (University), 39, 52, 70, 80,
376n63, 378n3

parable(s), 87, 186, 196; of the sower, 196
Parliament(ary), 44, 48, 279, 293, 295,
368, 378
passivity, 101, 108, 110–11; *see also* immediate revelation(s), passive reception of
the Word
Pennsylvania, 25, 294
perception, 37, 118, 193
persecution, 28, 42,–43, 45–48, 59,
67–68, 111, 174–75, 184, 191, 196,
222, 227–29, 239, 259, 285, 293, 300,
301–2, 304, 324, 327, 330, 333, 336,
368n81, 378n38
Petition of Right, 39; petition to Parliament, 293, 295

philosophy, 35–36, 50, 58–59, 118,
170, 184–85, 283, 402n32; new, 34;
Barclay's cautions regarding, 124–25,
380n68
plague, 46, 258
plain dress, 173, 182, 324, 327, 330, 333,
336, 375n29
plain speech, 67–68, 172, 324, 327, 329,
333, 335, 396n32; *see also* plain style;
pronominal usage
plain style, 56, 152, 362–63n85; *see also*
plain speech
poor, 42, 93, 95, 106, 125, 170, 289, 296
popery/popish, 94, 175–76
power: evil/satanic, 195, 240, 250,
273–74, 291, 307; Quaker use of,
6, 14, 21, 26, 62, 64, 68–72, 74, 76,
81–86, 89, 91, 95–102, 104, 106,
109–10, 119, 123–28, 136–37, 140,
159, 161–62, 164, 169, 172–74, 178,
180, 190, 193, 197, 208–211, 214–15,
218, 220, 222, 231, 233–35, 237–43,
246, 248–52, 254, 259–60, 262–65,
268, 272–76, 281, 284, 286, 289–91,
295–96, 299–301, 305, 307–8, 312,
323, 326, 332, 335, 348–49, 351–52,
354, 393n7; religious, 37, 39, 43, 48,
56, 228, 297; rhetorical, 49, 187,
360n40, 398n77, 401n11; secular, 228,
239, 368n84, 382n5
praemunire, 47, 228, 231
pray(ed)/praying, 22, 56, 68, 72, 85, 94,
108–10, 128, 134, 136, 150, 165, 170,
180, 192, 218, 222, 261, 265, 268,
271, 277, 290, 408n23
prayer(s), 40–41, 108, 126, 133, 150, 167,
176, 180, 192, 232, 281, 283, 288–89,
298, 316, 321, 374n19, 389n43,
408n23, 413n24; Book of Common
Prayer, 46, 94, 189; Lord's Prayer
(Paternoster), 94; vocalized, 108, 126
preacher as: conduit, 102; matchmaker,
14, 396n30; medium, 187, 396n30;
midwife, 187, 202, 396n30; oracle, 28,
96–97, 101, 110, 120, 128, 149, 202,
204–5, 231, 257, 267, 280, 296, 312,
338, 340, 342, 344, 360n37, 380n81;